The West

Encounters and Transformations
Volume A: From the Beginnings of Civilization to the Late Middle Ages

Fourth Edition

Brian Levack

University of Texas at Austin

Edward Muir

Northwestern University

Meredith Veldman

Louisiana State University

PEARSON

Boston Columbus Indianapolis New York San Francisco Upper Saddle River
Amsterdam Cape Town Dubai London Madrid Milan Munich Paris Montréal Toronto
Delhi Mexico City São Paulo Sydney Hong Kong Seoul Singapore Taipei Tokyo

Editor-in-Chief: Dickson Musslewhite
Executive Editor: Jeff Lasser
Editorial Project Manager: Rob DeGeorge
Director of Marketing: Brandy Dawson
Executive Marketing Manager: Wendy Albert
Marketing Assistant: Stephanie Toronidis
Production Project Manager: Mirella Signoretto
Senior Managing Editor: Ann Marie McCarthy
Senior Operations Supervisor: Mary Ann Gloriande
Senior Art Director: Maria Lange
Text Design: Red Kite Project
Cover Design: Maria Lange/Red Kite Project
Manager, Visual Research & Permissions: Beth Brenzel
Editorial Assistant: Maureen Diana
Cover Illustration: Matteo Ricci, by Paul Chung / © GL Archive / Alamy
Media Director: Brian Hyland
Media Project Manager: Claudine Bellanton
Program Manager: Emily Tamburri
Media Editor: Thomas Scalzo
Composition/Full-Service Project Management: S4Carlisle Publishing Services
Printer/Binder: RR Donnelley/Willard
Cover Printer: Lehigh-Phoenix Color/Hagerstown

This book was set in Minion Pro Regular 10.5/13

Credits and acknowledgments borrowed from other sources and reproduced, with permission, in this textbook appear on page C-1 or on the appropriate page within the text.

Library of Congress Cataloging-in-Publication Data
Levack, Brian P.
The West : encounters & transformations / Brian Levack, Edward Muir, Meredith Veldman. — Fourth edition, Combined volume.
pages cm
Includes bibliographical references and index.
ISBN-13: 978-0-205-94715-7 (paperback : combined volume : alkaline paper)
ISBN-10: 0-205-94715-8 (paperback : combined volume : alkaline paper) 1. Civilization, Western—History—Textbooks.
I. Muir, Edward. II. Veldman, Meredith. III. Title.
CB245.W455 2013
909'.09821—dc23

2013004227

Combined Volume
ISBN 10: 0-205-94715-8
ISBN 13: 978-0-205-94715-7

Volume 1
ISBN 10: 0-205-94859-6
ISBN 13: 978-0-205-94859-8

Volume 2
ISBN 10: 0-205-94858-8
ISBN 13: 978-0-205-94858-1

Instructor's Review Copy
ISBN 10: 0-205-97274-8
ISBN 13: 978-0-205-97274-6

Volume 1 A La Carte
ISBN 10: 0-205-94921-5
ISBN 13: 978-0-205-94921-2

Volume 2 A La Carte
ISBN 10: 0-205-94922-3
ISBN 13: 978-0-205-94922-9

Volume A
ISBN 10: 0-205-98768-0
ISBN 13: 978-0-205-98768-9

Volume B
ISBN 10: 0-205-98769-9
ISBN 13: 978-0-205-98769-6

Volume C
ISBN 10: 0-205-98770-2
ISBN 13: 978-0-205-98770-2

2 3 4 5 6 7 8 9 10 V092 18 17 16 15

PEARSON

BRIEF CONTENTS

1 The Beginnings of Civilization, 10,000–1150 B.C.E. 10

2 The Age of Empires: The International Bronze Age and Its Aftermath, ca. 1500–550 B.C.E. 43

3 Greek Civilization 78

4 Hellenistic Civilization 111

5 The Roman Republic 138

6 Enclosing the West: The Early Roman Empire and Its Neighbors, 31 B.C.E.–235 C.E. 169

7 Late Antiquity: The Age of New Boundaries, 250–600 201

8 Medieval Empires and Borderlands: Byzantium and Islam 232

9 Medieval Empires and Borderlands: The Latin West 262

10 Medieval Civilization: The Rise of Western Europe 296

11 The Medieval West in Crisis 328

CONTENTS

Maps viii
Documents ix
Preface xvii
About the Authors xxi

What Is the West? 1
THE SHIFTING BORDERS OF THE WEST 1
CHANGING IDENTITIES WITHIN THE WEST 3
WESTERN VALUES 5
ASKING THE RIGHT QUESTIONS 5

1 The Beginnings of Civilization, 10,000–1150 B.C.E. 10
DEFINING CIVILIZATION, DEFINING WESTERN CIVILIZATION 11
Making Civilization Possible: The Food-Producing Revolution 12
The First Food-Producing Communities 13
Transformations in Europe 15
MESOPOTAMIA: KINGDOMS, EMPIRES, AND CONQUESTS 17
The Sumerian Kingdoms 18
The Akkadian Empire of Sargon the Great 19
The Ur III Dynasty and the Rise of Assyria 21
Assyria and Babylonia 21
Cultural Continuities: The Transmission of Mesopotamian Cultures 22
JUSTICE IN HISTORY: Gods and Kings in Mesopotamian Justice 26
EGYPT: THE EMPIRE OF THE NILE 29
Egypt's Rise to Empire 29
DIFFERENT VOICES: Explaining Evil in Ancient Times 34
The New Kingdom: The Egyptian Empire in the Late Bronze Age 35
CONCLUSION: Civilization and the West 40

2 The Age of Empires: The International Bronze Age and Its Aftermath, ca. 1500–550 B.C.E. 43
THE DYNAMISM OF THE INTERNATIONAL BRONZE AGE 44
Zones of Power Within the International Bronze Age 45
ENCOUNTERS AND TRANSFORMATIONS: A Diplomatic Revolution 49
The Club of the Great Powers 51
Crisis and Collapse: The End of the International Bronze Age 54
RECOVERY AND REBUILDING: EMPIRES AND SOCIETIES IN THE AFTERMATH OF THE INTERNATIONAL BRONZE AGE 56
Before and Between the Empires 57
Empire Strikes Back: Neo-Assyrian and Neo-Babylonian Dominance 60
THE CIVILIZATION OF THE HEBREWS 65
The Early History of the Hebrews 65
Israel: From Monarchy to Exile 66
The Hebrew Religious Legacy 69
DIFFERENT VOICES: Holy War in the Ancient World 70
JUSTICE IN HISTORY: Crime and Punishment in a King's Court 74
CONCLUSION: International Systems, Ancient Empires, and the Roots of Western Civilization 75

3 Greek Civilization 78
GREECE REBUILDS, 1100–479 B.C.E. 79
Writing and Poetry During the Archaic Age 79
Political Developments During the Archaic Age 80
Contrasting Societies of the Archaic Age 84
THE GREEK ENCOUNTER WITH PERSIA 87
Cyrus the Great and Persian Expansion 87
DIFFERENT VOICES: Liberty and Despotism in Ancient Persia 89

Persia Under Darius the Great 90
The Persian Wars, 490–479 B.C.E. 91
THE CLASSICAL AGE OF GREECE, 479–336 B.C.E. 93
The Rise and Fall of the Athenian Empire 94
Social and Religious Life in the Classical Age 96
Cultural and Intellectual Life in Classical Greece 100
JUSTICE IN HISTORY: The Trial and Execution of Socrates the Questioner 105
CONCLUSION: The Cultural Foundations of the West 109

4 Hellenistic Civilization 111

THE IMPACT OF ALEXANDER THE GREAT 113
The Rise of Macedon Under King Philip 113
The Conquests of Alexander the Great 114
DIFFERENT VOICES: The Achievement of Alexander the Great 118
HELLENISM IN THE EAST AND WEST 119
The Hellenistic Successor States 119
Encounters with Foreign Peoples 121
HELLENISTIC SOCIETY AND CULTURE 126
Urban Society 126
New Opportunities for Women 128
Art and Architecture 128
Literature 129
JUSTICE IN HISTORY: Divine Justice in the Hellenistic World 130
HELLENISTIC PHILOSOPHY AND SCIENCE 131
Philosophy: The Quest for Peace of Mind 132
Explaining the Natural World: Scientific Investigation 133
CONCLUSION: Defining the West in the Hellenistic Age 136

5 The Roman Republic 138

THE NATURE OF THE ROMAN REPUBLIC 139
Roman Origins and Etruscan Influences 139
Establishing the Roman Republic 141
Roman Law 142
JUSTICE IN HISTORY: A Corrupt Roman Governor Is Convicted of Extortion 143
ROMAN TERRITORIAL EXPANSION 144
The Italian Peninsula 145
The Struggle with Carthage 147
The Macedonian Wars 149
ENCOUNTERS AND TRANSFORMATIONS: Roman Citizenship 151
THE CULTURE OF THE ROMAN REPUBLIC 151
The Encounter Between Hellenistic and Roman Culture 152
Art and Architecture 153
Philosophy and Religion 153
Rhetoric 155
SOCIAL LIFE IN REPUBLICAN ROME 156
Patrons and Clients 156
Pyramids of Wealth and Power 157
The Roman Family 157
THE END OF THE ROMAN REPUBLIC 158
The Gracchi 159
War in Italy and Abroad 160
DIFFERENT VOICES: The Catiline Conspiracy 161
The First Triumvirate 162
Julius Caesar and the End of the Republic 164
CONCLUSION: The Roman Republic and the West 166

6 Enclosing the West: The Early Roman Empire and Its Neighbors, 31 B.C.E.–235 C.E. 169

THE IMPERIAL CENTER 170
Imperial Authority: Augustus and After 170
The City of Rome 174
The Agents of Control 175
LIFE IN THE ROMAN PROVINCES: ASSIMILATION, RESISTANCE, AND ROMANIZATION 177
The Army: A Romanizing Force 177
Occupation, Administration, and Commerce 177
The Cities 178
The Countryside 179
Law, Citizenship, and Romanization 180
DIFFERENT VOICES: Roman Rule: Bane or Blessing? 182
THE FRONTIER AND BEYOND 183
Rome and the Parthian Empire 184
Roman Encounters with Germanic Peoples 184
Economic Encounters Across Continents 186
ENCOUNTERS AND TRANSFORMATIONS: The Battle of Teutoburg Forest 186
SOCIETY AND CULTURE IN THE IMPERIAL AGE 188
Upper and Lower Classes 188

Slaves and Freedmen 189
Women in the Roman Empire 189
Literature and Empire 191
Science in the Roman Empire 192
Religious Life 192
JUSTICE IN HISTORY: The Trial of Jesus in Historical Perspective 196
CONCLUSION: Rome Shapes the West 199

7 Late Antiquity: The Age of New Boundaries, 250–600 201
CRISIS AND RECOVERY IN THE THIRD CENTURY 202
The Breakdown of the Imperial Government 203
The Restoration of the Imperial Government 203
TOWARD A CHRISTIAN EMPIRE 206
Constantine: The First Christian Emperor 206
The Spread of Christianity 208
NEW CHRISTIAN COMMUNITIES AND IDENTITIES 211
The Creation of New Communities 212
Access to Holiness: Christian Pilgrimage 217
DIFFERENT VOICES: Christian Attitudes Toward Sexuality, Contraception, and Abortion 218
Christian Intellectual Life 219
THE BREAKUP OF THE ROMAN EMPIRE 222
The Fall of Rome's Western Provinces 222
The Survival of Rome's Eastern Provinces 224
JUSTICE IN HISTORY: *Two Martyrdoms:* Culture and Religion on Trial 228
CONCLUSION: The Age of New Boundaries 230

8 Medieval Empires and Borderlands: Byzantium and Islam 232
BYZANTIUM: THE SURVIVAL OF THE ROMAN EMPIRE 234
An Embattled Empire 234
Byzantine Civilization 236
The Macedonian Renaissance 242
THE NEW WORLD OF ISLAM 244
The Rise of Islam 245
ENCOUNTERS AND TRANSFORMATIONS: Ships of the Desert: Camels from Morocco to Central Asia 247
DIFFERENT VOICES: Christian and Muslim Justifications for Holy War 249
The Umayyad Caliphate 250
JUSTICE IN HISTORY: "Judgment Belongs to God Alone": Arbitration at Siffin 251
The Abbasid Caliphate 255
Islamic Civilization in Europe 256
CONCLUSION: Three Cultural Realms 259

9 Medieval Empires and Borderlands: The Latin West 262
THE BIRTH OF LATIN CHRISTENDOM 264
Germanic Kingdoms on Roman Foundations 264
Different Kingdoms, Shared Traditions 266
The Spread of Latin Christianity in the New Kingdoms of Western Europe 269
THE CAROLINGIANS 273
The Leadership of Charlemagne 273
The Division of Western Europe 277
INVASIONS AND RECOVERY IN THE LATIN WEST 278
The Polytheist Invaders of the Latin West 278
The Rulers in the Latin West 280
JUSTICE IN HISTORY: Revealing the Truth: Oaths and Ordeals 282
The Conversion of the Last Polytheists 285
THE WEST IN THE EAST: THE CRUSADES 287
The Origins of Holy War 287
DIFFERENT VOICES: Christian and Muslim Accounts of the Atrocities Crusaders Committed During the Fall of Jerusalem in 1099 289
Crusading Warfare 290
The Significance of the Crusades 291
ENCOUNTERS AND TRANSFORMATIONS: Legends of the Borderlands: Roland and El Cid 292
CONCLUSION: An Emerging Unity in the Latin West 294

10 Medieval Civilization: The Rise of Western Europe 296
TWO WORLDS: MANORS AND CITIES 298
The Medieval Agricultural Revolution 298
The Growth of Cities 301
THE CONSOLIDATION OF ROMAN CATHOLICISM 304
The Task of Church Reform 304
Discovering God in the World 310
JUSTICE IN HISTORY: Inquiring into Heresy: The Inquisition in Montaillou 314
STRENGTHENING THE CENTER OF THE WEST 316
The Monarchies of Western Europe 316

DIFFERENT VOICES: The Trial of the Knights Templar 319
MEDIEVAL CULTURE: THE SEARCH FOR UNDERSTANDING 319
Revival of Learning 320
Courtly Love 323
The Center of Medieval Culture: The Great Cathedrals 323
CONCLUSION: Asserting Western Culture 326

11 The Medieval West in Crisis 328
A TIME OF DEATH 329
Famine 330
The Black Death 330
A COLD WIND FROM THE EAST 334
The Mongol Invasions 335
The Rise of the Ottoman Turks 337
ENCOUNTERS AND TRANSFORMATIONS: The Silk Road 338
ECONOMIC DEPRESSION AND SOCIAL TURMOIL 341
The Collapse of International Trade and Banking 342
Workers' Rebellions 343
AN AGE OF WARFARE 344
The Fragility of Monarchies 344
The Hundred Years' War 345
JUSTICE IN HISTORY: The Trial of Joan of Arc 348
The Military Revolution 349
A TROUBLED CHURCH AND THE DEMAND FOR RELIGIOUS COMFORT 351
The Babylonian Captivity of the Church and the Great Schism 351
DIFFERENT VOICES: The Struggle over the Papal Monarchy 352
The Search for Religious Alternatives 353
THE CULTURE OF LOSS 355
Reminders of Death 355
Pilgrims of the Imagination 356
Defining Cultural Boundaries 358
CONCLUSION: Looking Inward 360

Glossary G-1
Suggestions for Further Reading R-1
Notes N-1
Photo Credits C-1
Index I-1

Each chapter concludes with the following: Making Connections, Taking It Further, Chapter Review, and Time Line.

MAPS

1 Core Lands of the West 6
1.1 The Beginnings of Civilization 12
1.2 The Beginnings of Food Production 13
1.3 Neolithic Cultures in Europe 16
1.4 Kingdoms and Empires in Southwest Asia 18
1.5 Egypt: The Old, Middle, and New Kingdoms 30
2.1 The International Bronze Age, ca. 1500–1100 B.C.E. 45
2.2 Southwest Asia in the Iron Age 58
2.3 Phoenician Expansion, ca. 900–600 B.C.E. 59
3.1 The Expansion of Greece in the Archaic and Classical Ages 82
3.2 The Persian Empire at Its Greatest Extent 88
3.3 The Peloponnesian War 96
4.1 The Conquests of Alexander the Great 116
4.2 Major Successor Kingdoms ca. 290 B.C.E. 120
4.3 Hellenistic Trade and Exploration 123
4.4 Celtic Expansion, Fifth to Third Century B.C.E. 125
5.1 Rome's Expansion in Italy 147
5.2 Roman Conquest During the Republic 150
6.1 The Roman Empire at Its Greatest Extent 171
6.2 The City of Rome, ca. 212 C.E. 174
6.3 Languages and Agriculture in the Roman Empire 178
6.4 The Silk Road 187
6.5 Palestine Under Roman Rule 194
7.1 The Roman Empire in Late Antiquity 205
7.2 Empire of the Huns 224
7.3 The Byzantine Empire at the Death of Justinian, 565 227
8.1 The Byzantine Empire, ca. 600 237
8.2 The Expansion of Islam: The Umayyad Caliphate, ca. 750 245
8.3 Christian Reconquest of Muslim Spain 259
9.1 Europe, ca. 750 264
9.2 Carolingian Empire 274
9.3 Invasions of Europe, Seventh Through Eleventh Centuries 278
9.4 The Major Crusades 288
10.1 European Fairs and Trade Routes 303
10.2 Universal Monarchy of Pope Innocent III 308
10.3 Western European Kingdoms in the Late Twelfth Century 317
11.1 Spread of the Black Death 331
11.2 The Mongol Empire, 1206–1405 335
11.3 The Ottoman Empire 339
11.4 The Hundred Years' War 346

DOCUMENTS

Note: The following documents are referenced in the margins of the text and are available at **www.myhistorylab.com**. Document titles bearing a red speaker are available with audio.

CHAPTER 1

A Visitor from the Neolithic Age 11
A Need to Remember 12
Redefining Self: From Tribe to Village to City 13
Sumerian Law Code: The Code of Lipit-Ishtar 19
Excerpts from the *Epic of Gilgamesh* 26
The Code of Hammurabi 28
An Egyptian Hymn to the Nile 29
Workings of *Ma'at*: The Tale of an Eloquent Peasant 30
Praise of the Scribe's Profession: An Egyptian Letter 32
Elders' Advice to Their Successors 32
Papyrus of Ani: The Egyptian Book of the Dead 39

CHAPTER 2

Ancient Egyptian and Hittite Voices 45
Hittite Law Code: Excerpts from the Code of the Nesilim 47
Homer: Debate among the Greeks at Troy 50
Mission to Byblos: The Report of Wenamun 59
The Babylonian Chronicles: The Fall of Nineveh Chronicle 63
Judaism Overview 69
Suffering Explained 75

CHAPTER 3

Homer *Iliad* (Eighth Century B.C.E.) 80
Aristotle: The Creation of the Democracy in Athens 86
Histories (400 B.C.E.) Herodotus 92
Pericles' Funeral Oration by Thucydides, ca. 420 B.C.E. 95
Education and the Family in Sparta, ca. 100 C.E. 98
Aristotle on Slavery (Fourth Century B.C.E.) 99
Aristophanes Argues Against the War, 411 B.C.E. 101
Herodotus on the Egyptians (Fifth Century B.C.E.) 103
Thucydides on Athens (Fifth Century B.C.E.) 103
Plato, *The Republic*, The Philosopher-King 104

CHAPTER 4

Maccabees: Resistance to Hellenization in the Hellenistic Period, ca. 100 B.C.E. 124
Polybius: Why Romans and Not Greeks Govern the World, ca. 140 B.C.E. 131

CHAPTER 5

Letters to Cicero, Fourteenth Century 155
Slaves in the Roman Countryside, ca. 150 B.C.E.–50 C.E. 157
Polybius: Why Romans and Not Greeks Govern the World, ca. 140 B.C.E. 167

CHAPTER 6

Excerpt from *The Roman Oration* by Aelius Aristides 170
Augustus on His Accomplishments 171
Slaves in the Roman Countryside 189
Juvenal, A Satirical View of Women 192
Judaism 195
Excerpt from the Gospel According to Luke 195
Christianity 196
Gnostic Teachings of Jesus, According to Irenaeus 198
Perpetua, The Autobiography of a Christian Martyr 198

CHAPTER 7

Eusebius of Caesarea, selections from *The Life of Constantine* 208
Pope Leo I on Bishop Hilary of Aries 209
Paulus Orosius, from *Seven Books of History Against the Pagans* 211
Benedict of Nursia, *The Rule* 215
Bishop Synesius of Cyrene, *Letter to His Brother* 221
Ammianus Marcellinus on the Huns 223
Sidonius Apollinaris, *Rome's Decay* and *A Glimpse of the New Order* 224
Excerpt from *The Governance of God* (5th Century C.E.) Salvian 224
Prologue of the *Corpus Juris Civilis*, ca. 530 226

CHAPTER 8

Ibn Fadlan's *Account of the Rus* 236
Liutprand of Cremona, *Report of His Mission to Constantinople*, 968 240

Epitome of the Iconoclastic Seventh Synod 754 241
The Qur'an 248
Al-Farabi on the Perfect State 254
Harun al-Rashid and the Zenith of the Caliphate 256
Ibn Khaldun, from the *Muqaddimah* 257

CHAPTER 9

Gregory of Tours, Sixth Century 265
The Confession of Saint Patrick 270
Bede, Conversion of England (582) 272
Excerpt from the Annals of St. Vaast (882–886) 279
Saga of Erik the Red (985) 280
Speculum Princips, "The Animal Life of Greenland and the Character of the Land in Those Regions" 280
Social Conditions in the Ninth Century 287

CHAPTER 10

Letter of Pope Gregory VII to the Bishop of Metz, 1081 306
The Battle of Hastings, 1066 317
The Magna Carta 318

CHAPTER 11

The Mongols: An Excerpt from the *Novgorod Chronicle*, 1315 337
Mehmed II (15th Century) Kritovoulos 340
An Ambassador's Report on the Ottoman Empire (1555) Ogier Ghiselin de Busbecq 341
Venetian Observations on the Ottoman Empire Late Sixteenth Century 341
Guilds: Regulating the Craft, 1347 343

Engage your students *beyond* the classroom . . .

. . . with MyHistoryLab and *THE WEST: Encounters and Transformations,* Fourth Edition

Would your students get more out of their introductory history course if you could engage them with history *beyond* the classroom? Would class discussion go farther if they were reading and writing more, working with primary sources, studying maps, and mastering key topics . . . *before* class meetings begin?

If your answer to these questions is yes, then it's time to consider how MyHistoryLab can help you meet these challenges. MyHistoryLab offers immersive content, tools, and experiences to engage students and help them succeed, enabling you to craft a better learning experience for them in your introductory survey course.

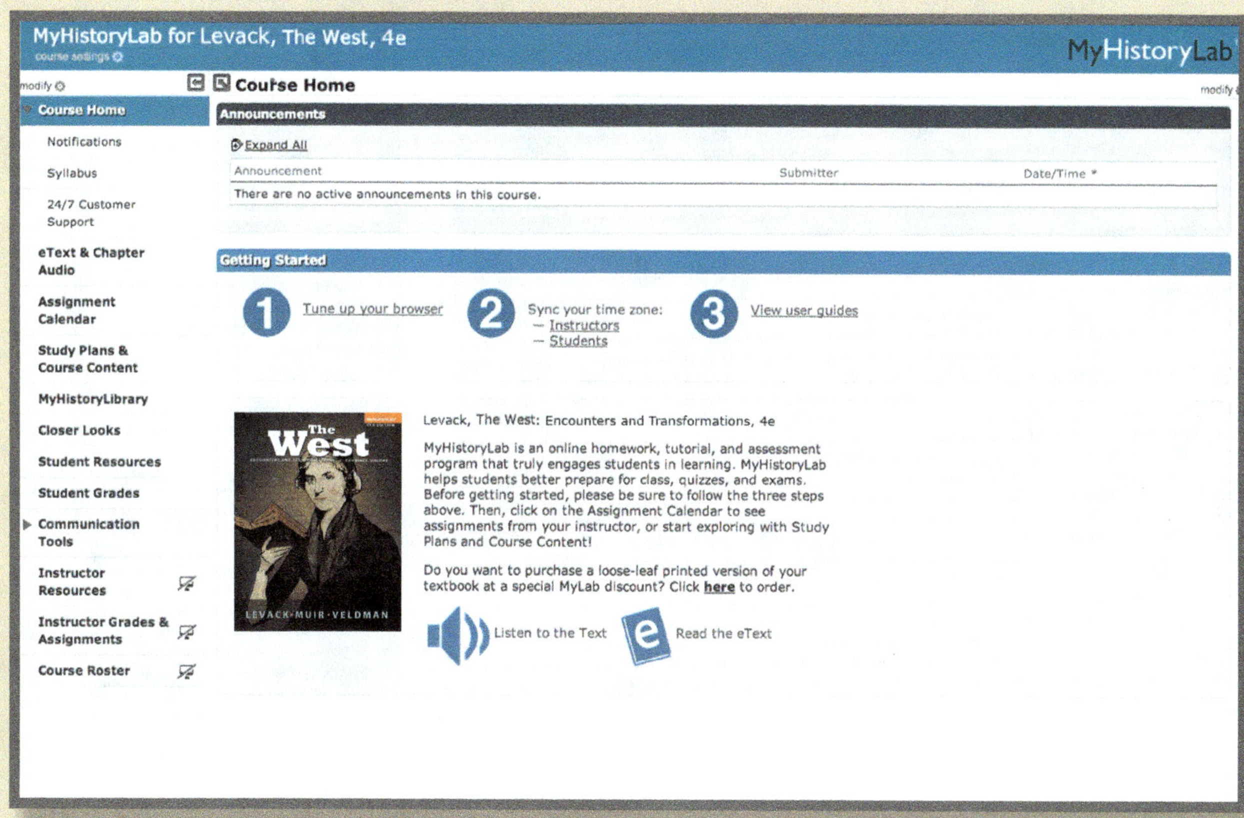

Prepare students on key topics with the MyHistoryLab Video Series

Are your introductory history students ready and eager to contend with a college textbook narrative? If not, help them get up-to-speed with the new MyHistoryLab Video Series: Key Topics in Western Civilization. Correlated to the chapters of *The West*, each video unit reviews key topics of the period, readying students to get the most from the text narrative. These engaging videos feature seasoned historians reviewing the pivotal stories of our past, in a lively format designed to demonstrate the power of historical narrative.

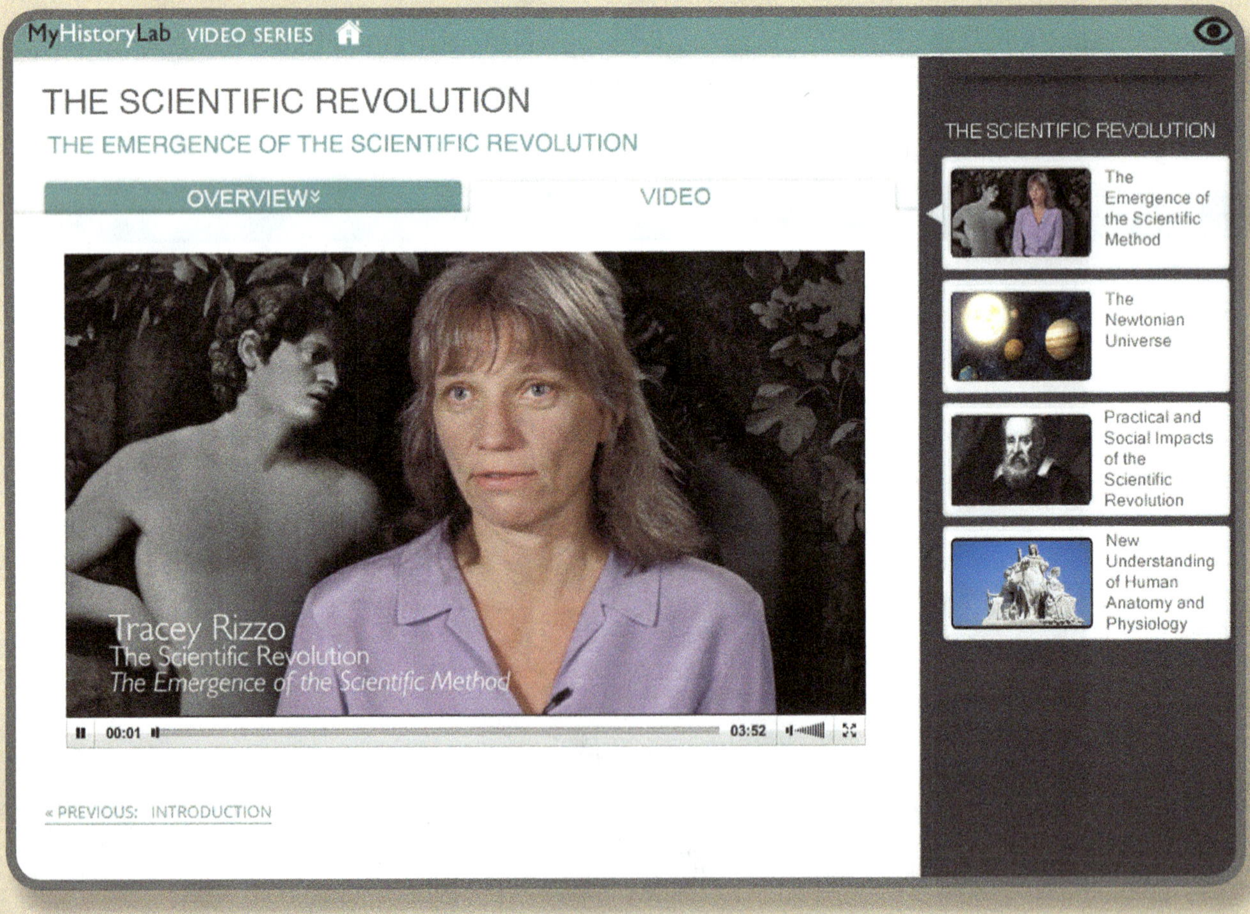

Drive your students into primary sources with the new MyHistoryLibrary

Now your students can read more than 200 of the most commonly assigned primary source documents, specially formatted in Pearson's powerful new eText. Students also have the option of listening to each reading in the accompanying Chapter Audio. Either way, students may access the text or the audio with various devices anytime they have access to the Internet.

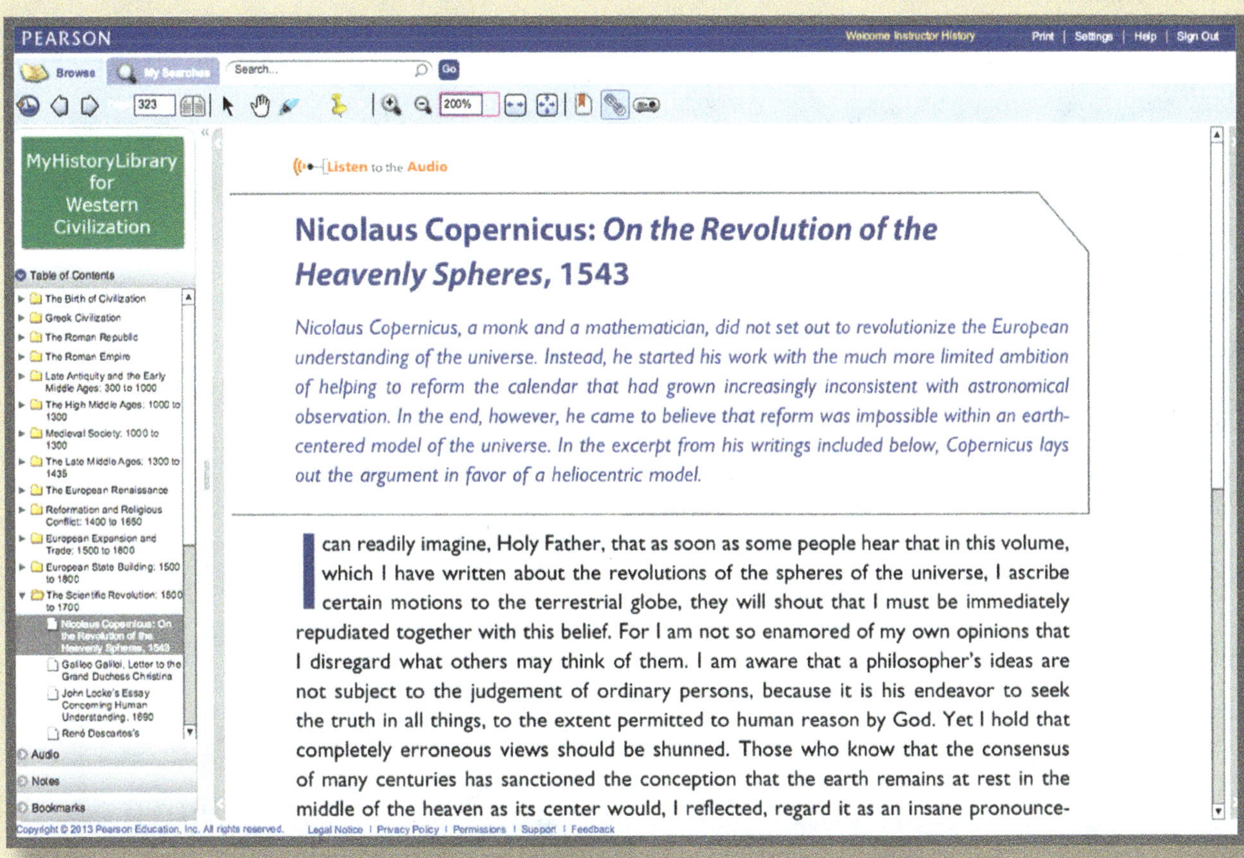

Immerse your students in a powerful eText deeply integrated with MyHistoryLab

Introductory survey teachers have long struggled to get students engaged in traditional textbooks. Now Pearson's MyHistoryLab offers a deeply immersive eText that transforms how students experience history. With a new pedagogically-driven design, it highlights a clear learning path through the material and offers a visually stunning learning experience in print or on a screen. With the Pearson eText, students can transition directly to MyHistoryLab resources such as primary source documents, videos, and Closer Look features. At last, history students can experience the eText they have been waiting for—one that comes alive on the screen.

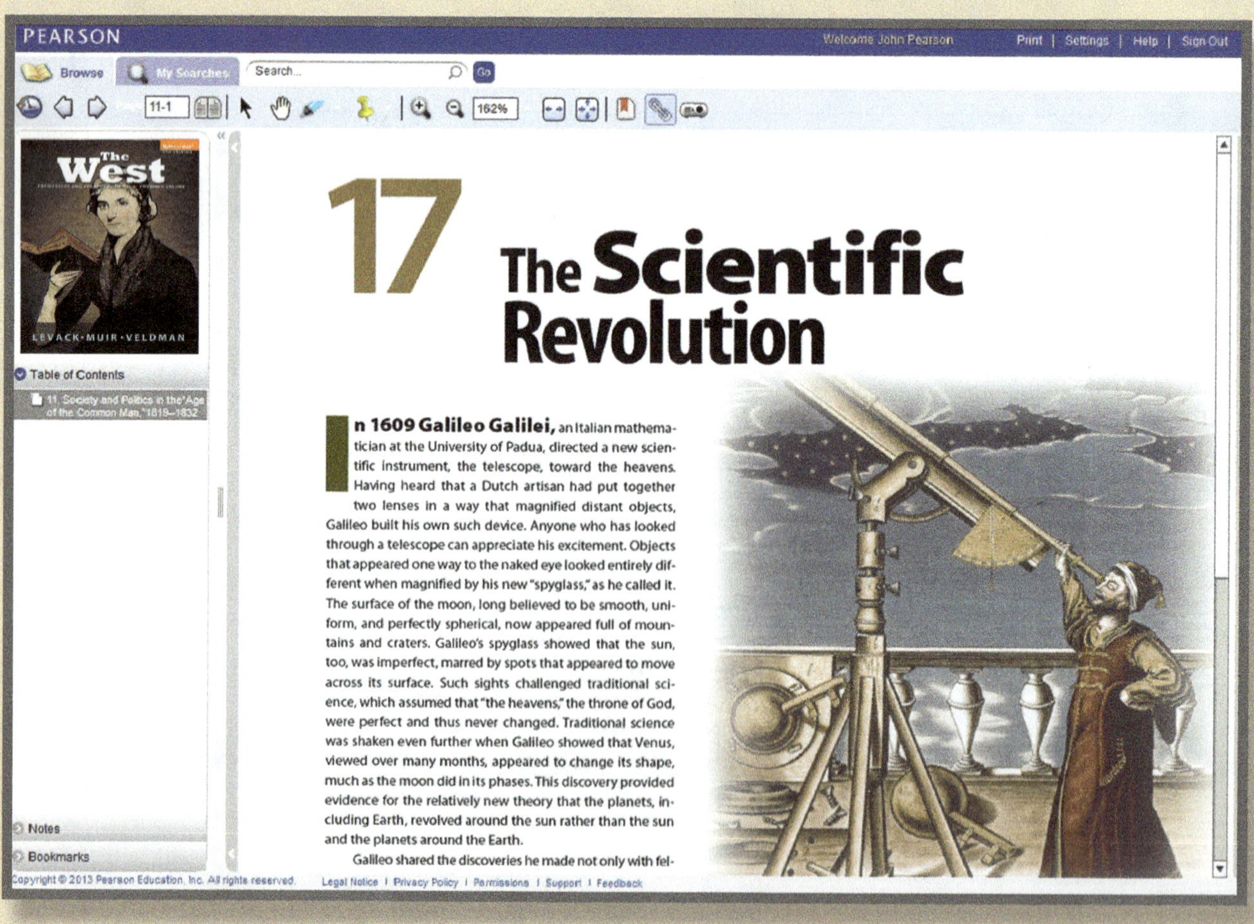

Key Supplements and Customer Support

Annotated Instructor's eText

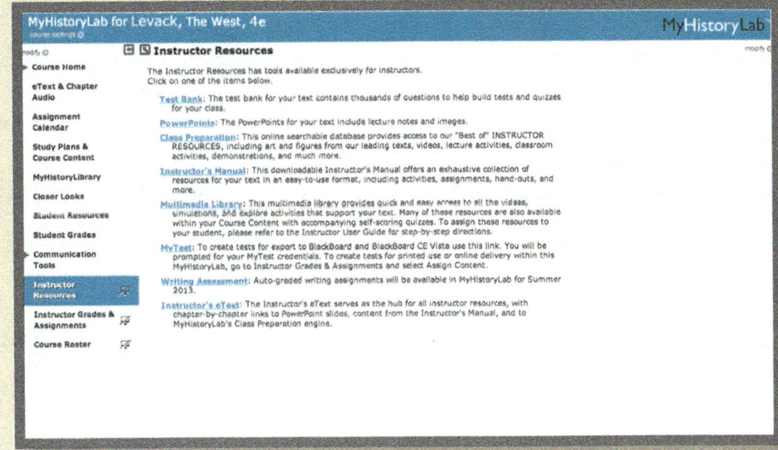

Contained within MyHistoryLab, the *Annotated Instructor's eText* for your Pearson textbook leverages the powerful Pearson eText platform to make it easier than ever for you to access subject-specific resources for class preparation. The *AI eText* serves as the hub for all instructor resources, with chapter-by-chapter links to PowerPoint slides, content from the Instructor's Manual, and *MyHistoryLab's* ClassPrep engine, which contains a wealth of history content organized for classroom use.

Instructor's Manual

The Instructor's Manual for *The West: Encounters and Transformations* contains learning objectives, a list of important themes discussed in the chapter, an overview of the Different Voices feature in the chapter, an annotated chapter outline with summaries of each section's content, suggestions for class activities, discussion questions, and suggestions for additional print and online resources for instructors. At the end of each chapter, MyHistoryLab Media Assignments catalog all of the MyHistoryLab resources for the chapter. The Instructor's Manual also contains a MyHistoryLab syllabus and suggestions for integrating MyHistoryLab into your course.

PowerPoint Presentations

Strong PowerPoint presentations make lectures more engaging for students. Correlated to the chapters of *The West*, each presentation includes a full lecture outline and a wealth of images, maps, and time lines from the textbook.

MyTest Test Bank

Containing a diverse set of multiple-choice, short-answer, and essay questions, the MyTest test bank supports a variety of assessment strategies. The large pool of multiple choice questions for each chapter includes factual, conceptual, and analytical questions, so that instructors may assess students on basic information as well as critical thinking.

Customer Support

Our dedicated team of local Pearson representatives will work with you not only to choose course materials but also to integrate them into your class and assess their effectiveness. Moreover, live support for MyHistoryLab users, both educators and students, is available 24/7.

Provide choices for your students through a variety of formats and price points

These alternatives to the traditional printed textbook are available for ***THE WEST: Encounters and Transformations,*** Fourth Edition.

>>> **MyHistoryLab with eTextbook** offers a full digital version of the print book and is readable on iOS and Android tablets. Students can get access to **MyHistoryLab** with the print book or save even more by purchasing on-line access at **www.myhistorylab.com**.

>>> **Books a la Carte** is a convenient, three-hole-punched, loose-leaf version of the traditional text at a discounted price—allowing students to carry only what they need to class. The Books a la Carte edition is also available with **MyHistoryLab** access.

>>> **Black & White Printed Textbook**, a discounted alternative, contains all the same content of the traditional text, rendered without color. To ensure full editorial integrity, some maps and illustrations in the Black & White edition have been redrawn. The Black & White edition is also available with **MyHistoryLab** access.

>>> **CourseSmart eTextbooks** offer the same content as the printed text in a convenient online format—with highlighting, online search, and printing capabilities. Learn more at **www.coursesmart.com**. **The CourseSmart eTextbook** is also available with **MyHistoryLab** access.

>>> **Pearson Custom Library** helps instructors build the perfect course solution. For enrollments of at least 25, create your own textbook by combining chapters from best-selling Pearson textbooks and reading selections. To begin building your custom text, visit **www.pearsoncustomlibrary.com**.

PREFACE

We wrote this textbook to answer questions about the identity of the civilization in which we live. Journalists, politicians, and scholars often refer to our civilization, its political ideologies, its economic systems, and its cultures as "Western" without fully considering what that label means and why it might be appropriate. The classification of our civilization as Western has become particularly problematic in the age of globalization. The creation of international markets, the rapid dissemination of ideas on a global scale, and the transmission of popular culture from one country to another often make it difficult to distinguish what is Western from what is not. *The West: Encounters and Transformations* offers students a history of Western civilization in which these issues of Western identity are given prominence. Our goal is neither to idealize nor to indict that civilization, but to describe its main characteristics in different historical periods.

The West: Encounters and Transformations gives careful consideration to two basic questions. The first is, how did the definition of the West change over time? In what ways did its boundaries shift and how did the distinguishing characteristics of its cultures change? The second question is, by what means did the West—and the idea of the West—develop? We argue that the West is the product of a series of cultural encounters that occurred both outside and within its geographical boundaries. We explore these encounters and the transformations they produced by detailing the political, social, religious, and cultural history of the regions that have been, at one time or another, a part of the West.

Considered as a geographical and cultural realm, *the West* is a term of recent origin, and the civilization to which it refers did not become clearly defined until the eleventh century, especially during the Crusades, when western European Christians developed a distinct cultural identity. Before that time we can only talk about the powerful forces that created the West, especially the dynamic interaction of the civilizations of western Europe, the Byzantine Empire, and the Muslim world.

Over the centuries Western civilization has acquired many salient characteristics. These include two of the world's great legal systems (civil law and common law), three of the world's monotheistic religions (Judaism, Christianity, and Islam), certain political and social philosophies, forms of political organization (such as the modern bureaucratic state and democracy), methods of scientific inquiry, systems of economic organization (such as industrial capitalism), and distinctive styles of art, architecture, and music. At times one or more of these characteristics has served as a primary source of Western identity: Christianity in the Middle Ages, science and rationalism during the Enlightenment, industrialization in the nineteenth and twentieth centuries, and a defense of individual liberty and democracy in the late twentieth century. These sources of Western identity, however, have always been challenged and contested, both when they were coming into prominence and when they appeared to be most triumphant. Western culture has never been monolithic; even today references to the West imply a wide range of meanings.

Defining the West

What is the West? How did it come into being? How has it developed throughout history? Many textbooks take for granted which regions or peoples of the globe constitute the West. They treat the history of the West as a somewhat expanded version of European history. While not disputing the centrality of Europe to any definition of the West, we contend that the West is not only a geographical realm with ever-shifting boundaries, but also a cultural realm, an area of cultural influence extending beyond the geographical and political boundaries of Europe. We so strongly believe in this notion that we have written the introductory essay "What Is the West?" to encourage students to think about their understanding of Western civilization and to guide their understanding of each chapter. Many of the features of what we call Western civilization originated in regions that are not geographically part of Europe (such as North Africa and the Middle East), while ever since the fifteenth century various social, ethnic, and political groups from non-European regions (such as North and South America, eastern Russia, Australia, New Zealand, and South Africa) have identified themselves, in one way or another, with the West. Throughout the text, we devote considerable attention to the boundaries of the West and show how borderlines between cultures have been created, especially in eastern and southeastern Europe.

Cultural Encounters

The definition of the West is closely related to the central theme of our book, which is the process of cultural encounters. Throughout *The West: Encounters and Transformations,* we examine the West as a product of a series of cultural encounters both outside the West and within it. We show that the West originated and developed through a continuous process of inclusion and exclusion resulting from a series of encounters among and within different groups. These encounters can be described in a general sense as external, internal, or ideological.

External Encounters

External encounters took place between peoples of different civilizations. Before the emergence of the West as a clearly defined entity, external encounters occurred between such diverse peoples as Greeks and Phoenicians, Macedonians and Egyptians, and Romans and Celts. After the eleventh century, external encounters between Western and non-Western peoples occurred mainly during periods of European exploration, expansion, and imperialism. In the sixteenth and seventeenth centuries, for example, a series of external encounters took place between Europeans on the one hand and Africans, Asians, and the indigenous people of the Americas on the other. Two chapters of *The West: Encounters and Transformations* (Chapters 13 and 18) and a large section of a third (Chapter 24) explore these external encounters in depth and discuss how they affected Western and non-Western civilizations alike.

Internal Encounters

Our discussion of encounters also includes similar interactions between different social groups *within* Western countries. These internal encounters often took place between dominant and subordinate groups, such as between lords and peasants, rulers and subjects, men and women, factory owners and workers, masters and slaves. Encounters between those who were educated and those who were illiterate, which recurred frequently throughout Western history, also fall into this category. Encounters just as often took place between different religious and political groups, such as between Christians and Jews, Catholics and Protestants, and royal absolutists and republicans.

Ideological Encounters

Ideological encounters involve interaction between comprehensive systems of thought, most notably religious doctrines, political philosophies, and scientific theories about the nature of the world. These ideological conflicts usually arose out of internal encounters, when various groups within Western societies subscribed to different theories of government or rival religious faiths. The encounters between Christianity and polytheism in the early Middle Ages, between liberalism and conservatism in the nineteenth century, and between fascism and communism in the twentieth century were ideological encounters. Some ideological encounters had an external dimension, such as when the forces of Islam and Christianity came into conflict during the Crusades and when the Cold War developed between Soviet communism and Western democracy in the second half of the twentieth century.

* * *

The West: Encounters and Transformations illuminates the variety of these encounters and clarifies their effects. By their very nature encounters are interactive, but they have taken different forms: They have been violent or peaceful, coercive or cooperative. Some have resulted in the imposition of Western ideas on areas outside the geographical boundaries of the West or the perpetuation of the dominant culture within Western societies. More often than not, however, encounters have resulted in a more reciprocal process of exchange in which both Western and non-Western cultures, or the values of both dominant and subordinate groups, have undergone significant transformation. Our book not only identifies these encounters, but also discusses their significance by returning periodically to the issue of Western identity.

Coverage

The West: Encounters and Transformations offers both comprehensive coverage of political, social, and cultural history and a broader coverage of the West and the world.

Comprehensive Coverage

Our goal throughout the text has been to provide comprehensive coverage of political, social, and cultural history and to include significant coverage of religious and military history as well. Political history defines the basic structure of the book, and some chapters, such as those on Hellenistic civilization, the age of confessional divisions, absolutism and state building, the French Revolution, and the coming of mass politics, include sustained political narratives. Because we understand the West to be a cultural as well as a geographical realm, we give a prominent position to cultural history. Thus, we include rich sections on Hellenistic philosophy and literature, the cultural environment of the Italian Renaissance, the creation of a new political culture at the time of the French Revolution, and the atmosphere of cultural despair and desire that prevailed in Europe after World War I. We also devote special attention to religious history, including the history of Islam as well as that of Christianity and Judaism. Unlike many other textbooks, our coverage of religion continues into the modern period. *The West: Encounters and Transformations* also provides extensive coverage of the history of women and gender. Wherever possible the history of women is integrated into the broader social, cultural, and political history of the period. But there are also separate sections on women in our chapters on classical Greece, the Renaissance, the Reformation, the Enlightenment, the Industrial Revolution, World War I, World War II, and the postwar era.

The West and the World

Our book provides broad geographical coverage. Because the West is the product of a series of encounters, the external areas with which the West interacted are of major importance. Three chapters deal specifically with the West and the world.

- Chapter 13, "The West and the World: The Significance of Global Encounters, 1450–1650"
- Chapter 18, "The West and the World: Empire, Trade, and War, 1650–1815"
- Chapter 24, "The West and the World: Cultural Crisis and the New Imperialism, 1870–1914"

These chapters present substantial material on sub-Saharan Africa, Latin America, the Middle East, India, and East Asia. Our text is also distinctive in its coverage of eastern Europe and the Muslim world, areas that have often been considered outside the boundaries of the West. These regions were arenas within which significant cultural encounters took place. Finally, we include material on the United States and Australia, both of which have become part of the West. We recognize that most American college and university students have the opportunity to study American history as a separate subject, but treatment of the United States as a Western nation provides a different perspective from that usually given in courses on American history. For example, this book treats America's revolution as one of four Atlantic revolutions, its national unification in the nineteenth century as part of a broader western European development, its pattern of industrialization as related to that of Britain, and its central role in the Cold War as part of an ideological encounter that was global in scope.

What's New to This Edition?

This edition of *The West: Encounters and Transformations* has been revised to reflect the latest developments in historical research and has added a host of new features to assist student learning. The most significant pedagogical innovation has been the seamless integration of documents, maps, videos, illustrations, and other resources from MyHistoryLab into the textbook. A new pedagogically driven design highlights a clear learning path through the material and offers a visually stunning learning experience in print or on a screen. With the Pearson eText, students can transition directly to MyHistoryLab resources such as primary source documents, videos, and maps.

Additionally, questions have been added to the captions of all the maps. The list of Suggested Readings has been revised and updated, and many of the terms in the Glossary have been edited to improve student comprehension.

Specific changes in the contents of this edition are as follows:

- Chapter 3 expands the discussion of Corinth and adds a new illustration linking the legendary wealth of that polis to its strategic geographical position.
- Chapter 4 refines the interpretation of Alexander the Great and directs the student to a Closer Look in MyHistoryLab that analyzes the famous mosaic of Alexander at the Battle of Issus.
- Chapter 5 uses new images from the Theater of Marcellus and the Parthenon to illustrate and clarify the differences between Greek and Roman architectural style.
- Chapter 7 refers students to several new documents about early Christianity in MyHistoryLab and a selection examining the role of religion in the fall of the Roman Empire.
- Chapter 8 clarifies the causes of the growing alienation between western and eastern rite Christians. It also discusses why, on the basis of the Qur'an, Muslims might disagree about the proper attitude they should take toward Jews and Christians.
- Chapter 9 revises the discussion of the differences between the status of Germanic and Roman women, providing a much more carefully nuanced picture. It takes account of the tremendous variation among the Germanic tribes in the status of women and pays more attention to class differences among women. The discussion of monastic life notes how monks did not just copy ancient texts but made their own significant intellectual contributions. The chapter offers an enriched discussion of Viking culture and technology.
- Chapter 10 expands the discussion of the papal monarchy.
- Chapter 11 employs the latest DNA research to revise the discussion of the epidemiology of the Black Death. Rather than leaving the cause of the Black Death as an open question, the new evidence gives greater support for the thesis that the high mortality came from a form of bubonic plague. The discussions of the Mongol Empire and the Silk Road have also been enriched, as has the account of medieval guilds.

Features and Pedagogical Aids

In writing this textbook we have endeavored to keep both the student reader and the classroom instructor in mind at all times. The text includes the following features and pedagogical aids, all of which are intended to support the themes of the book.

"What Is the West?"

The West: Encounters and Transformations begins with an essay to engage students in the task of defining the West and to introduce them to the notion of cultural encounters. "What Is the West?" guides students through the text by providing a framework for understanding how the West was shaped. Structured around the six questions of What? When? Where? Who? How? and Why?, this framework encourages students to think about their understanding of Western civilization. The essay serves as a blueprint for using this textbook.

"Encounters and Transformations"

These features, which appear in about half the chapters, illustrate the main theme of the book by identifying specific encounters and showing how they led to significant transformations in the cultures of the West. These features show, for example, how camels enabled encounters among nomadic tribes of Arabia, which led to the rapid spread of Islam; how the Mayans' interpretation of Christian symbols transformed European Christianity into a hybrid religion; how the importation of chocolate from the New World to Europe changed Western consumption patterns and the rhythms of the Atlantic economy; and how Picasso's encounter with African art contributed to the transformation of modernism. Each of these essays concludes with questions for discussion.

"Justice in History"

Found in every chapter, this feature presents a historically significant trial or episode in which different notions of justice (or injustice) were debated and resolved. The "Justice in History" features illustrate cultural encounters within communities as they try to determine the fate of individuals from all walks of life. Many famous trials dealt with conflicts over basic religious, philosophical, or political values, such as those of Socrates, Jesus, Joan of Arc, Martin Luther, Charles I, Galileo, and Adolf Eichmann. Other "Justice in History" features show how judicial institutions, such as the ordeal, the Inquisition, and revolutionary tribunals, handled adversarial situations in different societies. These essays, therefore, illustrate the way in which the basic values of the West have evolved through attempts to resolve disputes and conflict.

Each "Justice in History" feature includes two pedagogical aids. "For Discussion" helps students explore the historical significance of the episode just examined. These questions can be used in classroom discussion or as student essay topics. "Taking It Further" provides the student with a few references that can be consulted in connection with a research project.

"Different Voices"

Each chapter contains a feature consisting of two primary source documents that present different and often opposing views regarding a particular person, event, or development. An introduction to the documents provides the necessary historical context, identifies the authors of the documents, and suggests the different perspectives they take. A set of questions for discussion follows the two documents.

Questions for Discussion

This edition of *The West: Encounters and Transformations* offers many opportunities for students to address a variety of questions in each chapter.

- The main question that the chapter addresses appears after the introduction to each chapter.
- Each of the major sections of the chapter begins with the main question that the section addresses. These questions also appear at the bottom of the first page of the chapter under the "Learning Objectives" heading and are repeated in the Chapter Review at the end of the chapter.
- At the end of each chapter a set of questions under the heading "Making Connections" asks the student to think about some of the more specific issues discussed in the chapter.

- Each Encounters and Transformations, Justice in History, and Different Voices feature is followed by a set of questions under the heading "For Discussion."
- The caption for each map includes a question related to the map for which the text of the chapter provides an answer.

Maps and Illustrations

Artwork is a key component of our book. We recognize that many students often lack a strong familiarity with geography, and so we have taken great care to develop maps that help sharpen their geographic skills. Complementing the book's standard map program, we include maps focusing on areas outside the borders of Western civilization. More than 300 images of fine art and photos tell the story of Western civilization and help students visualize the past: the way people lived, the events that shaped their lives, and how they viewed the world around them.

Chronologies

Each chapter includes a varying number of chronologies in time line format that list the events relating to a particular topic discussed in the text. Chronologies present the sequence of events and can be helpful for purposes of review.

Key Terms and Glossary

We have sought to create a work that is accessible to students with little prior knowledge of the basic facts of Western history or geography. Throughout the book we have explained difficult concepts at length. For example, we present in-depth explanations of the concepts of Zoroastrianism, Neoplatonism, Renaissance humanism, the various Protestant denominations of the sixteenth century, capitalism, seventeenth-century absolutism, nineteenth-century liberalism and nationalism, fascism, and modernism. We have identified these concepts as key terms by printing them in bold in the narrative and defining them in the margins of the book. All key terms are listed in alphabetical order, together with their definitions, in the Glossary at the end of the book.

Suggested Readings

An annotated list of suggested readings for all the chapters appears at the end of the book. The items listed there are not scholarly works for the benefit of the instructor, but suggestions for students who wish to explore a topic in greater depth or to write a research paper. References to books or articles relevant to the subject of the "Justice in History" feature appear at the end of each feature under the heading "Taking It Further."

Chapter Reviews

At the end of each chapter, a Chapter Review revisits the questions that accompany each section heading and summarizes key concepts within the section that address these questions.

Time Lines

A time line at the end of each chapter lists important events discussed within the chapter.

A Note About Dates and Transliterations

In keeping with current academic practice, *The West: Encounters and Transformations* uses B.C.E. (before the common era) and C.E. (common era) to designate dates. We also follow the most current and widely accepted English transliterations of Arabic. *Qur'an*, for example, is used for *Koran; Muslim* is used for *Moslem.* Chinese words appearing in the text for the first time are written in pinyin, followed by the older Wade-Giles system in parentheses.

Acknowledgments

We are grateful to Jeff Lasser for guiding us through the long process of preparing the fourth edition and Rob DeGeorge for his help in selecting the illustrations and preparing the manuscript for publication.

We would like to thank the following reviewers for their helpful suggestions: Frank Biletz, Loyola University, Chicago; Julian Bourg, Boston College; Jace Crouch, Oakland University; Stephanie Annette Finley-Croswhite, Old Dominion University; Nichole Gotschall, Columbia Southern University; Derrick Griffey, Gadsden State Community College; Erik Heinrichs, Bridgewater State University; Carol Herringer, Wright State University; Stephanie Lamphere, Sierra College; Alison Williams Lewin, Saint Joseph's University; Erik Lindseth, Indiana University; Michael Martin, Fort Lewis College; Lindsey McNellis, University of Central Florida; Patricia O'Neill, Central Oregon Community College; Karen Sonnelitter, Purdue University; Tamrala Swafford, Columbia Southern University; Tom Ward, Spring Hill College; Bradley Woodworth, University of New Haven; and Terry Young, Patrick Henry Community College.

We would also like to thank the following friends and colleagues for their valuable advice and suggestions: Gabor Agoston, Catherine Clinton, Catherine Evtuhov, Wojciech Falkowski, Benjamin Frommer, Andrzej Kaminski, Adam Kozuchowski, Christopher Lazarski, David Lindenfeld, Suzanne Marchand, John McNeill, John Merriman, James Miller, Daria Nalecz, Karl Roider, Steven Ross, and Mark Steinberg. Finally, we wish to thank Graham Nichols for his telecommunications assistance and expertise.

ABOUT THE AUTHORS

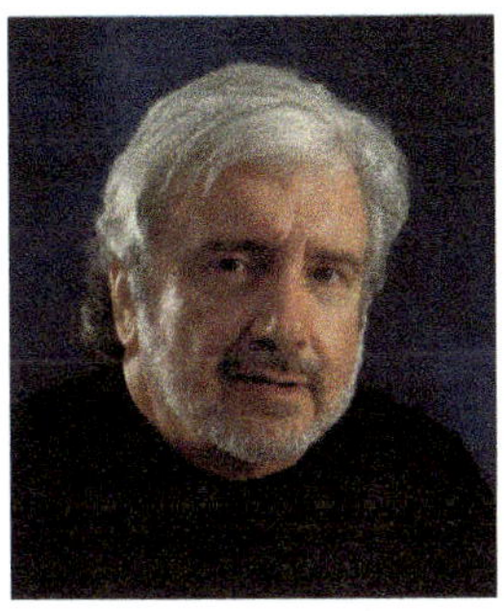

Brian Levack grew up in a family of teachers in the New York metropolitan area. From his father, a professor of French history, he acquired a love for studying the past, and he knew from an early age that he too would become a historian. He received his B.A. from Fordham University in 1965 and his Ph.D. from Yale in 1970. In graduate school he became fascinated by the history of the law and the interaction between law and politics, interests that he has maintained throughout his career. In 1969 he joined the history department of the University of Texas at Austin, where he is now the John Green Regents Professor in History. The winner of several teaching awards, Levack teaches a wide variety of courses on British and European history, legal history, and the history of witchcraft. For eight years he served as the chair of his department, a rewarding but challenging assignment that made it difficult for him to devote as much time as he wished to his teaching and scholarship. His books include *The Civil Lawyers in England, 1603–1641: A Political Study* (1973), *The Formation of the British State: England, Scotland and the Union, 1603–1707* (1987), *The Witch-Hunt in Early Modern Europe* (3rd edition, 2006), and *Witch-Hunting in Scotland: Law, Politics, and Religion* (2008).

His study of the development of beliefs about witchcraft in Europe over the course of many centuries gave him the idea of writing a textbook on Western civilization that would illustrate a broader set of encounters between different cultures, societies, and ideologies. While writing the book, Levack and his two sons built a house on property that he and his wife, Nancy, own in the Texas hill country. He found that the two projects presented similar challenges: It was easy to draw up the design, but far more difficult to execute it. When not teaching, writing, or doing carpentry work, Levack runs along the jogging trails of Austin and has recently discovered the pleasures of scuba diving.

Edward Muir grew up in the foothills of the Wasatch Mountains in Utah, close to the Emigration Trail along which wagon trains of Mormon pioneers and California-bound settlers made their way westward. As a child he loved to explore the broken-down wagons and abandoned household goods left at the side of the trail and from that acquired a fascination with the past. Besides the material remains of the past, he grew up with stories of his Mormon pioneer ancestors and an appreciation for how the past continued to influence the present. During the turbulent 1960s, he became interested in Renaissance Italy as a period and place that had been formative for Western civilization. His biggest challenge was finding the time to explore yet another new corner of Italy and its restaurants.

Muir received his Ph.D. from Rutgers University, where he specialized in the Italian Renaissance and did archival research in Venice and Florence, Italy. He is now the Clarence L. Ver Steeg Professor in the Arts and Sciences at Northwestern University and former chair of the history department. At Northwestern he has won several teaching awards. His books include *Civic Ritual in Renaissance Venice* (1981), *Mad Blood Stirring: Vendetta in Renaissance Italy* (1993 and 1998), *Ritual in Early Modern Europe* (1997 and 2005), and *The Culture Wars of the Late Renaissance: Skeptics, Libertines, and Opera* (2007). His books have also been published in Italian.

Some years ago Muir began to experiment with the use of historical trials in teaching and discovered that students loved them. From that experience he decided to write this textbook, which employs trials as a central feature. He lives beside Lake Michigan in Evanston, Illinois. His twin passions are skiing in the Rocky Mountains and rooting for the Chicago Cubs, who manage every summer to demonstrate that winning isn't everything.

Meredith Veldman grew up in the western suburbs of Chicago, where she learned to love winter and the Cubs—which might explain her preference for all things improbable and impractical. Certainly that preference is what attracted her to the study of history, filled as it is with impractical people doing the most improbable things. Veldman majored in history at Calvin College in Grand Rapids, Michigan, and then earned a Ph.D. in modern European history, with a concentration in nineteenth- and twentieth-century Britain, from Northwestern University in 1988.

As an associate professor of history at Louisiana State University, Veldman teaches courses in nineteenth- and twentieth-century British history and twentieth-century Europe, as well as the second half of "Western Civ." In her many semesters in the Western Civ. classroom, Veldman tried a number of different textbooks but found herself increasingly dissatisfied. She wanted a text that would convey to beginning students at least some of the complexities and ambiguities of historical interpretation, introduce them to the exciting work being done in cultural history, and, most important, tell a good story. The search for this textbook led her to accept the offer Levack and Muir made to join them in writing *The West: Encounters and Transformations.*

An award-winning teacher, Veldman is also the author of *Fantasy, the Bomb, and the Greening of Britain: Romantic Protest, 1945–1980* (1994) and *Margaret Thatcher: Shaping the New Conservatism* (2014). She and her family ride out the hurricanes in Baton Rouge, Louisiana. She remains a Cubs fan and she misses snow.

What Is the West?

Many of the people who influence public opinion—politicians, teachers, clergy, journalists, and television commentators—refer to "Western values," "the West," and "Western civilization." They often use these terms as if they do not require explanation. But what do these terms mean? The West has always been an arena within which different cultures, religions, values, and philosophies have interacted; any definition of the West will inevitably arouse controversy.

The definition of the West has always been disputed. Note the difference in the following two poems, the first by Rudyard Kipling (1865–1936), an ardent promoter of European imperialism who wrote "The Ballad of East and West" at the height of the British Empire:

> OH, East is East, and West is West, and never the twain shall meet,
> Till Earth and Sky stand presently at God's great Judgment Seat. . . .

The second, "East/West Poem," is by a Chinese-American living in Hawaii, Wing Tek Lum (1946–), who expresses the confusion caused by terms that designate both cultural traits and directions around the globe:

> O
> East is East
> and
> West is West.
> but
> I never did
> understand
> why
> in Geography class
> the East was west
> and
> the West was east
> and that no
> one ever
> cared
> about the difference.

This textbook cares about the difference. It also shows that East and West have, in contrast to Kipling's view, often "met." These encounters created the idea of the East and the West and helped identify the ever shifting borders between the two.

The Shifting Borders of the West

The most basic definition of the West is of a place. Western civilization is now typically thought to comprise the regions of Europe, the Americas, Australia, and New Zealand. However, this is a contemporary definition of the West. The inclusion of these places in the West is the result of a long history of European expansion through colonization and conquest.

This textbook begins about 10,000 years ago in what is now Iraq; the final chapter returns to discuss the Iraq War, but in the meantime the Mesopotamian region is only occasionally a concern for Western history. The history of the West begins with the domestication of animals, the cultivation of the first crops, and the establishment of long-distance trading networks in the Tigris, Euphrates, and Nile River valleys. Cities, kingdoms, and empires in those valleys gave birth to the first civilizations in the West. By about 500 B.C.E., the civilizations that were the cultural ancestors of the modern West had spread from southwestern Asia and north Africa to include the entire Mediterranean basin—areas influenced by Egyptian, Hebrew, Greek, and Roman thought, art, law, and religion. The resulting Greco-Roman culture created the most enduring foundation of the West. By the first century C.E. the Roman Empire drew the map of what historians consider the heartland of the West: most of western and southern Europe, the coastlands of the Mediterranean Sea, and the Middle East.

For many centuries, these ancient foundations defined the borders of the West. During the last century, however, the West came to be less about geography than about culture, identity, and technology. When Japan, an Asian country, accepted human rights and democracy after World War II, did it become part of the West? Most Japanese might not think they have adopted "Western" values, but the thriving capitalism and stable democracy of this traditional Asian country that was never colonized by a European power complicates the idea of what is the West. Or consider the Republic of South Africa, which the white minority—people descended from European immigrants—ruled until 1994. The oppressive white regime violated human rights, rejected full legal equality for all citizens, and jailed or murdered those who questioned the government. Only when democratic elections open to blacks replaced that government did South Africa fully embrace what the rest of the West would consider Western values. To what degree was South Africa part of the West before and after these developments?

THE TEMPLE OF HERA AT PAESTUM, ITALY Greek colonists in Italy built this temple in the sixth century B.C.E. Greek ideas and artistic styles spread throughout the ancient world, both from Greek colonists, such as those at Paestum, and from other peoples who imitated the Greeks.

Or how about Russia? Russia long saw itself as a Christian country with cultural, economic, and political ties with the rest of Europe. The Russians have intermittently identified with their Western neighbors, especially during the reign of Peter the Great (1682–1725), but their neighbors were not always sure about the Russians. After the Mongol invasions of the thirteenth and fourteenth centuries much of Russia was isolated from the rest of the West, and during the Cold War from 1949 to 1989 Western democracies considered communist Russia an enemy. When was Russia "Western" and when not?

Thus, when we talk about where the West is, we are almost always talking about the Mediterranean basin and much of Europe (and later, the Americas). But we will also show that countries that border "the West," and even countries far from it, might be considered Western in many aspects as well.

WHERE IS THE WEST? The shifting borders of the West have moved many times throughout history, but they have always included the areas shown in this satellite photo. These include Europe, north Africa, and the Middle East.

Changing Identities Within the West

In addition to being a place, the West is the birthplace of Western civilization, a civilization that encompasses a cultural history—a tradition stretching back thousands of years to the ancient world. Over this long period the civilization we now identify as Western gradually took shape. The many characteristics that identify it emerged over this time: forms of governments, economic systems, and methods of scientific inquiry, as well as religions, languages, literature, and art.

Throughout the development of Western civilization, the ways in which people identified themselves changed as well. People in the ancient world had no such idea of the common identity of the West, only of being members of a tribe, citizens of a town, or subjects of an empire. But with the spread of Christianity and Islam between the first and seventh centuries, the notion of a distinct civilization in these "Western" lands subtly changed. People came to identify themselves less as subjects of a particular empire and more as members of a community of faith—whether that community comprised followers of Judaism, Christianity, or Islam. These communities of faith drew lines of inclusion and exclusion that still exist today. Starting about 1,600 years ago, Christian monarchs and clergy began to obliterate polytheism (the worship of many gods) and marginalize Jews. From 1,000 to 500 years ago, Christian authorities fought to expel Muslims from Europe. Europeans developed definitions of the West that did not include Islamic communities, even though Muslims continued to live in Europe, and Europeans traded and interacted with the Muslim world. The Islamic countries themselves erected their own barriers, seeing themselves in opposition to the Christian West, even as they continued to look back to the common cultural origins in the ancient world that they shared with Jews and Christians.

MARINER'S COMPASS The mariner's compass was a navigational device intended for use primarily at sea. The compass originated in China; once adopted by Europeans, it enabled them to embark on long ocean voyages around the world.

During the Renaissance in the fifteenth century, these ancient cultural origins became an alternative to religious affiliation for thinking about the identity of the West. From this Renaissance historical perspective Jews, Christians, and Muslims descended from the cultures of the ancient Egyptians, Hebrews, Greeks, and Romans. Despite their differences, the followers of these religions shared a history. In fact, in the late Renaissance a number of Jewish and Christian thinkers imagined the possibility of rediscovering the single universal religion that they thought must have once been practiced in the ancient world. If they could just recapture that religion, they could restore the unity they imagined had once prevailed in the West.

The definition of the West has also changed as a result of European colonialism, which began about 500 years ago. When European powers assembled large overseas empires, they introduced Western languages, religions, technologies, and cultures to many distant places in the world, making Western identity a transportable concept. In some of these colonized areas—such as North America, Argentina, Australia, and New Zealand—the European newcomers so outnumbered the indigenous people that these regions became as much a part of the West as Britain, France, and Spain. In other European colonies, especially on the Asian continent, Western cultures failed to exercise similar levels of influence.

As a result of colonialism Western culture sometimes merged with other cultures, and in the process, both were changed. Brazil, a South American country inhabited by large numbers of indigenous peoples, the descendants of African slaves, and European settlers, epitomizes the complexity of what defines the West. In Brazil, almost everyone speaks a Western language (Portuguese), practices a Western religion (Christianity), and participates in Western political and economic institutions (democracy and capitalism). Yet in Brazil all of these features of Western civilization have become part of a distinctive culture in which indigenous, African, and European elements have been blended. During Carnival, for example, Brazilians dressed in indigenous costumes dance in African rhythms to the accompaniment of music played on European instruments.

Western Values

For many people today, the most important definition of the West involves adherence to "Western" values. The values typically identified as Western include democracy, individualism, universal human rights, toleration of religious diversity, ownership of private property, equality before the law, and freedom of inquiry and expression. These values, however, have not always been part of Western civilization. In fact, they describe ideals rather than actual realities; these values are by no means universally accepted throughout the West. Thus, there is nothing inevitable about these values; Western history at various stages exhibited quite different ones. Western societies seldom prized legal or political equality until quite recently. In ancient Rome and throughout most of medieval Europe, the wealthy and the powerful enjoyed more protection under the law than did slaves or the poor. Most medieval Christians were completely convinced of the virtue of making war against Muslims and heretics and curtailing the actions of Jews. Before the end of the eighteenth century, few Westerners questioned the practice of slavery and a social hierarchy of birth that remained powerful in the West through the nineteenth century; in addition, most women were excluded from equal economic and educational opportunities until well into the twentieth century. In many places women still do not have equal opportunities. In the twentieth century, millions of Westerners followed leaders who stifled free inquiry, denied basic human rights to many of their citizens, made terror an instrument of the state, and censored authors, artists, and journalists. The Holocaust, fascism, and communism were Western phenomena.

The values that define the West have not only changed over time, they also remain fiercely contested. One of the most divisive political issues today, for example, is that of "gay marriage." Both sides in this debate frame their arguments in terms of "Western values." Supporters of the legalization of same-sex marriages highlight equality and human rights: They demand that all citizens have equal access to the basic legal protections afforded by marriage. Opponents emphasize the centrality of the tradition of monogamous heterosexual marriage to Western legal, moral, and religious codes. What this current debate shows us is that no single understanding of "Western values," or of the West itself, exists. These values have always been contended, disputed, and fought over. In other words, they have a history. This text highlights and examines that history.

Asking the Right Questions

So how can we make sense of the West as a place and an identity, the shifting borders and definitions of the West, and Western civilization in general? In short, what has Western civilization been over the course of its long history—and what is it today?

Answering these questions is the challenge this book addresses. There are no simple answers to any of these questions, but there is a method for finding answers. The method is straightforward. Always ask the *what, when, where, who, how,* and *why* questions of the text.

The *What* Question

What is Western civilization? The answer to this question will vary according to time and place. In fact, for much of the early history covered in this book, "Western civilization" did not exist. Rather, a number of distinctive civilizations emerged in the Middle East, northern Africa, and Europe, each of which contributed to what later became Western civilization. As these cultures developed and intermingled, the idea of Western civilization slowly began to form. Thus, the understanding of Western civilization will change from chapter to chapter. The most extensive change in the place of the West was through the colonial expansion of the European nations between the fifteenth and twentieth centuries. Perhaps the most significant cultural change came with acceptance of the values of scientific inquiry for solving human and philosophical problems, an approach that did not exist before the seventeenth century but became one of the distinguishing characteristics of Western civilization. During the late eighteenth and nineteenth centuries, industrialization became the engine that drove economic development in the West. During the twentieth century, industrialization in both its capitalist and communist forms dramatically gave the West a level of economic prosperity unmatched in the non-industrialized parts of the world.

The *When* Question

When did the defining characteristics of Western civilization first emerge, and for how long did they prevail? Dates frame and organize the content of each chapter, and numerous short timelines are offered. These resources make it possible to keep track of what happened when. Dates have no meaning by themselves, but the connections *between* them can be very revealing. For example, dates show that the agricultural revolution that permitted the birth of the first civilizations unfolded over a long span of about 10,000 years—which is more time than was taken by all the other events and developments covered in this textbook. Wars of religion plagued Europe for nearly 200 years before Enlightenment thinkers articulated the ideals of religious toleration. The American Civil War—the war to preserve the union, as President Abraham Lincoln termed it—took place at exactly the same time as wars were being fought for national unity in Germany and Italy. In other words, by paying attention to other contemporaneous wars for national unity, the American experience seems less peculiarly an American event.

By learning *when* things happened, one can identify the major causes and consequences of events and thus see the transformations of Western civilization. For instance, the production of a surplus of food through agriculture and the domestication

MAP 1 CORE LANDS OF THE WEST These are the principal geographical features that will appear recurrently throughout this book.

of animals were prerequisites for the emergence of civilizations. The violent collapse of religious unity after the Protestant Reformation in the sixteenth century led some Europeans to propose the separation of church and state two centuries later. And during the nineteenth century many Western countries—in response to the enormous diversity among their own peoples—became preoccupied with maintaining or establishing national unity.

The *Where* Question

Where has Western civilization been located? Geography, of course, does not change very rapidly, but the idea of where the West is does change. By tracing the shifting relationships between the West and other, more distant civilizations with which it interacted, the chapters highlight the changing "where" of the West. The key to understanding the shifting borders of the West is to study how the peoples within the West thought of themselves and how they identified others as "not Western." During the Cold War, for example, many within the West viewed Russia as an enemy rather than as part of the West. In the previous centuries, Australia and North America came to be part of the West because the European conquerors of these regions identified themselves with European cultures and traditions and against non-European values.

The *Who* Question

Who were the people responsible for making Western civilization? Some were anonymous, such as the unknown geniuses who invented the mathematical systems of ancient Mesopotamia. Others are well-known—saints such as Joan of Arc, creative thinkers such as Galileo Galilei, or generals such as Napoleon. Most were ordinary. Humble people, such as the many millions who migrated from Europe to North America or the unfortunate millions who suffered and died in the trenches of World War I, also influenced the course of events.

Perhaps most often this book encounters people who were less the shapers of their own destinies than the subjects of forces that conditioned the kinds of choices they could make, often with unanticipated results. During the eleventh century when farmers throughout Europe began to employ a new kind of plow to till their fields, they were merely trying to do their work more efficiently. They certainly did not recognize that the increase in food they produced would stimulate the enormous population growth that made possible the medieval civilization of thriving cities and magnificent cathedrals. Answering the *who* question requires an evaluation of how much individuals and groups of people were in control of events and how much events controlled them.

The *How* Question

How did Western civilization develop? This is a question about processes—about how things change or stay the same over time. This book identifies and explores these processes in several ways.

First, woven throughout the story is *the theme of encounters and transformations.* What is meant by encounters? When the Spanish *conquistadores* arrived in the Americas some 500 years ago, they came into contact with the cultures of the Caribs, the Aztecs, the Incas, and other peoples who had lived in the Americas for thousands of years. As the Spanish fought, traded with, and intermarried with the natives, each culture changed. The Spanish, for their part, borrowed from the Americas new plants for cultivation and responded to what they considered serious threats to their worldview. Many native Americans, in turn, adopted European religious practices and learned to speak European languages. At the same time, Amerindians were decimated by European diseases, illnesses to which they had never been exposed. The native Americans also witnessed the destruction of their own civilizations and governments at the hands of the colonial powers. Through centuries of interaction and mutual influence, both sides became something other than what they had been.

The European encounter with the Americas is an obvious example of what was, in fact, a continuous process of encounters with other cultures. These encounters often occurred between peoples from different civilizations, such as the struggles between Greeks and Persians in the ancient world or between Europeans and Chinese in the nineteenth century. Other encounters took place among people living in the same civilization. These include interactions between lords and peasants, men and women, Christians and Jews, Catholics and Protestants, factory owners and workers, and capitalists and communists. Western civilization developed and changed, and still does, through a series of external and internal encounters.

Second, *features in the chapters* formulate answers to the question of how Western civilization developed. For example, each chapter contains an essay titled *Justice in History*. These essays discuss a trial or some other episode involving questions of justice. Some *Justice in History* essays illustrate how Western civilization was forged in struggles over conflicting values, such as the discussion of the trial of Galileo, which examines the conflict between religious and scientific concepts of truth. Other essays show how efforts to resolve internal cultural, political, and religious tensions helped shape Western ideas about justice, such as the essay on the *auto da fé*, which illustrates how authorities attempted to enforce religious conformity.

Some chapters include another feature as well. The *Encounters and Transformations* features show how encounters between different groups of people, technologies, and ideas were not abstract historical processes, but events that brought people together in a way that transformed history. For example, when the Arabs encountered the camel as an instrument of war, they adopted it for their own purposes. As a result, they were able to conquer their neighbors very quickly and spread Islam far beyond its original home in Arabia.

The *Different Voices* feature in each chapter includes documents from the period that represent contrasting views about a particular issue important at the time. These conflicting voices demonstrate how people debated what mattered to them and in the process formulated what have become Western values. During the Franco-Algerian War of the 1950s and early 1960s, for example, French military officers debated the appropriateness of torture when interrogating Algerian prisoners alleged to be insurgents. The debate about the use of torture against terrorist suspects continues today, revealing one of the unresolved conflicts over the appropriate values of the West.

The *Why* Question

Why did things happen in the way they did in history? This is the hardest question of all, one that engenders the most debate among historians. To take one persistent example, why did Hitler initiate a plan to exterminate the Jews of Europe? Can it be explained by something that happened to him in his childhood? Was he full of self-loathing that he projected onto the Jews? Was it a way of creating an enemy so that he could better unify Germany? Did he really believe that the Jews were the cause of all of Germany's problems? Did he merely act on the deeply seated anti-Semitic tendencies of the German people? Historians still debate the answers to these questions.

Such questions raise issues about human motivation and the role of human agency in historical events. Can historians ever really know what motivated a particular individual in the past, especially when it is so notoriously difficult to understand what motivates other people in the present? Can any individual determine the course of history? The *what, when, where, who,* and *how* questions are much easier to answer; but the *why* question, of course, is the most interesting one, the one that cries out for an answer.

This book does not—and cannot—always offer definitive answers to the *why* question, but it attempts to lay out the most likely possibilities. For example, historians do not really know what disease caused the Black Death in the fourteenth century that killed about one-third of the population in a matter of months. But they can answer many questions about the consequences of that great catastrophe. Why were there so many new universities in the fourteenth and fifteenth centuries? It was because so many priests had died in the Black Death, creating a huge demand for replacements. The answers to the *why* questions are not always obvious, but they are always intriguing; finding the answers is the joy of studying history.

1 The Beginnings of Civilization, 10,000–1150 B.C.E.

In 1991 hikers toiling across a glacier in the Alps between Austria and Italy made a startling discovery: a man's body stuck in the ice. They alerted the police, who soon turned the corpse over to archaeologists. The scientists determined that the middle-aged man had frozen to death about 5,300 years ago. Ötzi the Ice Man (his name comes from the Ötztal Valley where he perished) quickly became an international celebrity. The scientists who examined Ötzi believe that he was a shepherd leading flocks of sheep and goats to mountain pastures when he died. Grains of wheat on his clothing suggested that he lived in a farming community. Copper dust in his hair hinted that Ötzi may also have been a metalworker, perhaps looking for ores during his journey. An arrowhead lodged in his back indicated a violent death, but the circumstances remain mysterious.

Ötzi's gear was state-of-the-art for his time. His possessions showed deep knowledge of the natural world. He wore leather boots insulated with dense grasses chosen for protection against the cold. The pouch around his waist contained stone tools and fire-lighting equipment. The wood selected for his bow offered strength and flexibility. In his light wooden backpack, Ötzi carried containers to hold burning embers and dried meat and seeds to eat on the trail. The arrows in his quiver featured a natural adhesive that tightly bound bone and wooden points to the shafts. The most noteworthy find among Ötzi's possessions

LEARNING OBJECTIVES

1.1 What is the link between the food-producing revolution of the Neolithic era and the emergence of civilization?

1.2 What changes and continuities characterized Mesopotamian civilization between the emergence of Sumer's city-states and the rise of Hammurabi's Babylonian Empire?

1.3 What distinctive features characterized Egyptian civilization throughout its long history?

 Listen to Chapter 1 on MyHistoryLab

THE THINKER OF CERNEVODA While most surviving Neolithic art focuses on the central concerns of hunting and fertility, this terracotta sculpture depicts a figure deep in thought, Just 4½ inches high, this piece was created between 5250 and 4500 B.C.E. and found at a Neolithic site in Romania.

1.1
1.2
1.3

Watch the Video Series on MyHistoryLab

Learn about some key topics related to this chapter with the *MyHistoryLab Video Series: Key Topics in Western Civilization*

was his axe. Its handle was made of wood, but its head was copper, a remarkable innovation at a time when most tools were made of stone. Ötzi was ready for almost anything—except the person who shot him in the back.

Ötzi lived at a transitional moment, at the end of what archaeologists call the **Neolithic Age**, or "New Stone Age," a long period of revolutionary change lasting from about 10,000 to about 3000 B.C.E. in which many thousands of years of human interaction with nature led to food production through agriculture and the domestication of animals. This chapter begins with this most fundamental encounter of all—that between humans and the natural world.

Neolithic Age The New Stone Age, characterized by the development of agriculture and the use of stone tools.

A Visitor from the Neolithic Age

The achievement of food production let humans develop new, settled forms of communities—and then civilization itself. The growth of civilization also depended on constant interaction among communities that lived far apart. Once people were settled in a region, they began trading for commodities that were not available in their homelands. As trade routes extended over long distances and interactions among diverse peoples proliferated, ideas and technology spread.

This chapter focuses on two questions: How did the encounters between early human societies create the world's first civilizations? And, what was the relationship between these civilizations and what would become the "West"?

Defining Civilization, Defining Western Civilization

1.1 What is the link between the food-producing revolution of the Neolithic era and the emergence of civilization?

Anthropologists use the term **culture** to describe all the different ways that humans collectively adjust to their environment, organize their experiences, and transmit their knowledge to future generations. Culture serves as a web of interconnected meanings that enable individuals to understand themselves and their place in the world. Archaeologists define **civilization** as an urban culture with differentiated levels of wealth, occupation, and power. One archaeologist notes that the "complete checklist of civilization" contains "cities, warfare, writing, social hierarchies, [and] advanced arts and crafts."[1] With cities, human populations achieved the critical mass necessary to develop specialized occupations and a level of economic production high enough to sustain complex religious and cultural practices—and to wage war. To record these economic, cultural, and military interactions, writing developed. Social organization grew more complex. The labor of most people supported a small group of political, military, and religious leaders. These leaders controlled not only government and warfare, but also the distribution of food and wealth. They augmented their authority by building monuments to the gods and participating in religious rituals that

culture The knowledge and adaptive behavior created by communities that helps them to mediate between themselves and the natural world through time.

civilization The term used by archaeologists to describe a society differentiated by levels of wealth and power, and in which military, religious, economic, and political control are based in cities.

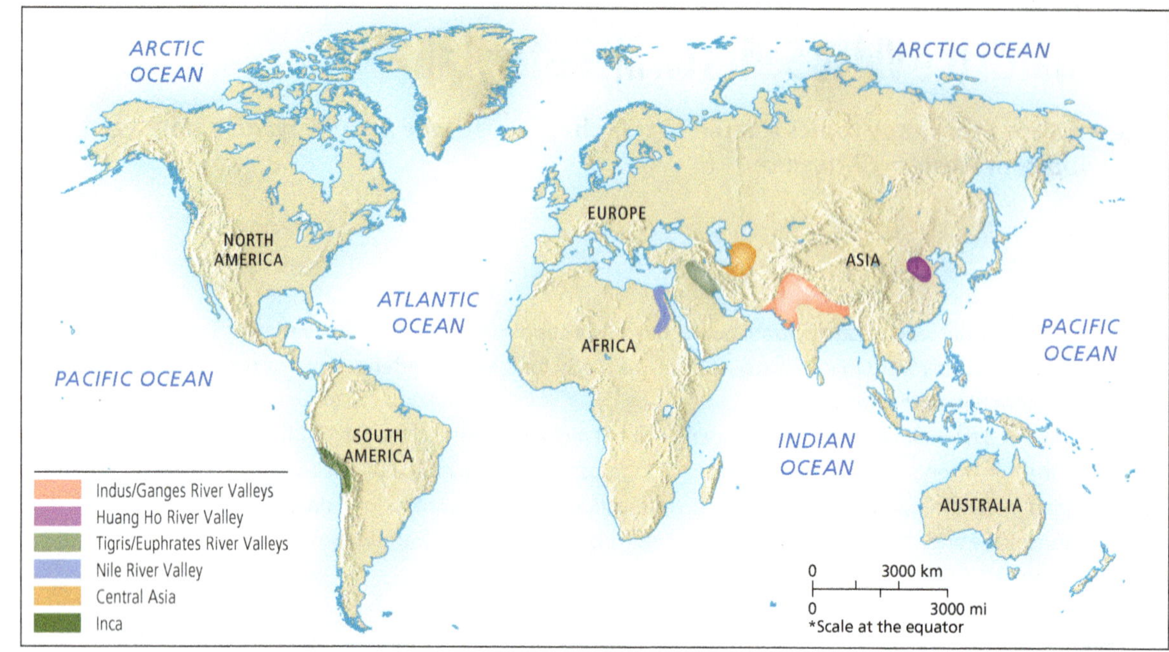

MAP **1.1** THE BEGINNINGS OF CIVILIZATION Civilizations developed independently in India, China, central Asia, and Peru, as well as in Egypt and southwest Asia. Western civilization, however, is rooted in the civilizations that first emerged in Egypt and southwest Asia. What five features make up the "complete checklist of civilization"?

linked divinity with kingship and military prowess. Thus, in early civilizations four kinds of power—military, economic, political, and religious—converged.

As **Map 1.1** shows, a number of civilizations developed independently of each other across the globe. This chapter focuses on the Mesopotamian and Egyptian civilizations because many of the characteristics of "Western civilization" originated in these areas. The history of Western civilization thus begins not in Europe, the core territory of the West today, but in what we usually call the Middle East and what ancient historians call the "Near East."* By 2500 B.C.E., when, as we will see, city-states in Mesopotamia formed a flourishing civilization and Egypt's Old Kingdom was well-developed, Europeans still lived only in scattered agricultural communities. Without the critical mass of people and possessions that accompanied city life, early Europeans did not develop the specialized religious, economic, and political classes that characterize a civilization.

Ideas

Making Civilization Possible: The Food-Producing Revolution

Homo sapiens sapiens Scientific term meaning "most intelligent people"; applied to physically and intellectually modern human beings that first appeared between 200,000 and 100,000 years ago in Africa.

A Need to Remember

For more than the first 175,000 years of their existence, modern humans, known as ***Homo sapiens sapiens*** ("most intelligent people"), did not produce food. Between 200,000 and 100,000 years ago, *Homo sapiens sapiens* first appeared in Africa and began to spread to other continents. Scientists refer to this stage of human history as the Paleolithic Age, or Old Stone Age, because people made tools by cracking rocks and using their sharp edges to cut and chop. These early peoples scavenged for wild food and followed migrating herds of animals. They also created beautiful works of art by carving bone and painting on cave walls. By 45,000 years ago, these humans had reached most of Earth's habitable regions.

*Terms such as the "Near East," the "Middle East," and the "Far East"—China, Japan, and Korea—betray their Western European origins. For someone in India, say, or Russia or Australia, neither Mesopotamia nor Egypt is located to the "east."

The end of the last Ice Age about 15,000 years ago ushered in an era of momentous change: the food-producing revolution. As the Earth's climate became warmer, cereal grasses spread over large areas. Hunter-gatherers learned to collect these wild grains and grind them up for food. When people learned that the seeds of wild grasses could be transplanted and grown in new areas, the cultivation of plants was underway.

People also began domesticating pigs, sheep, goats, and cattle, which eventually replaced wild game as the main sources of meat. The first signs of goat domestication occurred about 8900 B.C.E. in the Zagros Mountains in southwest Asia. Pigs, which adapt well to human settlements because they eat garbage, were first domesticated around 7000 B.C.E. By around 6500 B.C.E., domestication had become widespread.

Farming and herding were hard work, but the payoff was enormous. Even simple agricultural methods could produce about 50 times more food than hunting and gathering. Thanks to the increased food supply, more newborns survived past infancy. Populations expanded, and so did human settlements. With the mastery of food production, human societies developed the mechanisms not only to feed themselves, but also to produce a surplus, which allowed for economic specialization and fostered the growth of social, political, and religious hierarchies.

Read the Document

Redefining Self: From Tribe to Village to City

The First Food-Producing Communities

The world's first food-producing communities emerged in southwest Asia. People began cultivating food in three separate areas, shown on **Map 1.2**. Archaeologists have named the first area the **Levantine Corridor** (also known as the **Fertile Crescent**)—a 25-mile-wide strip of land that runs from the Jordan River valley of modern Israel and Palestine to the Euphrates River valley in today's Iraq.* The second region was the hilly land north of Mesopotamia at the base of the Zagros Mountains. The third was Anatolia, or what is now Turkey.

Levantine Corridor Also known as the Fertile Crescent, this arc of land stretching from the Jordan River to the Euphrates River was the place where food production and settled communities first appeared in southwest Asia (the Middle East).

Fertile Crescent Also known as the Levantine Corridor, this 25-mile-wide arc of land stretching from the Jordan River to the Euphrates River was the place where food production and settled communities first appeared in southwest Asia (the Middle East).

MAP **1.2** THE BEGINNINGS OF FOOD PRODUCTION This map shows early farming sites where the first known production of food occurred in ancient southwest Asia. What were the three areas in which people first began cultivating food?

*The term *Levant* refers to the eastern Mediterranean coastal region. "Levant" comes from the French: "the rising [sun]"—in other words, the territory to the east, where the sun rises.

The small settlement of Abu Hureyra near the center of the Levantine Corridor illustrates how agriculture developed. Humans first settled here around 9500 B.C.E. They fed themselves primarily by hunting gazelles and gathering wild cereals. But sometime between 8000 and 7700 B.C.E., they began to plant and harvest grains. Eventually they discovered that crop rotation—planting different crops in a field each year—resulted in a much higher yield. By 7000 B.C.E. Abu Hureyra had grown into a farming community, covering nearly 30 acres that sustained a population of about 400. A few generations later, the inhabitants of Abu Hureyra began herding sheep and goats to supplement their meat supply. These domesticated animals became the community's primary source of meat when the gazelle herds were depleted about 6500 B.C.E.

Families in Abu Hureyra lived in small, rectangular dwellings containing several rooms. Archaeological evidence shows that many women in the community developed arthritis in their knees, probably from crouching for hours on end to grind grains. Thus, we assume that while men hunted and harvested, women prepared food. The division of labor along gender lines indicates a growing complexity of social relations within the community.

Similar patterns of agricultural development characterized the early histories of other regions in southwest Asia. By 6000 B.C.E., for example, the Anatolian town of Çatal Hüyük (meaning "Fork Mound") consisted of 32 acres of tightly packed rectangular mud houses that the townspeople rebuilt more than a dozen times as their population expanded. About 6,000 people lived in houses built so closely together that residents could only enter their homes by walking along the rooftops and climbing down a ladder set in the smoke hole. Such a set-up, while physically uncomfortable, also strengthened Çatal Hüyük's security from outside attack. Archaeologists have

View the Closer Look Çatal Hüyük

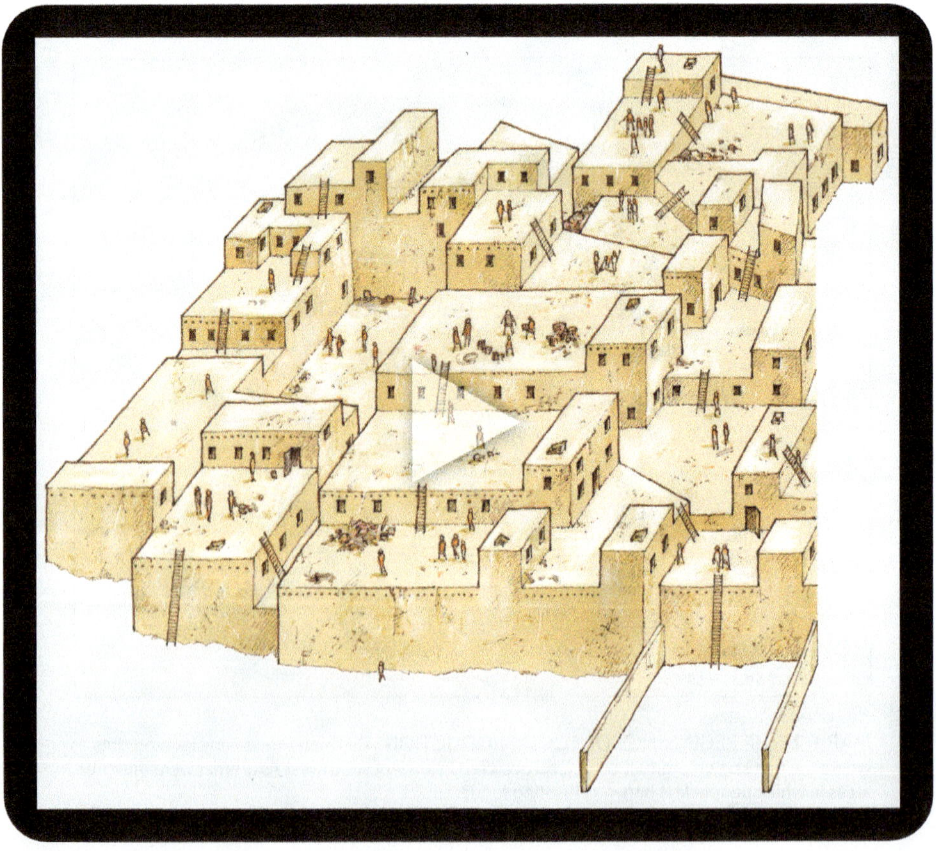

ÇATAL HÜYÜK This drawing illustrates archaeologists' reconstruction of Çatal Hüyük. In such a settlement, modern conceptions of privacy and self-determination would have been inconceivable.

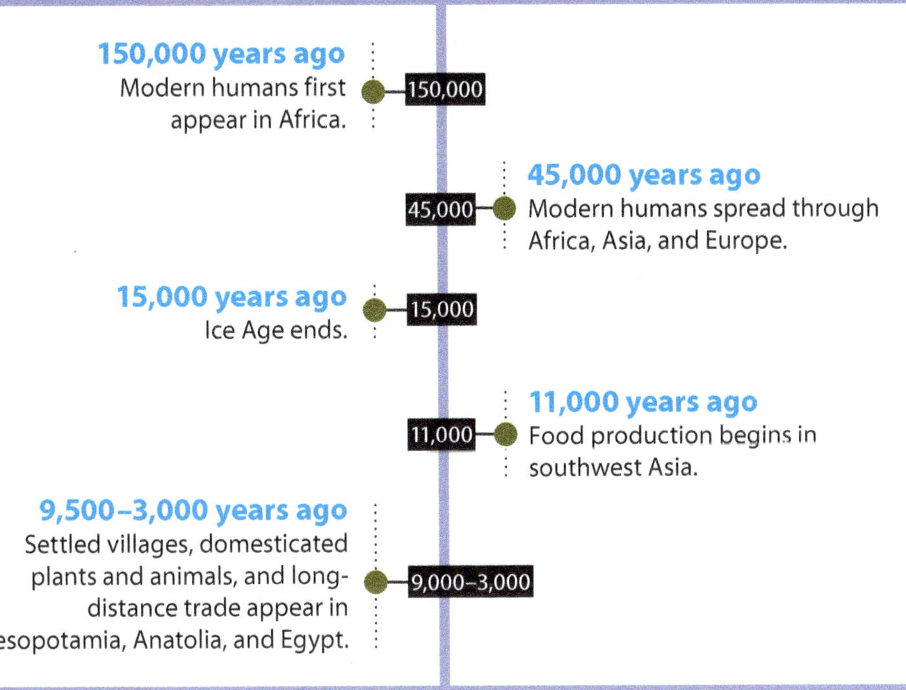

uncovered about 40 rooms that served as religious shrines. The paintings and engravings on the walls of these rooms focus on the two main concerns of ancient societies: fertility and death. In these scenes, vultures scavenge on human corpses while women give birth to bulls (associated with virility). These shrines also contain statues of goddesses whose exaggerated breasts and buttocks indicate the importance of fertility rites in the villagers' religious rituals.

Only a wealthy community could allow some people to work as artists or priests rather than as farmers, and Çatal Hüyük was wealthy by the standards of its era. Much of its wealth rested on trade in obsidian. This volcanic stone was the most important commodity in the Neolithic Age because it could be used to make sharp-edged tools such as arrowheads, spear points, and sickles for harvesting crops. Çatal Hüyük controlled the obsidian trade from Anatolia to the Levantine Corridor. With increasing wealth came widening social differences. While most of the burial sites at Çatal Hüyük showed little variation, a few corpses were buried with jewelry and other riches, a practice that indicates the beginning of distinctions between wealthy and poor members of the society.

The long-distance obsidian trade that underlay Çatal Hüyük's wealth also sped up the development of other food-producing communities in the Levantine Corridor, the Zagros Mountains, and Anatolia. These trade networks of the Neolithic Age laid the foundation for the commercial and cultural encounters that fostered the world's first civilization.

Transformations in Europe

In all of these developments, Europe remained far behind. The colder and wetter European climate meant heavier soils that were harder to cultivate than those in the Near East. The food-producing revolution that began in southwest Asia around 8000 B.C.E. did not spread to Europe for another thousand years, when farmers, probably from Anatolia, ventured to northern Greece and the Balkans. Settled agricultural communities had become the norm in southwest Asia by 6000 B.C.E., but not until about 2500 B.C.E. did most of Europe's hunting and gathering cultures give way to small, widely dispersed farming communities. (See **Map 1.3.**)

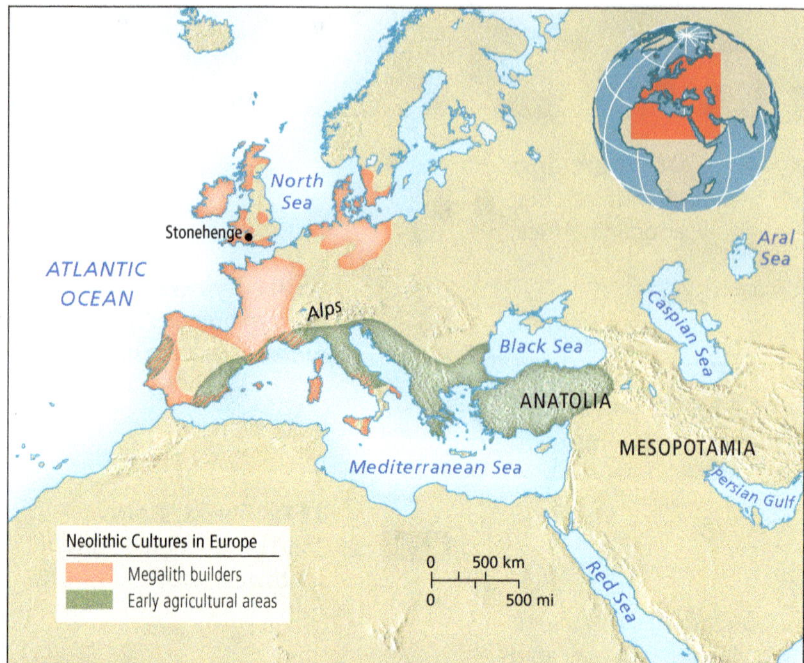

MAP **1.3** NEOLITHIC CULTURES IN EUROPE During the Neolithic period, new cultures developed as most of the peoples of Europe changed their way of life from hunting and gathering to food production. What features characterized these early European societies?

As farmers and herders spread across Europe, people adapted to different climates and terrain. A variety of cultures evolved from these differences but most shared the same basic characteristics: Early Europeans farmed a range of crops and herded domesticated animals. They lived in villages, clusters of permanent family farmsteads. Jewelry and other luxury goods left in women's graves might indicate that these village societies granted high status to women, perhaps because these communities traced ancestry through mothers.

Two important technological shifts ushered in significant economic and social change in these early European groups. The first was metallurgy, the art of using fire to shape metals. Knowledge of metallurgy spread slowly across Europe from the Balkans, where people started to mine copper about 4500 B.C.E. Jewelry made from copper and gold became coveted luxury goods. As trade in metals flourished, long-distance trading networks evolved. These networks provided the basis for the meeting and blending of different groups of peoples and different cultural assumptions and ideas.

The introduction of the plow was the second significant technological development for early Europe. The plow, invented in Mesopotamia in the late fifth or early fourth millennium B.C.E., became widely used in Europe around 2600 B.C.E. The use of plows meant that fewer people were needed to cultivate Europe's heavy soils. With more people available to clear forest lands, farming communities expanded and multiplied, as did opportunities for individual initiative and the accumulation of wealth.

As a result of these developments—and as had occurred much earlier in the Near East—the social structure within European villages became more stratified, with growing divisions between the rich and the poor. From the evidence of weaponry buried in graves, we know that the warrior emerged as a dominant figure in these early European societies. With the growing emphasis on military power, women's status may have declined.

These early Europeans constructed enduring monuments that offer tantalizing glimpses of their cultural practices and religious beliefs. Around 4000 B.C.E. Europeans began building communal tombs with huge stones called **megaliths**. Megaliths were constructed from Scandinavia to Spain and on islands in the western Mediterranean. The best-known megalith construction is Stonehenge in England. People began to

megalith A very large stone used in prehistoric European monuments between 5000 and 1500 B.C.E.

STONEHENGE This megalithic monument in southern England consists of two circles of standing stones with large blocks capping the circles. It was built without the aid of wheeled vehicles or metal tools, and the stones were dragged from many miles away.

build Stonehenge about 3000 B.C.E. as a ring of pits. The first stone circle of "bluestones," hauled all the way from the Welsh hills, was constructed about 2300 B.C.E. Only an advanced level of engineering expertise, combined with a high degree of organization of labor, made such construction possible.

The purpose of these magnificent constructions remains controversial. Some archaeologists argue that Stonehenge was used to measure the movement of stars, the sun, and the planets. Others view it as principally a place for religious ceremonies. Recent excavations suggest a third possibility: Stonehenge may have been a complex devoted to healing ceremonies. All three theories could be correct, for ancient peoples commonly associated healing and astronomical observation with religious belief and practice.

If we recall the "complete checklist" needed for a civilization—"cities, warfare, writing, social hierarchies, [and] advanced arts and crafts"[2]—we can see that by 1600 B.C.E., Europeans had checked off all of these requirements except cities and writing—both crucial for building human civilizations. The rest of this chapter, then, will focus not on Europe, but on the dramatic developments in southwest Asia and Egypt from the sixth millennium B.C.E. on.

Mesopotamia: Kingdoms, Empires, and Conquests

1.2 What changes and continuities characterized Mesopotamian civilization between the emergence of Sumer's city-states and the rise of Hammurabi's Babylonian Empire?

Long before the early Europeans living in Britain began to build Stonehenge, the first civilization and the world's first empires emerged on the Mesopotamian floodplain. Standing at the junction of the three continents of Africa, Asia, and Europe, southwest Asia became the meeting place of peoples, technologies, and ideas.

1.1

1.2

1.3

The Sumerian Kingdoms

About 5300 B.C.E. the villages in Sumer in southern Mesopotamia began a dynamic civilization that would flourish for thousands of years. The key to Sumerian civilization was water. Without a regular water supply, villages and cities could not have survived in Sumer. The name *Mesopotamia*, an ancient Greek word, means "the land between the rivers." Nestled between the Tigris and Euphrates Rivers, Sumerian civilization developed as its peoples learned to control the rivers that both enabled and imperiled human settlement.

The Tigris and Euphrates are unpredictable water sources, prone to sudden, powerful, and destructive flooding. Sumerian villagers first built their own levees for flood protection and dug their own small channels to divert floodwaters from the two great rivers to irrigate their dry lands. Then they discovered that by combining the labor force of several villages, they could build and maintain levee systems and irrigation channels on a large scale. Villages merged into cities that became the foundation of Sumerian civilization, as centralized administrations developed to manage the dams, levees, and irrigation canals; to direct the labor needed to maintain and expand the water works; and to distribute the resources that the system produced.

By 2500 B.C.E., about 13 major city-states—perhaps as many as 35 in all—managed the Mesopotamian floodplain in an organized fashion. (See **Map 1.4**.) In Sumer's city-states, the urban center directly controlled the surrounding countryside. Uruk, "the first city in human history,"[3] covered about two square miles and had a population of approximately 50,000 people, including both city-dwellers and the peasants living in small villages in a radius of about 10 miles around the city.

Sumer's cities served as economic centers where craft specialists such as potters, toolmakers, and weavers gathered to swap information and trade goods. Long-distance

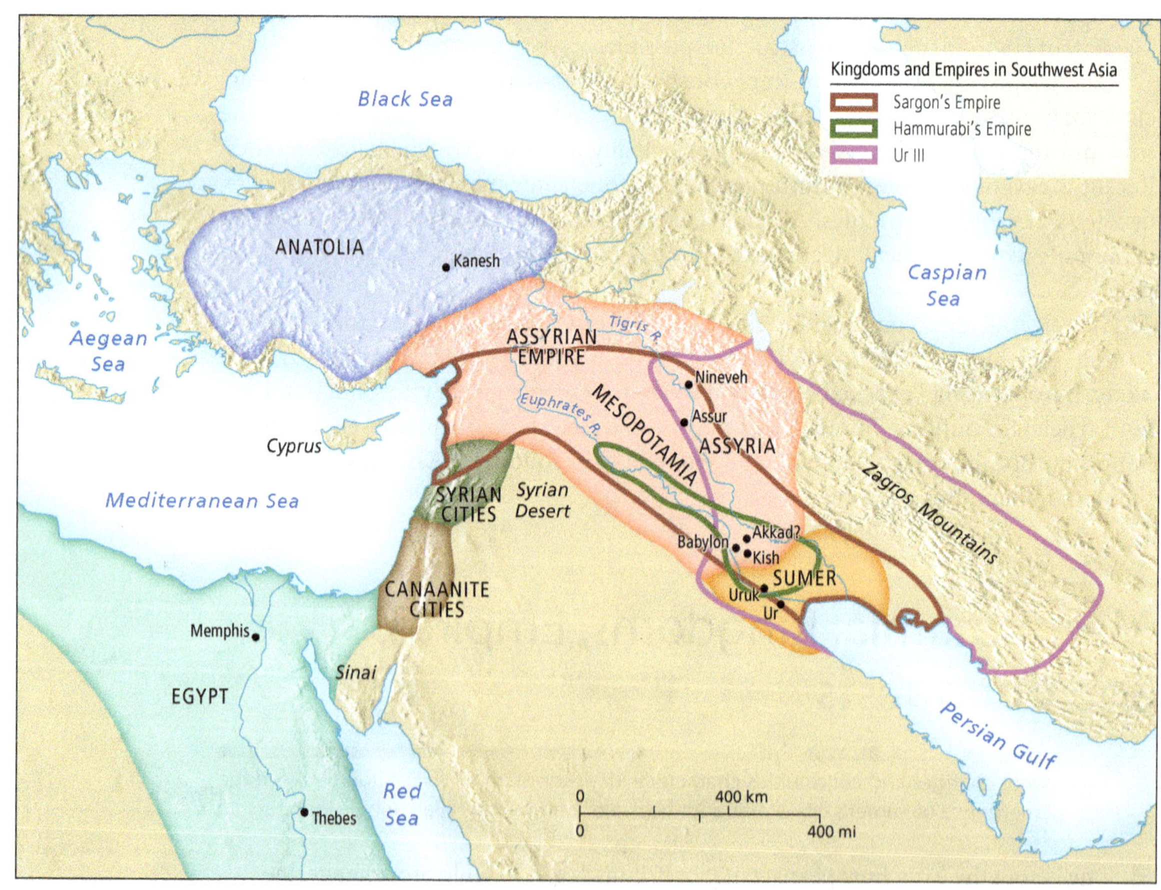

MAP **1.4** KINGDOMS AND EMPIRES IN SOUTHWEST ASIA Between 3000 and 1500 B.C.E., the Sumerian city-states, Sargon's Akkadian Empire, Hammurabi's empire in Babylon, and the Ur III dynasty emerged in southwest Asia. What features did these four different political entities share?

trade, made easier by the introduction of wheeled carts, enabled merchants to bring timber, ores, building stone, and luxury items unavailable in southern Mesopotamia from Anatolia, the Levantine Corridor, Afghanistan, and Iran.

Within each city-state, an elite group of residents regulated economic life. Uruk and the other Sumerian city-states were **redistributive economies**. In this type of economic system, the central authority (such as the king) controlled the agricultural resources and "redistributed" them to his people (in an unequal fashion!). Archaeologists excavating Uruk have found millions of bevel-rimmed bowls, all the same size and shape—and, as the archaeologist Robert Wenke notes, "surely one of the ugliest ceramic types ever made outside a kindergarten."[4] One theory is that the bowls were ration bowls—containers in which workers received their daily ration of grain. What is certain is that the bowls were mass-produced, and that only a powerful central authority could organize such mass production.

redistributive economies Type of economic system characteristic of ancient Mesopotamian societies. The central political authority controls all agricultural resources and their redistribution.

In the earliest era of Sumerian history, temple priests constituted this central authority. Sumerians believed that their city belonged to a god or goddess: The god owned all the lands and water, and the god's priests, who lived with him (or her) in the temple, administered these resources on the god's behalf. In practice, this meant that the priests collected exorbitant taxes in the forms of goods (grains, livestock, and manufactured products such as textiles) and services (laboring on city building and irrigation projects), and in return provided food rations for the workers from these collections.

As Sumer's city-states expanded, a new form of authority emerged. The ruins of monumental palaces as well as temples testify to the appearance of powerful royal households that joined the temple priesthood in managing the resources of the city-state. Historians theorize that as city-states expanded, competition for land increased. Such competition led to warfare, and during warfare, military leaders amassed power and, eventually, became kings.

The king's power rested on his military might. Yet to retain the people's loyalty and obedience, a king also needed religious legitimacy. Kingship, then, quickly became a key part of Sumerian religious traditions. Sumerians believed that "kingship descended from heaven," that the king ruled on the god's behalf. According to a Sumerian proverb, "Man is the shadow of god, but the king is god's reflection."[5] To challenge the king was to challenge the gods—never a healthy choice. The royal household and the temple priesthood thus worked together to exploit the labor of their subjects and amass power and wealth. Religious and political life were thoroughly intertwined.

Although the Sumerian city-states did not unite politically—and, in fact frequently fought each other—a number of factors created a single Sumerian culture. First, the kings maintained diplomatic relations with one another and with rulers throughout southwest Asia and Egypt, primarily to protect their trading networks. These trade networks also helped tie the Sumerian cities together and fostered a common Sumerian culture. Second, the city-states shared the same pantheon of gods. The surviving documents reveal that Sumerians in the different city-states sang the same hymns, used the same incantations to protect themselves from evil spirits, and offered their children the same proverbial nuggets of advice and warning. They did so, however, in two different languages—Sumerian, unrelated to any other known language, and Akkadian, a member of the Semitic language family that includes Hebrew and Arabic.

Read the Document

Sumerian Law Code: The Code of Lipit-Ishtar

The Akkadian Empire of Sargon the Great

The political independence of the Sumerian city-states ended around 2340 B.C.E. when they were conquered by a warrior who took the name Sargon ("true king") and built a capital city at Agade (or Akkad), the ruins of which may rest under the modern city of Baghdad. With the reign of Sargon (ca. 2340–ca. 2305 B.C.E.), the history of Mesopotamia took a sharp turn. Sargon created the first empire in history. The term **empire** identifies a kingdom or state that controls foreign territories, either on the same

empire Large political formation consisting of different kingdoms or territories outside the boundaries of the states that control them.

continent or overseas. Except for relatively brief periods of fragmentation, imperial rule became the standard form of political statehood in southwest Asia for millennia. Because an empire, by definition, brings together different peoples, it serves as a cauldron of cultural encounters. As we will see, such encounters often transformed not only the conquered peoples, but the conquerors themselves.

Map 1.4 shows that the empire Sargon built embraced a string of territories running far west up the Euphrates River toward the Mediterranean. Sargon was probably the first ruler in history to create a standing army, one that was larger than any yet seen in the Near East. This formidable fighting force certainly helps explain how he conquered so many peoples. To meld these peoples into an empire, however, required not only military power but also innovative organizational skills. The formerly independent Sumerian city rulers became Sargon's governors, and were required to send a portion of all taxes collected to Akkad. Akkadian became the new administrative language, and a standard measurement and dating system was imposed to make record-keeping more efficient.

Raising the revenues to meet the costs of running this enormous empire was vital. Akkadian monarchs generated revenues in several ways. They, of course, taxed their people. Hence, the Mesopotamian proverb: "There are lords and there are kings, but the real person to fear is the tax collector."[6] They also leased out their vast farmlands and required conquered people to pay regular tribute. In addition, Akkadian kings depended on the revenue generated by commerce. They placed heavy taxes on raw materials imported from foreign lands. In fact, most Akkadian kings made long-distance trade the central objective of their foreign policy. They sent military expeditions as far as Anatolia and Iran to obtain timber, metals, and luxury goods. Akkadian troops protected international trade routes and managed the maritime trade in the Persian Gulf, where merchants brought goods by ship from India and southern Arabia.

Akkadian troops also waged war. Warfare during this era changed with the use of two new military technologies. The composite bow boosted the killing power of archers. Multiple layers of wood from different types of trees as well as bone and sinew added to the tensile strength of the bow and so increased the distance an arrow could fly and the speed at which it did so. The second important military innovation was an

THE SUMERIANS AT WAR This Sumerian battle wagon, a heavy four-wheeled cart pulled by donkeys, appears on the "Standard of Ur" (ca. 2500 B.C.E.). Excavated in the 1920s, the "Standard" is actually a wooden box, about 8.5 × 20 inches, with an inlaid mosaic of shells, red limestone, and lapis lazuli. One panel of the mosaic depicts a Sumerian war scene, the other a banquet; hence, archaeologists have labeled the panels "War" and "Peace."

early form of the chariot, a heavy four-wheeled cart that carried a driver and a spearman. Mounted on fixed wheels (and so incapable of swift turns) and pulled by donkeys (the faster horse did not come into use until the second millennium), the early chariot must have been a slow, clumsy instrument. Yet it proved effective in breaking up enemy infantry formations.

The cities of Mesopotamia prospered under Akkadian rule. Even so, Akkadian rulers could not hold their empire together for reasons that historians do not completely understand. One older explanation is that marauding tribes from the Zagros Mountains infiltrated the kingdom and caused tremendous damage. More recent research suggests that civil war tore apart the empire. Regardless of the cause, Akkadian kings lost control of their lands, and a period of anarchy began about 2250 B.C.E. "Who was king? Who was not king?" lamented a writer during this time of troubles. After approximately a century of chaos, the kingdom finally collapsed. Sargon, however, lived on in the memories and folk tales of the peoples of southwest Asia as the model of the mighty king.

The Ur III Dynasty and the Rise of Assyria

With the fall of Akkad, the cities of Sumer regained their independence, but they were soon—and forcibly—reunited under Ur-Nammu (r. ca. 2112–ca. 2095 B.C.E.), king of the Sumerian city of Ur, located far to the south of Akkad. Ur-Nammu established a powerful dynasty that lasted for five generations.

The Ur III dynasty (as it is called) developed an administrative bureaucracy even more elaborate than that of Sargon. Like all bureaucracies, it generated vast amounts of documents—we have more documentary sources for the Ur III era than for any other in ancient southwest Asia. Local elites, who served as the king's governors, administered the empire's 20 provinces. To assure their loyalty, they were often bound to the king by ties of marriage. As governors, these locals controlled the temple estates, maintained the canal system, and acted as the highest judge in the province. Significantly, they did not control the military. Ur III's kings set up a separate military administration and made sure that the generals assigned to each province came from somewhere else. In this way, the king could be sure that the general owed his allegiance to the royal household, not to the local elite. Ur's kings also strengthened their power by assuming the status of gods. Royal officials encouraged the people to give their children names such as "Shulgi is my god" to remind them of the king's divine authority.

Despite their sophisticated bureaucratic apparatus and their claims to divinity, the kings of Ur proved unable to stave off political fragmentation indefinitely. Rebellions increased in size and tempo. About 2000 B.C.E., semi-nomadic peoples known as Amorites began invading Mesopotamia from the steppes to the west and north. The Amorites seized fortified towns, taking food and supplies and causing widespread destruction. Their invasions destabilized the economy. Peasants fled from the fields, and with no food or revenues, inflation and famine overcame the empire. Ur collapsed, and Mesopotamia shattered again into a scattering of squabbling cities.

Assyria and Babylonia

For a long period, the political unity Sargon forged in Mesopotamia remained elusive, as states and peoples fought each other for control. This period of political fragmentation allowed for an important development: a partial "privatization" of the Mesopotamian economy, as individuals began to trade on their own behalf. Not connected in any way to the temple or the palace and, therefore, outside the redistributive economy, many of these free people grew prosperous. Merchants traveling by land and sea brought

1.1

1.2

1.3

textiles, metals, and luxury items such as gold and silver jewelry and gems from lands bordering the Mediterranean and along the Persian Gulf and Red Sea.

Assyrian merchants, for example, developed an elaborate trade network linking the city-state of Assur with Anatolia. (See Map 1.4.) In Assur, they loaded up donkey caravans with tin and textiles for an arduous 50-day journey to the southern Anatolian city of Kanesh. (The surviving documentation is so detailed that we know that each donkey carried 150 pounds of tin or 30 textiles weighing about five pounds each.) Once they arrived in Kanesh, the merchants sold the donkeys, exchanged their merchandise for silver and gold, and headed back to Assur. Meanwhile, Assyrian merchants stationed in Kanesh sold the tin and textiles throughout Anatolia. The enterprise was risky—a storm, bandits, or a sick donkey could imperil it—but the profits were huge: 50 to 100 percent annually. Building on this economic prosperity, Assur (or Assyria) flourished as a powerful city-state until one of the most powerful empire-builders in the history of ancient southwest Asia reduced its power.

By 1780 B.C.E., the kingdom of Babylon had become a mighty empire under Hammurabi (r. 1792–1750 B.C.E.). Hammurabi never entirely conquered Assyria, but he dominated Mesopotamian affairs. Like Ur-Nammu and Sargon, Hammurabi developed a centralized administration to direct irrigation and building projects and to foster commerce throughout his realm. Both his law code (discussed later in this chapter) and his surviving letters to his royal agents reveal that no detail of economic life was too small for Hammurabi's notice. In one letter, for example, he ordered his agent to give "a fallow field that is of good quality and lies near the water, to Sin-imguranni, the seal-cutter."[7] Hammurabi did not, however, reverse the partial privatization of the economy that had developed during the era of political fragmentation. Babylonian society contained a prospering private sector of merchants, craftspeople, farmers, and sailors. Hammurabi liked to think of himself as a benevolent ruler, a kind of protective father. He declared, "I held the people of the lands of Sumer and Akkad safely on my lap."[8]

Nevertheless, Hammurabi and his successors imposed heavy taxes on their subjects. These financial demands provoked resentment, and when Hammurabi died, many Babylonian provinces successfully revolted. The loss of revenue weakened the Babylonian imperial government. By 1650, Hammurabi's empire had shrunk to northern Babylon, the territory Hammurabi had inherited when he first became king. Hammurabi's successors remained in control of northern Babylon for another five generations, but by 1400 B.C.E., a new people, the Kassites, ruled the kingdom.

Cultural Continuities: The Transmission of Mesopotamian Cultures

Although the rise and fall of kingdoms and empires punctuated the political history of Mesopotamia between the emergence of Sumerian civilization in 5300 B.C.E. and the collapse of Babylon in 1500 B.C.E., Mesopotamian culture exhibited remarkable continuity. Over these millennia, Sumerian religious values, architectural styles, literary forms, and other cultural concepts were absorbed, transformed, and passed on by the various peoples they encountered in both commerce and conquest.

THE MESOPOTAMIAN WORLDVIEW: RELIGION Religion—powerfully influenced by Mesopotamia's volatile climate—played a central role in the Sumerian and, hence, the wider Mesopotamian worldview. The Sumerians did not tend to think of their gods as loving or forgiving. Sumerian civilization arose on a floodplain subject to extreme and unpredictable climate conditions, with results ranging from devastating drought to torrential floods. Sumerians knew firsthand the famine and destruction that could result from sudden rainstorms, violent winds, or a flash flood They envisioned each of these natural forces as an unpredictable god who, like a human king or queen, was often unfair and had to be pleased and appeased:

> The sin I have committed I know not;
> The forbidden thing I have done I do not know.
> Some god has turned his rage against me;
> Some goddess has aimed her ire.
> I cry for help but no one takes my hand.[9]

Sumer's religion was **polytheistic**. Sumerians believed that many gods controlled their destinies. In the Sumerian pantheon, the all-powerful king Anu, the father of the gods, ruled the sky. Enlil was master of the wind and guided humans in the proper use of force. Enki governed the Earth and rivers and guided human creativity and inventions. Inanna was the goddess of love, sex, fertility, and warfare. These gods continued to dominate Mesopotamian culture long after Sumer's cities lost their political independence. After Hammurabi conquered most of Mesopotamia, Babylon's city-god Marduk joined the pantheon as a major deity.

polytheistic The belief in many gods.

Because the priests conducted the sacrifices that appeased the often-angry gods, the priesthood dominated Mesopotamian culture as did the temples in which they served and the gods to whom they sacrificed. In the center of every Sumerian city stood the temple complex, comprising temples to various gods, buildings to house the priests and priestesses, storage facilities for the sacrificial gifts, and looming over it all, the **ziggurat**. As the photograph of the ziggurat of Ur reveals, ziggurats were enormous square or rectangular temples with a striking stair-step design. Ur's ziggurat, built around 2100 B.C.E. by Ur-Nammu, had a 50-foot-high base, on which three stairways, each of 100 steps, led to the main gateways. The top of Ur's ziggurat did not survive, but in Ur-Nammu's time, a central staircase would have led upward to a temple.

ziggurat Monumental tiered or terraced temple characteristic of ancient Mesopotamia.

Ur-Nammu built Ur's ziggurat to house the chief god of the city. The Sumerians believed that one god or goddess protected each city, and that the city should serve as an earthly model of the god's divine home. Towering over the city, the deity's ziggurat reminded all the inhabitants of the omnipresent gods who controlled not only their commerce, but their very destiny.

THE MESOPOTAMIAN WORLDVIEW: SCIENCE Struggling to survive within an often hostile environment, Mesopotamians sought to understand and control their world through the practice of **divination**. To "divine"—to discern or to "read"—the future, a

divination The practice of discerning the future by looking for messages imprinted in nature.

ZIGGURAT OF UR Built of mud-brick, the Ziggurat of Ur was the focal point of religious life in the city. This vast temple was built by King Ur-Nammu of the Third Dynasty (2112–2095 B.C.E.) and restored by the British archaeologist, Sir Leonard Woolley, in the 1930s.

local wise woman or a priest looked for the messages imprinted in the natural world, such as in the entrails of a dead animal or in an unusual natural event. Once a person knew what the future was to hold, he or she could then work to change it. If the omens were bad, for example, a man could seek to appease the god by offering a sacrifice.

Divination and religious sacrifice seem to have little to do with science—and in Western culture in the twenty-first century, "religion" and "science" are often viewed as opposing or at least separate realms. Yet the Mesopotamian practice of divination helped shape a "proto-scientific" attitude toward the world. Much of divination consisted of "if . . . then . . ." equations:

> If a horse attempts to mount a cow, then there will be a decline in the land.
> If a man's chest-hair curls upward, he will become a slave.
> If the gallbladder [of the sacrificial sheep] is stripped of the hepatic duct, the army of the king will suffer thirst during a military campaign.[10]

Such statements seem silly, not scientific. Yet they rest on one of the fundamentals of modern science: close observation of the natural world. Only by observing and recording the *normal* processes of the natural world could Mesopotamians hope to recognize the omens embedded in the *abnormal*. Moreover, in the practice of divination, observation of individual events led to the formulation of a hypothesis of a general pattern—what we call **induction**, a crucial part of scientific analysis. In their effort to discern rational patterns in the natural world to improve the circumstances of their own lives, Mesopotamians were moving toward the beginnings of a scientific mentality—a crucial aspect of Western civilization.

induction The process of reasoning that formulates general hypotheses and theories on the basis of specific observation and the accumulation of data.

This proto-scientific understanding is even more evident in the technological, astronomical, and mathematical legacy of ancient Mesopotamia. Sumerians devised the potter's wheel, the wagon, and the chariot. They developed detailed knowledge about the movement of the stars, planets, and the moon, especially as these movements pertained to agricultural cycles, and they made impressive innovations in mathematics. Many Sumerian tablets show multiplication tables, square and cube roots, exponents, and other practical information such as how to calculate compound interest on loans. The Sumerians divided the circle into 360 degrees and developed a counting system based on 60 in multiples of 10—a system we still use to tell time.

THE DEVELOPMENT OF WRITING Perhaps the Sumerians' most important cultural innovation was writing. The Sumerians devised a unique script to record their language. Historians call the symbols that Sumerians pressed onto clay tablets with sharp objects **cuneiform**, or wedge-shaped, writing. The earliest known documents written in this language come from Uruk about 3200 B.C.E. Writing originated because of the demands of record-keeping. By around 4000 B.C.E., officials in Uruk were using small clay tokens of different shapes to represent and record quantities of produce and numbers of livestock. They placed these tokens in clay envelopes, and impressed marks on the outer surface of the envelopes to indicate the contents. By 3100 B.C.E., people stopped using tokens and simply impressed the shapes directly on a flat piece of clay or tablet with a pointed stick or reed.

cuneiform A kind of writing in which wedge-shaped symbols are pressed into clay tablets to indicate words and ideas. Cuneiform writing originated in ancient Sumer.

As commodities and trading became more complex, the number of symbols multiplied. Learning the hundreds of signs required intensive study. The scribes, the people who mastered these signs, became important figures in the royal and religious courts because their work enabled kings and priests to regulate the economic life of their cities. Sumerian cuneiform writing spread, and other peoples of Mesopotamia and southwest Asia began adapting it to record information in their own languages.

THE *EPIC OF GILGAMESH* Writing made a literary tradition possible. Sumerians told exciting stories about their gods and heroes. Passed on and adapted through the ages, these stories helped shape ideas about divine action and human response throughout Mesopotamian history.

CUNEIFORM TEXTS A Sumerian scribe in the city-state of Uruk wrote in cuneiform on this stone tablet around 3200 B.C.E.

One of the most popular of these stories concerned the legendary king Gilgamesh of Uruk. Part god and part man, Gilgamesh harasses his subjects. He demands sex from the young women and burdens the young men with construction tasks. The people of Uruk beg the gods to distract this bothersome hero. The gods send the beastly Enkidu to fight Gilgamesh, but after a prolonged wrestling match that ends in a draw, the two become close friends and set off on a series of adventures. The two heroes battle monsters and even outwit the gods. Finally the gods decide that enough is enough and arrange for Enkidu's death. Mourning for his stalwart friend, Gilgamesh sets out to find the secret to living forever. In the end, immortality eludes his grasp. A mere mortal, Gilgamesh becomes a wiser king, and his subjects benefit from his new wisdom. He realizes that while he must die, his fame may live on, and so he seeks to leave behind him a magnificent city that will live forever in human memory.

The *Epic of Gilgamesh* as we know it was recorded in Akkadian, but it is clear that the stories date from long before the rise of the Akkadian Empire. Recited and read by Mesopotamian peoples for millennia, the Gilgamesh story's influence extended beyond the borders even of the empires of Sargon or Hammurabi. Its themes, plots, and characters reappear in revised form in the literatures of such diverse peoples as the ancient Hebrews (recorded in the Hebrew Bible or Old Testament) and the early Greeks. These peoples, however, reworked the stories in accordance with their own cultural

1.1
1.2
1.3

Read the Document

Excerpts from the *Epic of Gilgamesh*

values. In its Sumerian form, the *Epic of Gilgamesh* demonstrates a Mesopotamian worldview: It emphasizes the capriciousness of the gods, the hostility of nature, and the unpredictability of human existence. It offers no hope of heaven, only resignation to life's unpredictability and the chance of finding some sort of reward during one's short time on Earth.

LAW AND ORDER Mesopotamian culture also made a lasting imprint on future societies through another important innovation: the code of law, preserved in written form. Archaeologists have so far uncovered three Sumerian law codes, the earliest dating to around 2350 B.C.E. The most famous lawgiver of the ancient world was the Babylonian empire-builder Hammurabi. The Law Code of Hammurabi—282 civil, commercial, and criminal laws—is the world's oldest complete surviving compendium of laws. We do not know to what extent these laws were actually implemented. Many scholars argue that the code was a kind of public relations exercise, an effort by Hammurabi both to present a social ideal and to persuade his people (and the gods) to view him as the "King of Justice." (See *Justice in History* in this chapter.)

What is clear is that Hammurabi's laws unveil the social values and everyday concerns of Babylonia's rulers. For example, many of the laws focus on the irrigation system that made Babylonian agriculture possible. One such law reads: "If a man has opened his channel for irrigation and has been negligent and allowed the water to wash away a neighbor's field, he shall pay grain equivalent to the crops of his neighbors"—or be sold as a slave.[11]

Hammurabi's law code buttressed Babylon's social hierarchy by drawing legal distinctions between classes of people. The crimes of aristocrats (called free men) were treated more leniently than were the offenses of common people, while slaves were given no rights at all. If an aristocrat killed a commoner, he or she had to pay a fine, whereas if a commoner killed an aristocrat, he or she was executed. But the code of Hammurabi also emphasized the responsibility of public officials and carefully regulated commercial transactions. If a home was robbed, and city officers failed to find the burglar, then the householder had the right to expect reimbursement for his losses from the city government. If a moneylender suddenly raised interest rates beyond those already agreed on, then he forfeited the entire loan.

Almost one-quarter of Hammurabi's statutes concern family matters. The laws' focus on questions of dowry and inheritance reflect the Mesopotamian view of marriage as first and foremost a business matter. The Sumerian word for *love* literally translates to "measure the earth"—to mark land boundaries and designate who gets

Justice in History

Gods and Kings in Mesopotamian Justice

Mesopotamian kings placed a high priority on ruling their subjects justly. Shamash, the sun god and protector of justice, named two of his children Truth and Fairness. In the preface to his law code, Hammurabi explained the relationship between his rule and divine justice:

> At that time, Anu and Enlil [two of the greatest gods], for the well-being of the people, called me by name, Hammurabi, the pious, god-fearing prince, and appointed me to make justice appear in the land [and] to destroy the evil and wicked, so that the strong might not oppress the weak, [and] to rise like Shamash over the black-headed people [the people of Mesopotamia].[12]

Mesopotamian courts handled cases involving property, inheritance, boundaries, sale, and theft. A special panel of

(continued on next page)

(continued from previous page)

royal judges and officials handled cases involving the death penalty, such as treason, murder, sorcery, theft of temple goods, or adultery. Mesopotamians kept records of trials and legal decisions on clay tablets so that others might learn from them and avoid additional lawsuits.

A lawsuit began when a person brought a dispute before a court. The court consisted of three to six judges chosen from among the town's leading men, such as merchants, scribes, and officials in the town assembly. The judges could speak with authority about the community's principles of justice.

Litigants spoke on their own behalf and presented testimony through witnesses, written documents, or statements made by leading officials. Witnesses took strict oaths to tell the truth in a temple before the statue of a god. Once the parties presented all the evidence, the judges made their decision and pronounced the verdict and punishment.

Sometimes the judges asked the defendants to clear themselves by letting the god in whose name the oath was taken make the judgment. The accused person would then undergo an ordeal or test in which he or she had to jump into a river and swim a certain distance underwater. Those who survived were considered innocent. Drowning constituted proof of guilt and a just punishment rendered by the gods.

The following account of one such ordeal comes from the city of Mari, about 1770 B.C.E. A queen was accused of casting spells on her husband. The maid forced to undergo the ordeal on her behalf drowned, and we do not know whether the queen received further punishment:

> Concerning Amat-Sakkanim . . . whom the river god overwhelmed. . . . : "We made her undertake her plunge, saying to her, 'Swear that your mistress did not perform any act of sorcery against Yarkab-Addad her lord; that she did not reveal any palace secret nor did another person open the missive of her mistress; that your mistress did not commit a transgression against her lord.' In connection with these oaths they had her take her plunge; the river god overwhelmed her, and she did not come up alive."[13]

THE LAW CODE OF HAMMURABI Hammurabi receives the law directly from the sun god, Shamash, on this copy of the Law Code.

SOURCE: Stele of Hammurabi. Hammurabi standing before the sun-god Shamash and 262 laws. Engraved black basalt stele. 1792–1750 B.C.E., 1st Babylonian Dynasty. Louvre, Paris, France. © Giraudon/Art Resource, NY.

This account illustrates the Mesopotamian belief that sometimes only the gods could make decisions about right and wrong. By contrast, the following trial excerpts come from a homicide case in which humans, not gods, made the final judgment. About 1850 B.C.E., three men murdered a temple official named Lu-Inanna. For unknown reasons, they told the victim's wife, Nin-dada, what they had done. King Ur-Ninurta of the city of Isin sent the case to be tried in the city of Nippur, the site of an important court. When the case came to trial, nine accusers asked that the three murderers be executed. They also requested that Nin-dada be put to death because she had not reported the murder to the authorities. The accusers said:

> They who have killed a man are not worthy of life. Those three males and that woman should be killed.

In her defense, two of Nin-dada's supporters pointed out that she had not been involved in the murder and therefore should be released:

> Granted that the husband of Nin-dada, the daughter of Lu-Ninurta, has been killed, but what had the woman done that she should be killed?

The court agreed, on the grounds that Nin-dada was justified in keeping silent because her husband had not provided for her properly:

> A woman whose husband did not support her . . . why should she not remain silent about him? Is it she who killed her husband? The punishment of those who actually killed him should suffice.

In accordance with the decision of the court, the defendants were executed.

This approach to justice—using witnesses, evaluating evidence, and rendering a verdict in a court protected by the king—demonstrated the Mesopotamians' desire for fairness. This court decision became an important precedent that later judges frequently cited.

For Discussion

1. How would a city benefit by letting a panel of royal officials make judgments about life-and-death issues? How would the king benefit?
2. How do these trials demonstrate the interaction of Mesopotamian religious, social, and political beliefs?

Taking It Further

Greengus, Samuel. "Legal and Social Institutions of Ancient Near Mesopotamia," in *Civilizations of the Ancient Near East,* ed. Jack M. Sasson, Vol. 1 (Peabody, MA: Hendrickson Publishers, 2001). Describes basic principles of law and administration of justice, with a bibliography of ancient legal texts.

1.1

1.2

1.3

patriarchy A social or cultural system in which men occupy the positions of power; in a family system, a father-centered household.

The Code of Hammurabi

what. Hammurabi's laws also highlight the **patriarchal** structure of Mesopotamian family life. In a patriarchal society, the husband/father possesses supreme authority in the family. Hence, Hammurabi's code declared that if a wife had a lover, both she and her lover would be drowned, while a husband was permitted extramarital sex. If a wife neglected her duties at home or failed to produce children, her husband had the right to divorce her. Yet Mesopotamian women, at least those in the "free" class, were not devoid of all rights. If a husband divorced his wife without sufficient cause, then he had to give her back her entire dowry. Unlike in many later societies, a married woman was an independent legal entity: She could appear in court and she could engage in commercial contracts. Some Babylonian women ran businesses, such as small shops and inns.

Many of Hammurabi's laws seem harsh: If a house caved in because of faulty workmanship and the householder died, then the builder was put to death. If a freeman hit another freeman's pregnant daughter and caused her to miscarry, he had to pay 10 silver shekels for the unborn child, but if his blow killed the daughter, then his own daughter was executed. Yet through these laws Hammurabi's Code introduced one of the fundamentals of Western jurisprudence: the idea that the punishment must suit the crime (at least in crimes involving social equals). The principle of "an eye for an eye" (rather than a life for an eye) helped shape legal thought in southwest Asia for a millennium. It later influenced the laws of the Hebrews and, thus through the Hebrew Bible (the Christian Old Testament), still molds western ideas about justice.

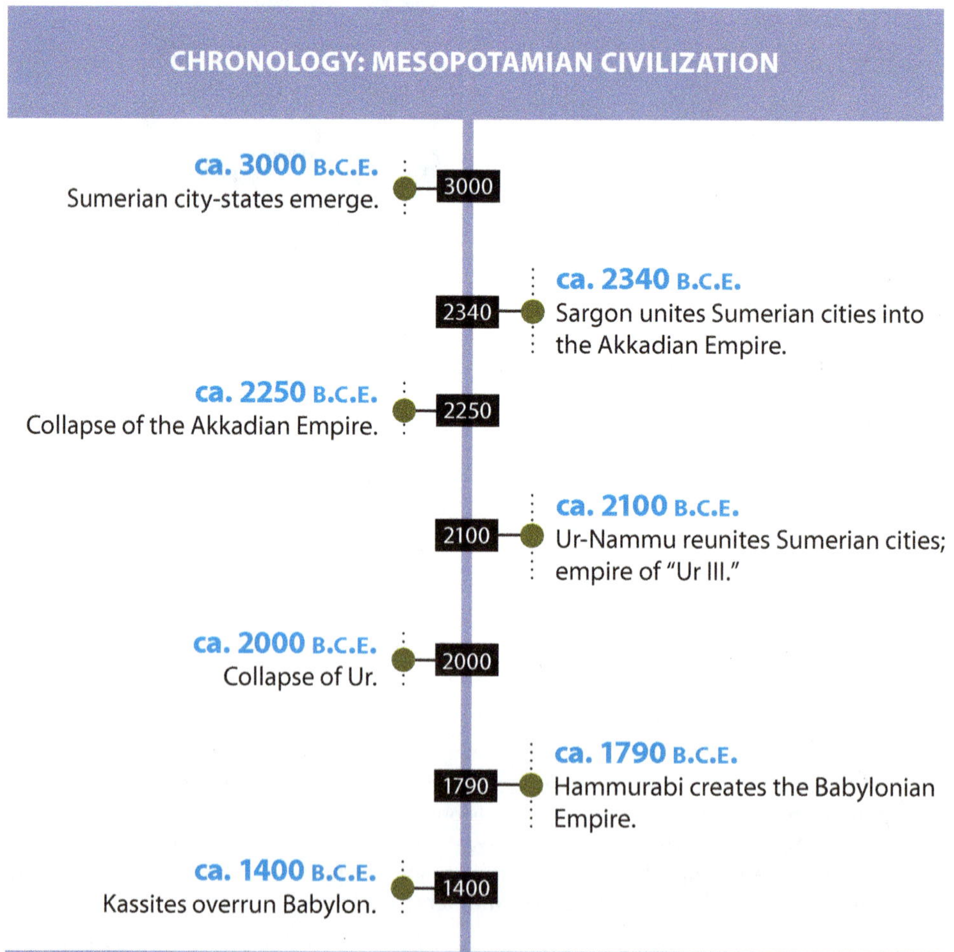

Egypt: The Empire of the Nile

1.3 What distinctive features characterized Egyptian civilization throughout its long history?

As the civilizations of Mesopotamia rose and fell, another civilization emerged far to the south: Egypt. A long and narrow strip of land in the northeast corner of Africa, Egypt depended for its survival on the Nile, the world's longest river, which flows north into the Mediterranean Sea from one of its points of origin in eastern Africa 4,000 miles away. The northernmost part of Egypt, where the Nile enters the Mediterranean, is a broad and fertile delta. The river flooded annually from mid-July to mid-October, leaving behind rich deposits of silt ideal for planting crops. Unlike in southwest Asia, the annual floods in Egypt came with clockwork regularity. For the Egyptians, nature was not unpredictable and random in its destruction, but a benevolent force, generous in sharing its riches.

An Egyptian Hymn to the Nile

Egypt was also fortunate in another of its physical features: It rested securely between two desert regions that effectively barricaded it from foreign conquest. Whereas Mesopotamia stood at the intersection of three continents, vulnerable to invading armies, Egyptian civilization emerged in a far more easily defended position. Egyptian history, then, is remarkable for its political stability. This stability, combined with the predictability and generosity of the Nile, may explain the confidence and optimism that marked Egyptian culture.

Historians organize the long span of ancient Egyptian history into four main periods: Predynastic and Early Dynastic (10,000–2680 B.C.E.), the Old Kingdom (ca. 2680–2200 B.C.E.), the Middle Kingdom (2040–1720 B.C.E.), and the New Kingdom (1550–1150 B.C.E.). Times of political disruption between the kingdoms are called *intermediate periods*. Despite these periods of disruption, the Egyptians maintained a remarkably stable civilization for thousands of years.

Egypt's Rise to Empire

Like the peoples of Mesopotamia, the Egyptians were originally hunter-gatherers who slowly turned to growing crops and domesticating animals. Small villages, in which people could coordinate their labor most easily, appeared along the banks of the Nile between 5000 and 4000 B.C.E. By 3500 B.C.E., Egyptians could survive comfortably through agriculture and herding. Small towns multiplied along the Nile, and market centers connected by roads emerged as hubs where artisans and merchants exchanged their wares.

Toward the end of the Predynastic period, between 3500 and 3000 B.C.E., trade along the Nile River resulted in a shared culture and way of life. Towns grew into small kingdoms whose rulers constantly warred with one another, attempting to grab more land and extend their power. The big consumed the small; by 3000 B.C.E., the towns had been absorbed into just two kingdoms: Upper Egypt in the south and Lower Egypt in the north. These two then united, forming what historians term the **Old Kingdom**. (See **Map 1.5**.)

Old Kingdom In ancient Near Eastern history, the period in Egyptian history from ca. 2680–2200 B.C.E., formed by the unification of the kingdoms of Upper Egypt and Lower Egypt.

THE KINGS AND THE GODS IN THE OLD KINGDOM In the new capital city of Memphis, the Egyptian kings became the focal points of religious, social, and political life. While in Mesopotamia, kings were regarded as the gods' representatives on Earth, Egyptian kings were acknowledged as gods who ruled Egypt on behalf of the other gods. Hence, Egyptians in the Old Kingdom called their king "the good god" (the label *pharaoh* was not used until the New Kingdom) and told tales that emphasized the divinity of the king. In one such story, the god Osiris, ruler of Egypt, was killed and chopped into bits

1.1
1.2
1.3

MAP **1.5** EGYPT: THE OLD, MIDDLE, AND NEW KINGDOMS
As this map shows, Egyptian power expanded from its base along the Nile delta, first southward along the Nile River, and then, through trade and conquest, into southwest Asia. Egypt's control of mineral resources, especially gold, turquoise, and copper, played an important role in its commercial prosperity. How did the New Kingdom compare to its predecessors? How does this map help explain the rivalry between New Kingdom Egypt and the Hittite Empire?

by his evil brother, Seth. Osiris's son, Horus, avenged his father by defeating Seth and reclaiming the Egyptian throne. All Egyptian kings, then, embodied Horus during their reign.

The story of Osiris, Seth, and Horus not only emphasized the divinity of the king, it also stressed the central theme of the Egyptian worldview: the struggle between the forces of chaos and of order. Seth embodied the forces of evil and disorder. In defeating Seth, Horus overcame chaos and restored what the Egyptians called *ma'at* to the world. The word *ma'at* has no English equivalent; in various contexts, it can mean truth, wisdom, justice, or stability. *Ma'at* was the way the gods had made the world—everything in its proper place, everything the way the gods wanted it to be. The king's essential task was to maintain ***ma'at***, to keep things in order and harmony. The king's presence meant that cosmic order reigned and that the kingdom was protected against forces of disorder and destruction.

Like the Mesopotamians, the Egyptians believed in many gods, but in Egypt the gods were not prone to punish men and women without reason. Because the Nile River flooded regularly and predictably, each year leaving behind rich soil deposits, the natural world seemed far less harsh and erratic to the Egyptians. They thus regarded their gods as largely helpful. Ordinary Egyptians tended to pray to minor household gods, such as Tauret, portrayed as a pregnant hippopotamus who protected women during childbirth. Official religion, however, centered on the major state gods, worshiped and housed in monumental temples across the kingdom. The sun god Re was one of the most important Egyptian deities. Re journeyed across the sky every day in a boat, rested at night, and returned in the morning to resume his eternal journey. By endlessly repeating the cycle of rising and setting, the sun symbolized the harmonious order of the universe that Re established. Evil, however, in the form of Apopis, a serpent god whose coils could trap Re's boat like a reed in the Nile, constantly threatened this order. Re's cosmic journey could continue only if *ma'at* was maintained.

ma'at Ancient Egyptian concept of the fundamental order established by the gods.

Read the Document

Workings of *Ma'at*: The Tale of an Eloquent Peasant

THE PYRAMIDS One spectacular feature of Egyptian religion in the Old Kingdom was the construction of pyramids. These elaborate monuments reflected Egyptian emphasis on the afterlife. The earliest pyramids, erected around 2680 B.C.E., were elaborate temples in which priests worshiped statues of the king surrounded by the enormous mud-brick monument. The pyramid contained compartments where the king could dwell in the afterlife in the same luxury he enjoyed during his life on Earth. King Djoser (2668–2649 B.C.E.) built the first pyramid complex, and the world's first monumental stone building, at Saqqara near Memphis. Known today as the Step Pyramid (pictured on p. 31), this structure rests above Djoser's burial place and rises high into the air in six steps, which represent a ladder to Heaven.

In the centuries after Djoser's reign, kings continued building pyramids for themselves and smaller ones for their queens, with each tomb becoming more architecturally sophisticated. The walls grew taller and steeper and contained hidden burial chambers and treasure rooms. The Great Pyramid at Giza, built around 2600 B.C.E. by King Khufu (or Cheops), was the largest human-made structure in the ancient world. It consists of more than two million stones that weigh an average of two and a half tons each. Covering 13 acres, it reaches over 480 feet into the sky.

Building the pyramid complexes was a long and costly task. In addition to the architects, painters, sculptors, carpenters, and other specialists employed on the site throughout the year, stone masons supervised the quarrying and transport of the colossal building blocks. Peasants, who were organized into work gangs and paid and fed

DJOSER'S STEP PYRAMID Djoser ascended to the throne of Egypt around 2668 B.C.E. and immediately ordered his vizier Imhotep to oversee the construction of his tomb. Up until this point, Egyptians constructed pyramids out of mud-brick, but Imhotep deviated from tradition and chose stone.

by the king, provided the heavy labor when the Nile flooded their fields every year. As many as 70,000 workers out of a total population estimated at 1.5 million sweated on the pyramids every day. Entire cities sprang up around pyramid building sites to house the workmen, artisans, and farmers. The construction of elaborate pyramids stopped after 2400 B.C.E., probably because of the expense, but smaller burial structures continued to be built for centuries.

THE SOCIAL AND POLITICAL ORDER IN THE OLD KINGDOM The king and the royal family stood at the top of the Old Kingdom's social and political hierarchy. As a god on Earth, the king possessed absolute authority. All of Egypt—all the land, every resource, every person—theoretically belonged to the king. Yet royal Egyptians were not free to act in any way they might choose. As we have seen, maintaining *ma'at*—ensuring that things remained in divine order—was central to the Egyptian worldview. For Egyptian kings, maintaining *ma'at* meant following carefully regulated rituals at almost all times. The rules that governed royalty differed from those for commoners. Kings, for example, had many wives and frequently married their daughters and sisters, whereas ordinary Egyptians were monogamous (a man took only one wife) and married outside the family.

Below the royal family stood the nobility, made up of priests, court officials, and provincial governors. Men in these ranks carried out the king's orders. Egypt, like the Mesopotamian empires, was a redistributive economy. The kings' officials collected Egypt's produce and redistributed it throughout the kingdom. The job of keeping records of the kings' possessions and supervising food production fell to the scribes, who were trained in **hieroglyphic** writing. *Hieroglyphs* (literally "sacred carvings")

hieroglyphic Ancient Egyptian system of writing that represented both sounds and objects.

1.1

1.2

1.3

represented both sounds (as in our alphabet) and objects (as in a pictorial system). Learning the hundreds of signs for literary or administrative purposes took years of schooling. It was worth the effort, however, for knowledge of hieroglyphs gave scribes great power. For 3,000 years, these royal bureaucrats kept the machinery of Egyptian government running despite the rise and fall of dynasties.

Read the Document

Praise of the Scribe's Profession: An Egyptian Letter

Ordinary Egyptians fell into three categories: skilled artisans, peasants, and slaves. Craftsmen and skilled workers such as millers and stone masons stood below the nobility on the social ladder. Employed in large workshops owned by the king or nobility, the craftsmen served the privileged classes above them. Below them were the peasants, who not only farmed, but also labored on public works such as temples, roads, and irrigation projects. As in medieval Europe, these peasants were tied to the land: They could not leave the estates that they farmed for the king or nobility, and if the land was sold, they were passed on to the new owner as well. Slaves occupied the bottom of the social ladder. They toiled on monumental building projects as well as within the temples and royal palaces. Slavery, however, was not dominant in the Egyptian economy. Free Egyptians did most of the work.

Free Egyptian women—whether from the nobility or the skilled artisans—possessed clear rights. They could buy and sell property, make contracts, sue in court, and own their own businesses. In a marriage, the husband and wife were regarded as equals. Women dominated certain occupations, such as spinning and weaving, and even worked as doctors.

WHERE IS *MA'AT*? THE COLLAPSE OF THE OLD KINGDOM Around 2200 B.C.E. the Old Kingdom collapsed, perhaps because terrible droughts lowered the level of the Nile. Famine followed. *Ma'at*—the divine harmony and order that stood at the center of the Egyptian worldview—had disappeared. For 200 years, anarchy and civil war raged in Egypt during what historians call the First Intermediate Period.

The chaos and disorder of the First Intermediate Period resulted in a significant religious and cultural shift. The optimism that had characterized Egyptian culture gave way to uncertainty and even pessimism as Egyptians wondered how to restore *ma'at* in a world so out of balance:

> Whom can I trust today?
> Hearts are greedy,
> And every man steals his neighbor's goods.[14]

In their quest to make sense out of the chaos, Egyptian writers began to emphasize rewards in the afterlife as recompense for righteous action here on Earth. In the Old Kingdom, Egyptians had sought to act justly in accordance with *ma'at* because they were confident that right action would be rewarded in the here and now. In the new climate of turmoil and hunger, however, they found comfort in the idea that although the good suffered in their earthly life, they would be rewarded in the life to come. During this period, the Egyptians developed the concept of a final judgment—the earliest known instance of such an idea in human history. After death, a person's heart would be weighed in the balance against *ma'at*. Those who tipped the scales—those who failed the test—would be consumed by the Devourer, a god with a crocodile's head. But those who passed would live like gods in the afterlife. (See *Different Voices* in this chapter.)

Read the Document

Elders' Advice to Their Successors

THE MIDDLE KINGDOM The First Intermediate Period ended when the governors of Thebes, a city in Upper Egypt, set out to reunify the kingdom. In 2040 B.C.E., Mentuhotep II (r. 2040–2010 B.C.E.) established a vigorous new monarchy, initiating the **Middle Kingdom**. (See Map 1.5.) He and his successors restored *ma'at* to Egypt: They rebuilt the power of the monarchy, reestablished centralized control, and repaired Egypt's commercial and diplomatic links to southwest Asia. Prosperity and stability returned.

Middle Kingdom In ancient Near Eastern history, refers to the period of Egyptian history from 2040 to 1720 B.C.E.

Yet the Middle Kingdom was not a reincarnation of the Old Kingdom. The chaos of the First Intermediate Period modified political ideas and social relations. The king was no longer an omnipotent god. Capable of making mistakes and even of being afraid, the Middle Kingdom monarch appeared in texts as a lonely figure, seeking to serve as a good shepherd to his people. With this new concept of kingship came a slightly altered social order, with the nobility possessing more power and autonomy than in the Old Kingdom.

New developments also marked religion. With the return of *ma'at*—with life on Earth more prosperous and stable—Egyptians began to see the final judgment as more of a problem that needed to be solved than as a source of comfort. How could one enjoy life and yet be assured of living like a god for eternity, rather than being consumed by the Devourer? To be sure that they passed the final judgment, Egyptians had themselves buried with special scarabs. A scarab is a small figure of a dung beetle, but these funeral scarabs featured human heads and carried magic incantations or charms. This powerful magic prevented the heart from testifying against the individual when it was weighed in the final judgment. In other words, it was a kind of false weight, a finger on the scales, a way to deceive the gods and ensure passage to the afterlife.

ENCOUNTERS WITH OTHER CIVILIZATIONS While Egypt's position between two deserts guaranteed its military security, it did not isolate Egypt from the rest of the ancient world. During both the Old and Middle Kingdoms, Egyptian kings forged an economic network that included trading cities in the Levant, Minoan Crete (see Chapter 2), the southern Red Sea area called Punt, and Mesopotamia. To protect the trade routes along which raw materials and luxury goods were imported, rulers did not hesitate to use force. They also, however, used diplomacy to stimulate trade.

Egyptian interactions with Nubia (modern Sudan) were particularly important. Rich in gold and other natural resources, Nubia also benefited from its location at the nexus of trade routes from central and eastern Africa. Agents of Egyptian rulers, called Keepers of the Gateway of the South, tried to protect this trade by keeping the peace with the warlike Nubian tribes. Slowly, Egyptian monarchs made their presence more permanent. King Mentuhotep II, whose reign marked the start of the Middle Kingdom, not only reunified Egypt but also gained control of Lower Nubia. This expansion of Egyptian control ensured the free flow of Nubian resources northward. Around 1900 B.C.E., King Amenemhet built 10 forts at strategic locations where trade routes from the interior of Africa reached the Nile River. These forts reinforced Egyptian access to Nubian gold, ivory, and other natural resources.

Attracted by Egypt's stability and prosperity, peoples from different lands settled in the Nile Valley. They took Egyptian names and assimilated into Egyptian culture. The government settled these immigrants, as well as war captives, throughout the kingdom where they could mix quickly with the local inhabitants. This willingness to accept newcomers into their kingdom lent Egyptian civilization even more vibrancy.

Immigrants from Canaan (modern-day Lebanon, Israel, and parts of Jordan and Syria) played a significant role in Egyptian history toward the end of the Middle Kingdom. Around 1720 B.C.E., centralized state control began to deteriorate (for reasons that remain unclear), and Canaanites began to seize political control over the regions in which they had settled. A century of political decentralization and chaos—the Second Intermediate Period—ensued, with even larger groups of Canaanite immigrants settling in Egypt's Delta region:

> Foreigners have become people [i.e., Egyptians] everywhere. . . .
> See now, the land is deprived of kingship by a few men who ignore custom.[15]

By approximately 1650 B.C.E., one of these Canaanite groups had established control over the entire northern delta region and forced the Egyptian rulers there to pay them tribute. The era of Hyksos rule had begun. Although *Hyksos* meant "rulers of

1.1

1.2

1.3

Different Voices

Explaining Evil in Ancient Times

The gap that separates twenty-first-century Western readers from the inhabitants of ancient Mesopotamia or Egypt is huge, and yet some of their questions sound familiar: Why do the good and the just suffer? Where do we turn for hope when life seems hopeless? The two documents that follow offer different responses to evil times. The first is an excerpt from a lengthy poem inscribed on four tablets during the Akkadian Empire in Mesopotamia. The Akkadian era was generally prosperous, but as this document shows, daily survival remained difficult for many. The second document comes from the tumultuous intermediate period following the collapse of Egypt's Old Kingdom. The writer may have been king of one of the fragmented states that emerged as the Old Kingdom disintegrated. In The Instructions for Merikare, *he shares with his son the lessons he has learned in a world gone mad.*

I. From Mesopotamia: I Will Praise the Lord of Wisdom

I turn around, but it is bad, very bad;
My ill luck increases and I cannot find what is right.
I called to my god, but he did not show his face,
I prayed to my goddess, but she did not raise her head.
Even the diviner with his divination could not make
 a prediction,
And the interpreter of dreams with his libation could not
 elucidate my case. . . .
What strange conditions everywhere!
When I look behind [me], there is persecution, trouble.
Like one who has not made libations to his god,
Nor invoked his goddess when he ate,
Does not make prostrations nor recognize [the necessity
 of] bowing down,
In whose mouth supplication and prayer are lacking,
Who has even neglected holy days, and ignored festivals . . .
Like one who has gone crazy and forgotten his lord,
Has frivolously sworn a solemn oath by his god, [like such
 a one] do I appear.
For myself, I gave attention to supplication and prayer;
My prayer was discretion, sacrifice my rule.
The day for worshipping the god was a joy to my heart;
The day of the goddess's procession was profit and gain to me.
The king's blessing—that was my joy. . . .
I wish I knew that these things would be pleasing to one's god!
What is good for oneself may be offense to one's god,
What in one's own heart seems despicable may be proper
 to one's god.
Who can know the will of the gods in heaven?
Who can understand the plans of the underworld gods?
Where have humans learned the way of a god?
He who was alive yesterday is dead today. . . .
As for me, exhausted, a windstorm is driving me on!
Debilitating Disease is let loose upon me;
An Evil Wind has blown [from the] horizon,
Headache has sprung up from the surface of the underworld. . . .
Feebleness has overcome my whole body,
An attack of illness has fallen upon my flesh.

II. From Egypt: The Instruction for Merikare

DO JUSTICE WHILST THOU ENDUREST UPON THE EARTH. Quiet the weeper; do not oppress the widow; supplant no man in the property of his father; and impair no officials at their posts. Be on thy guard against punishing wrongfully. Do not slaughter: it is not of advantage to thee. . . .

THE COUNCIL [OF GODS] WHICH JUDGES THE DEFICIENT, thou knowest they are not lenient on that day of judging the miserable. . . . they regard a lifetime as (but) an hour. A man remains over after death, and his deeds are placed beside him in heaps*. However, existence yonder is for eternity, and he who complains of it is a fool. (But) as for him who reaches it without wrongdoing, he shall exist yonder like a god, stepping out freely like the lords of eternity.

. . . .

Well directed are men, the cattle of the god. He made heaven and earth according to their desire, and he repelled the water-monster. He made the breath of life (for) their nostrils. . . . He has slain the treacherous of heart among them, as a man beats his son for his brother's sake. For the god knows every name.

For Discussion

1. What picture of Akkadian religious practice can we draw from the first document?
2. In this excerpt from *I Will Praise the Lord of Wisdom*, the anonymous author files a sort of cosmic complaint. What grievance does he present?
3. In the second excerpt, what advice does the king offer to his son Merikare? What does he want his son to understand?
4. How does *The Instruction for Merikare* demonstrate the new religious concepts that the Egyptians developed in response to the disappearance of political stability and economic prosperity during the First Intermediate Period?
5. Each of these documents reveals timeless existential concerns, but how do they point to the specific historical contexts in which they were written?

SOURCE: I. James B. Pritchard (ed.), *The Ancient Near East: Supplementary Texts and Pictures Relating to the Old Testament*, 597–598. II. "The Instruction for King Meri-kare." James B. Pritchard, *Ancient Near Eastern Texts Relating to the Old Testament* (Princeton: Princeton University Press, 1950), p. 415 (right column), p. 417 (right column).

*"his deeds are placed beside him in heaps": the Council of Gods weighs his wrongdoing.

foreign lands" in Egyptian, the Hyksos dynasty (ca. 1650–1540 B.C.E.) quickly assimilated Egyptian culture. They used Egyptian names and symbols, worshiped Egyptian gods, and employed native Egyptians to staff their bureaucracies and keep their state records—in Egyptian hieroglyphs.

But the Hyksos, and the Canaanite immigrant community from which they emerged, not only absorbed Egyptian ways, they also transformed them. Canaanite immigrants brought with them into Egypt a vital skill: the ability to make bronze. An alloy of copper and tin, bronze is much harder and lasts much longer than either copper or tin alone. From about 3500 B.C.E. when people living in northern Syria and Iraq began making bronze, the technology spread slowly throughout southwest Asia. Archaeologists talk about the "Early Bronze Age" (roughly 3500–2000 B.C.E.), the "Middle Bronze Age" (ca. 2000–1550 B.C.E.), and the "Late Bronze Age" (ca. 1500–1100 B.C.E.). It was in the Middle Bronze Age, then, that Canaanite immigrants introduced bronze to Egypt. Bronze meant new possibilities in agriculture, craft production—and war.

In particular, bronze made possible the horse-drawn light chariot. This advanced military technology was already revolutionizing warfare throughout southwest Asia, Anatolia, and Greece when the Hyksos brought it to Egypt. Unlike earlier chariots, the Bronze Age model featured only two wheels fixed to an axle for easier maneuvering. Bronze spokes made the wheels more durable. Two men wearing bronze chain-mail armor rode into battle on each chariot, one driving the horses, the other shooting bronze-tipped arrows at the enemy. Troops of trained charioteers and bowmen easily outmaneuvered the traditional massed infantry forces and inflicted terrible casualties on them from a distance.

Chariot warfare reshaped the economic policies and foreign relations of Egypt, its rivals, and its allies. Imperial systems of governing and revenue collection became more sophisticated and centralized as rulers sought to meet the expenses of training and supplying armies of charioteers by expanding their economic resources. As a result, empires flourished as never before. Archaeologists thus see the period after approximately 1500 B.C.E. as a new era, the "Late Bronze Age," a period of unprecedented imperial stability and international exchange. In Chapter 2, we will examine the international structures of this period in detail. In the following section, we continue the story of Egypt as it reemerged as a great power.

The New Kingdom: The Egyptian Empire in the Late Bronze Age

Egypt's **New Kingdom** began about 1550 B.C.E., when King Ahmose I (r. ca. 1550–ca. 1525 B.C.E.) expelled the Hyksos from Egypt. During the New Kingdom, Egypt's kings first took the title **pharaoh**, which means "great house"—or master of all Egyptians. As Map 1.5 shows, Ahmose's new dynasty not only reasserted the monarch's authority and rebuilt the power of the central state, it also pushed Egypt's territorial boundaries into Asia as far as the Euphrates River.

New Kingdom In ancient Near Eastern history, the period in Egyptian history from 1550 to 1150 B.C.E. During the New Kingdom, Egyptian kings first took the title of pharaoh and established an empire that reached to the Euphrates River.

pharaoh Title for the Egyptian king, used during the New Kingdom period.

BUILDING AN EMPIRE: MILITARY CONQUEST AND TERRITORIAL EXPANSION A large standing army made the New Kingdom conquests possible. Trained in the new chariot warfare and equipped with the composite bow (long known in Mesopotamia, but introduced into Egypt during the New Kingdom), Egypt's army was a mighty fighting force. One man in every 10 was forced into military service. Egyptian officers supplemented these troops with both mercenaries hired abroad and soldiers recruited in conquered regions of Palestine and Syria.

Egyptian attitudes toward non-Egyptians also encouraged the imperial expansion of the New Kingdom. Egyptians divided the world into two groups: themselves (whom they referred to as "The People") and everyone else. Egyptians believed that forces of chaos

1.1

1.2

1.3

resided in foreign lands where the pharaoh had not yet imposed his will. Thus, it was the pharaoh's responsibility to crush all foreign peoples and bring order to the world.

In their drive to establish order in the world, Egyptian rulers in the New Kingdom clashed with kingdoms in Anatolia and Mesopotamia. Under the dynamic leadership of Thutmose I (r. 1504–1492 B.C.E.), the armies of Egypt conquered southern Palestine. A coalition of Syrian cities slowed further advance, but by the end of the reign of the great conqueror, Thutmose III (r. 1458–1425 B.C.E.), Egypt had extended its control over the entire western coast (see Map 1.5). Thutmose III led his armies into Canaan 17 times and strengthened the empire's hold on it and Syria. Canaan proved an economic asset, both because of its own natural resources and because it was a vital trading center with ties to Mesopotamia and beyond.

The New Kingdom also regained control over Nubia about 1500 B.C.E. To strengthen their grip on the area, pharaohs encouraged Egyptians to establish communities along the Nile River there. These Egyptian colonies exploited the fertile river lands in Nubia for the benefit of the pharaoh.

KEEPING AN EMPIRE: ADMINISTRATIVE AND DIPLOMATIC INNOVATION The Egyptians amassed a vast empire with military might. They maintained it with administrative skill and diplomatic innovation. In the New Kingdom, the pharaoh's bureaucracy divided Egypt into two major administrative regions: Upper Egypt in the south, governed from the city of Thebes, and Lower Egypt in the north, ruled from the city of Memphis. Regional administrators raised taxes and drafted men to fight in the army and work on the pharaoh's building projects. The chief minister of state, the **vizier**, superintended the administration of the entire kingdom. Every year he decided when to open the canal locks on the Nile to irrigate farmers' fields. He supervised the Egyptian treasury and the warehouses into which produce was paid as taxes.

vizier The chief minister of state in New Kingdom Egypt, the vizier supervised the administration of the entire kingdom.

New Kingdom pharaohs also relied on diplomacy to control their vast realm. They corresponded frequently with their provincial governors, the leaders of their vassal states, and the rulers of other great states. These letters testify that the Egyptian monarchs used trade privileges and political benefits as much as military coercion to control restless subordinates and interact with neighboring realms.

CONTINUITY IN THE NEW KINGDOM During the New Kingdom, many of the characteristics of life under the Old and Middle Kingdom continued unchanged. The basic social hierarchy remained intact, with village-based peasants laboring on the land owned by the royal family, priests of the major temples, and nobility. Both the pharaoh's government and the major temples continued to administer the redistributive economy by collecting taxes in the form of produce and paying the peasants who labored on their building projects and estates from their storehouses. The temple of the god Amun at Karnak, for example, controlled over 100,000 workers.

In the New Kingdom, as in the Old and Middle Kingdoms, monumental architecture remained a focal point of political and religious life. Amenhotep III (r. 1388–1350 B.C.E.) constructed both an enormous palace for himself and a gigantic burial temple, with a large open solar court as its sanctuary and two 64-foot-high statues of the pharaoh flanking the entryway. Ramesses II (r. 1279–1212 B.C.E.) ornamented his long reign by building the Great Temple at Abu Simbel in Nubia. Four 65-foot-high statues of the pharaoh guard the entrance to the temple. The sanctuary penetrates over 200 feet into the mountainside, where four gigantic statues of the four gods sit. Twice a year (on February 21 and October 21), the rising sun shines directly through the entrance and falls right on three of the statues; the fourth, the god of the underworld, remains in the shadows.

Watch the Video

Ramesses II: Abu Simbel

Women maintained their position in Egyptian society in the New Kingdom. They had complete equality with men in matters of property, business, and inheritance.

Some women held priesthoods. The most powerful, the "God's Wife of Amun," was often a member of the royal family. This priestess had administrative responsibilities as well as the obligation to perform religious rituals.

CHANGE IN THE NEW KINGDOM While there was much continuity between the New Kingdom and its predecessors, at two points in its history the New Kingdom took a new direction. In the first, Egypt came under the rule of a remarkable woman; in the second, of a religious visionary.

In 1479 B.C.E. the pharaoh Thutmose II (ca. 1491–1479 B.C.E.) died. His son—by a subordinate wife—and successor, Thutmose III, was a child, so Thutmose II's chief wife and half-sister, Hatshepsut, became regent for the child-king. While Hatshepsut at first kept the titles often associated with the pharaoh's wife, such as "God's Wife," within two years she claimed the title of pharaoh. Evidence indicates that women had ruled Egypt on four earlier occasions, but these women may have been only regents and so not recognized as kings. In contrast, Hatshepsut clearly claimed to be, and was acclaimed as, pharaoh.

Because pharaohs had always been men, all of the images of kingly power were male, and the elaborate royal rituals presumed a male ruler. Hatshepsut adapted her image to these expectations. For example, in most inscriptions she is referred to by masculine titles and pronouns, and most of her statues depict her as a man, complete with a ceremonial beard. On some statues, however, Hatshepsut does appear as a woman, and in some inscriptions she is called "Daughter [rather than Son] of Re."

Hatshepsut ruled for over 20 years. Like most male pharaohs, she waged war when necessary, including a major campaign in Nubia, but most of her reign was peaceful. When she died about 1458 B.C.E., Thutmose III took the throne. Late in his 30-year reign, he ordered that Hatshepsut's name be chiseled off monuments throughout Egypt and all her statues be destroyed. Why he did so is a mystery. Because Thutmose waited so long to try to erase the evidence of Hatshepsut's rule, it seems unlikely that he was angry at her for becoming king. A more convincing explanation is that Thutmose

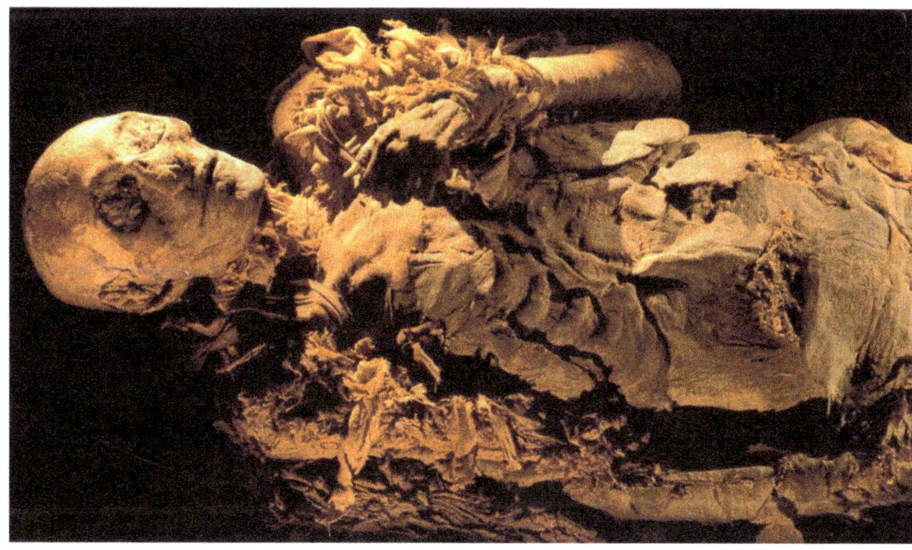

HATSHEPSUT: IMAGE AND REALITY Although she was a woman, tradition required that Hatshepsut be depicted as a man, as in this statue where she wears the pharaoh's customary beard. In 2007, archaeologists discovered Hatshepsut's mummy. Research revealed that the queen was between ages 45 and 60 when she died, that she had cancer, and that she was quite obese.

SOURCE: Head from an Osiride Statue of Hatshepsut. Egypt, New Kingdom, 18th dynasty, joint reign of Hatshepsut and Thutmose III. Ca. 1473–1458 B.C.E. From Deir-el-Bahri, Thebes. Limestone, H. 124.5 cm (49 in.). Rogers Fund, 1931 (31.3.157). The Metropolitan Museum of Art, New York, NY, U.S.A. Image © The Metropolitan Museum of Art/Art Resource, NY.

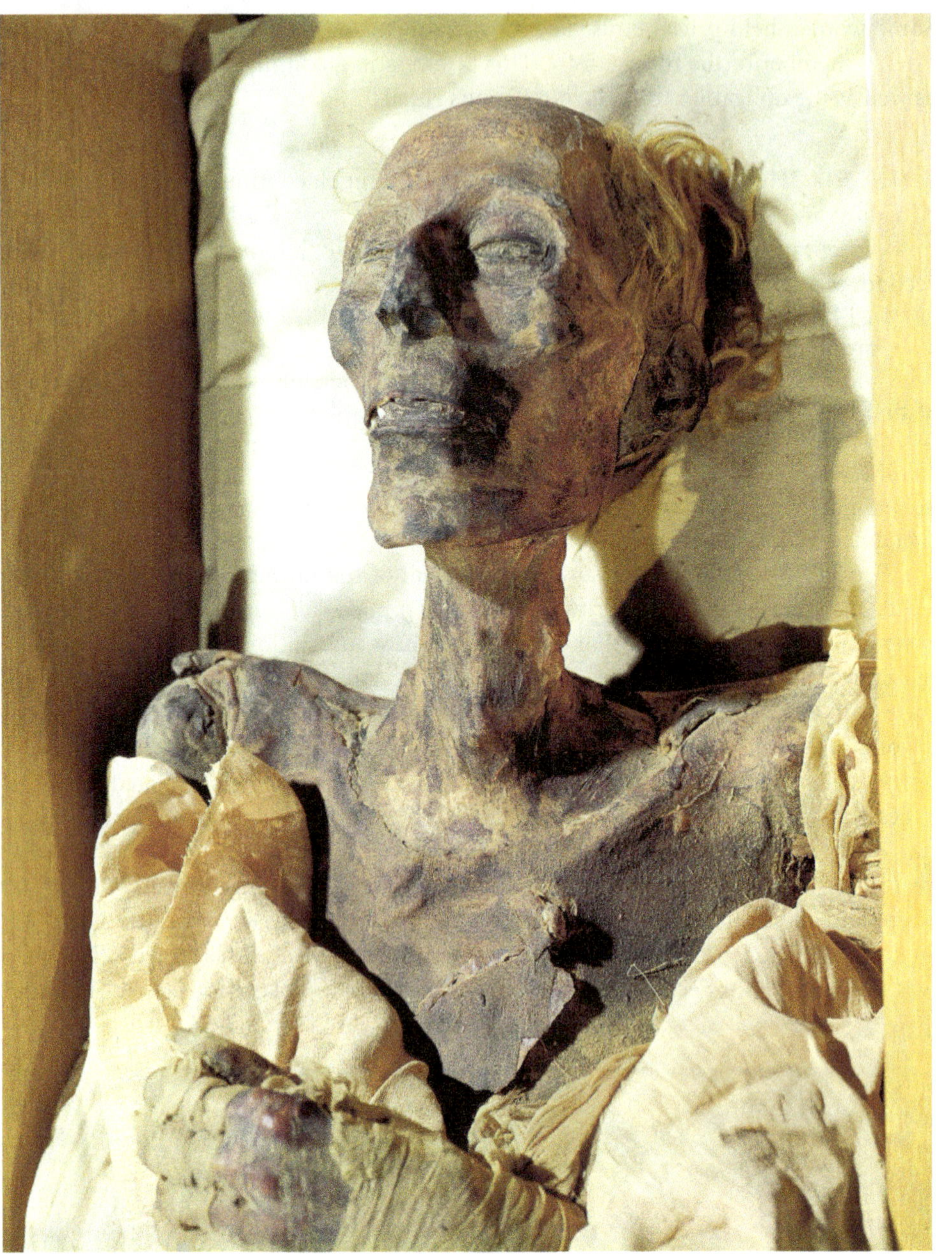

MUMMY OF RAMESSES II Both a science and an art, mummification preserved the body of King Ramesses II (r. 1279–1213 B.C.E.) for more than 3,000 years. Using a metal hook, embalmers extracted the brains through the nostrils. Sometimes they filled the skull with linen cloth and resin. Through an incision below the ribs, they removed all the organs except for the heart, which represented a person's life and would be examined by the gods on Judgment Day. The embalmers then dried the corpse by packing it with natrum, a natural compound of sodium carbonate and bicarbonate. After adding hairpieces and artificial eyes, the embalmers applied a layer of resin over the face and body, followed by a coat of paint—red for men and yellow for women.

was attempting to fulfill his basic duty as Egypt's king: to maintain *ma'at.* Hatshepsut's reign may have seemed too disorderly, too much of a change from the proper way of doing things. And so, to inform the gods that Egypt had returned to "proper" male kingship, Thutmose III ordered Hatshepsut erased from history.

Thutmose may have regarded the memory of Hatshepsut's reign as a danger to *ma'at.* It was, however, a stable era, in contrast to the second point at which the New Kingdom took a short, sharp change in direction. During the reign of Amenhotep IV (r. 1351–1334 B.C.E.), Egypt experienced a religious revolution. His father, Amenhotep III (r. 1388–1351 B.C.E.), had emphasized worship of Aten, the solar disc associated with the sun god Re, during his years on the throne. Building on this emphasis, Amenhotep IV changed his own name to Akhenaten ("one useful to Aten") and declared that Aten was not just the supreme god, but the only god.

Akhenaten attacked the worship of other gods, dismissed priests, closed temples, and appropriated their wealth and lands for himself. He forbade the celebration of ancient public festivals to the other gods and even the mention of their names, which his agents chiseled from monuments and buildings. Full of religious enthusiasm, Akhenaten and his queen, Nefertiti, abandoned the capital of Thebes and built a new city where no temple had ever stood. The modern name for this site is Tell el-Amarna and so historians refer to this period of religious ferment as the Amarna Period.

Because Akhenaten forbade the worship of other gods, some historians have argued that the Egyptians in the Amarna Period were the first people in history to develop **monotheism**, the idea of a single, all-powerful god. Yet this ignores the importance of pharaoh worship in Akhenaten's new religion. Akhenaten insisted that he and Nefertiti be worshiped as gods. Rather than inventing monotheism, then, Akhenaten may have been trying to restore the Old Kingdom conception of the king as a divine being.

monotheism The belief in only one god, first attributed to the ancient Hebrews. Monotheism is the foundation of Judaism, Christianity, Islam, and Zoroastrianism.

Whatever Akhenaten's intentions or personal beliefs, his religious revolution proved short-lived. Because ordinary Egyptians were unwilling to abandon the many traditional gods who played an important role in their daily lives, the priests whose power Akhenaten had undermined succeeded in arousing opposition to the reforms. After Akhenaten's death, the royal court returned to Memphis. The new pharaoh, Tutankhamun (r. 1334–1325 B.C.E.), rebuilt the temples destroyed by Akhenaten's agents and returned the revenue that Akhenaten had appropriated from the priests. Egypt turned back to its traditional religious beliefs and practices, and *ma'at* was restored.

Read the **Document**

Papyrus of Ani: The Egyptian Book of the Dead

In the twelfth century B.C.E., however, Egypt slipped into a long decline. Drought, poor harvests, and inflation ruined the Egyptian economy, while weak rulers struggled to hold the kingdom together. But as we will see in Chapter 2, however, domestic developments alone do not explain the collapse of the New Kingdom.

THE SUN GOD BLESSES AKHENATEN AND NEFERTITI In this panel that once decorated an altar, the Sun God Aten beams his blessing down onto Akhenaten and his wife, Nefertiti, as they play with their daughters.

CHRONOLOGY: CIVILIZATION IN EGYPT

ca. 2680 B.C.E. Earliest pyramids built; Old Kingdom emerges.

ca. 2200 B.C.E. Collapse of the Old Kingdom; First Intermediate Period begins.

ca. 2040 B.C.E. Mentuhotep II reunites Egypt; Middle Kingdom begins.

ca. 1720 B.C.E. Disintegration of the Middle Kingdom; Second Intermediate Period begins.

ca. 1650 B.C.E. Hyksos rule begins.

ca. 1550 B.C.E. Ahmose I expels the Hyksos; New Kingdom begins.

ca. 1480 B.C.E. Hatshepsut rules as female pharaoh.

ca. 1351 B.C.E. Amenhotep IV (Akhenaten) attempts a religious revolution.

ca. 1150 B.C.E. Collapse of the New Kingdom.

Around 1150 B.C.E., the interconnected societies of Anatolia, Mesopotamia, and the eastern Mediterranean coast, as well as Egypt, experienced economic hardship and political fragmentation. The prosperity and stability of the Late Bronze Age abruptly disappeared. In the next chapter we will look closely at the factors that shaped this period of prosperity, the developments that brought it to an end, and the kingdoms that emerged in its aftermath.

CONCLUSION

Civilization and the West

During the millennia covered in this chapter, early Europeans such as Ötzi the Ice Man learned to control and capitalize on nature in many ways—cultivating crops, domesticating animals, and smelting copper. Linked by trade networks, their villages were growing larger and their societies more stratified and specialized. Even so, most of Europe did not make the leap into civilization during the third and second millennia B.C.E., and "the West" did not yet exist. The idea of "Western civilization" as both a geographic and cultural designation emerged much later, with the Greeks (see Chapter 3) who used the term *Europe* to designate the West—and who, like us, were often unclear about the West's actual boundaries.

Yet in areas that we often regard as outside the boundaries of the West, in Iraq and in Egypt, Western civilization had its beginnings. From the ancient Mesopotamian and Egyptian civilizations, the West inherited such crucial components as systems of writing and numeracy, and the core of its legal traditions. These civilizations also left a treasury of religious stories and ideas that, adapted and revised by a small, relatively powerless people called the Hebrews, became the foundational ethic of Western civilization. That development, within the context of the collapse of the International Bronze Age, is one of the main themes of Chapter 2.

MAKING CONNECTIONS

1. Each of the cultures studied in this chapter developed a distinctive architectural form: the megalith, the ziggurat, and the pyramid. What do they tell us about the societies that built them?
2. Sargon was the first empire builder in history. How did he do it? Why did he do it? How did his methods of empire building compare to those of later Mesopotamian and Egyptian empire makers?
3. How and why did Mesopotamian and Egyptian cultural and religious patterns differ? Which is the more striking, the differences between them or the parallels?

TAKING IT FURTHER

For suggested readings, see page R-1.

On MyHistoryLab

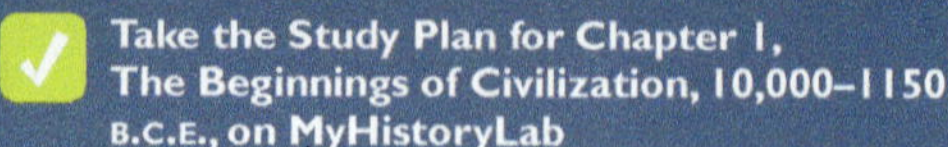

Chapter Review

Defining Civilization, Defining Western Civilization

1.1 What is the link between the food-producing revolution of the Neolithic era and the emergence of civilization?

When hunter-gatherers began farming and herding, food surpluses previously unknown in those societies allowed more newborns to live past infancy. The resulting population growth contributed to the spread of human settlements, and allowed for economic specialization and the development of social, political, and religious hierarchies, all of which are key ingredients for civilization.

Mesopotamia: Kingdoms, Empires, and Conquests

1.2 What changes and continuities characterized Mesopotamian civilization between the emergence of Sumer's city-states and the rise of Hammurabi's Babylonian Empire?

Although punctuated by the rise and fall of kingdoms and empires, Mesopotamian culture maintained a remarkable continuity over thousands of years. Constant features included the redistributive economic system that used the agricultural labor of the masses to sustain the religious and political hierarchy, and a religion marked by efforts to appease the many gods who, like the Tigris and Euphrates Rivers, were unpredictable and often destructive. Tales of these gods, written in the Akkadian language were adapted and passed on through the many Mesopotamian empires.

Egypt: The Empire of the Nile

1.3 What distinctive features characterized Egyptian civilization throughout its long history?

Both Egypt's sheltered geographic position and the predictability of the Nile River contributed to a civilization characterized by remarkable prosperity, stability, and continuity. Egyptians saw their kings as divine-like beings whose role was to ensure *ma'at*, the basic order and balance of the world. Both slaves and freemen labored to build the monumental architecture that displayed the dominance of the kings and made manifest Egyptians' faith in their gods. Empire-building was also an important Egyptian characteristic, as Egyptian rulers expanded their political dominion both southward into Africa and eastward toward Mesopotamia. Like its Hittite and Mesopotamian rivals, Egypt was a redistributive economy, with village-based peasants laboring on the land owned by the royal family, priests of the major temples, and nobility.

Chapter Time Line

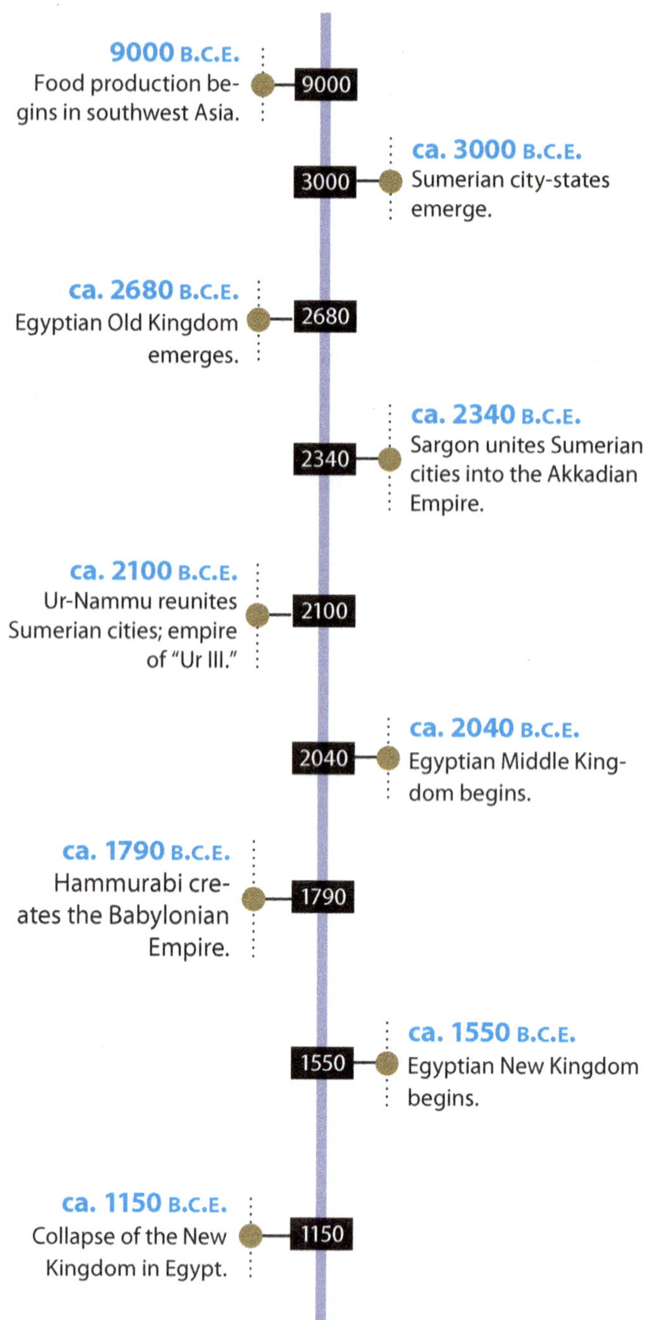

2 The Age of Empires: The International Bronze Age and Its Aftermath, ca. 1500–550 B.C.E.

In 1984, scuba-diving archaeologists began to excavate the wreck of a merchant ship that sank about 1300 B.C.E. at Uluburun, off the southern coast of Turkey. Its cargo included ostrich eggshells, elephant tusks, a trumpet carved from a hippopotamus tooth from Egypt, a ton of scented resin from southwest Asia, and pomegranates packed in finely painted storage jars from the island of Cyprus. The ship's hold also contained 354 flat copper bars, each weighing about 50 pounds, and several bars of tin.

The Uluburun ship's cargo highlights two defining features of the **Late Bronze Age** (1500–1100 B.C.E.). First, the ship carried copper and tin, the metals needed to make bronze, one of the most desired commodities of this era. Because substantial deposits of tin and copper were rarely found in the same region, merchants—such as those who contracted with the Uluburun ship owner—traded over long distances and across political boundaries to obtain both ores. In turn, monarchs devoted military and diplomatic resources to fostering and protecting this trade, the foundation of much of their prosperity and power. Thus, a second defining feature of the Late Bronze Age was its unprecedented degree of international

HOUSE OF THE ADMIRAL (Detail)
Created about 1500 B.C.E., this lively wall painting is about 22 feet long and a foot and a half high and comes from the so-called House of the Admiral on the island of Thera, midway between Crete and Greece. The scenes of busy maritime activity outside a harbor town provide a glimpse of the international connections that created the "International Bronze Age."

LEARNING OBJECTIVES

2.1 What elements made up the international system of the Late Bronze Age and why did it collapse?

2.2 What developments shaped southwest Asian and Mediterranean societies after the collapse of the International Bronze Age?

2.3 What beliefs and institutions shaped Hebrew civilization and its legacy?

Listen to Chapter 2 on MyHistoryLab

Watch the Video Series on MyHistoryLab

Learn about some key topics related to this chapter with the *MyHistoryLab Video Series: Key Topics in Western Civilization*

Late Bronze Age The period from 1500 to 1100 B.C.E., characterized by an unprecedented degree of international trade and diplomatic exchange.

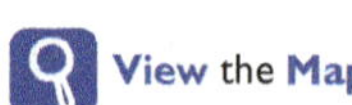

International Trade Routes in the Bronze Age

trade and diplomatic exchange. The Uluburun ship could not have stopped at so many ports and picked up such a diverse cargo had monarchs not worked together to construct a stable international structure. Trade networks, an international diplomatic system, and cultural exchanges made the Late Bronze Age the "International Bronze Age."

The International Bronze Age collapsed suddenly and somewhat mysteriously between (roughly) 1200 and 1100 B.C.E. Like a wrecked cargo ship, once-vibrant cultures sank into a dark age of invasions, migrations, and political fragmentation. In the aftermath of these turbulent events, two of the most powerful empires the world has ever known, the Neo-Assyrian and the Neo-Babylonian, rose to dominate the ancient world. Regarding themselves as the heirs of the Sumerian, Akkadian, and Old Babylonian civilizations examined in Chapter 1, the rulers of these new empires consciously sought to preserve and pass on Mesopotamian traditions. Thus, the continuity of Mesopotamian culture remained unbroken, despite the political tumult of these centuries.

While mighty empires dominated the International Bronze Age and its aftermath, for the history of the West the most important development of this period occurred on the fringes of empire, amidst a relatively small and powerless people. Called the Israelites or the Hebrews, these people developed the world's first monotheistic religion and created the ethical framework of Western civilization.

A key question for this chapter, then, is how did the varied encounters of the International Bronze Age and its aftermath shape not only diplomatic and trade relations but also cultural assumptions and values?

The Dynamism of the International Bronze Age

2.1 What elements made up the international system of the Late Bronze Age and why did it collapse?

Trade in not only tin and copper for the making of bronze but also luxury goods and princess brides, ships and chariots, and even architectural styles and religious ideas created the International Bronze Age—and numerous sources for the historian to study. Rulers used the wealth generated by trade to erect palaces and temples, the remains of which provide archaeological evidence. These rulers also employed numerous scribes who recorded their economic agreements, diplomatic maneuvers, and military accomplishments. Inscribed on clay tablets rather than written on perishable parchment or paper, many of these documents survived across the millennia. In 1887, for example, an Egyptian peasant woman uncovered a collection of over 370 cuneiform tablets, the diplomatic and imperial correspondence of the pharaohs from the mid-fourteenth century B.C.E. These Amarna Letters, as they are called (because they were found at Tell El-Amarna), include correspondence between the pharaoh and rulers of other empires, and communications sent to the pharaoh by the leaders of his vassal states in Canaan. Written in Akkadian (the Mesopotamian language used for international communication), the Amarna Letters offer detailed evidence about the international system of the Late Bronze Age.

Read the Document

Ancient Egyptian and Hittite Voices

Zones of Power Within the International Bronze Age

The economic and diplomatic network of the International Bronze Age covered five separate but interconnected zones. **Map 2.1** highlights these zones: to the south, the New Kingdom in Egypt; to the north, the Hittite Empire in Anatolia; to the east, the Assyrian and Babylonian empires in Mesopotamia; to the west, the eastern Mediterranean kingdoms of the Minoans on Crete and the Mycenaeans on mainland Greece; and finally, several small kingdoms along the Syrian–Canaanite coast.

View the Map

Map Discovery: Bronze Age Trade

THE HITTITE KINGDOM OF HATTI In Chapter 1, we explored the history of the first zone of power in the International Bronze Age: New Kingdom Egypt. The second zone of power lay in the rich plateau of Anatolia (modern Turkey). By about 1650 B.C.E., an **Indo-European** people called the Hittites had established control over this region. "Indo-European" is a linguistic term: Armenian, Persian, and a majority of European languages share similarities in vocabulary and grammar inherited from an Indo-European parent language. Distinguished, then, from the Semitic and other peoples of southwest Asia by the language they spoke, the Hittites' origins remain obscure. Some scholars argue that they originated in northern India. Others believe that

Indo-European Parent language of a majority of modern European languages as well as modern Armenian and Persian; sometimes used to refer to the people who spoke this language.

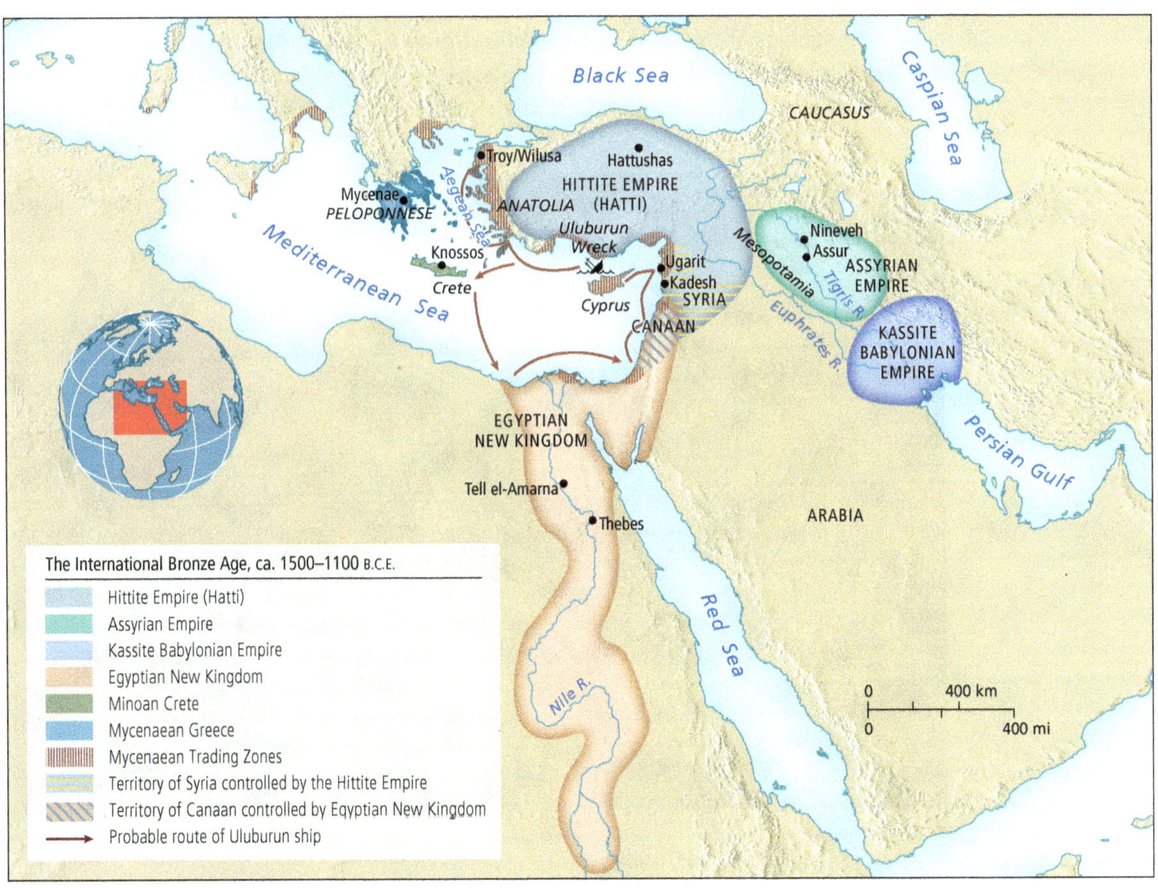

MAP **2.1** THE INTERNATIONAL BRONZE AGE, CA. 1500–1100 B.C.E. For 500 years, networks of commerce and diplomacy tied together the distinct cultures of Egypt, Greece, Anatolia, and southwest Asia. What were the five zones of power that shaped the International Bronze Age?

Indo-Europeans traveled from a homeland in the Caucasus to populate not only Anatolia but also modern-day India, Europe, and Iran. Still other scholars contend that Indo-Europeans existed in Anatolia from prehistory on.

Whatever their origins, by 1650 B.C.E. the Hittites had established a prosperous kingdom in central Anatolia called Hatti. The once-prominent idea that the Hittites invented the process of smelting iron and that their power rested on this secret skill has now been debunked. But even without iron, Hittite power gradually expanded from Anatolia into western Mesopotamia and Syria, and, by the fourteenth century B.C.E., into Canaan.

This expansion meant that the Hittite Empire and New Kingdom Egypt were soon competing for the same territories. Competition erupted into outright war at a number of points and finally produced an epic yet curiously indecisive military encounter: the Battle of Kadesh of 1274 B.C.E. (See *Encounters and Transformations* in this chapter.) Drained by this battle and those that succeeded it, Pharaoh Ramesses II and Hittite King Hattusili III turned to a diplomatic solution: They agreed that the Hittites would control northern Syria while Egypt kept its Canaanite territories. This treaty transformed long-term enemies into allies and marked a crucial step in stabilizing international relations.

Imperial expansion brought many diverse peoples under Hittite rule and reshaped Hittite religious practice. The Hittites rightly called their country "the land of a thousand gods." To unify its peoples, the Hittite monarchy transported its subjects' gods to its capital city of Hattusha and built many temples for them. Called the "Great King," the Hittite monarch played the role of chief priest of all the gods worshiped by the many different communities under his control. The new gods were simply added to the Hittite pantheon, regardless of any overlap or duplication of function. Thus, Hittite religion contained numerous sun gods, father gods, warrior deities, and fertility goddesses, and countless contradictory religious legends.

Just as they embraced new gods, the Hittites adopted other aspects of different cultures—such as architecture, diet, medical practices, and folklore—and transmitted these cultural borrowings to other peoples. By passing ancient Mesopotamian ideas to the Greeks, the Hittites played an important role in shaping what became Western

GODS ON PARADE This bas-relief of a procession of gods of the Underworld comes from Yazilikaya (literally "inscribed rock"), a rock sanctuary in modern Turkey that in Hittite times housed an elaborate religious site dedicated to the Hittite Storm God (also called the Weather God). A natural alcove of rocks, Yazilikaya comprises two roofless chambers that feature numerous carved rock reliefs. In the larger chamber, 64 gods join in a procession that culminates in the meeting of the Storm God with his consort the Sun Goddess. In Hittite myth, the Storm God's rains caused the Sun Goddess to conceive.

civilization. The Greek myth of Hercules likely resulted from this process of cultural transmission. The survival of the *Epic of Gilgamesh* in Hittite archives reveals that the Hittites adopted this Mesopotamian story (see Chapter 1), which they then passed on, via trade and conquest, to the Greeks. Over centuries of cultural transformation, Gilgamesh, the quintessential Mesopotamian hero, became Hercules. Similarly, Mesopotamian mathematical concepts probably made their way into Greek (and, hence, Western) culture via the Hittites.

Some scholars argue that the Hittites also deserve credit for creating the concept of history. In the Hittite kingdom, official proclamations often contained lengthy introductions that set the subject of the proclamation—a decree, perhaps, or a treaty—in context by reciting the past events that made it necessary or possible. These historical narratives demonstrate that the Hittites believed human beings could and should learn from history. Hittite kings, for example, were willing to acknowledge the incompetence or sins of past kings (something unthinkable in Egyptian annals in which the god-king could do no wrong), and to link such misbehavior to current misfortunes. Hittite historical accounts show that the Hittites sought to understand the present in terms of the past and saw history as the result of human action as well as divine whim.

Hittite Law Code: Excerpts from the Code of the Nesilim

KASSITE BABYLON AND ASSYRIA The third zone of power during the International Bronze Age lay in Mesopotamia. Around 1600 B.C.E. people known as Kassites infiltrated Mesopotamia as raiders, soldiers, and laborers. Their language and precise place of origin are unknown, but by 1400 B.C.E. they had gained control of most of southern Mesopotamia. For the next 250 years, Kassite monarchs maintained order and prosperity in Babylonia, establishing the longest ruling dynasty in ancient southwest Asian history.

During these centuries, Babylonia enjoyed a golden age. Kassite kings unified Babylonia's many cities through a highly centralized administration that controlled both urban centers and the countryside. The Kassite kings gained a reputation for fair rule by giving land to individuals of all ranks and by spending lavishly on temples, public buildings, and canals throughout the kingdom. Political stability and economic prosperity enabled Kassite Babylonia to become a renowned center of literature and learning. Seeking to overcome their outsider origins, Kassite kings claimed the Mesopotamian cultural legacy as their own. They ordered their scribes to copy and thus preserve Sumerian and Akkadian works.

Babylonia's chief rival for dominance in the Mesopotamian region during the International Bronze Age lay to the north: Assyria. Around 1360 B.C.E., the Assyrian kingdom began a new phase of expansion that culminated in the reign of the mighty Tukulti-Ninurta I (r. 1244–1208 B.C.E.), who led his armies to victory over Babylonia itself. By the time of Tukulti-Ninurta's death, Assyria controlled all the lands from northern Syria to southern Iraq.

THE MEDITERRANEAN CIVILIZATIONS: MINOAN CRETE AND MYCENAEAN GREECE The fourth zone of power in the International Bronze Age lay to the east, with the Mediterranean civilizations of Minoan Crete and Mycenean Greece. Although not as large and powerful as Egypt's New Kingdom or the Mesopotamian empires of Kassite Babylon and Assyria, these seafaring civilizations played a vital role in the international system that shaped the Late Bronze Age. They were also the predecessors of ancient Greece.

Minoan civilization emerged about 2600 B.C.E. when small urban communities on the island of Crete began to trade with Egypt and to import copper and tin from the eastern Mediterranean. By 1700 B.C.E., the Minoans had developed a magnificent palace-centered culture. These palaces served as political, economic, and religious centers. Unlike the symmetrical monumental buildings of Mesopotamia and Egypt, Minoan palaces were so sprawling that the Greeks later termed them "labyrinths." Ordinary Minoans lived in houses built around the palace. Some of these palace-centered communities were actually small cities. Knossos, for example, housed approximately 25,000 people.

2.1

2.2

2.3

Minoan prosperity rested on its sea trade and the export of luxury goods—jewelry, painted vases, and delicate figures carved in the deep blue gemstone called lapis lazuli. The Minoans developed a merchant navy that traded with Greece, Egypt, and the coastal communities of the eastern Mediterranean. High-prowed and sturdy, Minoan vessels were well-suited for sailing the Mediterranean Sea.

Although their language was evidently Indo-European, the Minoans learned their pictographic script from the Egyptians. Called "Linear A," Minoan script has yet to be fully deciphered. As a result, what we know about the Minoans comes from art and architecture, rather than texts. The lack of military fortifications around Minoan palaces—in contrast to the strong defenses that ringed other Late Bronze Age centers—and the many images of women on the wall paintings from Minoan palaces have provoked speculation about Minoan social life. Some scholars argued that Minoan society was unusually peace-loving and **matriarchal** (female-dominated). Later discoveries of weapons collections and the strong evidence for the existence of bull worship—a practice usually linked with patriarchal societies—call these arguments into question. The dominance of female images in the paintings more likely points to an emphasis on fertility, while the lack of defensive fortifications probably indicates that the Minoans possessed a navy strong enough to make them feel secure on their island home.

matriarchal A social or cultural system in which family lineage is traced through the mother and/or in which women hold significant power.

 **View** the **Map**

Map Discovery: Greece in the Bronze Age

This security ended abruptly and mysteriously. Minoan prosperity and power disappeared around 1400 B.C.E. Archaeologists do not know whether invaders caused the collapse of Minoan power or whether Minoan Crete was destroyed by a natural disaster, perhaps a tidal wave linked to a volcanic eruption on the nearby island of Thera.

In the wake of the Minoan collapse, the balance of economic power in the eastern Mediterranean shifted to the mainland of Mycenaean Greece. The term *Mycenaean* refers both to the kingdom of Mycenae (located in the Peloponnese, the southern peninsula of mainland Greece) and, more generally, to the culture of Greece during the

LEAPING THE BULL Scholars used to think that this Minoan mural ca. 1500 B.C.E. depicted a sporting event, perhaps similar to the contests staged between animals and men in the Roman Colosseum centuries later. Scientists now tell us that it is impossible to somersault over a charging bull, so perhaps the mural has religious or astrological significance. What is clear is the undeniable Minoan artistry, able to communicate power and grace across the millennia.

Encounters and Transformations

A Diplomatic Revolution

To greedy and ambitious rulers, the lands stretching from western Syria down the Canaanite corridor (today's Lebanon, Israel, and Palestine) offered numerous temptations—timberlands, agricultural fields and pasture lands, hills heavy with metals, and port cities with international commercial connections. In the thirteenth century B.C.E., this region became the site of an important encounter between the Hittite and Egyptian empires, one that transformed not only Great Power alignments for the next century, but also diplomacy itself.

During the fourteenth century B.C.E., the Hittite Empire had expanded southward. By the turn of the century, however, Egypt under the New Kingdom had regained enough power to challenge Hittite control of Syria and Canaan. For two decades, the two empires jostled for advantage. Then, Ramesses II (1279–1212 B.C.E.) succeeded to the throne of New Kingdom Egypt. Determined to push the Hittites out of Canaan and Syria, Ramesses spent five years gathering troops for battle. In 1274 B.C.E. he led his army northward. Muwatalli II (ca. 1295–1272) awaited him with a Hittite and mercenary army of 37,000 infantry and 3,500 chariotry. The stage was set for a decisive battle between the two empires.

As the Egyptians under Ramesses drew near to the Syrian city of Kadesh, they captured two supposed deserters from the Hittite army. These men reported that Muwatalli, alarmed by Ramesses's advance, had retreated with his army about 200 miles to the north. Delighted with the news, Ramesses decided to press on to Kadesh with just one division in the hopes of capturing the city before the Hittites moved south again. This decision left the Egyptian army strung out over several miles. Moreover, the "deserters" were actually Muwatalli's spies: Ramesses had fallen into a carefully set trap. The Hittite army launched a surprise attack on Ramesses's poorly situated forces.

Panic-stricken, the Egyptians broke—but then Ramesses himself led a chariot charge. Inspired by the pharaoh's personal bravery (or so Ramesses's account of the battle insisted), his men rallied. In addition, both Hittite lack of discipline—Hittite soldiers turned to plunder the Egyptian camp rather than press their advance—and the lucky arrival of a force of allied Canaanite charioteers helped swing the day in the Egyptians' favor. Yet Egypt did not win the battle. Muwatalli lost almost all of his chariots, but the next day his infantry withstood Ramesses's attacks. Deciding enough was enough, Ramesses turned around and went home. Once back in Egypt, he boasted of a great victory. Although no such victory had occurred, Ramesses's less-than-accurate version of the battle was inscribed on pillars across the land.

The struggle over Syria and Canaan continued. Over the next several years, Ramesses and his army fought a number of battles against the forces of Muwatalli and his successors. Neither, however, possessed the strength to annihilate the other because the Battle of Kadesh had depleted the resources of both Great Powers. And while they were busy draining each other dry, Assyria was amassing military power and economic strength. This new player could seize control of the entire game if the two seasoned veterans did not switch strategy.

In 1258 B.C.E., Ramesses II and the Hittite King Hattusili III (ca. 1267–1237 B.C.E.) signed an innovative treaty. Ramesses abandoned claims to northern Syria and Hattusili acknowledged Egyptian control over Canaan. Yet the treaty did more than end the fighting. It also created an alliance: The two powers agreed to aid one another in case of invasion or rebellion. The treaty demonstrated that diplomatic ties could serve Great Power interests. This diplomatic innovation survived long after both the Hittite Empire and the New Kingdom had disappeared into history.

For Discussion

Despite Ramesses's grandiose claims to the contrary, Egypt did not win a great victory in the Battle of Kadesh. Why, then, is this battle seen as historically significant?

International Bronze Age. Mycenae dominated the Peloponnese, but did not rule all of Greece. Instead, the Mycenaean kingdoms traded with and warred against each other.

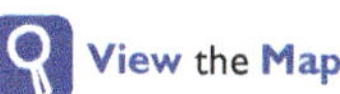

Map Discovery: Mycenean Trade and Contacts

In the century before the Minoan collapse, the Mycenaeans interacted extensively with Minoan Crete and adapted many of its cultural practices, including its palace-centered economy and a script related to Linear A. Called "**Linear B**," it is the earliest written form of Greek. Unfortunately, the surviving palace records, written on clay tablets, all relate to economic matters—landholding records, lists of broken equipment, inventories of available storage space, and the like. None of the tablets contains a story or religious hymn or battle chronicle.

"Linear B" The earliest written form of Greek, used by the Mycenaeans.

Although we have no literary record of Mycenaean values or beliefs, the archaeological evidence, particularly Mycenaean burial sites, reveals a prosperous and militaristic culture. Mycenaean merchants extended Minoan commercial routes as far west as Spain and northern Italy. The line between trading and raiding was never very solid, however, and the Mycenaeans earned a well-deserved reputation for piracy.

2.1

2.2

2.3

CITY-STATES AND COASTAL COMMUNITIES: SYRIA AND CANAAN As Map 2.1 shows, the final zone of power in the International Bronze Age consisted of the regions of Syria and Canaan (or Palestine). The political fragmentation of this region and its key location made it the battleground on which the Hittite, Mesopotamian, and Egyptian empires fought for supremacy. Often reduced to pawns in imperial power plays, smaller states throughout Syria and Canaan nevertheless played an active role in fostering trading relations, shaping diplomatic patterns, and initiating cultural innovation.

The city-state of Ugarit, for example, appears frequently in Late Bronze Age texts. A port city, Ugarit controlled a kingdom of about 2,000 square miles blessed with rich natural resources. The fertile plain offered arable land for grape vines, olive trees, and grains, while the surrounding hill forests provided timber for shipbuilding and construction. Ugarit's greatest asset was a natural harbor that made the city a hub of international trade. Merchant ships, such as the one that sank at Uluburun, sailed to Ugarit from across the Mediterranean, while caravans laden with goods arrived from Mesopotamia, the Hittite lands, and Canaan. People from all these places settled in Ugarit, whose population was estimated at about 6,000–8,000 inhabitants. Perhaps another 25,000 people lived as farmers in about 150 villages in the Ugarit countryside. Its natural resources and strategic location, however, made Ugarit a natural target for acquisitive empires. By the thirteenth century B.C.E., the Hittite emperor chose the occupant of Ugarit's throne.

Ugarit was fairly typical of the city-states of Syria and Canaan during the International Bronze Age. In scattered cities throughout the region, urban culture thrived as a result of the flourishing international trade (and heavy exploitation of the rural agricultural populations). Continued prosperity, however, demanded that Syrian and Canaanite rulers walk a diplomatic tightrope, allying first with this empire and then with that, negotiating for survival in an age of imperial might.

TROY: A CITY OF LEGEND The five zones of power that we have delineated provide the parameters of the International Bronze Age. Scattered among these zones were small city-states and kingdoms, sometimes swallowed up by one of the large empires, sometimes independent. One of these, the Anatolian city-state of Troy, has captured the popular imagination for 3,000 years, ever since it was immortalized as the site of the Trojan War in Homer's epic poem, the *Iliad*, which recounts the final year of the tragic clash between the Greeks and the Trojans. According to the *Iliad*, the war began when Paris of Troy kidnapped the beautiful Helen, queen of the Greek city-state of Sparta, and ended with the total destruction of Troy.

Homer: Debate among the Greeks at Troy

The *Iliad* was put into written form about 750 B.C.E., yet most scholars agree that it came out of an oral tradition extending back to the Late Bronze Age. The name "Troy" does not appear in Bronze Age documents, but many archaeologists argue that a conflict between Mycenae and a city-state called Wilusa in ancient texts may have sparked the oral tradition that became Homer's story of the war between the Greeks and Trojans—although if so, the point of contention was probably something dull, such as the question of safe passage for merchant ships, rather than the raging passion stirred up by a beautiful queen.

Archaeologists have identified the likely site of Troy/Wilusa on the northwestern Anatolian coast. Excavations there reveal that Troy prospered in the Late Bronze Age. Numerous distinct layers of occupation and construction tell us that generations of inhabitants rebuilt the city time and time again from about 3000 to 1000 B.C.E. Like the Troy of Homer's story, Troy VI (the sixth layer of occupation) was a grand city. It featured monumental gateways and a royal palace compound containing many mansions. But sometime around 1300 B.C.E., the city was destroyed—not by an enemy army, as in the legend of Troy, but probably by an earthquake. Troy's inhabitants rapidly rebuilt, but this new city (Troy VIIa) was smaller and poorer, not at all like the glorious civilization of Homer's tale.

So is Homer's Troy purely fiction? Perhaps . . . but perhaps not. We know that around 950 B.C.E. something decimated the city (Troy VIIb3) and left it a pile of rubble.

THE "DEATH MASK OF AGAMEMNON" This thin gold mask, about 11 inches long, was found at the citadel of Mycenae in the tomb of a ruler who died about 1550 B.C.E. Heinrich Schliemann, whose excavations were the first to show that Troy did exist in history as well as legend, mistakenly jumped to the conclusion that it was the death mask of King Agamemnon, who led the Greek forces during the Trojan War, as told in Homer's *Iliad*.

Enemy raids could have caused Troy's final destruction. Possibly the memory of these events fused with earlier tales of the grand civilization of Troy VI and its conflicts with Mycenaean Greeks and eventually took the form of Homer's *Iliad*. Like the *Epic of Gilgamesh*, the *Iliad* is a verbal version of an archaeological site, with many different layers of "occupation."

The Club of the Great Powers

Historians have used the label "the Club of the Great Powers" to describe the international network that shaped the Late Bronze Age. As the word *club* indicates, these Great Powers interacted closely and, in so doing, developed concepts and tools of international diplomacy and interchange that survived long after the Great Powers themselves had collapsed.

GREAT POWER RELATIONS AND EXCHANGES Great Power rulers knew who was in their club, who was leveraging for entrance, and who was vulnerable for expulsion. In the beginning of the Late Bronze Age, for example, Assyria was still too small and weak to be a member. By around 1330 B.C.E., however, Assyrian power was expanding and King Assur-Uballit I decided it was time to join the Great Powers' Club. He sent lavish gifts and a letter to the pharaoh that dared address the Egyptian ruler as an equal: "Up to now, my predecessors had not written: today I write to you."[1] In many ways, Great Power rulers acted as if they all belonged to the same extended (if somewhat dysfunctional) family. They addressed each other as "Brother," exchanged boastful letters, and traded gifts to celebrated enthronements, military conquests, and marriages (often to each others' daughters and sisters).

The gift exchanges among the Great Powers were highly formalized. Rulers did not hesitate to correct colleagues who failed to abide by the rules. For example, the Hittite king, Hattusili III, lectured the king of Assyria when he failed to send a suitable gift:

> It is the custom that when kings assume kingship, the kings, his equals in rank, send him appropriate gifts of greeting, clothing befitting kingship, and fine oil for his anointing. But you did not do this today.

Abiding by the rules of gift exchange was more than a matter of reciprocal greed. First, these exchanges signaled that each ruler recognized the legitimacy of the other, and so helped maintain the stability of international relations. Second, the rules of gift-giving were, for Great Power rulers, part of the definition of "civilization," and therefore one of the characteristics that differentiated them from barbarians. To be a member of the Club of Great Powers was to be a part of the civilized world. And third, gift-giving served as a disguised form of trade. One king would send a "gift" to another, and then demand a "gift" of equal value in return. In this way, luxury goods and other items in high demand circulated throughout the International Bronze Age economy. Egypt, for example, was the source of most of the Near Eastern gold supply as well as ivory, ebony, and alabaster.

Gift exchanges were confined to the Great Power kings and their queens, but Great Power rulers also actively fostered and protected trade in its wider forms. Much of their correspondence concerned the safety of caravan routes and shipping lanes. A ruler was responsible for the security of his realm. If bandits attacked a merchant's caravan, the ruler of the region in which the attack occurred was expected to make restitution. Trade was important to Great Power rulers both for the wealth it produced and for the taxes it generated. Moreover, international trade brought together the tin and copper needed to make bronze.

CONQUEST AND CLIENT STATES We saw in Chapter 1 that bronze was the key component of the light chariot, the central military technology of International Bronze Age empires. Because of the expense of maintaining armies of trained charioteers, Great Power rulers were constantly on the lookout for new sources of income. In addition to relying on trade to generate revenue, rulers depended on the spoils they claimed from military conquests and the tribute they collected from client states. War in the International Bronze Age was thus a business venture.

After conquest, most states became vassals or client-states of the conquering Great Power. Client-states provided their Great Power overlord with annual tribute and often with auxiliary troops. The relationship between a client-state and a Great Power was clearcut. A Great Power monarch writing to the ruler of one of his client-states would begin, "My servant." A client king's salutation to his overlord made the relationship even plainer:

> My king, my lord, my sun god, I prostrate myself at the feet of my lord, my sun god, seven times and seven times.[2]

COMMONALITIES AMONG THE GREAT POWER CULTURES The Egyptian, Hittite, Assyrian, Babylonian, and Minoan-Mycenean societies occupied different agricultural spaces; the fertility of the Nile delta, for example, contrasted with the aridity of most of Anatolia. They also possessed different histories, religions, and customs. Nevertheless, the Great Power societies in the International Bronze Age shared the same basic socioeconomic structures and militaristic values.

Archaeologists and historians use the term **palace system** to describe Late Bronze Age societies. In this system, wealth and power concentrated in the hands of the small ruling elite, who lived separated from the laboring masses in monumental fortified palaces. Sometimes constituting entire cities, these palaces were set apart from the neighborhoods of ordinary people. In Assur, capital city of the Assyrian Empire, for example, all the palaces and temples stood within the walled inner city, far from the areas where the rest of the city's populace lived.

palace system Late Bronze Age social system that concentrated religious, economic, political, and military power in the hands of an elite, who lived apart from most people in monumental fortified compounds.

The Minoan palace at Knossos exemplifies the International Bronze Age palace system. The palace occupied three acres. At its center stood a courtyard surrounded by hundreds of rooms that served as living quarters for the political and religious elite, administrative headquarters, and shrines for religious worship. Frescoes (plaster painted while it is still wet) of sea creatures, flowers, acrobats, and scenes of daily life adorned the walls. The residents enjoyed indoor plumbing and running water, comforts that most people in the West would not enjoy until the nineteenth century C.E.

Two distinct social hierarchies delineated International Bronze Age societies: the palace dependents and the free people in the villages. The first group comprised the military officers, religious officials, scribes, craftsmen, and agricultural laborers within the palace system. Paid with rations, in the case of lower ranked laborers and craftsmen, and with royal land grants in the upper ranks, they ensured the continuity of imperial administration and the luxurious lifestyle of the royal family. At Knossos, the palace dependents' rations were stored in warehouses that could hold more than a quarter million gallons of wine or olive oil. The regularity of such rations meant that the palace dependents were probably better off than the free villagers in the countryside. Obliged to pay taxes and to labor on royal building projects for a part of every year, these villagers practiced mixed farming, scraping out a living growing grains, cultivating fruit trees, and grazing sheep and goats. In bad times, they were forced to borrow from wealthier neighbors. If they could not pay back the debt, they were forced into slavery.

At the top of all Bronze Age societies stood the royal family, the members of which lived in luxury beyond the comprehension of most of their subjects—and of most of us today. Thirty royal graves uncovered at Mycenae contain skeletons nearly six feet tall—taller than the average Mycenaean and clear evidence that the kings enjoyed better nutrition than their subjects. The many gold and silver drinking vessels and pieces of jewelry found in the graves further demonstrate the luxury in which not only Mycenaean but all Bronze Age rulers lived.

All Late Bronze Age cultures glorified military conquest and so placed the warrior high on the social scale. Kings personally led annual military campaigns; hence, battle accounts dominate royal chronicles. In Mycenaea, the graves of warriors contain not only their bodies, but also their armor, weapons, and even their chariots. The burial of such prized items indicates the prestige of the warrior class. To be manly was to be a warrior, as this account of a Hittite ritual for inducting troops into the army makes clear:

> They bring the garments of a woman, a distaff [for spinning cloth] and a mirror, they break an arrow and you speak as follows: "Is not this that you see here garments of a woman? We have them here for [the ceremony of taking] the oath. Whoever breaks these oaths and does evil to the king and the queen and the princes, let these oaths change him from a man into a woman!" . . . Let them break the bows, arrows, and clubs in their hands and let them put in their hands distaff and mirror![3]

THE INTERNATIONAL MONUMENTAL STYLE Many Late Bronze Age kings constructed new capital cities as a way to proclaim their power to their people and to their potential rivals at home and abroad. In constructing these palaces and cities, kings borrowed from each other's cultures to such a degree that a single "international style" in monumental building emerged, as these Hittite and Mycenaean fortress gates illustrate. The entrance gate to the Hittite capital of Hattusha and the gate into the citadel of Mycenae both feature massive stone lions, the symbol of royal strength in many Bronze Age societies.

Crisis and Collapse: The End of the International Bronze Age

The diplomatic, cultural, and economic connections between Egypt, southwest Asia, Anatolia, and Greece broke between 1200 and 1100 B.C.E. These civilizations plummeted into a dark age marked by invasions, migrations, and the collapse of stable governments. On the Greek mainland, the Greek language and some religious beliefs endured, but the population declined by an estimated 75 percent; the crafts, artistic styles, and architectural traditions of Mycenaean life were forgotten. Drought, famine, and invasion dominate the surviving records. A later text, *The Epic of Erra*, recalled this era as a time of horror:

> Sealand shall not spare Sealand . . . nor Assyrian Assyrian.
> Nor shall Elamite spare Elamite, nor Kassite Kassite . . .
> Nor country country, nor city city,
> Nor shall tribe spare tribe, nor man man, nor brother brother, and they shall slay one another.[4]

THE SEA PEOPLES What happened to cause the end of the International Bronze Age? Ancient texts point to raids and invasions by wandering migrants as a key cause. Around 1100 B.C.E., for example, the king of Ugarit warned the king of another Syrian kingdom, "The ships of the enemy have been coming. They have been burning down my villages and have done evil things to the country."[5] Egyptian accounts, which called these invaders the **Sea Peoples**, described their coming in dramatic terms:

Sea Peoples Name given by the Egyptians to the diverse groups of migrants whose attacks helped bring the International Bronze Age to an end.

> No land could stand before their arms. . . . They desolated its people, and its land was like that which had never come into being. They were coming forward into Egypt, while the flame was prepared for them.[6]

Who were these "Sea Peoples" and were they responsible for the collapse of the International Bronze Age system? Scholars have yet to reach agreement on an answer to this key question. One set of explanations focuses on events in Mycenaean Greece and the Hittite Empire. We know that warfare among the many Mycenaean kingdoms resulted in the breakdown of its palace-centered economic system by about 1150 B.C.E. Searching for the means of survival, many Greeks migrated. Approximately 50 years later, a deadly combination of famine, civil war, and international invasion triggered the collapse of the Hittite imperial government. As in Mycenaea, economic chaos followed and desperate peasants fled.

The fall of the Mycenaean kingdoms and the Hittite Empire contributed to destabilizing migrations throughout the eastern Mediterranean. Displaced groups plundered cities and brought destruction to the entire eastern Mediterranean as they moved southward. By 1170 B.C.E., the Egyptian Empire had lost control of Syria and Canaan, and Ugarit fell. Groups of raiders settled on the Mediterranean coast and extended their power inland. Organized political life in Canaan soon disintegrated.

View the Map

Map Discovery: The Sea Peoples

SYSTEMIC INSTABILITY The story of the Sea Peoples is dramatic and compelling; it does not, however, fully explain the sudden end of the International Bronze Age. A second set of explanations for this collapse focuses on the internal instability of the Late Bronze Age palace system and its exploitation of agricultural laborers. Struggling to survive, peasants took out loans, and then, when they were unable to pay their debts, were forced into slavery. Facing enslavement, many peasants fled to mountainous regions or inaccessible marshes, places where they could eke out a living outside the palace system. They became ***habiru***. The term *habiru* is often translated as "robber," "bandit," or "mercenary," and many of the habiru were one or all of those things, forced into such a life by the harshness of the socioeconomic order. For Great Power governments, the *habiru* were a constant problem, not only because of the threat of criminality and social disorder, but more fundamentally, because the flight of peasants worsened agricultural labor shortages and so threatened to undercut the entire palace system.

habiru Peasants who existed outside the palace system of the Late Bronze Age; often seen as bandits.

By the twelfth century B.C.E., this key weakness in the palace system helped destroy it. Many areas appear to have suffered from a lengthy drought, which heightened demands on laborers and escalated the numbers of *habiru*. In turn, those left behind found the demands placed on them even more arduous—and so even more peasants

2.1

2.2

2.3

CHRONOLOGY: INTERNATIONAL BRONZE AGE

ca. 1700 B.C.E.	Minoan civilization flourishes on Crete.
ca. 1650–1600 B.C.E.	Hittite Kingdom emerges.
ca. 1550 B.C.E.	New Kingdom begins in Egypt.
ca. 1450 B.C.E.	First palaces built at Mycenae in Greece.
ca. 1400 B.C.E.	Kassites gain control of Babylonia.
ca. 1360 B.C.E.	Assyria begins period of expansion.
ca. 1200–1100 B.C.E.	International Bronze Age ends.

fled. Moreover, when bands of Sea Peoples appeared, many *habiru* were more than happy to join them in ransacking the palaces and temples, the symbols of their oppression. While ancient texts tend to portray the Sea Peoples as outside invaders, recent archaeological and historical research demonstrates that many of them were already settled in the lands they attacked—they were, in other words, rebels rather than invaders, and their rebellion helped to destroy the International Bronze Age.

Recovery and Rebuilding: Empires and Societies in the Aftermath of the International Bronze Age

2.2 What developments shaped southwest Asian and Mediterranean societies after the collapse of the International Bronze Age?

After the collapse of the International Bronze Age, the peoples of southwest Asia and the Mediterranean gradually rebuilt their world. Three important changes distinguished this new era from what had come before. First, the sophisticated international diplomatic and economic networks of the Late Bronze Age had disappeared, as had principal players in that network. Second, the disruption of Late Bronze Age trade routes resulted in an important metallurgical shift. No longer able to obtain both the tin and the copper necessary to create bronze, people began turning to a resource more plentiful and nearer to hand: iron. Ancient peoples had long been familiar with iron, but unforged iron is not very durable. Sometime after 1200 B.C.E., however, metalsmiths figured out how to smelt iron: By repeatedly heating the metal in a charcoal furnace, and then cold-hammering it, they created carbon steel, a sturdy metal that could outfight bronze. The **Iron Age** was born. By 1000 B.C.E. iron was widely used throughout the Mediterranean region, and by the ninth century B.C.E., throughout Mesopotamia and Egypt. As we will see, iron enabled the kings of Neo-Assyria and Neo-Babylonia to field armies far larger than ever before—and so to rule empires of unprecedented size.

A third change that distinguishes this era from the Late Bronze Age was the use of the domesticated camel for transport and travel. Camels began to appear in Near Eastern artwork and texts around 1100 B.C.E., although they had probably been domesticated centuries before. Because they can travel on little water, camels opened up desert routes to merchants. Rather than having to take roundabout roads that skirted the desert, they could opt for the direct—therefore, quicker and more profitable—route. As the camel trade became a significant factor in ancient economies, the Arab peoples began to play a larger role in southwest Asian cultures, usually as objects of fear. The ability of Arab raiders to plunder a caravan or to sack a city and then to disappear into the desert became legendary.

Iron Age Historical period following the Bronze Age; marked by the prevalent use of iron.

View the Map

Empires of the Ancient Near East

Before and Between the Empires

In the so-called "Dark Age" between the collapse of the International Bronze Age and the reemergence of Assyria as an imperial power (roughly 1100–950 B.C.E.), the weakening or disappearance of Great Powers allowed smaller kingdoms and city-states in Mesopotamia and the Levantine Corridor to flourish. As we will see later in this chapter, this period of transition saw the Israelite or Hebrew culture emerge in Canaan. **Map 2.2** shows that the Hebrew states of Israel and Judah rested within a network of Iron Age kingdoms and city-states. For over 600 years, these states formed shifting coalitions and alliances with and against each other and eventually the resurgent Assyrian and Babylonian empires as well.

NEW PEOPLES OF THE LAND: THE ARAMEANS Within the kaleidoscope of peoples, tribes, and migrants that surged through Syria and the Levant, the Arameans played a dominant role. Originally semi-nomadic pastoralists from northern Syria, Aramean tribes expanded into Assyrian and Babylonian territories during the waning years of the Late Bronze Age. Their raids helped weaken these kingdoms and loosen their hold on their empires. During the subsequent Iron Age, Arameans spread throughout the Near East; by the ninth century B.C.E. Aramean tribes dominated the whole of inland Syria and much of the Mesopotamian countryside, where Aramaic became the language of ordinary people.

The most important Aramean state was Aram-Damascus, centered on the city of Damascus (see Map 2.2). Occupied long before the Arameans emerged in the region, Damascus may be the oldest continuously inhabited city in the world. Damascus prospered and grew powerful during the Iron Age in part because of its location as a key trading post along one of the most economically vital "highways" in the ancient world: the camel caravan route from the Arabian desert to the Mediterranean Sea.

NEW PEOPLES OF THE SEA: THE PHOENICIANS Like the Arameans, the Phoenicians entered the historical record in the final centuries of the Late Bronze Age. Egypt's Late Bronze Age empire included Phoenician city-states along the northern Syrian coast (what is now Lebanon). In the tumult that accompanied the collapse of the International Bronze Age, these cities gained their independence. By 1000 B.C.E., the Phoenicians had developed a dynamic maritime civilization, based in eastern Mediterranean

2.1
2.2
2.3

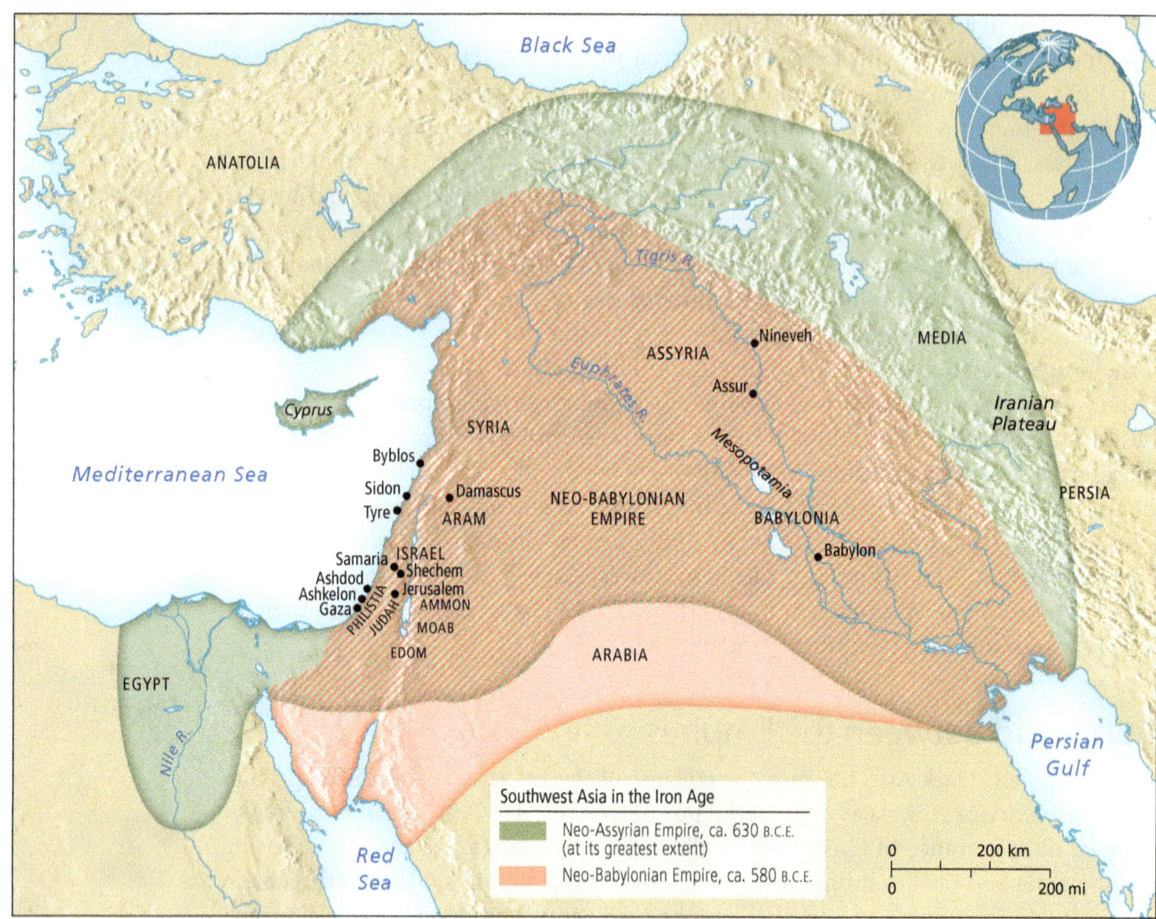

MAP **2.2** SOUTHWEST ASIA IN THE IRON AGE The economic and social crisis that accompanied the end of the International Bronze Age brought with it surges of migration, resulting in new peoples settling throughout southwest Asia and the coalescence of indigenous peoples into new tribal groups. Free (for a time) of Great Power control, Syria and Canaan splintered into small kingdoms and city-states. What were some of these smaller kingdoms and city-states? How did the rise of the Neo-Assyrian and Neo-Babylonian Empires change both the political map and the political realities of southwest Asia?

port cities such as Byblos, Tyre, and Sidon. By following old Minoan and Mycenaean trade routes, the port cities created a large commercial sphere of influence.

The Phoenicians, however, ventured beyond these old Bronze Age routes, even sailing into the Atlantic Ocean, as **Map 2.3** shows. The most dramatic Phoenician voyage occurred when Pharoah Necho II (610–595 B.C.E.) hired a Phoenician crew to circumnavigate the African continent—almost 2,000 years before Europeans would do so. Their sailing experience explains why the Phoenicians were probably the first peoples to develop the *bireme*, a ship with two sets of oars that could, therefore, achieve more speed and power when used in battle.

When the writers of the Hebrew Bible wanted to demonstrate the fabled wealth of King Solomon, they wrote that he contracted with King Hiram of Tyre for luxury goods and that he imported timber from Byblos. These biblical references to Phoenician city-states highlight Phoenician commercial dominance in the Iron Age. Renowned for their artisanal skills, the Phoenicians traded in weapons, jewelry, woodcraft, and the prized reddish-purple cloth for which the Phoenicians were named. (The word *Phoenician*, a Greek coinage, translates as "people of the purple cloth.") Map 2.3 shows that the search for metal ores also motivated much of Phoenician exploration and commerce.

To protect and expand their trade, the Phoenicians established overseas trading posts that grew into self-governing Phoenician colonies. These colonies extended as

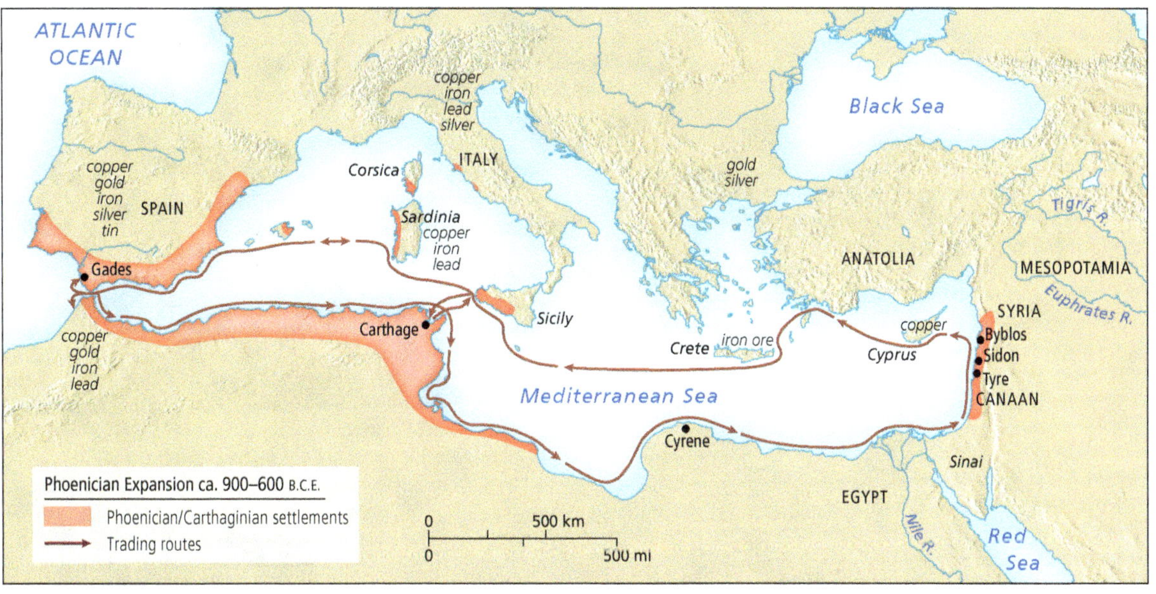

MAP **2.3** PHOENICIAN EXPANSION, CA. 900–600 B.C.E. Impelled by the quest for commerce—and particularly for control of the lucrative metals trade—Phoenicians developed a commercial empire across the Mediterranean Sea. Initially, the Phoenician settlements were only trading posts, but in many areas, these expanded into colonial settlements. By 600 B.C.E. Carthage had become the chief Phoenician city in the western Mediterranean. It controlled the resources of north Africa and parts of Spain. Why was the metals trade so important in this era? How did the Phoenicians serve as economic and cultural conduits, linking Asian, African, and European regions?

far as the coast of Spain, but the most important was Carthage ("New City") on the northern coast of modern Tunisia. Because of its magnificent harbor and strategic location, Carthage controlled trade between the eastern and western Mediterranean.

Their economic connections with lands that would later become the center of Western civilization meant that the Phoenicians served as cultural conduits between Near Eastern civilizations and Europe. Through trade and colonization, Phoenicians brought Asian and Egyptian artistic styles, many of them Bronze Age survivals, to western Mediterranean lands. One of the most important of these survivals was the phonetic alphabet. The principle of the phonetic alphabet seems to have been discovered around 1900 B.C.E. by Canaanites working in Egypt. The Canaanites simplified the complex Egyptian hieroglyphic system, keeping fewer than 30 signs, each representing a single consonant. The resulting "Proto-Canaanite" alphabet evolved into the alphabet used by the Phoenicians, who spread this efficient system of writing throughout the Mediterranean world, where the Greeks and then the Romans adopted it. In this way it became the source of all alphabets and writing in the West.

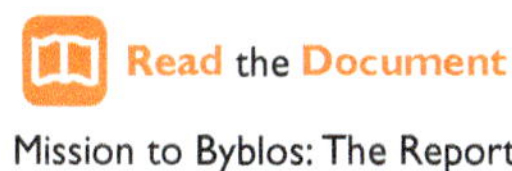

Mission to Byblos: The Report of Wenamun

CANAANITE CULTURES AND CONTINUITIES With the collapse of Egyptian imperial control at the end of the International Bronze Age, Canaan entered a period of instability, with semi-nomadic peoples moving through the region and new states coalescing. Map 2.2 shows that by around 1000 B.C.E., political power was dispersed among the coastal city-states of the Philistines and the small inland kingdoms of Ammon, Moab, and Edom, as well as Israel and Judah (discussed in the next section).

Many archaeologists argue that the Philistines originated as Aegean "Sea Peoples" who made their way to the Canaanite coast after living for some time in Egypt. One of the names of these peoples, the Peleset, may be the origin of the name "Palestine." By 1000 B.C.E. the Philistines inhabited five coastal city-states, each governed by a king. Loosely joined in a confederation, the Philistines became a major Canaanite power.

In contrast to the Philistines, most of the inhabitants of the Iron Age inland kingdoms were, archaeologists believe, indigenous Canaanites. They worshiped variations

TABLET AND PARCHMENT; CUNEIFORM AND ALPHABET This Neo-Assyrian relief from the Southwest Palace at Nineveh (ca. 630–620 B.C.E.) shows Assyrian scribes making an inventory of the booty from a military campaign against Babylonia. Significantly, one scribe holds a clay tablet and is writing in Akkadian cuneiform, whereas the second scribe is writing in Aramaic (and therefore in a phonetic alphabet script) on papyrus. By the seventh century B.C.E. both papyrus and parchment were widely used, but few of these fragile documents have survived.

of the pre-Bronze Age Canaanite gods El and Ba'al and their wives, the fertility goddesses Asherah and Ashtart (Astarte). Iron Age Canaanites also continued the ancient practice of worshiping their gods through non-figural sacred objects, such as standing stones, obelisks, and special trees. These sacred objects were often located on hilltops (called the "high places" in the Hebrew Bible or Old Testament). The core of Canaanite religious life remained, as it had been for millennia, the quest for fertility, both human and agricultural. The effort to ensure the birth of healthy children and abundant harvests accounts for the sensational features of Canaanite religious practices, such as cultic prostitution, in which the sexual union of the worshiper and priest or priestess reenacted the union of Ba'al and Ashtart, and child sacrifice, in which a couple offered their baby to the gods.

Empire Strikes Back: Neo-Assyrian and Neo-Babylonian Dominance

The independence of the small kingdoms and city-states of southern Anatolia, Syria, and Canaan did not last. Beginning in about 1000 B.C.E., the Assyrian and then the Babylonian imperial regimes began to regain control over their territories, reestablish their commercial power, and reconquer neighboring lands.

NEO-ASSYRIAN IMPERIALISM Even during the worst period of Aramean incursions and economic breakdown, Assyrian rulers never lost control of the Assyrian heartland, the rich agricultural region north and east of the city of Assur. As Map 2.2 shows, from about 1000 B.C.E. on, Assyria began again to exert control over the lands around this central zone. The reign of Ashurnasirpal II (883–859 B.C.E.) marked a key step in Assyrian imperial resurgence. Ashurnasirpal II campaigned throughout Syria and the Levant, gradually picking off the smaller city-states. He reasserted Assyrian power all the way to the Mediterranean coast, with the Phoenician city-states voluntarily paying tribute and accepting vassal status rather than facing the onslaught of the Assyrian military machine. Reviving and expanding Hittite imperial practice, Ashurnasirpal used mass deportations to punish conquered peoples, terrify potential enemies, and supply labor for monumental building projects such as his new, more glorious capital city.

CULTURAL CONTINUITIES: BA'AL ACROSS THE CENTURIES This thirteenth-century B.C.E. bronze statuette of the Canaanite god Ba'al comes from Ugarit. The worship of Ba'al was a feature of Canaanite religion throughout both the Bronze and Iron Ages. A gold foil overlay distinguishes the head and face, and silver on the chest, arms, and legs perhaps represents armor.

Source: Réunion des Musées Nationaux/Art Resource, NY.

Subsequent Assyrian monarchs extended and consolidated Ashurnasirpal's conquests. During the reign of Tiglath-Pileser III (r. 745–727 B.C.E.), the empire expanded rapidly. Ascending to the throne after four decades of rebellions and epidemics, Tiglath-Pileser reorganized the army and deployed it to quell rebellious subjects, annex parts of Canaan, and make himself king of Babylon. His achievements ushered in a century of Assyrian dominance—even, for a time, over Egypt. The Neo-Assyrian Empire was the first in history to control the Tigris, Euphrates, and Nile River valleys.

Administering such a large empire posed problems, especially in the realm of communication. Provincial governors ruled on the king's behalf, but if the king's orders took months to arrive, provinces could develop dangerous autonomy. To solve this problem, the Assyrians developed an early version of express mail. They erected road stations at intervals of about 20 to 30 miles (a day's march) along every major route (called "royal roads"). At these stations, the king's messengers would find supplies and fresh horses and mules for their chariots, so that they could travel from one end of the empire to the other in a matter of days.

The Assyrians fielded a standing army that was massive for the age—at least 100,000 men. All Assyrian men were required to serve in the military (although the wealthy could pay for substitutes), but the government also conscripted soldiers from the peoples it conquered. To pay for this army and for royal building projects, the Assyrian state imposed high taxes on its peoples, demanded tribute from its vassal states, and plundered the lands it conquered. Annual military campaigns, therefore, were an economic necessity.

Assyria's military successes rested in part on its innovative approach to fighting. The Assyrians invented mobile battering rams and siege towers to assault enemy cities, and pontoon bridges to transport heavy equipment across rivers. They also created the world's first cavalry unit. Ranks of highly skilled horsemen proved more adept than even the light chariot at breaking an infantry line, and unlike chariot forces, could conduct reconnaissance and fight in mountainous regions.

View the Closer Look Enemies Crossing the Euphrates to Escape Assyrian Archers

ASSYRIAN MILITARY INNOVATIONS: THE CAVALRY Ashurnasirpal II (883–859 B.C.E.) chose what had once been a minor provincial town, Kalhu, as the site of his new capital city. Proclaiming his greatness with monumental architecture, Ashurnasirpal built the Northwest Palace, a magnificent stone structure decorated with massive stone reliefs celebrating the king's triumphs. This photograph of a segment of one of those reliefs shows one of the most important Assyrian military innovations: use of cavalry troops.

With its great size and its innovative technologies, the Assyrian army developed a deserved reputation for terror. If a city or region resisted Assyrian control, its inhabitants met with no mercy. The Assyrians tortured, raped, mutilated, and skinned alive their defeated enemies. The survivors of these brutal conquests were then rounded up, forced to march for hundreds of miles, and dumped in strange lands to serve as an Assyrian labor source. By treating resistors and rebels with such cruelty, the Assyrians avoided having to fight very often: News of Assyrian atrocities spread to neighboring areas, which quickly and understandably surrendered to avoid such a fate. Hence, historians have described the Assyrian policy as "calculated frightfulness."[7]

Despite its ferocity, the Neo-Assyrian Empire played a crucial role in preserving and transmitting ancient Mesopotamian culture for future generations. Although the Assyrians ruled over Babylonia during the eighth and seventh centuries B.C.E. and even sacked the city of Babylon during the reign of Sennacherib (704–681 B.C.E.), they also recognized their cultural debt to Babylon and to its Akkadian and Sumerian predecessors. They treasured this cultural legacy and sought to collect and preserve scientific and literary works. During the Neo-Assyrian period, the final editions of the Akkadian creation story (the *Enuma Elish*) and the *Epic of Gilgamesh*—the versions that we know today—were written down.

The most remarkable effort in cultural collecting occurred during the reign of Asshurbanipal (668–627 B.C.E.). A warrior like all Assyrian kings, Asshurbanipal also

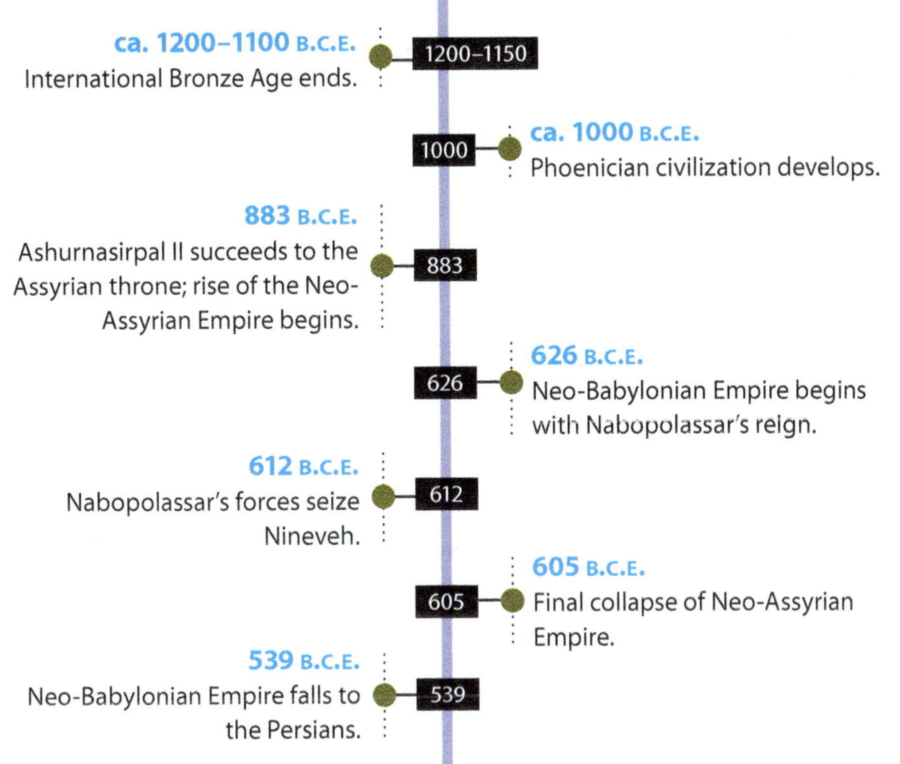

fancied himself a scholar. At his palace in the city of Nineveh he aimed to build a library that would contain every bit of Mesopotamian literature and learning produced up to his time. In perhaps the first known instance of what librarians call "collection development," Asshurbanipal sent representatives throughout the empire to purchase—or confiscate—tablets and texts. Back in Nineveh scribes copied and catalogued these tablets, and then shelved them in rooms divided by subject area. Classified documents such as spy reports and records of secret state affairs were stored in the deepest, least accessible rooms. Over 30,000 tablets, containing perhaps 10,000 different texts (many of them mere fragments), survive from Asshurbanipal's library.

Mighty as it was, the Assyrian Empire came to a sudden end. In the final decades of the seventh century B.C.E., a series of succession crises and revolts fatally weakened the empire. "Calculated frightfulness" produced such bitter resentment that subject peoples rebelled. The most significant of these rebels was the Babylonian king Nabopolassar in southern Mesopotamia (r. 626–605 B.C.E.). The self-described "son of a nobody," Nabopolassar fought for 10 years to free Babylon from Assyrian control. He then took the war into Assyria itself. In 616 B.C.E., after a three-month siege, Nineveh fell to the invaders. The victorious Nabopolassar proclaimed,

> I slaughtered the land of Subartu [Assyria]. . . . The Assyrian, who since distant days had ruled over all the peoples, and with his heavy yoke had brought injury to the people of the Land, his feet from Akkad I turned back, his yoke I threw off.

The Babylonian Chronicles: The Fall of Nineveh Chronicle

For some years Assyrians fought on with the assistance of Egyptian forces, but by 605 B.C.E., when Nabopolassar died, the Neo-Assyrian Empire had entirely collapsed.

THE NEO-BABYLONIAN EMPIRE Nabopolassar became the founder of the Neo-Babylonian (or Chaldean) Empire, which lasted until 539 B.C.E. Conflict with Egypt dominated the early years of the empire as the two Great Powers scrambled to fill the power vacuum left by Assyria's collapse. In the course of this conflict, the brilliant general Nebuchadnezzar II (r. 604–562 B.C.E.) seized Syria, the Phoenician city-states, and the kingdom of Judah. (See Map 2.2.)

The Neo-Babylonians continued the Assyrian practice of deporting conquered peoples, both as a weapon of terror and as a means of filling labor shortages. The deported upper classes of conquered peoples often were allowed to live at the royal court, where they were treated well, as long as they accepted Babylonian rule. Most of the deportees, however, lived in villages, where they were required to turn over most of their harvests to their landlords and to pay the temple taxes.

While agricultural laborers endured conditions of extreme exploitation, the Babylonian economy flourished. Neo-Babylonian rulers devoted resources to restoring roads and canals and to expanding the irrigation system. Private trading houses financed commercial expeditions and exchanges, and Babylon became a center of imperial and international trade. Political boundaries and war did not seem to matter. Egyptian merchants, for example, were welcome throughout Babylonian territories, as were their goods, even during periods of warfare between the two empires.

With the wealth acquired from both conquest and trade, Neo-Babylonian kings made their capital city of Babylon into one of the wonders of the ancient world. According to tradition, Nebuchadnezzar built the "Hanging Gardens of Babylon" for a favorite wife who missed her mountainous homeland. Splendid flowers and plants cascaded down the slopes of a terraced hillside that, from a distance, seemed to float in the air. A moat flooded with waters from the Euphrates River surrounded Babylon's eight miles of walls. As the following illustrations show, brightly colored tiles

THE ISHTAR GATE The magnificently tiled Ishtar Gate provided a dramatic entrance to Babylon, capital city of the Neo-Babylonian Empire. Babylonian artists used brightly colored tiles to create complex three-dimensional depictions of animals and warriors. The gate now rests in a museum in Berlin. An artist's reconstruction shows what the gate may have looked like during the empire's heyday.

decorated the Ishtar Gate, which opened onto a grand avenue leading to the temple of Marduk, Babylon's greatest god.

In addition to their architectural achievements, the Neo-Babylonians compiled an impressive record in astronomical research and observation. Confident that such research could uncover the will of the gods, Babylonian astronomers recorded the movements of the stars, the planets, and the moon. They kept a continuous log of observations between 747 B.C.E. and 61 C.E., an astonishing achievement. By 500 B.C.E., they had accumulated so much astronomical data that they could perform complex mathematical computations to predict eclipses of the moon and sun. These astronomers' calculations, which Persians and Greeks would later adopt, helped lay the foundation of Western science. The Neo-Babylonians also gave the West the names of many constellations, the zodiac, and many mathematical models of astronomical phenomena.

The Neo-Babylonians looked not only to the stars but also to the past to orient themselves in their world. Like the rulers of the Neo-Assyrian Empire, the kings of Babylon regarded themselves as heirs and custodians of a long and valuable cultural tradition. Although Aramaic was now the language of everyday life, Akkadian remained the language of state affairs, and Babylonian kings even sought to revive archaic expressions and script. They also worked to preserve artworks from past generations and to restore ruined temples and palaces. King Nabonidus (555–539 B.C.E.) has been called "the first archaeologist" because of his restoration of holy places in Sumer and Akkad and his interest in collecting and identifying ancient artifacts, which he kept in a museum in his daughter's palace in Ur.

Nabonidus was also a deeply religious man, the son of a priestess to the moon goddess Sin. During his reign, Nabonidus's devotion to Sin alienated many Babylonians, who believed that he jeopardized Babylonian prosperity by neglecting the worship of Marduk. This alienation at least partly explains why, in 539 B.C.E., the Neo-Babylonian Empire quickly fell under Persian control. The end of the Neo-Babylonian dynasty, however, did not destroy Babylon's economic networks or cultural traditions. Both continued to flourish under Persian rule, which we will examine in Chapter 3.

The Civilization of the Hebrews

2.3 What beliefs and institutions shaped Hebrew civilization and its legacy?

One of the most influential civilizations in the West has been that of the Hebrews, a people who originated in Canaan in the tumultuous era at the end of the Late Bronze Age. The history of the Hebrews—or Israelites—took shape within the context of the events we have examined in this chapter: the International Bronze Age and its collapse, the emergence of several small states in Canaan and Syria, and the resurgence of the Assyrian and Babylonian empires after 1000 B.C.E.

The Early History of the Hebrews

The history of the early Hebrews is one of the most controversial subjects in the study of the ancient Near East. Our primary textual source for this history is the Hebrew Bible, or what Christians call the Old Testament. Drawn from a variety of oral and written sources, and composed many centuries after the events they describe, the Hebrew biblical texts condense a complex process of migration, settlement, and religious development. These texts are not historical narratives, in the sense that twenty-first century readers understand history. Some scholars, in fact, argue that these texts can tell us little about early Hebrew history. They point out that the books that make up the Hebrew Bible were first written down in the seventh and sixth centuries B.C.E., some 400 to 600 years after many of the events that they describe. According to these scholars, the apparent history in these texts is almost entirely fictional, a myth of origins composed to give meaning, solace, and identity to an oppressed people. The majority of scholars, however, argue that although the biblical texts first achieved written form centuries after the events they narrate, these documents were based on oral traditions, some of which go back to the original episodes. The biblical texts, then, are not "history" but, when checked against the archaeological evidence, can be used as an important source for uncovering that history.

The people who became the Hebrews first appear in the historical record in Canaan around 1200 B.C.E. at the end of the Late Bronze Age. Archaeological evidence points to a dramatic growth in the numbers of small settlements in the hill country of inland Canaan, on the margins of established urban society. Certain features distinguish these hamlets from others in the area. The houses were grouped in clusters of three or four, with common walls and courtyards. These material remains confirm the portrait of early Israelite culture that we receive from the Hebrew Bible: a largely self-sufficient agricultural society, with a strong emphasis on family and community life.

But from where did these new hill-dwellers come? Many centuries later, the biblical book of Exodus explained that a leader called Moses led them from slavery in Egypt to freedom in Canaan. The archaeological and linguistic evidence, however, indicates that these "proto-Israelites" were indigenous Canaanites, most likely a coalescence of semi-nomadic peoples and urban refugees who fled to the hills to escape the economic disarray and political tumult that accompanied the collapse of the International Bronze Age. Yet we need not discard the Exodus narrative entirely. Sea Peoples raided Egypt in the thirteenth century B.C.E. and many of these peoples wound up in Canaan and Syria. One of these groups, then, may have mixed with indigenous Canaanites to form what became the Hebrews; their story, told and retold, may have come to stand for the identity of the entire group.

Israel: From Monarchy to Exile

With the collapse of the Late Bronze Age empires, a power vacuum existed in Canaan. The Philistines and the Israelites competed for advantage. The Philistines controlled the Mediterranean coastal plain in Canaan and pushed relentlessly at the Hebrews living in the inland hills. According to traditions recorded in the Bible, the desperate Hebrews decided that a king would give them stronger leadership. Such a turn to kingship marked a sharp break in Hebrew culture. If historians are correct in locating early Hebrew origins at least in part in the flight of oppressed city-dwellers to the hill country, then much of Hebrew identity was rooted in opposition to centralized political power. In the biblical texts, anti-royalism—resistance to kingship and the corresponding exploitation of the agricultural masses—constitutes a powerful and repeated theme.

THE UNITED MONARCHY According to the biblical record, the Israelites chose Saul to be their first king around 1020 B.C.E. Some 20 years later, a popular warrior named David (ca. 1005–970 B.C.E.) succeeded Saul, defeated the Philistines, and built a prosperous, centralized kingdom with Jerusalem, an old Canaanite city, as its capital. (See Map 2.2.) David created a royal court complete with a harem; established a census as the basis for tax collection, military conscription, and forced labor; and set up a centralized bureaucracy run by professional soldiers, administrators, and scribes. (See *Justice in History* in this chapter.)

The Bible tells us that David's son Solomon (ca. 970–931 B.C.E.) raised Israel to the pinnacle of its power and prosperity. One of Solomon's greatest achievements was the construction of a grand temple in Jerusalem. Built with the technical assistance of Phoenician architects and artisans and the forced labor of Solomon's subjects, the Jerusalem temple became the focal point of Israel's religious worship. Highlighting Solomon's wealth and his wisdom, the biblical text paints a picture of a monarch forging long-distance economic and diplomatic relationships throughout the ancient world. He married foreign princesses to cement diplomatic agreements, controlled the trade routes running from Egypt and Arabia to Syria, and established economic ties with kingdoms as far away as that of Sabaea (Sheba) in Yemen.

Like almost every aspect of early Hebrew history, however, this history of what we now call the United Monarchy is extremely controversial. No other ancient texts bear witness to the monarchies of David and Solomon, and scholars disagree about the meaning of the archaeological evidence. Three main sets of explanations exist. A minority of scholars contends that David and Solomon never existed at all. A larger group of specialists argues that the biblical story of the United Monarchy blends tenth-century B.C.E. realities and later events. In this view, the historical David and Solomon were relatively poor, rough tribal chieftains of the tenth century (B.C.E.), while the kingly details of the biblical narrative reflect the conditions of the seventh and sixth centuries B.C.E. The mainstream of historical scholarship, however, insists that the United Monarchy did exist in the tenth century. Extra-biblical textual and archaeological evidence testifies that by the tenth century B.C.E., Canaan was politically divided among small kingdoms—including, it seems likely, the United Monarchy of Israel.

THE DIVIDED MONARCHY The monarchy built by David and Solomon did not last long. The Bible tells us that after Solomon died, the northern Israelites rebelled. Dissatisfied with Solomon's policies of high taxes and forced labor, they refused to acknowledge the kingship of Solomon's son and broke away to form a separate northern kingdom. They kept the name "Israel" for this northern state, but moved its capital to the city of Shechem (and later, Samaria). Solomon's successors retained the throne in Jerusalem and ruled over the smaller southern kingdom that remained, now called Judah (see Map 2.2). Solomon's death thus ushered in the period of the Divided Monarchy or the "successor kingdoms."

The fate of the Divided Monarchy became entangled with the rise of the Neo-Assyrian and Neo-Babylonian empires. Judah, as the smaller and poorer of the two kingdoms, was less attractive to invaders and therefore more politically stable. David's descendants remained on the throne throughout Judah's history and enjoyed relatively strong support from their people. In contrast, Israel experienced a number of revolutions and succession shifts, often a result of the meddling of outside powers. The northern state entered its period of greatest strength around 885 B.C.E., when an army commander named Omri (ca. 885–875 B.C.E.) seized power. Omri's son and successor Ahab (ca. 873–852 B.C.E.) built on his father's legacy to make Israel into one of the most formidable powers in Canaan.

Israel and Judah Eighth Century B.C.E.

INTO EXILE The emergence of the Neo-Assyrian Empire, however, meant Israel's independence could not last. As we saw earlier in this chapter, in 745 B.C.E. Tiglath-Pileser III succeeded to the throne and expanded the Assyrian Empire. In just over a decade, Israel, like many of the smaller Syrian and Canaanite kingdoms, found itself an Assyrian vassal. And, like so many of the peoples under Assyrian control, the Israelites quickly grew weary of imperial demands. In 722 B.C.E., Israel's King Hoshea (ca. 731–722 B.C.E.) led a rebellion against Assyrian domination. In keeping with their policy of "calculated frightfulness," the Assyrians responded with brutality. The following year they wiped Israel off the map by annexing the territory outright and dividing it into four Assyrian provinces. Nearly 30,000 Israelites were deported to Mesopotamia. Today known as the Lost Ten Tribes of Israel, these deportees eventually forgot their cultural identity in their new homes and disappeared from history. Many of the remaining inhabitants of Israel took refuge in Judah (nearly doubling its population).

Although the destruction of its larger, more powerful northern neighbor increased Judah's regional importance, this small state survived during the age of empires only as an imperial vassal, first, of the Neo-Assyrians, then the Egyptians, Neo-Babylonians, and

Persians. Judahite kings who attempted to shrug off vassal status had little success. King Hezekiah (ca. 727–697 B.C.E.), for example, made the mistake of joining a Canaanite–Phoenician coalition against the mighty Assyrian monarch, Sennacherib. When the Assyrian army surrounded Jerusalem, Hezekiah surrendered and pledged his loyalty to his Assyrian overlord. The costs of survival were high: According to Sennacherib,

> Hezekiah himself, overwhelmed by the terror-inspiring splendor of my lordship . . . sent me in Nineveh, my lordly city, . . . elephant hides, ivory tusks, ebony-wood, boxwood, all kinds of valuable treasures, as well as his daughters, concubines, male and female musicians. He sent a personal messenger to deliver the tribute and render homage as a slave.[8]

Hezekiah's successors were not so fortunate. In 586 B.C.E., when King Zedekiah (ca. 597–586 B.C.E.) led another revolt, Babylonian forces burned Jerusalem to the

ASSYRIAN TORTURE TACTICS This Assyrian relief shows Assyrian soldiers impaling prisoners from Judah. In 701 B.C.E. the emperor Sennacherib and his army marched into Judah to put down a rebellion. They besieged the city of Lachish and then brutally tortured its inhabitants. They later besieged Jerusalem, but King Hezekiah's surrender saved the capital city.

ground and demolished Solomon's temple, the spiritual and political center of Judah. About 20,000 people were deported to Babylon, an event called the **Babylonian Exile.**

Unlike the inhabitants of Israel, however, the Hebrews deported from Judea retained their cultural and religious identity during their years in exile—and some were able to return to Judah. In 538 B.C.E., King Cyrus of Persia, now ruler of the Neo-Babylonian Empire as well, permitted all peoples exiled by the Babylonians to return to their homelands. Two generations later the Judahites finished building a new temple in Jerusalem, called the Second Temple. For the next 500 years this restored temple worship was the center of Hebrew religious life. Historians call the Hebrews who lived after the completion of the Second Temple *Jews* and their religion *Judaism*.

Babylonian Exile The period of Jewish history between the destruction of Solomon's temple in Jerusalem by Babylonian armies in 587 B.C.E., and 538 B.C.E, when Cyrus of Persia permitted Jews to return to Palestine and rebuild the temple.

Read the Document
Judaism Overview

The Hebrew Religious Legacy

Were it not for this religion, Western civilization textbooks would barely mention Israel under the United Monarchy or the successor kingdoms of Israel and Judah. Like Ammon or Moab, Israel and Judah were minor Canaanite states, fairly insignificant players in the imperial power game. But unlike Ammon and Moab, Israel and Judah possessed and passed on a powerful religious legacy, one that shaped the very heart of Western cultural identity.

EARLY SYNCRETISM Early Hebrew religious practice, like all of early Hebrew history, remains controversial. The existing evidence indicates that as they coalesced as a people in the hill country of Canaan, the proto-Israelites combined Canaanite religious practices with the worship of the god Yahweh (written as "Jehovah" or "the Lord" in

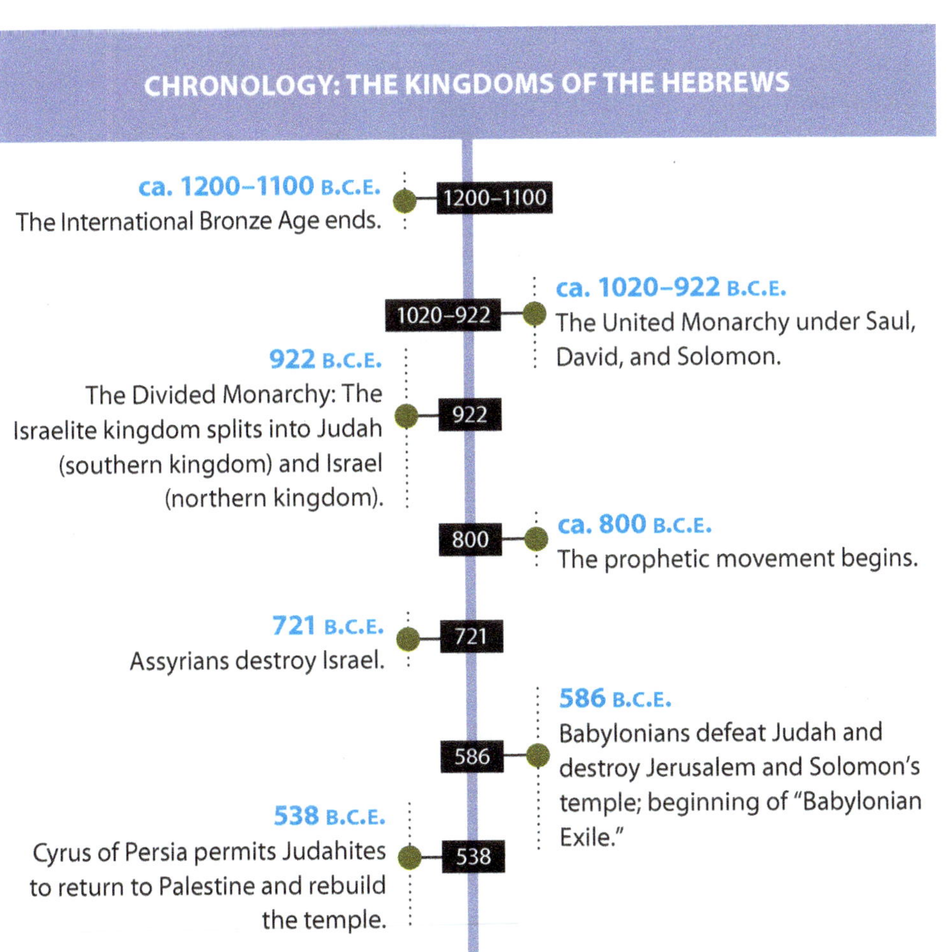

syncretism The practice of blending foreign religious beliefs with an indigenous religious system; a common practice throughout the Roman Empire.

Yahwism The worship of Yahweh ("Jehovah"); the form of early Israelite religious belief.

English Bibles), a deity likely brought to Canaan by migrants from Midian, a desert region north of the Arabian peninsula. Belief in Yahweh became central to Hebrew identity but the early Israelites also continued to worship the head Canaanite god El, his consort Asherah, and the fertility deity Ba'al.

By the time of the United Monarchy, **syncretism**—the practice of fusing foreign beliefs to an indigenous system—molded Israelite religion into what we call **Yahwism** (the worship of Yahweh). The Israelites now identified early Canaanite shrines to El as places where Yahweh revealed himself to his people. Yahwism also adopted Canaanite liturgical practices, such as the celebration of the harvest (Succoth, in later Judaism) and the New Year (Rosh Hashanah), and the Canaanite belief in cherubim—winged, semi-divine beings with human heads and the bodies of bulls or lions that frequently guarded the thrones of gods and kings.

Different Voices

Holy War in the Ancient World

The peoples of the ancient world drew no distinction between religion and politics. No king could rule without the gods' blessing and warfare served not only to expand the king's territory but also to glorify the gods and to demonstrate the divine power that upheld the political and social order. The accounts of "holy war" in these excerpts cannot be read as journalists' reports or historians' reconstructions. They are religious texts that allow us glimpses of the deepest motivations and aspirations of the societies that produced them.

I. The Annals of Assurnasirpal II of Assyria

One of the most famous Assyrian documents, The Annals of Assurnasirpal II, *provides detailed year-by-year records of the military campaigns of King Assurnasirpal (r. ca. 883–859).*

> Assur, my great lord, who called me by name and made great my kingship over the kings of the four quarters [of the world], had made my name exceeding great, and . . . had commanded me to conquer, to subdue and to rule; trusting in Assur, my lord, I marched by difficult roads over steep mountains with the hosts of my army, and there was none who opposed me. . . .
>
> While I was staying in the land of Kutmuhi, they brought me the word: "The city of Suru of Bit-Halupe has revolted . . . and Ahia-baba, the son of a nobody . . . they have set up as king over them." With the help of . . . the great gods who have made great my kingdom, I mobilized [my] chariots and armies and marched. . . .
>
> To the city of Sura of Bit-Halupe I drew near, and the terror of the splendor of Assur, my lord, overwhelmed them. The chief men and the elders of the city, to save their lives, came forth into my presence and embraced my feet, saying: "If it is thy pleasure, slay! If it is thy pleasure, let live! That which thy heart desireth, do!"
>
> Ahiababa, the son of nobody . . . I made captive. In the valor of my heart and with the fury of my weapons I stormed the city. All the rebels they seized and delivered them up. My officers I caused to enter into his palace and his temples. His silver, his gold . . . a great hoard of copper, alabaster, tables with inlay, the women of his palaces, his daughters, the captive rebels together with their possessions, the gods together with their possessions, precious stone from the mountains, his chariots with equipment, his horses . . . garments of brightly colored wool and garments of linen, goodly oil, cedar, and fine-scented herbs . . . his wagons, his cattle, his sheep, his heavy spoil, which like the stars of heaven could not be counted, I carried off. . . . I built a pillar over against his city gate, and I flayed all the chief men who had revolted, and I covered the pillar with their skins; some I walled up within the pillar, some I impaled upon the pillar on stakes, and others I bound to stakes round about the pillar; . . . and I cut off the limbs of the officers, of the royal officers who had rebelled. Ahiababa I took to Nineveh, I flayed him, I spread his skin upon the wall of Nineveh. My power and might I established over the land of Lake. . . . I increased the tribute and taxes and imposed upon them. . . .
>
> At that time I fashioned a heroic image of my royal self, my power and my glory I inscribed thereon, in the midst of his palace I set it up. I fashioned memorial steles and inscribed thereon my glory and prowess, and I set them up by his city gate.

II. The Book of Numbers: The Israelites' War Against Midian

The Old Testament's Book of Numbers (titled in the Hebrew Bible, In the Wilderness) *tells the story of the Israelites after their exodus from Egypt and before their settlement in Canaan. Like the rest of the Pentateuch (the first five books of the Bible), Numbers is likely based on oral traditions first written down about 950* B.C.E. *This early account was then revised, expanded, and edited over subsequent centuries, probably achieving final form in the sixth century* B.C.E.

(continued on next page)

(continued from previous page)

While Israel dwelt in Shittim the people began to play the harlot with the daughters of Moab. These invited the people to the sacrifices of their gods, and the people ate and bowed down to their gods. So Israel yoked himself to Ba'al of Pe'or. And the anger of the Lord was kindled against Israel. *[The Lord sends a plague.]* . . . those that died by the plague were twenty-four thousand.

And the Lord said to Moses, "Harass the Midianites and smite them; for they . . . beguiled you in the matter of Pe'or." . . . And Moses said to the people, "Arm men from among you for the war, that they may go against Midian, to execute the Lord's vengeance on Midian. You shall send a thousand from each of the tribes of Israel to the war." So there were provided . . . twelve thousand armed for war. And Moses sent them to the war, a thousand from each tribe, together with Phinehas the son of Eleazar the priest. . . . They warred against Midian, as the Lord commanded Moses, and slew every male. . . . And the people of Israel took captive the women of Midian and their little ones; and they took as booty all their cattle, their flocks, and all their goods. All their cities in the places where they dwelt, and all their encampments, they burned with fire. . . . Then they brought the captives and the booty and the spoil to Moses, and to Eleazar the priest, and to the congregation of the people of Israel, at the camp on the plains of Moab by the Jordan at Jericho.

Moses, and Eleazar the priest, and all the leaders of the congregation, went forth to meet them outside the camp. And Moses was angry. . . . Moses said to them, "Have you let all the women live? Behold, these caused the people of Israel . . . to act treacherously against the Lord in the matter of Pe'or, and so the plague came among the congregation of the Lord. Now therefore, kill every male among the little ones, and kill every woman who has known man by lying with him. But all the young girls who have not known man by lying with him, keep alive for yourselves." . . . And Moses and Eleazar the priest received the gold from the commanders . . . and brought it into the tent of meeting, as a memorial for the people of Israel before the Lord.

SOURCES: I. D. D. Luckenbill, *Ancient Records of Assyria and Babylonia*, Vol. I (Chicago, IL: University of Chicago Press, 1926), 141, 144–145; II. Numbers 25: 1–3, 9, 16–18; Numbers 31: 3–18, 52–54.

For Discussion

1. How does the first excerpt illustrate the Assyrian policy of "calculated frightfulness"?
2. Compare these accounts: What motivated these holy wars? Who received credit and why? What do the differences between these accounts reveal about these different cultures?

ASTARTE WORSHIP IN JUDAH Archaeologists uncovered these small statues (called Astarte figurines after the most important Canaanite fertility goddess) in the remains of a number of private houses in what was the kingdom of Judah. Dating from about 800–600 B.C.E., these figurines provide evidence for the continuation of Canaanite religious practices among the Hebrews.

2.1

2.2

2.3

prophetic movement An important phase in the development of what became Judaism. In the ninth century B.C.E., Hebrew religious reformers, or prophets, demanded the transformation of religious and economic practices to reflect ideals of social justice and religious purity.

THE PROPHETIC MOVEMENT In the ninth century B.C.E., Yahwism took a new turn, a revolutionary move of marked significance for Western history. In the years after the formation of the monarchy, the gap between rich and poor widened. The centralization and growth of the state increased the tax burden on peasants, many of whom fell into debt and lost their land. They cried out for justice and a return to what they remembered as a more egalitarian society. From these roots emerged the **prophetic movement**, a call for social justice and religious purity that eventually transformed Yahwism into the world's first monotheistic religion.

The prophet Elijah led the initial movement. He and his followers demanded that Israelites worship *only* Yahweh, and thus called for purifying Yahwism of Canaanite religious beliefs and practices. Speaking on behalf of the downtrodden with words they believed Yahweh had given to them, these social critics condemned the religious and moral corruption of landowners and kings. They linked the worship of Yahweh (and only Yahweh) to a social ideal of community, in which exploitation of the poor was seen as a sin against Yahweh's plan for humanity.

Over the next century, prophets such as Amos, Hosea, Isaiah, and Micah continued to denounce the economic inequalities of Israel and Judah and to call for the worship of only Yahweh. They also began to articulate a vision of religion as a heartfelt spiritual practice resulting in social action, rather than a matter of placating the gods through ritual. In a revolutionary statement, Micah presented Yahweh as rejecting typical religious worship:

> With what shall I come before the Lord, and bow myself before God on high? . . .
> Will the Lord be pleased with thousands of rams, with ten thousands of rivers of oil?
> Shall I give my first-born for my transgression, the fruit of my body for the sin of my soul?
> He has showed you, O man, what is good; and what does the Lord require of you but to do justice, and to love kindness, and to walk humbly with your God?[9]

YAHWEH ALONE: THE EMERGENCE OF MONOTHEISM The destruction of the northern kingdom of Israel in 721 B.C.E. persuaded many within Judah of the truth of the prophets' message. They concluded that Yahweh had chosen the Assyrians as his means of punishing Israel for its sins. A mood of religious reform spread throughout the southern state. King Hezekiah sought to purify Judah's religious practice by destroying the shrines and sacred sites dedicated to Ba'al and Asherah, and by centralizing the worship of Yahweh in the Temple in Jerusalem.

Hezekiah's successor, Manasseh (697–642 B.C.E.), tried to reverse his father's reforms and return to traditional practices, but this counter-reformation proved short-lived. Manasseh's successor was assassinated after only two years on the throne, clearing the way for the boy king, Josiah (640–609 B.C.E.), during whose reign the most thoroughgoing reform of Hebrew religion occurred. In 622 B.C.E., when Josiah was 26 years old, workers repairing the Temple uncovered a scroll called the "Book of the Law" (an early version of what we know as Deuteronomy, the fifth book of the Bible), ostensibly written by Moses and containing the basic principles by which the Hebrews should live. Deuteronomy in its earliest written form dates not from the time of Moses (i.e., 1300s B.C.E.), but from the 600s (B.C.E.). Inspired by this supposed "archaeological find," Josiah implemented a host of reforms, all of them based on the central theme of Deuteronomy: the "Covenant," or sacred contract, between Yahweh and the Israelites. According to the terms of this Covenant, Yahweh designated Israel as his chosen people, and in return, the Israelites were to worship only him and to seek to abide by his law.

Stirred by this religious reformation, one of Josiah's subjects used the ideal of the Covenant to reinterpret the Hebrew past by writing the "Deuteronomistic History," an early version of the biblical books of Joshua, Judges, Samuel, and Kings. This history projects the vision of Yahweh as the true God of Israel back onto the earliest days of the Hebrew people, and recasts the story of the Israelites as a struggle between the true followers of Yahweh and those who strayed to worship other gods. In its narrative, the History emphasized the intertwined concepts of Land and Law: Yahweh had given his chosen people the land of Israel, but on the condition that they worshiped him as his law, spelled out in Deuteronomy, demanded.

Josiah's religious reformation ended in 609 B.C.E. when Egyptian forces captured and killed him. Within decades Judah had fallen to Babylonian conquest, Jerusalem was destroyed, and the period of the Babylonian Exile had begun. As they struggled to make sense of these horrific events, the Hebrew exiles took the final step toward monotheism. Grappling with the lessons of their history and the meaning of their religious faith now that the Temple was destroyed, they came to a revolutionary understanding of the divine. They came to see Yahweh as unbounded by time and space, not confined to a temple. The one and only God, he ruled not only Israel and Judah, but all people in all places and in all time—and even beyond time. This idea of the one eternal and transcendent God would have a powerful impact on Western culture.

The Babylonian Exile also resulted in a number of other important developments in Hebrew religion. First, the fear of losing their identity as Hebrews as they lived in a foreign land amid foreign gods led to a new emphasis on religious purity. Hebrew leaders developed a complex code of ethical and ritual requirements designed to reinforce the separate identity of the Hebrew people. For example, Hebrews could no longer marry non-Hebrews and they had to observe strict dietary laws.

This new emphasis on purity resulted in significant but contradictory changes for Hebrew women. On the one hand, they found their religious role more restricted: Childbirth and menstruation made women "unclean" and therefore unfit for public worship. On the other hand, many of the dietary and ritualistic requirements took place within the home, in the family context, and so gave women central responsibility in sustaining Hebrew identity.

A second important religious development during the Babylonian Exile was the compilation of the basic texts of the Hebrew Bible. During this era Hebrew leaders added to Deuteronomy a number of texts written earlier or preserved in oral tradition. Edited and compiled, these texts with Deuteronomy became the **Pentateuch** or the **Torah**—the first five books of the Bible. Exiled Hebrews also produced a second edition of the Deuteronomistic History, one that particularly emphasized the central role of the now-destroyed Temple and its priesthood in the life of the Israelites.

Pentateuch The first five books of the Hebrew Bible.

Torah Most commonly, the first five books of the Hebrew Bible; also used to refer to the whole body of Jewish sacred writings and tradition.

By emphasizing the priesthood and Temple sacrifices, the editors of this later version of the Deuteronomistic History (who probably were themselves priests) tried to make correct religious practice the key to Hebrew faith and identity. This stress on religious ritual, however, ignored the social concerns that the prophets had placed at the heart of Yahweh's Law. The period of the Exile, then, saw a continuation of the prophetic movement, as new prophets arose to challenge the priestly emphasis on right ritual and instead demanded social justice. The prophet Ezekiel, for example, depicted Yahweh as a shepherd with a special love for the weakest in his flock:

> I myself will be the shepherd of my sheep . . . says the Lord God. . . . Behold, I judge between sheep and sheep. Is it not enough for you to feed on the good pasture, that you must tread down with your feet the rest of your pasture; and to drink of clear water, that you must foul the rest with your feet? . . . Behold, I, I myself will judge between the fat sheep and the lean sheep.[10]

The tension between the prophetic call for social justice, implemented through practical action, and the priestly demand for religious purity, demonstrated through ritual practices, would never be fully reconciled, either in Judaism or in the monotheistic religions of Christianity and Islam, which, like Judaism, drew on ancient Hebrew roots.

2.1

2.2

2.3

THE HEBREW LEGACY From those Hebrew roots grew many characteristic features of Western civilization. The notion of the "chosen people" shaped not only Christian theology but also modern expressions of nationalism. "Manifest destiny"—the idea that the United States had the right and responsibility to extend its political control across the North American continent—is rooted in this ancient Hebrew idea. Western culture also draws on the Hebrew ideal of the Law. In Hebrew tradition, Yahweh's Law stands supreme: Every king, even God's chosen ruler, will be judged on how well he implements God's Law and how fairly he treats God's people. This idea provides the seeds of the key Western legal and political principle that no ruler or leader stands beyond the law. The summary of Yahweh's Law found in the Ten Commandments remains for many the foundation of Western ethics, while the Hebrew Bible still provides some of the most powerful and poetic narratives in the Western tradition.

Most important, the belief in an all-powerful, all-encompassing God who transcends space and time, and yet intervenes in human history to take care of his people, has had a powerful influence on Western societies. Seeing the hand of God in history allowed Western cultures to adopt a notion of human history as linear, as meaningful movement through time, rather than an endless repetition or a steady degradation, and so helped make possible the idea of progress. Similarly, the concept of a transcendent

Justice in History

Crime and Punishment in a King's Court

Around 990 B.C.E., "in the spring of the year, the time when kings go forth to battle," Israel's King David sent his troops against the Ammonites. Although a renowned warrior, David stayed behind in Jerusalem. One afternoon he took a walk on his roof after he woke from his nap. (An afternoon siesta was then, like now, common in Mediterranean cultures, and the roof constituted the coolest part of the building.) From his rooftop David saw a woman bathing, "and the woman was very beautiful." When the king discovered that the woman was Bathsheba, wife of Uriah the Hittite* who was serving in the war against Ammon, he ordered her brought to him. In the spare vocabulary of the biblical text, David "took her, and she came to him, and he lay with her." This action set in motion a sequence of events that ultimately divided the Israelite kingdom.

The story of David and Bathsheba is part of the "Court History of David," found in the Old Testament books of II Samuel and I Kings.** Some scholars insist that the Court History originates from the time of King Josiah in the seventh century B.C.E. Other scholars, however, date the earliest version of the Court History to Solomon's reign in the tenth century B.C.E. and argue that this first version was then combined with other stories during Josiah's religious reformation (and then revised again after the Babylonian Exile). But no matter what its origins, the History reflects the values that propelled Josiah's reforms and promotes a revolutionary idea of social justice.

David, the handsome warrior and popular hero whom the Lord chose to lead his people, sowed the seeds of national tragedy. A few weeks after his sexual encounter with Bathsheba, the king received a message from her: "I am with child." Caught in adultery, David scrambled to cover up his crime. Assuming that Uriah, like most soldiers on leave, would want sex, David ordered Bathsheba's husband home from the battlefield. If Uriah slept with Bathsheba, then everyone would assume he was the baby's father. But the Hittite soldier refused to violate the rules of purity that required a soldier engaged in holy war to abstain from sex. Even when David invited him to dinner and plied him with so much wine that he became drunk, Uriah resisted the temptation to bed his lovely wife.

Frustrated, David sent Uriah back to the battle, along with a message for his commander, Joab: "Set Uriah in the forefront of the hardest fighting, and draw back from him, that he may be struck down and die." Joab obeyed. Uriah and several of Israel's mightiest fighters died in a hard-fought engagement with the Ammonites. Shortly after, David added Bathsheba to his stable of wives. The king thought he had gotten away with murder. But, the Court History tells us, "the thing that David had done displeased Yahweh."

*"Hittite" here does not refer to the Hittite Empire, which disintegrated over one century earlier, but rather to a small Canaanite kingdom or tribe.

**II Samuel 9–20 and I Kings 1–2 of the Christian Old Testament.

(continued on next page)

(continued from previous page)

A short time later, Yahweh's prophet, Nathan, arrived at court and told the king a story:

> There were two men in a certain city, the one rich and the other poor. The rich man had very many flocks and herds; but the poor man had nothing but one little ewe lamb, which he had bought. And he brought it up, and it grew up with him and with his children; it used to eat of his morsel, and drink from his cup, and lie in his bosom, and it was like a daughter to him. Now there came a traveler to the rich man, and he was unwilling to take one of his own flock or herd to prepare for the wayfarer who had come to him, but he took the poor man's lamb, and prepared it for the man who had come to him.

Infuriated by this injustice, David insisted, "As the Lord lives, the man who has done this deserves to die." Nathan replied, "You are the man."

Nathan's parable forced David to see himself as the selfish rich man who stole everything, including life itself, from Uriah. David recognized his crime and confessed, "I have sinned against Yahweh." But his confession did not mean he could evade the consequences of his actions. Nathan warned, "The sword shall never depart from your house. . . . Thus says Yahweh, 'Behold, I will raise up evil against you out of your own house.' "

David and Bathsheba's baby boy soon sickened and died. Bathsheba's second son by David, Solomon, inherited his father's throne, but only after the royal household endured a series of tragedies, including incestuous rape, murder, a civil war that forced David to flee his capital city, and the deaths of two more of David's sons (with a third executed by Solomon shortly after he took power). Solomon's reign may have marked the high point of the Hebrew monarchy, but his decision to continue the heavy taxation and forced labor policies of his father meant that resentment against the Davidic royal house festered among the people. This resentment finally burst into rebellion after Solomon's death and divided the kingdom.

By linking these unfolding tragedies to David's crime, the Court History revealed an idea of justice new to the ancient world. Because the kingdom belonged to Yahweh, not to David or any of his sons, Yahweh's Law applied to all. Although a mighty king, David was expected to obey the same laws that governed the behavior of an ordinary peasant. His failure to do so shattered his family, weakened his reign, and tarnished his legacy.

This emphasis on actions and consequences highlights a second important feature of the Court History: the importance of human action in a world under Yahweh's control. Although the History contains no miracles, no angels, no points of supernatural intervention in the natural world, the tragedies that unfold do not just happen by chance. Yahweh is in charge. Yet David and his sons are not pawns in a divine chess game. Their choices have consequences. What each person does matters. Justice, then, is individual as well as social, a working of Yahweh's will for the world in both communal and personal life.

For Discussion

1. How does the idea of kingship and justice revealed in the Court History differ from that of other Bronze and Iron Age monarchies?
2. How does the concept of justice revealed in this story strengthen and/or challenge the values that underlay the prophetic movement?

Taking It Further

Michael Dever, *What Did the Biblical Writers Know and When Did They Know It?* Grand Rapids, MI: Wm. B. Eerdmans Publishing Co., 2002. A clear and engaging introduction to the sources of the books of the Old Testament.

Israel Finkelstein and Neil Asher Silberman. *David and Solomon: In Search of the Bible's Sacred Kings and the Roots of the Western Tradition*. New York: Free Press, 2006. A more radical approach to the historical accuracy of the biblical picture of the United Monarchy than Dever's.

God contributed to the Western scientific tradition. Because God transcends rather than permeates the natural world, nature itself is not sacred. Human beings can study it; they can also use it, manipulate it, and transform it.

Suffering Explained

CONCLUSION

International Systems, Ancient Empires, and the Roots of Western Civilization

The International Bronze Age marked an early but crucial phase in the formation of Western civilization. Within a geographical area centered on the eastern Mediterranean but stretching far beyond its shores, a network of political, commercial, and cultural ties emerged among cities and kingdoms that had lived in relative isolation from each other. Long before it was possible to identify what we now call the West, the exchange of commodities, the spread of religious ideas, the growth of common political traditions, the dissemination of scientific and technological techniques, and the borrowing of one language from another created a complex pattern of cultural diffusion over a vast geographical area.

When the international system of the Late Bronze Age collapsed, these elements did not all disappear. The cultural inheritance of the Sumerians and Akkadians passed on to the Neo-Assyrian and Neo-Babylonian empires, consciously preserved in libraries and literary collections. The diplomatic innovations, most clearly seen in the treaty between Ramesses II and Hattusili III in 1258 B.C.E., became an important feature of international affairs. The proto-Canaanite alphabet survived, to be passed on to the Western world by the Phoenicians via the Greeks. And most important of all, in the midst of the collapse of Great Powers and the rise of new empires, a small, seemingly insignificant people with a still controversial origin encountered the divine in ways that continue today to influence, comfort, challenge, and transform peoples of the West and around the world.

MAKING CONNECTIONS

1. Review the key characteristics of Mesopotamian culture outlined in Chapter 1. Compare and contrast these characteristics with those of the Great Power cultures of the International Bronze Age and the later Neo-Assyrian and Neo-Babylonian societies. What is more important, cultural continuity or cultural transformation?
2. Consider this argument: "Empires dominated southwest Asia in the millennium from 1500 to 500 B.C.E.—and yet the developments of greatest significance for Western history and culture occurred not in the imperial systems, but in the smaller states, in the areas on the periphery of power." In what ways is this argument accurate? In what ways must it be modified or rejected?
3. How does the history of the Hebrews illuminate the central patterns of southwest Asian history in the period after the collapse of the International Bronze Age?

TAKING IT FURTHER

For suggested readings, see page R-1.

On MyHistoryLab

Take the Study Plan for Chapter 2, The Age of Empires: The International Bronze Age and Its Aftermath, ca. 1500–550 B.C.E., on MyHistoryLab

Chapter Review

The Dynamism of the International Bronze Age

2.1 What elements made up the international system of the Late Bronze Age and why did it collapse?

Complex economic and diplomatic networks connected five geographic areas, known as zones of power. Called the "Club of Great Powers" by historians, they developed shared concepts and tools of international exchange and diplomacy. The end of the Late International Bronze Age was likely caused by a combination of factors, including large-scale migrations in the wake of the collapse of: the Mycenean and Hittite kingdoms, prolonged drought conditions, and growing numbers of laborers fleeing the heavy economic demands of the palace system.

Recovery and Rebuilding: Empires and Societies in the Aftermath of the International Bronze Age

2.2 What developments shaped southwest Asian and Mediterranean societies after the collapse of the International Bronze Age?

The end of the Great Powers' sophisticated diplomatic and economic networks meant that smaller city-states and kingdoms, with their shifting coalitions and alliances, were allowed to grow and thrive. The rise of the Neo-Assyrian and Neo-Babylonian empires, however, put an end to this period of small-state independence. Changing political partnerships cut off the supply of resources to create bronze, and forced ancient peoples to explore the use of iron and to develop new trade routes, both overseas and on land.

The Civilization of the Hebrews

2.3 What beliefs and institutions shaped Hebrew civilization and its legacy?

As Hebrew civilization evolved out of polytheism through Yahwism to monotheism, it also developed in tension between the prophetic emphasis on social justice and the priestly insistence on proper ritual, and between communal ideals and an all-powerful monarchy. The Western legal principle that no leader stands beyond the law can be traced back to the Hebrew ideal that every king is judged on how well he implements God's Law and how fairly he treats his people.

Chapter Time Line

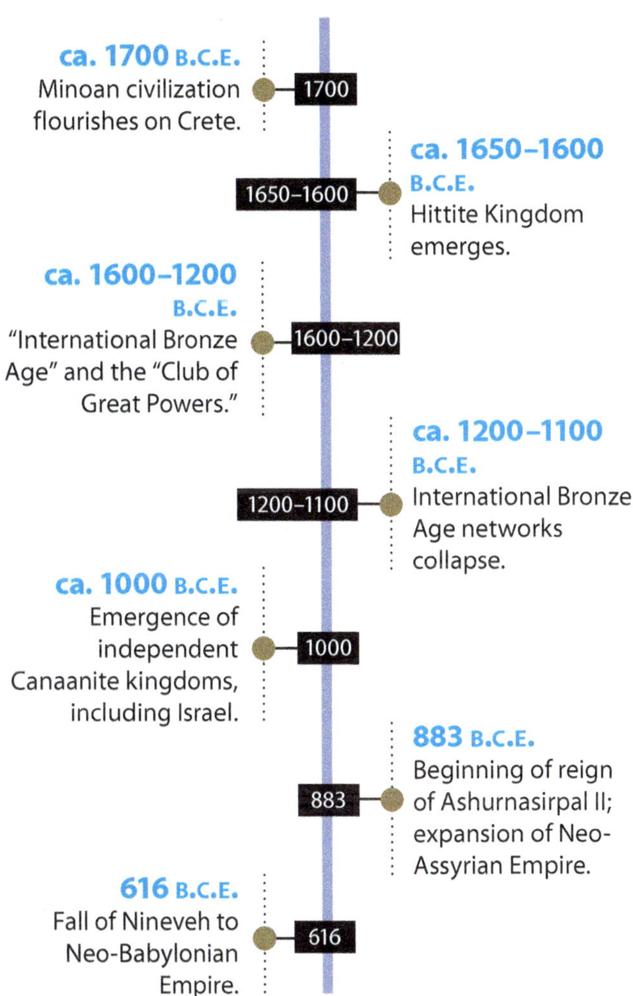

3 Greek Civilization

THE BATTLE OF SALAMIS, 480 B.C.E. This victory of the Athenian navy over Persia ended a major threat to Greek independence. This nineteenth-century painting of the battle accurately depicts the closeness of naval engagements in ancient times.

In 480 B.C.E. Xerxes, the great king of Persia (r. 485–465 B.C.E.), launched a massive invasion of Greece by leading 150,000 troops across the Hellespont, the narrow strait known today as the Dardanelles that separates Asia from Europe. Xerxes's intention was to conquer Greece and make it part of the largest and most powerful empire the world had ever known. Against all odds 31 Greek city-states, which had formed an alliance to repel the invaders, prevailed. In September of that year the highly maneuverable Athenian navy defeated the Persian fleet off the coast of the island of Salamis, forcing Xerxes to withdraw most of his forces to Anatolia for the winter. At the Battle of Plataea early the next year the combined Greek armies, led by Sparta, routed the troops that Xerxes had left behind. The surviving Persians were driven out of Greece, never to return.

The victories of the Greeks over the Persian colossus at Salamis and Plataea mark a milestone in the history of the West. They gave Greece, most notably the city-state of Athens, the security within which it could develop its political institutions as well as its philosophy,

LEARNING OBJECTIVES

3.1 How did Greek city-states develop their culture and political institutions during the Archaic Age?

3.2 How did the Persian Empire bring the peoples of the Near East together in a stable realm, and what elements of Persian religion and government have influenced Western thought?

3.3 What were the intellectual, social, and political innovations of Greece in the Classical Age?

Listen to Chapter 3 on MyHistoryLab

Watch the Video Series on MyHistoryLab

Learn about some key topics related to this chapter with the *MyHistoryLab Video Series: Key Topics in Western Civilization*

science, literature, and art. The resulting achievements of Greek civilization, which continued to interact with those of other states in the Mediterranean region, became the bedrock of Western civilization.

It would be misleading, however, to celebrate the Greek victory over Persia as a triumph of the West over the East. The location of Greece in Europe and Persia in Asia suggests such a contrast. But as we have seen, the terms *the West* and *the East* refer to more than geography; they also designate a constellation of cultural traditions. Some of the political, religious, and scientific traditions that we identify as Western can be traced back to the Persian Empire; many of them were the products of cultural encounters between Greece and Persia.

This chapter will discuss the growth of Greek civilization in the context of its relationship with the Persian Empire. The main question it will address is:

What role did both Persia and Greece play in the making of the West?

Greece Rebuilds, 1100–479 B.C.E.

3.1 How did Greek city-states develop their culture and political institutions during the Archaic Age?

As we saw in Chapter 2, Greek civilization entered a period of economic and political decline at the end of the International Bronze Age. The years from about 1100 to 750 B.C.E, known as the Dark Age, were followed by a period of economic growth at home and encounters with Phoenicians and Persians abroad. The revival of Greece during the Archaic Age, which lasted until 479 B.C.E, set the stage for Greece's cultural achievements during its Classical Age.

During the Dark Age, Greece endured economic, political, and cultural stagnation that contrasted with the wealth and splendor of the Mycenaean states that had flourished during the Bronze Age. Few new settlements were established on the Greek mainland, and urban life disappeared. Maritime trade declined sharply and the economies controlled by the palaces collapsed. Because there was no longer a need for scribes to record inventories, Linear B writing disappeared. A serious decline in agriculture led to a steep decrease in food production and population.

A slow economic recovery began in the Greek world about 850 B.C.E., when the population began to grow and trade became brisker. Because of the harsh living conditions on the mainland during the Dark Age, many Greeks moved to a region called Ionia on the coasts and islands of western Anatolia. Relatively isolated from other Greek communities, these pioneers developed their own dialect of the Greek language. By 800 B.C.E. the Ionian Greeks were regularly interacting with the Phoenicians in the eastern Mediterranean.

Writing and Poetry During the Archaic Age

Between about 750 and 650 B.C.E., fresh ideas poured into Greece from the Near East through contact with the Phoenicians and other peoples. Encounters with Near Eastern poets, merchants, artisans, refugees, doctors, slaves, and spouses brought innovations to Greece. These included new economic practices (such as charging interest on loans), new gods and goddesses (such as Dionysos, the god of wine), and inventions of convenience (such as parasols to provide shade).

The most valuable import from the Phoenicians was the alphabet. As we saw in Chapter 2, the Phoenicians, who had been using an alphabet of 22 letters for at least three centuries, introduced the system to Greece around 750 B.C.E. The adoption of the alphabet, to which the Greeks added vowels, was one of the developments that marked the beginning of the Archaic Age. Because an alphabet records sounds, not words, it can be adjusted easily for any language. Greeks soon recognized the potential of the new system and learned to write and read, first for business and then for pleasure. They began to record their oral traditions, legends, and songs. At the same time, they began to compose a new literature and write down their laws.

Two of the greatest works of Western literature, the *Iliad* and the *Odyssey,* were soon written down in the new alphabet. A Greek poet named Homer, who probably lived around 750 B.C.E., is credited with composing these poems, but they were not entirely his invention. In writing the poems, Homer drew on oral tales about the legendary Trojan War that wandering poets had been reciting for centuries. The poets had elaborated on the stories so many times that they lost their historical accuracy. Nevertheless, many details in the poems, especially about weapons and armor no longer used in Homer's day, suggest that the earliest versions of the poems were first recited in the Bronze Age and may be loosely based on events of that time.

The *Iliad* and the *Odyssey* were part of a larger body of stories that told how an army of Greek warriors sailed to Troy, a wealthy city on the northwest coast of Anatolia, to recover a beautiful Greek princess, Helen, who had been abducted by a Trojan prince. After 10 years of savage fighting, the Greeks finally stormed Troy and won the war, though their greatest fighters had died in battle. When the surviving heroes returned to Greece, they were met with treachery and bloodshed.

Homer's genius lay in his retelling of these old stories. He did not relate the entire saga of the Trojan War because he knew that his audiences were familiar with it. Instead, he selected certain episodes, and in fresh ways he emphasized aspects of human character and emotion in the midst of violent conflict. In the *Iliad,* for example, he describes how the hero Achilles, the mightiest of all the Greeks fighting at Troy, grows angry when his commander in chief, Agamemnon, steals his favorite concubine. In a rage, Achilles withdraws from the battle and returns to fight only to avenge his best friend, who had been killed by Hector, the main Trojan hero. Achilles eventually slays Hector, but does not relinquish his fury until Hector's father, Priam, the king of Troy, begs him to return his son's corpse for proper burial. Achilles relents and weeps, his humanity restored after so much killing. In Homer's hands, the story of Achilles's anger becomes a profound investigation into human alienation and redemption.

Read the Document

Homer *Iliad* (Eighth Century B.C.E.)

polis A self-governing Greek city-state.

acropolis The defensible hilltop around which a polis grew. In classical Athens, the Acropolis was the site of the Parthenon (Temple of Athena).

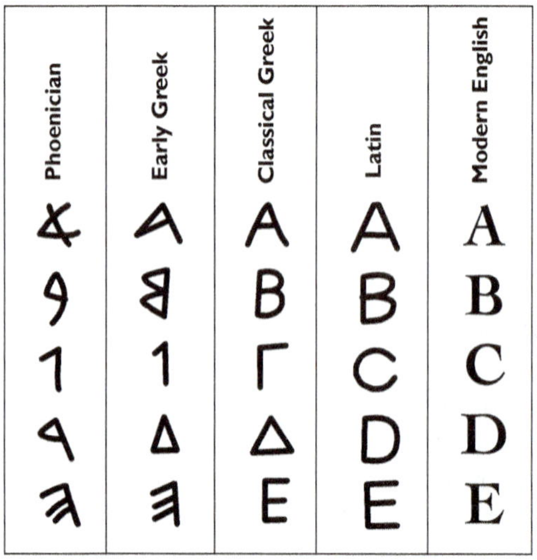

Phoenician	Early Greek	Classical Greek	Latin	Modern English
𐤀	A	A	A	A
𐤁	ᗺ	B	B	B
𐤂	1	Γ	C	C
𐤃	Δ	Δ	D	D
𐤄	∃	E	E	E

CHART OF THE DEVELOPMENT OF THE ALPHABET
This chart shows how the first five letters of the Phoenician alphabet developed into the first five letters of the English alphabet.

Political Developments During the Archaic Age

Greeks in the Archaic Age also experimented with new forms of social and political life. They developed a new style of community called the **polis** (plural *poleis*), or city-state. A polis was a self-governing community consisting of an urban center with a defensible hilltop, called an **acropolis**, and all the surrounding land farmed by citizens of the polis. Greek cities varied in size from a few square miles to several hundred. All contained similar institutions: an assembly in which the male citizens of the community gathered to discuss—and in some instances decide—public business; a council of male elders (usually aristocrats) who advised on public matters and in many cities made laws; temples to gods who protected the polis and on whose goodwill the community's prosperity depended; and an open area in the center of town called an **agora**, which served as a market and a place for informal discussions.

agora An open area in the town center of a Greek polis that served as a market and a place for informal discussion.

Living in a polis provided an extremely strong sense of community. A person could be a citizen of only one polis, and every citizen was expected to place the community's interests above all other concerns. Even the women, who were citizens but not permitted to play a role in public life, felt powerful ties to their polis. While only citizens had full membership in a polis, enjoying the greatest rights and bearing the greatest responsibilities, every city had noncitizens from other communities. Some of these noncitizens had limited rights and obligations, whereas slaves had no rights at all.

THE OLYMPIC GAMES AND GREEK UNITY During the Archaic Age Greeks also began to develop a sense of Greek unity that had been absent during the Dark Age. Athletic contests called panhellenic games, so named because they drew participants from the entire Greek world, became one of the means by which Greeks cultivated this new sense of Greek identity. The panhellenic games became a mainstay of aristocratic Greek culture in the Archaic Age. As many as 150 cities regularly offered aristocratic men the chance to win glory through competition in chariot-racing, discus-throwing, wrestling, footracing, and other field events. Through sports the Greeks found a common culture that allowed them to express their Greek identity and honor the gods at the same time because the games were also religious festivals.

Greek Athletics

The **Olympic Games**, which originated in 776 B.C.E., carried the most prestige. Every four years Greek athletes from southern Italy to the Black Sea gathered in the sacred grove of Olympia in the central Peloponnese to take part in games dedicated to Zeus, the chief Greek god. The rules required the poleis to call truces to any wars, even if they were in the middle of battle, and allow safe passage to all athletes traveling to Olympia. Records show the naming of champions at Olympia from 776 B.C.E to 217 C.E. The Roman emperor Theodosius I, who was a Christian, abolished the games in 393 C.E. because they involved the worship of Greek gods.

Olympic Games Greek athletic contests held in Olympia every four years between 776 B.C.E and 217 C.E.

COLONIZATION AND THE SETTLEMENT OF NEW LANDS A population boom during the Archaic Age forced Greeks to emigrate because the rocky soil of the mainland could not provide enough food. From about 750 to 550 B.C.E., cities such as Corinth and Megara on the mainland and Miletos in Ionia established more than 200 colonies around the Mediterranean and Black Seas.

Greek emigrants sailed to foreign shores. Many colonists settled on the Aegean coast north into the Black Sea region, which offered plentiful farmlands. The important settlement at Byzantium controlled access to the agricultural wealth of these Black Sea colonies. Greeks established many new cities in Sicily and southern Italy as well as on the southern coast of France and the eastern coast of Spain. By 600 B.C.E. Greeks had founded colonies in North Africa in the region of modern Libya and on the islands of Cyprus and Crete. Greek merchants also set up a trading community on the Syrian coast and another in the Egyptian delta, with the pharaoh's permission (see **Map 3.1**).

Although all Greek colonies maintained formal religious ties with their mother city-states, or *metropoleis,* they were self-governing and independent. Some colonies grew rich and populous enough to establish their own colonies. Because the Greek colonists seized territory by force and sometimes slaughtered the local inhabitants, relations with the people already living in these lands were often tense.

The Greek adoption of coinage spurred commercial activity. Coinage first replaced barter as a medium of exchange in the kingdom of Lydia in western Anatolia about 630 B.C.E. Minted from precious metals—gold, silver, copper, bronze—and uniform in weight, coins helped people standardize the value of goods, a development that revolutionized commerce. During the sixth century B.C.E., Greeks living in Ionia and on the Greek mainland began to mint their own coins. Each polis used a distinctive emblem to mark its currency. When Athens became the dominant economic power in

MAP **3.1** THE EXPANSION OF GREECE IN THE ARCHAIC AND CLASSICAL AGES During the Archaic and Classical Ages, Greek cities spread from Greece to the shores of the Black Sea and as far west as Italy and southern France. This map shows the Greek heartland: the mainland, the islands of the Aegean Sea, and Ionia. Although never unified politically in the Archaic and Classical Ages, the people in these cities spoke Greek, worshiped the same gods, and shared a similar culture. What prevented them from uniting politically?

the Aegean during the second half of the fifth century B.C.E., Athenian silver coinage became the standard throughout the Greek world and far beyond.

Greek colonization played a critical role in shaping Western civilization by creating wealthy centers of Greek culture in Italy and the western Mediterranean. Sometimes overshadowed in the historical record by city-states of the Greek mainland, such as Athens, Sparta, and Corinth, the impressive new poleis spread Greek civilization, language, literature, religion, and art far beyond Greece itself. The colony of Syracuse in Sicily, for example, grew to be larger than any city in Greece. Greek communities deeply influenced local cultures and made a significant impact on Etruscan and Roman civilization in Italy, as we will see in Chapter 5.

THE HOPLITE REVOLUTION The new wealth flowing through the Greek world facilitated the introduction of a new type of fighting force known as **hoplites**. These were units of well-armed, well-drilled infantry that entered the battlefield in massed ranks, four to eight deep, in a formation called a **phalanx**. Inspired by military developments in Assyria, Greek city-states came to realize that large infantry units were more effective than individual aristocratic warriors. Hoplite warfare required more soldiers than the aristocracy could provide, so the poleis had to recruit them from among the general population. Because the new recruits had to be wealthy enough to purchase their own armor and swords, hoplites generally came from the middle ranks of society.

In hoplite warfare each man relied for protection on the man to his right, whose shield protected his own sword arm. Cooperation was all-important, for if the line

hoplites Greek soldiers in the Archaic Age who could afford their own weapons. Hoplite tactics made soldiers fighting as a group dependent on one another. This contributed to the internal cohesion of the polis and eventually to the rise of democracy.

phalanx The military formation favored by hoplite soldiers. Standing shoulder to shoulder in ranks often eight men deep, hoplites moved in unison and depended on one another for protection.

broke, the individual soldier became more vulnerable. Hoplite fighting generated a sense of common purpose that had political consequences, as hoplites demanded a political voice in the communities for which they fought. Their growing confidence challenged aristocratic families who traditionally controlled community decision-making. Military organization thus contributed to political change.

THE RISE OF THE TYRANTS In many poleis new political leaders arose to champion the cause of the hoplite citizenry. These political leaders were known as **tyrants**, a word borrowed from the Near East that did not bear the negative connotation of cruel and arbitrary rule that it carries today. Originally the word *tyrant* meant someone who seized power in a polis rather than acquiring it by heredity, election, or some legal process. Tyrants were typically aristocrats, but they found their political support among the hoplites and the poor who felt left out of the political life of the community. Tyrants usually served the interests of the community as a whole, not just the aristocrats. They promoted overseas trade, built harbors, protected farmers, and began public works projects to employ citizen workers and to beautify their cities. They also cultivated alliances with tyrants in other poleis to establish peace and prosperity. Most important, the tyrants' authority enabled a broad range of citizens to participate in government for the first time.

tyrants Rulers in Greek city-states, usually members of the aristocracy, who seized power illegitimately rather than acquiring it by heredity or election. Tyrants often gained political support from the hoplites and the poor.

But tyrannies contained a fatal flaw. The power of the tyrant was handed down from father to son, and the successors rarely inherited their fathers' qualities of leadership. As a result, tyrannies often became oppressive and unpopular, especially among the hoplites and poor who had supported the tyrants in the first place. Few tyrannies lasted more than two generations.

The most famous of the early Greek tyrannies arose in the large and immensely wealthy and powerful polis of Corinth in the mid-seventh century B.C.E. For many years an aristocratic family, the Bacchiads, had dominated Corinth. In 657 B.C.E., however, the tyrant Cypselus, who had been born into this family, seized power with popular support. He ruthlessly suppressed his aristocratic rivals but maintained his popularity with the people. Disenchantment, however, set in with the rule of Cypselus's son, Periander, who succeeded his father in 625 B.C.E. Periander's brutal methods of rule, which included the systematic execution or banishment of his political opponents and the murder of his wife, lost him the support of the people. Soon after his succession by a third tyrant, in 585 B.C.E., Corinth replaced the tyranny with an aristocratic form of government.

CORINTH: CITADEL AT THE CROSSROADS One of the reasons for the legendary wealth of Corinth was its strategic position dominating the narrow land passage between the Peloponnese and mainland Greece and the crossing of ships over the Isthmus.

Contrasting Societies of the Archaic Age

The two most important poleis on the Greek mainland, Sparta and Athens, developed very different political and social systems during the Archaic Age. Both city-states experienced hoplite revolutions, and both resisted the rule of tyrants, but they nonetheless developed in different directions. Sparta became an **oligarchy**, which means government by a few. Athens, on the other hand, developed into a **democracy**, a word meaning rule by the people. Democracy is a form of political organization in which the people share equally in the government of their communities, devise their own political institutions, and select their own leaders.

oligarchy A government consisting of only a few people rather than the entire community.

democracy A form of government in which citizens devise their own governing institutions and choose their leaders; began in Athens, Greece, in the fifth century B.C.E.

SPARTA: A MILITARIZED SOCIETY Cut off from the rest of Greece by mountain ranges to the west and north, Sparta dominated the Peloponnese, the southernmost part of Greece. Until about 700 B.C.E. Spartans lived much like other Greeks except that their hoplites, who called themselves "the Equals," achieved political power without the aid of tyrants. Sparta was formally a monarchy, ruled by two hereditary kings, each from one of the city-state's prominent aristocratic families. The two kings were equal in authority, which meant that one could veto the decisions of the other, except in time of war, when one of the kings was chosen commander in chief. Effective political power in this polis, however, resided in the *gerousia*, a council of 28 elders whom the assembly of Spartan citizens, known as the *damos*, elected for life. The damos, which comprised only hoplites, had little effective power. It elected the members of the gerousia by acclamation and could only vote to accept or reject policies that this council proposed.

Rapid expansion in the Peloponnese prompted Spartans to develop a highly militarized society, especially after 700 B.C.E., when the Spartans conquered Messenia, a fertile region in the western Peloponnese. To control the Messenians, who vastly outnumbered them, the Spartans reduced the Messenians to the status of **helots** or serfs. Technically free, helots were nevertheless bound to the land and forced to farm it for the Spartans who owned it. If a Spartan master sold the land to another Spartan, the helots stayed with the land. Helots paid half of their produce to their Spartan masters, who could and did kill them with impunity. Controlling the helots through terror became the Spartans' preoccupation.

helots The brutally oppressed subject peoples of the Spartans. Tied to the land they farmed for Spartan masters, they were treated little better than beasts of burden.

In Sparta's social hierarchy free subjects stood one level above the helots. They included merchants, manufacturers, and other businessmen who lived in communities throughout Spartan territories. Free subjects paid taxes and served in the army when necessary, but they were not Spartan citizens.

The male and female citizens of Sparta stood at the top of the social pyramid. The greatest responsibility of all Spartan citizens was to fulfill the military needs of the polis. From early childhood, boys trained to become soldiers and girls trained to become the wives and mothers of soldiers. Boys left home at age 7 to live in barracks, where they mastered the skills of battle. They were periodically beaten to make them able to endure pain without flinching. Their comrades-in-arms played a more important role in their lives than their own families. Young married Spartan men were not permitted to live with their wives, but had to sneak away from their barracks at night to visit them.

Contempt for pain and hardship, blind obedience to orders, simplicity in word and deed, and courage were the chief Spartan virtues. Cowardice had no place in this society. Before sending their men to war, wives and mothers warned, "Come home with your shield—or on it!" Sparta's armies won a reputation as the most ferocious fighting force in all of Greece.

After its conquest of Messenia, Sparta organized the Peloponnesian League, an informal alliance of most of the other poleis in the Peloponnese, which it dominated. Spartans avoided wars far from home, but they and their allies joined with the Athenians and other Greeks in resisting Persia's aggression against Greece, as we will see shortly.

ATHENS: TOWARD DEMOCRACY Athens, the best known polis of ancient Greece, made an incalculably rich contribution to the political, philosophical, artistic, and literary traditions of Western civilization. The first democracy in the ancient world, Athens developed principles of government that remain alive today. Athens's innovative form of government and the flowering of its intellectual life stemmed directly from its response to tyranny and Persian aggression.

In the eighth and seventh centuries B.C.E., the Athenians settled Attica, the territory surrounding their city, rather than sending colonists abroad. In this way, Athens gained more land—about 1,000 square miles, the size of Rhode Island—and a larger population than any other polis on the Greek mainland. By the beginning of the sixth century, aristocrats controlled most of the wealth of Attica, and many of the Athenian peasants became heavily indebted to them. They risked being sold into slavery abroad if they could not repay their debts.

To forestall civil war between the debt-ridden peasantry and the aristocracy, both segments of the population of Attica agreed to let Solon, an Athenian statesman known for his practical wisdom, reform the political system. In 594 B.C.E. Solon (ca. 650–570 B.C.E.) enacted several reforms that limited the authority of the aristocracy and enabled all male citizens to participate more fully in public life. These reforms created the institutions from which democracy eventually developed. Solon cancelled debts, eliminated debt-slavery, and bought the freedom of Athenians who had been enslaved abroad. Taking advantage of a rise in literacy, Solon directed scribes to record his new laws on wooden panels for the whole community to read. This policy diminished aristocratic control of the interpretation of Athenian law and ensured that the laws would be enforced fairly for all Athenian citizens, regardless of their status.

Solon next organized the population into four political groups based on wealth. Only men in the two richest groups could hold the highest administrative office of *archon* and be elected to the highest court, traditionally a base of aristocratic authority. The third group could hold lower political office. The fourth group, the landless *thetes*, who could not afford hoplite weapons, did not hold any offices in the polis. All four groups, however, were represented in the council or **boule** of 400 male citizens (100 from each class), which served as an advisory body for the general assembly of all male citizens. Finally, men of any class could serve on a new court that Solon established. Women, slaves, and foreigners had no voice in government at all.

boule A council of 400 male citizens established by Solon in Greece in the sixth century B.C.E. It served as an advisory body for the general assembly of all male citizens.

The changes introduced by Solon did not end social discontent or achieve political stability. Small farmers continued to become impoverished despite his cancellation of agricultural debt; many of them lost their land to their creditors. Solon's political compromises satisfied no one. The aristocracy felt that Solon had given away too much of their power, whereas the merchants, shopkeepers, and artisans who occupied the third political group were unhappy because they had not received more political power. Most of the elected offices remained in the hands of the aristocracy.

Capitalizing on this widespread discontent, a nobleman named Peisistratus (ca. 590–528 B.C.E.) seized power in 561 and ruled Athens as a tyrant from 547 until his death in 528 B.C.E. Like other tyrannies in Greece, Peisistratus's regime initially enjoyed wide support. He alleviated the plight of the small landowners by giving them land that he had seized from aristocrats. He sponsored building works, supported religious festivals, encouraged trade and economic development, and supported the arts. He initiated a vigorous tradition of Athenian intellectual life by inviting artists and poets to come to Athens from all over Greece. His sons, however, abused their power, and jealous aristocrats, assisted by Sparta, toppled the family's rule in 510. Peisistratus's surviving son fled to Persia.

Two years later, the assembly selected a nobleman named Cleisthenes to reorganize Athenian political institutions. By cleverly rearranging the basic political units of Attica into 10 artificial tribes, Cleisthenes unified this territory and made Athens the center of all important political activity. Building upon Solon's reforms, he set the basic

3.1

3.2

3.3

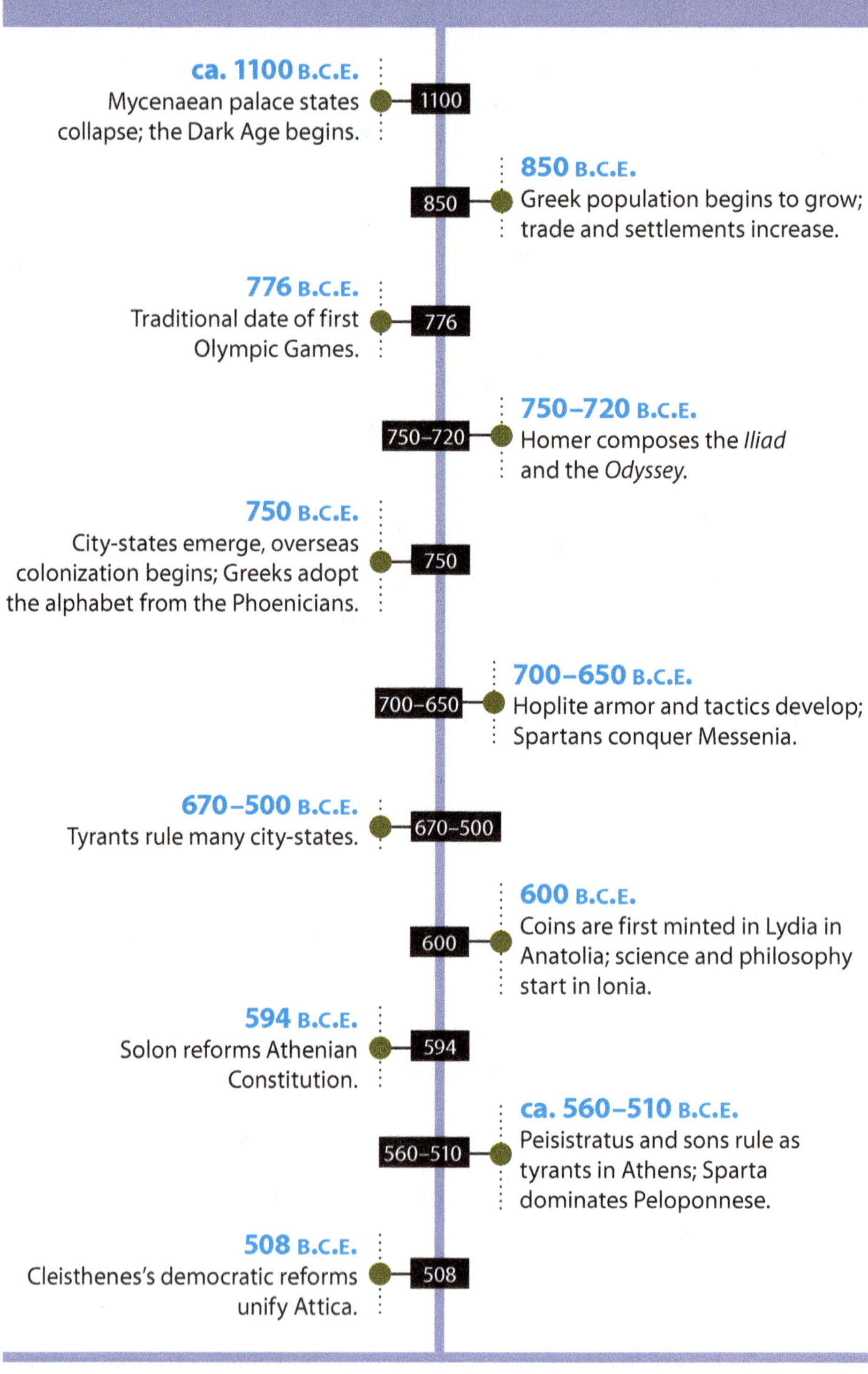

institutions of democracy in place with a new boule of 500 male citizens, in which each of the tribes chose 50 members by lot. The boule heard proposals from citizens and on this basis made up the agenda for the assembly, which consisted of all adult male citizens. All these male citizens could also hold public office. In this way Cleisthenes broke the power of aristocratic families and set up the lasting, fundamental structures of Athenian democracy.

Read the Document

Aristotle: The Creation of the Democracy in Athens

The Greek Encounter with Persia

3.2 How did the Persian Empire bring the peoples of the Near East together in a stable realm, and what elements of Persian religion and government have influenced Western thought?

Persian history began about 1400 B.C.E., when small groups of herdsmen started migrating into western Iran from areas north of the Caspian Sea. Over 500 years these settlers slowly coalesced into two closely related groups, the Medes and the Persians.

By about 900 B.C.E., the Medes had established mastery over all the peoples of the Iranian plateau, including the Persians. In 612 B.C.E., with the assistance of the Babylonians, the Medes conquered the Assyrians. They then pushed into central Anatolia (modern Turkey), Afghanistan, and possibly farther into Central Asia. In the sixth century, under the leadership of Cyrus the Great (r. 550–530 B.C.E.), Persia broke away from Median rule and soon conquered the kingdom of the Medes. Under the guidance of this brilliant monarch and his successors, the Persians acquired a vast empire. They followed a monotheistic religion, Zoroastrianism, and governed their subjects with a combination of tolerance and firmness.

Cyrus the Great and Persian Expansion

After ascending to the Persian throne Cyrus (r. ca. 550–530 B.C.E.) embarked on a dazzling 20-year career of conquest. His military genius and organizational skills transformed the small kingdom into a giant multiethnic empire that stretched from India to the Mediterranean Sea. Cyrus's swift victory over the Medes put Persia at the center of the Near East and thrust it into encounters with a diverse array of peoples.

Cyrus, who took the title of Great King, expanded his empire in several stages. In 546 B.C.E. he conquered Anatolia, where he first came into contact with Greeks. After his victories over these Greek cities, he installed loyal Greek rulers. Next he defeated the kingdom of Babylonia in 539 B.C.E., thus gaining control of Mesopotamia. Then he overran Afghanistan and fortified it against the raids of the Scythian nomads who lived on the steppe lands to the north. These fierce warriors posed a perpetual threat to the settled territories of Persia.

After Cyrus died in 530 B.C.E., his son Cambyses II (r. 529–522 B.C.E.) continued his father's policy of expansion by subduing Egypt and the wealthy Phoenician port cities of the Levant. Control of Phoenician naval resources enabled Persia to extend its empire overseas to Cyprus and the islands of the Aegean. Within barely 30 years, Persia had become the mightiest empire in the world, with territorial possessions spanning Europe, the Near East, and North Africa (see **Map 3.2**).

To ensure that they could easily communicate with their subjects, the Great Kings of Persia developed an elaborate system of roads that their Assyrian predecessors had begun to link their provinces. Officials maintained supply stations at regular intervals along these roads. The chief branch of this system, called the Royal Road, stretched between Anatolia and the Persian homeland in Iran. Persian roads not only facilitated the transportation of soldiers and commercial goods from one part of the empire to another, but they also made possible the flow of ideas and the transmission of cultural traditions.

The key to maintaining power over such a diverse empire lay in the Persian government's treatment of its many ethnic groups. The highly centralized Persian government wielded absolute power, but it rejected the brutal model of the Assyrian and Babylonian imperial system in favor of a more tolerant approach. After conquering Babylonia Cyrus allowed peoples exiled by the Babylonians, including the Hebrews, to return to their homelands. Subject peoples could worship freely and enjoy local

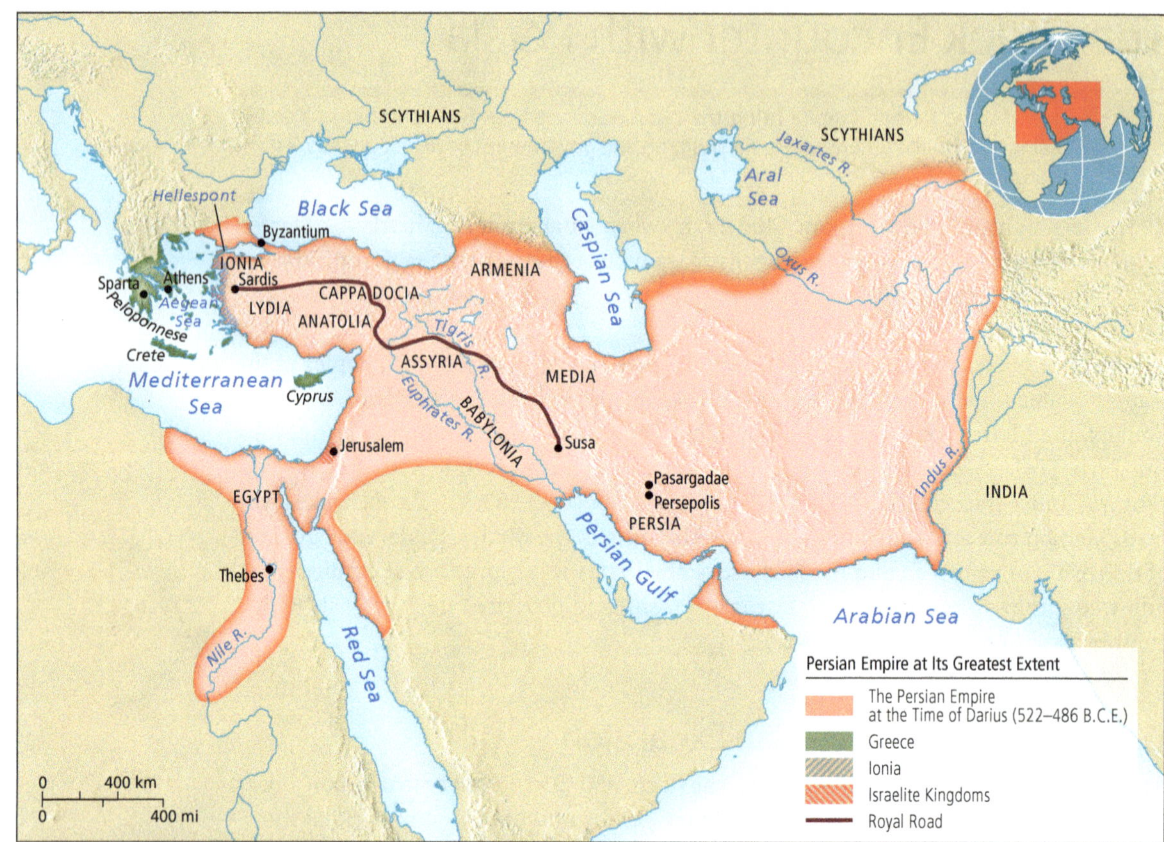

MAP **3.2** THE PERSIAN EMPIRE AT ITS GREATEST EXTENT The Persian Empire begun by Cyrus about 550 B.C.E. grew to include all of the Middle East as far as India, Egypt, and northern Greece. This multiethnic, multireligious empire governed its many peoples firmly but tolerantly. How did Persia try to hold this vast empire together?

autonomy if they acknowledged the political supremacy of the Great King. (See *Different Voices* in this chapter.)

Zoroastrianism The monotheistic religion of Persia founded by Zoroaster that became the official religion of the Persian Empire.

ZOROASTRIANISM: AN IMPERIAL RELIGION The Great Kings of Persia and the Persian people followed **Zoroastrianism**, a monotheistic religion that still has followers around the world today. Its founder, the prophet Zarathustra, known more commonly by his Greek name Zoroaster, lived and preached sometime between 1400 and 900 B.C.E. His message spread throughout Iran for many centuries before it became Persia's chief faith.

Persians transmitted Zoroaster's teachings, known collectively as the *Avesta*, through oral tradition until scribes recorded them in the sixth century C.E. According to Zoroaster, Ahura Mazda (Lord Wisdom), the one and only god of all Creation, is the cause of all good things in the universe. He represents wisdom, justice, and proper order among all created things. Another supernatural being, Angra Mainyu (or Ahriman), the spirit of destruction and disorder, opposes Ahura Mazda and threatens his benevolent arrangement of creation. The conflict between good and evil supernatural powers means that Zoroastrianism is a **dualistic** but not a polytheistic religion, because Angra Mainyu does not possess divine status.

dualistic A term used to describe a philosophy or a religion in which a rigid distinction is made between body and mind, good and evil, or the material and the immaterial world.

In Zoroastrian belief, Ahura Mazda will eventually triumph in this struggle with the forces of evil, leaving all creation to enjoy a blissful eternity. Until then, the cosmic fight between Ahura Mazda's forces of light and Angra Mainyu's forces of darkness gives meaning to human existence and lays the foundation for a profoundly ethical way of life. Ahura Mazda requires humans to contribute to the well-being of the world. Everyone must choose between right and wrong actions.

Different Voices

Liberty and Despotism in Ancient Persia

During the Persian Wars (490–479 B.C.E.), Greeks developed an image of Persia as a despotic state that denied its subjects the liberty that Greeks enjoyed in their poleis. The voices of Cyrus the Great King of Persia in the sixth century B.C.E. and the Greek historian Herodotus in the fifth century B.C.E. reveal how misleading those stereotypes could be. On the day of his coronation as king of Babylon in 539 B.C.E., Cyrus issued a proclamation assuring the Babylonian people that he would rule peacefully, repeal the oppressive burdens imposed on them by the tyrant Nabonidus, and restore the images of the Babylonian and Sumerian gods that Nabonidus had banished from their sanctuaries. Cyrus appeals to Marduk, the Babylonian god, to legitimize his rule. It is misleading to consider this proclamation the "first charter of human rights," a claim based on an inaccurate translation made in 1971. Nonetheless, Cyrus, known as "The Lawgiver," did use this opportunity to guarantee Babylonians freedom of religious worship and end the despotic rule of Babylon's last king.

The Greek historian Herodotus, who grew up in Ionia while it was under Persian control, also challenged the prevailing Greek stereotype of Persian despotism. In this excerpt from The Histories, *Herodotus claimed that Persia had discussed the merits and drawbacks of the three forms of government—monarchy, oligarchy, and democracy—when Darius I (r. 522–486 B.C.E.) succeeded Cyrus as Great King. Darius decided in favor of maintaining monarchical rule, but he reputedly defended his position on the grounds that the king had given Persians their "freedom" and only he could preserve that liberty.*

Cyrus Ends the Despotism of a Babylonian Tyrant

When I went as harbinger of peace i[nt]o Babylon I founded my sovereign residence within the royal palace amid celebration and rejoicing. Marduk, the great lord, bestowed on me as my destiny the great magnanimity of one who loves Babylon, and I every day sought him out in awe. My vast troops marched peaceably in Babylon, and the whole of [Sumer] and Akkad had nothing to fear. I sought the welfare of the city of Babylon and all its sanctuaries. As for the population of Babylon [. . . , w]ho as if without div[ine intention] had endured a yoke not decreed for them, I soothed their weariness, I freed them from their bonds(?). Marduk, the great lord, rejoiced at [my good] deeds, and he pronounced a sweet blessing over me, the king who fears him, . . . From [Shuanna] I sent back to their places . . . the gods who lived therein, and made permanent sanctuaries for them. I collected together all of their people and returned them to their settlements, and the gods of the land of Sumer and Akkad which Nabonidus—to the fury of the lord of the gods—had brought into Shuanna, at the command of Marduk, the great lord, I returned them unharmed to their cells, in the sanctuaries that make them happy. May all the gods that I returned to their sanctuaries, every day before Marduk and Nabu, ask for a long life for me, and mention my good deed.

SOURCE: http://www.britishmuseum.org/explore/highlights/article_index/c/cyrus_cylinder_-_translation.aspx. Excerpts from the translation of the *Cyrus Cylinder* by Irving Finkel are used by permission. Copyright © by The Trustees of the British Museum.

Herodotus Recounts Persia's Rejection of Democracy

Otanes recommended that the management of public affairs should be entrusted to the whole nation. "To me," he said, "it seems advisable, that we should no longer have a single man to rule over us—the rule of one is neither good nor pleasant. . . . How indeed is it possible that monarchy should be a well-adjusted thing, when it allows a man to do as he likes without being answerable? Such license is enough to stir strange and unwonted thoughts in the heart of the worthiest of men. Give a person this power, and straightway his manifold good things puff him up with pride . . . leading on to deeds of savage violence. . . . He sets aside the laws of the land, puts men to death without trial, and subjects women to violence. The rule of the many, on the other hand . . . is free from all those outrages which a king is wont to commit. . . . I vote, therefore, that we do away with monarchy, and raise the people to power."

Megabyzus spoke next, and advised the setting up of an oligarchy: "In all that Otanes has said to persuade you to put down monarchy," he observed, "I fully concur; but his recommendation that we should call the people to power seems to me not the best advice. For there is nothing so void of understanding, nothing so full of wantonness, as the unwieldy rabble. It were folly not to be borne, for men, while seeking to escape the wantonness of a tyrant, to give themselves up to the wantonness of a rude unbridled mob. . . . Let the enemies of the Persians be ruled by democracies; but let us choose out from the citizens a certain number of the worthiest, and put the government into their hands. For thus both we ourselves shall be among the governors, and power being entrusted to the best men, it is likely that the best counsels will prevail in the state." . . .

After him Darius came forward, and spoke as follows: "All that Megabyzus said against democracy was well said, I think; but about oligarchy he did not speak advisedly; for take these three forms of government—democracy, oligarchy, and monarchy—and let them each be at their best, I maintain that monarchy far surpasses the other two. What government can possibly be better than that of the very best man in the whole state? . . . Contrariwise, in oligarchies, where men vie with each other in the service of the commonwealth, fierce enmities are apt to arise between man and man, each wishing to be leader, and to carry his own measures; whence violent quarrels come, which lead to open strife, often ending in bloodshed. Then monarchy is sure to follow; and this too shows how far that rule surpasses all others. . . .

Lastly, to sum up all in a word, whence, I ask, was it that we got the freedom which we enjoy? Did democracy give it us, or oligarchy, or a monarch? As a single man recovered our freedom for us, my sentence is that we keep to the rule of one.

SOURCE: Herodotus, *The Histories,* trans. by George Rawlinson III. 80-1. (New York: Dutton, London: Dent, 1962). Reprinted by permission of Everyman's Library, Random House UK.

(continued on next page)

(continued from previous page)

For Discussion

1. Was the edict issued by Cyrus in 539 B.C.E. really a charter of human rights? What practical political considerations might have led him to issue this edict?
2. Did Darius's criticism of democracy and defense of monarchy have any merit, or were they merely rhetorical justifications of Darius's own desire for power?

Zoroastrianism: An Ancient Religion in Modern Times

At the Day of Judgment, sinners who have not listened to Ahura Mazda's instructions, such as those succumbing to the "filth of intoxication," will suffer eternal torment in a deep pit of terrible darkness. Those who have lived ethical lives will live forever in a world purged of evil. In a period of transformation called "the Making Wonderful," the dead will be resurrected, and all will live together in the worship of Ahura Mazda.

The Great Kings of Persia believed themselves to be Ahura Mazda's earthly representatives, responsible for fighting the forces of disorder in their world. Zoroastrianism thus provided an ideological support for the Persian Empire's wars of conquest and rule. The Great Kings lavishly supported the Zoroastrian church, and its priests, called magi, established the faith as the empire's official religion. They built grand temples with sacred fires throughout the empire. Although the Persian Empire tolerated other religions, Zoroastrianism became the official religion that supported the Great Kings.

Zoroastrian beliefs played an important role in shaping the three great Western religions: Judaism, Christianity, and Islam. The Zoroastrian belief that a powerful spirit of evil opposed God contributed to the Jewish belief in Satan, who appears in the later books of the Hebrew Bible as a demon with a distinct personality. In the first century C.E. Christians transformed Satan, whom they also called the Devil, into a cosmic force of evil. The Christian belief in a final struggle against the Devil, followed by the establishment of the kingdom of God on Earth, also originated in Zoroastrianism. The Zoroastrian idea of a final judgment, followed by an afterlife in Heaven or Hell, became a central concept in Christianity and Islam, although it was later downplayed within Judaism.

Persia Under Darius the Great

In 522 B.C.E. Darius, a Persian nobleman related to the royal family, seized the imperial throne by murdering one of the sons of Cyrus the Great. Assuming the status of the new Great King, Darius I inaugurated a new period of territorial expansion and cultural activity that lasted until the Macedonian conqueror Alexander the Great overwhelmed Persia in 330 B.C.E.

Darius controlled an efficient administration. He expanded and improved Persia's roads, set up a postal system, and standardized measures and coinage. He also reorganized Cyrus's system of provincial government, dividing the empire into 20 provinces called satrapies. Each province paid an annual sum to the central government based on its productivity. From the provincial capitals the governors, Persian noblemen called satraps, collected these taxes, gathered military recruits, and oversaw the bureaucracy.

Persepolis: A Royal City

By 513 B.C.E. Darius had greatly expanded his empire. On his northeastern frontier he annexed parts of India as far as the Indus River. To facilitate commerce he built a canal in Egypt that linked the Mediterranean and Red Seas. His conquests on the northwestern frontier of the Persian Empire, however, had the greatest impact on Western civilization because they brought Persia into direct contact with the Greeks. Eager to conquer Greece, Darius sent troops across the Hellespont to establish military bases in the north of Greece. Such incursions along the Greek frontier were only a small part of Darius's grand imperial strategy, but to the Greeks the growing Persian

DARIUS THE GREAT GIVING AN AUDIENCE In this carved panel from the Treasury of the Palace at Persepolis, the Great King Darius I (r. 522–486 B.C.E.) is shown receiving a dignitary. Darius is seated on his throne and holds a staff of office. Subject kings from all over the Persian Empire also came to court to pay their respects and bring tribute.

presence caused profound anxiety. The stage was set for the confrontation between the Persians and the Greeks, a conflict that demonstrated the limits of Persian imperialism.

Around 510 B.C.E. Darius conquered the Ionian Greek poleis. The Persians ruled their new subjects with a light hand, but the Ionian Greeks nevertheless revolted in 499 B.C.E. and asked Sparta and Athens for military assistance. The Spartans, who were further away from Ionia, refused, but the Athenians sent an expeditionary force that helped the rebels burn Sardis, a Persian provincial capital. The Persians crushed the rebellion in 494 B.C.E., but they did not forget Athens's intervention in it.

The Persian Wars, 490–479 B.C.E.

In 490 B.C.E., after four years of meticulous planning, a Persian army crossed the Aegean Sea in the ships of their Phoenician subjects. They landed at the beach of Marathon, some 26 miles from Athens. The area around Marathon was the traditional stronghold of the family of Peisistratus, the former Athenian tyrant. The Persians planned to install Peisistratus's son Hippias as the new tyrant of Athens.

To save their city, the Athenians marched to Marathon, and with the aid of troops from a neighboring polis (Spartan reinforcements arrived too late) defeated the Persians. The surprising Greek victory demonstrated that a force of heavily armed hoplites could defeat a more numerous but more lightly armored body of Persian infantry. Pride in this Greek victory also unified Athenians by making it unpopular to advocate a treaty or an alliance with Persia, as many had done before the battle.

After Marathon, Athens embraced even more dramatic reforms. A new political leader, Themistocles (ca. 523–ca. 458 B.C.E.), persuaded his fellow citizens to spend the proceeds from a rich silver mine in Attica on a new navy and port. By 480 B.C.E. Athens possessed nearly 200 warships, called **triremes**. With three banks of oars manned by the poorest citizens of the polis, who were paid to row them, the triremes transformed Athens

triremes Greek warships with three banks of oars. Triremes manned by the poorest people of Athenian society became the backbone of the Athenian Empire.

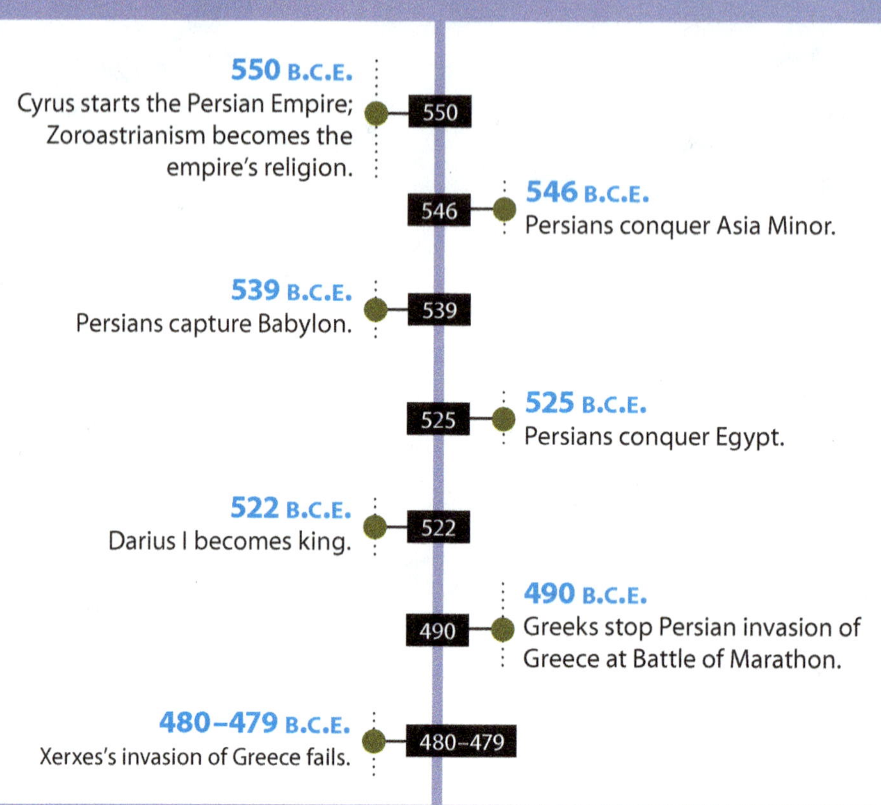

into a naval powerhouse. The entire male citizen body of Athens, not just the aristocrats and hoplites, could now be called to arms. The Athenian navy embodied Athenian democracy in action in that every male citizen had an obligation to defend his homeland.

Marathon dealt a blow to the Persians' pride that they resolved to avenge, but a major revolt in Egypt and Darius's death in 486 B.C.E. prevented them from invading Greece again for nearly a decade. In 480 B.C.E., Xerxes I, the new Great King, launched a massive invasion of Greece. He brought an overwhelming force of some 150,000 soldiers, a navy of nearly 700 mostly Phoenician vessels, and ample supplies. His troops crossed from Asia into Europe by means of a bridge of boats over the Hellespont, while the navy followed by sea in order to supply the troops. They intended to smash Athens.

Terrified by the size of the Persian army, fewer than 40 of the more than 700 Greek poleis joined the defensive coalition that had formed in anticipation of the invasion. Under the leadership of Sparta, the Greek allies planned to hold back the Persian land force in the north, while the Athenian navy would attack the invaders at sea. Leonidas, the Spartan king, led the coalition. A Greek force under his command stopped the Persians at the pass of Thermopylae until a traitor revealed an alternate path through the mountains that allowed the Persians to attack the Greeks from the rear. On the last day of the battle Leonidas, his entire force of 300 Spartans, and perhaps 1,200 allies died fighting.

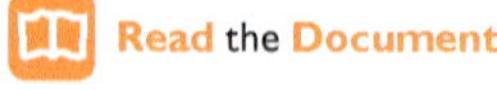

Histories (400 B.C.E.) Herodotus

Their sacrifice was not in vain. Thermopylae gave the Athenians precious time to evacuate their city and station their highly maneuverable fleet in the narrow straits of Salamis, just off the Athenian coast. In a stunning display of naval skill, the Athenian triremes defeated the Persian navy in a single day of heavy fighting. Xerxes returned to Persia, although he left a large army in central Greece.

Early in 479 B.C.E. a combined Greek army once again stopped the Persians at the Battle of Plataea, north of Attica. In this battle a large contingent of Spartans led the

LEONIDAS MONUMENT, THERMOPYLAE This monument celebrating the heroism of Leonidas and the Spartans at the Battle of Thermopylae in 480 B.C.E. was commissioned in 1955 by King Paul of Greece.

decisive final charge. The surviving Persian troops were driven out of Greece. That same year, the combined Greek naval force again defeated the Persian navy off the Ionian coast. Xerxes gave up the attempt to conquer Greece.

The Classical Age of Greece, 479–336 B.C.E.

3.3 What were the intellectual, social, and political innovations of Greece in the Classical Age?

The defeat of mighty Persia by a handful of Greek cities shocked the Mediterranean world. Xerxes's failure did not seriously weaken Persia, but it greatly strengthened the Greeks' own position in the Mediterranean and enhanced what we would now call their self-image. After the defeat of the Persians, the Greeks exhibited immense confidence in their ability to shape their political institutions and to describe and analyze their society and the world around them. The emboldened Athenians created a powerful empire that made them the dominant power in the Greek world while democratic institutions flourished in the polis. Yet Athens's very success sowed the seeds of its demise. After alienating many of the other Greek poleis, Athens lost the long and bitter Peloponnesian War with Sparta.

The distinguishing feature of the Classical Age was its remarkable creativity, especially in drama, science, history writing, philosophy, and the visual arts. Despite the turmoil of the Persian and Peloponnesian Wars, Greek society remained rigidly hierarchical with strictly defined gender roles and many slaves who did much of the heavy work. The structures of Greek society provided many male citizens with leisure time for debating public affairs in a democratic fashion, attending plays, and speculating about philosophical issues. The numerous Greek gods became the subject of much Greek art. Greeks worshiped these gods in temples in the Classical style, which the Romans and other Western peoples later imitated. None of the Greek cities produced

3.1

3.2

3.3

as many creative men as Athens, which makes its experience as an empire and a democracy particularly revealing.

The Rise and Fall of the Athenian Empire

With the Persian threat to Greece nearly eliminated, Athens began a period of rapid imperial expansion. This aggressive foreign policy eventually backfired. It created resentment among the other Greek city-states that led to war and the collapse of the Athenian Empire.

Delian League The alliance among many Greek cities organized by Athens in 478 B.C.E. in order to fight Persian forces in the eastern Aegean Sea. The Athenians gradually turned the Delian League into the Athenian Empire.

FROM DEFENSIVE ALLIANCE TO EMPIRE After the Battle of Plataea, the Greek defensive alliance set out to evict the Persians from the Ionian coast. The Spartans soon grew disillusioned with this campaign and withdrew their troops, leaving Athenians in charge. In the winter of 478 B.C.E., Athens reorganized the alliance, creating the **Delian League**, named for the small island of Delos where the members of the league met. Athens contributed approximately 200 warships to continue attacks against the Persians, while the other members supplied either ships or funds to pay for them. The league ultimately gathered a naval force of 300 ships. By 469 B.C.E. it had driven the last Persians from the Aegean.

With the Persians ousted, several poleis tried to leave the league, but the Athenians forced them to remain in it. The Athenians were rapidly turning the Delian League into an Athenian Empire organized for their own benefit. In subsequent decades the Athenians established garrisons in many cities of the league and intervened in their political life by imposing heavy taxes and financial regulations. Several revolts broke out, but no polis in the empire could overcome Athens's might. In 460 B.C.E. Athens sent approximately 4,000 men and 200 warships to assist an Egyptian revolt against Persia, but Persia destroyed the expedition. Sobered by this debacle, the Athenians moved the treasury of the Delian League from Delos to Athens, claiming that they were protecting it from Persian retaliation. In fact, the Athenians spent the league treasury on public buildings in Athens, including the Parthenon. Athens had become indifferent to the original purpose of the league, but the revenues it generated by exploiting the other cities in the league simultaneously enabled democracy to flourish in Athens itself.

WARFARE AT SEA In the Classical world, navies relied on long-rowed vessels with bronze battering rams to attack enemy ships. This painting of a war galley was made about 550 B.C.E. and shows soldiers, oarsmen, and a man at the helm. Athenians perfected the war galley. Their ships could reach a speed of more than nine nautical miles per hour for short distances.

DEMOCRACY IN THE AGE OF PERICLES The chief designer of the Athenian Empire was Pericles (ca. 490–429 B.C.E.), an aristocrat who dominated Athenian politics from 461 B.C.E. until his death. During the so-called "Age of Pericles," Athenian democracy at home and empire abroad reached their peak.

During the Age of Pericles, Athens had about 40,000 male citizens. Only free men over age 18 could participate in the city's political life. Women, foreigners, slaves, and other imperial subjects had no voice in public life.

The representative council of 500 men established by Cleisthenes continued to administer public business. The citizen assembly met every 10 days and probably never had more than 5,000 citizens in attendance, except on the most important occasions. The assembly decided issues of war, peace, and public policy by majority vote. Because men gained political power through debate in the assembly, a politician's rhetorical skills were crucial in convincing voters.

Ten officials called *generals* were elected every year by popular vote to handle high affairs of state and direct Athens's military forces. Generals typically were aristocrats of proven expertise. Pericles, for example, was reelected general almost continually for more than 20 years.

The vast increase in public business required to run the empire multiplied the number of administrators. By the middle of the fifth century, Athens had about 1,500 officials in its bureaucracy. Boards of assessors determined how much money the members of the Delian League had to pay. Legal disputes among cities in the league forced Athens to increase the number of its courts. Because of the constant need for jurors and other officeholders, Pericles began paying wages for public service, the first such policy in history. Jurors were chosen by lot, and trials lasted no more than a day to expedite cases, save money, and prevent jury tampering.

Pericles' Funeral Oration by Thucydides, ca. 420 B.C.E.

Pericles also gave women a more important role in Athenian society. Before 451 B.C.E. children born to Athenian men and their foreign wives became full citizens. Pericles allowed citizenship only if both parents were Athenian citizens. As a result, Athenian women took pride in giving birth to the polis's only legitimate citizens. Nevertheless, Athenian female citizens could not speak or vote in the assembly, hold public office, or serve on juries.

THE PELOPONNESIAN WAR AND THE COLLAPSE OF ATHENIAN POWER Sparta and its allies felt threatened by growing Athenian power. Between 460 and 431 B.C.E., Athens and a few allies skirmished intermittently with Sparta and the Peloponnesian League it dominated. Full-scale war broke out between the two poleis in 431 B.C.E., dragging on until 404 B.C.E. (see **Map 3.3**). In the early stages of the conflict, which was called the Peloponnesian War, the Spartans repeatedly invaded Attica in the hope of defeating Athenian forces in open battle.

Thanks to Athens's fortifications, the Athenians endured these invasions. Safe behind their fortifications, they relied on their navy to deliver food and supplies from cities in the Athenian Empire. They also launched attacks against Spartan territory from the sea. Although plague struck the overcrowded city in 430 B.C.E., killing almost one-third of the population including Pericles, the Athenians fought on.

In 421 B.C.E., Sparta and Athens agreed to a 50-year truce, but a mere six years later war broke out again. The reckless policies of Alcibiades (ca. 450–404 B.C.E.), a young Athenian general, started a new round of warfare. A nephew of Pericles, Alcibiades lacked his uncle's wisdom. In 415 B.C.E. he persuaded the Athenians to send an expeditionary force of 5,000 hoplites to invade Sicily and seize the rich resources of the city of Syracuse for the war effort. Just as the fleet was about to sail, Alcibiades's enemies accused him of profaning a religious festival, and he fled to Sparta. After two years of heavy fighting, the Athenian expedition ended in utter disaster. Every Athenian ship was captured, and Athenian soldiers were killed or sold into slavery.

MAP **3.3** THE PELOPONNESIAN WAR During this long conflict that lasted from 431 to 404 B.C.E., the forces of Athens and its allies struggled with Sparta and its allies for control of mainland Greece. Though Sparta defeated the Athenian Empire, Athens survived as an influential force in Greek social, political, and economic life. How did the struggle for financial resources influence the outcome of the war?

The Peloponnesian War dragged on for another 10 years, but Athens never recovered from the catastrophic loss of men and ships in Sicily. At the suggestion of Alcibiades, the Spartans established a permanent military base within sight of Athens, which enabled them to control Attica. When 20,000 slaves in the Athenian silver mines escaped to freedom under the Spartans, Athens lost its main source of revenue. The final blow came when Lysander, the Spartan commander in chief, used money from Persia to build a navy strong enough to challenge Athenian sea power. At the Battle of Aegospotami on the Hellespont, Lysander's navy destroyed every Athenian ship. Athens surrendered in 404 B.C.E.

The victorious Spartan forces pulled down Athens's long walls stretching to Piraeus, but they refused to burn the city to the ground as some of its enemies demanded, because Athens had been Sparta's valiant ally in the Persian Wars. Instead, the Spartans set up an oligarchy in place of democracy. Led by the "Thirty Tyrants," a violent and conservative political faction, the oligarchy soon earned the hatred of Athenian citizens. Within a year the Athenians overthrew the tyrants and restored democracy.

Social and Religious Life in the Classical Age

During the Classical Age, the Greek poleis developed a way of life in which gender and social status determined one's position in society and politics. Greek men and women lived very different lives, guided by strict rules of behavior. A hierarchy of gender roles determined a person's access to public space, legal rights, and opportunities to work. In this emphatically patriarchal society, only men held positions of public authority, controlled wealth and inheritance, and participated in political life. Women were restricted to domestic activities that mostly took place out of sight of nonfamily members. At the bottom of society slaves of both sexes were completely subject to their masters.

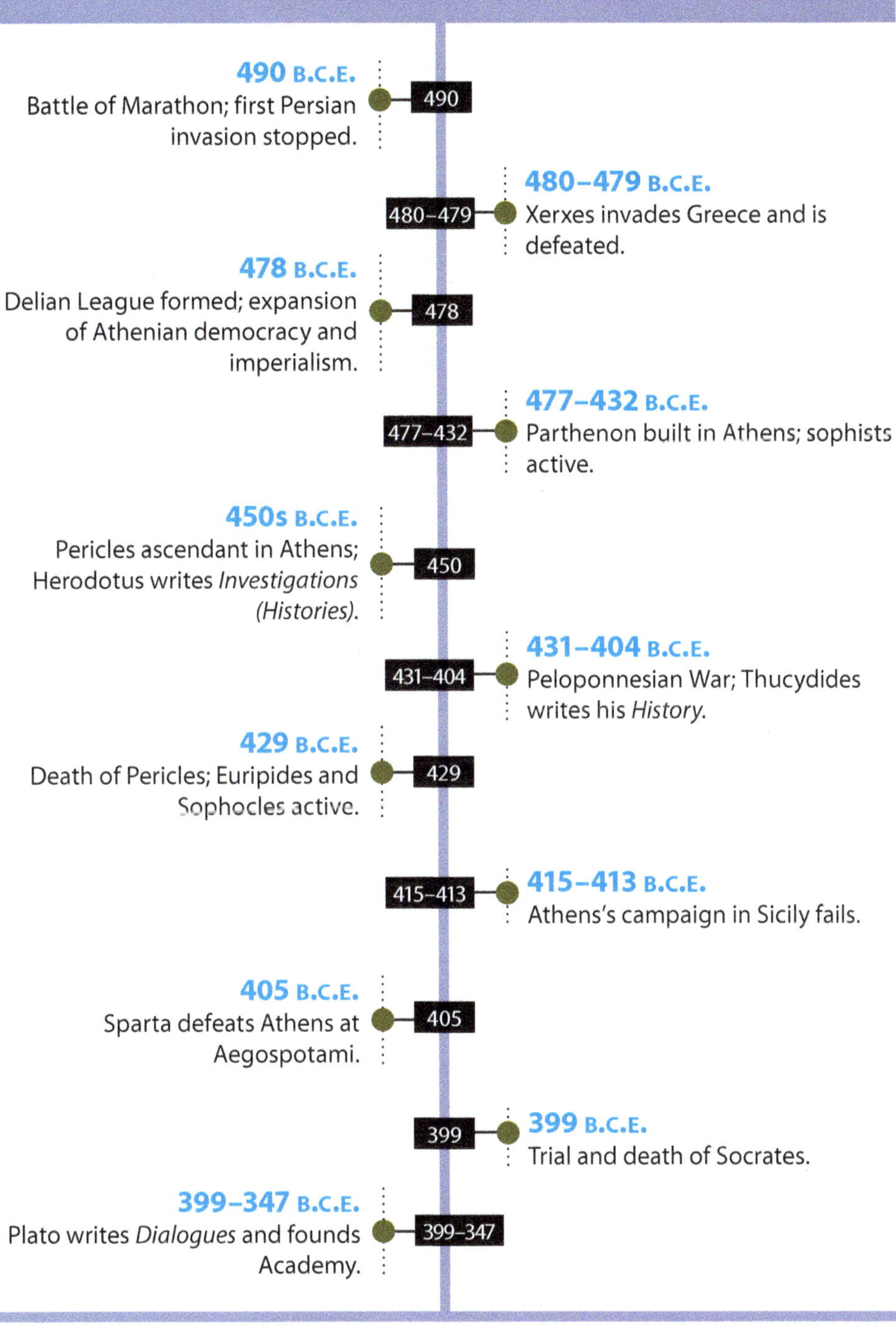

GENDER ROLES Greek women were expected to marry early in puberty, typically to men at least 10 years older than they were. Through marriage legal control of women passed from father to husband. In the case of divorce, which only men could initiate, the husband had to return his wife's dowry to her father. Most Greek houses were small and usually divided into two parts. In the brighter front rooms husbands entertained their male friends at dinner and enjoyed social interaction with other males. Wives spent most of their time in the more secluded part of the house, supervising the household slaves if there were any, raising children, dealing with their mothers-in-law, and weaving cloth.

3.1

3.2

3.3

GREEK MALE VIEW OF WOMEN In male-dominated Greek communities men idealized passive women. This Athenian vase of the fifth century B.C.E. reflects Greek men's view of a properly subordinate woman. In the image, the wife bids goodbye to her young husband, who is going off to war. Her place is at home, tending to chores until his return.

Greek men feared that their wives would commit adultery, which carried the risk of illegitimate offspring and implied that husbands could not control their possessions or access to their homes. Consequently, men strictly controlled women's sexual activity. Because men considered females powerless to resist seduction, respectable women rarely ventured out in public without a chaperone. Whenever possible, slaves went to market and ran errands. To the typical Greek husband, the ideal wife stayed out of public sight and dutifully obeyed him. She was not supposed to mind if he had relations with prostitutes or adolescent boys. Above all, she was expected to produce legitimate children, preferably sons, who would continue the family line and honorably serve the polis.

Women who worked outside the home did so primarily in three capacities: as vendors of farm produce or cloth in the marketplace, as priestesses, and as prostitutes. Female vendors in the marketplace came from the lower classes. Their skills in weaving cloth and making garments, as well as in growing vegetables, enabled them to supplement the family income.

Priestesses served the temples of goddesses such as Hera in Argos and Athena in Athens. In classical Athens, more than 40 publicly sponsored religious cults had female priests. These women gained high prestige in their communities. Greeks believed that some women possessed a special spirituality that made them mediums through whom the gods spoke. Such women served as oracles, as in the temple of Apollo at Delphi. They attracted visitors from all over the Mediterranean world who wanted to discern the gods' wishes or learn what the future might bring.

  Read the Document

Education and the Family in Sparta, ca. 100 C.E.

All Greek cities had prostitutes, but unlike priestesses, their profession was considered shameful. In Athens, most prostitutes were foreign slaves. Some women worked as elite courtesans called **hetairai**. Because Greek men did not think it possible to have intellectual conversations with their spouses, they hired hetairai to accompany them to social gatherings and to discuss politics, philosophy, and the arts. Like ordinary prostitutes, hetairai also were expected to be sexually available for pay.

hetairai Elite courtesans in ancient Greece who provided intellectual as well as sexual companionship.

The most famous of all hetairai was Aspasia, who came to Athens from the Ionian city of Miletus. She became Pericles's companion, and their son gained Athenian citizenship by special vote of the assembly. Aspasia participated fully in the circle of scientists, artists, and intellectuals who surrounded Pericles and made Athens "the school of Greece." According to legend, she taught rhetoric, wrote many of Pericles's speeches, and regularly conversed with the philosopher Socrates.

The Athenian orator Demosthenes famously summed up Greek attitudes toward women with these words: "We have hetairai for the sake of pleasure, regular prostitutes to care for our physical needs, and wives to bear legitimate children and be loyal custodians of our households."[1]

In classical Greece, where men considered women intellectually and emotionally inferior, some men, especially prominent members of society, believed that the best sort of friendship was found in male relationships and took adolescent boys as lovers. In these relationships, which were publicly acknowledged, the older man often assumed the role of mentor to his younger companion. Some poleis institutionalized such relationships. In the city of Thebes, for example, the elite "Sacred Band" of 150 male couples led the city's hoplites into battle during the fourth century B.C.E. These men were considered the best warriors because they would not endure the shame of showing cowardice to their lovers. The Sacred Band could defeat even Spartan warriors.

SLAVERY: THE SOURCE OF GREEK PROSPERITY Slaves had no political, legal, or personal rights. Masters could kill them without serious penalty and could demand sexual favors at any time. Slavery existed in every polis and at every social level. The slave population expanded in the period after 600 B.C.E. as poleis prospered and demands for labor increased.

Most information about Greek slavery comes from Athens, which was the first major slave society that is well documented. Between about 450 and 320 B.C.E., Athens had a total population of perhaps 250,000 people, one-third of whom were enslaved. The proportion of slaves to free people was similar in other poleis. In the Archaic Age the Athenian aristocracy had begun to rely on slave labor to work their large landed estates. Most of these slaves had fallen into bondage for debt, but after Solon made the enslavement of Athenian citizens illegal in 594 B.C.E., the wealthy bought slaves outside Attica. Many slaves were captured during the Persian Wars, but most slaves were either the children of slaves or purchased from the thriving slave trade in non-Greek peoples from around the Aegean.

Slaves performed many tasks. The city of Athens owned public slaves who served as a police force, as executioners, as clerks in court, and in other capacities. Most slaves, however, were privately owned. Some were highly skilled artisans and businessmen who lived apart from their owners but were required to pay them a high percentage of their profits. Most Greek households had male and female slaves who performed menial tasks such as cooking and cleaning. Some rich landowners owned gangs of slaves who worked in the fields. Others rented slaves to the polis to labor in the silver mines, where they were worked to death under hideous conditions.

Slavery did not necessarily last until a person's death. For example, a few slaves were freed by their owners. Others saved enough money from their trades to buy their freedom. Freed slaves could not become citizens, however. Instead, they lived as resident foreigners in the polis of their former masters and often maintained close ties of loyalty and obligation to them.

Slavery was so widespread in Athens because it was profitable. The Athenian political system evolved to permit and support the exploitation of slaves to benefit the citizen class. The slaves were primarily responsible for the prosperity of Athens and gave the aristocrats the leisure to engage in intellectual pursuits and create the rich culture that became part of the core of Western civilization.

Aristotle on Slavery (Fourth Century B.C.E.)

RELIGION AND THE GODS Religion permeated Greek life. Greeks worshiped many gods, whom they asked for favors and advice. Every city kept a calendar of religious observances established for certain days. Festivals marked phases in the agricultural year, such as the harvest or sowing seasons, and initiation ceremonies marked a person's transition from childhood to adulthood.

Above all, Greeks gave their devotion to the gods who protected their city. For instance, during the annual Panathenaea festival in Athens, the entire population, citizens and noncitizens alike, honored the city's patron goddess Athena with a grand procession and sacrifices. Every fourth year, the celebration was expanded to include athletic and musical competitions. In a joyous parade, the citizens would convey a robe embroidered with mythological scenes to the statue of Athena in her temple, called the Parthenon, or House of the Virgin Goddess, that stood on the Acropolis in the center of the city.

Although every polis had its own set of religious practices, people throughout the Greek world shared ideas about the gods. Like the Greek language, these shared religious beliefs gave Greeks a common identity. They also distinguished them from so-called barbarians who worshiped strange gods in ways the Greeks considered uncivilized.

Most Greeks believed that immortal and powerful gods and goddesses were all around them. These deities often embodied natural phenomena such as the sun and moon, but Greeks attributed human personalities and desires to them. Because these divine forces touched every aspect of daily life, human interactions with them were unavoidable and risky, for the gods could be as harmful as they were helpful to humans.

The Greeks believed that the 12 greatest gods lived on Mount Olympus in northern Greece as a large, dysfunctional family. Zeus was the father of some of the gods and king of them all. Hera was his sister and wife. Aphrodite was the goddess of sex and love. This jealous clan also included Apollo, god of the sun, prophecy, and medicine; Poseidon, god of the sea; and Athena, the goddess of wisdom. Greek mythology developed a set of stories about the Olympian gods that have passed into Western literature and art.

In addition to their home on Mount Olympus, the gods also maintained residences in cities. Temples served as the gods' living quarters. Worship at Greek temples consisted of offerings and sacrifices. Outside, in the open air, worshipers offered the gods small gifts, such as a small bouquet of flowers, a pinch of incense, or a small grain cake. On especially important festivals the Greeks sacrificed live animals to their gods on altars in front of the temples. Priests and priestesses supervised these rituals. The god inside the temple supposedly watched the priests prepare the sacrifice, heard the sacrificial animals bleat as their throats were slit, and listened to women howl as blood poured from the beasts. Finally, the god smelled the aroma of burning meat as the victim was cooked over the flames. Satisfied, the god awaited the next sacrifice while the cooked meat was usually distributed to the worshipers.

The Greeks also took pains to discern the future. Religious experts analyzed dreams and predicted the future based on the examination of the internal organs of sacrificed animals. Greeks and non-Greeks alike traveled to consult the priestess of Apollo, the so-called Oracle of Delphi, at a shrine in central Greece. If the god chose to reply to a query, he spoke through the mouth of his oracle, a priestess who would lapse into a trance. Priests recorded and explained the oracle's utterances, which could have more than one interpretation. When King Croesus of Lydia (r. 560–547 B.C.E.) supposedly asked the oracle what would happen if he went to war with the Persians, Apollo told him that "a great kingdom will fall." Croesus never dreamed it would be his own.

Cultural and Intellectual Life in Classical Greece

In the Classical Age, Greeks investigated the natural world and explored the human condition with astonishing freshness and vigor. Their legacy in drama, science, philosophy, and the arts has inspired people for many subsequent centuries. The term *renaissance,* which is applied to several cultural movements in later periods, refers to attempts to recapture the intellectual vitality of the Greek Classical Age and of the Romans, which drew heavily from it.

DRAMA Greek men and women examined their society's values through public dramatic performances. Athenian drama had its origins in an annual festival dedicated to Dionysus, the god of wine, which Peisistratus, the tyrant of Athens, introduced in 535 B.C.E. Plays, which included choral dancing, became part of these festivals, and authors entered their work in competition for a prestigious prize. Dramatic productions soon became a mainstay of Greek life. In their plays, usually set in the mythical past, the playwrights explored issues relevant to contemporary society. Above all, Greeks who attended the plays could expect to be educated and entertained. Fewer than 50 plays of the hundreds that were written during the Greek classical period have survived, but they count among the most powerful examples of Western literature.

In tragedies Athenian men watched stories about the terrible suffering underlying human society. In many of these plays a fatal personal flaw beyond one's ability to control led to the destruction of an important aristocrat or ruler. With an unflinching gaze, playwrights examined conflicts between violent passion and reason and between the laws of the gods and those of human communities. Their dramas depicted the terrible consequences of vengeance, the brutality of war, and the relationship of the individual to the polis. In the plays of the three great Athenian tragedians—Aeschylus, Sophocles, and Euripides—the audience learned vital lessons through the sufferings of the characters.

Aeschylus (525–456 B.C.E.) believed that the gods were just and that suffering stemmed directly from human error. His most powerful works include a trilogy called the *Oresteia.* These three plays express the notion that a polis can survive only when courts made up of citizens punish criminals, rather than leaving justice to family vendettas.

In the plays of Sophocles (ca. 496–406 B.C.E.), humans are free to act, but they are trapped by their own weaknesses, their history, and the will of the gods. In *Antigone,* a young woman buries her outlaw brother in accordance with divine principles but in defiance of her city's laws against burying rebels, knowing that she will be executed for her brave act. The misguided king who made the law and ordered her death realizes too late that a polis will prosper only if human and divine laws come into proper balance. In *Oedipus the King,* Oedipus unknowingly kills his father and marries his mother. When he learns what he has done, he blinds himself. Although he knows that fate caused his tragedy, he understands that he was the one who committed the immoral acts.

The plays of Euripides (ca. 484–406 B.C.E.) portray humans struggling against their fates. In these works, the gods have no human feeling and are capable of bestial action against humans. Euripides showed remarkable sympathy for women, who often fall victim to war and male deceit in his plays. At the end of *The Trojan Women,* the despairing Trojan queen Hecuba stands amid the smoldering ruins of her vanquished city, lamenting the cruel life as a slave that awaits her: "Lead me, who walked soft-footed once in Troy, lead me a slave where earth falls sheer away by rocky edges, let me drop and die withered away with tears."[2]

In addition to the tragedies, Greeks delighted in irreverent comedies. Performances of comedy probably began in the seventh century B.C.E. as lewd sketches associated with Dionysos, the god of wine and fertility. The playwright Aristophanes of Athens (ca. 450–388 B.C.E.) proved a master at presenting comedy as social commentary. No person, god, or institution escaped his mockery. Although committed to Athenian democracy, Aristophanes had no patience for hypocritical politicians or self-important intellectuals. His comic plays are full of raunchy sex, sarcasm, puns, and allusions to contemporary issues. Audiences howled at the fun, but these plays always carried a thought-provoking message. *The Birds* is an apt example. In this satire, Aristophanes tells the story of two down-on-their-luck Athenians who flee the city looking for peace and quiet. On their trek they have to deal with an endless stream of Athenian bureaucrats and frauds, whom Aristophanes mercilessly skewers. Finally the travelers seize power over the Kingdom of the Birds—and then transform it into a replica of Athens. This satire of Athenian imperialism shows Athenians helpless to avoid their own worst instincts.

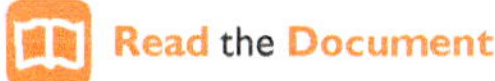
Read the Document

Aristophanes Argues Against the War, 411 B.C.E.

SCIENTIFIC THOUGHT Greek science began about 600 B.C.E. in the cities of Ionia, when a handful of men began to ask new questions about the natural world. Living

3.1

3.2

3.3

on the border with Near Eastern civilizations, these Greek thinkers encountered the vigorous Babylonian scientific and mathematical traditions that still flourished in the Persian Empire. Carefully observing the natural world and systematically recording data, these men began to reconsider traditional Greek explanations for natural phenomena. They rejected the idea that gods arbitrarily inflicted floods, earthquakes, and other disasters on humanity. Instead, they looked for natural causes of such phenomena. To these investigators, the natural world was orderly, knowable through careful inquiry, and therefore ultimately predictable. These scientists inquired about the physical composition of the natural world, tried to identify the general principles that explained why change occurs, and began to think about proving their theories logically.

Thales of Miletus (ca. 625–547 B.C.E.), the first of these investigators, theorized that the Earth was a disk floating on water. When the Earth rocked in the water, he proposed, the motion caused earthquakes. Thales traveled to Egypt to study geometry and established the height of the pyramids by calculating the length of their shadows. Perhaps influenced by Egyptian and Babylonian teachings, he believed that water gave rise to everything else. His greatest success as an astronomer came when he predicted a solar eclipse in 585 B.C.E.

One of Thales's students, Anaximander (ca. 610–547 B.C.E.), wrote a pioneering essay about natural science called *On the Nature of Things*. Anaximander became the first Greek to create a map of the inhabited world. He also argued that the universe was rational and symmetrical. In his view, it consisted of Earth as a flat disk at its center, held in place by the perfect balance of the limitless space around it. Anaximander also believed that change occurred on Earth through tension between opposites, such as hot versus cold and dry versus wet.

A third great thinker from Miletus, Anaximenes (ca. 545–525 B.C.E.), suggested that air is the fundamental substance of the universe. Through different processes, air could become fire, wind, water, earth, or even stone. His conclusions, along with those of Thales and Anaximander, may seem odd and unsatisfactory today, but these men were pioneers in the scientific exploration of the natural world. Their willingness to remove the gods from explanations of natural phenomena, and their effort to defend their theories, established the foundations of modern scientific inquiry and observation.

These Milesian thinkers sparked inquiry in other parts of the Greek world. Heraclitus of Ephesus (ca. 500 B.C.E.) argued that fire, not gods, provided the true origin of the world. Leucippus of Miletus (fifth century B.C.E.) and Democritus of Abdera (ca. 460–370 B.C.E.) proposed that the universe consisted of an endless number of minute particles called atoms that floated everywhere. When the atoms collided or stuck together, they produced the elements of the world we live in, including life itself. These atomists had no need for gods to explain the natural world.

HISTORY The Western tradition of writing history has its roots in the work of Herodotus (ca. 484–420 B.C.E.), who grew to adulthood in the Ionian city of Halicarnassus. Herodotus sought to find the general causes of human events, not natural phenomena. He called his work *Investigations* (the original Greek meaning of the word *history*), and he attempted to explain the Persian Wars, which he considered the greatest wars ever fought.

Gods appear in Herodotus's narrative but do not cause events to occur. Instead, Herodotus attempted to show that humans always act in accordance with the general principle of reciprocity; that is, people predictably respond in equal measure to what befalls them. He described reciprocal violence in legends, such as that of the Trojan War, and recounted the conquest of Lydia by Cyrus the Great in the sixth century. He tells how the Greeks became involved in Persian affairs and finally triumphed over Persian aggression.

Herodotus traveled widely and made the description and analysis of foreign cultures an integral part of his "investigations." He frequently visited Athens, where he read portions of his history of the Persian War to appreciative audiences. He also went to Egypt, Babylonia, and other foreign lands, gathering information about local religions and customs. Herodotus relished the differences among cultures, and his narrative brims with vivid descriptions of exotic habits in far-off lands.

Although he considered Greeks superior to other peoples, Herodotus raised basic questions about cultural encounters that still engage us today. Are one culture's customs better than another's? Can we evaluate a foreign culture on its own terms or are we doomed to view the world through our own eyes and experiences?

Read the Document

Herodotus on the Egyptians (Fifth Century B.C.E.)

Western civilization also owes an incalculable debt to Thucydides of Athens (d. ca. 400 B.C.E.). His brilliant *History of the Peloponnesian War* is perhaps the single most influential work of history in the Western tradition because it provides a model for analyzing the causes of human events and the outcomes of individual decisions. In it he combines meticulous attention to detail with a broad moral vision. To Thucydides, the Peloponnesian War was a tragedy. At one time under the leadership of Pericles, Athens epitomized all that was good about a human community. Its culture and political achievement had made it the "school of Greece." Unfortunately Athenians, like all humans, possessed a fatal flaw—the unrelenting desire to possess more. Never satisfied, they followed unprincipled leaders after Pericles's death, embarking on foolhardy adventures that eventually destroyed them.

In Thucydides's analysis, humans, not the gods, are entirely responsible for their own triumphs and defeats. As an analyst of the destructive impact of uncontrolled power on a society, Thucydides has no match. Even more than Herodotus, he set the standard for historical analysis in the West.

Read the Document

Thucydides on Athens (Fifth Century B.C.E.)

PHILOSOPHY The Greeks believed that their communities could prosper only when governed by just political institutions and fair laws. They questioned whether political and moral standards were rooted in nature or whether humans had invented them and preserved them as customs. They wondered whether absolute standards should guide polis life or whether humans are the measure of all things. No one has answered these questions satisfactorily to this day, but one of the legacies of classical Greece is that they were asked.

During the fifth century B.C.E., a group of teachers known as **Sophists**, or wise men, traveled throughout the Greek-speaking world. They shared no common doctrines, and they taught everything from mathematics to political theory with the hope of instructing people to lead better lives. The best-known Sophist was Protagoras (ca. 485–440 B.C.E.), who questioned the existence of gods and absolute standards of truth. All human institutions, he argued, were created through human custom or law and not through nature. Thus, because truth is relative, a person should be able to defend either side of an argument persuasively.

Sophists Professional educators who traveled throughout the ancient Greek world, teaching many subjects. Their goal was to teach people the best ways to lead better lives.

Socrates (469–399 B.C.E.) challenged the Sophists' notion that there were no absolutes to guide human life. He tried to help his fellow Athenians understand the basic moral concepts that governed their lives by relentlessly questioning them. Because Socrates wrote nothing himself, we know of his ideas chiefly through the accounts of his student, Plato (ca. 428–347 B.C.E.), who made his teacher the central figure in his own philosophical essays. (See *Justice in History* in this chapter.)

Plato established a center called the Academy in Athens for teaching and discussion, and earned a towering reputation among Greek philosophers. Like Socrates, he rejected the notion that truth and morality are relative concepts. Plato taught that absolute virtues such as goodness, justice, and beauty do exist, but on a higher level of reality than human existence. He called these eternal, unchanging absolutes **Forms**. In Platonic thought, the Forms constitute reality. Like shadows that provide only an outline of an object, what we experience in daily life merely approximates this reality.

Forms In the philosophical teachings of Plato, these are eternal, unchanging absolutes such as Truth, Justice, and Beauty that represent true reality, as opposed to the approximations of reality that humans encounter in everyday life.

SYMPOSIUM At drinking parties called *symposia,* men would gather to enjoy an evening meal, complete with dancing girls, musicians, and wine. After dinner they often discussed serious issues, including philosophy and ethics. This cup, painted in Athens about 480 B.C.E., shows a young man reclining on a couch while a young woman dances for his pleasure.

Plato's theories about the existence of absolute truths and how humans can discover them continue to shape Western thought. In particular, Platonic theory emphasizes how the senses deceive us and how the truth is often hidden. We can discover truth only through careful, critical questioning rather than through observation of the physical world. As a result, Platonic thought emphasizes the superiority of theory over scientific investigation.

According to Plato, humans can gain knowledge of the Forms because we have souls that are small bits of a larger eternal Soul that enters our bodies at birth, bringing knowledge of the Forms with it. Our individual bits of Soul always seek to return to their source, but they must fight the constraints of the body and physical existence that obstruct their return. Mortals can aid the Soul in its struggle to overcome the material world by using reason to seek knowledge of the Forms. This rational quest for absolutes, Plato argued, is the particular responsibility of the philosophers, but all of us should embark on this search.

In his great political work, *The Republic,* Plato described how people might construct an ideal community based on the principles he had established. In this ideal state, educated men and women called the Guardians would lead the polis because they alone were capable of comprehending the Forms. They would supervise the brave Auxiliaries who defended the city. At the bottom of society were the Workers who produced the basic requirements of life, but were the least capable of abstract thought.

 **Read the Document**

Plato, *The Republic,*
The Philosopher-King

Justice in History

The Trial and Execution of Socrates the Questioner

In 399 B.C.E. the people of Athens tried and executed Socrates, their fellow citizen, for three crimes: not believing in Athenian gods, introducing new gods, and corrupting the city's young men. The charges were paradoxical, because Socrates had devoted his life to investigating how to live ethically and morally. Although Socrates could have escaped, he chose to die rather than betray his fundamental beliefs. Socrates wrote nothing down, yet his ideas and the example that he set by his life and death make him one of the most influential figures in the history of Western thought.

Born in Athens in 469 B.C.E., Socrates fought bravely during the Peloponnesian War. Afterward he openly defied the antidemocratic Thirty Tyrants whom the Spartans had installed in Athens. Socrates did not seek a career in politics or business. Instead he spent his time thinking and talking, which earned him a reputation as an eccentric. His friends, however, loved and respected him.

Socrates did not give lectures. Instead, he questioned people who believed they knew the truth. By asking them such questions as "What is justice? Beauty? Courage?" and "What is the best way to lead a good life?" Socrates revealed that they—and most people—did not truly understand their basic assumptions. Socrates did not claim to know the answers, but he did believe in the relentless application of rational argument to elicit answers. This style of questioning, known as the Socratic method, infuriated complacent men because it made them seem foolish. But it delighted people interested in taking a hard look at their most cherished beliefs.

Socrates attracted many followers. His brightest student was the philosopher Plato, to whom Socrates was not only a mentor but a hero. Plato wrote a number of dialogues, or dramatized conversations, in which Socrates appears as a questioner, pursuing the truth about an important topic. Four of Plato's dialogues—*Euthyphro, Apology, Crito,* and *Phaedo*—involve Socrates's trial and death.

SOCRATES ON TRIAL Many sculptors made portraits of Socrates in the centuries after his death. Though Socrates was viewed as a hero who died for his beliefs, this sculptor did nothing to glamorize him. Socrates was famous for the beauty of his thoughts—and the ugliness of his face.

The trial began when three citizens named Lycon, Meletus, and Anytus accused Socrates before a jury of 501 men. After hearing the charges, Socrates spoke in his own defense, but instead of showing remorse, he boldly defended his method of questioning. Annoyed by Socrates's stubbornness, the jury convicted him.

Athenian law permitted accusers and defendants to suggest alternative penalties. When the accusers asked for death, Socrates responded with astonishing arrogance. He suggested instead that Athens pay him for making the city a better place. Outraged by this response, the jury chose death by an even wider margin. Socrates accepted their verdict calmly.

While Socrates sat in prison waiting for his execution, a friend named Crito offered to help him escape. Socrates refused to flee. He told Crito that only a man who did not respect the law would break it, and that such a man would indeed be a corrupting influence on the young. Socrates pointed out that he had lived his life as an obedient Athenian citizen and would not break the law now. Human laws may be imperfect, he admitted, but they allow a society to function. Private individuals should never disregard them. To the end he remained a loyal citizen.

On his final day, with his closest friends around him, Socrates drank a cup of poison and died bravely. Plato wrote, "This is the way our dear friend perished. It is fair to say that he was the bravest, the wisest, and the most honorable man of all those we have ever known."[3]

Historians and philosophers have discussed Socrates's case since Plato's time. Were the accusations fair? What precisely was his crime? In the matter of corrupting Athens's youth, there is no doubt that at least two of his most fervent young followers, Alcibiades and Critias, had earned terrible reputations. Alcibiades had betrayed his city in the Peloponnesian War. Critias was one of the most violent of the Thirty Tyrants. Many Athenians suspected Socrates of

(continued on next page)

(continued from previous page)

influencing them, even though these men represented everything he opposed.

Charges of impiety were harder to substantiate, but Athenians took them seriously. Socrates always participated in Athenian religious life. But during his defense he admitted that his religious views were not exactly the same as those of his prosecutors. His claim to have a divine *daimon* or "sign" who sat on his shoulder and gave him advice was eccentric though not actually sacrilegious. Many Athenians thought this daimon was a foreign god rather than Socrates's metaphor for his own mental processes.

The reasons for Socrates's prosecution lie deeper than the official charges indicate. His trial and execution emerged from an anti-intellectual backlash arising from the frustrations of Athens's defeat in the Peloponnesian War and in the Thirty Tyrants' rule. Even though Athenians had restored democracy, deep-seated resentments sealed Socrates's fate. In many societies throughout history, especially democratic ones like that of Athens that grant freedom to explore new ideas, people who fear change and creativity often attack artists, intellectuals, and innovators in times of stress. Athenians resented Socrates because he challenged them to think. He wanted them to live better lives, and they killed him.

For Discussion

1. What does this trial reveal about the nature of Athenian justice?
2. What does this trial tell us about the attitude of Athenians toward philosophy?
3. Was the execution of Socrates a failure or a logical consequence of Athenian democracy?

Taking It Further

Brickhouse, Thomas C., and Nicholas D. Smith. *Socrates on Trial.* 1989. A thorough analysis of Socrates's trial.

Stokes, Michael. *Plato: Apology, with Introduction, Translation, and Commentary.* 1997. The best translation, with important commentary.

Plato and his student Aristotle (384–322 B.C.E.) were the two greatest thinkers of classical Greece. Aristotle founded his own school in Athens, called the Lyceum. Unlike Plato, Aristotle did not envision the Forms as separate from matter. In his view, form and matter are completely bound together. For this reason, we can acquire knowledge of the Forms by observing the world around us and classifying what we find. Following this theory, Aristotle investigated many subjects, including animal and plant biology, aesthetics, psychology, and physics. His theories regarding mechanics (the study of motion) and his argument that the sun and planets revolve around the Earth acquired great authority among ancient and medieval thinkers and were not effectively challenged until the Scientific Revolution of the late sixteenth and seventeenth centuries.

Aristotle's political ideas were equally influential. Unlike Plato, who described an ideal state, Aristotle analyzed the political communities that actually existed in his day, the Greek poleis. This empirical approach to politics, which paralleled his study of the natural world, led him to conclude that human beings were by nature "political animals" who had a natural tendency to form political communities. By living in such societies they learned about justice, which was essential to the state and was its guiding principle. Aristotle's view that the people themselves, not the gods, established the state was immensely important in the history of Western thought. It has survived in modern democracies, especially in the United States, where the Constitution proclaims that the people themselves established the government and determined how it should be structured.

THE ARTS: SCULPTURE, PAINTING, AND ARCHITECTURE Like philosophers and dramatists during the Classical Age, Greek sculptors, painters, and architects pursued ideal beauty and truth. Classical artists believed the human body was beautiful and was the most appropriate subject of their attention. They also valued the human capacity to represent in art the ideals of beauty, harmony, and proportion found in nature. Greek men celebrated their ability to make rational judgments about what was beautiful and to create art that embodied those judgments.

To create a statue that was an image of physical perfection, sculptors copied the best features of several human models while ignoring their flaws. They strove to depict the muscles, movement, and balance of the human figure in a way that was both lifelike in its imitation of nature and yet idealized in the harmony and symmetry of the torso

View the Closer Look The Erechtheum: Porch of the Maidens Athens

THE ERECHTHEUM, LOCATED ON THE NORTH SIDE OF THE ACROPOLIS The Erechtheum was a temple to the goddess Athena in her oldest form as Athena Polias, the protector of the city.

and limbs. This balance between realism and idealism, as well as the belief that the human male body came closest to perfection and that men embodied the most admirable virtues, explains the proliferation of male statues—many of them nude—throughout the Greek world.

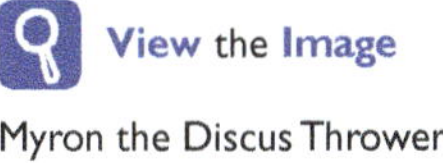

View the Image
Myron the Discus Thrower

Greek painters explored movement of the human body as well as colors and the optical illusion of depth. The figures that they depicted on vases and walls became increasingly lively and realistic as the Classical Age unfolded. Artists portrayed every sort of activity from religious worship to erotic fun, but regardless of the subject, they shared a similar goal: to create a lifelike depiction of the human figure.

In a similar effort to capture ideals of perfection, Greek architects designed their buildings, especially temples, to be symmetrical and proportional. They used mathematical ratios that they observed in nature to shape their designs. The buildings they created show a grace, balance, and harmony that have inspired architects for more than two millennia.

The temple of the goddess Athena in Athens, called the Parthenon, stood as the greatest triumph of classical Greek architecture. Built on the Acropolis of Athens, the temple symbolized Athens's imperial glory. Using funds appropriated from the Delian League, Athenians built the huge temple between 447 and 432 B.C.E. and dedicated it to the city's divine protector. The architects Ictinus and Callicrates achieved a superb

THE MALE NUDE IN GREEK SCULPTURE: POLYCLITUS'S SPEAR-CARRIER This Roman replica of a bronze statue of a warrior, probably the hero Achilles from the *Iliad,* by the Greek sculptor Polyclitus of Argos, reflects the desire of Greek artists to depict the ideal man. The spear-carrier's anatomy is perfectly proportioned, and his muscles indicate discipline and preparation for battle. He is the perfect male citizen, balanced and controlled yet poised to fight. The original statue has not survived.

example of structural harmony, perfectly balancing all the building's elements according to mathematical proportions copied from nature. For the Parthenon's sacred inner room, Phidias, a friend of Pericles, sculpted a statue of Athena made of gold and ivory over a wooden core and decorated it with gems and other precious metals. The temple also displayed an elaborate series of carved and brightly painted marble panels depicting the mythology of Athena. The Parthenon remained nearly intact until 1687 C.E., when powder kegs stored inside exploded, causing irreparable damage and leaving the structure much the way it appears today.

CONCLUSION

The Cultural Foundations of the West

Under the leadership of Athens, Greek city-states made the most enduring contributions of the ancient world to Western civilization. The influence of Greek philosophy, literature, science, art, and architecture remains evident even today in Europe and the lands Europeans settled. The most distinctive contribution of the Greeks to politics, the theory and practice of democracy, also thrives in many parts of the Western world. None of these political and cultural legacies of Greece, however, has come down through the ages without modification, alteration, and mixture with other non-Greek or nonclassical traditions. Greek culture underwent a process of modification in the Mediterranean lands, especially in Italy and in Asia during the Hellenistic period, as we will see in Chapter 4. The Greco–Roman culture that emerged from that process of cultural encounter and exchange has undergone further adaptation, revival, and modification in Europe during the past two thousand years.

This process of cultural encounters between Greek and non-Greek peoples in the ancient world becomes even more complicated when we consider the cultural exchanges that took place between Persia and Greece. Many of these encounters occurred as Persians transmitted older Near Eastern traditions of science, mathematics, astronomy, and religion to the Greeks and the people of the western Mediterranean, North Africa, and eventually Europe. An even more durable Persian influence on the West occurred after a Macedonian ruler, Alexander the Great, conquered Greece and then defeated the Persian Empire in the fourth century B.C.E. Alexander promoted Greek culture in the lands he conquered, but he also assumed the powers of the Persian Great King, which were antithetical to the principles of Athenian democracy. Alexander combined a theory of divinely authorized absolute monarchy with a tradition of Persian imperial rule that had a lasting impact on Western civilization. To the complex and sometimes contradictory political and cultural encounters of the Hellenistic age we now turn.

MAKING CONNECTIONS

1. Like modern-day Iran, Persia is usually considered part of Asia or the East. What role did ancient Persia play in the development of the West?
2. What were the lasting contributions of Greek civilization to the West?
3. Why did the three great poleis of Greece—Corinth, Athens, and Sparta—follow different paths of political development?
4. What were the differences between Athenian and Spartan women?

TAKING IT FURTHER

For suggested readings see page R-1.

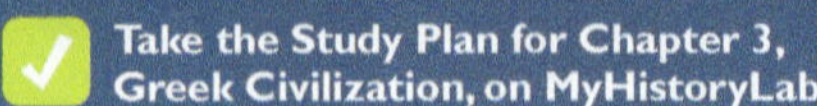

Chapter Review

Greece Rebuilds, 1100–479 B.C.E.

3.1 How did Greek city-states develop their culture and political institutions during the Archaic Age?

Encounters with people from the Near East led to the adoption of an alphabet, which Greeks used to record oral traditions and laws, and eventually to develop a new literature that includes some of the greatest works in the Western tradition. The establishment of the polis, or city-state, emphasized a strong sense of community among the Greeks who inhabited them, and the Olympic Games fostered a sense of Greek identity across city-states. The colonization that was a result of the population boom of the Archaic Age led to new commercial activity and the adoption of coinage, which in turn offered the means to develop advances in military technique and fighting.

The Greek Encounter with Persia

3.2 How did the Persian Empire bring the peoples of the Near East together in a stable realm, and what elements of Persian religion and government have influenced Western thought?

The Persians acquired a vast empire that they governed with a combination of tolerance and firmness. Conquered peoples were allowed to worship and live freely as long as they acknowledged the political supremacy of the king. An elaborate system of roads allowed for not only commercial trade and military transport, but also the transmission of cultural ideas and traditions. Their monotheistic religion, Zoroastrianism, played an important role in shaping the three great Western religions: Judaism, Christianity, and Islam.

The Classical Age of Greece, 479–336 B.C.E.

3.3 What were the intellectual, social, and political innovations of Greece in the Classical Age?

The social structures of Greek society, including strict gender roles and the institution of slavery, gave many male citizens the leisure time for attending plays, speculating about philosophical issues, and debating democratic ideals. Marked by creativity in drama, science, history writing, philosophy, and the visual arts, the cultural innovations of the Classical Age continue to influence the Western world even today. The Greek's legacy of the theory and practice of democracy continues to thrive in many parts of the world.

Chapter Time Line

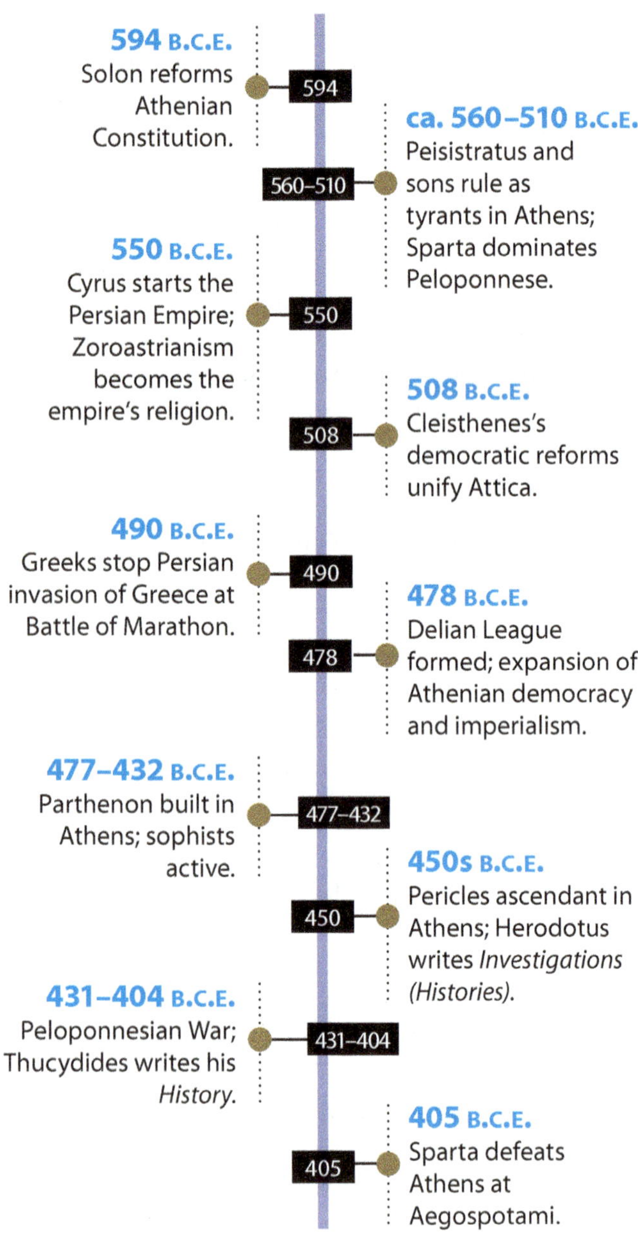

4 Hellenistic Civilization

In 323 B.C.E. an unprecedented succession of military victories by the young Macedonian monarch, Alexander the Great, came to an end. In the space of a mere 11 years Alexander had gained control of all of Greece and conquered the mighty Persian Empire. Slashing through what is today Iran and Afghanistan, he defeated the Indian ruler Poros and reached northwest India. Only then did his soldiers, suffering from fatigue and homesickness, refuse to advance farther. After consulting an omen that told him it was inauspicious to cross the rain-swollen River Beas, Alexander ordered a retreat. At Susa in southwest Iran he married his second and third wives (while still married to his first wife, Roxanna) and made plans for further conquests from India to the Atlantic. But Alexander's apparent ambition to establish a "universal monarchy" covering most of the known world was not to be realized. In June 323 B.C.E. he died, just two months shy of his thirty-third birthday. After his death his empire—the largest the world had ever known—collapsed and was divided into a number of smaller kingdoms, which acquired their own hereditary dynasties and continued the type of monarchical rule that Alexander had exercised.

The conquests of Alexander the Great marked the beginning of the Hellenistic period of Western civilization. Greeks called themselves *Hellenes*, and thus historians use the term **Hellenistic** to

LEARNING OBJECTIVES

4.1 How did Alexander the Great create a large empire in which Greek civilization flourished in the midst of many diverse cultures?

4.2 What was the relationship between Greeks and non-Greeks in the lands that Alexander conquered and those with whom Greeks came into contact after his death?

4.3 What were the distinguishing features of Hellenistic society and culture, and what was the result of encounters between Greeks and non-Greeks?

4.4 What did Hellenistic thinkers contribute to philosophy and the scientific investigation of the natural world?

Listen to **Chapter 4** on **MyHistoryLab**

CELT AND WIFE This dramatic statue epitomizes the mixing of cultures in the Hellenistic Age. The statue is a Roman copy in marble of a bronze original made at Pergamum in Anatolia by a Greek sculptor. The artist tells the tragic story of a defeated Celt (Gaul). Rather than be captured alive, he has just killed his wife and is at the precise moment of taking his own life. In typically Hellenistic style, the artist combines anatomical accuracy with psychological agony.

Watch the Video Series on MyHistoryLab

Learn about some key topics related to this chapter with the *MyHistoryLab Video Series: Key Topics in Western Civilization*

Hellenistic The word used to describe the civilization, based on that of Greece, that developed in the wake of the conquests of Alexander the Great.

barbarians A term used by Greeks to describe people who did not speak Greek and who were therefore considered uncivilized.

describe the complex cosmopolitan civilization, based on that of Greece, that developed in the wake of Alexander's conquests. This civilization offered a rich variety of goods, technologies, and ideas to those who knew the Greek language. Just as people throughout the world today study English because it is the primary language used in science and technology, global business, and international politics, people in the Hellenistic period used Greek as the common tongue in trade, politics, and intellectual life. Greek culture also became the standard by which civilized people identified themselves. Convinced of their intellectual and cultural superiority over inferior people—an idea promoted by the philosophy of Aristotle, Alexander's tutor—civilized people referred to those who did not speak Greek as **barbarians**, a term derived from the Greeks' description of these people's language as "ba-ba," meaning unintelligible to Greeks.

Hellenistic culture thrived within Alexander's successor kingdoms. It also spread far beyond the lands he conquered, mainly to the western Mediterranean, where it had a profound influence on the civilizations of North Africa and Europe, especially Rome. Romans, Jews, Persians, Celts, Carthaginians, and other peoples all absorbed elements of Greek culture—its philosophy, religion, literature, and art. Hellenism gave a common language of science and learning to diverse peoples speaking different languages and worshiping different gods. Hellenism thus provided a cultural unity to an area stretching from Europe in the west to Afghanistan in the east. Large parts of this cultural realm ultimately became what historians call the West.

The spread of Hellenistic culture over this vast area involved a series of cultural exchanges. Greek culture had great prestige and possessed a powerful intellectual appeal to non-Greek peoples, but it also threatened their local, traditional identities. Instead of simply accepting Greek culture, these non-Greek peoples engaged in a process of cultural adaptation and synthesis. In this way Hellenism, which throughout this period remained open to outside influences, absorbed foreign scientific knowledge, religious ideas, and many other elements of culture. These were then transmitted to the greater Hellenistic world. Some of the basic components of Western civilization originated in these cultural encounters between Greek and non-Greek peoples. These include the seven-day week, beliefs in Hell and Judgment Day, the study of astrology and astronomy, and technologies of metallurgy, agriculture, and navigation.

The Hellenistic era and the age of independent Hellenistic kingdoms came to a close in 30 B.C.E., when the Roman ruler Octavian brought an end to the Ptolemaic dynasty, which had ruled Egypt since the death of Alexander. Rome now controlled almost all the states that had been established in the lands that Alexander had conquered. The end of Ptolemaic Egypt therefore marked the end of the Hellenistic Age, but it did not put an end to the influence of Hellenism. As we will see in Chapter 5, Rome rose to power during the Hellenistic period and blended Greek culture with its own. The resulting Greco–Roman cultural synthesis, which Rome transmitted to the lands that it controlled, became the bedrock of Western civilization. This chapter will address the question:

How did Hellenism achieve its dominant position within the West?

The Impact of Alexander the Great

4.1 How did Alexander the Great create a large empire in which Greek civilization flourished in the midst of many diverse cultures?

The Hellenistic Age had its roots in Macedon, a kingdom to the north of Greece that was rich in timber, grain, horses, and fighting men. Most Macedonians lived in scattered villages and made a living by engaging in small-scale farming, raiding their neighbors, and trading over short distances. Relentless warfare against wild Thracian and Illyrian tribes to the north and east kept Macedonians constantly ready for battle.

Macedonians spoke a dialect of Greek, but their customs and political organization differed from those of the urbanized Greek communities that lay to their south. Unlike democratic Athens, Macedon had a hereditary monarchy. Cutthroat struggles for ascendancy in the royal family trained Macedonian kings to select the best moment to deliver a lethal blow to an enemy. Maintaining control over their territory was a constant problem for Macedon's kings because independent-minded nobles resented their rule. Only the army of free citizens could legitimize a king's reign. In return for their support, the soldiers demanded the spoils of war. As a result, Macedonian kings had to wage war continually to obtain that wealth and keep their precarious position on the throne.

The Rise of Macedon Under King Philip

Throughout most of the Classical Age of Greece these fierce Macedonian highlanders seemed like savages to the sophisticated Greeks. When cities started to appear in Macedon in the fifth century B.C.E., Macedonian noblemen began to emulate the culture of classical Greece. The members of the Macedonian royal family, for example, claimed the mythical Greek hero Heracles, son of the god Zeus, as their ancestor. This claim won them the right to compete in the Olympic Games, which were open only to Greeks. Macedonian kings also offered Greek playwrights and scholars large sums of money to lure them to their capital city of Pella.

In the political realm, however, Macedon shrewdly avoided involvement in Greek affairs. During the Persian Wars (490 B.C.E. and 480–479 B.C.E.), Macedonian kings pursued a cautious and profitable policy of friendship with the Persian invaders. During the convulsions of the Peloponnesian War (431–404 B.C.E.) and its turbulent aftermath, Macedon refrained from exploiting Athens, Sparta, and the other Greek cities as they bled to exhaustion. The lack of Greek entanglements, however, could not ease the tensions between kings and nobles in Macedon itself. In 399 B.C.E., Macedon slid into 40 years of anarchy. Just as Macedon was on the verge of disintegration, King Philip II (r. 359–336 B.C.E.) transformed the Macedonian kingdom.

A ruthless opportunist with a gift for military organization, the one-eyed Philip consolidated his power by eliminating his rivals, killing many of them in battle. He unified the unruly nobles who controlled different regions of Macedon by demonstrating the advantages of cooperation under his leadership. As Philip led the nobles to victory after victory over hostile frontier tribes and shared his plunder with them and with the common soldiers, the Macedonians embraced his leadership.

Philip created a new army in which the nobles had a special role as cavalry armed with heavy lances. Called the **Companions**, these cavalrymen formed elite regiments bound to their king by oaths of loyalty. Philip reorganized the infantry, or foot soldiers, who were recruited mainly from the rural peasantry, into phalanxes.

Companions Elite regiments of cavalrymen armed with heavy lances formed by Philip of Macedon in the fourth century B.C.E.

These Macedonian phalanxes, unlike those of the Greek hoplites, used long lances to hold off the enemy while the cavalry attacked the enemy formations from the rear. This new strategy, which Philip probably learned about when he was a hostage in Thebes, gave his armies an enormous tactical advantage over traditional Greek hoplite formations. After seizing the gold and silver mines of the north Aegean coast of Greece, Philip also had ample funds to hire additional armies of mercenaries to augment his Macedonian troops.

With Macedon firmly under his control, its borders secure, and his army eager for loot, Philip stood poised to strike at Greece. In 349 B.C.E. he seized several cities in northern and central Greece, inaugurating a decade of diplomacy, bribery, and threats as he maneuvered to dominate the rest of the Greek poleis.

Recognizing that Philip represented a threat to Greek liberty, the brilliant Athenian orator Demosthenes (384–322 B.C.E.) organized resistance among the city-states. In 340, when Philip attempted to seize the Bosporus, the narrow water link between the Aegean Sea and Athens's vital Black Sea trade routes, Demosthenes delivered a series of blistering speeches against Philip known as "the Philippics" and assembled an alliance of cities. In 338 B.C.E., however, Philip crushed the allied armies at the Battle of Chaeronea. Philip's 18-year-old son Alexander led the Companions in a cavalry charge that won the day for the Macedonians.

Philip then set up a coalition of Greek cities called the League of Corinth under his leadership. He also stationed Macedonian garrisons at strategic sites in Greece and forbade Greek cities to change their form of government without his approval. For the Greek poleis, the age of independence was over.

Philip next cast his eyes on the Persian Empire. In 337 B.C.E. he cloaked himself in the mantle of Greek culture and announced that he would lead his armies and those of the Greek cities against the Persians. His goal was to avenge Persia's invasion of Greece in the previous century. Philip's shrewd linking of classical Greek civilization with Macedonian military might now became a rallying cry for imperialist expansion under his direction. But as Philip laid plans for his assault on Persia in 336 B.C.E., one of his bodyguards assassinated him at the wedding of one of his daughters. Alexander, the son of Philip and Olympias, the king's bitterly estranged wife whom he had forced into exile the previous year, succeeded Philip as king and continued his father's plans to invade Persia. While Alexander honored his slain father, Olympias hung the sword that the assassin had used to kill him in the temple of Apollo and proceeded to murder Philip's son and daughter and his wife, Cleopatra Eurydice.

The Conquests of Alexander the Great

A man of immense personal charisma and political craftiness, Alexander (r. 336–323 B.C.E.) won the support of his soldiers by demonstrating fearlessness in combat and military genius on the battlefield. He combined a predatory instinct for conquest and glory with utter ruthlessness in the pursuit of power. These traits proved to be the key to his success. By the time of his death, Alexander had won military victories as far east as India, creating a vast empire. His successes made him a legend during his lifetime, and millions of his subjects worshiped him as a god. Historians consider him a pivotal figure in Western civilization because his conquests led to the spread of Hellenistic culture in lands that were to become important components of the West.

After brutally consolidating power in Macedon and Greece following his father's death, Alexander launched an invasion of Persia. With no more than 40,000 infantry and 5,000 cavalry, he crossed the Hellespont and marched into Persian territory in 334 B.C.E. The young Macedonian king won his first great victory over Persian forces at

View the **Closer Look** Alexander and Darius at the Battle of Issus

ALEXANDER THE GREAT Detail of a Roman mosaic depicting Alexander the Great at the Battle of Issus, where he defeated the Persian army in 333 B.C.E. The empire he established by the time of his death in 323 B.C.E. defined the main boundaries of the Hellenistic world.

the Battle of the Granicus River, giving him control over Anatolia with its rich Greek coastal cities. He then marched into Syria, where he broke the main Persian army near the town of Issus in 333 B.C.E. Here, just as he had done at Granicus River, Alexander led the Macedonian cavalry's victorious charge into the teeth of the enemy. From this victory Alexander gained control of the entire eastern coast of the Mediterranean Sea and the Persian naval bases located there.

When Alexander captured the port city of Tyre in 332 B.C.E., Darius panicked and offered the young Macedonian his daughter in marriage and all of his empire west of the Euphrates River in return for peace. Alexander rejected the offer and marched into Egypt, where the inhabitants welcomed him as a liberator from their Persian masters and crowned him as Pharaoh. From Egypt he advanced into Mesopotamia, where he crushed Darius again on the battlefield at Gaugamela near the Tigris River.

When Alexander entered Babylon in triumph after Gaugamela, he again received an enthusiastic welcome as a liberator. From Babylon his forces ventured southeast to Persepolis, the Persian palace city, which fell in January 330 B.C.E. There Alexander ordered his soldiers to kill all the adult males, enslave the women, loot the palace's vast treasures, and burn it to the ground. The enormous wealth Alexander acquired from Persepolis and other Persian treasure centers paid for all of his military activities for the next seven years and invigorated the entire Macedonian economy. Darius III, the Great King of Persia (r. 335–330 B.C.E.), escaped to the east, but was soon murdered by his own nobles. The once-powerful Persian Empire, which covered one million square miles and had a population of 50 million people, lay in ruins.

Alexander had fulfilled his father's pledge to gain vengeance against Persia, but he had no intention of stopping his march of conquest (see **Map 4.1**). He pushed past the tribesmen of the harsh Afghan mountain ranges to penetrate central Asia. Then in 327 B.C.E. he entered what is today Pakistan through the Khyber Pass, the narrow route that separates central Asia from the south Asian subcontinent. At the Battle of the Hydaspes River, Alexander defeated the Indian king Poros, who had assembled a formidable army of 6,000 cavalry, 30,000 infantry, and 200 war elephants. But Alexander's exhausted armies refused to advance farther into India, and he was forced to retreat. The route he chose for his return westward passed through a scorching desert, where many of his soldiers died, and Alexander himself suffered nearly fatal wounds. While recuperating at Babylon in 323 B.C.E., where he had begun to plan more conquests, Alexander succumbed to fever after a drinking bout. He had never lost a battle.

The Conquests of Alexander the Great

In strategic locations through the lands he had conquered, Alexander established cities as garrisons for his troops. More than a dozen of these cities received the name *Alexandria* in his honor. Thousands of Greeks migrated east to settle in the new cities to take advantage of the expanded economic opportunities for trade and farming. These Greek settlers became the cultural and political elite of the new cities.

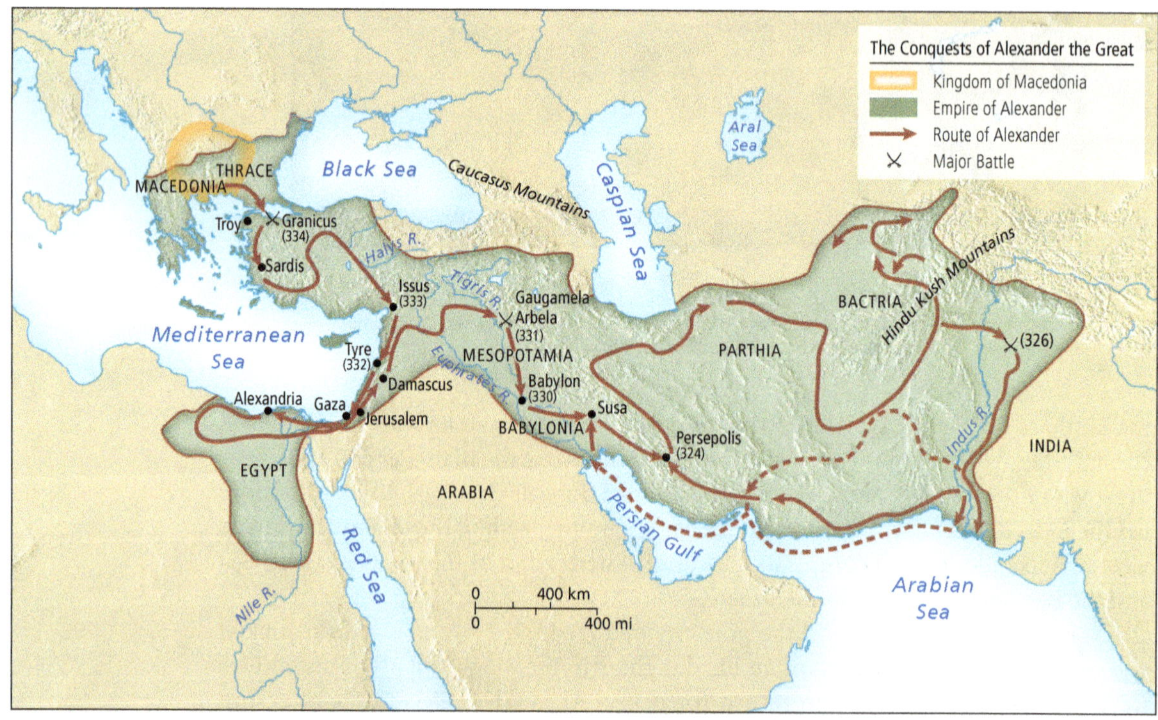

MAP **4.1** THE CONQUESTS OF ALEXANDER THE GREAT Alexander led troops from his Macedonian homeland as far east as the Indus Valley. He defeated the Persian Empire and incorporated it into his own empire. This map shows Alexander's march of conquest and the sites of his most important victories. Why was Macedonia unable to profit fully from these conquests?

CHRONOLOGY: ALEXANDER THE GREAT AND THE GREEK EAST

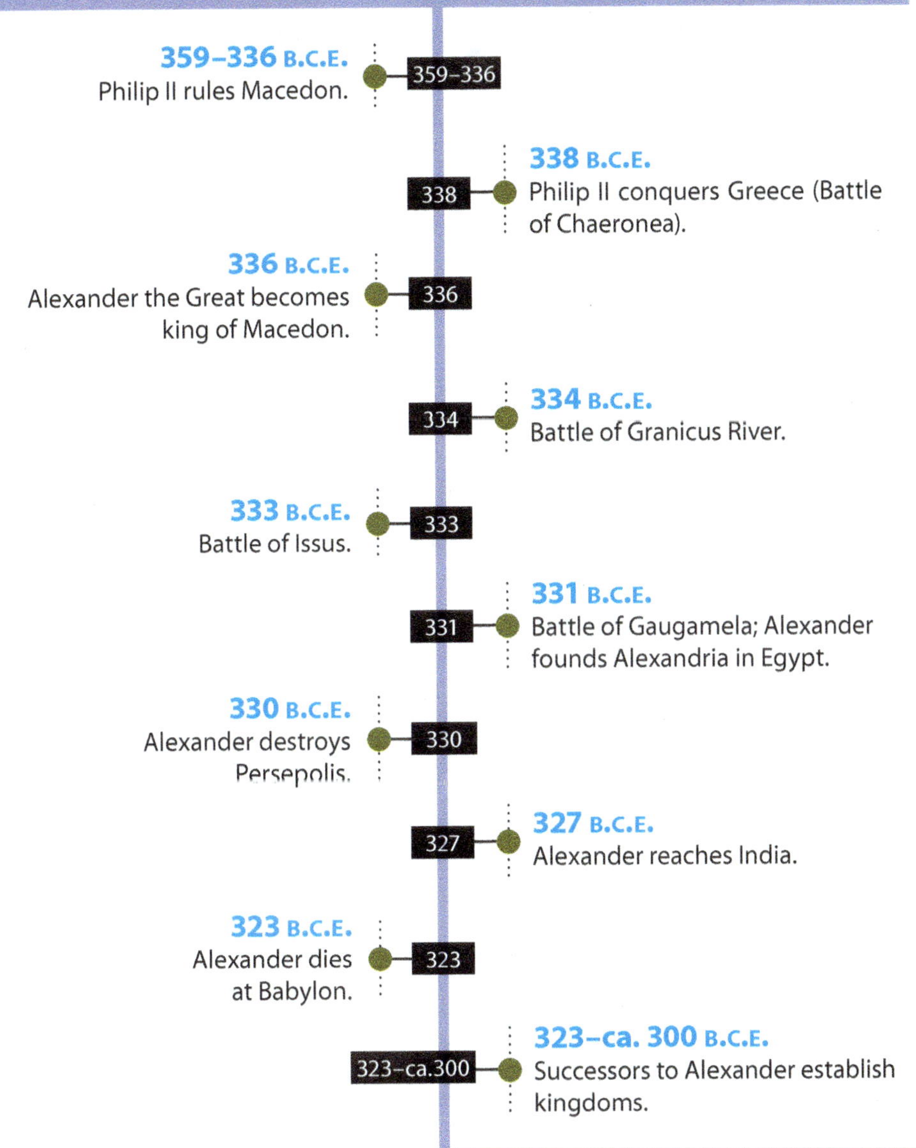

Governing an empire of this size proved to be a difficult challenge. The Macedonian kingdom that Alexander led was geared to seizing land and plundering cities. It was another task entirely to create the infrastructure and discipline necessary for ruling an immense territory that had little linguistic or cultural unity. Alexander recognized that the only model of rule suitable to such a diverse empire was that which his Persian predecessors had devised: a Great King presiding over a hierarchy of nobles who governed Persian territory and some non-Persian provinces, and subject kings who ruled other non-Persian regions.

Necessity thus forced Alexander to bring his Macedonian troops and his new Persian subjects together in an uneasy balance. To that end, he persuaded his army to proclaim him "King of Asia"—that is, the new Great King. With his Companions he simply took over the government of the former Persian Empire from the top. He included a handful of loyal Persians in his administration by making them regional governors or **satraps**, while offering other Persian noblemen minor roles in his regime. These

satraps Persian provincial governors who collected taxes and oversaw the bureaucracy.

Different Voices

The Achievement of Alexander the Great

The conquests of Alexander the Great lent themselves to different interpretations that depended to a large extent on whether one focused on the diffusion of Greek culture in Asia and Europe or on the brutal methods Alexander employed in subjecting different people to his rule. The Greek biographer Plutarch (ca. 46 C.E.–120 C.E.), writing during the Roman Empire, credited Alexander with facilitating the reception of Greek philosophy and culture in the lands that he conquered. In a speech celebrating these achievements Plutarch claimed that Alexander had gained a wider acceptance of Greek philosophy among the people whom he had conquered than the Greeks themselves had achieved during the Classical Age. One can attribute Plutarch's claim that Alexander promoted the unity of mankind to the rhetorical excesses of his speech. It is unlikely that Plutarch himself actually subscribed to such a noble interpretation of Alexander's relentless quest to establish a universal monarchy. The Jews, who had been conquered by Alexander, understandably had a far less positive view of his legacy. The Jewish author of the biblical book 1 Maccabees, written in the second century B.C.E., saw Alexander's reign as a period of violence and instability.

A Greek Biographer Celebrates the Cultural Achievement of Alexander the Great

But if you consider the effects of Alexander's instruction, you will see that he educated the Hyrcanians to contract marriages, taught the Arachosians to till the soil, and persuaded the Sogdians to support their parents, not to kill them, and the Persians to respect their mothers, not to marry them. Most admirable philosophy, which induced the Indians to worship Greek gods, and the Scythians to bury their dead and not to eat them! We admire the power of Carneades, who caused Clitomachus, formerly called Hashdrubal and a Carthaginian by birth, to adopt Greek ways. We admire the power that persuaded Diogenes the Babylonian, to turn to philosophy. Yet when Alexander was taming Asia, Homer became widely read, and the children of the Persians, of the Susianians and the Gedrosians sang the tragedies of Euripides and Sophocles. And Socrates was condemned by the sychophants in Athens for introducing new deities, while thanks to Alexander Bactria and the Caucasus worshipped the gods of the Greeks. Plato drew up in writing one ideal constitution but could not persuade anyone to adopt it because of its severity, while Alexander founded over 70 cities among barbarian tribes, sprinkled Greek institutions all over Asia, and so overcame its wild and savage manner of living. . . . Those who were subdued by Alexander were more fortunate than those who escaped him, for the latter had no one to rescue them from their wretched life, while the victorious Alexander compelled the former to enjoy a better existence. Alexander's victims would not have been civilized if they had not been defeated. . . . If, therefore, philosophers take the greatest pride in taming and correcting the fierce and untutored elements of men's character, and if Alexander has been shown to have changed the brutish customs of countless nations, then it would be justifiable to regard him as a very great philosopher. . . .

Believing that he had come as a god-sent governor and mediator of the whole world, he overcame by arms those he could not bring over by persuasion and brought men together from all over the world, mixing together, as it were, in a loving-cup, their lives, customs, marriages, and ways of living. He instructed all men to consider to be their native land and his camp to be their acropolis and their defense, while they should regard as kinsmen all good men, and the wicked as strangers. The difference between Greeks and barbarians was not a matter of cloak or shield, or of a scimitar or Median dress. What distinguished Greekness was excellence, while wickedness was the mark of the barbarian; clothing, food, marriage and the way of life they should all regard as common, being blended together by ties of blood and the bearing of children.

SOURCE: Plutarch, *On the Fortune or Virtue of Alexander*, in Michel Austin (ed.), *The Hellenistic World from Alexander to the Roman Conquest*, 2006, 57–58.

A Jewish Writer Describes the Misery Caused by Alexander the Great

After Alexander son of Philip, the Macedonian, who came from the land of Kittim, had defeated King Darius of the Persians and the Medes, he succeeded him as king; he had already become king of Greece. He fought many battles, conquered strongholds, and put to death the kings of the earth. He advanced to the ends of the earth, and plundered many nations. When the earth became quiet before him, he was exalted, and his heart was lifted up. He gathered a very strong army and ruled over countries, nations, and princes, and they became tributary to him. After this he fell sick and perceived that he was dying. So he summoned his most honored officers, who had been brought up with him from youth, and divided his kingdom among them while he was still alive. And after Alexander had reigned twelve years, he died. Then his officers began to rule, each in his own place. They all put on crowns after his death, and so did their descendants after them for many years; and they caused many evils on the earth.

SOURCE: *1 Maccabees 1–9.*

For Discussion

1. What criteria did Plutarch and the author of 1 Maccabees use to evaluate the achievement of Alexander the Great?
2. Did Alexander bring "civilization" to the lands he conquered?
3. How might the author of 1 Maccabees have responded to Plutarch's claim that Alexander brought men together from all over the world?

practical steps promised to bring order to the empire. By adopting the elaborate Persian ceremonial role of the Great King, Alexander demonstrated to his foreign subjects that his regime stood for security and continuity of orderly rule.

Alexander's proud Macedonian soldiers, however, ultimately stymied his efforts to achieve this balance. They refused to prostrate themselves before him, as Persian royal ceremony dictated. Alexander may well have thought of himself as a god, but his soldiers refused to worship him. Instead, they saw Alexander's recruitment of 30,000 Persian troops into their army as a threat to the traditional relations between Macedonian soldiers and their king. They also resented the marriages with the daughters of Persian noblemen that Alexander forced on them in order to unite Macedonians and Persians—although no Persian nobles received Greek or Macedonian wives. The Macedonian troops expected to keep all the spoils of victory for themselves. They wanted to be conquerors, not partners in a new government. They failed to understand that men of other cultures within the new empire might be equally loyal to Alexander and thus deserve a share of power and honor. Alexander's charismatic personality held his conquests together, but his death destroyed any dreams of cooperation between Persians and Greeks.

Alexander's adoption of the powers and symbolism of Persian kingship, even though it was unpopular with his Macedonian soldiers, was the product of an encounter between Macedonian and Persian styles of rule. The political culture that emerged from this encounter had a lasting influence on Western civilization. In contrast to the democratic and republican culture that had flourished in classical Athens, Alexander offered a model of royal and imperial rule that gave the king absolute power and identified that power, if not his own person, with that of the gods. Both traditions—democratic republicanism and divine-right absolutism—competed with each other throughout the history of the West. The competition became evident in classical Rome, which began as a republic but was later transformed into an empire in which the ruler had unrivalled power. The tension between the two ideologies persisted throughout the Middle Ages and into the Renaissance, when the Italian state of Florence revived the republican culture of ancient Greece and Rome at the same time that the duke of Milan revived the aspirations of the Roman Empire.

Hellenism in the East and West

4.2 What was the relationship between Greeks and non-Greeks in the lands that Alexander conquered and those with whom Greeks came into contact after his death?

The Hellenistic Successor States

Alexander left no adult heir, and the Macedonian nobles who served as his generals fought viciously among themselves to control his conquered territory. Eventually, these generals created a number of kingdoms out of lands Alexander had acquired (see **Map 4.2**). One general, Ptolemy (r. 323–286 B.C.E.), established the Ptolemaic dynasty in Egypt, which lasted until 30 B.C.E. Antigonus "the One-Eyed" (r. 306–301 B.C.E) gained control of the Macedonian homeland, where his descendants established the Antigonid dynasty, which survived until Rome overthrew the last of these monarchs in 167 B.C.E. The largest portion of Alexander's conquests, comprising the bulk of the old Persian Empire, fell to his general Seleucus (r. 312–281 B.C.E.). But the territory controlled by Seleucus's successors constantly shrank, and in the mid-third century B.C.E. the Parthians, a people from northeastern Persia, shook off Seleucid rule and created a vigorous new state in what is today Iran. By 150 B.C.E. the Seleucids ruled only Syria, Palestine, and a small portion of southeastern Anatolia.

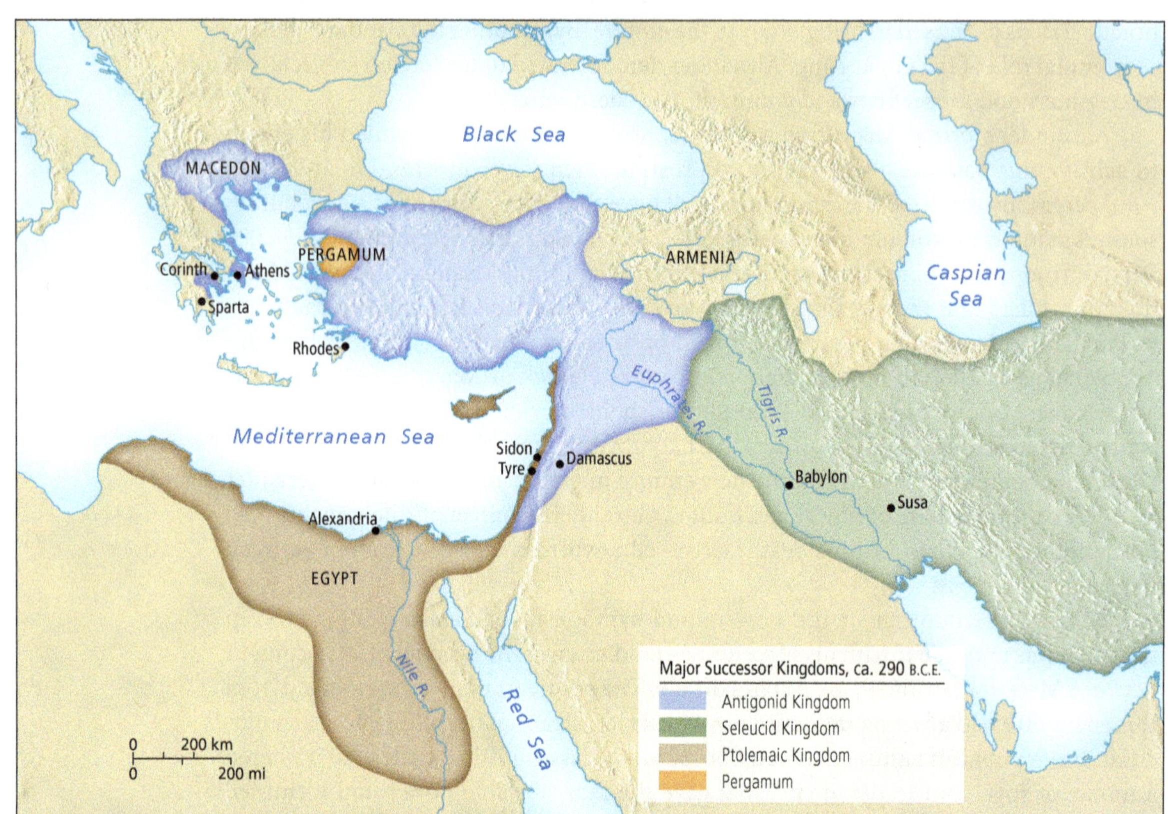

MAP **4.2** MAJOR SUCCESSOR KINGDOMS CA. 290 B.C.E. After Alexander's death, his generals divided his empire into several kingdoms. This map shows the boundaries of the Antigonid, Seleucid, and Ptolemaic kingdoms about 290 B.C.E. The Antigonids acquired control of the old kingdom of Macedon in 294 B.C.E., although this control was not secured until the reign of Antigonus II (r. 276–239 B.C.E.). The city of Pergamum in Anatolia became a kingdom under Attalus I around 230 B.C.E. How did the rulers of these kingdoms maintain their power?

Following the example of Macedon itself, the Hellenistic successor states all maintained a monarchical form of government in which a king ruled the people with the support of the army and highly regimented bureaucracies. The leading administrators and bureaucrats were all Greeks and Macedonians. Indigenous people were not recruited into the ruling elite. Greek was the language of government and the elite in the successor kingdoms. The talented queen Cleopatra VII (r. 51–30 B.C.E.), who was the last descendant of Ptolemy to rule in Egypt, was the first of her line ever to speak Egyptian. Greek-speaking monarchs nonetheless knew that they needed to cultivate the goodwill of their non-Greek-speaking subjects. As one monarch asked in a Hellenistic political dialogue, "How can I accommodate myself to all the different races in my kingdom?" A subject answered: "By adopting the appropriate attitude to each, making justice one's guide."

The king towered over Hellenistic society, holding authority over all his subjects and bearing ultimate responsibility for their welfare. Following the example of Alexander, the Hellenistic monarch earned legitimacy by leading his troops into wars of conquest. The king embodied the entire community that he ruled. He was at once the ruler, father, protector, savior, source of law, and god of all his subjects. His garb reinforced his elevated position—the king arrayed himself in battle gear with a helmet or Macedonian sombrero, a crown, purple robes, a scepter, and a special seal ring. The monarch earned the loyalty of his subjects and glorified his own rule by founding cities, constructing public buildings, and rewarding his inner circle.

Ptolemy II, who ruled in Egypt from 283 to 246 B.C.E., exemplified these notions of Hellenistic kingship. Ptolemy expanded his dominions by conquering parts of Anatolia and Syria from the Seleucids. He also expanded the bureaucracy, refined the tax system, and funded new towns for his soldiers and veterans. With his support, merchants established new posts on the Red Sea, where they traded with merchants from India and other eastern lands. Ptolemy patronized the arts and sciences by building research institutes and libraries. He transformed Egypt's capital city of Alexandria, the port founded by Alexander in Egypt in 331 B.C.E., into the leading center of Greek culture and learning in the Hellenistic world. To reinforce his authority and majesty, Ptolemy II encouraged his subjects to worship him as a god the way earlier Egyptians had worshiped the pharaohs.

This worship of Hellenistic monarchs drew from indigenous traditions throughout the Near East, but in its Hellenistic form it had more political than religious significance. People worshiped their kings as a spontaneous expression of gratitude for the protection and peace that good government provided. For example, when the Antigonid king Demetrius "the Besieger" captured Athens in 308 B.C.E., the pragmatic Athenians sang a song in honor of their new master: "The other gods either do not exist or are far off, either they do not hear, or they do not care; but you are here and we can see you, not in wood and stone but in living truth."[1] Deification legitimized a king's rule and helped secure his subjects' loyalty.

Hellenistic monarchs depended on large professional armies to maintain their authority and defend their territories. These rulers fought wars over much larger territories than those that had led to squabbles among Greek city-states in previous centuries. The conquest of such territories required an increase in the size of field armies. The Athenian hoplites had numbered about 10,000 men in the fifth century B.C.E., but Hellenistic kings routinely mustered armies of between 60,000 and 80,000 men. Many soldiers came from military colonies that the kings established. In return for land, the men of these Greek-speaking colonies had to serve generation after generation in the king's army and police the native, non-Greek populations.

PTOLEMAIC KING OF EGYPT This golden ring depicts Ptolemy VI, who ruled Egypt from 176 to 145 B.C.E. Although he and his court spoke only Greek, he is depicted as a pharaoh wearing a double crown, the age-old symbol of Egyptian monarchy. The image on the ring demonstrated the integration of old and new political symbols in Egypt during the Hellenistic Age.

Encounters with Foreign Peoples

During the Hellenistic Age, Greeks encountered many foreign peoples; the effects of these interactions laid some of the foundations of the West. The encounters took place when Greeks explored regions in Africa and Europe where they had not penetrated before; when Hellenistic Babylonians, Egyptians, Persians, Afghans, and Hebrews resisted or adopted Hellenistic culture; and when Celtic peoples migrated to the boundaries of the Hellenistic world in Europe and Anatolia.

EXPLORING THE HELLENISTIC WORLD A spirit of inquiry—combined with a hunger for trade and profit—drove men to explore and map the unknown world during the Hellenistic Age (see **Map 4.3** on page 123). Explorers supported by monarchs ventured into the Caspian, Aral, and Red Seas. By the second century B.C.E., Greeks had established trading posts along the coasts of modern Eritrea and Somalia in east Africa, where merchants bought goods, particularly ivory, transported from the interior of Africa. Hellenistic

THE ROYAL LIBRARY OF ALEXANDRIA The cosmopolitan city of Alexandria, the capital of Egypt founded by Alexander in 331 B.C.E., became the leading center of Greek culture in the Hellenistic world. Its famous library, depicted here in a nineteenth-century German engraving, functioned as a major center of scholarship until the first century B.C.E.

people also craved pepper, cinnamon, cloves, and other spices and luxury goods from India, but Arab middlemen made direct trade between the Hellenistic world and India nearly impossible. One intrepid navigator named Eudoxus tried to find a sea route to India by sailing around Africa, but he never got farther southwest than the coast of Morocco.

The most ambitious and successful of all Hellenistic explorers was Pytheas of Marseilles (ca. 380–306 B.C.E.). Setting out from the Carthaginian city of Gades (the modern Spanish port of Cadiz) in about 310 B.C.E., he sailed north around Britain and reported the existence of either Iceland or Norway. He may have even reached the Vistula River in Poland by sailing through the Baltic Sea. Throughout his journeys Pytheas contributed much to navigational knowledge by recording astronomical bearings and natural wonders such as the northern lights. He is the first person known to have reported the midnight sun and polar ice.

As these explorers expanded geographical horizons, Greeks developed a condescending interest in the peoples of the world. Greeks considered themselves culturally superior to non-Greek-speaking peoples who lived beyond the borders of Hellenistic kingdoms, including Jews, Babylonians, Celts, steppe nomads, and sub-Saharan Africans. Greeks considered all of these peoples barbarians. Despite this prejudice,

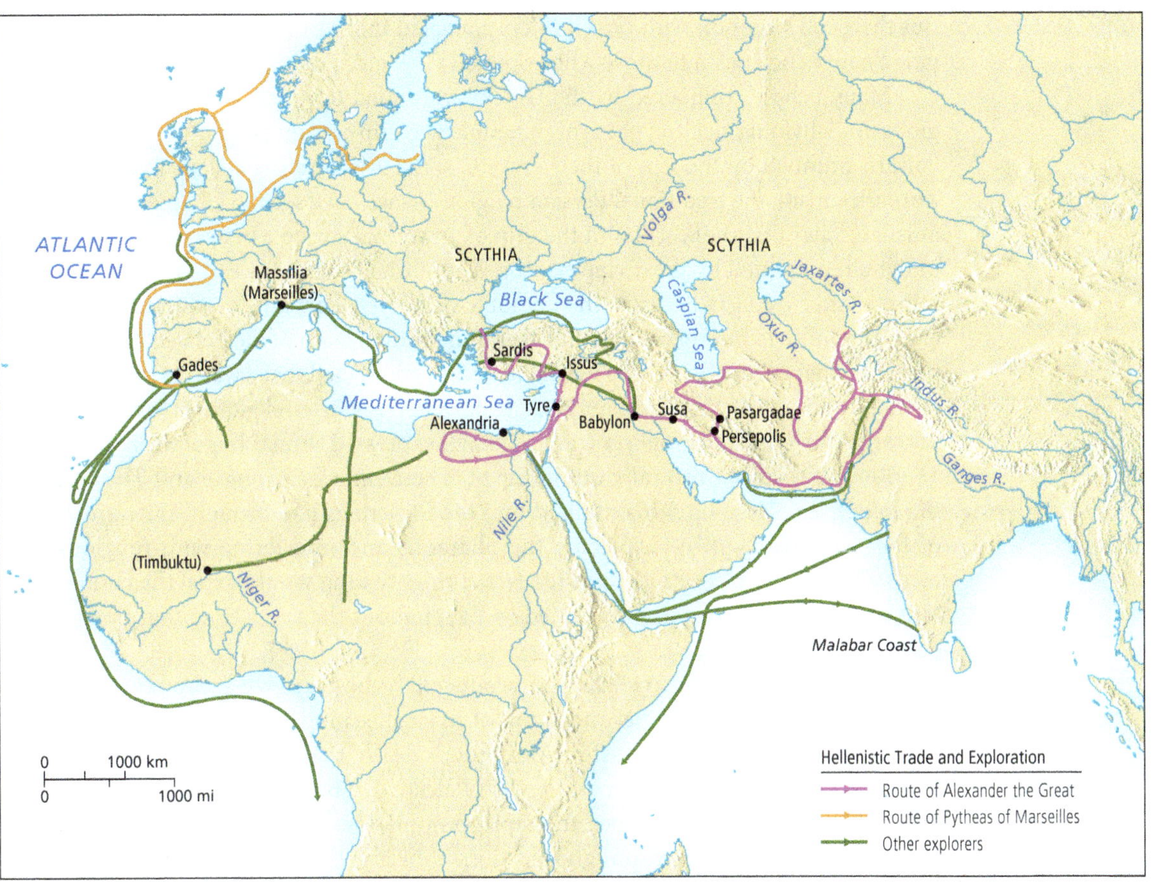

MAP **4.3** HELLENISTIC TRADE AND EXPLORATION During the Hellenistic Age, merchants traveled widely across the breadth of the Mediterranean and throughout the Near East. They sailed into the Persian Gulf and Indian Ocean on commercial ventures. Some explorers sailed along the east and west coasts of Africa as well as Europe's Atlantic coast, reaching Britain and the North Sea. What impact did these voyages have on the dissemination of Hellenistic culture?

educated men and women throughout the Hellenistic world enjoyed reading accounts in Greek of foreign peoples' customs, myths, natural history, and forms of government.

Knowledge about different peoples often came from non-Greek intellectuals who translated their accounts into Greek. For example, Berosus, a Babylonian priest, wrote a history of his people that also provided Greek readers with extensive astronomical knowledge. Manetho, an Egyptian priest, composed a history of his land. Hecataeus of Abdera, a Greek, wrote a popular history arguing that Egypt was the site of the origin of civilization. Most of what the West believed it knew about India until the Middle Ages derived from the reports of Megasthenes, a Seleucid diplomat who served as ambassador in India. Information about the histories and belief systems of their non-Greek neighbors entertained Greek intellectuals and helped Hellenistic rulers govern their conquered peoples.

RESISTANCE TO HELLENISTIC RULE Despite this curiosity among educated Greeks about foreign customs, barriers of mutual incomprehension, suspicion, and resentment separated Greeks from their subjects. Language was one such barrier. In most kingdoms, administrators conducted official business only in Greek. Few Greek settlers in the cities or even in isolated military colonies bothered to learn the local languages, and only a small percentage of the local populations learned Greek. Many communities ignored their Greek rulers completely. In Mesopotamia and Syria, Aramaic remained the dominant language, not Greek. Some non-Greeks, however, hoped to rise in the service of their Greek masters. They made an effort to learn Greek and assimilate into Hellenistic culture.

But their collaboration with Greek rulers alienated them from their own people and divided native societies into those who accepted Hellenistic culture and those who did not.

Many people conquered by the Greeks continued to practice their traditional religions. In Babylonia, age-old patterns of temple worship continued uninfluenced by Greek culture. Stunned by the loss of their empire, some aristocratic Persians found solace in Zoroastrianism, the traditional Persian religion. As we have seen in Chapter 3, Zoroastrianism teaches that the world is in the grip of an eternal struggle between the good forces of light, represented by the divine creator, Ahura Mazda, and the evil forces of darkness, represented by Angra Mainyu, the demonic destroyer. Persian Zoroastrianians considered Alexander to be Angra Mainyu's agent. In the aftermath of the Persian defeat, an important religious text (written in Greek, ironically) predicted that a warrior messiah would soon overthrow the Seleucid kings and restore Persia's true religion and rulers. A book known as the *Dynastic Prophecy* (ca. 300 B.C.E.) expressed similar hopes for Babylonians.

Resentful voices also rang out in Egypt. The *Demotic Chronicle* and *The Oracle of the Potter* (ca. 250 B.C.E.) maintained that the Ptolemies had brought the punishment of the gods to Egypt by displacing the pharaohs and interfering with religious customs. One day, the books assured readers, a mighty king would expel the conquerors. Not coincidentally, rebellions erupted in Egypt about the same time that these works gained popularity.

The Jewish response to Hellenism produced the best-known account of resistance, preserved in the First and Second Book of Maccabees in the Hebrew Bible. (See *Different Voices* in this chapter.) After Alexander's death, first the Ptolemies and then the Seleucids controlled Jerusalem and Jewish Palestine. The Ptolemaic monarchs at first tolerated Judaism and welcomed the rapid assimilation of Jerusalem's priestly aristocracy into Greek culture. Although traditional Jewish worship at the temple in Jerusalem continued, a gymnasium and other elements of Greek culture first appeared in Jerusalem during the rule of these Hellenized Jewish priests.

In 167 B.C.E., however, the Seleucid king Antiochus IV Epiphanes (r. 175–164 B.C.E.) tried to make the city more Hellenistic. When the Jews resisted, his soldiers put up statues of Greek gods in the Temple, an abomination in Jewish eyes. Initially, Antiochus had intended to advertise his own strength, not to suppress Judaism, but his plan backfired. A family of Jewish priests, the Maccabees, began a religious war of liberation. They drove the armies of Antiochus out of Palestine, purified the Temple in Jerusalem, and established an autonomous Jewish kingdom under their rule. Later, when Jewish writers sought to explain these actions to the Greek-speaking Jews of Alexandria, they described them in terms of resistance to Hellenism. However, the Maccabeans themselves soon adopted many Greek customs and used Greek names, causing deep rifts within Jewish society.

Maccabees: Resistance to Hellenization in the Hellenistic Period, ca. 100 B.C.E.

CELTS ON THE FRINGES OF THE HELLENISTIC WORLD In addition to the Greek culture that spread throughout the Mediterranean and Near East, Celtic civilization flourished in Europe during the Hellenistic Age. The Celts, who lived in tribes that were never politically unified on a large scale, shared common dialects, metal- and pottery-making techniques, and agricultural and home-building methods. They were the ancestors of many Europeans today.

Through trade and war, Celts influenced the northern margins of the Hellenistic world from Anatolia to Spain. Trade routes with the Celts from the Mediterranean were established as early as the eighth century B.C.E., but war often interrupted commerce. The military activities of Celtic tribes restricted the expansion of Hellenistic kingdoms in Macedon and Anatolia, thereby pressuring these kingdoms to strengthen their military capacities.

Hallstatt culture The first Celtic civilization in central Europe; from about 750 to about 450 B.C.E., Hallstatt Celts spread throughout Europe.

Archaeologists call the first Celtic civilization in central Europe **Hallstatt culture**, because of excavations of Celtic settlements in Hallstatt, Austria. Around 750 B.C.E., Hallstatt Celts started to spread from their homeland into Italy, the Balkans, Ireland,

Spain, and Anatolia, conquering local peoples on the way. These early Celts left no written records, so we know little of their political practices. The luxury goods and weapons they buried in graves, however, indicate a stratified society led by a warrior elite. Hallstatt sites were heavily fortified, suggesting frequent warfare. Men gained status through the competitive exchange of gifts, raiding, and valor in battle. In southern France, Celts encountered Hellenistic civilization at the Greek city of Massilia (modern Marseilles). There they participated in lively trade along the Rhône River for Greek luxury goods, including wine and drinking goblets.

In the mid-fifth century B.C.E. a new phase in Celtic civilization began. It is called **La Tène culture**, which takes its name from a site in modern Switzerland. More weapons were found in La Tène tombs than in the Hallstatt period, possibly indicating intensified warfare. La Tène Celts developed new centers of wealth and power, especially in the valleys of the Rhine and Danube Rivers. They also founded large, fortified settlements in these regions and in present-day France and England.

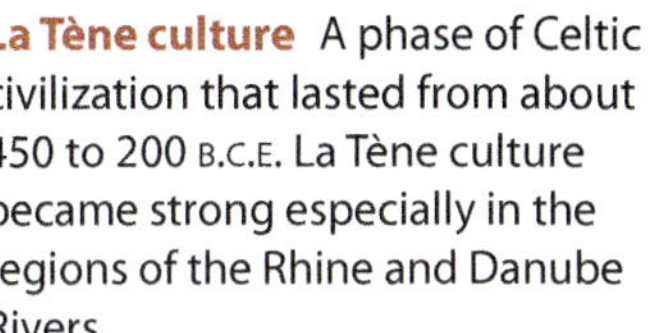

La Tène culture A phase of Celtic civilization that lasted from about 450 to 200 B.C.E. La Tène culture became strong especially in the regions of the Rhine and Danube Rivers.

La Tène craftsmen benefited from new trade routes across the Alps to northern Italy, the home of Etruscan merchants and artisans (see Chapter 5). Etruscans traded bronze statuettes to the Celtic north, and they may have also introduced the two-wheeled fighting chariots found in aristocratic Celtic tombs. Greek styles in art reached the Celts through these Etruscan intermediaries, but Celtic artists developed their own distinctive style of metalwork and sculpture. Many Celtic communities began to use coinage, which they adopted from the Greeks.

For about a century relations between the Celtic and Mediterranean peoples centered on trade, but around 400 B.C.E. overpopulation in central Europe caused massive migrations of Celtic tribes (see **Map 4.4**). In 387 B.C.E. one migrating group of

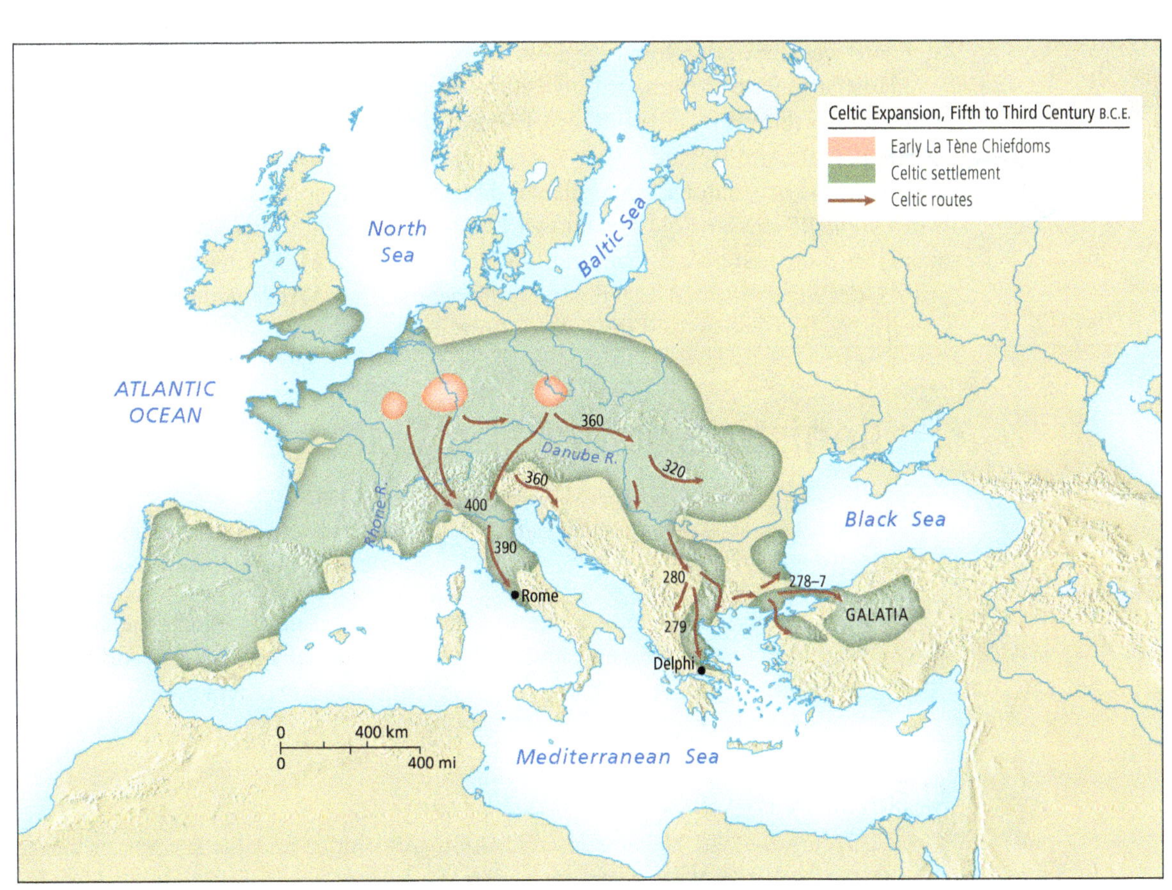

MAP **4.4** CELTIC EXPANSION, FIFTH TO THIRD CENTURY B.C.E. During the Hellenistic Age, Celtic peoples migrated into many parts of Europe and Asia Minor. This map shows their routes. What prevented Celts from uniting and forming an empire?

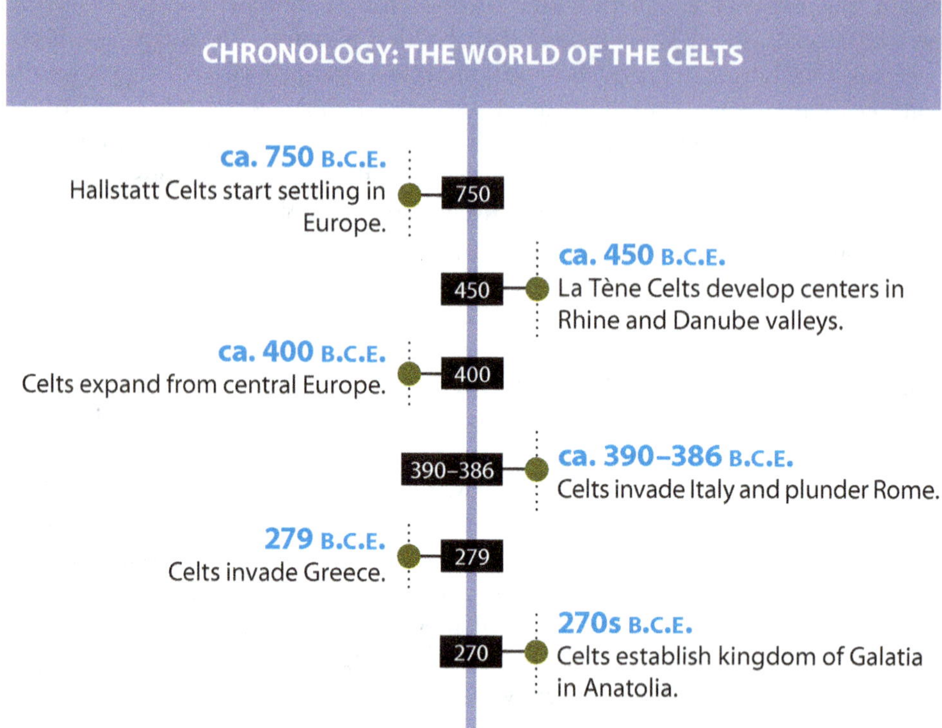

Celts, called Gauls, sacked the city of Rome. Their invasion had an unexpected effect on Roman military technology: The highly effective Celtic short sword became the standard weapon of the Roman legions.

Hostile migrations lasted until 200 B.C.E. Some Celts traveled to lands that are Slavic today (Slovakia and southern Poland), while others settled in northern Italy, Spain, Britain, and Ireland. Other Celts invaded the Balkans, plundered Greece, and finally settled in Anatolia, where they established a kingdom called Galatia (from the word *Gauls*). Galatian soldiers, known for their bravery and cruelty, became mercenaries in the constant wars among the Hellenistic successor kingdoms. Ultimately, most Celts were absorbed, together with the peoples in the Hellenistic kingdoms in the eastern Mediterranean, into the Roman Empire.

Hellenistic Society and Culture

4.3 What were the distinguishing features of Hellenistic society and culture, and what was the result of encounters between Greeks and non-Greeks?

Chronic warfare among monarchs made political unity among the Hellenistic kingdoms impossible. Nevertheless, the social institutions and culture of Greek-speaking people in all these kingdoms gave them a unity that their monarchs could not achieve.

Urban Society

Greek city life defined Hellenistic civilization. Alexander and his successors seized dozens of Greek city-states scattered across the eastern Mediterranean and founded dozens of new cities in all the territories they conquered. Hellenistic cities were much more than garrisons established to enforce the conquerors' power. They continued traditions of learning, art, architecture, and citizen participation in public life that had flourished in the classical poleis. Most important, people in cities throughout the Hellenistic world spoke a standard version of Greek called **Koine** that gave them a sense of common identity.

Koine The standard version of the Greek language spoken throughout the Hellenistic world.

On the surface, many of the institutions of the classical poleis remained the same: magistrates, councils, and popular assemblies ran the cities' affairs, and some form of democracy or election to office remained the norm in local government. Yet beneath the surface, the poleis had undergone radical changes. Because kings wielded absolute power, once-independent cities such as Athens and Corinth lost their freedom to make peace or wage war. Although they chose their own local governments, these cities now served as the bureaucratic centers that administered their rulers' huge kingdoms.

As we saw in Chapter 3, citizenship in the city-states of classical Greece was a carefully limited commodity that gave people a sense of identity, guaranteed desirable rights and privileges, and demanded certain responsibilities. The territories that any city-state controlled were relatively small, yet even Athens at the height of its empire in the fifth century B.C.E. never considered giving Athenian citizenship to all the people it ruled, even within Attica. In contrast, during the Hellenistic Age, large kingdoms containing many cities were the basic political units. People were both subjects of a king and citizens of their particular cities. To be sure, some philosophers played with the idea of a universal citizenship of all humankind, but there was no notion of a citizenship that all the people in one kingdom would share. Citizenship lost its political force because individual cities had lost their political autonomy. In a sharp break with earlier practice, important men sometimes gained the honor of citizenship in more than one city, which Greeks in the Classical Age would have found inconceivable.

To maintain the illusion of the cities' independence, Hellenistic kings permitted considerable autonomy in local government. Nonetheless, while democracies had developed in Greece during the Archaic and Classical periods to protect the interests of the poor as well as the rich, in the Hellenistic Age the wealthy dominated society and government, and the condition of the poor deteriorated. Rich men appointed or approved by the king controlled all the courts, held all the magistracies, and represented all the cities at the court of the kings, who in return showered these civic leaders with honors and rewards. Through land grants, tax immunities, and other favors, the monarchs developed networks of personal ties that bound civic leaders to them. In return, these urban elites served their king and spent their vast fortunes building magnificent temples, gymnasiums, and other structures for their fellow citizens.

Hellenistic kings and aristocrats turned their cities into showcases of art and design. Distinctive styles of building and ornamentation quickly spread from the east to Carthage, Rome, and other communities in the western Mediterranean. The most distinctive architectural innovations in the cities were vast palace complexes, which were built to accommodate the Hellenistic monarchs and their entourages in the successor kingdoms. Laying out streets on a grid plan became standard in the Mediterranean world, lending a sense of order to urban space. Stone theaters for plays and spectacles, council halls, and roofed colonnades called *stoas* sprang up everywhere, as did public baths with heated pools and gymnasium complexes with sports facilities, libraries, and lecture halls.

Hellenistic cities contained more diverse populations than had classical poleis. Alexandria, Egypt's largest and most cosmopolitan Greek city, boasted large communities of Macedonians, Greeks, Jews, Syrians, and Egyptians. Although these groups lived in different areas of the city and often fought violently with one another, they all participated to varying degrees in Alexandria's culture. For example, Alexandrian Jews who spoke Greek translated the Hebrew Bible into Greek, a version called the **Septuagint**, so that Jews who had lost their command of Hebrew could understand it. The Septuagint later provided early Christians, many of whom spoke and read Greek, with their knowledge of the Hebrew Bible, which Christians refer to as the Old Testament.

Septuagint The Greek translation of the Hebrew Bible (Old Testament).

APHRODITE OF MELOS Aphrodite, the goddess of sexual love, displayed the perfection of the female form. This marble statue of her, which was found on the Greek island of Melos, was sculpted in the middle of the second century B.C.E. Popularly known by her Italian name, Venus di Milo, the goddess is half-nude. She rests on her right foot and seems to step forward toward the viewer. Originally one of her missing arms was probably raised to cover her breasts in a gesture of modesty. Her facial expression is serene. The garment draped loosely around her hips allowed the sculptor to explore the play of thin cloth over her thighs, expressing his delight in movement and physicality. More sedate than other voluptuous representations of Aphrodite from the Hellenistic period, this statue portrays a male vision of a perfect woman, highly sexual but also charmingly modest.

New Opportunities for Women

One measure of the status of women in a society is the level of female infanticide. Greek parents in the Classical Age routinely abandoned unwanted female babies, leaving them to die. Hellenistic families, however, particularly those of the Ptolemaic nobility, raised more baby girls than before. Greek women in Egypt and other Hellenized lands enjoyed full citizenship and held religious offices. Many owned land and property, paying taxes as men did, but they could only enter into business contracts of minimal value on their own.

Some aristocratic Hellenistic women wielded considerably more power than had been conceivable in the classical Greek period. The wives of Hellenistic kings were models of the new, more powerful Hellenistic woman. Inscriptions praise Hellenistic queens for demonstrating such traditional female virtues as piety and for producing sons. As public benefactors, these women built temples and public works, sponsored charioteers at the Olympic Games, and provided dowries for poor brides. Queens sometimes exerted real authority, at times supporting and commanding armies. For example, Arsinoë II (r. 276–270 B.C.E.), sister and wife of Ptolemy II, directed the Egyptian armies and navies of the Ptolemaic kingdom in their conquest of Phoenicia and much of the coast of Anatolia. Egyptian sources refer to her as Pharaoh, a royal title usually reserved for men, and she was often identified with the goddess Isis.

To a lesser extent, opportunities for non-aristocratic Greek women also increased during the Hellenistic Age. In Alexandria young women were taught dancing, music, reading and writing, and scholarship and philosophy. Often the daughters of scholars became scholars themselves. We know that non-aristocratic Greek women wrote about astronomy, musical theory, and literature, and many female poets competed for honors. In addition, a few Hellenistic women distinguished themselves as portrait painters, architects, and harpists. Despite these accomplishments, women still had fewer rights and opportunities than men, and they remained under the supervision of their male relatives. In Egypt, a woman could not travel overnight without her husband's permission.

Art and Architecture

Art and architecture during the Hellenistic period changed as Greek civilization was introduced into the successor kingdoms. Artists and architects continued to use classical motifs and themes, but instead of simply imitating classical models, they used them in new ways. This creative development of Greek classicism resulted from both the freedom that artists experienced working in a new environment and from the influences of native cultures. The most notable stylistic innovation of the Hellenistic age was the **baroque** style, which suggested movement rather than repose and often appealed to the emotions.

The baroque style was evident in many of the Hellenistic temple precincts, where the designers created sweeping vistas across carefully planned terraces and grand stairways. Some of the finest examples of Hellenistic baroque architecture have survived in Pergamum, a Greek city on the southern coast of modern Turkey, close to the Aegean Sea. To commemorate the victory of Pergamum over the Celts and the Seleucids, King Attalus I (241–197 B.C.E.) commissioned a series of monuments. The Acropolis in Athens provided the classical model for this work, but the commission of native craftsmen to create these monuments helps to explain their baroque features, most notably their vast scale and their many different focal points, which lead the viewer's eye across the façades of the buildings.

Hellenistic sculptors also took classical Greek forms in new directions. Turning away from representations of ideal perfection, Hellenistic artists delighted in exploring the movement of the human body and varieties of facial expression. Their subjects ranged from alluring love goddesses to drunks and haggard old boxers. Artists enjoyed portraying the play of fabrics across the human body to accentuate the contours of male and female flesh. The statue of Nike of Samothrace, probably carved on the island of Rhodes about 200 B.C.E., depicts this Greek goddess as if she has just landed on the bow of a ship, with her wings outstretched and her garment blowing in the wind. Sometimes painted in bright colors, these statues explored human frailty and homeliness as often as they celebrated beauty and lofty emotions. The statue of the Celt and his wife, also carved in Pergamum in the third century B.C.E. (see page 111), conveys not only physical movement, but also the depth of human emotions experienced by the man who is committing suicide.

baroque A dynamic style in art, architecture, and music that was intended to elicit an emotional response. Baroque buildings were massive, imposing structures with sweeping façades. The baroque style represented a development of Greek classicism in the Hellenistic period. In the seventeenth century the baroque style was closely associated with royal absolutism.

 View the Closer Look

Aspects of Hellenism in Gandharan Sculpture

Literature

Much Hellenistic literature has vanished, but surviving works give a glimpse of creativity and originality that often combined urbanity and scholarship. Hellenistic poets turned to frivolous themes because the repressive political climate discouraged them from questioning authority. Light comedy became immensely

PERGAMUM ALTAR OF ZEUS The buildings at Pergamum in northwest Anatolia (present-day Turkey) were constructed in the Hellenistic baroque style. They were based on classical Greek models but had sweeping facades that presented the viewer with multiple focal points. The Altar of Zeus at Pergamum, shown here in a twentieth-century reconstruction, is positioned on a massive stone podium with a 371-foot colonnade (a porch with a line of columns). Like many baroque buildings, the altar was opulently decorated. The two long friezes below the colonnade depict the life of the Greek mythological figure Telephos, son of Heracles, who was believed to be the founder of the city of Pergamum.

Justice in History

Divine Justice in the Hellenistic World

The widespread belief that personal misfortunes, such as illness, accidents, or destruction of one's property, indicated divine displeasure frequently led people in the Hellenistic world to confess their crimes. These offenses included secular crimes such as theft, slander, bodily injury, sorcery, and adultery, as well as religious crimes such as violating dietary rules, insulting the gods, or entering a sanctuary without cleansing the body or one's clothes. It did not matter whether the person had committed such an offense intentionally. The crucial factor was the sign of the gods' displeasure. When offenders became convinced of their guilt, they often went to the local sanctuary to discover the cause of the gods' anger and learn how they could atone for their misbehavior. Their objective was to receive signs from the gods through oracles or in dreams while they slept.

Inscriptions in the temple of the goddess Demeter at Knidos in Anatolia during the late second and first centuries B.C.E. reveal that the wronged party would sometimes initiate the judicial process by depositing an inscribed stone tablet at a sanctuary. The inscription would identify the alleged culprit and ask the gods to force the offender to come to the sanctuary to confess the crime. One of these inscriptions in a case of slander reads: "I dedicate to Demeter and Kore [another goddess, Demeter's daughter] the man who has made imputations against me, [claiming] that I made a poison against my own man; may he come up to the sanctuary of Demeter, with his entire family, burning [with fever] and confessing." Such inscriptions resembled the writing on "curse tablets" that people in the Hellenistic world occasionally inscribed to bring misfortune on an enemy. The purpose of these "confession inscriptions," however, was not to cause harm to another human being but to call the gods' attention to an act of injustice and to motivate those gods to pressure the guilty party to confess. The confessions were prayers for divine justice that would give the aggrieved party moral satisfaction or possibly revenge.

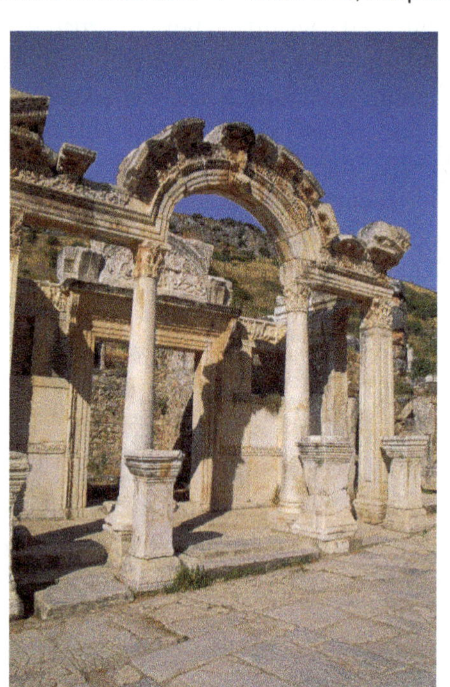

TEMPLE OF APHRODITE This temple near Denizli, in modern-day Turkey, built in the first century B.C.E., was the preeminent temple of the goddess Aphrodite in Anatolia. People asking for divine assistance in eliciting confessions to crimes would often enter sanctuaries such as this.

People suspected of crimes could also appeal to the gods to establish their innocence. When a woman named Tatias heard rumors that she had given her son-in-law a magical potion that had driven him insane, she went to the local sanctuary and "deposited curses in the temple." This public ceremony, which differed from the writing of a malevolent curse in private, was her way of demonstrating to the community that she was innocent. Unfortunately for Tatias, her relatives publicly annulled her curses, leaving her guilty in the eyes of society.

Ideally the only parties involved in this process were the accusers, the confessing criminals, and the gods, but the priests in the sanctuary often played a crucial role in the process as well. They would receive or perhaps even solicit accusations from the victims of crime, assist in writing the confessions, and interpret the supposed signs of the divine will. In many cases they attempted to show that the afflictions that brought people to the sanctuary in the first place were punishments for their offenses. The priests did not, as historians once believed, inflict corporal punishment, but they did advise those who confessed how they might atone for their transgressions. Sometimes they interrogated an afflicted person who came to the sanctuary to determine the cause of the gods' wrath. Thus, the priests played a role usually assigned to judges in actual trials. The procedures followed in the sanctuaries were not trials in the proper sense of the word because they did not involve the testimony of witnesses or the delivering of verdicts. But the inscriptions often used legal language, which the priests probably suggested, and the procedure served the same purpose as a trial, which was to resolve conflict in society. Like trials, these proceedings involved encounters between the priest serving in a quasi-judicial capacity and the person who came to the sanctuary, as well as between that person and the god who was believed to have spoken through an oracle or a dream.

The involvement of priests in a process that resembled a trial of both secular and religious crimes reveals that Hellenistic societies drew no firm line between the secular and the religious spheres. Crimes that were prosecuted in the secular courts could also be dealt with in religious sanctuaries. Without the assistance of the priests, who controlled access to the sanctuaries and helped formulate the confessions, the process could not have functioned properly. The dedication of appeals and confessions to the gods also shows that the gods in these polytheistic societies were believed to play an active role not only in the resolution of problems of everyday life, but also in the administration of justice.

For Discussion

1. Why might a person in a Hellenistic kingdom go to a local sanctuary and later confess to a religious or secular offense?
2. How did Hellenistic religious beliefs influence prevailing notions of justice?

Taking It Further

Angelos Chaniotis, "Under the Watchful Eyes of the Gods," in S. Colvin (ed.), *The Greco-Roman East: Politics, Culture, Society* (2006). A study based on more than 140 confessions inscribed in stone.

popular, especially in the hands of the playwright Menander of Athens (ca. 300 B.C.E.). This clever author delighted audiences with escapist, frothy tales of temporarily frustrated love and happy endings. These plays, known now as New Comedy, developed from the risqué satires of classical Athens. They featured vivid street language and a cast of stock characters: crotchety parents, naive young men, silly young women, clever slaves, and wicked pimps.

Theocritus (ca. 300–ca. 260 B.C.E.), who came from the city of Syracuse in Sicily but wrote in Alexandria, invented a new genre called pastoral poetry. His verses described idyllic life in the countryside, but his rustic herdsmen reflected the sadness and tensions of city life. Of all the Hellenistic poets, Theocritus has had the most wide-ranging and enduring influence, providing a model for pastoral verse in Rome, Shakespeare's England, and even nineteenth-century Russia. The other great poet of Alexandria, Callimachus (ca. 305–240 B.C.E.), combined playfulness with extraordinary learning in works ranging from *Collections of Wonders of the World* to his moving love poems, the *Elegies.* His poetry provides the best example of the erudite style known as **Alexandrianism**, which demonstrated a command of meter and language and appealed more to the intellect than to the emotions.

The most accomplished historian of the Hellenistic period was Polybius (ca. 202–120 B.C.E.), a native of the Greek city of Megalopolis. Polybius devoted the latter part of his life to writing a history of Rome's meteoric rise to power within the Mediterranean region. As a work of literature, Polybius's *Histories* cannot compete with those of the great Greek historians Thucydides and Herodotus; his leaden style prevented him from capturing the drama of events. The strength of *Histories* lies in its comprehensive coverage of events in all the countries of the Mediterranean world and its adherence to high standards of accuracy and impartiality, both of which were noticeably absent in the works of his predecessors.

NIKE OF SAMOTHRACE This statue of Nike, the winged Greek goddess of victory, found on the Greek island of Samothrace, captures the sensation of her flight through the air by portraying her wings outstretched and the wind blowing the folds of her garment. The statue was situated on the sculpture of a bow of a ship, where Nike has just landed.

Alexandrianism A style of Hellenistic poetry that demonstrated a command of meter and language and appealed more to the intellect than the emotions.

  Read the Document

Polybius: Why Romans and Not Greeks Govern the World, ca. 140 B.C.E.

Hellenistic Philosophy and Science

4.4 What did Hellenistic thinkers contribute to philosophy and the scientific investigation of the natural world?

Hellenistic philosophers distinguished between three branches of their discipline: logic, the study of abstract reasoning; ethics, the study of how one should conduct one's life; and physics, the study of the natural world. In the Middle Ages educated people began to refer to physics as natural philosophy; since the eighteenth century they have identified this type of investigation as science.

COMEDY MOSAIC FROM POMPEII Many brilliant decorative mosaics have survived from the Hellenistic world. Often derived from Greek paintings that have been lost, these scenes give a vivid glimpse into everyday life. This mosaic is based on a scene from a comedy performed in a theater.

During the Hellenistic period all three branches of philosophy remained anchored in the works of Plato and Aristotle, but philosophy acquired its own distinctive features.

Philosophy: The Quest for Peace of Mind

The Hellenistic contribution to philosophy was most striking in the study of ethics. Three of the philosophical groups that emerged during this period—the Epicureans, the Stoics, and the Cynics—shared the common goal of acquiring an inner tranquility or peace of mind. According to Xenocrates (d. 314 B.C.E.), the head of the Platonic Academy in Athens, the purpose of studying philosophy "is to allay what causes disturbance in life." This quest for personal tranquility did not disregard the needs of other people. Its goal was to determine which ways of interacting with other people were right and which were wrong.

Epicureans Followers of the teachings of the philosopher Epicurus (341–271 B.C.E.). Epicureans tried to gain peace of mind by choosing pleasures rationally.

The first of these philosophical schools, the **Epicureans**, was founded by Epicurus of Samos (341–271 B.C.E.). Known by its meeting place in Athens, the Garden, this school was open to women and slaves as well as free men. Because Epicurus believed that "the entire world lives in pain," he urged people to gain tranquility through the rational choice of pleasure. The word *epicurean* today denotes a person of discriminating taste who takes pleasure in lavish eating and drinking, but the pleasure Epicurus sought was intellectual, a perfect harmony of body and mind. To achieve this harmony, Epicurus recommended a virtuous and simple life, characterized by plain living and withdrawal from the stressful world of politics and social competition. Epicurus also reassured his students that they should fear neither death nor the gods. There was no reason to fear death because the soul was material; hence, there was no afterlife. Nor was there any reason to fear the gods, who lived happily, far from Earth, unconcerned with human activity. Freed from these fears, humans could find inner peace.

The main rival to Epicureanism was Stoicism, the school established by Zeno of Citium (ca. 335–ca. 263 B.C.E.) at Athens in 300 B.C.E. Taking its name from the Stoa Poikile (the Painted Portico) where Zeno and his successors taught, Stoicism remained influential well into the time of the Roman Empire. **Stoics** believed that all human beings have an element of divinity in them and therefore participate in one single indissoluble cosmic process. They could find peace of mind by submitting to that cosmic order, which Stoics identified with nature or fate. Thus, the word *stoic* today denotes a person who responds to pain or misfortune without showing emotion. Stoics believed that wise men did not allow the vicissitudes of life to distract them. Rather than calling for withdrawal from the world, like the Epicureans, Stoicism encouraged people to participate actively in public life. Because Stoicism accepted the status quo, many kings and aristocrats embraced it. They wanted to believe that their success formed part of a cosmic, divine plan.

Stoics Followers of the philosophy developed by Zeno of Citium (ca. 335–ca. 263 B.C.E.) that urged acceptance of fate while participating fully in everyday life.

Cynics took a different approach to gaining peace of mind. The word *cynic* today usually refers to a person who sneers at the sincerity of human motives and behavior. But the ancient Cynics, inspired by Antisthenes (ca. 445–360 B.C.E.), a devoted follower of Socrates, taught that the key to happiness was the rejection of all needs and desires. To achieve this goal, Cynics abandoned all possessions to lead a life of rigorous asceticism. Diogenes (ca. 412–324 B.C.E.), the chief representative of this philosophy, made his home in an empty barrel. Cynics showed contempt for the customs and conventions of society, including wealth, social position, and prevailing standards of morality. One prominent Cynic, Crates of Thebes (ca. 328 B.C.E.), caused a public scandal when he did the unthinkable: He took his wife, the philosopher Hipparchia, out for a meal in public instead of leaving her at home, where respectable women belonged. Some Cynics took the example of Diogenes to further extremes by satisfying, rather than denying, their simplest natural needs. Their behavior, which included public masturbation and defecation, gave them their name, which derived from the Greek word for dog. Their rejection of prevailing social values, coupled with their offensive public behavior, explains why their teachings failed to have a lasting impact.

Cynics Followers of the teachings of Antisthenes (ca. 445–360 B.C.E.) who rejected pleasures, possessions, and social conventions to find peace of mind.

ZENO OF CITIUM Zeno, the Athenian founder of Stoicism, argued that one should submit to the cosmic order, otherwise defined as nature or fate, in one's search for inner peace. Stoicism had considerable influence among Roman politicians and writers.

Explaining the Natural World: Scientific Investigation

While Athens remained the hub of philosophy in the Hellenistic Age, the Ptolemaic kings made Alexandria the center of scientific learning. There King Ptolemy I founded the Museum, an institution

4.1

4.2

4.3

4.4

named after the Muses, goddesses of the arts and knowledge, that sponsored research and lectures on the natural world. Nearby, the royal Library housed hundreds of thousands of texts in an attempt to organize the entire body of knowledge of the world.

In addition to summarizing the work of previous scholars, scientists in Alexandria and throughout the Hellenistic world sought to describe the natural world as it actually was. This emphasis on scientific realism involved the rejection of some of the more speculative notions that had characterized classical Greek science. Theophrastus (ca. 371–287 B.C.E.), a disciple of Aristotle who is often considered the first scientist of the Hellenistic period, rejected the philosophical view of Aristotle that nature was static rather than dynamic and could be explained in terms of philosophical "first principles." Theophrastus's nine-volume *Enquiries into Plants* led him to the conclusion that plants had not devolved or "degenerated" from animals, as Aristotle had claimed.

In mathematics, Euclid (ca. 300 B.C.E.) produced a masterful synthesis of geometry in his work, *Elements,* which remained the standard geometry textbook until the twentieth century. Euclid demonstrated how one could attain knowledge of a subject by rational methods alone—by mathematical reasoning through the use of deductive proofs and theorems. Equally famous as a mathematician was Archimedes of Syracuse (ca. 287–212 B.C.E.), who calculated the value of *pi* (the ratio of a circle's circumference to its diameter) and measured the diameter of the sun. A sophisticated mechanical engineer, Archimedes reputedly said: "Give me a fulcrum and I will move the world." Archimedes put his scientific knowledge to work in wartime. During the Roman siege of Syracuse in 212 B.C.E., he reportedly built a huge reflecting mirror that focused the bright Sicilian sun on Roman warships, burning holes in their sails.

View the Image

Archimedes's Mirror

Knowledge of astronomy also advanced during the Hellenistic Age. In their research, Hellenistic investigators borrowed from the long tradition of observation of the heavens that Babylonian and Egyptian scholars had established. This intersection of Greek and Near Eastern astronomical work produced one of the richest new areas of knowledge in the Hellenistic world. For example, Heraclides of Pontus (ca. 388–312 B.C.E.) anticipated a heliocentric (sun-centered) theory of the universe when he observed that the planets Venus and Mercury orbit the sun, not Earth. Aristarchus of Samos (ca. 310–230 B.C.E.) established the idea that the planets revolve around the sun while spinning on their own axes. Eratosthenes of Cyrene (ca. 276–194 B.C.E.) made a calculation of the Earth's circumference that came within 200 miles of the actual figure.

The sun-centered view never won wide acceptance, however, because of fierce opposition from the followers of Aristotle, whose geocentric (Earth-centered) theories had become canonical. To support Aristotle's **cosmology** (a map of the universe), Hipparchus of Nicaea (ca. 190–127 B.C.E.) produced the first catalog of stars and insisted that they encircled the Earth. The geocentric view of the universe prevailed until the sixteenth century C.E., when the Polish astronomer Nicholas Copernicus, who had read the work of Heraclides and Aristarchus, provided mathematical data to support the sun-centered theory (see Chapter 17).

cosmology A theory concerning the structure and nature of the universe such as those proposed by Aristotle in the fourth century B.C.E. and Copernicus in the sixteenth century.

Medical theory and research also flourished in the great Hellenistic cities. Diocles, a Greek doctor of the fourth century B.C.E. who combined theory and practice, wrote the first handbook on human anatomy and invented a spoon-like tool for removing arrowheads from the human body. Doctors during this period believed that both human behavior and health were products of the balance of fluids, called humors, in the body. They argued about whether to categorize the humors as hot, cold, wet, and dry or as blood, phlegm, yellow bile, and black bile. Praxagoras of Cos (late fourth century B.C.E.) argued that the body contained more than a dozen kinds of humors. He also studied the relation of the brain to the spinal cord. Other doctors, such as Herophilus and Erasistratus, who lived in Alexandria in the fourth century B.C.E., systematically dissected human cadavers. They also may have practiced vivisection, operating on living subjects to study their organs. There is some evidence that they conducted

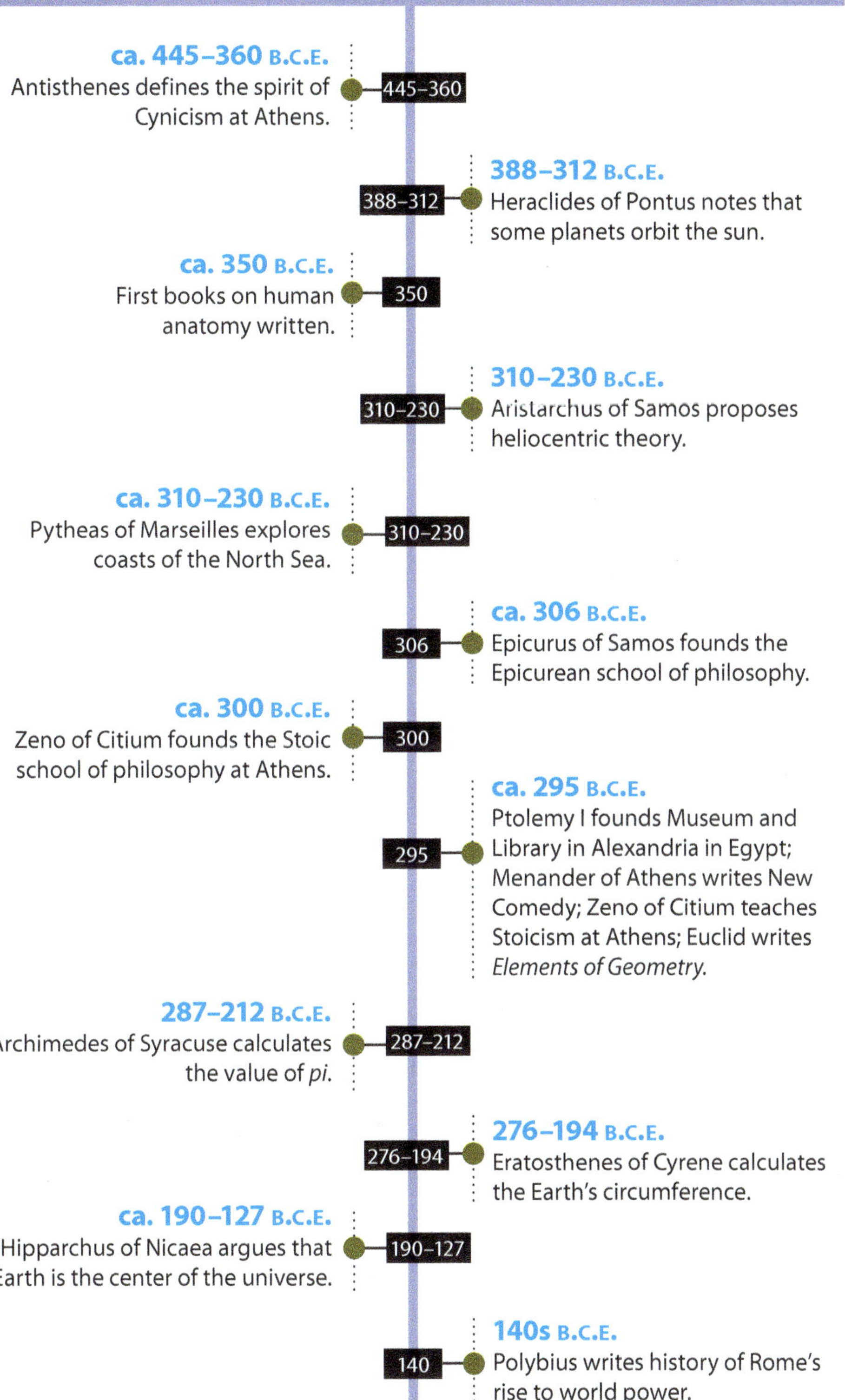
CHRONOLOGY: HELLENISTIC LITERATURE, SCIENCE, AND PHILOSOPHY
ca. 445–360 B.C.E.
Antisthenes defines the spirit of Cynicism at Athens.
445–360
388–312 B.C.E.
Heraclides of Pontus notes that some planets orbit the sun.
388–312
ca. 350 B.C.E.
First books on human anatomy written.
350
310–230 B.C.E.
Aristarchus of Samos proposes heliocentric theory.
310–230
ca. 310–230 B.C.E.
Pytheas of Marseilles explores coasts of the North Sea.
310–230
ca. 306 B.C.E.
Epicurus of Samos founds the Epicurean school of philosophy.
306
ca. 300 B.C.E.
Zeno of Citium founds the Stoic school of philosophy at Athens.
300
ca. 295 B.C.E.
Ptolemy I founds Museum and Library in Alexandria in Egypt; Menander of Athens writes New Comedy; Zeno of Citium teaches Stoicism at Athens; Euclid writes *Elements of Geometry*.
295
287–212 B.C.E.
Archimedes of Syracuse calculates the value of *pi*.
287–212
276–194 B.C.E.
Eratosthenes of Cyrene calculates the Earth's circumference.
276–194
ca. 190–127 B.C.E.
Hipparchus of Nicaea argues that Earth is the center of the universe.
190–127
140s B.C.E.
Polybius writes history of Rome's rise to world power.
140

experiments on condemned criminals who had not yet been executed, a practice outlawed today. Through dissection, whether of the dead or the living, these physicians learned a great deal about the human nervous system, the structure of the eye, and reproductive physiology.

CONCLUSION

Defining the West in the Hellenistic Age

During the Hellenistic Age the cultural and geographical boundaries of what would later be called the West began to take shape. These boundaries encompassed the regions where Hellenistic culture had a lasting influence. The lands within the empire of Alexander the Great, all of which lay to the east of Greece and Egypt, formed the core of this cultural realm, but the Hellenistic world also extended westward across the Mediterranean, embracing the lands ruled by Carthage from North Africa to Spain. Hellenism also reached the edges of the lands inhabited by the Celts. In all these areas Greek culture interacted with those of the indigenous peoples it penetrated, and the synthesis that resulted from these encounters became one of the main foundations of Western civilization.

As the next chapter shows, the encounter between Greek culture and the culture of non-Greek lands during the Hellenistic period was most creative in Rome, a small republic that eventually conquered the Hellenistic kingdoms and established its own hegemony over the lands that lay both to the west and the east of the Italian peninsula. When the Roman politician and military commander Octavian (later known as Caesar Augustus) won control of the Mediterranean world, the Near East, Egypt, and parts of Europe in 30 B.C.E., the Hellenistic Age came to an end. This political achievement, and the resulting transformation of the Roman Republic into the Roman Empire at the same time, did not, however, put an end to the influence of Hellenistic culture. By forging a new, more resilient civilization in which Greeks, Romans, and many other peoples intermingled in peace, the Romans created their own version of Hellenism.

MAKING CONNECTIONS

1. What were the main differences between the political institutions of the Hellenistic successor states and those in Greece during the Classical Age?
2. In what ways did Hellenistic culture modify or change the culture of Greece during the Classical Age?
3. Why did the Hellenistic successor states fail?

TAKING IT FURTHER

For suggested readings see page R-1.

On MyHistoryLab

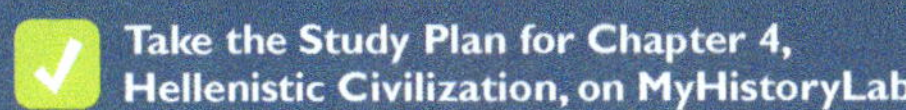

Chapter Review

The Impact of Alexander the Great

4.1 How did Alexander the Great create a large empire in which Greek civilization flourished in the midst of many diverse cultures?

A combination of diplomacy, bribery, and threats helped Phillip II position Macedonia to crush the allied armies of the city-states and set up a coalition of Greek cities under his leadership. Philip shrewdly linked classical Greek civilization with a rallying cry for imperialist expansion when he rallied the Greek people to avenge their invasion by Persia in the previous century. After Phillip's death, Alexander the Great honored his father's legacy by winning a series of victories in Asia. To hold together this vast kingdom, Alexander adopted the powers and symbolism of Persian kingship.

Hellenism in the East and West

4.2 What was the relationship between Greeks and non-Greeks in the lands that Alexander conquered and those with whom Greeks came into contact after his death?

Since the ruling elite was composed of Greeks and Macedonians and not indigenous peoples, Greek was the language of the government. To maintain the goodwill of their non-Greek subjects, Hellenistic monarchs founded cities, constructed public buildings, and maintained security by building and maintaining large professional armies. In return, kings were worshiped for the protection and peace that the government provided. While educated Greeks were curious about the cultures and traditions of the non-Greeks they encountered, few Greek settlers in new lands bothered to learn the local languages, and native resistance sometimes resulted when Greeks tried to force Hellenistic traditions on these cultures.

Hellenistic Society and Culture

4.3 What were the distinguishing features of Hellenistic society and culture, and what was the result of encounters between Greeks and non-Greeks?

Characterized by Greek city life, Hellenistic society emphasized the traditions of learning, visual arts, and citizen participation in public life. Cities, however, lost much of their independence in the Hellenistic successor kingdoms, and the wealthy acquired greater power and influence. Hellenistic cities had more diverse populations than in the classical Greek period, and the wealthy acquired a more dominant role in society and government. Some aristocratic women wielded greater power than in the classical period. Artists and architects continued to use classical motifs and themes but introduced the more highly ornamented baroque style.

Hellenistic Philosophy and Science

4.4 What did Hellenistic thinkers contribute to philosophy and the scientific investigation of the natural world?

The study of ethics was a lasting contribution of Hellenistic thinkers, as the different philosophical schools shared the common goal of acquiring an inner tranquility, or peace of mind. Scientists throughout the Hellenistic world placed an emphasis on scientific realism when it came to investigating the natural world, and the field of mathematics was marked by Euclid's demonstration of how knowledge can be attained by mathematical reasoning and Archimedes's calculation of the value of *pi*. Medical theory and research also flourished in the great Hellenistic cities.

Chapter Time Line

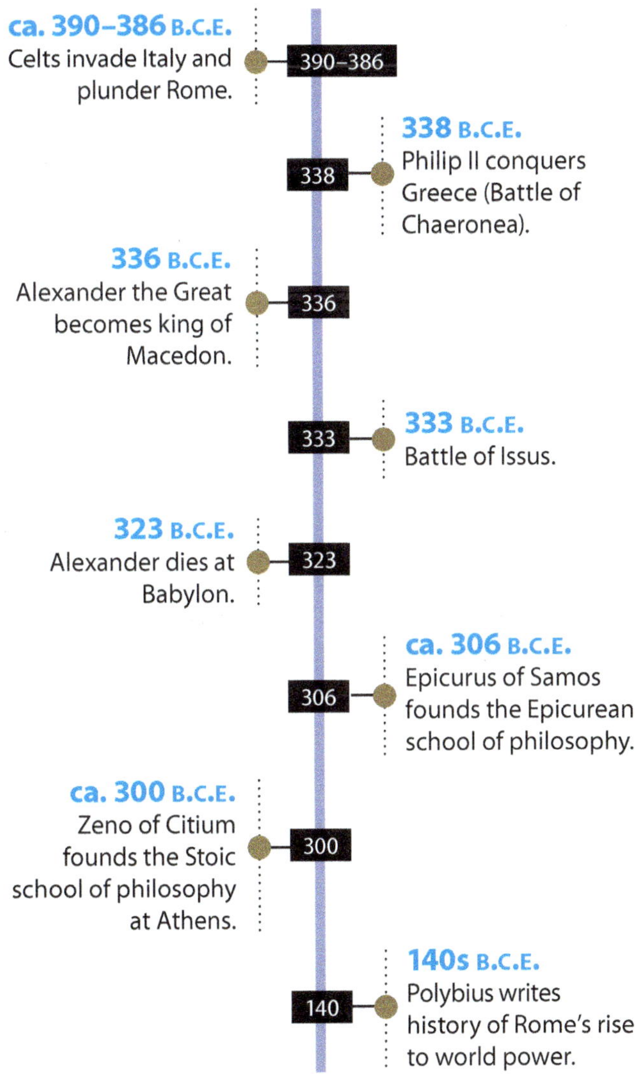

5 The Roman Republic

In 146 B.C.E. the Roman general Lucius Mummius led a large military force into the Greek city of Corinth, about 50 miles west-southwest of Athens. Mummius had just won a victory over the forces of the Achaean League, a confederation of Greek cities. Corinth was the most powerful city in this federation. Recognizing that their cause was hopeless, most Corinthians fled before the Romans reached the city gates, and Mummius entered the city unopposed. The Romans killed the men who remained, enslaved the women and children, plundered the city's treasures, and then burned Corinth to the ground. Thus ended a long chapter in the history of a Greek city known for its international trade, wealth, and the luxury in which many of its residents lived. The cities in the Achaean League came under the direct control of Rome and later became part of the Roman province of Achaea.

The sack of Corinth had a broader significance than the destruction of this once powerful Greek city. It marked the final step in the establishment of Rome as the dominant power in the Mediterranean world. The significance of this event was not lost on contemporaries. The Greek historian Polybius, who had tried to prevent the Achaean League from aligning itself with the kingdom of Macedon against Rome in 171 B.C.E., concluded his narrative of the rise of Rome in the Mediterranean with an account of this final blow to Greek independence. After the destruction of Corinth Rome continued its

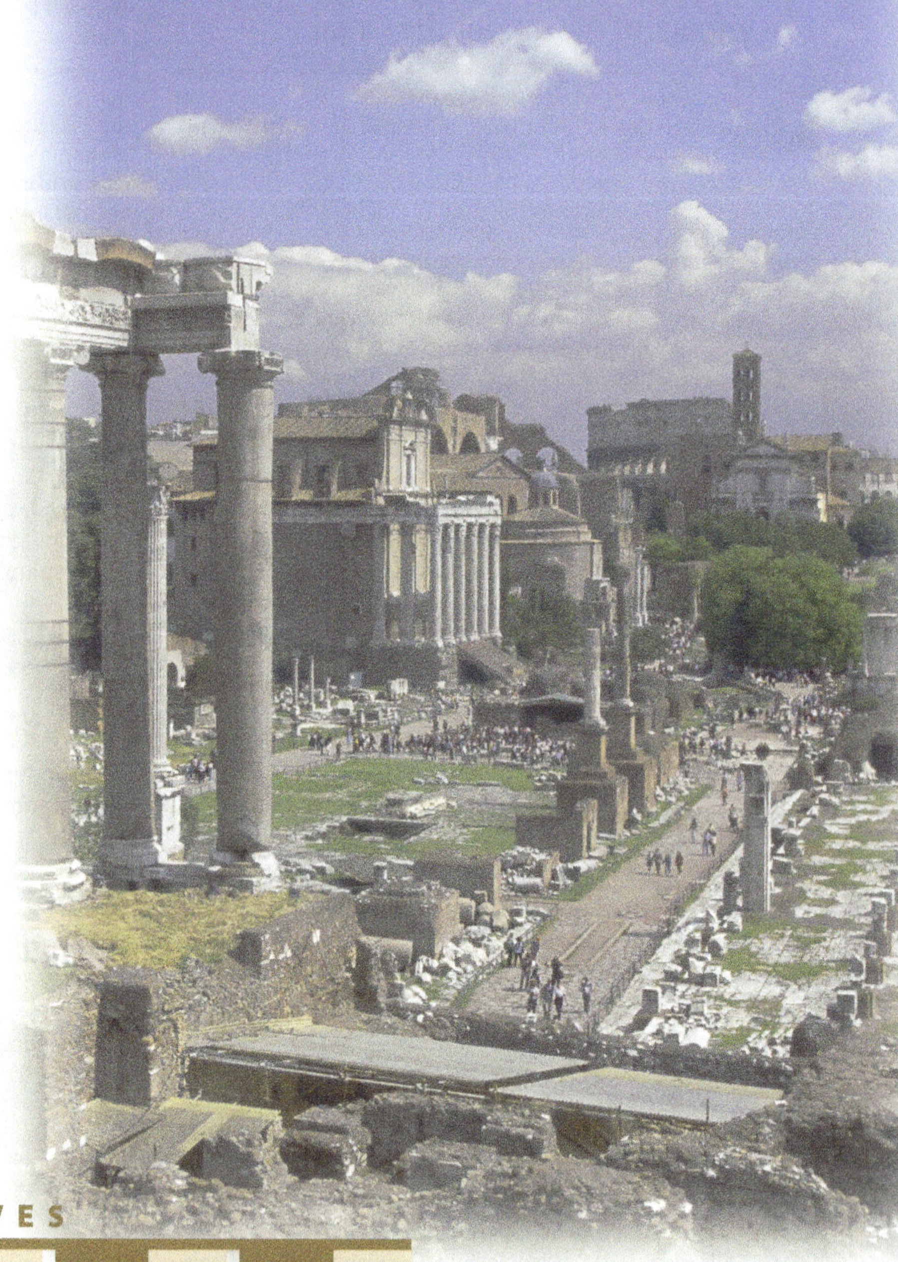

VIEW OF THE FORUM FROM CAPITOLINE HILL This view of the Forum was taken from the site of the temple of Jupiter, Rome's mightiest god. All victory processions after a successful war would have ended at this temple, where sacrifices were made. Now tourists visit the remains of buildings from which Rome ruled an international empire.

LEARNING OBJECTIVES

5.1 What type of government did Rome establish when it eliminated kingship?

5.2 How did the Roman Republic come to dominate the Mediterranean world during the Hellenistic Age?

5.3 How did the Roman encounter with Greek culture lead to the forging of a durable cultural synthesis?

5.4 How was Roman society structured, and what relationships existed within the Roman family?

5.5 Why did the Roman Republic end?

Listen to Chapter 5 on MyHistoryLab

Watch the Video Series on MyHistoryLab

Learn about some key topics related to this chapter with the *MyHistoryLab Video Series: Key Topics in Western Civilization*

meteoric rise. Within little more than a century, Rome would gain control of the entire Mediterranean world, most of western Europe, and many of the Asian territories that Alexander the Great had conquered in the fourth century B.C.E. The lands that came under Roman rule would mark the geographical boundaries of what would later become the West. Rome also developed political and cultural traditions that became central to Western identity. These traditions were largely based on those of Greece, but they had a distinctive Roman imprint. The Greco–Roman culture that resulted from this encounter was then transmitted to the many lands that came under Roman rule. Greco–Roman culture, in which Latin, rather than Greek, was the dominant language in politics, diplomacy, commerce, and literature, thus became the most enduring foundation of Western civilization.

This chapter will address the question:

How did this small republic on the Italian peninsula rise to power within the Hellenistic world and thus lay the foundations of the geographical and cultural realm that we call the West?

The Nature of the Roman Republic

5.1 What type of government did Rome establish when it eliminated kingship?

From Rome's Capitoline Hill a tourist today can look down on the Roman Forum and see a field of broken buildings and monuments. These remains lie at the heart of what was once an enormous empire extending from northern England to the Black Sea and from Morocco to Mesopotamia. On the western slope of the neighboring Palatine Hill, archaeologists have uncovered hut foundations from Rome's earliest occupants in the tenth century B.C.E. How the Roman Empire emerged from this crude village above a swamp remains one of the most remarkable stories in the history of the West.

During the Hellenistic Age, Rome expanded from a relatively small city-state with a republican form of government into a vast and powerful empire. As it conquered the peoples who ringed the Mediterranean—the Carthaginians, the Celts, and the Hellenistic kingdoms of Alexander's successors—Rome incorporated these newcomers into the political structure of the Republic (see **Map 5.1** on p. 147). Trying to govern these sprawling territories with institutions and social traditions suited for a city-state overwhelmed the Roman Republic and led to the establishment of a new form of government, the Roman Empire, by the end of the first century B.C.E.

Roman Origins and Etruscan Influences

Interaction with outsiders shaped the story of Rome from its beginning. Resting on low but easily defensible hills covering a few hundred acres above the Tiber River, Rome lies at the intersection of north-south and east-west trade routes that had been used

RAPE OF THE SABINE WOMEN In the legendary history of Rome, the first generation of Roman men acquired wives from the Italian tribe of Sabines, who inhabited the region around Rome. When the Sabines refused, the Romans supposedly abducted the Sabine women and then asked them to accept Roman husbands. The legend, which has no factual basis, was enshrined in the literary works of Livy and Plutarch. The word *rape* in this context refers to abduction, not sexual violation. The rape of the Sabine women became a popular subject for artists in the sixteenth and seventeenth centuries. This depiction of the rape was painted by Pietro da Cortona between 1627 and 1629.

in Italy since the Neolithic Age. Romans used these same routes to develop a thriving commerce with other peoples, many of whom they eventually conquered and absorbed.

Settlements began in Rome about 1000 B.C.E., but we know little about the lives of these first inhabitants. So small was the scale of village life that clusters of huts on the different hills may have constituted entirely different communities. What would one day be the Forum—the place of assembly for judicial and other public business—was a marsh that villagers used as protection and burial grounds.

Control of the Tiber River crossing and trade allowed Rome to grow quickly. Excavated graves from the eighth century B.C.E. reveal that a wealthy elite had already emerged. Women evidently shared the benefits of increased prosperity. One grave contained a woman buried with her chariot, a symbol of authority and status. During the seventh century Rome's population increased rapidly. Extended families or clans became a force in Roman life. Throughout this early period, according to Roman legend, kings ruled the city.

Historians think that Latin, the Roman language, was only one of at least 140 distinct languages and dialects spoken by Italy's frequently warring communities during the first four centuries of Rome's existence. During this period, Romans developed their military skills to defend themselves against their neighbors. Nevertheless, the Romans had amicable relations with some neighbors—particularly the Etruscans, who lived northwest of Rome.

In the seventh and sixth centuries B.C.E., Etruscan culture strongly influenced Rome. By 800 B.C.E. Etruscans, whose origins remain unknown although they may have migrated to Italy from Anatolia, were firmly established in Etruria (modern Tuscany), a region in central Italy between the Arno and Tiber Rivers. By the sixth century B.C.E. they controlled territory as far south as the Bay of Naples and east to the Adriatic Sea. The Etruscans maintained a loose confederation of independent cities that often fought against other Italian peoples.

Etruscans carried on a lively trade with Greek merchants, exchanging native iron ore and other resources for vases and other luxury goods. Commerce became the conduit through which Etruscans and later Romans absorbed many aspects of Greek culture. The Etruscans, for example, adopted the Greek alphabet and subscribed to many Greek myths, which they later transmitted to the Romans.

During the sixth century B.C.E., the Etruscans ruled Rome. Although the Etruscans and Romans spoke different languages, a common culture deriving from native Italian, Etruscan, and Greek communities gradually evolved, especially in religious practice. The three main gods of Rome—Jupiter, Minerva, and Juno—were first worshiped in Etruria. (The Greek equivalents were Zeus, Athena, and Hera.) Etruscan seers taught Romans how to interpret omens, especially how to learn the will of the gods by examining the entrails of sacrificed animals. Etruscans also gave the Romans a distinctive temple architecture that differed from that of the Greeks. Etruscan and later Roman temples had much deeper porticos, covered porches supported by colonnades.

Establishing the Roman Republic

By about 600 B.C.E. Romans had prospered sufficiently to drain the marsh that became the Forum. They also began to construct temples and public buildings, including the first Senate house, where the elders met to discuss community affairs. Under the rule of its kings, some of whom were of Etruscan origin, Rome became an important military power in Italy. Only free male inhabitants of the city who could afford their own weapons voted in the citizen assembly, which made public decisions with the advice of the Senate. Poor men could fight but not vote. Thus began the struggle between rich and poor that would plague Roman life for centuries.

Topographical Map: Ancient Rome, ca. Eighth Century B.C.E.

About 500 B.C.E., when Rome had become a powerful city with perhaps 35,000 inhabitants, the Romans put an end to kingship and established a **republic**, a state in which political power resides in the people or their representatives rather than in a monarch. According to legend, in 509 B.C.E. Lucius Junius Brutus, a member of the ruling dynastic family, overthrew the tyrannical Etruscan king, Tarquin the Proud.

republic A state in which political power resides in the people or their representatives rather than in a monarch.

After the monarchy was abolished, Rome established several new institutions that structured political life for 500 years. An assembly comprising Rome's male citizens, called the Centuriate Assembly, managed the city's legislative, judicial, and administrative affairs. As in the Greek poleis, only men participated in public life. Each year, the assembly elected two chief executives called consuls, who could administer the law but whose decisions could be appealed to the assembly. In time, the assembly also elected additional officers to deal with legal and financial responsibilities. The Senate, comprising about 300 Romans who had held administrative offices, advised the consuls, though the senators had no formal authority. Priests performed religious ceremonies on behalf of the city. Hatred of kings, which became a staple of Roman political thought, prevented any one man from becoming too prominent. A relatively small group of influential families held real power within the political community by monopolizing the main offices and working behind the scenes. As we saw in Chapter 3, this kind of government is known as an oligarchy, or the rule of the few.

To celebrate the end of the monarchy, the people of Rome built a grand new temple to Jupiter on the Capitoline Hill, looking down on the Forum. They also established the community of Vestal Virgins, priestesses who served as caretakers of the sacred fire and hearth in the Temple of Vesta, one of Rome's most ancient religious sites. In such ways the welfare of Rome became a shared public concern.

Tensions between social groups shaped Roman political life during the Republic. At the top of the social hierarchy stood the **patricians**, a wealthy elite who traced their ancestry back to royal Rome. These families claimed to have toppled the monarchy. Because they monopolized the magistracies and the priesthoods, patricians occupied most of the seats in the Senate. Other rich landowners and senators with lesser pedigrees, as well as the prosperous farmers who made up the army's ranks, joined the patricians in resisting the **plebeians**, the general body of Roman citizens. The plebeians generally occupied the lower ranks of Roman society, although some of them managed to acquire

patricians In ancient Rome, patricians were aristocratic clans with the highest status and the most political influence.

plebeians The general body of Roman citizens.

significant wealth. The plebeians demanded more political rights, such as a fair share of distributed public land and freedom from debt bondage. These efforts of poor Romans to acquire a political voice, called the **Struggle of the Orders**, accelerated during the fifth century B.C.E., when Rome experienced a severe economic recession.

Struggle of the Orders The political strife between patrician and plebeian Romans beginning in the fifth century B.C.E. The plebeians gradually won political rights and influence as a result of the struggle.

The main weapon that the plebeians had in this struggle was the threat, realized on only three occasions, of literally leaving the city, thereby bringing economic life to a standstill and depriving the army of its soldiers. The first victory in the plebeians' struggle came in 494 B.C.E., when they won the right to elect two tribunes each year as their spokesmen. Tribunes could veto magistrates' decisions and so block arbitrary judicial actions by the patricians. In 471 B.C.E., a new Plebeian Assembly gave plebeians the opportunity to express their political views in a formal setting, although without the authority to enact legislation.

In 445 B.C.E., a new law permitted marriage between plebeians and patricians. This enabled wealthy plebeians to marry into patrician families. In 367 B.C.E., politicians agreed that one of each year's two consuls should be a plebeian. The plebeians now were fully integrated into Roman government. Moreover, Romans also limited the amount of public land that could be distributed to any citizen. The new arrangement prevented patricians from seizing the lion's share of conquered territories and enabled poor citizen soldiers to receive captured land. The last concession to the plebeians came in 287 B.C.E., when the decisions of the Plebeian Assembly became binding on the whole state.

When Polybius chronicled the meteoric rise of Rome to world power, he attributed the success of the Republic to its mixture of the three forms of government identified by Aristotle: monarchy, aristocracy, and democracy. In the Roman Republic, two consuls represented monarchy; the Senate represented aristocracy (those considered most fit to rule); and the assemblies, which included both patricians and plebeians, represented democracy. According to Polybius, this republican mixture of the three forms of government was supposed to prevent the evils that threatened to emerge from each: despotism from monarchy, oligarchy from aristocracy, and mob-rule from democracy. As it turned out, aristocracy tended to prevail in the Roman Republic because the two consuls were almost always rich senators and because patricians usually had the upper hand in the assemblies. It is true that the plebeians in the assembly could check the power of the patricians, and to that extent the Roman constitution was "balanced." But wealthy plebeians, who represented the "democratic" element in the Roman constitution, joined the patricians to form a new ruling elite. The government of the Roman Republic was therefore not as balanced as Polybius boasted. His description of that government, however, had a lasting impact on the efforts of later Western regimes to establish a form of government in which representatives of "the one," "the few," and "the many" all had a voice.

Roman Law

The conflict between the patricians and the plebeians during the early Republic resulted in the formulation of a body of law governing relations between individuals (private law) and between individuals and the government (public law). When the Republic was first established, legal disputes were settled by appealing to a body of unwritten customs that were believed to have originated in the distant past. When the application of these ancient customs in a specific case was unclear, a body of patricians known as the pontiffs would interpret the law. When plebeians began to participate in the political life of the Republic, they recognized that the patricians might interpret the law in favor of their social class. The assembly therefore demanded that the law be put in writing so that decisions by the pontiffs had to be based on an authoritative and publicly known text. Accordingly, a commission appointed in 451 B.C.E. produced a body of written law known as the **Law of the Twelve Tables**, which was inscribed on 12 bronze tablets and posted in the Forum. This legislation, which was supposedly modeled on the Athenian law of Solon, was actually a written summary of existing customary law, not new law being handed down for the first time.

Law of the Twelve Tables A Roman law code inscribed on 12 bronze tablets and published in 451 B.C.E. This summary of existing law was the first body of written law in Rome.

Justice in History

A Corrupt Roman Governor Is Convicted of Extortion

Governors sent by the Roman Senate to rule the provinces wielded absolute power, which often corrupted them. One such man was Gaius Verres, who was convicted in 70 B.C.E. in a court in Rome for his flagrant abuse of power while governor of Sicily. The courtroom drama in which Verres was found guilty reveals one of the deepest flaws of the Roman Republic: the unprincipled exploitation of lands under Roman control. It also reveals one of Rome's greatest strengths: the presence of men of high ethical standards who believed in honest government and fair treatment of Roman subjects. The trial and its result reveal republican Rome at its best and worst.

While governor from 73 to 71 B.C.E., Verres had looted Sicily with shocking thoroughness. In his pursuit of gold and Greek art, Verres tortured and sometimes killed Roman citizens. His outraged victims employed the young and ambitious lawyer Marcus Tullius Cicero (106–43 B.C.E.) to prosecute Verres. They could not have chosen a better advocate.

The prosecution of Verres marks the beginning of Cicero's illustrious career as one of the most active politicians and certainly the greatest orator of the Republic. Cicero also stands as one of the most influential political philosophers of Western civilization, one who hated the corruption of political life and opposed tyranny in any form. His many literary works have influenced political thinkers from antiquity to the present.

In the Roman Republic, only senators and equestrians, the two ranks of the Roman aristocracy, between ages 30 and 60 could serve on juries for civil crimes such as those Verres committed. All adult male citizens had the right to bring a case to court, but women had less freedom to do so. After swearing oaths of good faith, accusers would read the charges in the presence of the accused, who in turn agreed to accept the decision of the court.

When a trial actually began, the prosecutor was expected to be present, but the accused could decline to attend. The prosecution and the defense both produced evidence, then cross-examined witnesses. Because a Roman lawyer could discuss any aspect of the defendant's personal or public life, character assassination became an important—and amusing—rhetorical tool.

After deliberating, the jury delivered its verdict and the judge gave the penalty required by law, generally fines or periods of exile. No provisions for appeal existed, but the assembly could grant a pardon by means of a legislative act.

Cicero worked this system to his advantage in his prosecution of Verres. He quashed an attempt to delay the trial until 69 B.C.E., when the president of the court would be a crony of Verres. Then, with a combination of ringing oratory and irrefutable evidence of Verres's crimes, Cicero made his case. The following excerpt from his speech shows Cicero's mastery of persuasive rhetoric:

> Judges: At this grave crisis in the history of our country, you have been offered a peculiarly desirable gift. . . . For you have been given a unique chance to make your Senatorial Order less unpopular, and to set right the damaged reputation of these courts. A belief has taken root which is having a fatal effect on our nation—and which to us who are senators, in particular, threatens grave peril. This belief is on everyone's tongue, at Rome and even in foreign countries. It is this: That in these courts, with their present membership, even the worst criminal will never be convicted provided that he has money. . . . And at this very juncture Gaius Verres has been brought to trial. Here is a man whose life and actions the world has already condemned—yet whose enormous fortune, according to his own loudly expressed hopes, has already brought him acquittal! Pronounce a just and scrupulous verdict against Verres and you will keep the good name which ought always to be yours. . . . I spent fifty days on a careful investigation of the entire island of Sicily; I got to know every document, every wrong suffered either by a community or an individual. . . .
>
> For three long years he so thoroughly despoiled and pillaged the province that its restoration to its previous state is out of the question. . . . All the property that anyone in Sicily still has for his own today is merely what happened to escape the attention of this avaricious lecher, or survived his glutted appetites. . . . It was an appalling disgrace for our country.
>
> . . . In the first stage of the trial, then, my charge is this. I accuse Gaius Verres of committing acts of lechery and brutality against the citizens and allies of Rome, and many crimes against God and man. I claim that he has illegally taken from Sicily sums amounting to forty million sesterces. By the witnesses and documents, public and private, which I am going to cite, I shall convince you that these charges are true.[1]

Cicero's speech was persuasive, and the jury found Verres guilty. Verres went into exile in Marseilles to avoid his sentence, but he did not avoid punishment altogether. Justice—relentless and ironic—caught up with him years later during the civil wars that followed Julius Caesar's death in 44 B.C.E. Mark Antony, who was also a connoisseur of other people's wealth, wanted Verres's art collection for himself and so put Verres's name on a death list to obtain it. The former governor of Sicily was murdered in 43 B.C.E.

In his prosecution of Verres, Cicero delivered more than an indictment of one corrupt man. He revealed some of the deepest flaws of the Roman Republic. The trial inspired short-term reforms, but not until the reign of Emperor Caesar Augustus (r. 27 B.C.E.–14 C.E.) did Roman administration of provincial populations become more just.

SOURCE: From *Selected Works: Against Verres 1; Twenty-Three Letters; The Second Philippic Against Antony; On Duties, 111; On Old Age* by Cicero, translated by Michael Grant (Penguin Classics 1960, second revised edition, 1971.)

(continued on next page)

(continued from previous page)

For Discussion

1. What does the trial of Verres reveal about weaknesses in the Roman Republic?
2. Cicero's speech illustrates his disdain for corruption and tyranny. What are the tensions between personal morality and the requirements of governing a large empire?

Taking It Further

Gruen, Erich S. *The Last Generation of the Roman Republic.* Berkeley: University of California Press, 1974. A magisterial analysis of the republic's decline, with emphasis on legal affairs.

Rawson, Elizabeth. *Cicero: A Portrait.* Ithaca: Cornell University Press, 1975. This book gives a balanced account of Cicero's life.

The original text of the Law of the Twelve Tables has not survived, but references in later legal documents provide a fairly good idea of its broad outlines. It covered such matters as the proper protection of women ("Women shall remain under the guardianship [of a man] even when they have reached legal adulthood") and debt bondage ("Unless he pays his debt or someone stands surety for him in court, bind him in a harness, or in chains . . ."). The value of the text to the plebeians resided not so much in the substance of the law, which was in many respects unfavorable to them, but in the legal procedures it spelled out. With the law now published, citizens discovered how to start a legal proceeding, which in civil cases (those involving property) meant they would bring the charge before a magistrate, who would then appoint a private citizen to examine witnesses and reach a decision. Only in serious criminal cases, such as homicide, would the magistrate take the initiative in prosecuting the case by himself. Because the Roman Republic did not have a large bureaucracy, the Twelve Tables encouraged citizens to settle cases among themselves, even in criminal cases involving serious physical injury.

The Twelve Tables governed civil and criminal disputes among Roman citizens. The frequency of disputes involving noncitizens, especially as Rome acquired distant lands, led to the establishment of another body of law, the *jus gentium* or law of nations. Because this law was based on what was considered to be the law of all civilized people, it was often equated with **natural law**, a system of justice believed to be inherent in nature rather than prescribed by human beings. The *jus gentium* became, in effect, the first body of international law.

natural law A law that is believed to be inherent in nature rather than established by human beings.

Roman law developed significantly during the later years of the Roman Republic and the empire, and in the sixth century C.E. the Roman emperor Justinian promulgated a massive legal code known as the *Corpus Juris Civilis* (Body of Civil Law). This legal code later became the foundation of the legal systems of most European countries. But Romans never failed to recognize that the Law of the Twelve Tables lay at the core of this comprehensive legal code. Thus, the law written down at the behest of plebeians in the early Roman Republic became the foundation of the legal culture of the West.

Roman Territorial Expansion

5.2 How did the Roman Republic come to dominate the Mediterranean world during the Hellenistic Age?

Under the Republic, Rome conquered and incorporated all of Italy, the vast Carthaginian Empire in North Africa, Spain, and many of the Celtic lands to the north and west of Italy (see **Map 5.2** on p. 150). As a result of these conquests, the Roman state had to change the methods of government established in the fifth century B.C.E.

The Italian Peninsula

The new political and military institutions that developed in Rome enabled the Romans to conquer the entire Italian peninsula by 263 B.C.E. In the process the Romans learned the fundamental lessons necessary for ruling larger territories abroad. Romans began to expand their realm by allying with neighboring cities in Italy. For centuries, Rome and the other Latin-speaking peoples of Latium (the region of central Italy where Rome was situated) had belonged to a loose coalition of cities called the Latin League. Citizens of these cities shared close commercial and legal ties and could intermarry without losing citizenship rights in their native cities. More important, they forged close military alliances with one another.

In 493 B.C.E. Rome led the Latin cities in battle against fierce hill tribes who coveted Latium's rich farmlands. From the success of this venture, Rome learned the value of political alliances with neighbors. Rome and its allies next confronted the Etruscans. In 396 B.C.E. the Romans overcame the Etruscan city of Veii through a combination of military might and shrewd political maneuvering. From this experience, the Romans discovered the uses of careful diplomacy.

A temporary setback to Rome's expansion occurred in 389 B.C.E., when a raiding band of Celts from the north of Italy defeated a Roman army and plundered the city of Rome. Only after a generation did Romans recover from this disaster and reassert their preeminence among their allies. Still, they had learned that tenacity and discipline enabled them to endure even a serious military defeat.

The next major step in Rome's expansion came in 338 B.C.E., when Roman troops suppressed a three-year revolt of its Latin allies, who had come to resent Rome's overlordship. The peace settlement of this **Latin War** set the precedent for Rome's future expansion: Rome gave defeated peoples either partial or full citizenship depending on the treaty it struck with each community. (See *Encounters and Transformations* in this chapter.) The conquered allies were permitted to retain their own customs and were not forced to pay tribute. Rome asked for only two things in return: loyalty and troops. All allied communities had to contribute soldiers to the Roman army in wartime. With the huge new pool of troops, Rome became the strongest power in Italy.

Latin War A war that the Latin peoples of Italy waged against the Roman Republic between 340 and 338 B.C.E.

In return for their military service and support of Rome, the newly incorporated citizens, especially wealthy landowners from the allied communities, received a share of the profits of war. They also received the guarantee of Roman protection from

RUINS OF ROMAN THEATER IN AOSTA, ITALY The Greek city of Aosta in southern Italy, which flourished during the Hellenistic period, fell to Rome in the third century B.C.E. Romans built theaters in many of the cities they conquered.

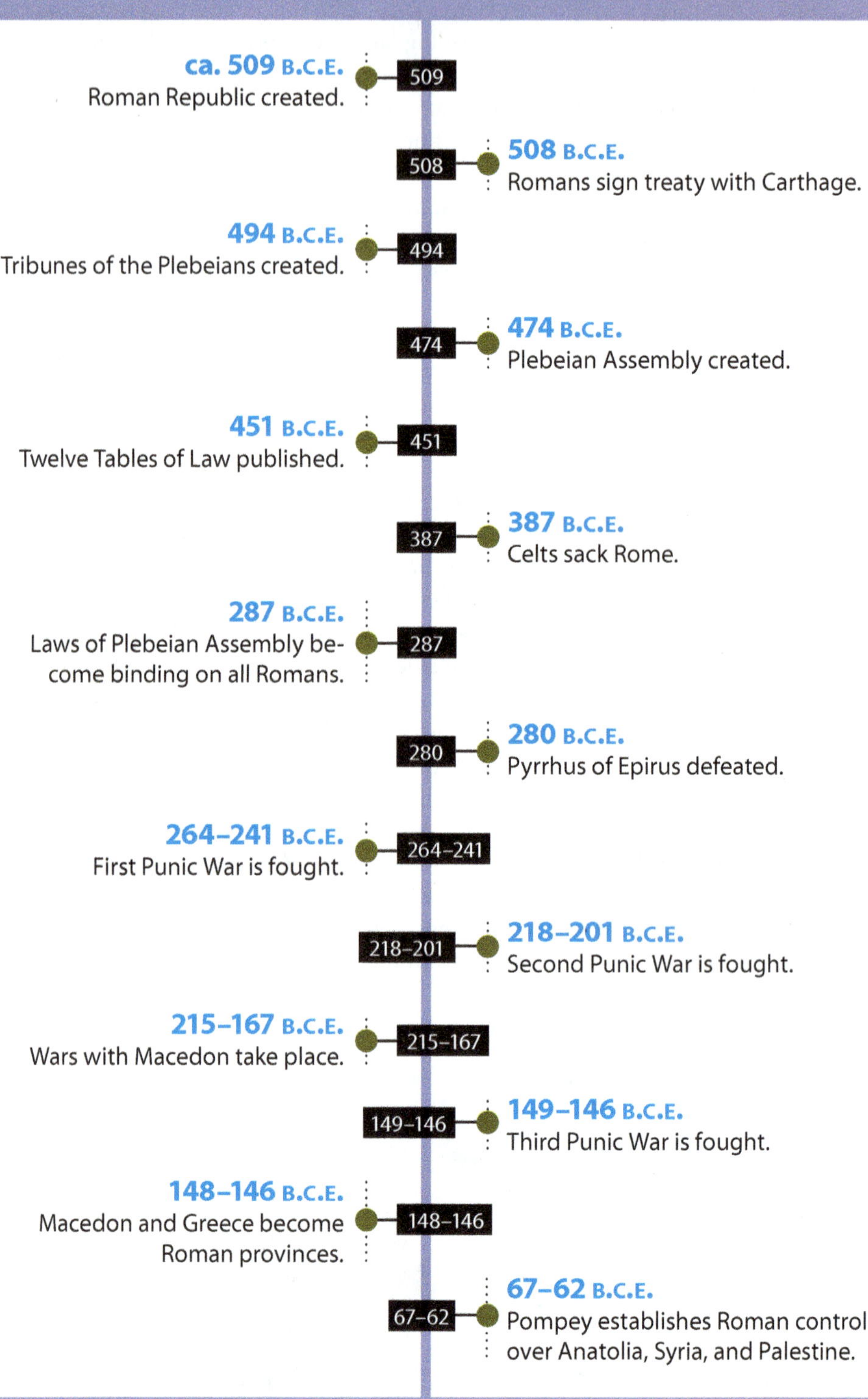

internal dissension or outside threats. Those communities not granted full Roman citizenship could hope to earn it if they served Roman interests faithfully. Some communities joined the Roman state willingly. Others, particularly the Samnites of south central Italy, resisted bitterly, but to no avail.

Romans then became embroiled in the affairs of Greek cities of the "toe" and "heel" of the boot-shaped Italian peninsula. Some of these Greek cities invited King

Pyrrhus of Epirus (r. 318–275 B.C.E.), a Hellenistic adventurer from the western Balkans, to wage war against Rome on their behalf. Pyrrhus invaded southern Italy with 25,000 men and 20 elephants. Though he defeated Roman armies in two great battles in 280 B.C.E., he lost nearly two-thirds of his own troops and withdrew from Italy. "Another victory like this and I'm finished for good!" he said to a comrade, giving rise to the expression "a Pyrrhic victory," which is a win so costly that it is ruinous. Without Pyrrhus's protection, the Greeks in southern Italy could not withstand Rome's legions, and by 263 B.C.E. Rome ruled all of Italy.

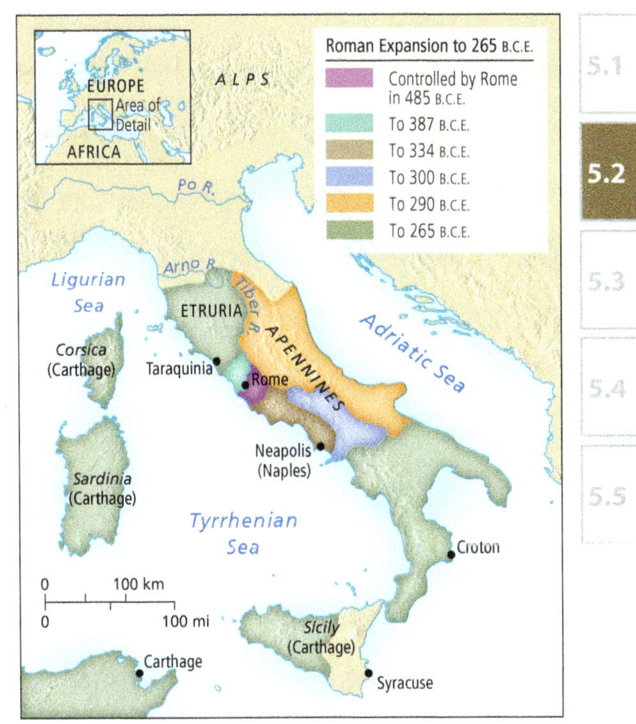

MAP **5.1** ROME'S EXPANSION IN ITALY Rome acquired control of Italy gradually over the course of more than 200 years. By 265 B.C.E. it had control of almost the entire Italian peninsula. How did Rome acquire these various lands?

The Struggle with Carthage

By the third century B.C.E., imperial Carthage dominated the western Mediterranean region. From the capital city of Carthage located on the North African coast near modern Tunis, Carthaginians held rich lands from modern Algeria to Morocco, controlled the natural resources of southern Spain, and dominated the sea lanes of the western Mediterranean. Phoenician traders had founded Carthage in the eighth century B.C.E., and the city's energetic merchants carried on business with Greeks, Etruscans, Celts, and eventually Romans.

Hellenistic culture influenced Carthage as it did other Mediterranean and Near Eastern cities. During the Classical Age, Carthaginian trade with the Greek cities in Sicily, and probably with Greek artisans in North Africa, introduced many aspects of Greek culture to Carthage. For example, Carthaginians worshiped the Greek goddess of agriculture, Demeter, and her daughter, Kore (also called Persephone), in an elegant temple. By the fourth century B.C.E. the Carthaginian Empire was playing an integral role in the economy of the Hellenistic world by exporting agricultural products, raw materials, metal goods, and pottery.

Rome and Carthage were old acquaintances. At the beginning of the Republic, the two had signed a commercial treaty. More than two centuries of wary respect and increasing trade followed. But in 264 B.C.E., just as Rome established power throughout the Italian peninsula, a war between Greek cities in Sicily drew Rome and Carthage into conflict. When a Carthaginian fleet went to help a Greek city in Sicily, another city, controlled by soldiers of Italian descent, asked Rome for assistance in dislodging the Carthaginians. The Senate refused, but the Plebeian Assembly, eager for the spoils of war, voted to intercede. Rome invaded Sicily, setting off the First Punic War, so called because the word *Punic* comes from the Latin word for *Phoenician.*

The First Punic War between Rome and Carthage for control of Sicily lasted from 264 to 241 B.C.E. During this time the Romans, who persisted in the conflict despite costly defeats, learned how to fight at sea, cutting off the Carthaginian supply lines to Sicily. In 241 B.C.E. Carthage signed a treaty in which it agreed to surrender Sicily and the surrounding islands and to pay a war indemnity over the course of a decade. Roman treachery, however, wrecked the agreement. While the Carthaginians struggled to suppress a revolt of mercenary soldiers, Rome seized Corsica and Sardinia, over which Carthage had lost effective control, and demanded larger reparations. Roman bad faith stoked Carthaginian desire for revenge.

War did not resume for another two decades. Under the able leadership of Hamilcar Barca (270–228 B.C.E.), Carthage developed resources in Spain, while Rome campaigned against Celts in north Italy and fierce tribes on the Adriatic coast. During these years trade between Rome and Carthage expanded. The growth of Carthaginian power in Spain, however, led to renewed conflict with Rome. The Second Punic War (218–201 B.C.E.)

erupted when Hamilcar's son, Hannibal (247–182 B.C.E.), 25 years old and eager for vengeance, ignored a Roman warning and captured Saguntum, a Spanish town with which Rome had formal ties of friendship. In a daring move, Hannibal then launched a surprise attack on Italy from the north by marching from Spain and crossing the Alps. With an army of nearly 25,000 men and 18 elephants, he crushed the Roman armies sent against him. In the first major battle, at the Trebia River in the Po Valley, 20,000 Romans died. At Lake Trasimene in Etruria in 217 B.C.E., another 25,000 Romans fell. In the same year at Cannae, Rome lost 50,000 men in its worst defeat ever.

Despite these staggering losses, the Romans persevered and eventually defeated the Carthaginian general. They succeeded, first of all, because Hannibal lacked sufficient logistical support from Carthage to capitalize on his early victories to besiege and take the city of Rome. Second, most of Rome's allies in Italy remained loyal. They had often seen Romans prevail in the past and knew that the Romans took fierce revenge on disloyal friends. Thus, the Roman policy of including and protecting allies

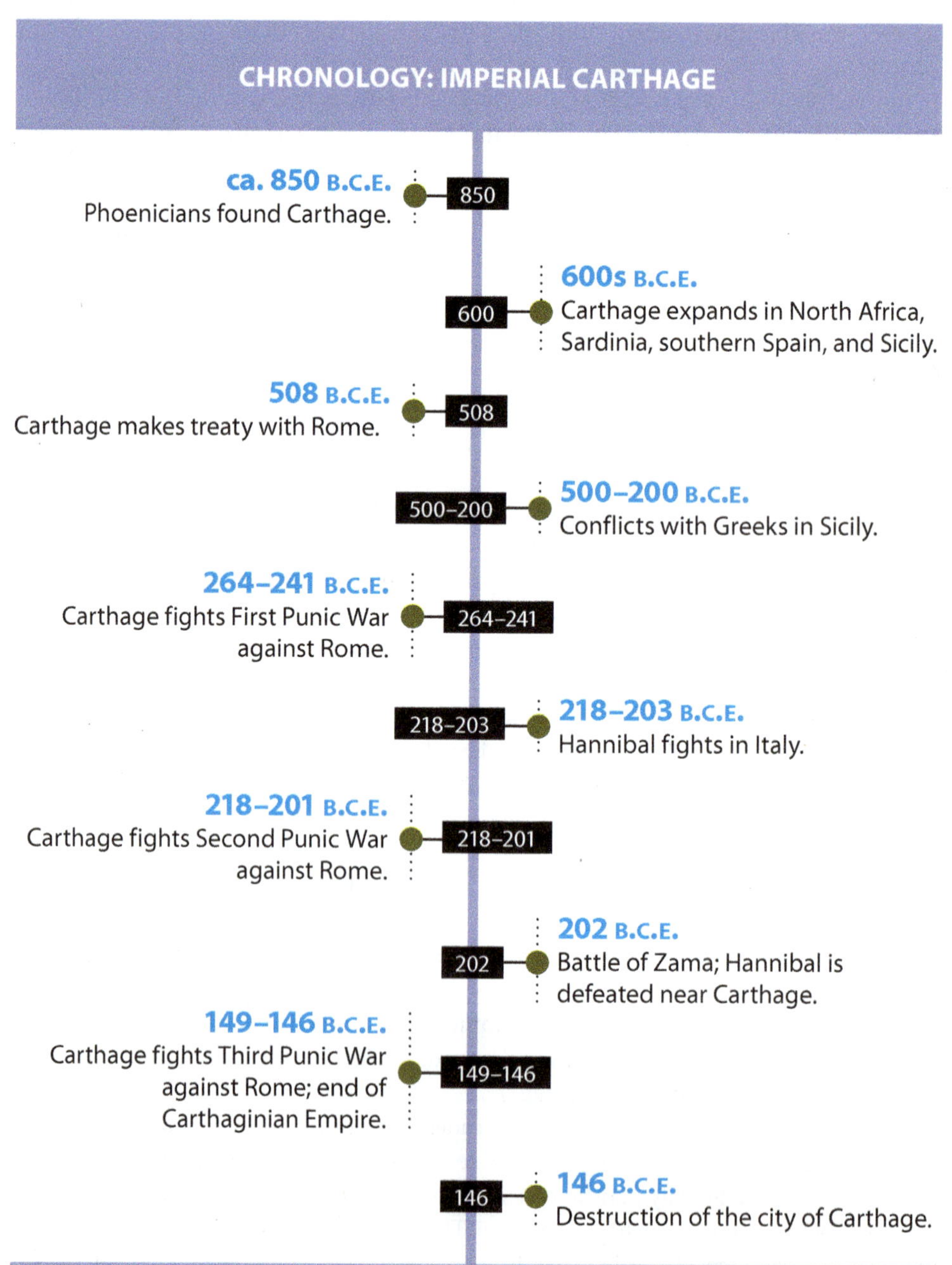

paid off. A third reason for Hannibal's defeat was the indomitable Roman spirit. Finally, no matter how many times they were defeated, the Romans simply refused to stop fighting.

The turning point in the war came when Roman commanders adopted a new strategy. After incurring so many defeats, the army dared not face Hannibal in open battle. Instead, Quintus Fabius Maximus (d. 202 B.C.E.), the Roman commander in Italy, avoided direct confrontation on the battlefield and used guerilla tactics to pin down Hannibal in Italy, thereby earning the nickname "the Delayer." At the same time Publius Cornelius Scipio, later called Africanus (237–187 B.C.E.), took command of the Roman forces in Spain. Within a few years he defeated the Carthaginian forces there, preventing reinforcements from reaching Hannibal. In 204 B.C.E., Scipio led Roman legions into Africa, forcing Carthage to recall Hannibal from Italy to protect the city.

At the Battle of Zama near Carthage in 202 B.C.E., fortune finally deserted Hannibal. Scipio triumphed, and Hannibal fled into exile. Hannibal had won every battle but his last. Though Scipio did not destroy Carthage, the city lost all of its overseas territories to Rome.

Because the battles against Hannibal had been so costly, many vengeful Romans wanted the total destruction of Carthage. In particular, the statesman Marcus Porcius Cato (234–149 B.C.E.), who ended every public utterance with the demand "Carthage must be destroyed!", goaded Romans to resume war with their old adversary. The Third Punic War (149–146 B.C.E.) resulted in the destruction of Carthage. Survivors were enslaved, and the city was burned to the ground. Its territories became the Roman provinces of Africa.

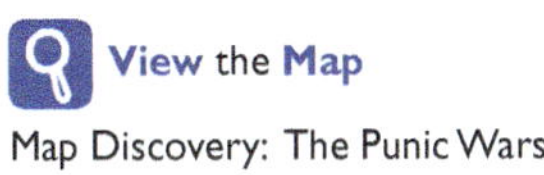

Map Discovery: The Punic Wars

Roman casualties in the struggle against Carthage resulted in a temporary change in the position of women in Roman society. Roman losses in the Battle of Cannae were so great that according to the historian Livy, "There was not one matron who was not bereaved." The inheritance of the slain soldiers' wealth by widows and children increased the fortunes of many Roman women, some of whom openly displayed their newfound wealth. In 215 B.C.E., to help pay the staggering cost of the war, the government passed the Oppian Law, which restricted the amount of gold that any single woman or widow could hold and forbade them to wear certain articles of clothing. In 195 B.C.E. a group of wealthier Roman women demonstrated in favor of repealing the Oppian Law. The women's participation in these demonstrations—the first of their kind in the West—marked the growing independence of women in the Republic.

The Macedonian Wars

By the end of the Punic Wars, Rome had also become involved in the affairs of the Hellenistic kingdoms of the East. Initially reluctant to take direct control of these regions, Roman leaders gradually assumed responsibility for maintaining order in the region and eventually established absolute control over the entire eastern Mediterranean region.

Rome waged three wars against Macedon between 215 and 167 B.C.E. that resulted in Rome's gaining mastery of Macedon and Greece. The First Macedonian War (215–205 B.C.E.) began when the Macedonian king, Philip V (r. 221–179 B.C.E.), made an alliance with Hannibal after the Roman defeat at the Battle of Cannae. The results of the conflict were inconclusive. Rome entered a second war with Macedon (201–196 B.C.E.) because Philip and the Seleucid king Antiochus III of Syria (r. 223–187 B.C.E.) had agreed to split the eastern Mediterranean between them. The poleis of Greece begged Rome for help, and Rome responded by ordering Philip to cease meddling in Greek affairs. Philip refused, and Roman forces easily defeated him with the support of Greek cities. In 196 B.C.E. the Roman general Titus Quinctius Flamininus declared the cities of Greece free and withdrew his forces.

MAP **5.2** ROMAN CONQUEST DURING THE REPUBLIC Armies of the Roman Republic conquered the Mediterranean world during the Hellenistic Age, overcoming the Carthaginian Empire, the Hellenistic successor kingdoms, and many Celtic peoples in Spain and Gaul. What was the key to Roman military success?

These cities were not truly free, however. Rome installed oligarchic governments, on whose support the Romans could rely. These unpopular regimes reflected the class distinctions of Rome itself. When Antiochus III sent an army to free Greece from Roman control, Rome defeated him in 189 B.C.E. Rome imposed heavy reparations but took no territory, preferring to protect the newly freed Greek cities of Anatolia and Greece from a distance.

Encounters and Transformations

Roman Citizenship

In the early Roman Republic, citizenship, as in classical Athens, was a privilege granted to relatively few men. Roman citizens had the full protection of the law and could vote and hold political office. All legitimate male children of Roman citizens acquired the status of their fathers at birth. Neither slaves nor women possessed the rights of citizenship, but freed slaves acquired a limited form of citizenship upon their emancipation, and the sons of freed slaves became citizens.

The nature of Roman citizenship changed as the result of Roman encounters with the inhabitants of the territories in Italy that Rome conquered and absorbed into the Roman state. At the end of the Latin War (340–338 B.C.E.) Rome granted a limited form of citizenship to the former members of the Latin League that had attempted to acquire independence from the Republic. These new citizens acquired rights of property and the right to migrate to a different city within the lands the Republic controlled, but they could not enter into a lawful marriage with full Roman citizens. This form of limited citizenship, known as Latin right, gradually became a legal category that was extended beyond former members of the Latin League.

Citizens of states that were allied with Rome, known as *socii*, could acquire certain legal rights of citizenship in exchange for military service. Dissatisfaction with such arrangements was one of the causes of the Social War of 91–88 B.C.E. During this war the Senate passed a law, known as *Lex Julia*, that granted citizenship to all Italian and *socii* states that were not involved in the war or who would be willing to cease hostilities. Thus, the offer of citizenship became a tool of Roman military and foreign policy. At the end of the war Rome extended full Roman citizenship to all *socii* and those possessing Latin Right.

The *Lex Julia* marked a significant step in establishing the principle that one acquired citizenship by birth in a territory or state. This *lex solis* (law of territory) eventually became the main basis for determining nationality and citizenship in the West, although it has often had to accommodate the *lex sanguinis* (law of blood), in which one acquires citizenship from a parent or other relative. Both principles, for example, have a role in determining citizenship in the United States today. The original form of Roman citizenship, as a privilege granted to certain individuals, continued to determine the status of "freemen" in European cities until the nineteenth century, but the basis of Western nationality that prevails today has deep roots in the Roman law of citizenship passed in the first century B.C.E.

For Discussion

1. How did military and diplomatic needs change the Roman law of citizenship?
2. To what extent does the definition of American citizenship today reflect the Roman inheritance?

Rome's policy of control from a distance changed after a third war with Macedon (172–167 B.C.E.), when a new Macedonian king tried to supplant Rome as protector of Greece. After a smashing victory, Rome divided Macedon into four separate republics and forbade marriage and trade among them. Roman troops ruthlessly stamped out all opposition, destroying 70 cities and selling 150,000 people into slavery. The same fate awaited the Achaean cities that turned against Rome, most notably Corinth, whose destruction at the hands of the Roman general Mummius was described at the beginning of this chapter.

The Culture of the Roman Republic

5.3 How did the Roman encounter with Greek culture lead to the forging of a durable cultural synthesis?

During five centuries of republican rule, Rome created a new cultural synthesis by mixing elements of its own culture with that of Greece. The resulting synthesis, which Rome later disseminated throughout its empire, became a major foundation of Western identity. Much of the Greek culture that Rome assimilated and modified originated in the Hellenistic period, and the main impetus of this cultural exchange was Roman territorial expansion within the Hellenistic world.

The Encounter Between Hellenistic and Roman Culture

Romans had interacted with Greek culture for centuries, first indirectly through Etruscan intermediaries, and then through direct contact with Greek communities in southern Italy and Sicily. During the second century B.C.E., when Rome acquired the eastern Mediterranean through its wars with Macedon and the Seleucids, Hellenism's intellectual influence on Rome accelerated. In addition to fine statues and paintings, Greek ideas about literature, art, philosophy, and rhetoric poured into Rome after the Macedonian wars.

This Hellenistic legacy challenged many Roman assumptions about the world. But there was a paradox in how Roman patricians reacted to Hellenism. Many noblemen in Rome felt threatened by the novelty of Hellenistic ideas. They preferred to maintain their conservative traditions of public life and thought. They wanted to preserve the image of a strong and independent Roman culture, untainted by foreign influences. Thus, during the second century B.C.E., Romans occasionally tried to expel Greek philosophers from Rome because they worried that Greek ideas might undermine traditional Roman values. Yet many Roman aristocrats also admired the sophistication of Greek political thought, art, and literature and wished to participate in the Hellenistic community.

Consequently many members of the Roman elite learned Greek, but refused to speak it while on official business in the East. While Latin remained the language spoken in the Senate house, senators hired Greek tutors to instruct their sons at home in philosophy, literature, history, and rhetoric, and Greek intellectuals found a warm welcome from Rome's upper class. Cato the Censor, the senator who had insisted that Rome destroy Carthage, embodied the paradox of maintaining public distance from Greek culture while privately cherishing it. He cultivated an appearance of forthrightness and honesty, traditional Roman values that he claimed were threatened by Greek culture. He publicly denounced Greek oratory as unmanly,

CIRCULAR TEMPLE This circular temple from the city of Rome near the Tiber River dates to the late second century B.C.E. It is the earliest surviving marble temple in Rome. The plan of the temple and the original marble of the columns and much of the rest of the building came from Greece.

while drawing upon his deep knowledge of Greek rhetoric and literature to write his speeches praising Roman culture.

Before their exposure to the Hellenistic world in the second century B.C.E., Romans had little interest in literature. Their writing consisted mainly of inscriptions of laws and treaties on bronze plaques hung from the outer walls of public buildings. Families kept records of the funeral eulogies of their ancestors, while priests maintained simple lists of events and religious festivals. By about 240 B.C.E., Livius Andronicus, a former Greek slave, began to translate Greek dramas into Latin. In 220 B.C.E., a Roman senator, Quintus Fabius Pictor, wrote a history of Rome in Greek—the first major Roman prose work.

Hellenistic culture also had a major impact on Roman drama. Two Roman playwrights, Plautus (ca. 250–184 B.C.E.) and Terence (ca. 190–159 B.C.E.), took their inspiration from Hellenistic New Comedy and injected humor and wit into Roman literature. Their surviving works, which were always set in the Greek world, offer entertaining glimpses into the pitfalls of everyday life while also reinforcing the patrician values of the rulers of Rome's vast new domains.

Art and Architecture

The massive infusion of Hellenistic art to Rome following the Macedonian wars inevitably affected public taste. The most prestigious works of art decorated public shrines and spaces throughout the city. Many others went to private collectors, including Gaius Verres, the corrupt governor of Sicily who plundered the artistic treasures of that province when he was governor between 73 and 71 B.C.E. (See *Justice in History* in this chapter.) Ironically Cicero, who prosecuted Verres, was himself an avid collector of Greek art. The mania for Greek art became so intense that Greek artists soon moved to Rome to enjoy the patronage of wealthy Romans.

In Rome these artists often produced copies of Greek originals. In many cases only these Roman copies have survived. If it had not been for the Greek artists in Rome, therefore, many treasures of Greek art would have been lost to posterity. The encounter between Greece and Rome was not, however, limited to the imitation of Greek works. In portrait sculpture, for example, a realistic style developed in Rome that unflinchingly depicted all the wrinkles of experience on a person's face. In this way the venerable Roman tradition of making ancestral masks merged with Greek art.

The development of Roman architecture during the Republic tells a similar story. The early Roman works of architecture were essentially copies of Greek originals, complete with the three orders of Doric, Ionic, and Corinthian capitals on the columns. The main contributions that Romans made to architecture were structural, as in the construction of arches, vaults, and domes, rather than in artistic design. In the first century B.C.E., however, the magnificent temple of Fortune at Praeneste, a town near Rome, combined Italian and Hellenistic concepts in a genuinely Greco-Roman style. By the end of the Republic, Romans had gained enough confidence to adopt the intellectual heritage of Greece and use it to serve their own ends without fear of seeming "too Greek."

Philosophy and Religion

Many educated Romans found Greek philosophy attractive. The theory of matter advanced by the Hellenistic philosopher Epicurus, whose ethical philosophy we discussed in Chapter 4, gained wide acceptance among Romans. Epicurus believed that everything has a natural cause: that "nothing comes from nothing." Romans learned about Epicurus's theories of matter and the infinity of the universe from the poem, *On the Nature of the Universe*, by the Roman poet Lucretius (d. ca. 51 B.C.E.), who wrote in Latin. The Hellenistic ethical philosophy that held the greatest appeal to Romans, however, was Stoicism, because it encouraged an active public life. Stoic emphasis on mastering human difficulties appealed to patrician Romans' sense of duty and dignity. Cicero, in particular, combined Stoic ideas in a personal yet fully Roman way. He stressed moral behavior in political life while urging the attainment of a broad education. Cicero's high-minded devotion to the Republic won him the enmity of unscrupulous politicians. He was murdered in 43 B.C.E. after making public speeches accusing Mark Antony of being a threat to republican freedom.

The encounter between Roman and Hellenistic religion provides a striking example of the Greco–Roman cultural synthesis. Contact with Greek civilization during the Hellenistic period led to the development of a closer correspondence between many Roman and Greek gods. Thus, the powerful Roman god Jupiter acquired many of the characteristics of the Greek god Zeus. The Roman god of war, Mars, resembled the Greek god Ares, and the Roman goddess of hunting, Diana, acquired many of the attributes of Artemis. But the mythical personalities and activities of Roman gods were never the same as those of their Greek counterparts. Jupiter, for example, was not as sexually voracious as Zeus, while the Roman goddess Venus combined many of the features of the Greek goddess Aphrodite with those of the Etruscan deity Turan. All in all, Roman gods were much better behaved and more dignified than the group that Homer bequeathed to the Greeks.

Romans also recognized the local gods of the territories they conquered and absorbed. A decision by the Roman Senate to import the image of the foreign nature

ROMAN AND GREEK COLUMNS The Theater of Marcellus in Rome, completed in the late first century B.C.E., used columns with Doric, Ionic, and Corinthian capitals modeled on those in Greek architecture. Three of these columns with Corinthian capitals are shown to the left. Doric capitals, modeled on those of the Greek Parthenon, shown to the right, were often used in Roman architecture. In the classical revival of the eighteenth century C.E., the Doric order connoted seriousness of purpose, and in the United States it symbolized republican virtue.

goddess Cybele to Rome in 204 B.C.E. illustrates the ease with which Rome acquired new deities. The cult of Cybele, known as the Great Mother, flourished in the Hellenistic kingdom of Pergamum, where devotees worshiped her in the form of an ancient and holy rock. During the war with Hannibal, the Senate imported the rock to Rome to inspire and unify the city. A committee of leading citizens brought the sacred boulder to a new temple on the Palatine Hill amid wild rejoicing. When the ship carrying the rock got stuck in the Tiber River, legend has it that a noble lady, Claudia Quinta, towed the ship with her sash. Not only did Rome defeat Hannibal soon after the arrival of Cybele's sacred stone, but the move cemented Roman relations with Pergamum.

STATUE OF CYBELE, THE GREAT MOTHER Romans worshiped the Great Mother (*Magna Mater*) after her cult was introduced in Rome during the Second Punic War against Hannibal. People had worshiped this goddess throughout the eastern Mediterranean since remote antiquity. This statue represents her majestic power.

The recognition of imported gods resulted in a proliferation of Roman deities. In 27 B.C.E. the government constructed a new temple, the Pantheon (literally a "temple of all the gods"), to honor the hundreds of gods that the people recognized. With so many different gods, the Republic developed a policy of tolerating a wide variety of religious practices. This leniency, however, had its limits. The governing class viewed with suspicion any religious practice that was not conducted publicly, threatened public order, or challenged conventional standards of morality. In 186 B.C.E. the consuls received reports that a new cult of the god Dionysos, whom the Romans called Bacchus, had spread from Erturia to Rome, conducting nocturnal orgies. The members of this cult were allegedly engaging in "the promiscuous intercourse of free-born men and women" and "debaucheries of every kind." They also were accused of "poison and secret murders" that went undetected because the "loud shouting and the noise of drums and cymbals" drowned out the cries of the victims. The government responded to these reports, which were almost certainly exaggerated, by demanding the arrest of the participants, declaring that no religious ceremonies should take place in private, and forbidding such assemblies in the future.

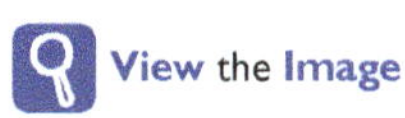

View the Image

The Interior of the Dome of the Pantheon, Rome

Rhetoric

The Roman passion for oratory, exemplified in the speeches of Cicero, also reflected the Roman adoption of a Greek tradition. As we saw in Chapter 3, Athenians developed the art of oratory to a high level. Romans had great admiration for this Greek tradition and imitated Athenian oratorical style. To some extent, Romans suffered from an inferiority complex regarding their oratorical skills. The great Roman rhetorician Quintilian (35–100 C.E.) admitted that Roman orators could never be as elegant or as subtle as the Greeks, but he argued that they could be "blunter" and "weightier." By emphasizing the power of persuasive speech, employed mainly in politics and law, Romans developed a style of oratory that was more effective, if not as sophisticated, as that of Greece.

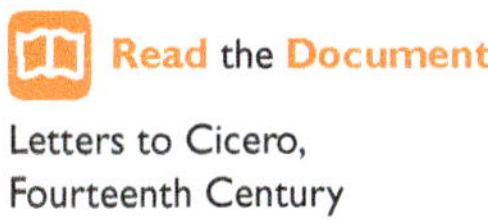

Read the Document

Letters to Cicero, Fourteenth Century

As in many other areas of culture, the Roman achievement in oratory proved to be more durable than that of the Greeks, mainly because Romans developed a tradition of rhetorical instruction that had a lasting influence on Western education. Learning how to give classical orations became a skill once again during the Renaissance of the

TABLE **5.1** ROMAN GODS AND THEIR GREEK COUNTERPARTS

Roman God	Greek God	Association
Apollo	Apollo	the sun, prophecy, medicine
Bacchus	Dionysos	wine, agriculture, festivity
Ceres	Demeter	plants, maternal love
Diana	Artemis	hunting, the moon, fertility
Jupiter	Zeus	light, the sky
Juno	Hera	women
Mars	Ares	war
Mercury	Hermes	trade
Minerva	Athena	wisdom
Neptune	Poseidon	the sea
Victoria	Nike	Victory
Pan	Pan	herds, forests
Proserpina	Persephone or Kore	Fertility
Pluto	Hades	the underworld and the dead
Venus	Aphrodite	love, sex, beauty

fifteenth and sixteenth centuries, especially in Italy, which revived the Greco–Roman culture that had flourished in the Roman Republic. Educators in Renaissance Europe, as in ancient Rome, placed a premium on one's ability to inspire citizens to political or military action. Rhetoric, the art of persuasion, became more important, at least for members of the educated elite, than the attainment of philosophical wisdom. Thus, the knowledge of and training in rhetoric became one of the cultural legacies that the Roman Republic bequeathed to the West.

Social Life in Republican Rome

5.4 How was Roman society structured, and what relationships existed within the Roman family?

Under the Republic a few influential families dominated political life, sometimes making decisions about war and peace from which they could win wealth and prestige. The Roman Republic remained strong because these ruling families took pains to limit the power any one man or extended political family could attain.

Patrons and Clients

The ruling families of Rome established political networks that extended their influence throughout Roman society. These relationships depended on the traditional Roman institution of **patrons and clients**. By exercising influence on behalf of a social subordinate, a powerful man (the patron) would bind that man (the client) to him in anticipation of gaining future support. In this way complex webs of personal interdependency influenced the entire Roman social system. The patron-client system operated at every level of society. It was customary for a man of influence to receive his clients at his home the first thing in the morning. In a modest household the discussion between patron and client might involve everyday business such as shipping fish, arranging a marriage, or making a loan. But in the mansion of a Roman patrician a patron might be more interested in forging a political alliance. When several patron-client groups joined forces, they became significant political factions under the leadership of one powerful patron.

patrons and clients In ancient Roman society, a system in which a powerful man (the patron) would exercise influence on behalf of a social subordinate (the client) in anticipation of future support or assistance.

Pyramids of Wealth and Power

Like its political organization, Rome's social organization demonstrated a well-defined hierarchy. By the first century B.C.E. a new, elite class of political leaders had emerged in Rome, composed of both the original patrician families and wealthy plebeians who had attained membership in the Senate through their service in various public offices. The men of this leadership class dominated the Senate and formed the inner circle of government. From their ranks came most of the consuls. They set foreign and domestic policy, led armies to war, held the main magistracies, and siphoned off the lion's share of the Republic's resources.

Beneath this elite group came the equestrian class. Equestrians normally abstained from public office but were often tied to political leaders by personal obligation. They were primarily well-to-do businessmen who prospered from the financial opportunities that Rome's territorial expansion provided. For example, during the Republic, equestrian businessmen could bid on contracts to collect taxes from the provinces. The man awarded such a contract had few restraints on the methods by which he raised the revenue. After paying the treasury the amount agreed upon in the contract, he could keep any surplus as profit. Many equestrians accumulated fortunes in this way.

Next in rank came the large body of citizens who were known as plebeians. As we have seen, this group had acquired political representation and influence, but the Plebeian Assembly had gradually come under the control of politicians who were the clients of patrician patrons. These wealthy plebeian politicians, who had become members of a new ruling elite, had little interest in the condition of other plebeians, who now had no direct means to express their political will. Army service kept many plebeians who had small farms away from their land for long periods of time. Consequently, many plebeian farmers went bankrupt. Rich investors seized this opportunity to create huge estates by grabbing the bankrupt farms and replacing the free farmers with slaves. Sometimes impoverished plebeians became dependent tenant farmers on land they had once owned themselves. As a result, these plebeians increasingly turned to leaders who promised to protect them and give them land.

Rome's Italian allies had even fewer rights than the plebeians, despite their service in the Roman armies. Although millions of allies inhabited lands controlled by Rome, only a privileged few of the local elites received Roman citizenship. The rest could only hope for the goodwill of Roman officials.

At the bottom of the Roman hierarchy were slaves. By the first century B.C.E., about two million slaves captured in war or born in captivity lived in Italy and Sicily, amounting to about one-third of the population. Like Greeks, Romans considered slaves to be pieces of property, "talking tools," whom their owners could exploit at will. Freed slaves owed legal obligations to their former masters and were their clients. The brutal inequities of this system led to violence. The slave gangs who farmed vast estates in Sicily revolted first. In 135 B.C.E. they began an ill-fated struggle for freedom that lasted three years and involved more than 200,000 slaves.

Slaves in the Roman Countryside, ca. 150 B.C.E.–50 C.E.

Thirty years later another unsuccessful outburst began in southern Italy and Sicily because slave owners refused to comply with a senatorial decree to release any slaves who once had been free allies of Rome. During this outburst, 30,000 slaves took up arms between 104 and 101 B.C.E. The most destructive revolt occurred in Italy from 73 to 71 B.C.E. An army of more than 100,000 slaves led by the Thracian gladiator Spartacus (gladiators were slaves who fought for public entertainment) battled eight Roman legions, totaling about 50,000 men, before being crushed by the superior Roman military organization.

The Roman Family

A Roman *familia* typically included not just the husband, wife, and unmarried children, but also their slaves and often freedmen and others who were dependent on the household. Legitimate marriages required the agreement of both husband and wife. Women usually married at puberty, as had been the practice in classical Athens, and men did so in their twenties. In most families only two or three children survived infancy. It was fairly common and socially acceptable for men to live with unmarried women (concubines) before they were married or after their wives had died, but not while they were married. Married men seeking extramarital sex generally turned to their slaves or engaged the services of prostitutes, a practice that was legal in republican Rome.

The Roman family mirrored the patterns of authority and dependency found in the political arena. Just as a patron commanded the support of his clients regardless of their status in public life, so the male head of the household directed the destiny of all his subordinates within the *familia.* A man ruled his *familia* with full authority over the purse strings and all of his descendants until he died. The head of the family, the *paterfamilias,* theoretically held power of life and death over his wife, children, and slaves, though few men exercised such power. In practice, women and grown children often enjoyed considerable independence, and patrician women often influenced political life, though always from behind the scenes.

Upper-class Romans placed great value on the continuity of the family name, family traditions, and control of family property through the generations. For these reasons they often adopted males, even of adult age, to be heirs, especially if they had no legitimate sons of their own. Legitimate offspring always took the name of their father, and in case of divorce, which could be easily obtained, continued to live with him. Illegitimate offspring stayed with their mother.

With few exceptions Roman women remained legally dependent on a male relative. In the most common form of marriage, a wife remained under the formal control of the *paterfamilias* to whom she belonged before her marriage—in most cases, her father. In practice this meant that she retained control of her own property and the inheritance she had received from her father. A husband in this sort of marriage would have to be careful to avoid angering his wife's father or brothers, and so he might treat his wife more justly. Another, older form of marriage brought the wife under the full control of her husband after the wedding. She had to worship the family gods of her husband's household and accept his ancestors as her own. If her husband died, one of his male relatives became her legal protector.

Slaves could not achieve the stability of family life through the generations that free Romans desired. Former female slaves (freedwomen) remained tied to their former masters with bonds of dependency and obligation. Roman law did not recognize marriage between slaves. Some Roman handbooks, explaining how to use slaves to maximum advantage, advocated letting slaves establish conjugal arrangements. Owners could, however, shatter such unions by selling either of the enslaved partners or their offspring.

The End of the Roman Republic

5.5 Why did the Roman Republic end?

The inequalities of wealth and power in Roman society eventually destroyed the Republic. The rapid acquisition of territories and the enormous wealth that the Roman elite accumulated from overseas conquest heightened those differences. Those who profited the most from imperial rule—politicians, governors, generals, and businessmen—fiercely resisted reformers' efforts to achieve a more equitable distribution of resources. The ruling elite sought personal glory and political advantage even if it came at the Republic's expense. Their quest for political prominence through military adventure, coupled with flaws in Rome's political institutions, eventually overwhelmed the republican constitution and brought about a revolution—a decisive, fundamental change in the political system.

The Gracchi

During the second century B.C.E., more and more citizen farmers in Italy lost their farms to powerful landholders, who replaced them with gangs of slaves. Some members of the political elite feared the danger inherent in these developments. If citizen farmers could no longer meet the property requirements for military service and pay for their own weapons, as they were required to do, Rome would lose its supply of recruits for its legions.

Two young brothers, Tiberius and Gaius Gracchus, attempted reforms. Although their mother was a patrician (the daughter of Scipio Africanus), she had married a wealthy plebeian. Thus, the brothers were legally plebeian, and they sought influence through the tribunate, an office limited to plebeians. As a tribune, Tiberius Gracchus (162–133 B.C.E.) convinced the Plebeian Assembly to pass a bill limiting the amount of public land that one man could possess. Excess land from wealthy landholders was to be redistributed in small lots to poor citizens. While the land redistribution was in progress, conservative senators ignited a firestorm of opposition to Tiberius Gracchus. He responded by running for a second term as a tribune, which was a break with precedent. Fearing revolution, a clique of senators in 133 B.C.E. clubbed Tiberius to death. Land redistribution did not cease, but a terrible precedent of public violence had been set.

A decade later, when Tiberius's brother Gaius Gracchus became a tribune in 123 B.C.E., he turned his attention to the problem of extortion in the provinces. With no checks on their authority, many corrupt governors who came from the ranks of the Senate forced provincials to give them money, valuable goods, and crops. Gaius Gracchus attempted to stop these abuses. To dilute the power of these corrupt provincial administrators and to win the political support of equestrians in Rome, he permitted equestrian tax collectors to operate in the provinces and to serve on juries that tried extortion cases. Gaius also tried to speed up land redistribution. But when he attempted to give citizenship to Rome's Italian allies to prevent Romans from confiscating their land, he lost the support of the Roman people, who did not wish to share the benefits of citizenship with non-Romans. In 121 B.C.E. Gaius committed suicide rather than allow himself to be murdered by a mob sent by his brother's senatorial foes.

The ruthless suppression of the Gracchus brothers and their supporters lit the fuse of political and social revolution in Rome. By attempting to effect change through the Plebeian Assembly, the Gracchus brothers unwittingly paved the way for less scrupulous politicians to seek power by falsely claiming to represent the interests of the poor. Their violent deaths signaled the end of political consensus among the oligarchy. Rivalry among the elite combined with the desperation of the poor was an explosive blend, with the army as the potentially decisive factor. If an unscrupulous politician were to join forces with poverty-stricken soldiers, the Republic would be in peril.

Gaius Marius (157–86 B.C.E.) became the first Roman general to use the army for political ends. He rose to power when the angry Roman poor made him their champion. Despite his equestrian origins, this experienced general won the consulship in 107 B.C.E. A special law of the Plebeian Assembly put him in command of the legions fighting King Jugurtha of Numidia in North Africa; and he brought the war to a quick and successful conclusion. Then he crushed Germanic tribes seeking to invade Italy.

In organizing his armies Marius made radical changes. He eliminated the property requirement for enlistment, thereby opening the ranks to the poorest citizens in the countryside and in Rome. These soldiers swore an oath of loyalty to their commander in chief, who in return promised them farms after a victorious campaign. Marius's reforms put generals in the middle of the long-running political struggle between the Senate and the Plebeian Assembly, the two institutions authorized to allocate lands won in war.

Marius achieved great personal power, but he did not use it against the institutions of the Republic. When he left Italy because of his unpopularity among the elite, the Roman Republic lurched ahead to its next major crisis: a revolt of the Italian allies.

War in Italy and Abroad

Social War The revolt of Rome's allies against the Republic in 90 B.C.E., in which they demanded full Roman citizenship.

In 90 B.C.E. Rome's loyal allies in Italy could no longer endure being treated as inferiors when it came to distribution of land and booty. They launched a revolt against Rome known as the **Social War** (from the Latin word *socii,* which means "allies"). The confederation of allies demanded not independence but participation in the Roman Republic. They wanted full citizenship rights because they had been partners in Rome's wars and thus felt entitled to share in the fruits of victory. The allies lost the war, but soon afterward Rome granted citizenship to all Italians. These new citizens tilted the political scales away from the wealthy in Rome toward the population of Italy in general.

The Social War in Italy was followed by wars abroad. The patrician Lucius Cornelius Sulla (138–78 B.C.E.), consul in 88 B.C.E., was setting out with an army to put down a serious provincial revolt in Anatolia when the Plebeian Assembly turned command of his troops over to Marius, whose military reforms had aided the poor. In response, Sulla marched from southern Italy to Rome and placed his own supporters in positions of authority in the Senate, the Plebeian Assembly, and the magistracies.

Only a year later, however, while Sulla was still in Anatolia, Marius and the other consul, Cinna, won back political control of Rome. They declared Sulla an outlaw and killed many of his supporters in what became known as the Marian massacres. When Sulla returned to Italy in 82 B.C.E., at the head of a triumphant and loyal army, he seized Rome after a battle in which about 60,000 Roman soldiers died. He then murdered

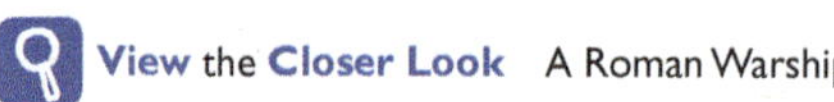
View the Closer Look A Roman Warship

A ROMAN WARSHIP This relief depicts a Roman battleship. Rome became a naval power later in its history when it defeated Carthage and went on to rule the Mediterranean.

Different Voices

The Catiline Conspiracy

In 63 B.C.E. Lucius Sergius Catilina, known in English as Catiline, staged a conspiracy to bring down the government of the Roman Republic. Catiline was a member of a patrician family whose fortunes had declined. He had a distinguished military career, but the Senate dismissed him on trumped up charges of debauchery in 71 B.C.E. The conspiracy originated after he failed to become consul once again in 64 B.C.E. The conspirators planned to murder a large number of senators and assassinate Cicero, who was serving as consul that year. That plot failed. Catiline was killed in a battle with republican forces, and four co-conspirators were executed.

The account of the conspiracy by the Roman historian Sallust (ca. 86–35 B.C.E.) involves an analysis of the social and moral decline that proved fertile ground for Catiline in plotting to overthrow the government. Cicero was more concerned with exposing Catiline's bad character. In his first oration denouncing Catiline, Cicero attacked the man for his perfidy.

A Roman Historian's Analysis of the Catiline Conspiracy

At this period the empire of Rome appears to me to have been in an extremely deplorable condition; for though every nation, from the rising to the setting of the sun, lay in subjection to her arms, and though peace and prosperity, which mankind think the greatest blessings, were hers in abundance, there yet were found, among her citizens, men who were bent, with obstinate determination, to plunge themselves and their country into ruin; for, notwithstanding the two decrees of the senate, not one individual, out of so vast a number was induced by the offer of reward to give information of the conspiracy; nor was there a single deserter from the camp of Catiline. So strong a spirit of disaffection had, like a pestilence, pervaded the minds of most of the citizens.

Nor was this disaffected spirit confined to those who were actually concerned in the conspiracy; for the whole of the common people, from a desire of change, favored the projects of Catiline. This they seemed to do in accordance with their general character; for, in every state, they that are poor envy those of a better class, and endeavor to exalt the factious; they dislike the established condition of things, and long for something new; they are discontented with their own circumstances, and desire a general alteration; they can support themselves amidst revolt and sedition, without anxiety, since poverty does not easily suffer loss.

As for the populace of the city, they had become disaffected from various causes. In the first place, such as everywhere took the lead in crime and profligacy, with others who had squandered their fortunes in dissipation, and, in a word, all whom vice and villainy had driven from their homes, had flocked to Rome as a general receptacle of impurity. In the next place, many, who thought of the success of Sulla, when they had seen some raised from common soldiers into senators, and others so enriched as to live in regal luxury and pomp, hoped, each for himself, similar results from victory, if they should once take up arms. In addition to this, the youth, who, in the country, had earned a scanty livelihood by manual labor, tempted by public and private largesses, had preferred idleness in the city to unwelcome toil in the field. To these and all others of similar character, public disorders would furnish subsistence. It is not at all surprising, therefore, that men in distress, of dissolute principles and extravagant expectations, should have consulted the interest of the state no further than as it was subservient to their own. Besides, those whose parents, by the victory of Sulla, had been proscribed, whose property had been

(continued on next page)

CICERO ATTACKS CATILINE In this nineteenth-century representation of a session of the Roman Senate, Cicero gives one of his orations against Catiline, who is sitting alone to the right. From a fresco in Palazzo Madama, Rome, house of the Italian Senate.

SOURCE: Gaius Sallustius Crispus, *Conspiracy of Catiline*, Translated by J. S. Watson. New York: Harper & Brothers, 1867.

(continued from previous page)

confiscated, and whose civil rights had been curtailed, looked forward to the event of a war with precisely the same feelings.

All those, too, who were of any party opposed to that of the senate, were desirous rather that the state should be embroiled, than that they themselves should be out of power. This was an evil, which, after many years, had returned upon the community to the extent to which it now prevailed.

Cicero, First Oration Against Catiline

When, O Catiline, do you mean to cease abusing our patience? How long is that madness of yours still to mock us? When is there to be an end of that unbridled audacity of yours, swaggering about as it does now? Do not the nightly guards placed on the Palatine Hill—do not the watches posted throughout the city—does not the alarm of the people, and the union of all good men—does not the precaution taken of assembling the senate in this most defensible place—do not the looks and countenances of this venerable body here present, have any effect upon you? Do you not feel that your plans are detected? Do you not see that your conspiracy is already arrested and rendered powerless by the knowledge which every one here possesses of it? What is there that you did last night, what the night before—where is it that you were—who was there that you summoned to meet you—what design was there which was adopted by you, with which you think that any one of us is unacquainted?

Shame on the age and on its principles! The senate is aware of these things; the consul sees them; and yet this man lives. Lives! aye, he comes even into the senate. He takes a part in the public deliberations; he is watching and marking down and checking off for slaughter every individual among us. And we, gallant men that we are, think that we are doing our duty to the Republic if we keep out of the way of his frenzied attacks.

You ought, O Catiline, long ago to have been led to execution by command of the consul. That destruction which you have been long plotting against us ought to have already fallen on your own head.

SOURCE: *The World's Famous Orations*, 1906.

For Discussion

1. On what grounds did Sallust and Cicero condemn Catiline's conspiracy?
2. If Catiline had the support of the various groups of Romans that Sallust identified, why did his conspiracy fail?

3,000 of his political opponents. The Senate named Sulla dictator in 81 B.C.E., thereby giving him complete power. With the support of the Senate, whose authority he hoped to restore, Sulla restricted the power of tribunes to propose legislation because they had caused so much political instability for 50 years. After restoring the peace and the institutions of the state, and after becoming consul in 80 B.C.E, Sulla surprised many people by resigning the following year. Like Marius, Sulla was unwilling to destroy the Republic's institutions for the sake of his own ambition. It was enough for him to have restored peace and the preeminence of the Senate. Nevertheless, he had set a precedent for using armies in political rivalries. In the next 50 years the Senate conspicuously failed to restrain generals backed by their armies, thereby contributing to the collapse of the Republic.

The First Triumvirate

Three men provoked the Roman Republic's final downward spiral: Pompey (Gnaeus Pompeius, 106–48 B.C.E.), Marcus Licinius Crassus (ca. 115–53 B.C.E.), and Gaius Julius Caesar (100–44 B.C.E.). Pompey, the general who suppressed a revolt in Spain, and Crassus, the wealthiest man in Rome who had been one of Sulla's lieutenants, joined forces to crush the slave revolt of Spartacus in 71 B.C.E. Backed by their armies, they then became consuls for 70 B.C.E., even though Pompey was legally too young and had not yet held the prerequisite junior offices.

During their consulships, Pompey and Crassus made modest changes to Sulla's reforms. They permitted the tribunes to propose laws again and let equestrians serve on juries. After their year in office they retired without making further demands. Pompey continued his military career. In 67 B.C.E. he received a special command to clear pirates from the Mediterranean to protect Roman trade. The following year Pompey crushed the ongoing rebellion in Anatolia and reorganized the Near East, creating new provinces and more client kingdoms subservient to Rome.

When Pompey returned to Rome, he asked the Senate to grant land to his victorious troops. The Senate, jealous of his success and afraid of the power he would gain as the patron of so many veteran troops, refused. To gain land for his soldiers and have his political arrangements in the Near East ratified, Pompey made an alliance with two men even more ambitious than he: his old ally Crassus and Gaius Julius Caesar, the ambitious descendant of an ancient but poor patrician family. The three formed an informal alliance known as the **First Triumvirate**. No man or institution could oppose their combined influence. Caesar obtained the consulship in 59 B.C.E., despite the objections of many senators. By using illegal means that would return to haunt him, he directed the Senate to ratify Pompey's arrangements in the Near East and grant land to his troops. He resolved the financial problems of Crassus's clients, the equestrian tax collectors, at public expense.

First Triumvirate The informal political alliance made by Julius Caesar, Pompey, and Crassus in 60 B.C.E. to share power in the Roman Republic. It led directly to the collapse of the Republic.

As a reward for his efforts, the perpetually debt-ridden Caesar arranged to receive the governorship of the Po Valley and Illyricum for five years after his consulship

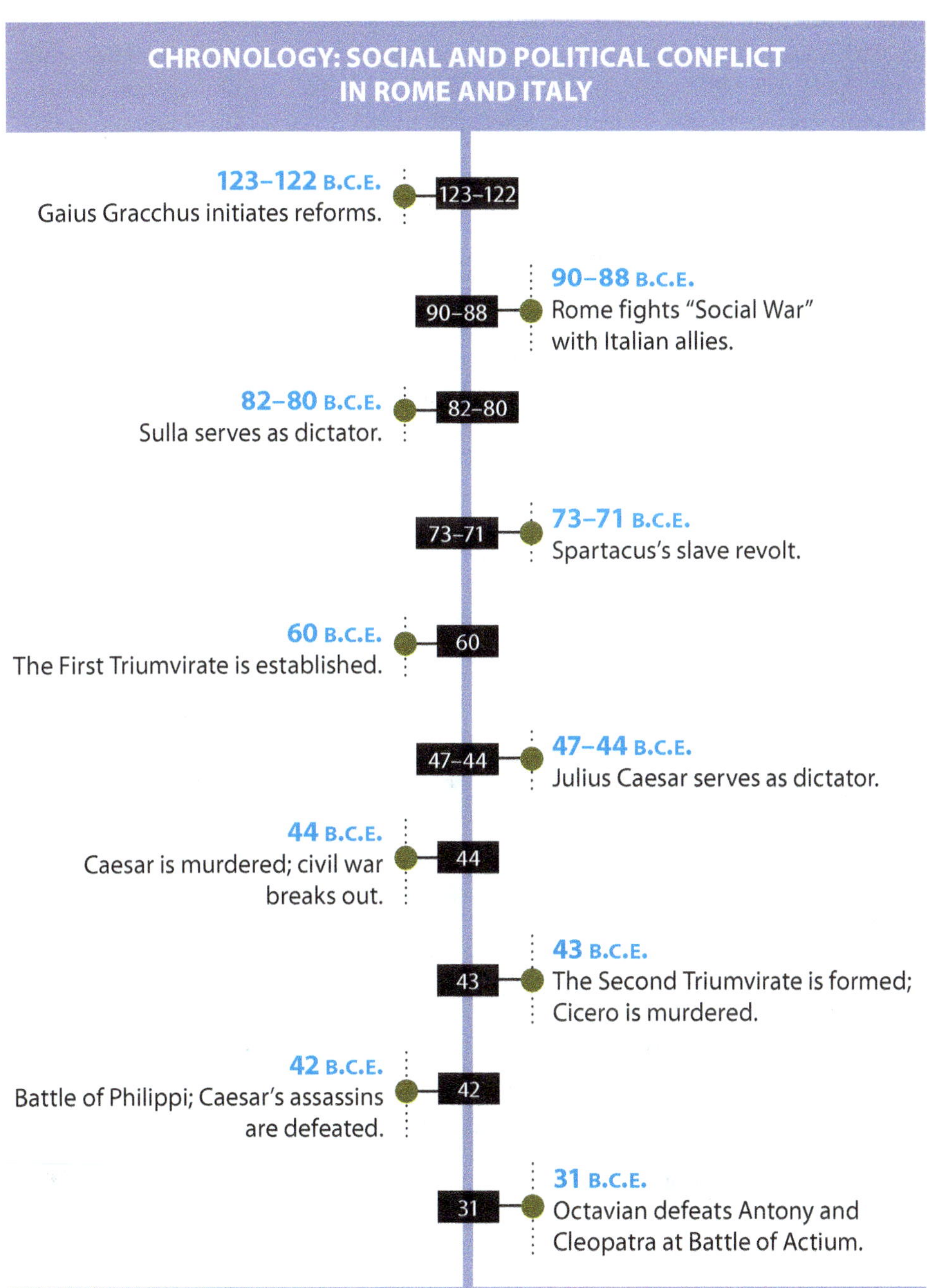

ended. Later he extended that term for 10 years. During this time, he planned to enrich himself at the expense of the provincials. As he set out for his governorship, however, he was given command of Transalpine Gaul (northwest of the Alps), where the German chieftain Ariovistus threatened Roman security. This change enabled Caesar to operate militarily in all of Gaul—and ultimately to conquer it.

Julius Caesar and the End of the Republic

Caesar's determination to conquer Gaul lay in his pursuit of personal political power. He knew that he could win glory, wealth, and prestige in Rome by conquering new lands, and to that end he promptly began a war (58–50 B.C.E.) against the Celtic tribes of Transalpine Gaul. A military genius, Caesar chronicled his ruthless tactics and victories in his *Commentaries on the Gallic War,* as famous today for its vigorous Latin as for its unflinching glimpse of Roman conquest, which resulted in the death or enslavement of about one million Celts. In eight years Caesar conquered the area of modern France, Belgium, and the Rhineland, turning these territories into Roman provinces. He even briefly invaded Britain. His intrusion into Celtic lands led to their eventual Romanization. The French language developed from the Latin spoken by Roman conquerors, as did the other "Romance" languages: Spanish, Italian, Portuguese, and Romanian.

Meanwhile, the other members of the triumvirate, Crassus and Pompey, also sought military glory. The wealthy Crassus failed to conquer the Parthians, the successors to the Persian Empire. In 53 B.C.E. the Parthians destroyed Crassus's army in Syria, killing Crassus himself and capturing the military insignia (metal eagles on staffs, called standards) that each legion proudly carried into battle. Pompey assumed the governorship of Spain, but stayed in Rome while subordinates fought Spain's Celtic inhabitants.

In Rome, a group of senators grew fearful of Caesar's power, ambitions, and arrogance. They appealed to Pompey for assistance, and he brought the armies loyal to him to the aid of the Senate against Caesar. The Senate then asked Caesar to lay down his command in Gaul and return to Rome. Caesar knew that if he complied with this request he would be indicted on charges of improper conduct or corruption as soon as he returned to Rome. Facing certain conviction, he refused to return for a trial. In

VERCINGETORIX SURRENDERS TO CAESAR The Gallic chieftain Vercingetorix, who raised an army of Gallic tribes against Roman legions under Julius Caesar's command, was trapped in the stronghold of Alesia, near modern Dijon, in 52 B.C.E. Reinforcements failed to break the siege, and Vercingetorix was forced to surrender. Five years later he was publicly beheaded. This scene of Vercingetorix throwing down his weapons was painted by L. Royer in 1899.

COIN FROM THE LATE ROMAN REPUBLIC The front of this silver coin depicts the god Janus (after whom the month of January is named), who looked in two directions. The reverse depicts a Roman galley.

49 B.C.E. he left Gaul and marched south with his loyal troops against the forces of the Senate in Rome. Recognizing the magnitude of his gamble ("The die is cast!" he said when he crossed the Rubicon River, the legal boundary between Gaul and the Roman territory under the direct control of the consuls), he deliberately plunged Rome into civil war. Because of his victories in Gaul and his generosity to the people of Rome, Caesar could pose as the people's champion while seeking absolute power for himself. Intimidated by Caesar's forces and public support, Pompey withdrew to Greece, but Caesar overtook and defeated him there at Pharsalus in 48 B.C.E. When Pompey fled to Egypt, high officials in the Ptolemaic court murdered him to win Caesar's favor.

It took Caesar more than two years to complete his victory over Pompey's supporters and return to Italy in 45 B.C.E. Back in Rome, Caesar had himself proclaimed dictator for life and assumed complete control over the government, flagrantly disregarding the traditions of the Republic. Because he did not live to fully implement his plan, Caesar's long-term goals for the Roman state remain unclear, but he probably intended to establish some version of Hellenistic monarchy.

View the Map

Map Discovery: Career of Julius Caesar

Once in power, Caesar permanently ended the autonomy of the Senate. He enlarged this body from 600 (its size at the time of Sulla) to 900 men, and then filled it with his supporters. He also established military colonies in Spain, North Africa, and Gaul to provide land for his veterans and to secure those territories. He adjusted the chaotic republican calendar by adding one day every fourth year, creating a year of 365.25 days. The resulting "Julian" calendar lasted in western Europe until the sixteenth century C.E. Caesar regularized gold coinage and urban administration and planned a vast public library. At his death, plans for a major campaign against Parthia were underway, suggesting that conquest would have remained a basic feature of his rule.

5.1

5.2

5.3

5.4

5.5

Caesar seriously miscalculated by assuming he could win over his enemies by showing them clemency and by making administrative changes that disregarded republican precedent. These changes earned Caesar the hatred of traditionalist senators who failed to recognize that the Republic was dead. On March 15, 44 B.C.E., a group of resentful and envious senators led by the idealistic Marcus Junius Brutus (85–42 B.C.E,) stabbed Caesar to death at a Senate meeting. The assassins claimed that they wanted to restore the Republic, but they had only unleashed another civil war.

Marcus Antonius (Mark Antony), who had been Caesar's right-hand man, stepped forward to oppose the conspirators. He was soon joined by Gaius Julius Caesar Octavianus (63 B.C.E.–14 C.E), Caesar's grandnephew and legal heir, who became known as Octavian. Though Octavian was only 19, he gained control of some of Caesar's legions and compelled the Senate to name him consul. Marcus Lepidus, commander of Caesar's cavalry, joined Mark Antony and Octavian to form the **Second Triumvirate** in 43 B.C.E. The new trio coerced the Senate into granting them power to rule Rome legally. By ruling without the active participation of the consuls and the Senate, the Second Triumvirate maintained Rome as a Republic in name only.

Second Triumvirate In 43 B.C.E. Octavian (later called Caesar Augustus), Mark Antony, and Lepidus made an informal alliance to share power in Rome while they jockeyed for control. Octavian emerged as the sole ruler of Rome in 31 B.C.E.

At the Battle of Philippi, a town in Macedonia, in 42 B.C.E., forces of the Second Triumvirate crushed the army of Brutus and the senators who had assassinated Caesar. But soon Antony, Octavian, and Lepidus began to struggle among themselves for absolute authority. Lepidus, who had taken control of Spain and North Africa, was forced out of office in 36 B.C.E.; Antony and Octavian agreed to separate the spheres of influence. Octavian took Italy and Rome's western provinces, while Antony took the eastern provinces.

In Egypt, Antony joined forces with Cleopatra VII, the last Ptolemaic monarch to rule there. Both stood to gain from this alliance: Antony secured control of the resources of Egypt while Cleopatra got territory and influence. In response to this alliance, Octavian launched a vicious propaganda campaign. Posing as the conservative protector of Roman tradition, he accused Antony of surrendering Roman values and territory to an evil foreign seductress. The inevitable war broke out in 31 B.C.E. At the Battle of Actium in Greece, Octavian's troops and fleet defeated Antony and Cleopatra's land and naval forces. The couple fled to Alexandria, in Egypt, where they committed suicide a year later.

As we saw in Chapter 4, the death of Cleopatra and the end of the Egyptian Ptolemaic dynasty in 30 B.C.E. marked the end of the Hellenistic Age, which had begun with the creation of successor kingdoms after the death of Alexander the Great in 323 B.C.E. The Battle of Actium and the subsequent Roman conquest of Egypt also effectively marked the end of the Roman Republic. Although Octavian, who was given the title Caesar Augustus by the Senate in 27 B.C.E., would preserve the forms of the Republic, he acquired effective absolute power in both Rome and the vast empire that Rome controlled. The transition from Republic to Empire also raised the question, which frequently recurred in the history of the West, whether republican political institutions were compatible with imperial power. The history of Athens and Rome suggests that they were not.

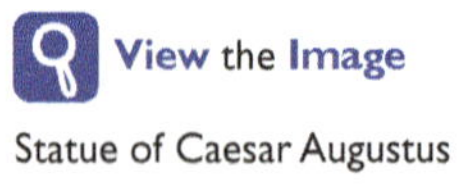

Statue of Caesar Augustus

CONCLUSION

The Roman Republic and the West

The Roman Republic made four great contributions to the geographical and cultural area that would later be identified as the West. The first was the institution of republican government. Although Rome made many changes in its political institutions over the course of more than 500 years, it bequeathed to the West a model of government that mixed features of the three forms of government identified by Aristotle and analyzed by Polybius: monarchy, aristocracy, and democracy. The Roman Republic served as a model of government for political communities in the West for the next two thousand years. Not least among them was the United States of America, which became a republic in the late eighteenth century when it declared its independence from Great

Britain. By vesting executive power in a president rather than a monarch, just as Rome had given executive power to consuls, and by dividing the legislature into a Senate and a House of Representatives, the new American republic drew inspiration from the history of the Roman Republic. The most important difference between the institutions of the two republics was that the aristocratic Roman Senate played a much greater role than its American counterpart in the government of the Republic. Although in theory the Roman Senate was mainly an advisory body that had little formal power, its influence over the consuls and other magistrates was considerable.

Second, the Roman Republic transmitted to the West the ideal of **civic virtue**, the belief that the success of a republic depended on its citizens' possession of personal traits that contributed to the common good. These traits included *gravitas* (which meant dignity, seriousness, and duty), piety, and justice. Aristotle had emphasized the importance of civic virtue in his claim that citizenship consisted in political duties rather than political rights. There was little discussion of civic virtue in the Hellenistic monarchies, but a revival and development of the concept took place in the Roman Republic. During the late years of the Republic, moral philosophers and historians blamed the loss of Roman liberty on the perceived loss of civic virtue. The idea of civic virtue modeled on that of republican Rome profoundly influenced the history of the West, especially during the Renaissance in the fifteenth and sixteenth centuries, the Enlightenment in the eighteenth century, and the early years of the United States in the late eighteenth and early nineteenth centuries.

The third legacy that Rome bequeathed to the West was its legal system. Based originally upon the Law of the Twelve Tables, and developed gradually through judicial interpretation and eventual codification in the late imperial period, Roman law became the basis of most Western legal systems. Roman law systems in the West were rivalled only by those that followed the English system of common law. Many of the legal traditions associated with both English and Roman law, however, including the participation of citizens in the legal process, originated in the Roman Republic.

The fourth and arguably the most important legacy of Rome to the West was Greco–Roman culture. This distinctive Roman version of Hellenism represented a creative synthesis of Greek and Roman culture. In art and philosophy Roman culture was largely derivative of that of Greece, but in architecture and literature it represented a creative adaptation of the cultures that Romans encountered. Greco–Roman culture also preserved a large body of Greek art and philosophy, much of which has survived only through Roman imitations and translations. Credit for the successful transmission of Greco–Roman culture to subsequent generations can be attributed to the long period of peace, the *Pax Romana*, which lasted from 31 B.C.E. to 180 C.E. To that period of Roman world dominance, the Roman Empire, we now turn.

Read the Document

Polybius: Why Romans and Not Greeks Govern the World, ca. 140 B.C.E.

civic virtue The belief that the success of a republic depended on its citizens' possession of personal traits that contributed to the common good.

MAKING CONNECTIONS

1. The Roman Republic rose to power during the Hellenistic period. In what sense were its political institutions and culture Hellenistic?
2. To what extent did Roman territorial expansion lead to the fall of the Roman Republic?
3. How did Romans model their society on that of classical and Hellenistic Greece? How did they modify or reject that cultural inheritance?
4. Compare the political institutions of the Roman Republic with those of the United States of America in the late eighteenth century.

TAKING IT FURTHER

For suggested readings see page R-1.

On MyHistoryLab

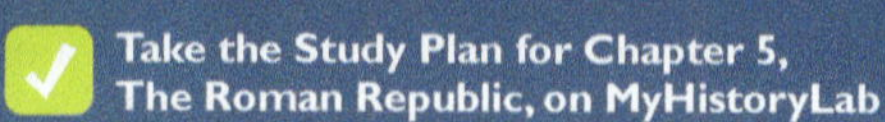

Chapter Review

The Nature of the Roman Republic

5.1 What type of government did Rome establish when it eliminated kingship?

Rome became a republic, a state in which political power resides in the people or their representatives rather than in a monarch. Tension between the elite and wealthy patricians and the plebeians, composed of rich landowners, the military, and the general populace, characterized Roman political life during the Republic.

Roman Territorial Expansion

5.2 How did the Roman Republic come to dominate the Mediterranean world during the Hellenistic Age?

New political and military institutions allowed Rome to conquer first the Italian peninsula, and then ally with neighboring cities in Italy. Building these alliances allowed the Romans to conquer nearby tribes, and later a combination of military might and diplomacy helped them defeat the powerful Etruscans. The attempt to assimilate conquered peoples included offering a limited form of citizenship in exchange for military service, and the growing army was then used to crush those, like Macedonia, who refused to submit to Rome's territorial ambitions. Victory over Carthage in the Third Punic War resulted in Rome's acquisition of all the territories ruled by Carthage.

The Culture of the Roman Republic

5.3 How did the Roman encounter with Greek culture lead to the forging of a durable cultural synthesis?

During the Roman territorial expansion within the Hellenistic world, Greek ideas about literature, art, philosophy, and rhetoric were adopted and adapted into Roman culture. Greek literature and art became the foundation of the Roman tradition in those areas, while elements of the Greek religion were transformed due to the Republic's toleration for a wide variety of religious practices. The educated elite emphasized the art of persuasion, or Rhetoric, over the attainment of philosophical wisdom, which became one of the Roman Republic's cultural legacies to the West.

Social Life in Republican Rome

5.4 How was Roman society structured, and what relationships existed within the Roman family?

At the top of the hierarchical structure of Roman society was an elite group of political leaders hailing from both pedigreed patrician families and some wealthy plebeians. Rich merchants from the equestrian class were next, and then general populace, or plebeians. As pieces of property, slaves were at the bottom of the hierarchy. The structure of the Roman family was similar, with the male head of the household exercising complete control over his family members. However, women and grown children often enjoyed considerable independence, and patrician women often wielded political power behind the scenes.

The End of the Roman Republic

5.5 Why did the Roman Republic end?

The inequitable distribution of resources in the Roman Republic eventually overwhelmed the republican constitution and caused a revolution. The rapid acquisition of territories allowed the ruling elite to become enormously wealthy, which only heightened the differences in wealth and power that characterized Roman society. This relentless pursuit of power and glory by the elite, coupled with flaws in Rome's political institutions, eventually caused a fundamental change in the political system.

Chapter Time Line

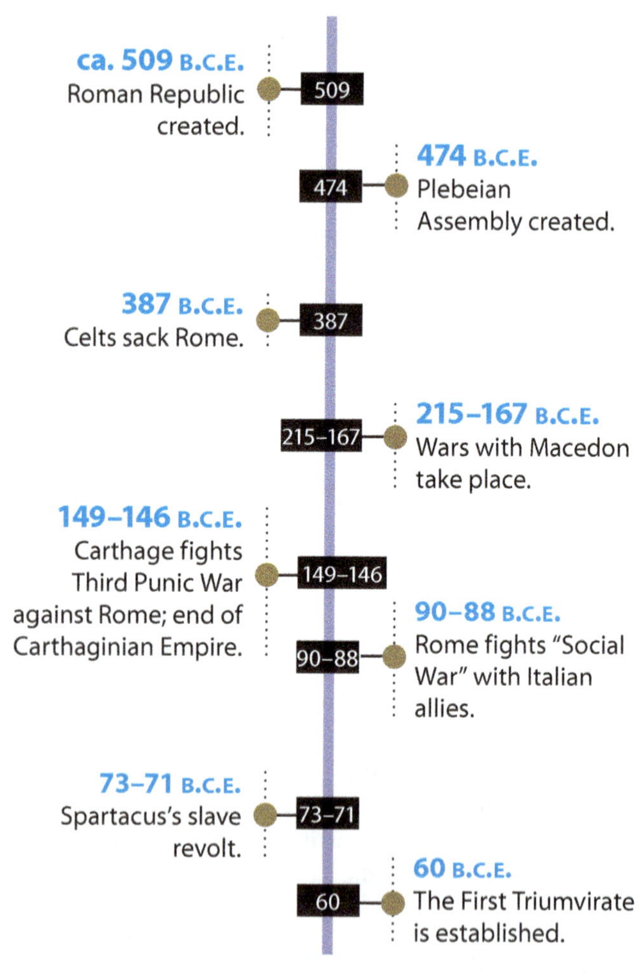

6 Enclosing the West: The Early Roman Empire and Its Neighbors, 31 B.C.E.–235 C.E.

In 155 C.E., Aelius Aristides, an aristocratic Greek writer who held Roman citizenship, visited Rome, where he gave a public oration in honor of the imperial capital. His words reveal what the Roman Empire meant to a wealthy, educated man from Rome's eastern provinces. According to Aristides, the trait "most worthy of consideration and admiration" in the Roman system was that "everywhere you have made citizens all those who are the more accomplished, noble and powerful people." A man might live thousands of miles from the city of Rome, and yet "neither does the sea nor a great expanse of intervening land keep one from being a citizen. . . . [Rome] has never refused anyone. But just as the earth's ground supports all men, so it too receives men from every land." Aristides's vision points to the key of the Romans' success—a willingness to assimilate their subjects into Rome's political and social life. Aristides believed that by transforming "non-Romans" into Romans, Rome's imperial expansion brought civilization to the world.

A HARBOR TOWN This first-century fresco, found in a Roman villa near Pompeii, offers us a glimpse of the lively seafaring trade that helped maintain the Roman Empire.

LEARNING OBJECTIVES

6.1 How did the Roman imperial system develop, and what roles did the emperor, Senate, army, and city of Rome play in this process?

6.2 How did provincial peoples assimilate to or resist Roman rule?

6.3 How did Romans interact with peoples living beyond the imperial borders?

6.4 What was the social and cultural response to the emergence and consolidation of the empire?

Listen to Chapter 6 on MyHistoryLab

6.1
6.2
6.3
6.4

Watch the Video Series on MyHistoryLab

Learn about some key topics related to this chapter with the *MyHistoryLab Video Series: Key Topics in Western Civilization*

Read the **Document**

Excerpt from *The Roman Oration* by Aelius Aristides

Pax Romana Latin for "Roman Peace," this term refers to the Roman Empire established by Augustus that lasted until the early third century C.E.

Aristides's praise demonstrates Rome's success in creating a sense of common purpose among its citizens. During its first 250 years of existence, the empire brought cultural unity and political stability to an area stretching from the Atlantic Ocean to the Persian Gulf. The imperial regime brought peace to the Mediterranean world for more than two centuries. Historians call this era the ***Pax Romana***, the Roman Peace. But for the slaves whose labor fueled the economy and the small farmers whose taxes supported the state, Roman rule meant oppression and impoverishment.

This chapter analyzes the Roman Empire as three concentric circles of power—the imperial center, the provinces, and the frontiers and beyond. In the imperial center stood not only the emperor but also the Roman Senate, the chief legal and administrative institutions, and the city of Rome itself, an important model of the Roman way of life. In the second circle, provincial populations struggled with the challenges posed by the imposition of Roman rule and, in the process, helped construct a new imperial culture. The outermost circle of the empire, its frontier zones and the lands beyond, included Romans living within the empire's borders and the peoples who lived on the other side, but interacted with Rome through trade and warfare. By exploring what it meant to be a Roman in each of these circles, this chapter seeks to answer a key question:

How did the encounters between the Romans and the peoples they conquered transform the Mediterranean world and create a Roman imperial culture?

The Imperial Center

6.1 How did the Roman imperial system develop, and what roles did the emperor, Senate, army, and city of Rome play in this process?

After civil wars destroyed the Roman Republic, a new political system emerged. Rome's form of government changed from a republic, in which members of an oligarchy competed for power, to an empire, in which one man, the emperor, held absolute power for life. Roman culture was now anchored by an imperial system based on force (see **Map 6.1**).

Imperial Authority: Augustus and After

As we saw in Chapter 5, Julius Caesar's heir, Octavian (63 B.C.E.–14 C.E.), wrenched the state from the spiral of civil war and claimed that he had restored normal life to the Republic. In fact, Octavian destroyed the Republic while pretending to preserve it. In his own eyes, and those of a people weary of war, Octavian was the savior of *republican* Rome. Yet behind a façade of restored republican tradition, Octavian created a Roman version of a Hellenistic monarchy. By neutralizing his political enemies in the Roman Senate, vanquishing his military rivals, and establishing an iron grip on every

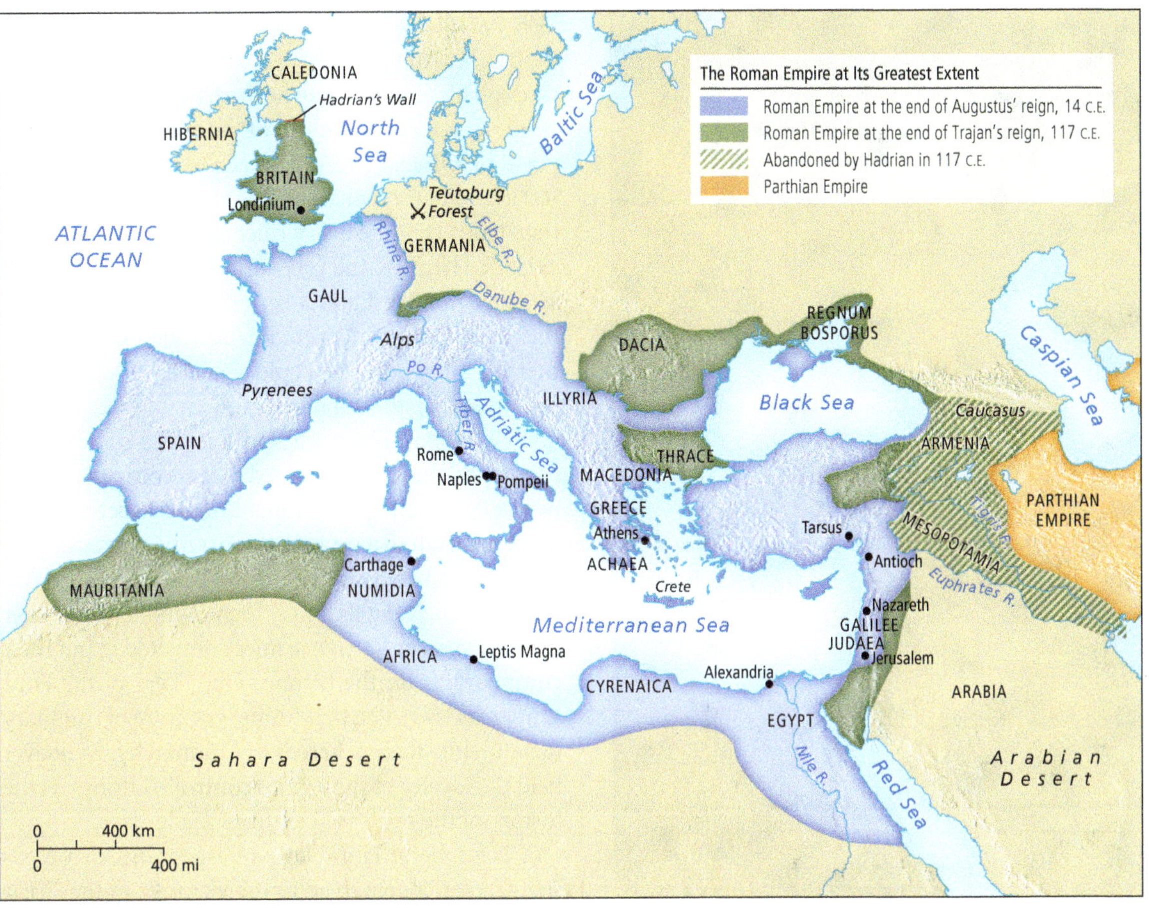

MAP **6.1** THE ROMAN EMPIRE AT ITS GREATEST EXTENT Stretching from the north of Britain to the Euphrates River, the empire brought together hundreds of distinct ethnic groups. When did the Empire reach its greatest extent? What forces compelled its contraction?

mechanism of power, Octavian succeeded where Julius Caesar and other republican politicians had failed: He achieved total mastery of the political arena at Rome. No one successfully challenged his authority.

To mask his tyranny, Octavian never wore a crown and modestly referred to himself as *Princeps*, or First Citizen. His position in Rome was all-powerful yet unobtrusive. In 27 B.C.E., as he boasted in the official account of his reign, he "transferred the Republic from his power into that of the Senate and the Roman people." This abdication was a sham and few people were fooled. Following Octavian's instructions, the Senate showered honors on him, including the name "Augustus" (which is how we will refer to him throughout the rest of this chapter). *Augustus* means "the revered" and implied an exalted, godlike authority. (It became the title of all subsequent emperors.) Augustus "accepted" the Senate's plea to remain consul and agreed to control the frontier provinces where the most troops were stationed, including Spain, Gaul, Germany, and Syria. The senators rejoiced, calling Augustus "sole savior of the entire empire."

In 23 B.C.E. Augustus renounced the consulship and was voted the powers of tribune for life. A tribune's power gave Augustus the right to conduct business in the Senate and veto legislation. It also conferred immunity from arrest and punishment. He could now legally interfere in all political and military affairs in the provinces. Augustus personally controlled Egypt, the richest province, as successor to the pharaohs, and soldiers swore an oath of allegiance to him. Other generals led legions into battle, but always in his name. Other magistrates officially administered the state, but no one was chosen without his approval.

Augustus on His Accomplishments

AUGUSTUS: A COMMANDING PRESENCE This statue of Augustus dating to 19 B.C.E. depicts him as a warrior making a gesture of command. His face is ageless, the carving on his armor celebrates peace and prosperity, and his posture is balanced and forceful.

THE PROBLEM OF SUCCESSION Like a Hellenistic monarch, Augustus hoped to pass power down through his family. When he died, his stepson Tiberius (r. 14–37 C.E.) took control of the empire without opposition. Officially Rome remained a republic, but in fact a hereditary monarchy was now in place. For more than half a century, every ruler came from Augustus's extended family—the **Julio-Claudian dynasty**. Some senators muttered about restoring the Republic, but this remained an idle—and dangerous—dream. Neither the army nor the people would have supported a Senate-led republican rebellion.

Hereditary monarchy promised to stave off the instability that accompanied open competition for power. But such open competition, and such instability, returned to Rome after the last of Augustus's line, Nero, committed suicide in the face of rebellion in 68. He left no heir, and four men claimed power over the next year, as Roman armies competed to put their commanders on the throne. This "Year of the Four Emperors" revealed that Rome was more of a military dictatorship than a hereditary monarchy: Whoever held the loyalty of the armies controlled Rome, as the history of the next two centuries made clear.

The general Titus Flavius Vespasianus, or Vespasian (r. 69–79), emerged as the victor from the "Year of the Four Emperors." The Flavian dynasty that he established lasted just 25 years, until the death of his last son, Domitian (r. 81–96). A conscientious and able monarch, Domitian nevertheless ruled with an openly autocratic style. He created a reign of terror among Rome's elite until a group of senators murdered him.

To avoid another succession crisis, the Senate cooperated with the army in choosing a new emperor, the elderly senator Nerva (r. 96–98). They hoped that this respected man who had no sons would ensure orderly government, and so he did. Under pressure from the military, Nerva adopted the general Trajan (r. 98–117) as his son and heir. He thus inaugurated the era historians call the **Antonine Age**. For almost a century (96–180), Rome enjoyed competent rule because Nerva's practice of adopting highly qualified successors continued. After Trajan adopted Hadrian (r. 117–138), Hadrian in turn adopted Antoninus Pius (r. 138–161), and Antoninus adopted Marcus Aurelius (r. 161–180) as his successor. The Roman historian Tacitus (ca. 55–120) praised these emperors for establishing "the rare happiness of times, when we may think what we please, and express what we think."

Julio-Claudian dynasty Established by Octavian Augustus, this hereditary monarchy drawn from members of his extended family ruled Rome until 68 C.E.

Antonine Age Almost one hundred years of political stability in the Roman Empire, inaugurated when Nerva adopted Trajan as his son and heir.

This time of peace ended with another imperial murder. Unlike his immediate predecessors, Marcus Aurelius had a son. So he abandoned the custom of picking a qualified successor, and instead was followed to the throne by his incompetent, cruel, and eventually insane son, Commodus (r. 180–192). Conspirators within the imperial palace arranged to have Commodus strangled in 192, triggering another civil war.

A senator from North Africa, Septimius Severus, emerged victorious from this conflict and assumed the imperial throne (r. 193–211). Septimius Severus exemplified the ascent of provincial aristocrats to the highest levels of the empire. The Severan dynasty lasted until 235. Septimius Severus was popular with the army—he raised its pay for the first time in more than 100 years. But when the last emperor of his

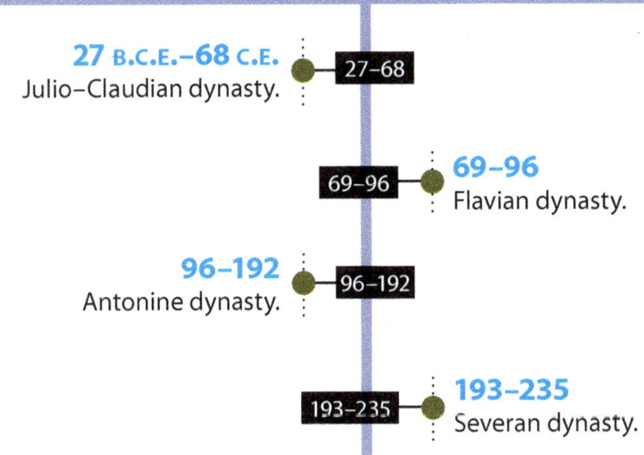

dynasty, Severus Alexander (r. 222–235), attempted to bribe the German tribes instead of fighting them, his own troops killed him because they wanted the cash for themselves. Again, the murder of an emperor provoked civil war. Fifty years of political and economic crises followed the end of the Severan dynasty. As we will see in Chapter 7, the imperial structure that emerged after this time of crisis differed significantly from the Augustan model.

THE EMPEROR'S ROLE: THE NATURE OF IMPERIAL POWER Under the Augustan imperial system, the emperor had four main responsibilities. First, he protected and expanded imperial territory. Only the emperor determined foreign policy, made treaties with other nations, and waged war, whether to protect the empire from its enemies or expand the empire with aggressive campaigns of conquest.

Second, the emperor administered justice and provided good government. In theory all citizens could appeal directly to him for justice. The emperor and his staff also responded to questions on points of law and administration from provincial governors and other officials who ruled in the emperor's name. Emperors provided emergency relief after natural disasters, looked after the roads and infrastructure of the empire, and financed public works in many provincial cities. During his long reign Augustus—the wealthiest individual in the empire—used his personal fortune to pay his soldiers, erect public buildings, and sponsor public spectacles such as gladiatorial contests.

The emperor's third responsibility stemmed from his religious role. As *Pontifex Maximus*, or High Priest, the emperor supervised the public worship of the gods of Rome, particularly Jupiter. Emperors and subjects alike believed that to fulfill Rome's destiny to rule the world, they needed to make regular sacrifices to the gods.

Finally, the emperor became a symbol of unity for the peoples of the empire. Inevitably, the emperor seemed more than human, even worthy of worship, for he was the guarantor of peace, prosperity, and victory for Rome, and had more power than any other living person.

Worship of the emperor began with Augustus. He was reluctant to call himself a god because Roman tradition opposed such an idea, but he permitted his spirit to be worshiped as a sort of *paterfamilias* or head of a universal family of peoples of the empire. He also referred to himself as the "son of a god"—in this case Julius Caesar, whom the Senate had declared divine. After Augustus, imperial worship became more pronounced, although few emperors, such as Domitian, emphasized their divinity during their lifetimes. Most were content to be worshiped after death. On his deathbed, Vespasian managed to joke, "I guess I'm becoming a god now."

In Rome's eastern provinces such as Egypt, where people for thousands of years had considered their kings divine, the worship of the emperor spread quickly. Each city's official calendar marked the emperor's day of ascession to the throne. Soon, cities across the empire worshiped the emperor on special occasions through games, speeches, sacrifices, and public feasts. This cult of the emperor provided a common focus of allegiance for the empire's diverse peoples. Although most people would never see their ruler, he was in their prayers every day.

He was also in their public spaces. Emperors built and restored roads, temples, harbors, aqueducts, and fortifications. These public works demonstrated the emperor's unparalleled patronage and concern for the public welfare. In turn, local aristocrats emulated his generosity by financing lavish building projects in their own cities.

Other elements of material culture also made the imperial presence real for the emperor's subjects. Coins, for example, provided a glimpse of the emperor's face and a phrase that characterized some aspect of his reign. Slogans such as "Restorer of the World," "Concord with the Gods," and "The Best Ruler—Sustenance for Italy" brought the ruler's message into every person's pocket. Statues of the emperor served a similar purpose. (One statue in Carthage in North Africa had a removable head, so that when a new emperor ascended the throne, the town leaders could save money by replacing only the head instead of the whole statue.)

Emperors also used military victories to celebrate their reigns. In the Republic, conquest had brought wealth and glory to generals. In the new imperial system, only the emperor could take credit for victory. Imperial propaganda described the emperor as eternally triumphant.

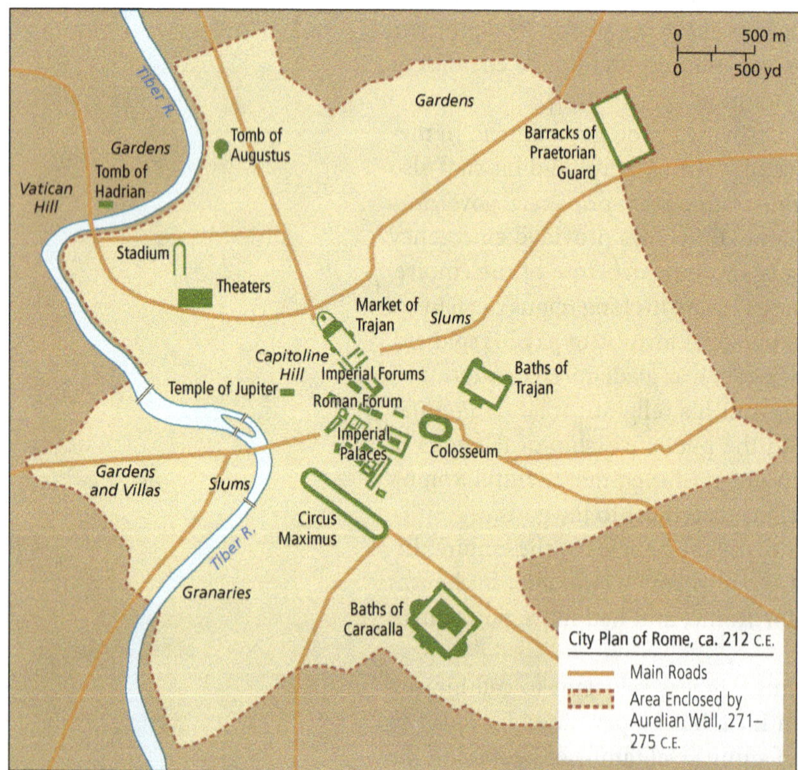

MAP **6.2** THE CITY OF ROME, CA. 212 C.E. This diagram shows the main public buildings of the imperial capital. Most cities elsewhere in the empire imitated this urban plan. How does the city plan illustrate the realities of power in imperial Rome?

The City of Rome

The city of Rome stood as a monument to the authority of the emperor. Augustus boasted that he had found Rome built of brick and left it made of marble. Though an exaggeration, this claim reveals the effect of monarchy on Rome's urban fabric. Every emperor wanted to leave his mark on the city as a testimony to his generosity and power. As Rome grew, it became the model for cities throughout the empire. Its public spaces and buildings provided a stage for imperial rule (see **Map 6.2**).

The center of political and public life in Rome was the Roman Forum, a field filled with imposing buildings that housed the treasury and records office, law courts, and the Senate House. Roman law, inscribed on gleaming bronze tablets and placed on the outer walls of these buildings, testified to the principles of justice and order that formed the framework of the Roman state. Basilicas, colonnaded halls in which Romans conducted public business ranging from finance to trials, crowded against the sides of the Forum.

Because public and religious life were intertwined, the Forum also contained temples of the gods who controlled Rome's destiny. Statues to the goddesses Victory and Concord stood in the Senate, while the huge marble temple of Jupiter "Best and Greatest," Rome's chief god, looked down on the Forum from the Capitoline Hill.

The Forum highlighted the emperor's power. Emperors built triumphal arches there. After a victorious military campaign, emperors and their troops paraded through the Forum on the Sacred Way, passed under the arches, and finished at the temple of Jupiter. Delighted crowds watched defeated kings pass by in chains and marveled at floats piled with loot and slaves carrying paintings depicting the war.

The emperor's might was on display throughout the city. Emperors spent gigantic sums on stadiums and additional forums. The huge arena called the Colosseum, built by Vespasian and his son Titus (r. 79–81), provided a spot in the heart of the city where 50,000 spectators could cheer the slaughter of men and animals.

View the Closer Look
The Roman Colosseum

Emperors also built and maintained luxurious public baths. Eleven aqueducts provided Rome with 300 million gallons of water every day for these baths, the city's many fountains, and those houses that had indoor plumbing.

To erect their monumental buildings, the Romans developed new architectural techniques. They were the first to build extensively in concrete (and may have invented it), which allowed them to develop new methods of construction such as the vault. The Pantheon, built by Hadrian in 126, is the largest ancient roofed building still standing today. With a diameter of 142 feet, its dome has no interior supports.

Emperors built their palaces on the Palatine Hill, which looked down on the Forum, and mansions covered nearby hills. Wealthy citizens lived in luxury that would not be equaled in the West for centuries. In contrast, the impoverished majority of Rome's inhabitants lived in filthy slums in the valleys between Rome's seven hills or along the Tiber River, where they crowded into apartment buildings up to six stories high. Lacking solid foundations, apartment buildings often collapsed and could become firetraps. (It is hardly a surprise, then, that Augustus established the first professional fire department in Western history.)

The Agents of Control

The emperor stood at the heart of the empire, but the imperial center included other agents of control, the most important of which were the Roman Senate and the army.

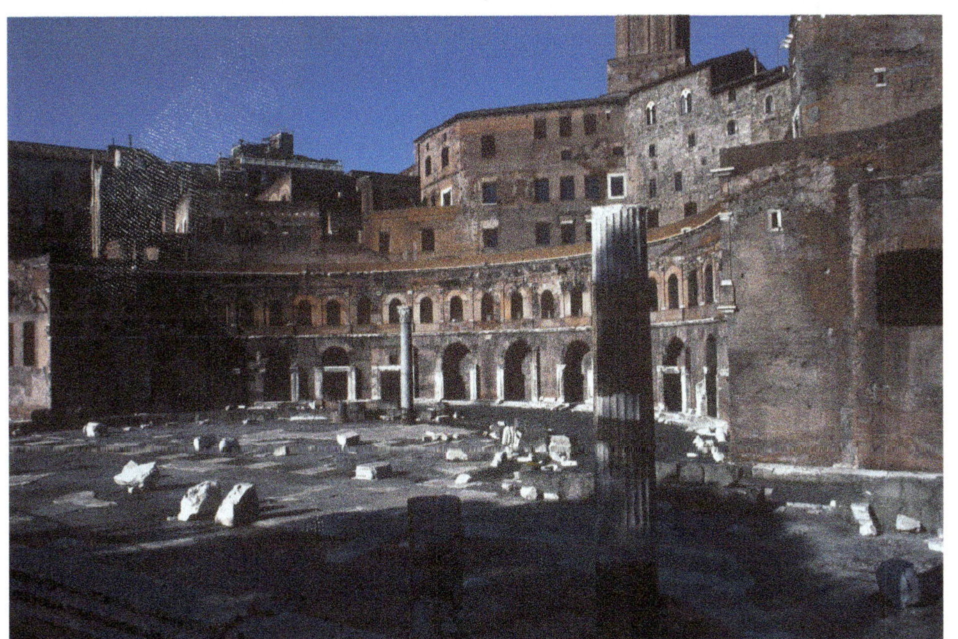

TRAJAN'S FORUM Built between 107 and 112, Trajan's Forum included libraries of Greek and Latin texts, an enormous basilica, a multistoried marketplace, and a marble column 125-feet high on which was carved the story of his conquest of Dacia (modern Romania).

THE ROMAN SENATE: FROM AUTONOMY TO ADMINISTRATION The Empire retained most of the basic machinery of government inherited from the Republic—but it operated in conformity with the emperor's wishes. The emperor, not the Senate, now controlled military, financial, and diplomatic policy. Free political debate was silenced. Because he wanted to avoid the competition for power that had destroyed the Republic, Augustus eliminated his opponents and filled the Senate with loyal supporters. Nevertheless, to maintain the illusion that he had saved rather than destroyed the Republic and because senators as a class were the wealthiest, most influential men in Rome, Augustus took pains to show respect for the Senate.

Deprived of its autonomy, the Senate became an administrative arm of imperial rule. Senators served as provincial governors, army commanders, judges, and financial officers. They managed the water and grain supplies of the city of Rome, and some of them served on the emperor's advisory council. Senators learned to serve the empire faithfully, even if they disliked the emperor personally.

Emperors often brought able new men into the Senate from the provinces. This practice gave provincial elites a stake in the imperial enterprise. By the end of the third century more than half of Rome's 600 or so senators came from outside Italy.

While the emperor's relationship with the Senate was of primary importance, other social ranks were also prominent in imperial administration. Many members of the equestrian class served in government positions. Emperors also employed freedmen and even slaves on their administrative staffs and benefited from their loyalty and competence.

THE ROMAN ARMY AND THE POWER OF THE EMPEROR The Roman army was another crucial component of imperial rule. The army could make or depose an emperor—something that every ruler understood. Without the army's support, Augustus would never have succeeded in remaking the Republican regime into his imperial system.

Augustus created a highly efficient professional army that served as the bulwark of the empire for nearly 250 years. His first step was to reduce the army from 60 legions to between 25 and 30 legions, so that the legionary troops now totaled 150,000 citizens. To solidify their loyalty, Augustus established regular terms of service and ample retirement benefits for veterans and their families.

auxiliary Soldiers in the Roman imperial army who were drawn from subject peoples. Auxiliaries received Roman citizenship after their term of service.

Soldiers drawn from subject peoples who were not citizens served as **auxiliary** troops. After completing their years of service, auxiliaries received Roman citizenship—an important incentive for recruitment. The combined legions and auxiliaries brought the military strength of the Roman army to 300,000 men.

Legionaries enlisted for 20 years of active service (with another five in reserve), but only about half survived to retirement. Short life expectancy rather than death in battle kept the survival figure low, although regular rations and medical care may have helped soldiers live longer than civilians. A soldier with special skills, such as literacy, could rise through the ranks and become an officer. For those who survived their service, Augustus established military colonies in Italy and the provinces. He rewarded more than 100,000 veterans with land. Later emperors continued this practice.

The imperial army epitomized Roman imperial values. It maintained a high degree of organization, discipline, and training—characteristics on which Romans prided themselves. To the Romans, strict military discipline distinguished their soldiers from disorganized barbarians. Military punishments were ferocious. For example, if a soldier fell asleep during sentry duty, his barrack mates were required to beat him to death. But tight discipline and vigorous training produced effective fighters. To keep in fighting shape, troops constantly drilled in weaponry, camp building, and battle formations. A Roman soldier was expected to march 20 miles in four hours—while carrying his 40-pound pack and swimming across rivers encountered along the way.

Life in the Roman Provinces: Assimilation, Resistance, and Romanization

6.2 How did provincial peoples assimilate to or resist Roman rule?

Beyond the city of Rome and the imperial center lay the second concentric circle of power, the Roman Empire's provinces. In these regions some people assimilated readily to Roman ways, while others resisted. Unlike the Greeks of the Classical Age, Romans in the imperial era were willing to assimilate the peoples they conquered into Rome's political and cultural life. Formal grants of Roman citizenship gave many people the legal rights and privileges of being Roman.

The Army: A Romanizing Force

The army played an important role in **Romanization**, the process by which subject peoples adopted and adapted Roman cultural and political practices. Provincial recruits learned Roman ways during their service. Latin, the language of command and army administration, provided another common bond to men whose mother tongues reflected the empire's ethnic diversity.

Romanization The process by which conquered peoples absorbed aspects of Roman culture, especially the Latin language, city life, and religion.

Each of the legions with a contingent of auxiliary troops was stationed as a permanent garrison in a province with an elaborate logistical infrastructure to provide weapons, food, and housing. Camp architecture and fortifications, as well as weapons, armor, and tactics, followed the same conventions across the empire, thus reinforcing the army's role as a Romanizing force. Generals and staff officers often had postings in different provinces during their careers and so developed a sense of shared enterprise.

Retired Roman soldiers who settled in the provinces also served as a Romanizing force. Until the end of the second century C.E., soldiers could not legally marry during their military service, but many men reared families anyway with local women. Sons born to such unions frequently followed their fathers into the army. At retirement, most soldiers stayed near the bases in which they had been stationed. Many towns arose full of former military personnel and their friends, families, and small businesses. These towns helped transmit Roman culture and values to provincial peoples.

Occupation, Administration, and Commerce

Romanization was neither quick nor unopposed. Revolts against Roman authority often followed soon after a subject people's initial defeat, while freedom was still a living memory. Roman force, however, usually—but not always—proved overwhelming.

One such uprising occurred in Britain. After the conquest of Britain in 43 C.E., several British kingdoms supplied troops to the Roman army in return for protection and a degree of autonomy. But in 60 Emperor Nero annexed one such kingdom, the Iceni. Emboldened by their new dominance, the Roman agents abused Queen Boudicca and raped her daughters. The queen then led the Iceni into open rebellion. With the aid of neighboring tribes who also resented the Romans, Boudicca destroyed a legion and leveled several cities. Resistance, however, ended quickly in 61 after Roman forces routed Boudicca's troops, and the queen took her own life. The Britons, like many other peoples before and after them, learned that resistance to Rome was futile.

The tension between Roman armies and provincial populations never entirely disappeared, but gradually the top layers of conquered populations became Romanized. They adapted Roman customs and in some cases entered Roman politics. Romanization transformed the provinces from occupied zones where shattered communities obeyed foreign masters to imperial territories in which variations of Roman culture flourished, and provincial elites came to think of themselves as Romans.

The Romanization of conquered peoples coincided with the absorption of conquered territories into the Roman provincial system. A governor ruled each province: He and a small staff administered justice, supervised tax collection, and orchestrated the flow of goods back to Rome. This structure of government created an administrative-military class that drew its members from the senatorial and the equestrian orders. In the service of the emperor, these men climbed the ladder of success through appointments in different provinces. Gnaeus Julius Agricola (40–93) is an apt example. The father-in-law of the historian, Tacitus, Agricola had a brilliant military career. As governor of Britain, however, he co-opted the defeated elites into the Roman way of life. (See *Different Voices* in this chapter.)

Transport and commercial networks connected the provinces to Rome. Soldiers marched on the 40,000 miles of paved roads crisscrossing the empire, but because transporting goods by land remained more expensive than moving them by water, rivers and the Mediterranean were the primary arteries of trade. With pirates quelled by Roman fleets, shipping flourished. Improved harbors, ports, and canals further encouraged long-distance trade.

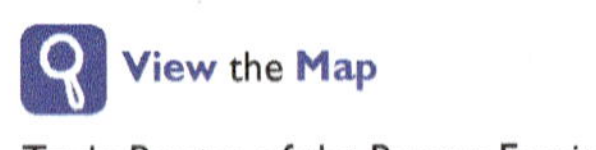

Trade Routes of the Roman Empire

The Cities

The Roman way of life manifested itself most noticeably in cities. Provincial cities became "little Romes." They served the empire by funneling wealth from its massive hinterland into imperial coffers. As centers for tax collection and law courts, cities were where the imperial administrators interacted with provincial aristocrats, who dominated the local population. More than 1,000 cities eventually dotted the imperial map (see **Map 6.3**).

In the West where urban traditions were largely absent, the Romans created new cities, such as Lugdunum (Lyons) in France and Eburacum (York) in Britain. These new urban centers imitated the city of Rome in their physical and architectural layout. All of them had a forum in their center, flanked by a council house (modeled on the Roman Senate), basilicas, and temples. The cities provided all the amenities and requirements of Roman urban life, such as bathhouses, brothels, arenas for gladiatorial combat and wild beast hunts, and slave markets. Main streets in the towns led to the Roman road system.

Such cities were an important Romanizing force. Local elites started to speak Latin, identify local gods with Roman gods, adopt Roman architecture and styles of art, and enjoy the Roman way of life. Often these elites also received the reward of Roman citizenship. Some even entered the Roman Senate.

Common patterns characterized urban life throughout the empire. Women held no administrative office and had no role in public decision making, although wealthy

MAP **6.3** LANGUAGES AND AGRICULTURE IN THE ROMAN EMPIRE The 50 million inhabitants of the Roman Empire spoke many different languages and lived in a variety of climates and agricultural zones. Which of the divisions noted on this map were the most important and why? What does the distribution of cities reveal about the extent and limits of Roman power?

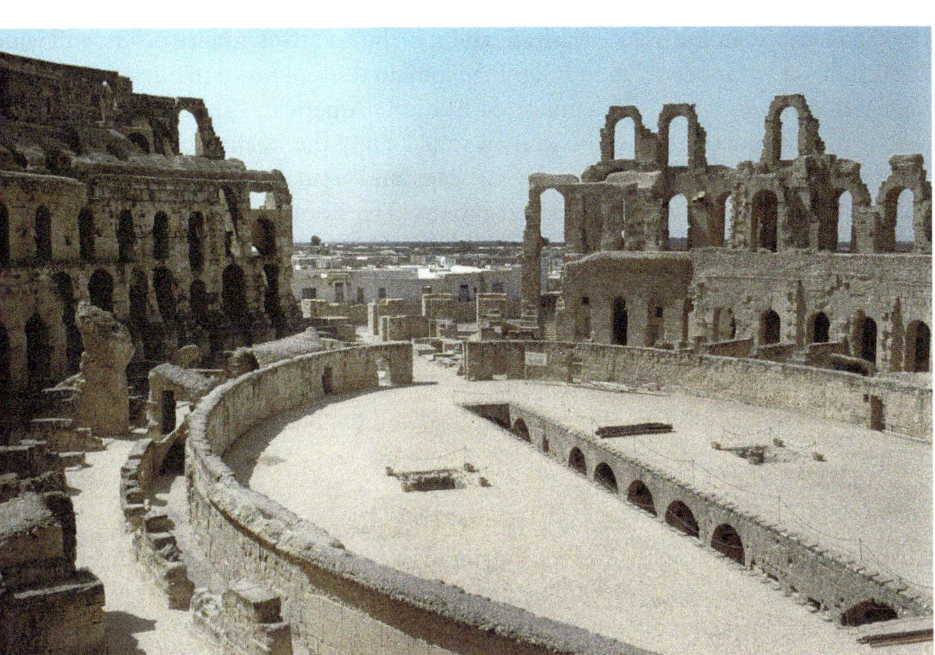

LITTLE ROMES Built in the early third century C.E., the amphitheater at the Tunisian town of El-Djem (the ancient city of Thysdrus) was one of the largest in the empire. Like the Colosseum in Rome, which it imitated, this arena sat thousands of spectators at gladiatorial fights and other entertainments.

women sometimes presided as priestesses in civic religious observances. The male citizens of each city voted on local issues and elected town officials. A city council modeled on the Roman Senate presided over each city's affairs. A handful of the community's wealthiest men served in the city council or as magistrates and priests. The councils managed the grain supply, arranged for army recruitment, supervised the marketplaces, administered justice in local law courts, and, most important of all, collected taxes for the central government. In imitation of the emperor, councilors paid out of their own pockets for the upkeep of public works, aqueducts, and baths, and funded religious festivals and public amusements.

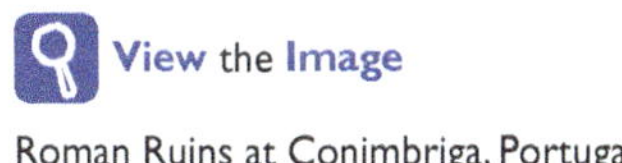

Roman Ruins at Conimbriga, Portugal

The Countryside

As Roman culture came to predominate in urban centers, the division between city and countryside widened. Provincial urban elites benefited from efficient and orderly government. In contrast, rural inhabitants, who formed most of the empire's population, faced economic exploitation and threats to their ways of life.

Despite the growth of trade, the Roman Empire was an agrarian state, and peasants performed the agricultural labor that drove the empire's economy. Some peasants rented their lands from landlords to whom they owed payment in the form of produce, money, or labor. If they failed to pay the rent, they could be punished or enslaved. Other peasants owned small farms sufficient to maintain their families, perhaps with the assistance of seasonal wage laborers or a few slaves. These landowning peasants faced the threat that a more powerful landowner might seize their fields by force. When this happened, peasants had little hope of getting their land back. The imperial system favored the wealthy and worked to the disadvantage of the rural poor. Rabbi Hanina ben Hama, who lived in Palestine about 240, stated bluntly that the empire established cities "to impose upon the people forced labor, extortion and oppression." Famine and natural disasters also posed a constant threat. A bad harvest could mean that peasants would have to sell their land or starve.

Despite these hardships, the peasantry managed to produce enough food to maintain the imperial system, especially the army. Indeed, agricultural productivity during this era was remarkable, considering the low yields of farms, the difficulty and expense of transportation, and the rudimentary technology. Some historians estimate that Europe did not see a comparable level of agricultural productivity again until the seventeenth century.

Food staples in the Mediterranean region included olives, grains, beans, and wine. Pasta had not yet appeared in Italy, and the tomato was unknown in Europe before the sixteenth century, when it was imported from the Americas. Wheat, often cooked in water to make porridge, was the Roman staple. Only the wealthy could afford to eat meat often. Most people relied on cheese, beans, and vegetables such as cabbage, garlic, and onions to supplement their wheat rations. The Romans did not have sugar, but most Romans seemed to enjoy sweets: They ate quantities of dates and honey.

Terrain, climate, and local farming customs determined the type of agriculture practiced. In Sicily and parts of southern Italy, chain gangs of slaves working on vast estates planted and harvested the crops. Migrant workers labored in the olive groves and wheat fields of Spain and North Africa, while seasonal movement of grazing animals predominated in the hilly regions of Italy and the Balkans.

Law, Citizenship, and Romanization

In the early empire, Roman law set Romans apart from the bulk of the population who followed their own laws. For example, Jews lived according to Jewish law or Athenians by Athenian law, as long as they paid their taxes to the emperor and did not cause trouble. If a Jew or an Athenian held Roman citizenship, however, he could also enjoy the rights and benefits of Roman law in addition to being the citizen of his native city. A Roman citizen possessed legally defined rights, including the guarantee of freedom from enslavement. Male citizens had the right to compete for public magistracies, vote in public assemblies, serve in the legions, and make an appeal in a criminal trial. No matter where they lived, Roman citizens took pride in their legal tradition and rights of citizenship.

Then, in 212, Emperor Caracalla (r. 211–217) issued what became known as the **Antonine Decree**, which granted citizenship to virtually all free men and women within the empire, perhaps to increase the tax base. Legal uniformity further strengthened provincial loyalty to Rome.

Antonine Decree In 212 C.E. the emperor Aurelius Antoninus, called Caracalla, issued a decree that granted citizenship to all the free inhabitants of the Roman Empire. The decree enabled Roman law to embrace the entire population of the empire.

Roman law made three important contributions to Western legal practices. First, the Romans created a standard feature of Western legal systems: the distinction between civil and criminal law. In Rome, civil law dealt with all aspects of family life, property and inheritance, slavery, and citizenship. It thus defined relations among different classes of Roman society and enabled courts to judge disputes among citizens. Criminal law addressed theft, homicide, sexual crimes, treason, and offenses against the government.

Second, Roman law influenced Western traditions of legal codification and interpretation. By the second century C.E., professional jurists (legal experts) directed imperial legal affairs under the supervision of the emperor. Far more than just imperial administrators, jurists such as Ulpian (d. 228) were legal scholars. They collected and analyzed earlier laws and judges' opinions, and wrote hundreds of commentaries that shaped the interpretation of Roman law for centuries, were passed on to the lawyers of medieval Europe, and still influence legal traditions. One such interpretative tradition is that under the principle of what the Romans called "equity," or fairness, judges should consider the spirit or intent rather than simply the letter of the law. According to Ulpian, "Law is the art of the good and the fair." On the basis of equity, Roman jurists argued that an accuser bears the burden of proof. A defendant does not have to prove he or she is innocent. Rather, he or she must be proven guilty.

Third, the Roman concept of "the law of nature" influenced Western ideas of justice. This concept stemmed in part from Stoicism (see Chapter 4), with its ideal of an underlying order to all things. From this ideal came the idea that certain principles of justice are part of nature itself, and thus that human laws should conform to natural law. Building on this Roman concept, later thinkers insisted that all human beings have inalienable rights and should be treated equally under the law.

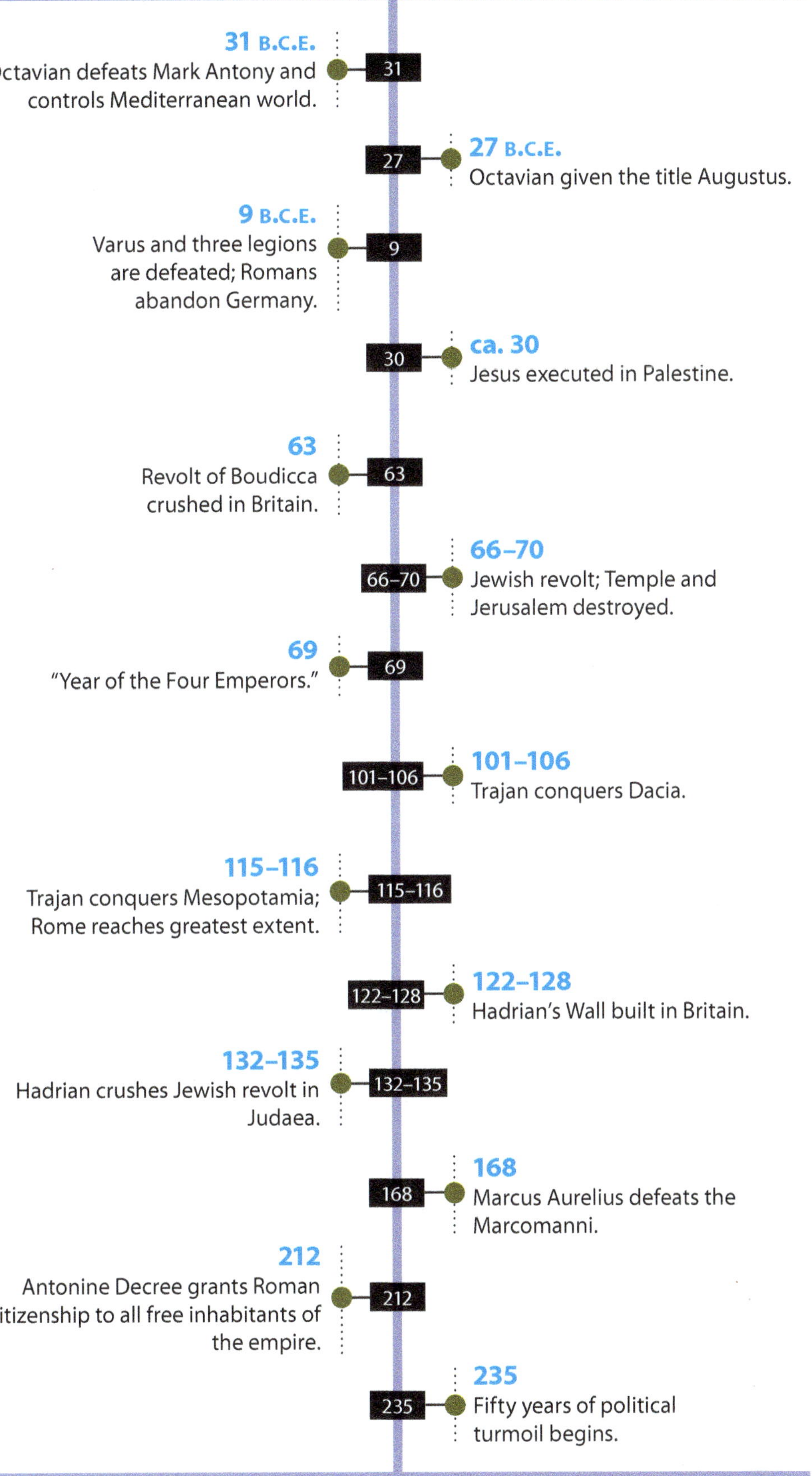
CHRONOLOGY: POLITICAL AND MILITARY EVENTS
31 B.C.E.
Octavian defeats Mark Antony and controls Mediterranean world.
31
27
27 B.C.E.
Octavian given the title Augustus.
9 B.C.E.
Varus and three legions are defeated; Romans abandon Germany.
9
30
ca. 30
Jesus executed in Palestine.
63
Revolt of Boudicca crushed in Britain.
63
66–70
66–70
Jewish revolt; Temple and Jerusalem destroyed.
69
"Year of the Four Emperors."
69
101–106
101–106
Trajan conquers Dacia.
115–116
Trajan conquers Mesopotamia; Rome reaches greatest extent.
115–116
122–128
122–128
Hadrian's Wall built in Britain.
132–135
Hadrian crushes Jewish revolt in Judaea.
132–135
168
168
Marcus Aurelius defeats the Marcomanni.
212
Antonine Decree grants Roman citizenship to all free inhabitants of the empire.
212
235
235
Fifty years of political turmoil begins.

Equality under the law did not, however, exist in the Roman imperial age. Roman citizens had more rights than noncitizens, but not all Roman citizens had the same rights. In the first century C.E. laws began to reflect the differences in wealth that divided citizens. By the third century, law, especially criminal law, distinguished between the wealthy upper class, generally called *honestiores* or "better people," and the poor, called *humiliores* or "humbler people." For example, *honestiores* could not be tortured to force them to give evidence, and if they were convicted of a capital crime, they received a quick death by sword. The "humbler people" received gruesome punishments, such as being burned alive or being thrown to wild animals in the arena.

As the legal distinctions between better and humbler peoples illustrates, Roman law shifted to mirror the new hierarchies of imperial Rome. Control of the law, which had rested with citizen assemblies and magistrates during the Republic, now lay with the emperor. The idea that the emperor's wishes had the force of law was widely accepted by the early third century.

Different Voices

Roman Rule: BANE OR BLESSING?

In his epic poem, the Aeneid, the poet Virgil (70–19 B.C.E.) provided Rome with a founding myth that identified the central features of Roman imperial pride:

> *Other men will shape molten bronze with greater artistry; . . . others will plead cases with more skill, . . . and will predict the rising constellations. You, Roman, do not fail to govern all people with your supreme authority. These will be your skills: to establish law and order within a framework of peace, to be merciful to those who submit, to crush in war those who are arrogant.*

As this quotation shows, Roman cultural identity centered on the belief that Romans had a genius for governing and therefore that the spread of Roman rule brought unparalleled benefits not only to Rome, but to those Rome conquered. Yet thoughtful Romans were aware that many peoples experienced Roman rule as oppressive. In the selections that follow, we see the struggles of one such Roman, the great historian Tacitus (ca. 55–120), to acknowledge the complex implications of the "Pax Romana." In addition to writing history, Tacitus climbed the political ranks, becoming consul under Nerva (r. 96–98) and governor of Asia about 112. Despite his political successes, Tacitus was a pessimist. He believed that the transformation from republic to empire had weakened Rome's moral character. Perhaps it is not surprising, then, that he was able to put himself in the position of not only the conqueror, but also the conquered. In the following excerpts, he gives us the voices of both.

A. In this section of his Histories, *Tacitus describes the aftermath of a failed revolt in Gaul in 70. The Roman general who has just suppressed the revolt addresses the defeated rebels:*

> Tyranny and war always existed in Gaul until you yielded to our authority. And we, although we have been provoked many times, have imposed upon you by right of conquest only this one demand: that you pay the costs of keeping peace here. For peace among different peoples cannot be maintained without troops, and troops cannot be maintained without pay, and pay cannot be found without taxation. In other respects, we are equals. You yourselves often command our legions and govern this and other provinces. You are in no respect excluded or shut out. Although you live far from Rome, you enjoy as much as we do the benefits of praiseworthy emperors; on the other hand, the cruel emperors threaten most those closest to them. . . . Perhaps you expect a milder type of government if Tutor and Classicus [leaders of the defeated revolt] assume power? Perhaps you think that they can equip armies to repel the Germans and the Britons for less tribute than you now pay us? But if the Romans are driven out—God forbid—what situation could exist except wars among all these races? The structure of our Empire has been consolidated by 800 years of good fortune and strict organization, and it cannot be torn apart without destroying those who tear it apart. And you especially will run the greatest risk, for you have gold and natural resources, which are the chief causes of war. Therefore love and cherish peace and the city of Rome which you and I, conquered and conqueror, hold with equal rights.

B. In 77 C.E. Tacitus married the daughter of Gnaeus Julius Agricola (40–93), a Roman general and administrator. Between 78 and 85, Agricola served as governor of Roman Britain and consolidated Roman rule over northern England and southern Scotland (which the Romans called Caledonia). In this excerpt from Tacitus's biography of his father-in-law, a chief named Calgacus attempts to rally the British against the Romans:

> Up until this day, we who live in this last strip of land and last home of liberty have been protected by our very

(continued on next page)

(continued from previous page)

remoteness. . . . Beyond us, there are no tribes, nothing except waves and rocks and, more dangerous than these, the Romans, whose oppression you have in vain tried to escape by obedience and submission. Plunderers of the world they are, and now that there is no more territory left to occupy their hands which have already laid the world waste, they are scouring the seas. If the enemy is rich, they are greedy; if the enemy is poor, they are power-hungry. Neither east nor west has been able to sate them. Alone of all men they covet rich nations and poor nations with equal passion. They rob, they slaughter, they plunder—and they call it "empire." Where they make a waste-land, they call it "peace."

C. In this section, Tacitus describes Agricola's policies of occupation.

For, to accustom to rest and repose through the charms of luxury a population scattered and barbarous and therefore inclined to war, Agricola gave private encouragement and public aid to the building of temples, courts of justice and dwelling houses, praising the energetic and reproving the indolent. Thus an honourable rivalry took the place of compulsion. He likewise provided a liberal education for the sons of the chiefs, and showed such a preference for the natural powers of the Britons over the industry of the Gauls that they who lately disdained the tongue of Rome now coveted its eloquence. Hence, too, a liking sprang up for our style of dress and the toga became fashionable. Step by step they were led to things which dispose to vice, the lounge, the bath, the elegant banquet. All this in their ignorance they called civilization, when it was but a part of their servitude.

For Discussion

1. How do Selections B and C illustrate the process of Romanization?
2. In two of the excerpts presented, Tacitus, like other ancient historians, quotes what he thought *might have been said*. How believable are these speeches? What sort of conclusions can we draw from them?
3. Tacitus used his historical writings to criticize many of the features of the Roman Empire. If history is written to promote a political objective, is it invalid?

SOURCE: A. Tacitus, *Histories*, 4.74; quoted in JoAnn Shelton, *As the Romans Did: A Sourcebook in Roman Social History* (Oxford: Oxford University Press, 1998), p. 288. B. Tacitus, *A Biography of Agricola*, 29–31; quoted in Shelton, p. 287. C. Tacitus, *A Biography of Agricola*, 21; from the *Complete Works of Tacitus*, edited by Moses Hadas, translated by Alfred John Church and William Jackson Brodribb (New York: The Modern Library, 1942).

The Frontier and Beyond

6.3 How did Romans interact with peoples living beyond the imperial borders?

In Virgil's *Aeneid*, Jupiter promises Rome "imperial rule without limit." But by the time of Hadrian's reign (117–138), the limits of the empire were clear. The third concentric circle of the Roman world consisted of the frontier—the outermost regions of the empire and the non-Roman world beyond. For the Romans, the lines drawn between the Roman Empire and the non-Roman world symbolized a cultural division between civilization and barbarism. Romans used this distinction to define their place in the world and to justify their conquests.

Like the generals of the Republic and the Hellenistic kings, Augustus set out to conquer as much land as possible to win glory and to demonstrate his power. He solidified Rome's control over Gaul and added large parts of the Danube River basin to the empire. His successors continued to add new lands to the empire. Britain fell to Rome in 43, and by 117 Trajan had annexed modern Romania, Mesopotamia, and parts of Arabia. At this point, the empire reached its greatest extent.

After Trajan, emperors turned their attention from conquest to consolidation. Trajan's successor, Hadrian, abandoned Mesopotamia and reorganized Rome's frontier with a series of fortifications, including the wall that still crosses the north of Britain and bears his name. His successors continued to fortify both the borders of the empire. By the early third century, regularly spaced military bases and fortresses dotted the empire's northern border while fleets patrolled the Rhine and Danube. In the East, another line of defenses extended from the Black Sea to the Nile. In North Africa, fortifications indicated the limits of cultivable land along the Sahara.

HADRIAN'S WALL Hadrian's massive fortification epitomizes the second-century-C.E. military concept of the fortified frontier. Stretched across northern Britain, it separated the Roman provinces to its south from the "barbarians" to the north.

Rome and the Parthian Empire

One of Rome's most formidable rivals was the Parthian (or Persian) Empire. Stretching from the Euphrates River to Pakistan, Parthia replaced the successor states of Alexander the Great in the mid-third century B.C.E. (see Chapter 4). The Parthian Empire was a powerful state that combined elements of Persian and Hellenistic culture. It survived until 224, when another Persian dynasty, the Sasanian, overthrew the last Parthian king.

The Romans knew the Parthians as fierce warriors. Parthia's specially bred battle horses, famous as far away as China, made heavily armed Parthian cavalrymen and archers worthy opponents of Rome's legions. Augustus—and most of the Roman emperors after him—shifted between war and diplomacy with Parthia. Trajan's conquest of Armenia and the Parthian provinces of Mesopotamia in 115–116 could not be sustained because they overextended Rome's resources.

The rivalry between Parthia and Rome, however, did not prevent commercial and technological exchanges. Romans prized Parthian steel and leather, and learned Parthian techniques of irrigation. In turn, Roman engineers and masons constructed roads and dams in Persia. Caravan routes that brought goods from India to Rome crossed Parthian territory. Most important, the Romans adopted the use of heavily armed cavalry from Parthia. By the fourth century, these units constituted the core of Roman military might.

Roman Encounters with Germanic Peoples

The peoples living north of the Rhine and Danube Rivers, not the Parthians, posed the greatest threat to Rome. Called "Germans" by the Romans, these peoples never used that term or thought of themselves as one group. Numbering in the millions, most of them spoke their own dialects and did not understand the language of other tribes. Led by aristocratic warriors, they often fought among themselves.

In the early years of Augustus's reign, Roman legions conquered large portions of "Germania" between the Rhine and Elbe Rivers. A revolt in 9 C.E. drove out the Romans, however, and Roman civilization never took root in the interior of northern Europe east of the Rhine. (See *Encounters and Transformations* in this chapter.) The Rhine and Danube Rivers became the boundary between Rome and its northern enemies. Most of Rome's legions were stationed along this key dividing line.

Tribes along the northern border sometimes fragmented into pro- and anti-Roman factions and occasionally formed loose confederations to invade the empire. For example, the *Marcomanni*, meaning "men of the borderlands," constituted one of these hostile confederations during the reign of Marcus Aurelius (161–180). Seeking booty, this confederation attacked the empire with more than 100,000 men.

During long periods of peace, the people on either side of the border interacted with one another through military service and trade. Germanic aristocrats developed a taste for Mediterranean luxuries, including wine and jewelry. Some lived in villas in imitation of Roman aristocrats. Germanic men served in the Roman army as auxiliary troops. Discharged after the standard 25 years of service, many of these men returned to their homes with Roman money in their purses, a smattering of Latin, and knowledge of the riches and power of the empire.

By 200, the weight of different peoples pressing on Rome's northern borders began to crack the imperial defenses. With the end of the Severan dynasty in 235, the empire entered 50 years of disasters. Invading groups from north of the Rhine and Danube Rivers pushed as far south as central Italy in search of plunder. The Romans ultimately repelled the invaders and restored the empire's security, but as we will see in the next chapter, the restored empire differed radically from the system Augustus inaugurated.

 **View the Closer Look** Marcus Aurelius and the Impending Invasion

THE EQUESTRIAN STATUE OF MARCUS AURELIUS IN PIAZZA DEL CAMPIDOGLIO IN ROME During his reign from 161–180 C.E., Marcus Aurelius campaigned against the barbarians that attempted to penetrate Rome's northern frontier.

Economic Encounters Across Continents

The Roman Empire was part of an almost global economic web. One Roman account from the first century C.E., *Voyage Around the Red Sea* (author unknown), describes a vast commercial network. Trade routes linked the Mediterranean basin, the East African coast, the Persian Gulf, and the Red Sea with southeast Asia and China.

ENCOUNTERS WITH CHINA Chinese documents from the first century C.E. mention ambassadors sent to Rome who reached as far as the Persian Gulf, and in 166, Roman merchants who claimed they were ambassadors from Emperor Marcus Aurelius went to China, but the two empires never established formal ties.

Silk, not diplomatic links, bound Rome and China together. Superior to wool and linen in texture and in its ability to retain colored dyes, silk was one of the most desired commodities in Roman society. The Chinese possessed a monopoly on silk production (until the sixth century C.E., when Western monks finally succeeded in smuggling the eggs of silkworms and the seeds of mulberry trees out of China).

In the Republican era, silk was so rare that even the wealthiest Romans could afford only small pieces, which they tended to wear as brooches. Then, during the age of Augustus, Romans learned to use the monsoon winds to travel from ports on the

Encounters and Transformations

The Battle of Teutoburg Forest

In September of 9 C.E., the Roman commander in Germania, Publius Quinctilius Varus, received word of an uprising some miles from his army's camp. The report came from Arminius, chief of one of the largest and most powerful German tribes. Arminius had fought for years in the Roman army as an auxiliary commander. His service to Rome earned him Roman citizenship and the rank of equestrian. Thus, when Arminius warned Varus of the rebellion, Varus believed him.

Already heading toward winter camp, Varus detoured into unfamiliar territory to quell the rebellion. After marching for hours, the troops at the head of the two-mile-long column of 18,000 men found themselves on a narrow track between a wooded hill and a bog. Here Arminius and his men, hidden amid the trees, attacked. The Romans were trapped. Packed so tightly that they could not lift their shields or fling their javelins, the soldiers could hardly defend themselves. Within hours, Arminius and his German troops annihilated three legions, along with six auxiliary infantry cohorts and three auxiliary cavalry units. Varus himself committed suicide.

The Battle of Teutoburg Forest, as the encounter between Varus's legions and Arminius's followers came to be known, transformed Roman imperial expectations and established the empire's boundaries in western Europe. Ever since Caesar's conquest of Gaul in 51 B.C.E., Roman forces had endeavored to move north and eastward into Germania. Moreover, in the decades before this momentous battle, Romans had come to view their army as unbeatable, particularly against "barbarians" such as the Germans. Varus's defeat changed all that. In panic, Roman troops abandoned the camps and fortresses that they had built beyond the Rhine. Most of these were never rebuilt. Except for brief punitive expeditions, Roman soldiers never again penetrated deep into Germania.

In 17 C.E. Augustus's successor Tiberius (r. 14–37) formally abandoned any effort to expand the empire across the Rhine. The Rhine River became an important cultural and political dividing line between the Roman and Germanic worlds. To the west and south of this line, Roman rule meant that people drank wine, followed Roman law, and spoke Latin—and eventually, the "Romance" (from "Roman") languages that derive from Latin. East of the Rhine, however, beer-drinking Germany followed a different cultural direction.

Yet Rome influenced that direction. In the decades *before* Varus's defeat, Germanic societies changed as they responded to the imposition of Roman rule over Gaul and the Rhineland. Inter-tribal exchanges and alliances increased—thus enabling these societies to coordinate a surprise attack on three of Rome's finest legions. Germanic societies also grew more hierarchical and militaristic, with mounted warriors gaining in wealth, power, and status. Arminius's victory accentuated these developments. Thus, the Battle of Teutoburg Forest not only halted the expansion of the Roman Empire in western Europe, it also accelerated the transformation of Germanic society that previous Germanic-Roman encounters had already begun.

For Discussion

How was the encounter of Arminius's followers and Varus's troops in 9 C.E. itself the product of a previous "encounter" and "transformation"? And what "transformation" followed the encounter in the Teutoburg Forest?

Red Sea coast of Egypt across the Indian Ocean to the west coast of India, a journey that took about 40 days. In India, merchants exchanged glass, gold, wine, copper, and other items for silk. By the time this trade occurred, the price of the silk would have multiplied several times, as payments were made to each middleman along the 5,000-mile "Silk Road" that ran from northern China across the sweltering deserts, towering mountains, and treacherous salt flats of central Asia and down through modern Afghanistan to the Indian coast (see **Map 6.4**). Yet silk was so precious that a successful journey guaranteed a Roman merchant a profit 100 times larger than his original investment.

Roman demand for silk, spices (especially pepper), and other luxury items from the Far East produced a trade imbalance. As early as the first century C.E., the Roman statesman and natural scientist Pliny the Elder (23–79) griped, "And by the lowest reckoning India, China, and the Arabian Peninsula take from our Empire many thousands of pounds of gold every year—that is the sum which our luxuries and our women cost us." Many historians view the drain of hard currency to the East to pay for luxury goods as a key economic weakness of the empire.

ENCOUNTERS WITH AFRICA Coins found in the interior of Africa suggest that the Romans may have had commercial dealings with peoples there. To the Romans, however, "Africa" was one of their provinces bordering the Mediterranean Sea—the region we know as North Africa today—not the vast continent that lay to the south, beyond the Sahara Desert. Only in the European Middle Ages would the name *Africa* come to stand for the entire continent.

The Romans knew little about sub-Saharan Africa. In 146 B.C.E., the Roman general Scipio Aemilianus sent the historian Polybius on an expedition down the west coast of Africa, which got as far as Senegal and a place Scipio called Crocodile River. In the first century C.E., a Roman military expedition that marched south from a base

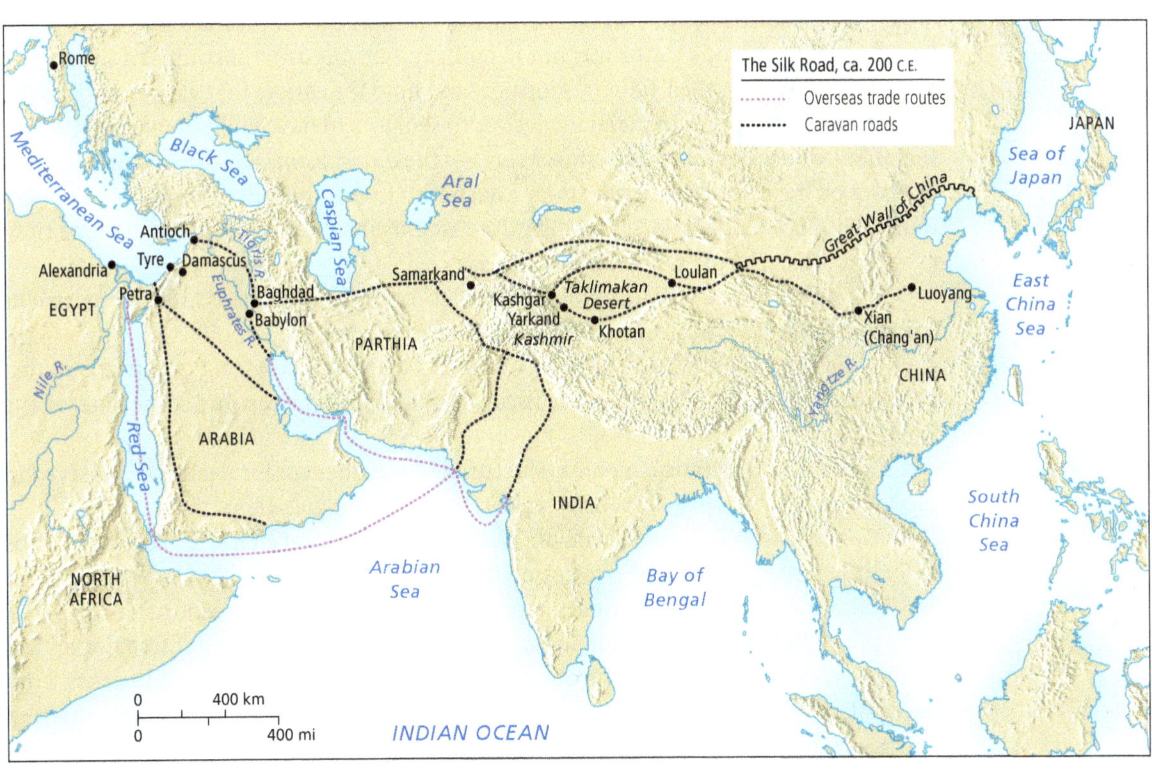

MAP **6.4** THE SILK ROAD The Silk Road linked Asian cultures and economies to those on the continent of Europe for hundreds of years. Why was the first-century C.E. development of sea routes to supplement the overland parts of the journey a significant development? What products made their way across these continents—and why?

in North Africa in pursuit of some raiders may have reached Chad. One hundred years later, an intrepid Roman officer named Julius Maternus traveled south for four months, reaching a place "where the rhinoceroses gather." He emerged in the Sudan, where he found the Nile and returned home.

The Romans used the word *Aethiopians* ("the People with Burned Faces") to refer to the peoples who lived south of the Sahara. Most of their knowledge of these peoples came from the Egyptians, who regularly traded for ivory, gold, and slaves with peoples living in what the Egyptians called Nubia (in modern Sudan), where sophisticated and powerful kingdoms had existed for centuries.

Society and Culture in the Imperial Age

6.4 What was the social and cultural response to the emergence and consolidation of the empire?

The central theme of Roman politics after Augustus—the illusion of continuity masking fundamental change—also characterized imperial society and culture. The basic social structure of the Republic survived the shift to empire, but important changes occurred. While writers and poets praised Rome's greatness, they also explored the ambivalence of life under stable but autocratic rule. The spread of religious cults promising salvation hinted that many people under Roman rule found life less than stable and looked outside the political sphere for safety.

Upper and Lower Classes

In the Roman Empire, aristocrats remained at the top of the social pyramid, enjoying the greatest wealth, power, and prestige. Three social groups, or orders, possessed aristocratic status. The first order, the senators of Rome, occupied the top of the social pyramid. The rank of senator was not hereditary, but Augustus encouraged the sons of senators to follow in their fathers' footsteps and hold the offices that gave entry into the Senate. He also offered financial incentives to senators to have children and perpetuate their family line. Despite these efforts, most of the oldest Roman senatorial families had died out by the end of the first century C.E.; new families from Rome and the provinces took their place. All senators, and their descendants for three generations, had the right to wear a broad purple stripe on their togas.

Below the rank of senators stood the larger order of equestrians. Many equestrians continued to follow business careers as they had during the Republic, but the expansion of the empire gave them new opportunities for public service. Equestrians staffed many of the posts in the diplomatic, fiscal, and military services, and some entered the Senate.

The third aristocratic order was the curiales, members of local elites who served in the councils of every provincial city. Like senators and equestrians, they were expected to be wealthy, as well as of respectable birth and good moral character. Yet many sons of wealthy freedmen became city councilors.

These three aristocratic orders represented only about 1 percent of the empire's population. Below them came the common people—Rome's poor but free underclass of citizens. Although excluded from political life, commoners received benefits from imperial rule. In the city of Rome, adult male citizens received a daily allotment of free grain, olive oil, and pork. Ordinary Romans also received a steady diet of free entertainment, such as gladiatorial combats in the Colosseum and chariot races in the Circus Maximus. The satirist Juvenal (ca. 55–140) described life in the city of Rome as a matter of "bread and circuses": free food and free entertainment.

Ordinary urban Romans needed bread and circuses to compensate not only for their loss of political power, but also for their poor living conditions. Crowded into slums with little light or ventilation, the poor lived in misery. Disease kept birth rates and life expectancies low. Probably more than a quarter of all infants died within their first five years, and a third of those who survived were dead by age 10. The average life expectancy for Roman men was 45 years and the average for women 34.

Poor people lived in similarly wretched conditions in every Roman city, but without the daily distributions of grain. Most rural Romans were farmers, who provided most of the troops in the Roman army.

Slaves and Freedmen

Slavery was a fact of life in every ancient society. When Augustus took control of Rome, slaves constituted 35 to 40 percent of the population of Italy. These millions of slaves held the lowest status in a society in which social and legal status meant everything. Ancient slavery was not based on race or skin color. Most slaves had been captured in war. Others, born of a slave mother, were enslaved from birth.

Ownership of slaves reflected a person's status. The emperor and wealthy aristocrats owned tens of thousands of slaves who labored on their estates throughout the empire. Artisans, teachers, shopkeepers, and freedmen, in contrast, might own a slave or two. Because slaves could earn money, even some slaves owned slaves.

Slaves used for domestic service or in commerce and crafts were the lucky ones. Many male slaves worked on plantations, or "latifundia," as part of slave gangs. They often labored in chains and slept in underground prisons. The male slaves sent to work in the mines, some of whom were convicts, experienced even worse conditions. Female slaves were spared the horrors of working in the fields and mines, but they were valued far less than male slaves.

Violence lay at the heart of the institution of slavery. Masters could physically or sexually abuse slaves with impunity. A slave's testimony in court was valid only if extracted by torture. In the face of such brutality, slaves had few options. They could try to escape, but if caught, they were branded on the forehead. No slave revolt succeeded in imperial or republican Rome.

Slaves, however, might obtain their freedom through manumission. Through this carefully regulated legal procedure, a master granted freedom to a slave as a reward for faithful service, good behavior, or even out of affection. Of course, manumission also worked to the best interests of the owner: The hope of freedom kept slaves docile. Moreover, Roman law established limits to manumission. No more than 100 slaves could be freed at the death of an owner, and the slave had to be at least 30 years old and the owner at least 25.

Former slaves made up only about 5 percent of Rome's population, but their enterprise and ambition made the freedmen an important class. Many worked in business or as skilled laborers, teachers, and doctors. A freedman had only partial citizen rights, but his or her children became full Roman citizens, who could freely marry other citizens.

Slavery remained a part of Mediterranean economic and social life until the early Middle Ages; however, in the second century C.E., the economic role of slaves diminished. As emperors concentrated on consolidating rather than expanding the empire, the supply of slaves from warfare dwindled and their cost rose. Slave owning may have become less economically viable.

Slaves in the Roman Countryside

Women in the Roman Empire

Women in the senatorial and equestrian ranks possessed more freedom than was usual in the ancient world, in part because of a gradual shift in marriage customs. By 250, the form of marriage by which a woman passed from the control of her father to

LADIES AND THEIR HAIRDRESSER A skilled slave styles the hair of a trio of wealthy women in this first century fresco from Pompeii.

that of her husband had nearly died out. Instead, a married woman legally remained under the control of her father or guardian. Because their husbands no longer controlled their dowries, this legal change gave women more freedom. Some women used this freedom to move into the public sphere, taking part in banquets, attending gladiatorial battles at the Colosseum and races at the Circus Maximus, and presiding over literary salons. Women owned property, made investments, and became public benefactors. Many high-ranking women were educated in the liberal arts and lived cultivated lives. Their portraits—carved in stone or painted on walls—reveal a restrained elegance. The portraits of wives and daughters of emperors even appeared on coins.

At the highest level of society, some women possessed political power, though expressed behind the scenes. Livia (58 B.C.E.–29 C.E.), married to Augustus for 52 years, wielded enormous political influence during his and her son Tiberius's reigns. The Emperor Hadrian may have received his throne in part because of the influence of his cousin Trajan's wife, Plotina (d. 121). At her funeral, Hadrian admitted, "She often made requests of me, and I never once refused her."

Most women, of course, were not immortalized in stone or coin and had no political power. We have scanty evidence about the lives of non-aristocratic women in the Roman Empire. We do, however, know of women moneylenders, shopkeepers, and investors. Some women became doctors or artists. Most women probably married and gave birth to three or four children.

Although literary evidence demonstrates that many aristocratic Roman men cherished their daughters, female infanticide remained common. The expected ratio of female to male births is 105 to 100. In second-century C.E. Rome, however, the rate was 100 to 131. Unwanted babies—not only girls but also the sick and malformed, and some born outside marriage—were left by the roadside to die or to be reared by strangers.

Literature and Empire

The prosperity and stability of the Roman Empire allowed the literary arts to flourish. Wealthy patrons, including the emperor, sponsored publications and provided an audience for new works. Yet imperial rule also limited free expression. Roman writers confronted the tensions of living in a society that had exchanged freedom for stability.

The career of the philosopher Seneca (ca. 4 B.C.E.–65 C.E.) illustrates the constraints facing writers in the imperial era. Seneca intended his writings to give advice to rulers. Influenced by Stoicism (see Chapter 4), he acknowledged how hard it was to live a moral life. Seneca's integrity and rhetorical brilliance earned him the unenviable task of being Nero's tutor when the emperor was still an impressionable 12-year-old. For eight years Seneca guided Nero, and the empire enjoyed good government. As Nero matured, however, he found other, less decent advisers. Seneca, appalled by his student's descent into corruption, was accused of plotting to kill Nero. To avoid execution, he killed himself.

HISTORY-WRITING IN AN AGE OF AUTOCRACY The work of the historian Livy (59 B.C.E.–12 C.E.) illustrates the fine line writers in this autocratic society walked. In his history Livy presented Rome's rise to world mastery as a series of moral and patriotic lessons. He showed how Rome's military and moral strength catapulted it to world power. Although proud of Rome's greatness, Livy believed that with power came decadence. He did not gloss over the ruthlessness with which Augustus waged the civil war that destroyed the Republic, nor did he veil his criticism of what he perceived as Rome's moral and political decline. Livy's open criticism displeased Augustus, yet the emperor did not punish the historian, perhaps because Livy also expressed the hope that Augustus would restore Rome's glory.

The historian Tacitus (ca. 55–ca. 120) belonged to a later generation. While Livy experienced the tumultuous transition from republic to empire, Tacitus lived and wrote when the imperial system was firmly in place. Although his own career flourished under both the tyrannical Domitian and the just Trajan, Tacitus hated political oppression. He never abandoned his love for the best of Roman ideals. In the *Agricola,* his biography of his father-in-law, Tacitus affirmed that good men could serve their country honorably, even under bad rulers such as Nero. The *Agricola* thus inadvertently revealed an important accomplishment of Augustus's imperial system: It had tamed Rome's aristocrats, transforming them into an efficient governing class.

IMPERIAL POETRY Poets, too, had to adapt to life in an autocracy. The tragic career of Ovid (43 B.C.E.–17 C.E.) demonstrated the risks of offending an emperor. Ovid's love poems had made him the darling of Rome. But his lighthearted descriptions of Roman sexual life violated Augustus's efforts to restore traditional family values, while his book *Metamorphoses,* with its themes of change and impermanence in Greek and Roman mythology, indirectly challenged the ideal of a stable state under Augustus's leadership. In 8 C.E., Ovid's erotic poem, "The Art of Love," along with a sexual scandal involving Augustus's granddaughter, earned him the hostility of the emperor. Augustus exiled Ovid to a village on the Black Sea where the poet remained for the rest of his life.

Horace (65–8 B.C.E.), son of a wealthy freedman, escaped Ovid's fate by avoiding political and sexual entanglements and maintaining close ties to Augustus. His poetry on public themes praised the emperor for bringing peace and the hope of a moral life to the world. Throughout his work, Horace urged appreciation of life's temporary joys. In his most famous verse, he sings,

> Be wise, taste the wine, and since our time is brief, be moderate in your aspirations. Even as we speak, greedy life slips away from us. Grasp each day (*carpe diem*) and do not pin your hopes on tomorrow.

Virgil also earned Augustus's favor. At Augustus's request Virgil composed the *Aeneid*, an epic poem that legitimized and celebrated the emperor's reign. The *Aeneid* tells the story of Aeneas, a Trojan prince who founds the city of Rome. Through a series of cinematic "flash-forwards," Virgil presented the entire history of the Roman people as culminating in the reign of Augustus. Yet Virgil was not just an imperial propagandist as the ending of the *Aeneid* shows. Tempted by his love for the Carthaginian queen Dido to abandon his mission of founding Rome, Aeneas overcomes his personal desire to fulfill his mission: He abandons Dido, who then commits suicide. At the end of the poem, Aeneas stands victorious—but he has sacrificed everything. Virgil makes his readers wonder about the costs of public service.

Juvenal also exposed the weaknesses of the imperial age. One of the most quotable of Roman poets, Juvenal's satires mocked overeducated women, duplicitous Greeks, and boring provincials. His favorite target, however, was daily life in Rome. His descriptions of the city's noise, smells, flimsy housing, crowded streets, and pervasive criminality emphasized the wide gap in lifestyles between privileged and ordinary folk, and so highlighted the corruption of republican ideals.

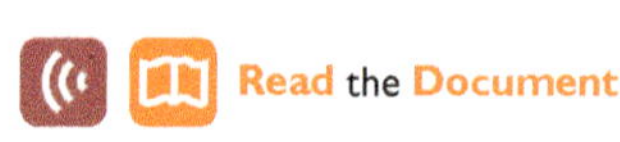

Juvenal, A Satirical View of Women

Science in the Roman Empire

The Hellenistic scientific tradition (see Chapter 4) flourished under Roman rule. Using the division of spheres into units of 60 first developed by the Sumerians and perfected by the Babylonians, Claudius Ptolemy (ca. 90–170) codified the Hellenistic theory that the sun revolves around the Earth. Western astronomers used Ptolemy's maps of the heavens for nearly 1,500 years, while his *Geography* remained the basis of cartography until the sixteenth century.

Roman medicine shaped Western practices for more than 1,500 years. The physician Galen (131–201) sought to make medicine a science. He insisted on the importance of dissection for understanding the body and stressed the need for experimentation. For most of his career, Galen worked in Rome, but he served for four years as physician to the gladiators in Pergamum in Anatolia, where he was able to study firsthand the impact of trauma on the human body.

Galen's main influence on Western medicine, however, was negative. Galen believed that an imbalance in the body's four "humors," or basic bodily fluids (blood, black bile, yellow bile, and phlegm), produced disease. Too much blood, for example, meant fever. To restore the balance, Galen taught, the physician should restore the balance by applying leeches or cutting open a vein, and thereby drain the patient of "excess" blood. A strong purgative or emetic to induce vomiting or diarrhea could drain "excess" bile. Bloodletting and purging, and the humoral theory on which they were based, remained central in Western medical practice into the early nineteenth century. Unfortunately, these treatments weakened or killed innumerable patients.

Religious Life

Because the imperial regime made no effort to regulate religion, people throughout the empire freely worshiped many gods and maintained their traditional rituals. Nevertheless, this era witnessed significant religious change, including the transformation of Judaism and the emergence of Christianity.

POLYTHEISM IN THE EMPIRE Syncretism, the practice of equating gods and fusing their cults, was a common feature of imperial religious life and helped unify the empire. The Romans often identified foreign gods with their own deities. Romans did not care that other peoples might worship Jupiter, Juno, or any other Roman god in different ways or give the gods different attributes.

Each city in the empire had its own gods, but some religious cults transcended their places of origin. Feeling lost in the sprawl of the empire's cities, slaves, freedmen, and the urban poor turned to religions that offered both community and salvation. Religions that promised victory over death or liberation from the abuses and pain of daily existence spread across the empire.

The goddess Isis, for example, who originated in Egypt, offered freedom from fate to her many followers. Her story revolved around the death and resurrection of her husband, Osiris (also called Serapis). Her worshipers believed that they, too, would experience life after death. Moreover, Isis—often depicted holding her baby son, Horus—represented the universal mother and so promised compassionate nurture. In *The Golden Ass,* the Roman writer Apuleius (ca. 125–170) described the goddess's protective power. Full of eroticism and magic, the story tells of Lucius, a young Romeo, who turns into a donkey after he is caught spying on a gorgeous witch. Lucius stumbles through misadventures until Isis restores him to human form. Lucius thanks her for caring "for the troubles of miserable humans with a sweet mother's love" and becomes her priest.

MUMMY WRAPPING FROM EGYPT A painted linen cloth, wrapped around a mummy in an Egyptian burial during the second century C.E., shows the Egyptian god Osiris (on the left) and the jackal-headed god Anubis (on the right). Between them is the dead man, dressed in Roman clothing. His portrait has been carefully painted and added separately. The wrapping and portrait demonstrate the continuity of ancient Egyptian religion during Roman imperial rule.

Another religion that promised salvation to its initiates was that of Mithras, a sun god. According to his followers, Mithras was killed by his enemies on December 21, the winter solstice, and rose from the dead on December 25. By worshiping Mithras, his followers believed they too could achieve life after death. Limited to men, worship of Mithras took place in underground chambers in which small groups celebrated a ceremonial meal that evoked Mithras's memory, recited lessons about the journey of the soul after death, and sacrificed to the god. Because this religion stressed courage and duty, it particularly attracted soldiers.

Worship of the Unconquered Sun (Sol Invictus) also spread throughout the empire. Originating in Syria, this deity was associated with Helios-Apollo, the Greco-Roman sun god, and with Mithras. When Elagabalus, the high priest of the Syrian sun god (El-Gabal), became Roman emperor (r. 218–222), he built a huge temple dedicated to his god in Rome, and designated December 25, the birth and resurrection day of Mithras, as a special day of worship to the deity. Within 50 years, the Unconquered Sun became the chief god of official worship.

THE ORIGINS OF RABBINIC JUDAISM Roman rule reshaped Judaism and the history of the Jewish people. In 37 B.C.E., the Roman Senate appointed Herod the Great (37–4 B.C.E.), a Roman ally from southern Palestine, as "King of the Jews." Despite this grand

MITHRAS SLAYS THE BULL Designed around 200 C.E., a wall painting from a shrine at Marino, south of Rome, shows the god Mithras in the sacred act of sacrificing a bull. Limited to men only, the worship of Mithras occurred throughout the empire. Scholars are unsure of the symbolic meaning of the dog, scorpion, and snake shown in this painting.

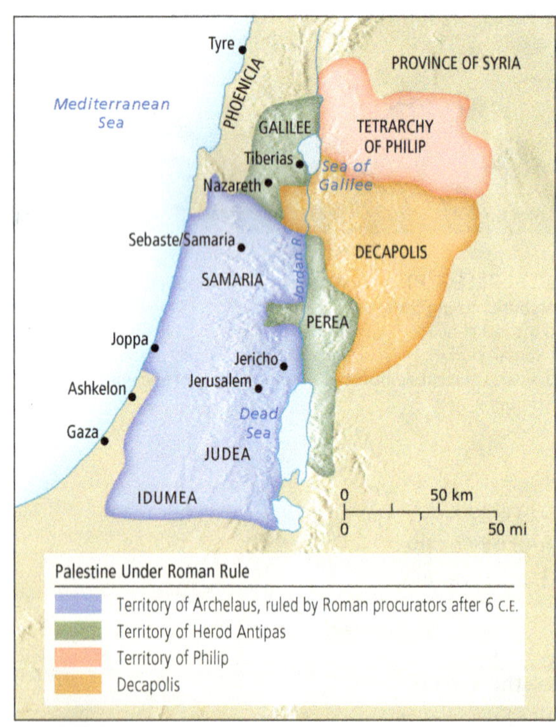

MAP **6.5** PALESTINE UNDER ROMAN RULE Herod the Great (73 B.C.E.–4 B.C.E.) ruled Palestine as a client king of Rome. After he died, however, the kingdom was divided among three of his sons. Just two years later, the Romans deposed Archelaus, the son who had inherited Judea, and assumed direct rule over his territories. How does this map illustrate the varieties of Roman administrative arrangements for governing the vast empire? How does it help explain why both Herod the Great and Herod Antipas play a role in the Gospel accounts of Jesus of Nazareth's birth, life, and death?

title, Herod ruled at the Romans' behest. Most Jews never regarded him as their rightful king. After Herod's death, his kingdom was divided among his three sons, but in 6 C.E., Augustus annexed the largest and most important of these kingdoms: Judea. The annexation of Judea meant that the Romans now directly controlled the city of Jerusalem, the spiritual center of Jewish life (see **Map 6.5**). Inept governors and heavy taxation caused Judea's economy to decline, famines and banditry became common, and a divide opened up among the Jews. The landed elite benefited from Roman rule. Ordinary Jews, however, viewed their leaders as collaborators with a godless power. They followed the scribes and rabbis ("my master" in Hebrew). These men of learning, who devoted their lives to copying religious texts and interpreting the scriptures, had little stake in Roman rule.

Sixty years of Roman mismanagement and the Jewish desire for independence led to revolt in Judea in 66. Jews formed their own government, appointed regional military commanders, abolished debt, and issued their own coinage. Internal divisions, however, weakened the rebellion. Imperial forces captured Jerusalem in 70, destroyed the Temple, and enslaved an estimated two million people.

Yet Judaism and the Jews survived. A new kind of religious life developed. Since the sixth century B.C.E., communities of Jews had lived outside Palestine, but after the Romans ransacked Judea, the **Diaspora** ("dispersion of population") characterized Jewish life. Jerusalem ceased to be the focus of Judaism's religious ceremony, although not of Jewish religious thought and hope. Animal sacrifice centered in the Temple disappeared. The rabbi replaced the priest

ARCH OF TITUS This marble relief from the Arch of Titus represents the loot from the Temple of Jerusalem carried in the triumphal parade in Rome after Titus crushed the Jewish revolt of 66–70. Soldiers display the Great Menorah, one of the holiest symbols of Judaism.

as religious instructor and community guide. Trained in the Jewish law, rabbis interpreted and taught the Torah and settled disputes. Synagogues developed into centers where Jews celebrated the Sabbath and prayed together.

The **Mishnah** emerged from this era. A collection of opinions, decisions, and homilies from both oral tradition and texts written to explain the Jewish law, the Mishnah was completed around 220. Each of the Mishnah's 63 books deals with a particular aspect of law, from ritual purity to crime. Among the moral principles the Mishnah stresses, saving life was paramount. To save a life, any person could break any Jewish religious law, except those forbidding idolatry, adultery, incest, or murder. Saving one life symbolized saving humanity.

Diaspora Literally "dispersion of population"; usually used to refer to the dispersion of the Jewish population after the Roman destruction of the Temple in Jerusalem in 70 C.E.

Mishnah Completed around 220, a collection of homilies and decisions to explain Jewish law.

Read the Document

Judaism

THE EMERGENCE OF CHRISTIANITY Over a century before the Mishnah was compiled, the new religion of Christianity grew from Jewish roots. Beginning around 28 C.E., Jesus of Nazareth (ca. 4 B.C.E.–ca. 30 C.E.), a Jew from Galilee in northern Palestine, traveled through Palestine with a band of followers, urging men and women to join together in God's Kingdom before the imminent end of this world (see Map 6.5). Jesus's followers believed him to be the messiah, an important figure in Jewish prophetic writings. In Jewish belief, the messiah's coming would inaugurate a new age of blessing for God's people.

Read the Document

Excerpt from the Gospel According to Luke

Sometime between 30 and 33 C.E., Jesus entered Jerusalem to preach his message. Roman authorities convicted him as a revolutionary and crucified him—the usual capital punishment for noncitizens in the empire. Jesus's followers, however, insisted that he rose from the dead and ascended into heaven, and that his spirit remained on Earth and guided their lives. Eventually called "Christians" (from the Greek word *Christ,* meaning "messiah" or "anointed one"), these men and women expected that Jesus would soon return and launch a new age of righteousness. They shared their possessions in common and—in a shocking violation of Roman and Jewish emphasis on family life—downplayed family and social ties. As the decades passed without Jesus's return, however, they focused on building their communities and preserving their distinctive faith.

But what defined this faith? Jesus's first followers were Jews who regarded him as a rabbi, a prophet, and eventually the messiah—all Jewish religious concepts. But as

Read the Document

Christianity

Christianity spread to non-Jews, and as Christians adjusted their expectations of Jesus's return, diverse and often clashing understandings of Jesus emerged.

In this process of religious debate and development, the work and teaching of Paul of Tarsus (d. ca. 65) were crucial. An educated Jew, Paul traveled throughout Anatolia and Greece, founding and developing Christian communities. Even more important, he wrote letters, or Epistles, that circulated among these communities. Written in the 50s, these letters taught that Jesus was not only the Jewish messiah, but also the Son of God who died on the cross as part of the divine plan. In Paul's letters, Jesus's brutal death became a loving sacrifice: By enduring the punishment that sinful men and women deserved, the sinless Son of God gave his followers eternal life in heaven after they died on Earth.

orthodox In Christianity, the term indicates doctrinally correct belief.

heresy A teaching or belief not considered orthodox.

New Testament The collection of texts that, together with the Hebrew Bible, or Old Testament, comprise the Christian Bible. New Testament texts include the Epistles (letters of Paul of Tarsus to early Christians), the Gospels (stories of Jesus Christ's life, death, and resurrection), and other early Christian documents.

Paul's version of Jesus's teaching became the foundation of **orthodox** Christianity. *Orthodox* means "right belief," and from the mid-third century on, Christians who promoted beliefs about Jesus that differed from those defined as orthodox faced the charge of **heresy**. *Heresy* literally translates as "choice." A heretic was someone who chose to believe wrong things. But in the 200 years after Jesus's death, orthodox Christianity did not yet exist, and neither did the **New Testament** (the collection of texts that, together with the Old Testament or Hebrew Bible, comprise the Christian Bible). Because Jesus himself wrote nothing, different groups with different ideas could each claim to be his true followers.

View the Closer Look

Early Christian Symbols

While Paul, for example, taught that non-Jewish Christian men did not need to be circumcised (a key Jewish initiation rite) and that non-Jews need not follow Jewish dietary restrictions, others of Jesus's followers insisted that all Christians had to abide by all Jewish laws. Still other early Christians, called Marcionites, rejected not only Jewish laws and customs, but also the Jewish Scriptures and even the Jewish God. In their view, Jesus was not the Jewish messiah, but rather the chosen messenger of a loving God who came to Earth to save people from the vengeful God of the Jews.

An even more divisive issue than the relationship of Christians to Judaism was the question of Jesus's divinity. "Adoptionist" Christians saw Jesus as fully human, a man that God adopted to be his special son and to carry out his mission, while "docetic" Christians argued that Jesus only appeared to possess a material body but was in fact divine and not human at all. A third group of Christians believed Jesus was fully God and fully human. In 325 (see Chapter 7), this third view became orthodox

Justice in History

The Trial of Jesus in Historical Perspective

In 30 C.E. imperial authorities in Jerusalem in the Roman province of Judea tried and executed a Jewish teacher known as Jesus of Nazareth. Although an insignificant event at the time, the trial of Jesus and its interpretation has had a profound impact on Western civilization.

Information about Jesus's trial comes from the New Testament books of Matthew, Mark, Luke, and John. These narratives, called the Gospels, were written 30 to 60 years after Jesus's death. They relate that during three years of teaching and miracles in Galilee and Judea, Jesus earned the resentment of the Jewish religious leadership by disregarding aspects of Jewish religious law. According to the Gospels, when Jesus entered the Temple precinct in Jerusalem, he angered the Jewish elites by denouncing their hypocrisy and overturning the tables of money changers. The priests then conspired to kill him. They paid one of Jesus's followers to reveal his whereabouts. Soldiers arrested Jesus on the night either before or of the Passover feast and brought him to the house of Caiaphas, the Jewish High Priest. There Jesus either had a private hearing before the High Priest and his father-in-law (according to the Gospel of John) or a trial before the Sanhedrin, the highest Jewish court. According

(continued on next page)

(continued from previous page)

to the Gospels of Matthew, Mark, and Luke, the Sanhedrin found Jesus guilty of blasphemy for claiming to be the messiah, the Son of God.

Lacking the authority under Roman rule to put Jesus to death, the Jewish leaders brought him before Pontius Pilate, the Roman governor, and demanded that he execute Jesus. Pilate hesitated, but the priests persuaded him by insisting that Jesus threatened the emperor's authority by claiming to be king of the Jews. Pilate's soldiers crucified Jesus, but according to the Gospels, the blame for Jesus's death lay with the Jews who demanded his execution. In all four Gospels, Jewish crowds in Jerusalem cry out, "Crucify him!" to a reluctant Pilate.

The Gospel accounts of Jesus's arrest, trial, and crucifixion pose problems for historians. Parts of these narratives conflict with what scholars understand about the conduct of trials by Jewish authorities and Roman administrators. For example, the historical evidence that we have indicates that the Sanhedrin did not hold trials at night. It did not meet in the house of the High Priest, nor convene on a feast day or the night before a feast.

Far more important than these issues, however, is the question of the crime of blasphemy. In first-century Judaism, the messiah was expected to be a kingly figure—but not God. If Jesus did identify himself as the messiah, he would not have been guilty of blasphemy. Some scholars, however, point out that the Jewish leaders would have regarded Jesus's claim to sit in God's presence (and thus to share in God's rule) as blasphemous.

Jesus's blasphemy remains unclear, but there is little debate about the importance of Jesus's confrontation with the Jewish elites in the Temple. Jesus committed a dangerous act by denouncing the priests in Jerusalem. These men, especially the High Priest himself, owed their power to the Roman overlords and were responsible for maintaining order. Many Jews in the Temple elite saw Jesus as an agitator who threatened their authority. According to Matthew, Mark, and Luke, the Temple guards, not Roman soldiers, arrested Jesus and brought him before the Sanhedrin. The Romans had appointed all 71 members of the court, including Caiaphas, who led it. These men knew that if they could not control Jesus, the Romans would replace them. The court could not execute Jesus, but it could send him before Roman magistrates on a charge that the Romans would prosecute—stirring up rebellion.

Jesus's popularity with the common people and the disturbance in the Temple precinct would have aroused Roman suspicion. Moreover, if Jesus had claimed to be the messiah, he was guilty of insurrection from a Roman standpoint, for the term had royal connotations, and no one within the empire could be called a king without the emperor's permission. Roman officials usually responded to real or imagined threats to the political order by crucifixion. In the eyes of Pontius Pilate, a cautious magistrate, Jesus was a threat to public order, and so deserved execution. Pilate would not have been reluctant to kill him.

Why, then, do the Gospels tend to shift the blame for Jesus's death from Pilate to the Jewish community? The Gospels began to be written down amid growing hostility and suspicion between Jews and Christians. Moreover, after Roman armies destroyed the Temple in the Jewish rebellion of 66–70, Christians wanted to disassociate themselves from Jews. They hoped to persuade Roman authorities to think of them not as rebels, but as followers of a lawful religion. Such concerns may have shaped the Gospel writers' tendencies to emphasize the role of Jewish leaders instead of Pilate in Jesus's death.

The Gospels also relate that before he died, Jesus predicted the destruction of the Temple. Many early Christians came to believe that the fall of the Temple and the savage repression of the Jewish rebellion were divine punishment for the Jews who had caused Jesus's death. These interpretations of Jesus's trial and execution, and of the destruction of the Jewish community in Palestine, helped poison Christian–Jewish relations for two millennia. From the first century through the twentieth, important segments of the Christian community blamed "the Jews" for Jesus's crucifixion.

For Discussion

1. What does Jesus's trial show about Roman methods of provincial administration—and about the limitations of these methods? Who had power in Judea?
2. In Christian theology, Jesus died for the sins of the world. In theological terms, then, all sinners—all human beings—bear responsibility for his death. Why does it matter if the Gospels blame Jesus's crucifixion on Jews instead of Romans?

Taking It Further

Borg, Marcus, and N.T. Wright. *The Meaning of Jesus: Two Visions.* 2007. Two leading New Testament scholars present their interpretations of the historical Jesus.

Crossan, John Dominic. *Who Killed Jesus: Exposing the Roots of Anti-Semitism in the Gospel Story of the Death of Jesus.* San Francisco: HarperSanFrancisco, 1997. An engaging and controversial investigation.

Sherwin-White, A. N. *Roman Society and Roman Law in the New Testament.* Eugene, OR: Wipf and Stock Publishers, 2004. A leading historian puts the New Testament in its Roman context.

doctrine, but in the first and second centuries, the Christian understanding of Jesus was far from set.

The question of Christianity's relationship with the material world also remained open in these centuries, as the emergence of **Gnostic** versions of Christianity illustrates. Gnostic beliefs varied widely (and not all Gnostics embraced Christianity), but in general Gnosticism taught that men and women are really spiritual beings who belong to God's realm, the world of the good, the world of the spirit. In contrast, the material world (including the human body) is not God's creation, but a fundamentally evil prison in which human spirits are trapped. In the Gnostic view, few humans recognize or *know* these truths. *Gnostic* comes from the Greek word

Gnostic Religious doctrine that emphasizes the importance of *gnosis*, or hidden truth, as a way of releasing spiritual reality from the prison of the essentially unreal or evil material world.

CHRIST AS THE GOOD SHEPHERD Carved in the second century C.E., this statue depicts Jesus as a good shepherd, a frequent motif in early Christian art. An image drawn from both the Hebrew Bible and Greek representations of the god Apollo, the Good Shepherd illustrates the blending of Greek and Hebrew ideas in Christianity.

gnosis, for knowledge. Gnosticism taught that only a few men and women possess the secret knowledge that will allow them to escape from the evil of this world and return to their rightful spiritual home. In Gnostic Christianity, then, Jesus is a kind of cosmic riddler who came not to save the world, but to save his few from the world. Gnosticism tended to promote disengagement from worldly affairs and detachment from physical needs and desires. While the solidification of orthodoxy in the third century meant that Gnostic Christians were labeled heretics, the question of the proper Christian attitude toward worldly concerns and bodily desires divides believers even today.

CHRISTIANITY WITHIN THE ROMAN WORLD Christianity drew many of its first converts from the urban "middle classes"—merchants, artisans, business owners—but it also appealed to socially marginalized groups, such as women, noncitizens, and slaves. Indeed, Jesus's message was revolutionary in the way it overturned boundaries of class, gender, and ethnicity. After Jesus's death, Paul encouraged a communal life in which all followers of Jesus were equal in the eyes of God. As he wrote to a small Christian community in Galatia in Anatolia, "For in Christ Jesus . . . there is no longer Jew or Greek, there is no longer slave or free, there is no longer male or female; for all of you are one in Christ Jesus."

Many of Christianity's core concepts, such as its ideas about personal salvation, the equality of individual men and women before God, and the redemption of humanity from sin, distinguished it from the empire's polytheistic faiths. Most strikingly, Christianity firmly rejected the existence of multiple gods and sought to convince followers of other religions that they stood in error. This conversionist impulse (called *proselytizing*), in addition to Christians' withdrawal from the public life of Roman culture, earned them suspicion—and sometimes death.

Until the mid-third century, persecutions of Christians tended to be local affairs, sparked by the hostility of a city magistrate or provincial governor. In 64, however, Emperor Nero blamed Christians for a fire that consumed central Rome. (Popular legend blamed him, equally wrongly.) Hundreds of Christians died in the arena before cheering crowds.

Christians called those who died rather than renounce their beliefs **martyrs**, or witnesses for their faith. The early Christian leader Tertullian (ca. 160–240) chided his Roman persecutors, "We multiply whenever we are mown down by you; the blood of Christians is [like] seed." But in 235 (the end date of this chapter), Christianity remained a minority movement within the Roman Empire.

Read the Document

Gnostic Teachings of Jesus, According to Irenaeus

  Read the Document

Perpetua, The Autobiography of a Christian Martyr

CONCLUSION

Rome Shapes the West

The map of the Roman Empire outlined the heart of the regions included in the West today. Rome was the means by which cultural and political ideas developed in Mediterranean societies and spread into Europe. This quilt of lands and peoples was acquired mostly by conquest. An autocratic government stitched the pieces together. Although Roman authorities permitted no dissent, they allowed provincial peoples to become Roman. Being Roman meant that one had specific legal rights of citizenship, not that one belonged to a particular race or ethnic group. Thus, in addition to conquering the empire and patrolling its borders, the Roman army brought a version of Roman society to subject peoples. By imitating Roman styles of architecture and urban life, the cities, too, spread Roman civilization. Moreover, the elites of these cities helped funnel the resources of the countryside into the emperor's coffers, and so sustained the imperial system.

Rome's civilization, including its legal system, its development of cities, and its literary and artistic legacy, became the basis of much of Western civilization. The legal precedents Roman jurists established remain valid in much of Europe. Latin and Greek literature of the early Roman Empire has entertained, instructed, and inspired Western readers for nearly 2,000 years. Until recently all educated people in the West could read Latin, and many could read Greek. Many of our public buildings and memorial sculptures adhere to Roman models. The Roman Empire was the most important and influential model of an imperial system for Europeans until modern times. Of equal importance, the monotheism and ethical teachings of Judaism and Christianity have shaped Western culture.

martyr In Christian tradition, believers who chose to die rather than to renounce or deny their Christian beliefs.

MAKING CONNECTIONS

1. Evaluate this argument: "Behind a carefully crafted façade of restored Republican tradition, Octavian created a Roman version of a Hellenistic monarchy, like those of Alexander the Great's successors in the eastern Mediterranean." What are the characteristics of a Hellenistic monarchy? Which of these characteristics did the Augustan system of imperial rule share? Why did Augustus seek to maintain the "façade of restored Republican tradition"?
2. How did the relationship between the Jewish population of Palestine and the Roman imperial government in the first century C.E. shape the early history of Christianity?

TAKING IT FURTHER

For suggested readings, see page R-1.

On MyHistoryLab

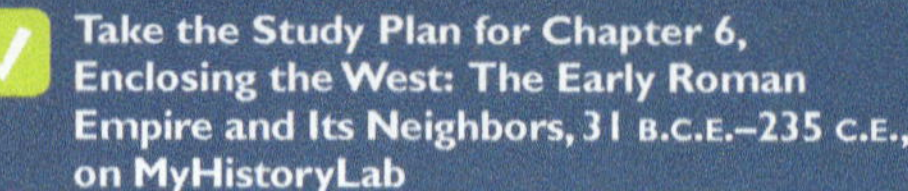

Chapter Review

The Imperial Center

6.1 How did the Roman imperial system develop, and what roles did the emperor, Senate, army, and city of Rome play in this process?

While Rome officially remained a Republic, a hereditary monarchy resulted when Augustus eliminated his enemies in the Roman Senate and defeated his military rivals. The role of the emperor included protecting and expanding territory, administering justice, supervising the public worship of Roman gods, and being a symbol of unity for the empire. The politically impotent Senate acted as an administrative arm of the emperor, and a loyal and large imperial army was crucial to maintaining his power. Finally, the city of Rome, including public works that demonstrated his power, was a testament to the authority of the emperor.

Life in the Roman Provinces: Assimilation, Resistance, and Romanization

6.2 How did provincial peoples assimilate to or resist Roman rule?

Provincial peoples were assimilated into imperial life when they joined the army as provincial recruits and adopted and adapted Roman culture. Revolts by conquered peoples were common soon after defeat, but were also short-lived and unsuccessful. New urban centers became smaller versions of Rome, where gradually the local elites learned Latin, worshiped Roman gods, adopted Roman visual arts, and were sometimes granted citizenship.

The Frontier and Beyond

6.3 How did Romans interact with peoples living beyond the imperial borders?

From commercial and technological exchanges with Parthia, to the trade of luxury items with China and contact with the Germanic and African peoples, a combination of trade, skirmishes, and cultural transmission marked Roman interaction with the peoples beyond their borders.

Society and Culture in the Imperial Age

6.4 What was the social and cultural response to the emergence and consolidation of the empire?

While the basic social structure of the empire appeared the same, with an elite group of the wealthy at the top of society and the lower classes living in poverty and squalor, a gradual shift in marriage customs gave women in the upper classes more autonomy and power. The arts continued to flourish despite imperial restrictions, with literature reflecting some of the inequalities of Roman life. The rise of religious cults, including Christianity with its message of personal salvation and equality of individuals, attested to the spread of social unrest and the fact many people under Roman rule were looking outside the political sphere for safety.

Chapter Time Line

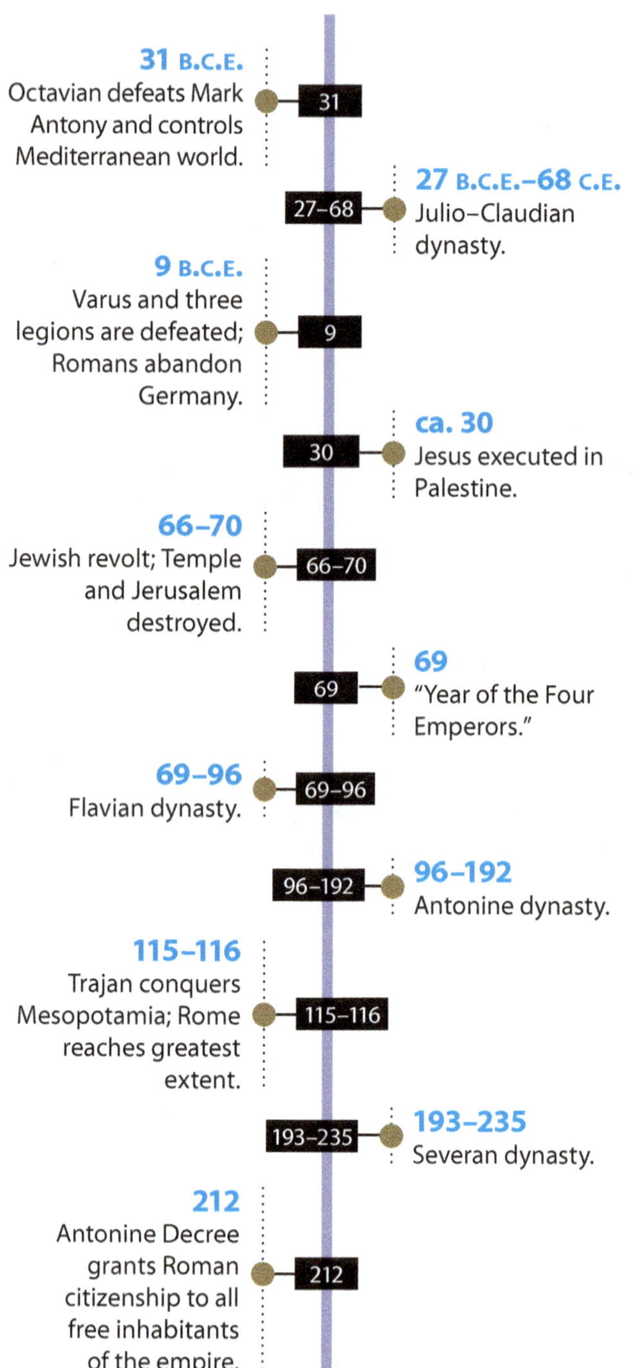

7 Late Antiquity: The Age of New Boundaries, 250–600

The events of the last week of August in 410 stunned the Roman World. A small army of landless warriors—no more than a few thousand men—led by their king, Alaric, forced their way into the city of Rome and plundered it for three days. For more than a year, Alaric had been threatening the city in an attempt to extort gold and land for his people. When his attempts at extortion failed, he attacked the city directly. Because Alaric's followers, the Visigoths, were Christian, they spared Rome's churches and took care not to violate the nuns. But that left plenty of loot—gold, silver, and silk—for them to cart away, and they did not hesitate to plunder the tombs of pagan emperors, including the Mausoleum of Augustus.

For these warriors and their families, who had first invaded the Roman Empire from their homelands in southern Russia 30 years earlier, pillaging the most opulent city in the Mediterranean world was a profitable interlude in a long struggle to secure a permanent home. For the Romans, however, the looting of Rome was an unfathomable disaster. They could scarcely believe that their capital city, the gleaming symbol of world rule, had fallen to an army of people they considered barbarian thugs. "If Rome is

View the Closer Look Tetrarchy: The Division of the Roman Empire Under Diocletian

THE TETRARCHS To depict their solidarity and readiness for war, the tetrarchs or co-emperors are presented as soldiers in military uniform, holding their swords with one hand and clasping their colleague's shoulder with the other. Each pair of figures shows one junior emperor and one senior emperor, who has more worry lines in his forehead as a sign of his greater responsibilities.

LEARNING OBJECTIVES

7.1 How did the Roman Empire successfully reorganize following the instability of the third century?

7.2 How did Christianity become the dominant religion in the Roman Empire, and how did it affect Roman society?

7.3 How did Christianity transform communities, religious experience, and intellectual traditions inside and outside the Roman Empire?

7.4 How and why did the Roman Empire in the West disintegrate?

Listen to **Chapter 7** on **MyHistoryLab**

Watch the Video Series on MyHistoryLab

Learn about some key topics related to this chapter with the *MyHistoryLab Video Series: Key Topics in Western Civilization*

sacked, what can be safe?" lamented the Christian theologian Jerome when he heard the news in far-off Jerusalem. His remark captured the outrage and astonishment felt by Roman citizens everywhere, Christian and non-Christian alike, who believed that their empire was divinely protected and would last forever.

How did the Visigoths manage to sack Rome? The answer is rooted in the radical and debilitating transformations of the Roman Empire during late antiquity, the period between about 250 and 600, which bridged the classical world and the Middle Ages. **Late antiquity** can be divided into three stages. The first stage consisted of the half-century crisis from 235 to 284 of near-fatal civil war, foreign invasion, and economic crisis. During the second stage Rome experienced nearly 100 years of political reform and economic revival that stabilized it during the fourth century. Yet during the fifth century, the third stage of late antiquity, the political unity of the Mediterranean world ended. The Roman Empire collapsed in the West, and new Germanic kingdoms developed in Italy, Gaul, Britain, Spain, and North Africa. In contrast, the Roman Empire in the East, centered on its new capital city of Constantinople (modern Istanbul), managed to survive and prosper. Until their empire fell to the Turks 1,000 years later in 1453, the inhabitants of this eastern realm considered themselves Romans. In both Constantinople (where Roman political administration was maintained) and the new kingdoms of the West (where it was not), Rome's cultural legacy continued in the Greek and Latin languages and some forms of Roman law.

late antiquity The period between about 250 and 600, which bridged the classical world and the Middle Ages.

During late antiquity Christianity emerged as the dominant religion throughout the Roman Empire. From there it spread beyond the imperial borders, bringing new notions of civilization to the peoples of northern Europe, North Africa, and the Middle East. Henceforth, Western civilization was for most people a Christian civilization, and the borders that separated peoples were not just political ones, as in the ancient world, but religious ones. The encounter between the Roman Empire and Christianity raised this question:

How did their mutual interactions transform both the culture of the empire and the practice of Christianity?

Crisis and Recovery in the Third Century

7.1 How did the Roman Empire successfully reorganize following the instability of the third century?

Between 235 and 284, the Roman Empire staggered from political and economic turmoil. The institutions of the army and the office of the emperor, which had made the Roman Empire the dominant power in the Mediterranean, seemed incapable of standing up to new threats. Generals competed for the throne, chronic civil war shook the empire's very foundation, and invaders hungry for land and plunder broke through the weakened imperial borders. However, by the end of the third century, Emperor Diocletian arrested the disintegration with drastic administrative and social reforms.

The Breakdown of the Imperial Government

After the assassination of Emperor Severus Alexander in 235, military coup followed military coup as ruthless generals with nicknames like "Sword-in-Hand" competed for the throne. In the latter half of the third century, not one of more than four dozen emperors and would-be emperors died a natural death. Most emperors held power for only a few months. Preoccupied with merely staying alive and on the throne, they neglected the empire's borders, leaving them vulnerable to attack.

This had dire consequences. Invaders attacked both eastern and western provinces. To the Romans' deep shame, Emperor Valerian was captured in battle by the Great King of Persia in 260. War bands from across the Rhine River reached as far south as Italy, forcing Emperor Aurelian to build a great wall around the city of Rome in 270. Other cities across the empire constructed similar defenses. As a consequence of the political turmoil in the empire, the seat of power shifted from Rome to provincial cities. Unlike their predecessors, the soldier-emperors of this era, who came mostly from frontier provinces, had little time to cultivate the support of the Roman Senate. Instead, they held court in cities close to the embattled frontiers. Towns far from Rome, such as York in Britain or Trier in Gaul, had long functioned as military bases and supply distribution centers. Now they served as imperial capitals whenever the emperor resided there. Some cities and provinces took advantage of the weakened government to try to break away from Roman control.

The Restoration of the Imperial Government

Near the end of the third century, Emperor Diocletian (r. 284–305) rescued the empire from its chaotic condition. Drawing on his brilliant organizational talents, he launched a succession of military, administrative, and economic reforms that had far-reaching consequences. Not since the reign of Augustus three centuries earlier had the Roman Empire been so transformed.

After ruling alone for two years, Diocletian recognized that the enormous responsibilities of imperial government overburdened a single emperor. So he divided the

SUBJUGATION OF VALERIAN Persian kings built their tombs in a cliff six miles north of Persepolis, the old Persian royal center. Here at Naqsh-i Rustam, a carving depicts the Great King Shapur I (239–272) on horseback holding the arm of his prisoner, the Roman emperor Valerian. The previous Roman emperor, Philip (known as "the Arab"), kneels in supplication.

THE WALLS OF ROME Emperor Aurelian built a 12-mile circuit of walls around Rome in the 270s to protect the city from Germanic invaders. The walls, 20 feet high and 12 feet thick, had 18 major gates. That Rome should need protective walls would have been unthinkable during the early days of the Roman Empire.

administration of the empire into two parts. In 286 he chose a co-ruler, Maximian, to govern the western half of the empire from Rome, while he continued to rule in the east. Then, in 293, Diocletian and Maximian further subdivided the empire by appointing two junior-level emperors. Each of these four co-emperors maintained a separate administrative system and his own army.

tetrarchy The government by four rulers established by the Roman emperor Diocletian in 293 C.E. that lasted until 312. During the tetrarchy many administrative and military reforms altered the fabric of Roman society.

Through this system of shared government called the **tetrarchy** or rule of four, Diocletian hoped not only to make the imperial government more efficient, but also to put an end to the bloody cycle of imperial assassinations. Although he had gained the throne by murdering his predecessor, he knew that the empire's survival depended on a reliable succession strategy. To that end, Diocletian dictated that the junior emperors were to step into the senior emperors' places when the seniors retired. Then these new senior emperors were to select two new talented and reliable men to be junior emperors and become their eventual replacements. As supreme power was handed down from capable ruler to capable ruler, the constant cycle of assassinations and civil wars would be broken. Diocletian further subdivided the empire into almost 100 provinces. By focusing the responsibilities of provincial governors on smaller regions, Diocletian encouraged more efficient administration. He grouped these provinces into dioceses, each administered by a vicar who supervised the provincial governors. When Christianity later became legal in the empire, it borrowed the diocese as its principal administrative unit.

To restore Roman military power, Diocletian reorganized the Roman army, raising its total size to about 400,000 men for all of the empire, an increase of 50,000 soldiers, making it a huge army for its time. To protect the empire from invaders, he stationed most of these troops along the borders and built new military roads. In this way, forces of heavily armed cavalry could race to trouble spots if enemies broke through the frontiers. Diocletian also sought to reduce the army's involvement in political affairs. Although he was a soldier himself, he recognized that the army had played a disruptive role in earlier decades by constantly engaging in civil wars. He created many new

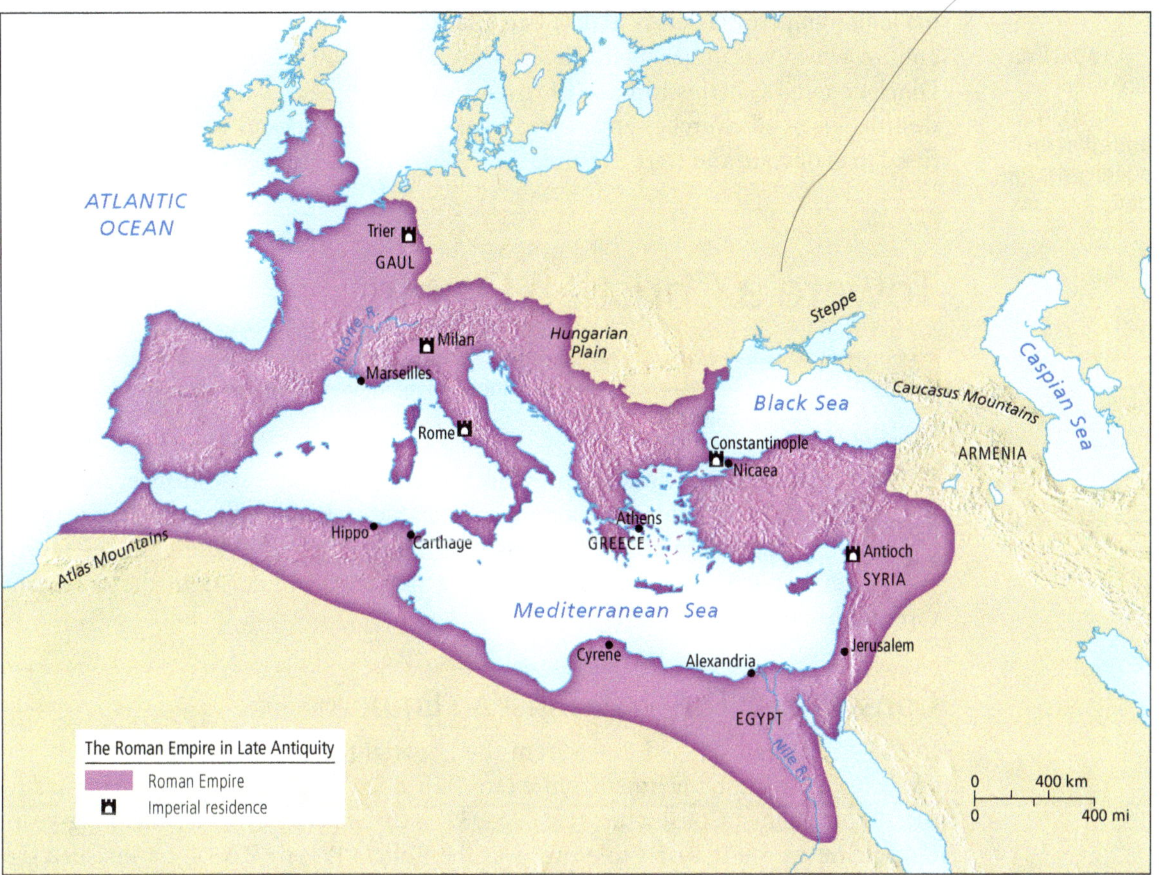

MAP **7.1** THE ROMAN EMPIRE IN LATE ANTIQUITY Following the reforms of Diocletian, the Roman Empire enjoyed a century of stable government, with the same borders as in earlier centuries. From this map, which areas of the West were most influenced by Roman civilization and which the least?

legions led by commanders who were loyal to him, but he reduced the size of each legion to limit its commander's power and to increase its maneuverability. With these military reforms in place, Diocletian was able to secure the empire's borders and suppress revolts (see **Map 7.1**).

Maintaining the expanded civilian and military apparatus created by the tetrarchy, especially in an era of rampant inflation, created new challenges. Diocletian had to make full use of the empire's financial resources and promote economic reforms. To halt the declining value of money, he attempted to freeze wages and prices by imperial decree. He also increased taxes and endeavored to make tax collection more effective by instituting a regular—and deeply resented—census to register all taxpayers. Although senators, army officers, and other influential citizens continued to be undertaxed or not taxed at all, the new tax system generated enough revenues to fund the enormous machinery of government.

The greatest tax burden fell on those least able to pay it: the peasants. The law required these agricultural workers to remain where the census registered them. Sons were supposed to follow their fathers. This attempt to maintain the agricultural tax base was successful, but it lessened social mobility, and the gap between rich and poor continued to grow. Many poor peasants turned to a few rich and powerful men for protection against the ruthless imperial tax collectors. In return, these peasants granted ownership of their farms to these wealthy patrons. The peasants, called *coloni,* continued to work the land but they gave up their freedom for security.

Diocletian's attempts to strengthen the empire led to religious persecution. He believed that failure to worship the traditional Roman gods had angered the deities and brought hardship to the empire. (See *Justice in History* in this chapter.) In 303, he and

7.1

7.2

7.3

7.4

Great Persecution An attack on Christians in the Roman Empire begun by Emperor Galerius in 303 C.E. on the grounds that their worship was endangering the empire. Several thousand Christians were executed.

his junior emperor Galerius initiated an attack on Christians in the eastern part of the empire, which was under their rule. In what is now known as the **Great Persecution**, Diocletian and Galerius forbade Christians to assemble for worship and ordered the destruction of all churches and sacred books. Several thousand women and men refused to cooperate and were executed.

Toward a Christian Empire

7.2 How did Christianity become the dominant religion in the Roman Empire, and how did it affect Roman society?

Diocletian left the eastern provinces of the empire, at least, stronger militarily, administratively, and economically than they had been for nearly a century. His attempt to eradicate Christianity, however, was a failure. In the fourth century Christians developed from a persecuted minority to the dominant force in the empire.

Constantine: The First Christian Emperor

In 305, Diocletian stepped down from the imperial throne and insisted that his co-emperor in the West, Maximian, retire too. Only one year later, the troops stationed in Britain proclaimed Constantine (ca. 280–337) a co-emperor. The 20-something-year-old general set out to assert sole rule over the Roman Empire. In 312 he smashed the army of his rival co-emperor in the West at the Battle of the Milvian Bridge over the Tiber River at Rome. Twelve years later he defeated the last tetrarch ruling in the East. Constantine then rejoined the western and eastern halves of the empire together with himself as absolute ruler. Thus, both the divided rule of the empire and the system of succession through co-emperors that Diocletian implemented came to an end.

In other ways, however, Constantine continued along Diocletian's reformist path. Under Constantine the empire's eastern and western sectors retained separate administrations. He retained Diocletian's emphasis on a large field army and heavily armored cavalry. The imperial bureaucracy and army remained immense, so taxes remained high. Under Diocletian coins had been losing their value, which contributed to the rampant inflation of prices and made the burden of taxes on the poor ever harder to sustain. To remedy the situation, Constantine reformed the coinage system. He recognized that the existing coins had become so debased they were effectively worthless, so he created a new gold coin—the *solidus*, which had a fixed gold content. The solidus stabilized the economy by restoring the value of currency. The new coin ended the inflationary spiral that had contributed so much to the political and social turmoil of the third century. It remained the standard coin in the Mediterranean world for 800 years.

Unlike Diocletian, Constantine embraced the new religion of Christianity. Most emperors had associated themselves with a divine protector. In fact, Constantine had chosen the sun god Apollo as his first divine companion. But the night before the pivotal Battle at the Milvian Bridge in 312, Constantine experienced a vision of the cross upon which Jesus had been crucified. After triumphing in battle, Constantine interpreted his vision as a sign from the Christian God who brought him the victory.

Because monotheistic Christianity repudiated rival gods and alternative forms of worship, Constantine's conversion led to the eventual triumph of Christianity throughout the empire. Constantine did not order his subjects to accept Christianity or forbid polytheist worship. He did, however, encourage widespread and public

THE COLOSSUS OF CONSTANTINE These fragments are all that remain of the colossal statue of Emperor Constantine, which stood 40-feet high in the apse of the Basilica of Maxentius in the Roman Forum. The co-emperor Maxentius began the basilica in 307 to glorify himself with a gigantic statue. After Constantine defeated Maxentius at the Battle of the Milvian Bridge in 312, Constantine had the head replaced with his own facial image. The emperor's head with its disproportionately large eyes that look toward heaven perhaps symbolized the Christian emphasis on the world to come over the transience of human life.

practice of his new faith. Before Constantine, Christian worship had often been conducted in the privacy of homes, but he lavished funds on church buildings. He obtained the gold for his new solidus coinage by looting the treasures that had been stored for centuries in polytheist temples. Now encouraged by the emperor, Christianity quickly gained strength and became a potent challenge to traditional modes of religious expression.

To create an entirely Christian new Rome, Constantine founded a second capital city, Constantinople, the "City of Constantine," on the site of the Greek city Byzantium in 324. Constantine's choice of location revealed a shrewd eye for strategy. The city lay at the juncture of two military roads that linked Europe and Asia and controlled communications between the Mediterranean and the Black Seas. From this strategic spot the emperor monitored the vast resources of the empire's eastern provinces. Like Diocletian, Constantine recognized that the wealth and power of the empire lay in the East.

7.1

7.2

Eusebius of Caesarea, selections from *The Life of Constantine*

7.3

7.4

View the Map

Spread of Christianity

Constantine's capital became a strongly fortified city. In response to the threat of attack by pirates, Emperor Theodosius II erected massive defensive walls around the city in 413. In future centuries these fortifications would protect the city—and indeed, the empire—from ruin on many occasions. With a new Senate formed on the model of that of the city of Rome, a steady supply of grain from Egypt to feed the capital's inhabitants, and plenty of opportunities for trade, Constantinople attracted people from all over the empire. The city rapidly grew in size, reaching perhaps several hundred thousand inhabitants by the early sixth century.

The Spread of Christianity

Before the fourth century Christianity had grown through missionaries who established congregations in most cities of the empire. After Constantine, successive emperors encouraged Christianity, which mushroomed throughout the empire through the spread of bishops who became local figures of great prestige. With imperial support, church leaders Christianized the look of cities by building churches and attacking polytheist temples.

THE RISE OF THE BISHOPS Part of the success of Christianity was due to the sophistication of its internal organization. In the early centuries of Christianity a distinction developed between the laity—the ordinary worshipers—and the priests, who led the worship, administered the sacraments, and acted as pastors for the laity. In imitation of the Roman urban administration, Christians developed their own administrative hierarchy. Just as an imperial official directed each city's political affairs with a staff of assistants, so each city's Christian community came to be led by a chief pastor, called a bishop, who in turn had a staff of subordinate priests and deacons. Just as a provincial governor controlled the political affairs of all of the cities and rural regions in his province, so the bishop of the main city of a province held authority over the other bishops and priests in the province. This main or head bishop came to be called a *metropolitan* (because he resided in the chief city, the metropolis, of the province) in the East, an *archbishop* in the West. This hierarchy of metropolitans/archbishops, bishops, priests, and deacons linked the scattered communities of believers together into what emerged as the Christian Church.

With this administrative structure, the Church grew quickly, and bishops became important authorities in their cities. A bishop supervised the religious life of his *see* or diocese, a unit based on Diocletian's administrative reforms. A diocese comprised not only the city itself, but also its surrounding villages and agricultural regions. Such supervision involved explaining Christian principles and teaching the Bible. Bishops soon became far more than religious teachers. As the Church grew wealthy from the massive donations of emperors such as Constantine and the humbler offerings of pious women and men throughout the empire, bishops used these resources to help the poor. The bishops cared for the general welfare of orphans, widows, sick people, prisoners, and travelers. When famine struck southern Gaul in the fifth century, for example, the bishop of Lyons sent so much food from his church estates that grain barges jammed the Rhône and Saône Rivers and carts full of grain clogged the roads going south.

Constantine permitted bishops to act as judges in civil actions, which made them agents of the imperial government. This policy soon entangled them in secular politics because litigants could choose to be tried before a bishop rather than a civil judge. The decisions of a bishop had the same legal authority as those rendered by civil judges. Using the rhetorical skills they had learned in Roman schools, bishops were also the advocates for their cities before provincial governors or the imperial court. In many ways they usurped the role of the traditional urban aristocracy. For example, when the people of Antioch in Syria rioted and smashed a statue of the emperor, the local bishop, not a local aristocrat, intervened to prevent imperial troops from massacring the city's people.

In the West, Rome became the most important see. Like all bishops, the bishop of Rome came to be called the "pope"—the papa or father of his flock. In his case the title stuck and eventually referred only to him. By the mid-fifth century the emperor formally recognized the pope's claim to have preeminence over other bishops. Two factors explain why the office of the bishop of Rome evolved into the **papacy**. First, together with Jerusalem, Rome was a site of powerful symbolic importance to Christians because the Apostle Peter, considered the first among Jesus's disciples, and Paul of Tarsus, the traveling teacher who took a leading role in spreading Christianity beyond its Jewish origins, died as martyrs in Rome. Second, early Christians considered Peter to have been the first bishop of Rome who passed on his authority to all subsequent popes in what is called the Doctrine of the Petrine Succession.

papacy The administrative and political institutions controlled by the Pope (Father), the bishop of the city of Rome. The papacy began to gain strength in the sixth century in the absence of Roman imperial government in Italy.

Popes claimed to be the chief bishops of the Christian world. They insisted that their spiritual authority took precedence over that of rival bishops in other important cities, especially Constantinople. The bishops (called patriarchs) of Constantinople often quarreled bitterly with the pope over matters of faith and politics. The tensions among these bishops led to divisions between the eastern and western parts of the empire that have lasted until the present day.

Through the authority of the bishops, the Church began functioning almost as an administrative arm of the government, although it still had its own internal organization. Indeed, when Roman rule collapsed in western Europe in the fifth century, the Church stepped in to fill the vacuum of public leadership.

Read the Document

Pope Leo I on Bishop Hilary of Aries

CHRISTIANITY AND THE CITY OF ROME Christianity transformed the appearance of Roman cities. Constantine set an example of public and private spending on churches, hospitals, and monastic communities that conformed to Christian values. One of the great churches that Constantine built in Rome was called "Saint Paul Outside the Walls." This imposing structure marked the supposed burial spot of Paul of Tarsus. Constantine also financed the construction of another grand church on the presumed site of Peter's martyrdom and burial, in an obscure cemetery on what was called the Vatican hill, just outside Rome's wall. St. Peter's Basilica was an imposing structure, with five aisles punctuated with marble columns. Its altar rested over Peter's grave. (Today the papal basilica of St. Peter stands on that same spot, in the heart of the Vatican, the city-state of the pope.) The construction of these churches signaled that Jesus's apostles Peter and Paul had replaced Rome's mythical founders Romulus and Remus as the city's sacred patrons. With the construction of Christian churches, spending and construction on traditional buildings such as temples, bathhouses, and public entertainment facilities such as the circuses declined. At the prompting of Rome's bishops, other public buildings, such as the large basilicas used for public business, including legal trials, were turned into churches.

With the proliferation of new Christian churches in Rome and other cities came new religious festivals and rituals, such as the anniversaries of the martyrdom of saints. Sometimes a Christian holiday (holy day) competed with a non-Christian holiday. For example, Rome's churchmen designated December 25 as the birthday of Christ to challenge the popular festival of the Unconquered Sun, which fell on the same day. By the early sixth century, the Church had filled the calendar with days devoted to Christian ceremonies. Christmas and Easter (which commemorates the resurrection of Jesus) and days for commemorating specific martyrs supplanted traditional Roman holidays. These festivals thus changed the patterns of urban community life throughout the empire. Not all of the traditional Roman holidays disappeared, however. Those that Christians considered harmless continued to be observed as civic holidays. These included New Year's Day, the accession days of the emperors, and the days that celebrated the founding of Rome and Constantinople.

One additional development in the Christian shaping of time was the use of the letters A.D. as a dating convention. A.D. stands for *anno domini*, or "in the year of our Lord," referring to the year of Jesus's birth. The convention began in 531, when a monk

BASILICA OF SAINT PAUL OUTSIDE THE WALLS The church of Saint Paul Outside the Walls was built by Emperor Constantine on the supposed burial spot of Paul of Tarsus. Like other late antique churches, Saint Paul's followed the plan of a Roman public building, a basilica, but added an altar in the semicircular apse at one end. The fifth-century mosaics of the triumphal arch portray the Apocalypse described in the prophecies of John the Revelator. In the middle is an image of Christ flanked by the 24 doctors of the church. At the left of the arch is Saint Paul pointing downward to his tomb.

in Rome established a simple system for determining the date of Easter every year. He began his calendar with the birth of Jesus in the year one (zero was unknown in Europe at this time) and started counting from there. Although he was probably a few years off in his determination of the year of Jesus's birth, his system came into general use by the tenth century. In many modern secular societies where belief in Christianity is not universal, the abbreviation A.D. has been replaced by C.E.—meaning "in the Common Era"—to designate years.

OLD GODS UNDER ATTACK Before Christianity became the dominant religion in the Roman Empire, people prayed to gods of all sorts. Different deities met different needs, and the worship of one did not preclude worship of another. To Christians, this diverse range of religious expression was intolerable. They labeled all polytheistic worship with the derogatory term **pagan** from the Latin word *paganus*, which meant "hillbilly," a reflection of the urban bias of early Christianity and the failure of Christianity to spread among country people.

pagan The Christian term for polytheist worship (worshiping more than one god). In the course of late antiquity, the Christian Church suppressed paganism, the traditional religions of the Roman Empire.

After converting to Christianity in 312, Constantine ordered the end of the persecution of Christians. Although Christianity did not become the "official" religion of the empire for nearly a century, tolerance for non-Christian beliefs and practices began to fade. In the fourth century, imperial laws forbade sacrificing animals on the altars outside the old gods' temples. State funding for polytheistic worship gradually stopped. Instead of temples, emperors built churches with money collected from the taxpayers. Bishops and monks, often in collusion with local administrators, led attacks on polytheist shrines and holy places.

Because polytheism was not a single, organized religion, it offered no systematic opposition to government-supported attacks, but there were influential opponents to the Christianization of the empire. In sharp contrast to the pious Christian court at Constantinople, the conservative aristocracy of the city of Rome clung hard to the old gods. In 384, their spokesman begged the emperor for tolerance. Quintus Aurelius Symmachus argued that Rome's greatness had resulted from the observance of ancient rites. His pleas fell on deaf ears. Emperor Theodosius I (r. 379–395) and his grandson Theodosius II (r. 402–450) forbade all forms of polytheistic worship, and non-Christian practice lost the protection of the law. By the mid-fifth century, the aristocracy of the city of Rome had accepted Christianity. (See *Justice in History* in this chapter.)

Many less influential people also struggled to maintain ancient forms of worship, but the pace of conversion accelerated in the fifth and sixth centuries. Emperor Justinian (r. 527–565) sponsored programs of forced conversion in the countryside of Anatolia, where many of his subjects still followed ancient ways. Eradicating polytheism in the Roman Empire meant far more than substituting one religion for another. In the pre-Christian world, polytheism lay at the heart of every community, influencing every activity, every habit of social life. To replace the worship of the old gods required a true revolution in social and intellectual life. Completing that revolution became the challenge of the new Christian communities.

FEMALE PRIEST This foot-high ivory panel shows a female priest making a sacrifice at an altar to an unnamed god or goddess. *Symmachorum* means "of the family of the Symmachi," an aristocratic Roman clan in which some members defended the old gods in the face of Christianity. Unlike the polytheist cults of late antiquity, Orthodox Christians did not allow women to serve as priests.

New Christian Communities and Identities

7.3 How did Christianity transform communities, religious experience, and intellectual traditions inside and outside the Roman Empire?

Christianity solidified community loyalties and allegiances by providing a shared belief system and new opportunities for participation in religious culture. Yet Christianity also opened up new divisions and gave rise to new hostilities over conflicting interpretations of the doctrines of the faith. Because Christians spoke Greek, Latin, Coptic, Syriac, Armenian, and other languages, different religious interpretations and rituals sometimes took hold among different language groups, creating distinct communities.

Read the Document
Paulus Orosius, from *Seven Books of History Against the Pagans*

The Creation of New Communities

Christianity fostered the growth of large-scale communities of faith by providing a well-defined set of beliefs and values. These basic beliefs and values had to be integrated with daily life and older ways of thinking. Thus, Christianity required followers to study and interpret the Bible. It also demanded allegiance to one God and a complex set of doctrines.

CHRISTIAN DOCTRINE AND HERESY Despite the institutionalization of the Church through the office of bishops, the theological controversies that had shaped Christianity from its very start continued and new controversies emerged. Councils of bishops met frequently to try to resolve doctrinal differences and produce statements of the faith that all parties could accept.

The persistent question was who was or is Jesus? Was he a man, God, or some combination of both? Like Jews, the followers of Christ believe that one God created and governs Heaven and Earth. If Jesus were just a man, as the adoptionist Christians discussed in Chapter 6 thought, then monotheism is preserved. If Jesus were a man that God adopted to be his special son and to carry out his mission, then Jesus was no different in his nature from any other man and could be subject to sin and error. If, however, Jesus were God who only appeared to possess the body of a man, as the docetic Christians believed, then other problems arose. For example, if Christ were entirely divine, then who did he pray to? This emphasis on Jesus's divinity made his death on the cross and his resurrection irrelevant, for God could not suffer and die. It also severed the links between Jesus and his human followers by emphasizing that Jesus was entirely "transcendent" or "other," entirely beyond human comprehension or human limitations.

A group of theologians developed the doctrine of the Trinity during the second and third centuries as an answer to these persistent questions about the nature of Jesus. They argued that the one God was to be understood as existing in three distinct "persons," each fully and absolutely God—God the Father, God the Son, and God the Holy Spirit—the Holy Trinity. This solution, however, did not entirely resolve the controversies. Church leaders continued to argue about the precise relation of the three persons within the Trinity. Were the Son and the Holy Spirit of the same essence as the Father? Were they equally divine? Did the Father exist before the Son?

These questions about the nature of the Trinity just continued the adoptionist–docetic debate in a different form, which came to be called the Arian–Athanasian dispute. The **Arians** followed Arius of Alexandria (ca. 250–336), a priest steeped in Greek philosophy. Arians asserted that God the Father created Jesus, so Jesus could not be equal to or of the same essence as God the Father. Arians argued that the Trinitarian idea that Jesus was both fully divine and fully human was illogical. The Athanasians, followers of Bishop Athanasius of Alexandria (293–373), were horrified by what they saw as the Arians' attempt to degrade Jesus's divinity. They argued that Christian truths were beyond human logic and that Jesus was fully God, equal to and of the same substance as God the Father, yet also fully human.

Arians Christians who believe that God the Father is superior to Jesus Christ his Son. Most of the Germanic settlers in western Europe in the fifth century were Arians.

The Arian–Athanasian dispute resulted in perhaps the most influential of the many church meetings held in late antiquity: the Council of Nicaea. As the first general council, Nicaea signaled the beginning of an empire-wide Church. In 325, Emperor Constantine summoned the quarrelling bishops to Nicaea, a town near Constantinople, to reach a decision about the relationship among the divine members of the Holy Trinity. The bishops produced the Nicene Creed, which is still recited in Christian worship today. The creed, in agreement with Athanasian belief, states that God the Son (Jesus Christ) is identical in nature and essence to God the Father. In 451 the Council of Chalcedon reinforced the Nicene Creed. The assembled bishops agreed that Jesus was both fully human and fully divine, and that these two natures were entirely distinct though united. Their position became the interpretation accepted to this day by Orthodox, Catholic, and Protestant Christians.

COMMUNITIES OF FAITH AND LANGUAGE The doctrinal differences between Christian groups helped cement different communal and even ethnic identities in late antiquity. Three geographic zones of Christians emerged that held different interpretations of Christian doctrine, each a testament to the remarkable variety of Christian cultures.

A central zone based in Constantinople and including North Africa, the Balkans, and much of western Europe contained Christians called **Chalcedonians**, or orthodox. (In the Latin-speaking western provinces, they were also called Catholics.) These believers followed the decision of the Council of Chalcedon that defined Christ's divine and human natures as equal but entirely distinct. Christ was both God and man at the same time, but his divine and human natures did not mix. In late antiquity, the emperors in Constantinople and the popes in Rome—as well as most of the population of the Roman Empire—were Chalcedonian Christians.

Chalcedonians Christians who followed the doctrinal decisions and definitions of the Council of Chalcedon in 451 C.E. stating that Christ's human and divine natures were equal, but entirely distinct and united in one person "without confusion, division, separation, or change." Chalcedonian Christianity came to be associated with the Byzantine Empire and is called Greek Orthodoxy. In western Europe it is known as Roman Catholicism.

Although the Christians in this first zone agreed on fundamental matters of doctrine, they differed culturally by producing Bibles, delivering sermons, and conducting religious ceremonies in their native languages—Latin in the western part of the central zone; mostly Greek (but also Syriac, Armenian, and Coptic) in the eastern part of the central zone. About 410, the monk Jerome finished a new Latin translation of the Bible that replaced earlier Latin versions. This translation, called the **Vulgate**, became the standard Bible in European churches until the sixteenth century.

Vulgate The Latin translation of the Bible produced about 410 by the monk Jerome. It was the standard Bible in western Christian churches until the sixteenth century.

The Western Church's use of Latin kept the door open for the transmission of all Latin texts into a world defined by Christianity. This ensured the survival of Roman legal, scientific, and literary traditions, even after Roman rule had evaporated in western Europe. Latin also forged a common bond among different political communities of the empire's western sector, where it served as an international language

THE VIENNA GENESIS The Greek text written in silver ink at the top of the page tells the story of Susanna at the Well from the book of Genesis in the Bible. Though the illustration at the bottom of the page tells a biblical story, certain details reflect conditions in late antiquity, such as fortified cities and the growing importance of camels in travel and commerce. The seated, semi-nude female in the lower left is derived from polytheist religion. She personifies the stream from which the more modestly dressed Susanna gathers water.

Latin Christendom The parts of medieval Europe, including all of western Europe, united by Christianity and the use of Latin in worship and intellectual life. Latin served as an international language among the ruling elites in western Europe, even though they spoke different languages in their daily lives.

among ruling elites, even though they spoke different languages in their daily lives. Thus, Church-based Latin served as a powerful unifying and stabilizing influence. The Latin language combined with Christianity to spur the development of **Latin Christendom**—the many peoples and kingdoms in western Europe united by their common religion and shared language of worship and intellectual life.

In the eastern provinces of the Roman Empire, Christianity had a different voice. There a Greek-based Church developed. Greek was the language of imperial rule and common culture in that region, and Greek became the language of the Eastern Christian Church. In addition to the New Testament, which had been originally written in Greek, eastern Christians used a Greek version of the Hebrew Bible (the Old Testament) called the Septuagint, which Greek-speaking Jews had prepared in Alexandria in the second century B.C.E. for their own community. The Septuagint combined with the Greek New Testament to become the authoritative Christian Bible throughout most of Rome's eastern provinces.

Monophysites Christians who do not accept the Council of Chalcedon (see Chalcedonians). Monophysites believe that Jesus Christ has only one nature, equally divine and human.

In a second zone in the eastern Mediterranean and beyond were Anti-Chalcedonians, usually known by the derogatory term of **Monophysites** (literally "one nature"). They did not accept the teaching of the Council of Chalcedon about the combination of the divine and the human in Christ as being "in two natures." Instead, they believed that Christ had one nature in which the human evolved into the divine. In Christ, human nature "dissolved like a drop of honey in the sea." He had a human body and a human "living principle," but the divine took over his thinking. Three anti-Chalcedonian communities had developed by the end of late antiquity—in Armenia in the Caucasus mountain region of eastern Anatolia; in Egypt, among the native Egyptian speakers, called Copts; and among the inhabitants of Syria who spoke Syriac. A vast literature of biblical interpretation, sermons, commentaries, and church documents was gradually created in the languages of each of these communities.

In addition to the Chalcedonian and anti-Chalcedonian regions in late antiquity, a third zone of Christians consisted of the Arians. As described earlier, Arians believed that Jesus was not equal to or of the same substance as God the Father because God had created Jesus. Arians saw themselves as more rigidly monotheistic than Chalcedonian Christians, whose belief in the Trinity they regarded as bordering on polytheism. Most of the people who followed Arian Christianity were the Goths and other Germanic settlers who converted to Christianity in the fourth century, when they still lived north of the Danube River and in southern Russia. When they invaded the Roman Empire in the fifth century, they seized political control of Rome's western provinces. While the Goths were still north of the Danube, a missionary named Ulfila devised a Gothic alphabet and used it to translate the Bible from Greek into Gothic, an early version of German. A Christian Gothic culture thrived in the western zone despite its minority status.

In these three zones, variations of the Christian faith expressed in different languages formed the seedbed of ethnic communities, some of which still flourish, such as the Armenians, Copts, and Greek-speaking Orthodox Christians. Yet the spread of Christianity weakened other local groupings. As language-based Christian communities spread inside and outside the empire, many local dialects and languages disappeared. Only the languages in which Christianity found textual expression survived.

asceticism The Christian practice of severely suppressing physical needs and daily desires in an effort to achieve a spiritual union with God. Asceticism is the practice that underlies the monastic movement.

THE MONASTIC MOVEMENT Near the end of the third century, a new Christian spiritual movement took root in the Roman Empire. Known today as **asceticism**, this movement called for Christians to subordinate their physical needs and desires to a quest for spiritual union with God. Asceticism both challenged the emerging connection between the political and Christian authorities and rejected the growing wealth of the Church.

The life of an Egyptian Christian, Antony, provided a model for future ascetics. Around 280 he sold all his property and walked away from his crowded village near the

Nile into the desert in search of a higher spirituality. A few decades later, Athanasius, the Bishop of Alexandria who had argued against the Arians, composed a biography, the *Life of Antony,* telling how Antony overcame all the temptations the Devil could conjure up, from voluptuous naked women to opportunities for power and fame. Vividly describing the struggle between asceticism ("the discipline") and the lures of everyday life ("the household"), Athanasius's work became one of the most influential books in Western literature. It inspired thousands of men and women to imitate Antony by rejecting the ties of the household and material world. Asceticism appealed to those who desired an alternative to political and especially family life with its coercive parental authority, marriage, sexuality, and children. These all distracted from the contemplation of God.

Ascetic discipline required harsh and often violent treatment of the body. The first ascetics, called anchorites (meaning "withdrawal") or hermits (meaning "of the desert"), lived alone in the most inaccessible and uncomfortable places they could find, such as a cave, a hole in the ground, or on top of a pillar. In addition to praying constantly in their struggle to overcome the Devil and empty themselves of human desires so that God could enter and work through them, these men and women starved and whipped themselves, rejecting every comfort, including human companionship.

Over time, however, many Egyptian ascetics began to construct communities for themselves. The result was the **monastic movement**. Because these communities, called monasteries, often grew to hold 1,000 or more members, they required organization and guidance. Leaders emerged to provide clear instructions for regulating monastic life and offer spiritual guidance to the members of the monasteries. (The male inhabitants of monasteries were called monks, or solitary men. Women were called nuns.)

monastic movement In late antiquity, Christian ascetics organized communities where men and women could pursue a life of spirituality through work, prayer, and asceticism. Called the monastic movement, this spiritual quest spread quickly throughout Christian lands.

Drawing from the ideas of these earlier monastic rules written in Greek, Benedict of Nursia (ca. 480–547) wrote a Latin *Rule* that became the foundation of monasticism in western Europe. Benedict built a monastery on Monte Cassino near Naples in 529. While he emphasized voluntary poverty and a life devoted to prayer, he placed more stress on labor. Fearing that the Devil could tempt an idle monk, Benedict wanted his monks to keep busy. He therefore ordered that all monks perform physical labor for parts of every day when they were not sleeping or praying.

In the western Roman Empire, monasticism played a central role in preserving classical learning and thus allowing its integration into Christian culture in later centuries. Much of the credit for preserving the classical intellectual tradition lay with the monasteries founded by Benedict. These monks, called the Benedictine order, established monasteries throughout western Europe, modeled on Benedict's original monastery of Monte Cassino. Benedict himself was wary of classical teaching, but he wanted the monks and nuns under his supervision to be able to read religious books. At least basic education in literacy had to become part of monastic life. The Benedictine definition of "manual labor" expanded to include copying ancient manuscripts, which supplied the libraries in the monasteries and preserved Latin literature.

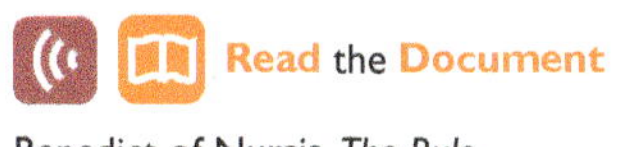

Benedict of Nursia, *The Rule*

MONASTICISM AND WOMEN The monastic movement opened new avenues for female spirituality and offered an alternative to marriage and childbearing. By joining monastic communities and leaving the routines of daily life behind, women could escape the obligations of the male-dominated society. As Christian monasticism spread, ascetic women began to create communities of their own. They lived as celibate sisterhoods of nuns, dedicated to spiritual quest and service to God.

The wives or daughters of wealthy and powerful families were typically the founders of female monastic communities. Such women wielded an authority and influence that would not have been available to them otherwise. For example, Melania the Younger (383–439), the daughter of a wealthy Roman senatorial family, decided to sell her vast estates and spend the proceeds in religious pursuits. When the Roman Senate objected to the breaking up of Melania's family estates, she appealed to the empress, who interceded with the legal authorities to enable her to dispose of her property. (Melania's slaves also objected because they did not want to be sold separately to raise cash for her religious projects, but she ignored them.) Melania spent her fortune building monasteries in the Holy Land of Palestine. Most women could not afford to make such dramatic gestures, but they could imitate Melania's accomplishment on a modest scale.

Despite the piety of women such as Melania, an increasingly negative view of women emerged in the writings of late antique churchmen. Christian writers branded women as disobedient, sexually promiscuous, innately sinful, and naturally inferior to men. They interpreted Genesis, the first book of the Bible, to mean that women bore a special curse. In their reading of the Genesis account, Eve, the first woman, seduced Adam, the first man. For this reason late antique Christians blamed Eve—and women collectively—for humanity's expulsion from the Garden of Eden and for all the woes human beings had suffered since. Yet Christians also believed that God would save the souls of women as well as men, and they honored Mary for her role in bringing Jesus, and therefore salvation, into the world. (See *Different Voices* in this chapter.)

JEWS IN A CHRISTIAN WORLD Until Christianity became the official religion of the Roman Empire, Jews had been simply one among hundreds of religious and ethnic groups who lived under Roman rule. Although polytheist Romans considered Jews eccentric because they worshiped only one god and refused to make statues of him, they still respected the Jewish people's faith. Before the fourth century, Jews had enjoyed full citizenship rights, practiced all professions, and belonged to all levels of society.

Christianity slowly erased all this. As we saw in Chapter 6, relations between Christians and Jews grew more hostile after the Jewish rebellion and the destruction of Jerusalem by the Roman army in 70. Christian theology mirrored this growing hostility. Christians taught that the Diaspora (the dispersion of Jews around the world after Jerusalem's destruction) was God's way of punishing the Jews for failing to accept Jesus as their messiah and for crucifying Jesus Christ.

Beginning in the fourth century, Roman laws began to discriminate against Jews, forbidding them to marry Christians, own Christian slaves, or accept converts to Judaism. With the support of Christian imperial officials, Church leaders sometimes forced entire communities of Jews to convert to Christianity on pain of death. Although organized resistance among scattered Jewish communities was impossible, many Jews refused to accept the deepening oppression. Their resistance ranged from acts of violence against Jews who had converted to Christianity to armed revolt against Roman authorities.

Individual Jewish communities continued to administer their own affairs under the leadership of rabbis—men who served as teachers and interpreters of Jewish law. We saw in Chapter 6 that the Mishnah, the final codification of Jewish oral law, was completed by the end of the third century. Rabbis incorporated the Mishnah into the **Talmud**, which included commentaries on the law, ethics, and Jewish history. The influential Jerusalem Talmud was compiled about 400, the Babylonian Talmud a century later. Rabbis and their courts now dominated Jewish communities. These learned men established academies of legal study in Roman Palestine and Persian Babylonia, where their interpretations guided everyday Jewish life.

Talmud Commentaries on Jewish law. Rabbis completed the Babylonian Talmud and the Jerusalem Talmud by the end of the fifth century C.E.

In rabbinic Judaism women continued to play an important role in the household, especially since Judaism emphasized the importance of moral behavior and religious practice rather than dogma. As a result, as wives and mothers, Jewish women had a more positive role in the practice of their religion than women did in Christianity, which considered married women and men morally inferior to celibate nuns and monks. Some Jewish women served as leaders of synagogues in late antiquity, but in public life as opposed to private life, rabbinic Judaism subordinated women. For example, Jewish women did not receive an education at the Jewish academies. Excluded

GREEK ZODIAC IN A SYNAGOGUE In late antiquity, Jews living in Palestine sometimes decorated their synagogues with mosaic floors depicting the zodiac. Although these mosaics appeared in synagogues and often contained Hebrew writing, the scenes and style of the mosaics were typical of Greek and Roman art. This blending demonstrates that members of the Jewish congregation also participated in the general non-Jewish culture of the province.

from the formal process of interpreting holy texts, Jewish women did not acquire highly prized religious knowledge.

Instead, men expected them to conform to submissive roles as daughters, wives, and mothers, much as women in other religious communities were expected to do.

Access to Holiness: Christian Pilgrimage

In late antiquity, Christians began to make religious journeys, or **pilgrimages**, to visit sacred places, especially those housing holy objects, known as **relics**. Christians believed these relics were inherently holy because they were physical objects associated with saints and martyrs or with Jesus himself. The most highly valued relics were bones from the venerated person. Christians believed that merely by touching something of a holy person, one could share in that holiness, which could cure them of an illness, heighten their spiritual awareness, or help them achieve eternal life.

The mortal remains of Christian martyrs provided the first relics for pilgrims; however, after the persecution of Christians ceased in 312, believers began to venerate the bodies of great bishops and ascetic monks and nuns. From the fourth century onward, Christians regularly dug up skeletons of saints, chopped them up, and

pilgrimages Religious journeys made to holy sites in order to encounter relics.

relics In Christian belief, relics are sacred objects that have miraculous powers. They are associated with saints, biblical figures, or some object associated with them. They served as contacts between Earth and Heaven and were verified by miracles.

7.1
7.2
7.3
7.4

Different Voices

Christian Attitudes Toward Sexuality, Contraception, and Abortion

Churchmen were hostile to sexuality and considered celibacy the superior way for Christians to live. There were numerous reasons for this hostility, but most of all Christians expected Christ to return at any moment, which made any pursuit except for spiritual purification seem irrelevant. In addition, one of the attractions of early Christianity was liberation from coercive family ties, which distracted believers from their higher obligations to God. Yet as time passed and Christ did not return, churchmen began to recognize the necessity for Christians to produce children for the faith to grow. The result was a double ethic that exalted celibacy and yet placed special obligations on those who were married to bear children. The following excerpts illustrate this double ethic. The first document, attributed to Saint Patrick from the mid-fifth century, shows how an Irish woman's decision to live a celibate life subjected her to persecution from non-Christians who thought her obligation was to bear children. The second comes from a sermon by Caesarius, bishop of Arles from 502 to 542.

St. Patrick

And there was also a blessed lady of native Irish birth and high rank, very beautiful and grown up, whom I baptized; and a few days later she found some reason to come to us and indicated that she had received a message from an angel of god, and the angel had urged her too to become a virgin of Christ and to draw near to God. Thanks be to God. . . . she most commendably and enthusiastically took up that same course that all virgins of God also do—not with their fathers' consent; no, they endure persecution and their own parents' unfair reproaches, and yet their number grows larger and larger. . . . But it is the women kept in slavery who suffer especially; they even have to endure constant threats and terrorization.

Caesarius of Arles

No woman should take drugs for purposes of abortion, nor should she kill her children that have been conceived or are already born. If anyone does this, she should know that before Christ's tribunal she will have to plead her case in the presence of those she has killed. Moreover, women should not take diabolical draughts with the purpose of not being able to conceive children. A woman who does this ought to realize that she will be guilty of as many murders as the number of children she might have borne. I would like to know whether a woman of nobility who takes deadly drugs to prevent conception wants her maids or tenants to do so. Just as every woman wants slaves born for her so that they may serve her, so she herself should nurse all the children she conceives, or entrust them to others for rearing. Otherwise, she may refuse to conceive children or, what is more serious, be willing to kill souls which might have been good Christians. Now, with what kind of a conscience does she desire slaves to be born of her servants, when she herself refuses to bear children who might become Christians?

For Discussion

1. What do these documents reveal about Christian views about women?
2. How do Caesarius's reasons for opposing contraception and abortion differ from the arguments of those who oppose these practices today?

SOURCES: *St. Patrick: His Writing and Muirchu's Life*, edited and translated by A.B.E. Hood, Arthurian Period Sources, vol. 9 (London: Phillimor, 1978), p. 50. *Saint Caesarius of Arles, Sermons*, vol. 1 (sermons 1-80), translated by Sister Mary Mageleine Mueller, O.S.F. (New York: Fathers of the Church, Inc., 1956), pp. 221–22.

distributed the pieces to churches. The more important the holy person, the fiercer the competition for the bones and other objects associated with him or her. Churches in the largest cities of the empire, such as Rome, Constantinople, Alexandria, and Jerusalem, acquired fine collections. Residents of Constantinople believed that the Virgin Mary's robe, kept in a church inside the city, drove away enemies when it was carried in procession along the battlements.

Emperors and important bishops acquired the greatest and most powerful relics of all—those that had reportedly touched Jesus himself. These included the crown of thorns he wore when crucified, the cross on which he died, and the nails that fastened him to the wood. Relics reminded Christians that the martyrdom of his followers symbolically repeated Jesus's own death. Hence, they constructed church altars, where followers celebrated the Eucharist (the rite in which bread and wine are offered as Jesus's body and blood in memory of his death) over the graves or relics of martyrs.

Traveling to touch a relic was the primary motive for a pilgrimage. Palestine became a frequent destination of Christian pilgrims because it contained the most sacred sites and relics associated with events described in the Bible and particularly with Jesus's life and death. Between the fourth and seventh centuries, thousands of earnest

Christian pilgrims flocked to Palestine to visit holy sites and pray for divine assistance and forgiveness for their sins. Helena, the mother of Emperor Constantine, made pilgrimage fashionable. In the early fourth century, she visited Jerusalem, where she reportedly found remnants of the cross on which Jesus was crucified, and identified many of the sites pertaining to Jesus's life. Inspired by his mother's journey, Constantine funded the construction of lavish shrines and monasteries at these sites and guest houses for pilgrims. Practically overnight Palestine was transformed from a provincial backwater to the spiritual focus of the Christian world. Religious men and women—rich and poor, old and young, sick and healthy—streamed to Palestine and Jerusalem.

Palestine did not have a monopoly on holy places, however. Pilgrims traveled to places throughout the Roman world wherever saints had lived and died and where their relics rested. Pilgrimages contributed to the growth of a Christian view of the world in three ways. First, because pilgrimage was a holy enterprise, Christian communities gave hospitality and lodging to religious travelers. This fostered a shared sense of Christian community among people from many lands. Second, Christians envisioned a Christian "map" dominated by spiritually significant places. Travel guides that explained this "spiritual geography" became popular among pilgrims. Most of all, pilgrims who returned home, enriched in their faith and perhaps cured in mind or spirit, inspired their home communities with news of a growing Christian world directly linked to the biblical lands they heard about in church.

Christian Intellectual Life

During the first three centuries after Jesus's death, when Christians were marginalized and at times persecuted, many Church leaders criticized classical learning. Churchmen argued that the learning of pagan intellectuals was false wisdom, that it distracted Christians from what was truly important—contemplation of Jesus Christ and the eternal salvation he offered—and therefore that it corrupted young Christians. Tertullian (ca. 160–240), for example, argued for the separation of Christianity from the learning and culture of the non-Christian world: "What has Athens to do with Jerusalem? What is there in common between the philosopher and the Christian?" Christians like Tertullian mistrusted the human intellect and stressed the need to focus on the divine revelation of the Christian Scriptures.

After Constantine's conversion, influential voices in the Church began to answer these questions. To them, classical learning no longer seemed as threatening as it had before. Many Church leaders now came from the empire's urban elite, where they had absorbed classical learning. Christian officials grudgingly approved secular education because they recognized that the traditional curriculum was useful for administering the Church and for the law. Training in classical rhetoric, grammar, and literature became an integral part of upper-class Christian life. By the fifth century, traditional schooling for Christians was accepted as a useful if risky enterprise. As Basil the Great (ca. 330–379), bishop of Caesarea in Cappadocia (in modern Turkey), explained to young men about to embark on their studies, classical learning had both benefits and dangers. Although pagan learning, he advised, had some spiritual value, the charm of words could poison the Christian's heart.

Augustine of Hippo (354–430) most fully took up the challenge of classical learning to Christianity. By examining the most troubling philosophical and historical questions in light of the scriptures, Augustine became the most influential Church Father among Latin-speaking Christians. The **Church Fathers** were writers from both the Greek- and Latin-speaking worlds who sought to reconcile Christianity with classical learning.

Church Fathers Writers in late antiquity from both the Greek- and Latin-speaking worlds who sought to reconcile Christianity with classical learning.

Born to parents of modest means, Augustine attended traditional Roman schools as a youth, an education that made him thoroughly familiar with the classics and

7.1

7.2

7.3

7.4

prepared him for a high position in public life. After his conversion to Christianity, Augustine became the influential bishop of the city of Hippo Regius in North Africa. He recounted his spiritual experiences and conversion in the *Confessions* (397), an autobiography written in his middle age. Drawing on the ideas of the Greek philosopher Plato and on Christian scriptures, Augustine in the *Confessions* meditated on the meaning of life, especially on sin and redemption. Augustine showed that intellect alone was incapable of bringing about the spiritual growth that he desired. God needed to intervene. For his spiritual conversion to be complete, Augustine believed he had to cleanse himself of the desires of the flesh, which led him to renounce sexuality completely. Using his episcopal office as a platform from which to defend Christianity from polytheist philosophers and to define all aspects of the Christian life, Augustine displayed a sincere respect for Roman cultural and intellectual accomplishments—especially rhetoric and history. But he always believed Christianity was superior. For

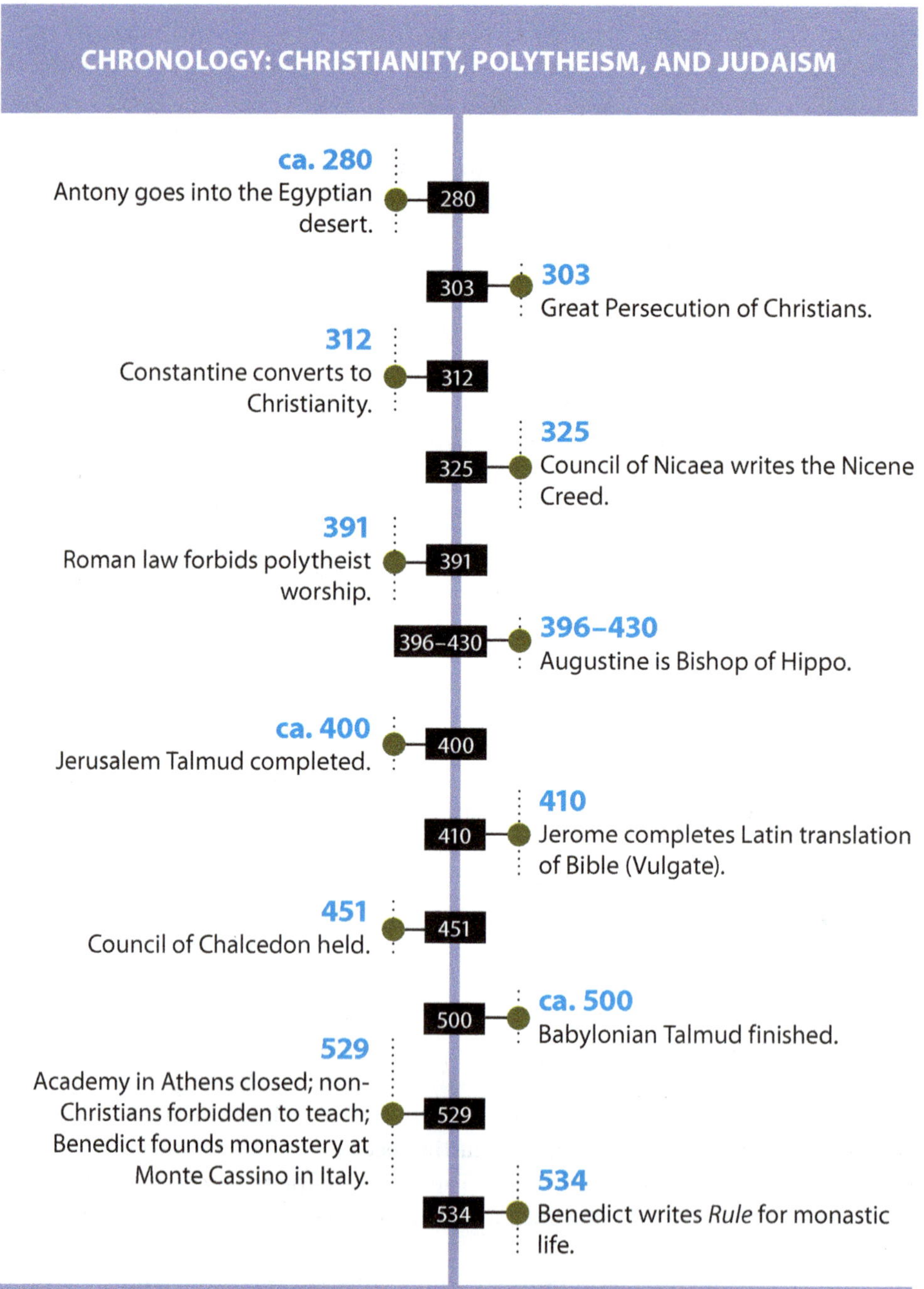

Augustine, the most dangerous enemy of all true Christians was "antiquity, mother of all evils"—the source of false beliefs.

In his book *The City of God*, completed in 423, Augustine developed a new interpretation of history. Augustine's historical theory disconnected Christian ideas of human destiny from the fate of the Roman Empire. In his view, the Roman Empire was just one among many that had existed and that would exist before Jesus's return. According to Augustine, the only dates humanity should view as spiritually significant were Jesus's time on Earth and the End of Days sometime in the future. Only God knew the significance of all events in between.

Augustine's theory proved timely. Within a few years of his death, the Vandals seized North Africa and the Roman Empire lost control of all of its provinces in western Europe. Augustine thus gave Roman Christians a new perspective with which to view this loss: Rome had contributed to world civilization and to the growth of the Christian Church, but now Christianity would grow on its own without the support of Roman emperors.

After the collapse of the Roman Empire in the western provinces, the challenge for Christian thinkers came less from reconciling Christianity with the power of classical learning than from keeping classical learning alive at all. Outside the monasteries, traditional schooling in the classics survived only as long as cities could afford to pay for teachers. In most of the towns of the western provinces of the empire, schools gradually disappeared during the fifth century as a result of the Germanic invasions. In the eastern provinces they survived until the seventh century, then faded away.

NEOPLATONISM AND CHRISTIANITY Greek and Roman philosophy remained influential in the late antique period. One branch of this tradition, called **Neoplatonism**, is associated with the thought of Plotinus (205–270), a non-Christian philosopher. His teachings greatly influenced Christianity, an example of how classical and Christian thought intertwined in late antiquity. Plotinus, who taught in Rome, traced his intellectual roots primarily to the works of Plato (ca. 429–327 B.C.E.). He also drew ideas from Aristotle (384–322 B.C.E.), Stoic philosophers (third century B.C.E.), and their followers.

Neoplatonism A philosophy based on the teachings of Plato and his successors that flourished in late antiquity, especially in the teachings of Plotinus. Neoplatonism influenced Christianity in late antiquity. During the Renaissance Neoplatonism was linked to the belief that the natural world was charged with occult forces that could be used in the practice of magic.

Plotinus argued that all things that exist, whether intangible ideas or tangible matter, originate in a single force called the One. Humans could reunite their souls with the One by overcoming their passions and physical desires that were governed by the body. Many Neoplatonists believed that by gaining the help of the gods through magical rites and studying divine revelations, the human soul could reconnect with the One and realize its fullest potential. Neoplatonism had many similarities to Gnosticism, which was discussed in Chapter 6 and which also guided some early Christians. The Gnostics, however, emphasized magic in a way that the sober, philosophical Neoplatonists such as Plotinus thought was the work of "imbeciles."

Neoplatonism appealed to many Christians. For them, the One was God, and the Bible provided the divine revelations that could lead to the salvation of the human soul and reunification with God. Gregory of Nyssa (331–395) in the Greek East and Augustine in the Latin West were only two of the many churchmen who incorporated Neoplatonism into their own works in the later fourth century. After Christian and non-Christian Neoplatonists argued over whether the identity of "the One" could be equated with the Christian God, Emperor Justinian closed Plato's Academy in Athens in 529 and forbade non-Christians to teach philosophy.

Nevertheless, Neoplatonic thought helped shape the Christian doctrine of the immortality of the human soul. It also reinforced the ascetic ideal practiced by monks and nuns. Thus, contempt for the material, temporal world and the physical body took deep root in Christian culture.

Read the Document

Bishop Synesius of Cyrene, *Letter to His Brother*

The Breakup of the Roman Empire

7.4 How and why did the Roman Empire in the West disintegrate?

During the fifth century, the Roman Empire split into two parts: the Latin-speaking provinces in western Europe, and the largely Greek- and Syriac-speaking provinces in the East. As the Roman government lost control of its western domains, independent Germanic kingdoms emerged. The eastern provinces remained under the control of the Roman emperor, whose capital city was not Rome, but Constantinople. The definitive split of the Roman Empire marked the end of late antiquity. In future centuries the legacy of the Roman Empire survived in the West through Latin culture and Latin Christianity. In the East, it survived as a political reality until its final collapse 1,000 years later in 1453.

The Fall of Rome's Western Provinces

Why Roman rule remained strong in the eastern Mediterranean while collapsing in western Europe is one of the most hotly debated subjects in history. Most Christians of the time attributed the collapse of Roman rule to God's anger at the stubborn persistence of polytheist worship. Polytheists, for their part, blamed Christians for destroying the temples of the gods who had protected Rome in the past. In later centuries, the explanations varied. Edward Gibbon, an eighteenth-century writer whose *Decline and Fall of the Roman Empire* has influenced all historians of Rome and remains one of the most widely read history books of all time, criticized the Catholic Church for diverting able men away from public service and into religious life. Other historians attributed Rome's collapse in the West to enormous waves of savage barbarian invasions. The reason the Romans lost their western provinces is, however, more complicated and less dramatic than any of these one-dimensional explanations.

LOSS OF IMPERIAL POWER IN THE WEST The end of Roman rule in western Europe came in a haphazard and gradual fashion as the cumulative result of unwise decisions, weak leadership, and military failure. During the first century, the Romans established the northern limits of their empire in Europe along the Rhine and Danube Rivers. From that time forward, Roman generals and emperors withstood invasions of many different northern tribes looking for plunder and new lands. The Roman legions maintained a relatively stable northern frontier through diplomacy as well as military might. Since the time of Augustus, Roman emperors had permitted newcomers to settle on Roman lands. Until the fourth century, the empire had always been able to absorb the settlers.

In the fourth century, the sudden appearance of the Huns, a fierce nomadic people from central Asia, in southern Russia set in motion events that helped bring about the collapse of Roman rule in western Europe. Unlike the settled farmers who lived in Europe, the Huns were nomads who herded their flocks over the plains (or *steppes*) that stretched from southern Russia to central Asia. Able to travel vast distances quickly on their rugged horses, the highly mobile Huns overran adversaries from settled agricultural communities. The Huns also earned a reputation for ferocity. Living under the specter of starvation, they lusted after the great riches and easy lifestyles they observed in the urbanized empires of Rome and Persia.

In 376, in what is now south Russia, an army of Huns drove a group of Visigoths from their farmlands. The Visigoth refugees gained permission from the Roman Emperor Valens to cross the Danube and settle in the Balkans in return for supplying troops to the Roman army. In the past, Roman rulers had frequently made this sort of arrangement. The Roman officials in charge of this resettlement, however, exploited the refugees by charging them exorbitant fees for food and supplies. In 378 the Visigoths revolted. At the Battle of Adrianople in Thrace they killed Valens and destroyed an entire Roman army.

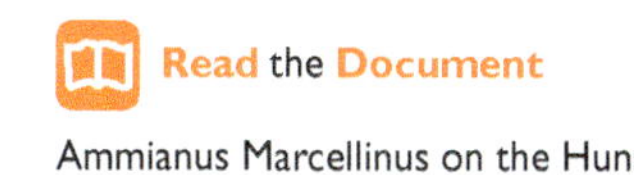

Ammianus Marcellinus on the Huns

7.1

7.2

7.3

7.4

The Visigoths' successful rebellion wounded the empire, but not fatally. Rome's response to the disaster, however, sowed the seeds for a loss of imperial power in the west. Necessity forced the new emperor, Theodosius the Great, to permit Visigothic soldiers to serve in the Roman army under their own Visigothic commanders. But allowing independent military forces of dubious loyalty to operate freely within the empire was a terrible mistake. The consequences of Theodosius's decision became all too clear in the mid-390s when Alaric, the new Visigothic king, began to plunder Roman cities in the Balkans and Greece. As discussed at the beginning of this chapter, in 401 Alaric and his troops sacked Rome for three days. Senators and citizens could only watch as the Visigoths rampaged through their streets.

The Visigoths' sack of Rome not only dealt a psychological blow to the empire's inhabitants, it also led indirectly to the loss of many of Rome's western provinces. To fight Alaric, Rome's armies withdrew from the empire's northwestern defenses, leaving the frontier in Britain and along the Rhine vulnerable. In Britain, Rome abandoned its control entirely after an ambitious general, styling himself Constantine III, led Britain's last legions across the English Channel in 407 in an unsuccessful attempt to grab the imperial throne. This left Britain defenseless, vulnerable to groups of Germanic tribesmen known as the Saxons already settled on British soil.

Elsewhere the chaos spread. Although the invading bands were small, the imperial government in the West no longer possessed the administrative capacity to marshal its military resources and push the invaders out. In December 406, the Rhine River froze, enabling migrating Germanic tribes to enter the empire with little opposition. Small bands of these marauding tribes roamed through Gaul, while the Vandals and their allies raided their way through Spain. In 429 the Vandals crossed to North Africa, where they soon established an independent kingdom. By 450 the Visigoths had formed a kingdom of their own in Gaul and Spain.

Overwhelming numbers of savage tribesmen did not invade the empire. In fact, their numbers were puny. For example, only 40,000 Vandals controlled North Africa, which had a population of several million Romans. And although the Germans plundered and pillaged, they could not hold on to imperial lands and settle there without the active cooperation of Roman administrators who thought they could bargain with the tribesmen. Once they put down roots, however, the Germanic invaders consolidated their strength and established their rule. By then, Roman authorities lacked both the organization and the strength to expel them.

Even though most of the western provinces had fallen to invaders by 450, the Romans held on to Italy for a while longer. The city of Rome remained the home of the Senate, while the emperor of the western provinces resided in Ravenna, a town on Italy's northeast coast. Warlords, however, held the real power in Italy, although they were formally subordinate to the emperor. These soldiers were usually not Romans by birth, but they adopted Roman culture and fought for Rome. In 476 one of these warlords, a Germanic general named Odovacar, deposed the last emperor in the west, a boy named Romulus Augustulus, and named himself king of Italy. For many historians the year 476 used to symbolize the end of the Roman Empire in the west. In fact, however, 476 is a date of little significance. The Romans' control of their western provinces had slipped away decades earlier (see **Map 7.2**).

CULTURAL ENCOUNTERS AFTER THE END OF ROMAN RULE By the mid-fifth century, when most fighting between Germanic invaders and Romans had ended, the two sides, as rulers and ruled, began an era of intense encounters. In Britain the Germanic invaders were polytheists who snuffed out the Christians. Yet legends hint at a fierce resistance against the invaders. The stories about King Arthur that have captivated English-speaking

7.1
7.2
7.3
7.4

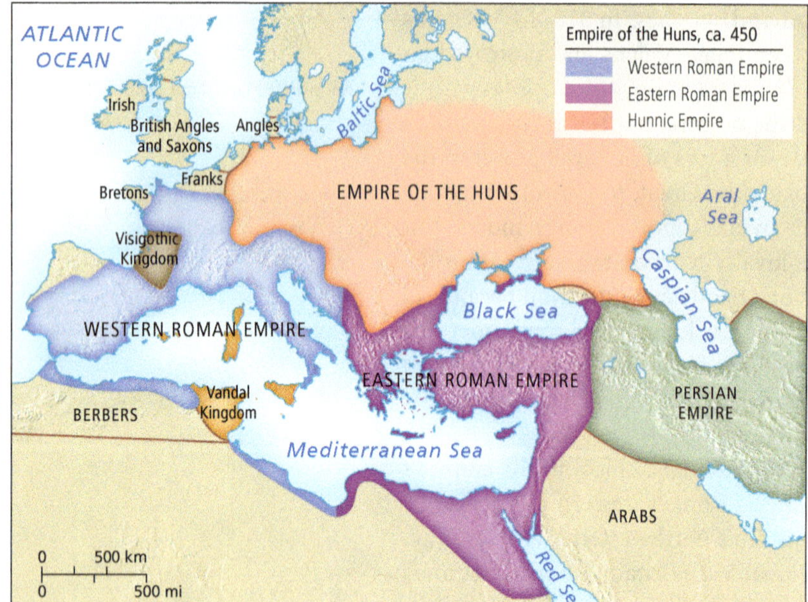

MAP **7.2** EMPIRE OF THE HUNS During late antiquity, the Huns established a powerful empire based in the Hungarian plain. These fierce horsemen terrified the settled peoples of the Roman world, but their empire broke up within a generation. Does the division of the Roman Empire into western and eastern halves indicate strength or weakness? Why?

audiences since the Middle Ages are based on memories of valiant resistance to the Saxon invaders in the mid-fifth century.

In Gaul, North Africa, Italy, and Spain, the new settlers followed Arian Christianity. The Roman inhabitants, on the other hand, followed Chalcedonian (Catholic) Christianity and thus saw the invaders as heretics. Although this religious difference caused friction between the two peoples, it also worked to their mutual advantage. Roman law forbade marriage with Arian Christians, so the conquerors remained a distinctive minority in their new domains. This enabled them to maintain a separate Arian clergy and separate churches.

Of all the former empire's western provinces, Italy prospered the most under Germanic rule, particularly under the long reign of Theodoric the Ostrogoth (r. 493–526). Theodoric murdered Odovacar, the German warrior who had deposed the last Roman emperor in the West, to obtain the throne of Italy. In politics, Theodoric sought to create mutual respect between Ostrogoths and Romans by maintaining two separate administrations—one for his Ostrogoths, the other for the Romans—so that both communities could manage their own affairs under his supervision. He also included aristocratic Romans among his closest advisers and most trusted administrators. Even in his religious policies Theodoric pursued mutual tolerance. As an Arian Christian, he supported the separate Arian clergy, but he also maintained excellent ties with the pope, leader of the Roman Christians. Theodoric united Visigothic kingdoms in Gaul with his own in Italy, ultimately wielding great influence throughout western Europe. Italy prospered under his rule, and the communities of Ostrogoths and Romans lived together amicably.

Read the **Document**

Sidonius Apollinaris, *Rome's Decay* and *A Glimpse of the New Order*

Although Theodoric had paid formal homage to the emperor in Constantinople, during his rule the western provinces' links to the Roman Empire in the East began to weaken. Most of the invaders, including Theodoric's Ostrogoths, continued their traditional practice of pledging obedience to a local chieftain. This tradition began to erode loyalty to the far-off Roman emperor in Constantinople. By pledging themselves to a Germanic king, men gained a place in the "tribe" of their new chieftain.

Roman culture did not abruptly end with the last vestiges of Roman rule. It remained a vital presence in most regions, but it took different forms in the lands now ruled by Germanic leaders. In Britain, Roman culture perhaps fared the worst and little of it survived into later ages. There the Germanic language of the Saxon invaders and their Anglo allies took hold and began developing into the English spoken today. In Gaul, Italy, and Spain, the Germanic settlers quickly learned Latin. Over time these Latin-based "Romance" (based on the Roman speech) languages grew into the early versions of French, Italian, Catalan, Spanish, and Portuguese. Latin continued as the language of literacy, and the settlers borrowed heavily from Roman literary forms. Writing in Latin, they produced histories of their tribal kingdoms in imitation of Roman historians. They also developed law codes composed in Latin influenced by Roman models.

Read the **Document**

Excerpt from *The Governance of God* (5th Century C.E.) Salvian

The Survival of Rome's Eastern Provinces

Despite the profound alterations wrought by Christianity and Rome's loss of the western provinces, the Roman Empire endured in the eastern Mediterranean without interruption. Constantinople, the imperial city founded by Constantine in 324, became the center of a remodeled empire that merged Christian and Roman characteristics. Historians call the remodeled Roman Empire in the East the **Byzantine Empire**, after Byzantium, the original Greek name of Constantinople.

Byzantine Empire The eastern half of the Roman Empire, which lasted from the founding of Constantinople in 324 to its conquest by the Ottoman Turks in 1453.

CHRISTIANITY AND LAW UNDER JUSTINIAN The most important amalgamation of Christian and Roman traditions took place during the reign of Emperor Justinian (r. 527–565). Born in the Balkans, Justinian was the last emperor in Constantinople to speak Latin as his native language. He combined a powerful intellect, an unshakable Christian faith, and a driving ambition to reform the empire. He defied convention by marrying Theodora, a strong-willed former actress, and included her in imperial decision making once he became emperor.

Justinian inaugurated changes that highlighted his role as a Christian emperor. First, he emphasized the position of the emperor at the center of society in explicitly Christian

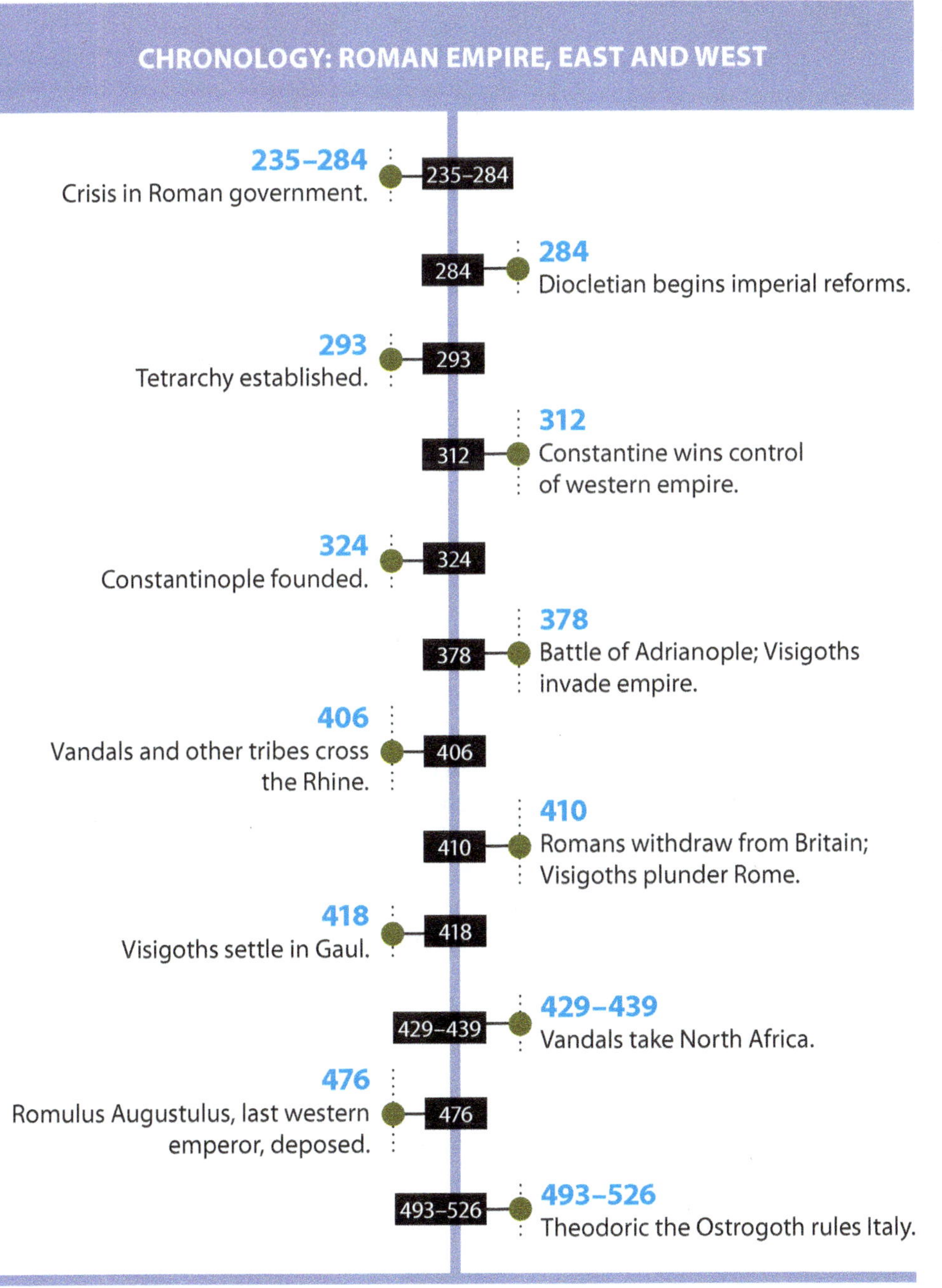

DIPTYCH OF A CONSUL This ivory panel celebrates a Roman consul at Constantinople in the sixth century. In his right hand he holds the *mappa*, a ceremonial cloth that symbolizes his office. Behind him stand personifications of Rome (on his left) and Constantinople (on his right). Such panels were given as gifts when consuls took office. This one demonstrates Roman traditions continuing in the new world of Byzantium.

Read the Document

Prologue of the *Corpus Juris Civilis*, ca. 530

terms. He was the first emperor to use the title "Beloved of Christ," and he amplified the emperor's role in Church affairs. Justinian considered it his duty as emperor to impose uniform religious belief throughout the empire by enforcing the decrees of the Council of Chalcedon as he interpreted them. In the East this meant stamping out the survival of polytheist worship and struggling to find a common ground with the anti-Chalcedonians. After Justinian reconquered some of the western domains of the empire, he had to deal with the Arian Vandals and Ostrogoths living there. In the East Justinian suppressed polytheism, but he never reached an agreement with the anti-Chalcedonian communities in Syria and Egypt. After the armies of Islam conquered these regions in the following century, the Christian churches there fell out of imperial control (see Chapter 8). In the West the bishops of North Africa and Italy resented Justinian's attempts to determine doctrine. As a result, a bitter division arose between Christian churches in the eastern and western Mediterranean over the rights of bishops to resist imperial authority on religious matters.

Justinian attempted to create a Christian society by using Roman law coupled with military force. Unlike rulers of Rome's early empire, who permitted subject peoples to maintain their own customary laws, Justinian suppressed local laws throughout his realm. He envisioned all of his subjects obeying only Roman law—law that he defined and that God approved. (Justinian was sure that if God did not approve of his legislative changes, God would not allow him to continue as emperor.)

Thus, in his God-given mission as emperor-legislator, Justinian reformed Roman law. To simplify the vast body of civil law, he ordered his lawyers to sort through all the laws that had accumulated over the centuries and determine which of them should still be enforced.

Justinian's codification of the law, which was completed in 534, and associated legal texts are now collectively called the *Corpus Juris Civilis*. The body of Roman law passed down to later generations primarily through this compilation. At the end of the eleventh century, scholars in Italy discovered manuscripts of Justinian's legal works in church libraries, and interest in Roman law revived. Thus, the *Corpus Juris Civilis* became a pillar of Latin-speaking European civilization.

RECONQUERING PROVINCES IN THE WEST Once he had reorganized the empire's legal system, Justinian turned his attention to Rome's fallen western provinces. He wanted to reestablish imperial control over these territories, now ruled by Germanic kings. Once the empire was restored to its former glory, Justinian's plan was to impose his version of Christian orthodoxy upon the Arian Vandals and Ostrogoths in his western domains. He would also force them to live under his version of Roman law and government.

In 533, Justinian sent a fleet of 10,000 men and 5,000 cavalry under the command of his general Belisarius to attack the Vandal kingdom in North Africa. It fell quickly, and within a year Belisarius celebrated a triumph in Constantinople. Encouraged by this easy victory, Justinian set his sights on Italy, where the Ostrogothic ruling family was embroiled in political infighting. This time Justinian underestimated his opponents. The Ostrogoths, who had won the support of the Roman population in Italy, mounted a fierce resistance to Belisarius's invasion in 537. Justinian failed to support Belisarius with adequate funds and soldiers. Bitter fighting dragged on for two decades. Justinian's armies eventually wrestled Italy back under imperial control, but the protracted reconquest had disastrous consequences. The years of fighting devastated Italy, and the financial burden drained the empire's resources (see **Map 7.3**).

One of the reasons Justinian's reconquest of Italy took decades was the visitation of a lethal plague that struck the empire in 542 and migrated swiftly to Italy, North Africa, and Gaul. The first onslaught took the lives of about 250,000 people, half the population of Constantinople. An estimated one-third of the empire's inhabitants died. With the population devastated, Justinian's army could not recruit the soldiers it needed to fight on several fronts.

The plague also weakened the economy. In many provinces, farms lay deserted and city populations shriveled. Commercial ties between the eastern and western

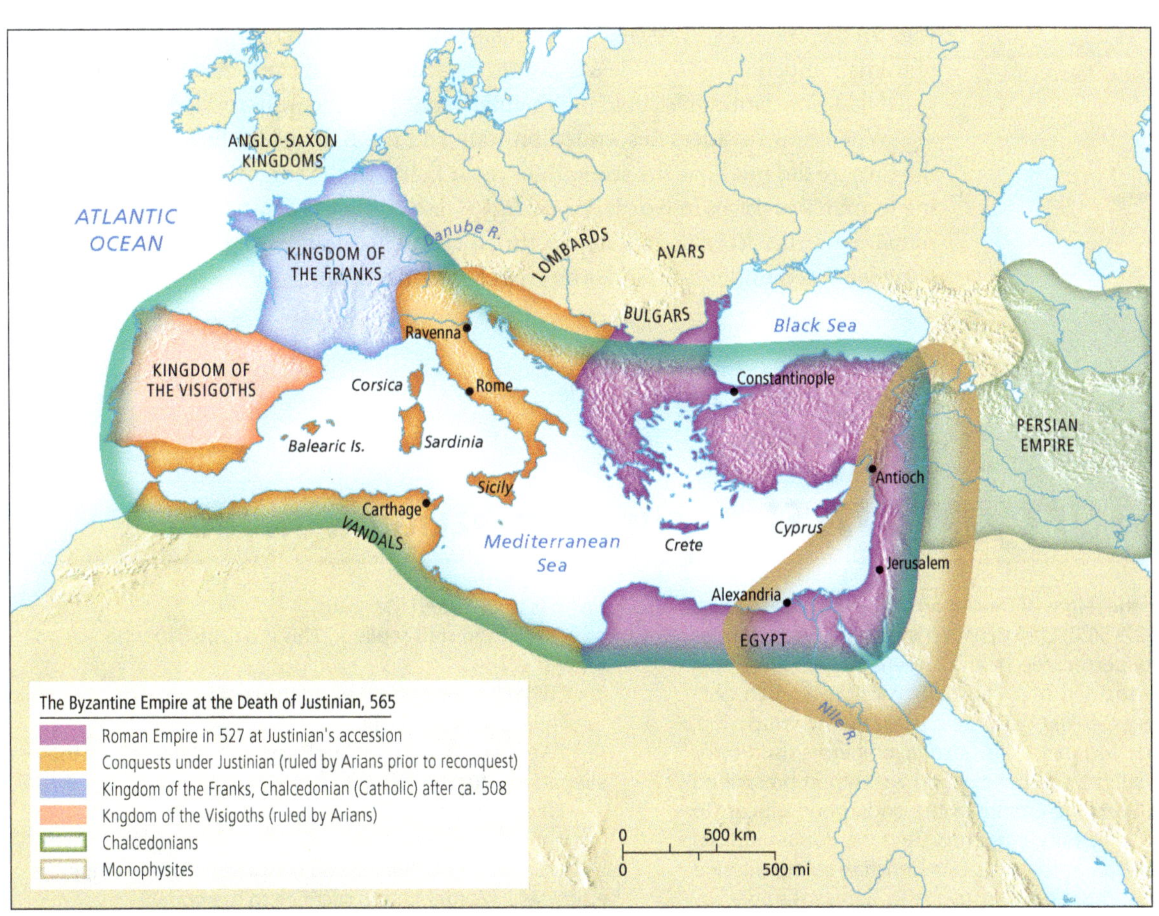

MAP **7.3** THE BYZANTINE EMPIRE AT THE DEATH OF JUSTINIAN, 565 When Justinian died in 565, Italy, North Africa, and part of Spain that had been lost in the fifth century had been restored, temporarily, to imperial rule. Under the dynamic Sasanian dynasty, the Persian Empire fought many wars with the Romans. Neither empire had an advantage because they were roughly the same size and possessed equivalent resources of wealth and manpower. Compare this map with Maps 7.1 and 7.2. What do these comparisons show about the decline of the Roman Empire?

Mediterranean declined. In the western provinces, economies became more "local" and self-sufficient.

THE STRUGGLE WITH PERSIA Although Justinian's greatest military successes were in the western Mediterranean, his most dangerous enemy was the Persian Empire (formerly Parthia) on his eastern flank. This huge, multiethnic empire, under the rule of the Sasanian dynasty (ca. 220–633), had been Rome's main rival throughout late antiquity. The tension stemmed chiefly from competition over Armenia, which was a rich source of troops, and Syria, which possessed enormous wealth. Though wars between Romans and Persians were frequent, neither side could win permanent superiority over the other.

Justinian fought several brutal wars with Persia. He gave top priority to this struggle by supplying it with more than half of his troops, led by his best generals. He also provided more financial resources to the struggle in the East than to the wars of reconquest in the West. Chosroes I (r. 531–579), the aggressive and ambitious Great King of Persia, proved a worthy adversary for Justinian. Chosroes repeatedly invaded the Byzantine Empire, causing great damage. In 540, for example, he sacked Antioch, the wealthiest city in Syria. Because war with Persia was extraordinarily expensive, Justinian bought peace by paying thousands of pounds of gold to the Persian monarch. Even this cost less than continuing to fight every year.

By the time of Justinian's death, the two empires had established an uneasy coexistence, but the basic animosity between them remained unresolved. For the next half century, Justinian's successors engaged in intermittent warfare with the Persians. By fighting expensive wars on the western and eastern flanks of his empire, Justinian hastened the disintegration of Roman imperial rule outside the eastern provinces. The overextension of resources ensured that Constantinople could not maintain control of the western Mediterranean.

When new invaders descended on Italy and the Balkans in the late sixth century, the Empire did not have the strength to resist them. In the seventh century the remaining Roman provinces in North Africa, Egypt, and Syria were lost. Nevertheless, in what remained of the Roman Empire, Justinian succeeded in creating a Christian–Roman society, united under one God, one emperor, and one law.

Justice in History

Two Martyrdoms: CULTURE AND RELIGION ON TRIAL

Between the reigns of Diocletian (r. 284–305) and Justinian (r. 527–565), Christians went from being a religious minority persecuted by the imperial government to a majority that persecuted non-Christians with the Roman government's backing. One thing did not change during this period, however. Whether polytheist or Christian, emperors used force to compel their subjects to believe and worship in prescribed ways, hoping to keep the empire in the gods' good graces. To ensure religious conformity, emperors used the Roman judicial system. A comparison of the trials of a Christian soldier named Julius in 303 with Phocas, an aristocrat in Constantinople accused of paganism in 529 and 545, illustrates the objectives and methods of the Roman government's religious prosecution.

In 303 officials brought a veteran soldier named Julius before the prefect Maximus. The following excerpt comes from a description of the trial:

"Who is this?" asked Maximus.

One of the staff replied: "This is a Christian who will not obey the laws."

"What is your name?" asked the prefect.

"Julius," was the reply.

"Well, what say you, Julius?" asked the prefect. "Are these allegations true?"

"Yes, they are," said Julius. "I am indeed a Christian. I do not deny that I am precisely what I am."

"You are surely aware," said the prefect, "of the emperors' edicts which order you to sacrifice to the gods?"

"I am aware of them," answered Julius. "I am indeed a Christian and cannot do what you want; for I must not lose sight of my living and true God."...

"If you think it a sin," answered the prefect Maximus, "let me take the blame. I am the one who is forcing you,

(continued on next page)

(continued from previous page)

so that you may not give impression of having consented voluntarily. Afterwards you can go home in peace, you will pick up your ten-year bonus, and no one will ever trouble you again. . . . If you do not respect the imperial decrees and offer sacrifice, I am going to cut your head off."

"That is a good plan," answered Julius, "Only I beg . . . that you execute your plan and pass sentence on me so that my prayers may be answered. . . . I have chosen death for now so that I might live with the saints forever."

The prefect Maximus then delivered the sentence as follows: "Whereas Julius has refused to obey the imperial edicts, he is sentenced to death."[1]

After Constantine's conversion to Christianity in 312, Christian officials began to attack polytheism with the government's support. Emperor Justinian launched three major persecutions of polytheists. In the first episode of persecution in 528–529, one year after Justinian ascended to the throne, a handful of government officials were charged with worshiping pagan gods.

JUSTINIAN This mid-sixth-century ivory panel depicts Emperor Justinian in a standard pose of Roman emperors. The panel sends the message that Justinian rules the world with the approval and support of God.

One of these men was Phocas the Patrician, an aristocratic lawyer with an illustrious career in the emperor's service. After serving at court, he was sent to Antioch to rebuild the city after a ruinous earthquake in 527. He was arrested during that first episode of persecution. Cleared of charges of practicing paganism in 529, Phocas continued to enjoy Justinian's trust and earn further promotions. In 532 he served for a year as Praetorian Prefect, the emperor's most powerful official with responsibility for administering the empire. Phocas raised revenue for the construction of the new Cathedral of Holy Wisdom in Constantinople and spent his personal funds in supporting smaller churches and ransoming hostages captured by Byzantium's enemies. Justinian next made him a judge and sent him on a mission to investigate the murder of a bishop. Part of Justinian's confidence in Phocas came from the fact that he was deeply learned and competent. Phocas and other victims had a deep commitment to traditional Roman culture. But that very commitment led to their downfall. Their "paganism" was not the furtive worship of old gods like Zeus or Apollo. Rather, Phocas was considered a pagan because he was loyal to classical philosophy, literature, and rhetoric, without any Christian overlay or interpretation.

Then, in 545–546, during the second wave of persecution, despite his publicly recognized activities in support of the Church and his faithful service to Justinian, Phocas was arrested again, one of many doctors, teachers, and government officials suddenly charged with paganism. Constantinople endured a time of terror. Officials accused of worshiping the old gods in secret were driven from public office, had their property confiscated by the emperor, and were executed. In a panic, some of the accused took their own lives. Phocas was one of them. Rather than undergo the humiliation of public execution, he committed suicide. The furious emperor ordered that Phocas's body be buried in a ditch like an animal, without prayer or ceremony of any sort.

Phocas thus missed the third purge of 562, when polytheists were arrested throughout the empire, paraded in public, imprisoned, tried, and sentenced. Zealous crowds threw thousands of non-Christian books into bonfires.

The official reason for persecuting Christians such as Julius was relatively simple: Christians broke the law by refusing to make sacrifices to the Roman gods. But why did Christian governments also later use such a heavy hand in persecuting polytheists? Men like Phocas who were attacked as pagans were highly educated in the traditional learning of the Greco–Roman world. Indeed, it was this learning that was really on trial. For Justinian, this sort of classical learning had no place in a Christian empire.

For Discussion

Why did both polytheist and Christian governments of Rome persecute adherents of nonofficial religions?

Taking It Further

Helgeland, John. *Christians in the Military: The Early Experience.* 1985, 64–65. An introduction to the persecutions of Christians in the Roman army and their depiction in Christian literature.

Maas, Michael. *John Lydus and the Roman Past: Antiquarianism and Politics in the Age of Justinian.* 1992. This book explains how Justinian's policies about religion also involved an encounter with the empire's classical heritage.

CONCLUSION

The Age of New Boundaries

During late antiquity the transformation of the Roman world into new political configurations with new boundaries helped create a new conception of the West. Henceforth, the West was closely associated with the legacy of Roman civilization filtered through the lens of Christianity. The most lasting development of the period came from the encounter between the civilization of the Roman Empire and Christianity, which before the fourth century had been the faith of a persecuted minority. As Christianity became the dominant religion throughout the Roman Empire, it was itself transformed, not the least through the attempts to reconcile Christian revelation with classical learning. Christian thinkers assimilated much of classical culture, and with the support of the Roman emperors, Christianity became the official religion. During this process of assimilation, Christians disagreed among themselves over how they explained the divinity of Jesus Christ, and these disagreements led to distinctive strains of Christian belief.

The Roman Empire itself was irreparably split into two parts, which became the foundations for two distinctive Christian civilizations. After Roman rule in the West collapsed, Germanic rulers established new kingdoms in the old Roman provinces. Some of these kingdoms spoke Romance languages derived from Latin, and all of them used Latin for religious worship, learning, and the law. From the western provinces of the Roman Empire during late antiquity, Latin civilization spread to parts of central, eastern, and northern Europe that had never been part of the Roman Empire. In the eastern Mediterranean, the Roman Empire survived as the Byzantine Empire (discussed in Chapter 8) and became the home of Orthodox Christianity. In Byzantium, Greek remained the dominant tongue of daily life, learning, and Christian worship.

When Islam emerged as a powerful religious and political entity at the end of the late antique period, as we will discuss in Chapter 8, classical learning and Roman institutions also influenced its adherents. But the Muslim and Christian empires became enemies, a tendency that created the most lasting divisions among the peoples who had once been citizens of the Roman Empire.

MAKING CONNECTIONS

1. Besides the Bible, what were the significant influences on early Christianity?
2. What were the differences between Roman and Germanic ideas of rulership in late antiquity?
3. Why did the Roman Empire survive in the East and not the West in late antiquity?

TAKING IT FURTHER

For suggested readings, see page R-1.

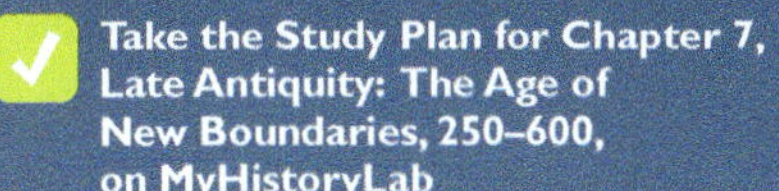

Chapter Review

Crisis and Recovery in the Third Century

7.1 How did the Roman Empire successfully reorganize following the instability of the third century?

Military, administrative, and economic reforms imposed organization on the previously chaotic Roman Empire. A system of shared government spread the heavy administrative responsibilities from one emperor to four, and ended the cycle of imperial assassinations by instituting a reliable succession strategy. New roads granted a significantly larger army the mobility to face invaders along the frontiers, and increased taxes and a regular census to register all taxpayers made the taxation system more profitable and efficient.

Toward a Christian Empire

7.2 How did Christianity become the dominant religion in the Roman Empire, and how did it affect Roman society?

After Constantine's conversion, successive emperors continued to encourage Christianity until it was finally the dominant religion in the empire. The internal organization of Christianity, including a clear distinction of power between the laity and the priests, imitated Roman urban administration and encouraged bishops to become important figures in Roman cities. These cities were transformed by public and private spending on churches, hospitals, and monastic communities that conformed to Christian values, and new religious festivals and rituals slowly replaced celebrations for polytheistic worship. Eventually, tolerance for any religions except Christianity waned.

New Christian Communities and Identities

7.3 How did Christianity transform communities, religious experience, and intellectual traditions inside and outside the Roman Empire?

Christianity supported the development of communities of faith by providing a well-defined set of beliefs and values that had to be integrated with daily life and older ways of thinking. At the same time, Roman laws began to discriminate against Jews as religious life in the empire became increasingly narrow. While Christians were historically wary of secular learning, training in classical rhetoric, grammar, and literature became an integral part of upper class Christian life, and monasticism played a central role in preserving classical learning.

The Breakup of the Roman Empire

7.4 How and why did the Roman Empire in the West disintegrate?

Poor decisions, weak leadership, and military failure contributed to the end of the Roman Empire. Permitting independent military forces of dubious loyalty to operate freely within the empire, and the inability of the imperial government to deal with multiple small invading bands of invaders, resulted in a tenuous hold over the West. The active cooperation of Roman administrators who thought they could bargain with the invading Germanic leaders led to these tribesmen settling down and consolidating their rule. Eventually, Roman authorities simply lacked the military strength and organization necessary to expel them.

Chapter Time Line

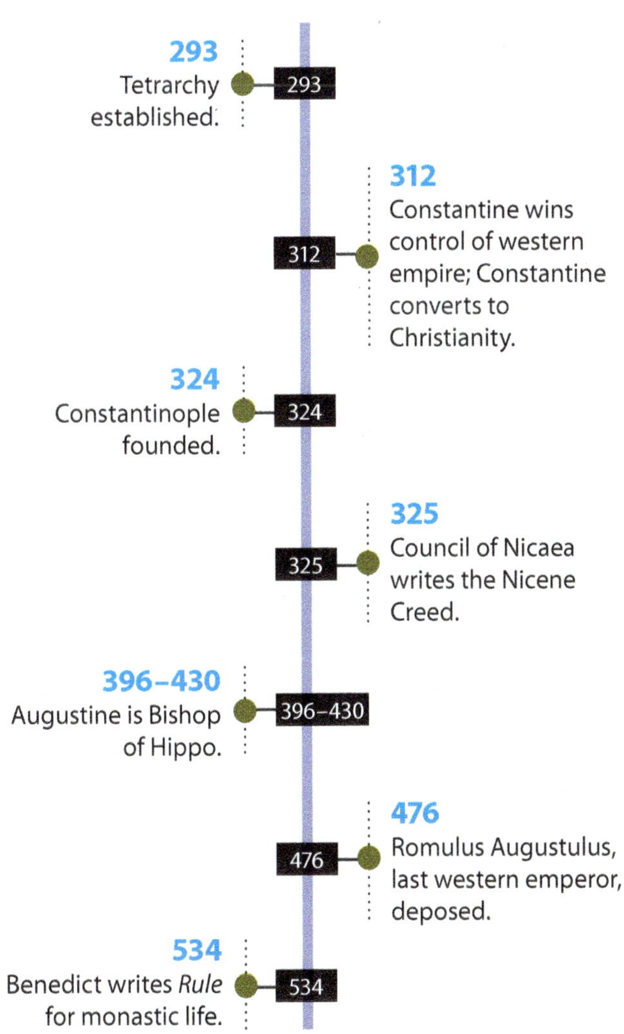

8 Medieval Empires and Borderlands: Byzantium and Islam

In 860 fierce Rus tribesmen aboard a fleet of sleek ships with prows shaped like dragons' heads raided the Byzantine villages along the shores of the Black Sea and then advanced to the gates of Constantinople, ready for pillage and rape. Panic gripped the inhabitants of the city. The Patriarch of Constantinople called on the people to repent of their sins to avoid God's wrath; when the Rus unexpectedly departed, the people of Constantinople interpreted it as an act of divine intervention.

Strategically located where the Black Sea meets the Sea of Marmara, Constantinople was the shining capital of the Byzantine Empire—and the largest and richest city in the world. Its Greek-speaking inhabitants considered the Rus savages, prone to the worst kinds of violence. Like so many other barbarian peoples, the Rus who were Vikings living in what is now Ukraine and Russia could not speak Greek, were not Christians, and did not recognize the authority of the Byzantine emperor, which the Greeks believed came directly from God. The leaders of Constantinople tried to keep these barbarians under control by signing treaties, which stipulated that no more than 50 Rus could enter the city at one time and they all had to leave by autumn. In exchange for civilized behavior, the Rus received free baths, food, provisions for a month, and equipment for their return to their homeland. By the ninth century the Rus had established a regular pattern. Each spring, after spending the winters

LEARNING OBJECTIVES

8.1 How did the Roman Empire's eastern provinces evolve into the Byzantine Empire?

8.2 How did Islam develop in Arabia, and how did its followers create a vast empire so quickly?

Listen to Chapter 8 on MyHistoryLab

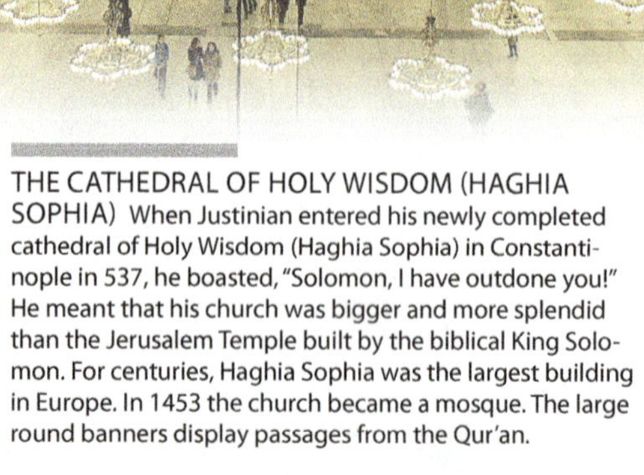

THE CATHEDRAL OF HOLY WISDOM (HAGHIA SOPHIA) When Justinian entered his newly completed cathedral of Holy Wisdom (Haghia Sophia) in Constantinople in 537, he boasted, "Solomon, I have outdone you!" He meant that his church was bigger and more splendid than the Jerusalem Temple built by the biblical King Solomon. For centuries, Haghia Sophia was the largest building in Europe. In 1453 the church became a mosque. The large round banners display passages from the Qur'an.

Watch the Video Series on MyHistoryLab

Learn about some key topics related to this chapter with the *MyHistoryLab Video Series: Key Topics in Western Civilization*

along the river valleys of the north collecting tribute from the Slavic tribes, the Rus set off in their boats, risking dangerous rapids and waterfalls on the Dnieper River and ambush from hostile tribes, to reach the Black Sea and the splendid emporium of the world, Constantinople, which they called simply the "Great City."

Accustomed to winter treks, grubby villages, and constant danger, they were dazzled by the sight of the Great City, with its half million inhabitants and 12 miles of fortifications. The gilded cupolas of its churches, the marble palaces of the aristocrats and emperor, and the cavernous wharves and warehouses of its merchants amazed these tribesmen. The people of Constantinople were equally astonished—and frightened—by the sun-worn, fur-clad Rus.

The Rus came to Constantinople to trade. The merchants of Constantinople traded Byzantine and Chinese silks, Persian glass, Arabic silver coins (highly prized by the Rus), and Indian spices for honey, wax, slaves, and musty bales of furs from Scandinavia and what is now northern Russia. Despite their sense of superiority, the Byzantines needed the barbarians. In the merchant stalls of Constantinople, traders from many cultures met, haggled, and came to know something of one another. None perhaps were more unlike the other than the rough Rus and the refined Byzantines, but their mutual desires for profit kept them in a persistent, if tentative, embrace. These repeated interactions among diverse peoples who traded, competed, and fought with one another offer clues for understanding the medieval world, also known as the Middle Ages.

The term *Middle Ages* refers to the period between the ancient and modern civilizations from about the fifth to fifteenth centuries. Medieval culture rested on the foundations of three great civilizations: the Greek Christianity of Byzantium; the Arabic-speaking Islamic caliphates of the Middle East, North Africa, and Spain; and the Latin Christian kingdoms of western and northern Europe. The dynamic interactions among these three civilizations, distinguished by religion and language, lay at the heart of medieval culture. From the seventh to the eleventh centuries, the most energetic and creative of these three civilizations was the Islamic world, whose armies threatened both Byzantium and the Latin Christian kingdoms. In the century after the death of its founder, the prophet Muhammad, in 632, Islam's followers burst from their home in Arabia to conquer an empire stretching from Spain to central Asia. Especially during the tenth and eleventh centuries, this Islamic empire produced important philosophical and scientific work and supported a thriving economy.

The most distinctive feature of the medieval period was that all these civilizations rested on monotheistic religions that shared basic beliefs about God. All struggled to eliminate polytheism either by persuasion or force. However, because each of these medieval civilizations defined itself as an exclusive community of faith, cultural boundaries developed between them that are still visible today. This chapter examines two of these civilizations, Byzantium and Islam. Chapter 9 discusses the Latin Christian kingdoms. The most important question raised by the two civilizations discussed here is this:

How did their different versions of monotheism sustain them as empires?

Byzantium: The Survival of the Roman Empire

8.1 How did the Roman Empire's eastern provinces evolve into the Byzantine Empire?

In late antiquity Constantinople and Rome had symbolized the two halves of the Roman Empire. Once joined in a common Christian culture, eastern and western Christians gradually grew apart, so that by the late ninth century, they began to constitute separate civilizations, one Byzantine and the other Latin. There were still cultural exchanges between them as merchants, pilgrims, and scholars crossed back and forth, but the two civilizations had ceased to understand one another. They held different opinions about religious matters, such as the dating of Easter, the rituals of the liturgy, the role of images in worship, and the extent of the pope's authority. They also spoke different languages. In the East, Greek was the language of most of the population, and Latin had been largely forgotten by the end of the sixth century. In the West, Latin or local dialects of it prevailed. Except in southern Italy and Sicily, few Westerners knew Greek.

Eastern Europe became an unstable borderland on the flanks of Byzantium inhabited by polytheist farmers and nomads. Rival missionaries practicing Greek and Latin forms of Christianity competed there for converts and allies. Greek missionaries were the most successful in converting the Slavic peoples to Orthodox Christianity, a faith that survived among the Slavs even after the collapse of Byzantium itself.

An Embattled Empire

After the reign of Emperor Justinian (r. 527–565), the Byzantine Empire was gradually reduced to a regional power struggling for survival against many enemies. In the west the Byzantines faced the Germanic kingdom of the Lombards who eroded the imperial rule over Italy that Justinian had reestablished. The threats in the Balkans came from nomadic tribes from the Eurasian steppes, such as the Avars, Slavs, and Bulgars, who permanently settled there within the empire. These peoples became the ancestors of some of the current inhabitants of the region, such as modern Bulgarians, Croats, and Serbs. To the east the Byzantines confronted their old rival, the Persian Empire. Defeating Persia in a series of wars from 603 to 629 took such a huge toll that Byzantium was too exhausted to resist a new threat out of the Arabian peninsula from the armies of Islam. The encounters between these diverse enemies and Byzantium were usually hostile, and their encirclement of Byzantium forced Byzantine administration and military policy to change and adapt.

The Byzantine emperors after Justinian tried to hold on to the western provinces by reorganizing the administration of North Africa and Italy into two new units called *exarchates*—the Exarchate of Carthage (which also administered southern Spain) and the Exarchate of Ravenna. Because of their long distance from Constantinople and the immediate press of the local problems they confronted, the two exarchates were somewhat independent from the rest of the Byzantine Empire. The exarchs (or governors) held both civilian and military authority in these territories—a break from Roman practice, which had kept these two spheres separate. This joint command signaled the gravity of the problems the exarchs faced.

This administrative overhaul did not save Byzantium's western territories. Southern Spain fell to the Visigoths in the 630s, and Muslim armies took Carthage in 698. In 751 the Lombards captured Ravenna and put an end to the exarchate, although Byzantine rule survived in southern Italy until the eleventh century.

The Byzantine hold on eastern Europe also proved fragile. In much of the Balkan peninsula from the late sixth through ninth centuries, Byzantine weakness created a power vacuum that made the settled inhabitants who were Christians and still considered themselves subjects of the Roman Empire vulnerable to polytheist invaders. Like so many others before and after them, raiders and migrants poured out of the Eurasian steppes, a band of grasslands that spread some 5,000 miles from what is now Hungary and Ukraine in Europe into central Asia. Nomads could easily cross the grasslands on horseback. Interactions with the Avars, Slavs, Bulgars, and Rus contributed to the contraction of Byzantine territory and influence.

The nomadic Avars, who suddenly appeared in the sixth century on the plains of present-day Hungary from the steppes north of the Black Sea, had a bone-chilling reputation for ferocity. From Hungary they raided central Europe and the Balkans. These tenacious warriors dominated the region until the early ninth century and threatened Byzantium and the new kingdoms taking shape in Italy, Germany, and France.

The Avars created an empire by forcing conquered peoples to serve in their armies. Some of these peoples were Slavs. Between about 400 and 600, Slavic societies had formed from a blend of many cultures and ethnic groups. The Slavic communities that developed in eastern Europe between the Baltic Sea and the Balkans lay outside Byzantium's borders. Their Avar conquerors ruled by brute force, and most Slavs could not win back their independence. However, a few Slavic communities managed to overthrow Avar rule. In the second half of the sixth century, bands of Slavs began to migrate south across the Danube River into the Balkans. Collaborating with marauding Avars, the Slavs settled in sparsely populated frontier lands in what is now Croatia and Serbia. As the Slavs pushed south, many Byzantines abandoned their cities to the invaders. By 600, Slavic and Avar groups had seized most Byzantine lands from the Danube to Greece.

By the ninth century, these tribes began to convert to one or another form of Christianity, and the patterns of those conversions have had lasting consequences. The tribes in eastern Europe were fragmented politically, which mirrored the intricate distribution of ethnic and linguistic groups. State-building was especially complicated because much of the region had never been under Roman rule and lacked the legacies of Roman cities, institutions, and law that made the survival of Byzantium possible and the Germanic kingdoms of western Europe viable. Conversion patterns exacerbated eastern European fragmentation because the religious dividing line between those who adhered to Roman Catholicism and those who followed Orthodox Christianity cut directly through the region. Religion, like ethnicity and language, became a source of disunity rather than cohesion.

Fast on the heels of the Avars and Slavs from the steppes came the nomadic peoples called the Bulgars, who established rule over the largely Slavic inhabitants of the Balkans by the eighth century. The Bulgars destroyed the surviving old Roman cities there, expelled what Christians remained, and attacked the Byzantine Empire. In 811, after annihilating a Byzantine army, the Bulgarian khan (the head of a confederation of clans) Krum (r. 803–814) lined the skull of the slain Byzantine emperor with silver and turned it into a drinking cup. With this symbolic act of debasement, the Bulgarians gained a fierce reputation as enemies of Christianity and Byzantium.

In 865, however, Khan Boris I (r. 852–889) accepted the Orthodox Christianity of his former enemies in Byzantium. His conversion illustrates the politics of the period. During the ninth century Christianity began to acquire a powerful allure among the polytheistic tribes. Their acceptance of Christianity opened the possibility for diplomatic ties and alliances with the Christian powers. For Boris, therefore, conversion was a way to ward off Byzantine hostility and make peace. For four years, Boris negotiated with Rome, Constantinople, and German missionaries, all of whom sought to convert the Bulgars. In the end, Boris got what he wanted—a Bulgarian Orthodox Church that recognized the ultimate authority of the patriarch of Constantinople but was essentially autonomous.

The autonomy of the Bulgarian Church was further guaranteed later in the ninth century by the adoption of a Slavic liturgy rather than a Latin or Greek liturgy. This was made possible by the missionary work in neighboring Moravia of Cyril (ca. 826–869) and his brother Methodius (815–885), who had invented an alphabet to write the Slavic language. They translated a Greek church liturgy into a version of the Slavic language now known as Old Church Slavonic. The acceptance of the Slavonic liturgy gradually led the ethnically and linguistically mixed peoples of Bulgaria to identify with Slavic culture and language. From a string of monasteries established by the Bulgarians, the Old Church Slavonic liturgy spread among the Serbs, the Romanians, and eventually the Russians, creating cultural ties among these widespread peoples that have survived to the present.

As we saw at the beginning of this chapter, Byzantium also faced assault from the northern Rus. The Rus established a headquarters at Kiev on the Dnieper River and extended their domination over the local Slav tribes. From among the merchant-warriors of the Rus arose the forebears of the princes of Kiev, who by the end of the tenth century ruled a vast steppe and forest domain through a loose collective of subject principalities. The term *Rus* (later *Russian*) came to be applied to all the lands the princes of Kiev ruled.

Kievan Rus reached its zenith under Vladimir the Great (r. 978–1015) and his son Iaroslav the Wise (r. 1019–1054). A ruthless fighter, Vladimir consolidated into a single state the provinces of Kiev and Novgorod, a city in the far north that had grown rich from the fur trade. Born a polytheist, Vladimir had seven wives and took part in human sacrifices. However, when offered a military alliance with Byzantium in 987, he abandoned his wives, married the Byzantine emperor's sister, and converted to Orthodox Christianity. He then forced the inhabitants of Kiev and Novgorod to be baptized and cast their idols into the rivers. The Byzantine Church established administrative control over the Rus Church by appointing an Orthodox archbishop for Kiev. The liturgy was in Old Church Slavonic, which provided a written language and the stimulus for the literature, art, and music at the foundations of Russian culture. Iaroslav employed scribes to translate Greek religious books into Old Slavonic and founded new churches and monasteries across the Kievan state (see **Map 8.1**). The religious and political connection between the Rus and Byzantium shaped Russian history and limited the eastward spread of Latin Christianity (Roman Catholicism).

Read the Document
Ibn Fadlan's *Account of the Rus*

Byzantine Civilization

In addition to assaults from so many directions, the Byzantine Empire faced turmoil from within. The loss of territories caused economic suffering, and religious controversies at times alienated the population from the government. But despite terrible losses, Byzantium endured. Three institutions held the empire together: the emperor, who set policies and safeguarded his subjects' welfare; the army, which defended the frontiers; and the Orthodox Church, which provided spiritual guidance.

IMPERIAL ADMINISTRATION AND ECONOMY Based at Constantinople, the emperor stood at the center of Byzantine society. His authority reached to every corner of the empire. This supreme ruler governed with the assistance of a large bureaucracy that he tightly controlled. In this hierarchical bureaucracy, elaborate titles and different clothing indicated different ranks. Only the emperor or members of his family, for example, could wear the color purple, a symbol of royalty. High dignitaries wore silk garments of distinctive colors encrusted with jewels. The higher the official, the more gems he was permitted to display. Bureaucrats and courtiers (members of the emperor's personal retinue) lined up in elaborate processions in order of their importance, as indicated by the color of their clothing and shoes. Through these ceremonies the emperor displayed the government to the people. Such processions were not just political propaganda.

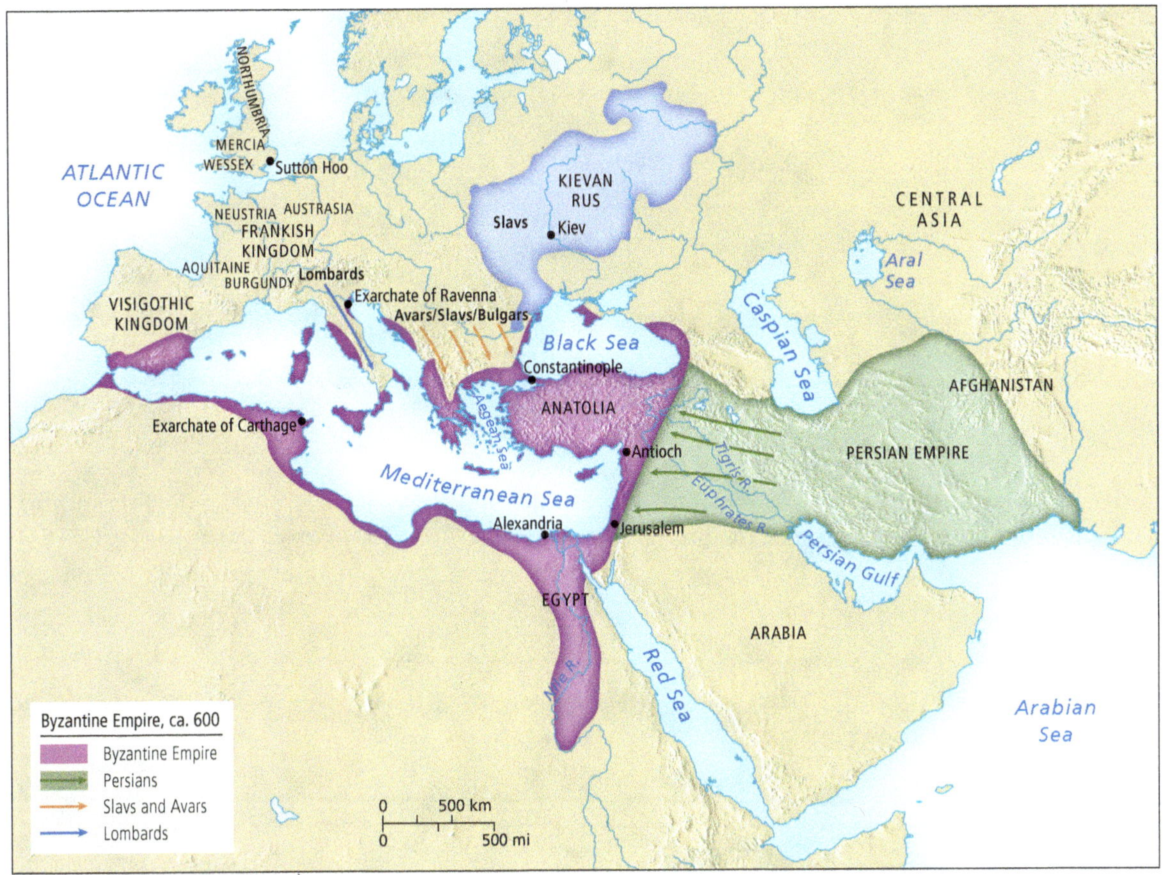

MAP **8.1** THE BYZANTINE EMPIRE, CA. 600 By 600 the Byzantine Empire consisted of Anatolia, Greece, part of the Balkans, Syria, Egypt, and some territories in North Africa and Spain. Until the rise of Islam, the Persian Empire remained Byzantium's greatest enemy. What parts of the Mediterranean were most influenced by Byzantine civilization?

They made the constitution of the empire evident through the hierarchic order of the procession. They also indicated the politics of the court as favored courtiers moved to a higher-ranked position in the procession, and those out of favor moved to a lower-ranked place or disappeared from the procession altogether.

Men fortunate or talented enough to obtain an office in the imperial government acquired wealth and influence. For this reason leading provincial families sent their sons to Constantinople to obtain positions in the bureaucracy. Through this method of recruitment, Constantinople remained in close touch with the outlying regions of the empire. This system gave provincial families a stake in the success of the empire and the provinces a voice in the capital. However, it was also vulnerable to corruption. Many men obtained their positions by bribing court officials. Other officeholders owed their jobs to family influence rather than talent. But even a corrupt system can be an effective form of government because official corruption made loyalty to the emperor more rewarding than opposition to him.

From his position at the head of this elaborate hierarchy, the emperor also controlled Byzantium's economy. The stable imperial coinage spurred a flourishing cash-based economy. Official monopolies controlled the production and distribution of specific commodities such as silk. These monopolies protected the interests of the emperor and those he favored by stifling competition. As long as the monopolies flourished, the government had a source of revenue through taxation.

By the end of the seventh century, however, when the rich provinces of Egypt and Syria and the wealthy cities of Alexandria, Antioch, Carthage, and others had fallen to the Arabs, the Byzantine economy stumbled. Thousands of refugees from

KING DAVID PLATE Nine silver plates made in Constantinople about 630 illustrate scenes from the career of the biblical King David. The largest plate (about 20 inches in diameter) shows David battling the giant Goliath. Though the subject matter is biblical, the style of representing clothing, human bodies, and spatial relationships comes directly from the classical tradition. The subject connected Byzantium's struggles with Persia to the Bible's heroic king.

SOURCE: Byzantine, early seventh century. Dish: David and Goliath. Silver, Syrian workmanship. D. 19 1/2 in. Found in Karavas, near Kyrenia, Cyprus, 1902. The Metropolitan Museum of Art, Gift of J. Pierpont Morgan, 1917.

lands conquered by Muslims streamed into the empire and strained its resources. In conquered Byzantine provinces, Muslim rulers set up their own monopolies and prevented Byzantine merchants from participating in long-distance commerce. Cut off from foreign markets, Byzantines stopped manufacturing goods for export and building new houses and churches. By 750, the standard of living in most Byzantine cities except Constantinople had fallen.

THE MILITARY SYSTEM OF THE THEMES In response to the many external threats, Byzantine society was reorganized for constant war. Emperors relied on their armies to protect Constantinople, the nerve center of the shrinking Byzantine state, and to defend the borders against invaders. By about 650 in Anatolia, which became the empire's main source of recruits for the army, emperors abandoned the late Roman system of relying on the provincial governors to protect the frontiers. To replace the old provinces, emperors created four military districts called *themes*. Each of the themes had its own army and administration commanded by a general chosen by the emperor. The themes' armies developed strong local identities and prided themselves on their military skills, a legacy the Byzantine Empire had inherited from the Roman legions. These military forces kept the empire from collapsing despite devastating losses to Islamic armies throughout the seventh century.

By 750 the themes had developed considerable autonomy from Constantinople and were the basis of further reorganization of the agricultural economy and procedures for recruitment. Soldiers and sailors who were once paid in cash from the emperor's tax revenues now were granted land on which to support themselves. Fighting men had to provide their own weapons from their income as farmers, and the theme system enabled the parts of the empire to function without direct support from the imperial treasury. The theme system created defensive flexibility for the empire. While it could no longer launch large-scale offensive conquests, Byzantium could at least attempt to defend its borders.

Over time the four original themes were subdivided and new ones added in other regions until, by the end of the eleventh century, there were 38 themes. The military strength of the empire came to depend on the theme system in which free, tax-paying soldier-farmers lived in villages under the supervision of a military commander who was also civil administrator. These soldier-farmers usually fought in their own districts, which meant they were defending their homes and families. As a result, they provided a formidable bulwark against invaders.

The Byzantine borders were especially harassed by Muslim enemies; however, from the first thrust of Muslim armies against Byzantium's frontier in the seventh century until its fall to the Turks in 1453, Constantinople held on. While the Persian Empire fell to Arab armies by the 630s, Byzantium survived. That fact is perhaps the most important measure of the success of Byzantium's military reorganization.

One of the lasting cultural fruits of these conflicts was legends of great heroes. These legends began as stories recited in verse to entertain Byzantine aristocrats whose ancestors had fought the Arabs. Several of these oral legends were eventually refashioned into popular epic poems. One such poem, *Digenes Akritas,* described the heroic feats of soldiers during the late eighth century on the eastern frontier of the empire, where Byzantines and Arabs both fought and cooperated. The father of the poem's hero was an Arab commander who abducted the daughter of a Byzantine general, married her, and converted to Christianity. The son of this mixed marriage was Digenes ("two-blooded"), a man of two peoples and two religions, who became a border fighter (an "akritas"). This greatest Byzantine hero, who lived between two cultures, was the poetic embodiment of the engagement between Byzantium and Islam. The legends surrounding *Digenes Akritas* had a profound influence on Greek literature. Later writers retold its stories again and again.

THE CHURCH AND RELIGIOUS LIFE Constantinople boasted so many churches and sacred relics that by 600 the Byzantines had begun to think of it as a holy city, protected by God and under the special care of the Virgin Mary. Churchmen taught that Constantinople was a "New Jerusalem" that would be at the center of events at the End of Days when God would bring history to an end and judge humanity.

One of the institutional pillars of the Orthodox Church in Byzantium was the clergy. They were organized hierarchically like the imperial bureaucracy. The patriarch, or chief bishop, of Constantinople headed several thousand clergymen in the capital and directed church affairs throughout the empire. Emperors generally controlled the appointment of patriarchs, and often the two worked closely together. The patriarch helped impose religious unity throughout the empire by controlling the network of bishops based in cities near and far. Each city's bishop supervised the veneration of the saints' relics housed in its churches. (Byzantines believed that sacred relics protected their communities, just as their polytheistic ancestors believed the gods had provided protection in the pre-Christian past.) Because bishops usually came from the city's elite, they were influential local leaders, responsible for administering many public policies, not just religious ones.

Monasteries played a significant role in the empire's life. Men and women went to separate monasteries to live a spiritual life, praying for their own salvation and that of others. People who needed help, such as orphans, the elderly, battered wives, widows, and the physically and mentally ill, found refuge in monasteries. Monks and nuns distributed food and clothing to the poor. Donors gave lavishly to fund these activities, and many monasteries grew wealthy through these gifts.

During the seventh and eighth centuries, Christian instruction under the supervision of the Church replaced the traditional Roman educational system. Pious Christians developed a suspicion of classical learning, with its references to ancient gods and to customs the Church condemned. Those few Byzantines who learned how to read did so by studying the Bible, not the classics of Greek antiquity. As a result of this general decline in learning, the Church monopolized culture and thought. Knowledge of classical literature, history, and science disappeared except in Constantinople, and even there the academic community was tiny.

Read the Document

Liutprand of Cremona, *Report of His Mission to Constantinople*, 968

ICONS AND THE ICONOCLASTIC CONTROVERSY The Orthodox Church created unity of faith and culture, but that unity was broken in the eighth century by controversy within the Church itself. As enemies tore at the borders of the empire, Byzantines wondered why God was punishing them. Their answer was that somehow they were angering God. Convinced that only appeasing God could save them, Emperor Leo III (r. 717–741) took action. To make Byzantium a completely Christian empire, he forcibly converted communities of Jews. His most important move, however, was to challenge the use of **icons**, the images of Christ and saints found everywhere in Byzantine worship.

icons The Christian images of God and saints found in Byzantine art.

Centuries before, the first Christians had refused to make images of Christ and other holy individuals. They had two reasons for banning such representations. First, the Hebrew Bible forbids creating representations of God, and they considered this prohibition still in effect for Christians. Second, they thought that Christians might start to worship their images the way that polytheists worshiped statues in their temples. "When images are put up, the customs of the pagans do the rest," wrote one church leader in the fourth century.

Despite such warnings, many Christians responded aesthetically to the beautiful polytheist statues and images that filled their cities. Christian sculptors and painters started to create a distinctive Christian art that combined religious images with the styles and techniques of classical art. After Constantine put an end to the persecution of Christians, this new art flourished. Artists routinely portrayed Christ and the saints in churches. During the sixth and seventh centuries, Byzantines used religious images with greater zeal than ever before. By 600, for example, the emperor placed a large image of Christ above the Bronze Gate, the main entrance to the imperial palace in Constantinople. Smaller icons became intensely popular in churches, homes, and monasteries.

Byzantine theologians defended icons as doorways through which the divine presence could make itself accessible to believers. Churchmen cautioned that God or saints do not actually reside within the icons, and so believers should not worship the images themselves. Rather, they should consider icons as openings to a spiritual world, enabling believers to encounter a holy presence. Thus, Byzantines treated icons with love and respect. Monks and nuns were particularly zealous in their veneration of icons.

However, by the eighth century, some Byzantine theologians thought icon veneration had gone too far and sought to revive the early Christian prohibitions against religious images. They advised Emperor Leo that icon veneration should be halted because uneducated believers confused the image of the icon with what it represented and worshiped icons as polytheists worshiped idols. When a volcanic eruption destroyed the island of Santorini in the Aegean, Leo concluded that these advisers were correct and that God was angered by icon veneration. In 726 Leo ordered the destruction of holy images (except for crucifixes) throughout the empire, but public resistance forced him to move carefully. For example, when he ordered workers to remove the image of Christ from the Bronze Gate at the imperial palace, the people of Constantinople rioted. Four years later, Leo renewed the general prohibition. The destruction of icons, known as **iconoclasm** (image breaking), divided Byzantine society until 842.

The veneration of icons was such a vital part of popular religious life that Leo found it difficult to enforce iconoclasm outside Constantinople. Revolts broke out in Greece and southern Italy when imperial messengers sought to destroy images. The iconoclastic controversy also affected international politics. Outraged by the emperor's prohibition of icons, which he considered heresy, Pope Gregory III, the dominant religious figure in the West, excommunicated Leo. In retaliation Leo deprived the papacy of religious authority over southern Italy, Sicily, and the Balkan coast of the Adriatic Sea, authority the popes had exercised since the fourth century. The popes never forgave the emperor because with the loss of religious authority came the loss of the principal source of papal revenues. This conflict contributed to a growing rift between Greek Orthodox and Latin Christianity. In the future, instead of relying on the Byzantine emperors for military protection, the Roman popes turned north to the Franks. The Iconoclastic Controversy created a lasting shift that allied the Roman pope with the kingdoms of western Europe.

iconoclasm The destruction of religious images in the Byzantine Empire in the eighth century.

Read the Document

Epitome of the Iconoclastic Seventh Synod 754

RESTORATION OF THE ICONS This sixteenth-century Cretan icon commemorates when Empress Theodora established an annual festival in 843 to mark the end of Iconoclasm. The image of the Virgin Mary at the top is the Virgin Hodegetria, the protector of the city of Constantinople.

After years of turmoil, two Byzantine empresses who were influenced by monks and who sympathized with their subjects' religious convictions restored icons to churches. In 787, the Empress Irene called a general church council that reversed Leo's condemnation of icons. After Irene was deposed in 802 iconoclasm revived, but in 843 Empress Theodora introduced a religious festival for commemorating images, which Orthodox Christians still celebrate annually. The Iconoclastic Controversy may have widened the gap between Greek Orthodoxy and Latin Christianity, but its resolution created even greater religious unity within the Byzantine world. A common religious culture also provided solace and a spiritual connection to Byzantium for many Christians who found themselves in the former Byzantine territories that Islamic rulers had conquered.

Macedonian Renaissance During the Macedonian dynasty's rule of Byzantium (867–1056), aristocratic families, the Church, and monasteries devoted their immense riches to embellishing Constantinople with new buildings, mosaics, and icons. The emperors sponsored historical, philosophical, and religious writing.

The Macedonian Renaissance

Byzantium's losses to external enemies were reversed during the Macedonian dynasty (867–1056), the term for a line of emperors from the Balkans that lasted six generations. Before the Macedonians, instability characterized the Byzantine imperial system because when an emperor died, powerful families struggled over who would become the new emperor. But after Basil I (r. 867–886), the first Macedonian, murdered his way to the throne, his family retained power by naming emperors' sons as co-emperors and encouraging the principle of dynastic succession.

THE BYZANTINE PORTRAIT This ivory plaque shows Emperor Constantine VII Porphyrogenitus (r. 913–959) being crowned by Christ. It was probably made in 944 to commemorate Porphyrogenitus's becoming the sole ruler of the empire. Under the emperor's left hand the inscription reads, "Emperor of the Romans."

Under the Macedonian emperors, Byzantine armies and fleets fought Muslims on several fronts. In the east the Byzantines pushed into Syria and Palestine almost to Jerusalem. A large part of the Mesopotamian river valley fell into their hands. They annexed the kingdom of Georgia and part of Armenia. In the Mediterranean, the Byzantines retook the islands of Crete and Cyprus and kept the Muslims from southern Italy, although they were unable to prevent the conquest of Sicily, which became a center of Muslim culture.

The economy of Constantinople thrived. Home to more than half a million people by the tenth century, the city became a great marketplace where traders exchanged goods from as far away as China and the British Isles. It was also a center for the production of luxury goods, especially the highly prized silk cloth and brocades traded throughout Europe, Asia, and North Africa. Aristocratic families, the Church, and monasteries became immensely rich and embellished the city with magnificent buildings, mosaics, and icons, creating the **Macedonian Renaissance**.

The Macedonian dynasty released creative energies by restoring the religious unity that the Iconoclastic Controversy had compromised. The most original work was religious, embodied in sermons, theological scholarship, and especially hymns; however, thanks to generous imperial patronage, Constantinople also became a center for philosophical study and the writing of history for the first time since the seventh century. The accumulation and study of ancient Greek manuscripts created an important cultural link between the ancient and medieval worlds.

The patriarch Photius (ca. 810–ca. 893) was one of the most eminent scholars in the history of Byzantium. Photius maintained a huge library, which became a center for the study of ancient Greek literature. He wrote important works, including the *Library*, an encyclopedic compendium of classical and Byzantine writers both religious and secular. Photius's summaries and analyses of these writers have remained especially vital because many of these books have subsequently been lost. Photius was also deeply involved in Church politics and was twice deposed from office because of political intrigue in Constantinople. His selection as patriarch by Emperor Michael III in 858 while still a layman met with strong opposition from the Roman pope. A bitter critic of the Latin Christians—Photius and the pope each excommunicated the other—Photius is often blamed for widening the gap between the two main branches of Christianity.

Under the Macedonian dynasty elaborate court ceremonies magnified the quasi-sacred office of the emperor. The historian Emperor Constantine VII Porphyrogenitus (r. 913–959) wrote the *Book of Ceremonies*, which became a model for royal ceremony in kingdoms from Spain to Russia. The *Book of Ceremonies* disseminated Byzantine concepts of rulership, which suggested that the emperor, like Christ, had two natures. One of these natures was human and fallible, but the other was derived from God, which gave the properly consecrated ruler divine authority over his subjects. Hence, Byzantine emperors were anointed with holy oil in a ceremony that was similar to the ordination of priests. The divine authority of monarchs represented by the emperor's or king's anointment became a central feature of political thought during the Middle Ages.

Even under the Macedonians, Byzantium remained under the threat of invasions. The empire's success in meeting these threats depended on two factors—the political stability guaranteed by the Macedonian dynasty, and the organization and recruitment of the army through the military districts of the themes. In the early eleventh century, however, the dynasty weakened and the army deteriorated.

When Emperor Basil II (r. 976–1025) died, Byzantine power and prosperity were at their peak, but he left no direct male heirs. His nieces and their husbands ruled until 1056, largely because Byzantines believed that the peace and prosperity of the empire depended on the dynasty. Basil's successors, however, were not strong leaders. Administration of the empire was highly centralized, with a tangled bureaucracy that supervised everything from diplomatic ceremony to the training of artisans. Without energetic leadership, the Byzantine bureaucracy degenerated into routine and failed to respond to new challenges.

The early Macedonian emperors' success in checking invasions had been largely the result of Byzantium's superior military capacities, guaranteed by the systematic organization of the army in the themes and the strength of the economy. As discussed earlier, the success of the themes depended on a system in which free, tax-paying soldier-farmers fought in their own districts, defending their homes and families. However, by the eleventh century deteriorating economic conditions threatened the independence of these soldier-farmers. Every time a crop failed or drought or famine struck, starving soldier-farmers in the themes were forced to surrender their land and their independence to one of the aristocrats who offered them food. As these great landowners acquired more land, the small farmers who were the backbone of the army began to disappear or lose their freedom. Because only free landholders could perform military service, the concentration of land in the hands of a few was disastrous for the army. Qualified soldiers with the land to support them became rare.

The late Macedonian emperors lacked the will to prevent this trend, and the army increasingly depended on foreign mercenaries. These emperors found themselves in a bind. Their income largely depended on their monopoly over industry and trade, but that control meant that land was the only profitable alternative form of investment for aristocrats. Opening up the economy might have hurt their own incomes, and so the emperors failed to do what was necessary to protect the empire. The situation was bleak; however, over succeeding centuries, enemies ate away at Byzantium until its final collapse in 1453.

8.1

8.2

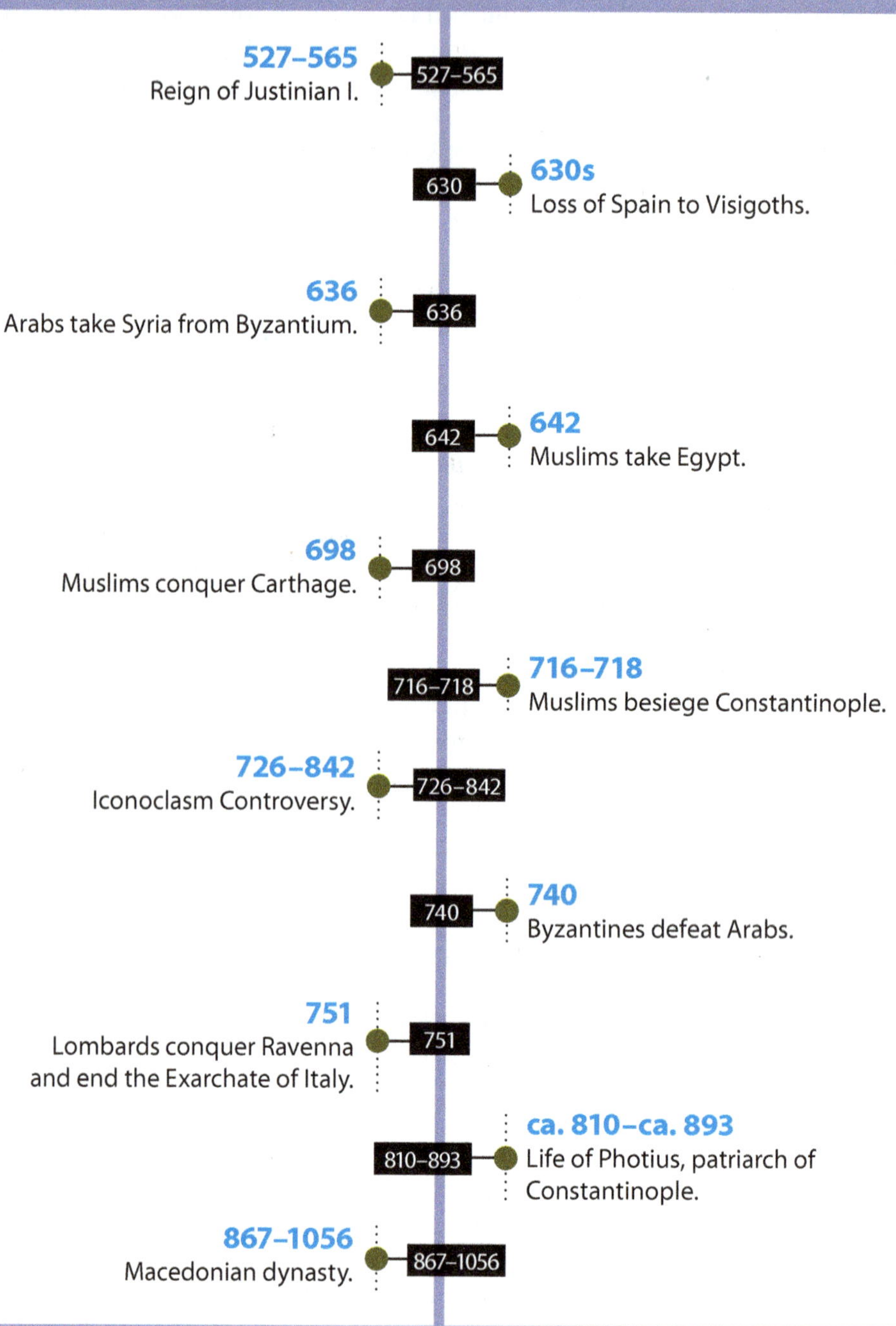

The New World of Islam

8.2 How did Islam develop in Arabia, and how did its followers create a vast empire so quickly?

The Muslim armies that battered Byzantium created a new civilization that transformed the Mediterranean world and created an empire that stretched from Spain to central Asia (see **Map 8.2**). Today there are more than one billion Muslims around the globe. This growing faith has left an indelible stamp not only on the West but also on the rest of the world.

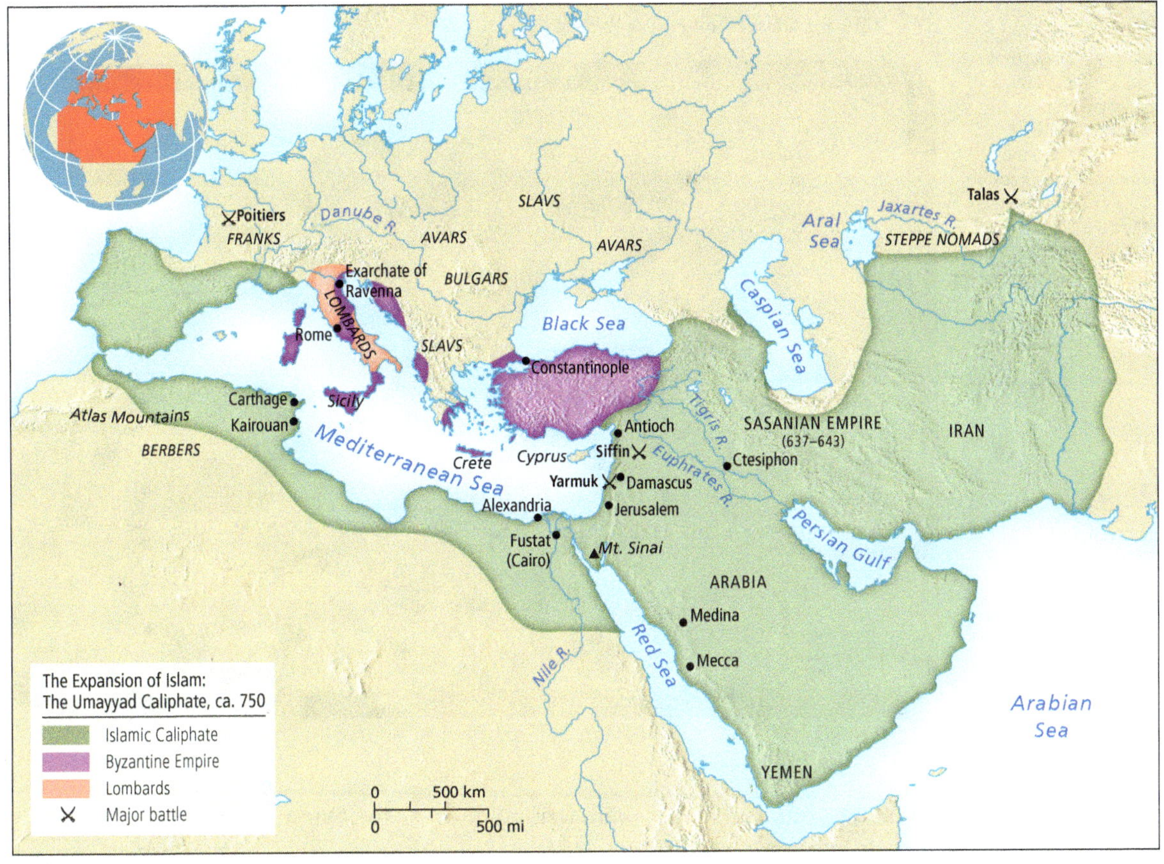

MAP **8.2** THE EXPANSION OF ISLAM: THE UMAYYAD CALIPHATE, CA. 750 By about 750 the Umayyad caliphate had reached its greatest extent. It provided political unity to territories stretching from central Asia to Spain. Islam became the dominant religion in this vast empire. Compare this map with Map 8.1. In what places did Islamic culture supplant Byzantine culture?

Islam originated in the early seventh century among the inhabitants of the Arabian peninsula. Arabs were tribal people. Many of them were nomads herding camels, goats, and sheep. (See *Encounters and Transformations* in this chapter.) In south Arabia, other Arabs farmed, lived in towns, and developed extensive commercial networks. Each tribe claimed descent from a common male ancestor. Tribal chiefs led by their own personal prestige and by the common consent of the tribesmen. Arab tribes, however, performed many of the functions of a state, which included protecting the lives and property of their members.

The Rise of Islam

Islam is based on the Qur'an and the sayings of the prophet Muhammad (ca. 570–632). Muhammad was born to the powerful Hashimite clan of the Quraysh tribe in the cosmopolitan and wealthy west Arabian trading city of Mecca. Mecca was the site of the Ka'aba, a sacred stone where polytheist Arabs worshiped many gods. As a young man Muhammad married a widowed businesswoman, Khadija, and worked as a caravan merchant, earning a reputation as a skilled arbitrator of disputes among tribes.

At about age 40, Muhammad reported that while he was meditating in solitude an angel appeared before him, saying, "Muhammad, I am Gabriel and you are the Messenger of God. Recite!" According to Muhammad's account, the angel gave him a message to convey to the people of Mecca. Muhammad's message was a call to all Arabs to worship the one true God (the god of Abraham) and to warn of the fires of hell if people failed to answer that call. Muhammad continued to recite his revelations

THE KA'ABA IN MECCA In pre-Islamic times, Arabs worshiped a large, black stone at the Ka'aba shrine in the center of Mecca. When Muhammad established Islam in Mecca in 629, he rejected the polytheist past and transformed the Ka'aba into the holiest place in the Islamic world, revered as the House of God. Muslims from all over the world make pilgrimages to the Ka'aba. These journeys foster a shared religious identity among them, no matter where their homelands lie.

for the rest of his life. They were written down as the Qur'an (meaning "recitation"), the holy book of Islam. Though Muhammad won followers among friends and family, the people of Mecca initially rejected his monotheist message.

In 622, Muhammad and his followers moved from Mecca to Medina, 200 miles to the north, where feuding tribes had invited him to settle their disputes. Muhammad's emigration to Medina, known as the *Hijra,* is the starting date of the Muslim calendar. The event marks a turning point in the development of Islam. For the first time Muhammad and his followers lived as an independent community. Accepted by his disciples as the prophet of God, Muhammad strictly regulated the internal affairs of his new community and its relations with outsiders, creating a society that was political as well as religious. At the center of this Islamic community lay the **mosque**, the place where his followers gathered to pray and hear Muhammad recite the Qur'an.

mosque A place of Muslim worship.

Initially, Muhammad enjoyed good relations with the Jews who controlled the markets in Medina. He and his followers even abided by Jewish rituals, such as turning toward Jerusalem while praying. But as his influence among the Arab tribes grew, he became involved in disputes with the Jewish tribes who refused to accept him as a prophet. Alienated from the Jews, Muhammad changed the direction of prayer to Mecca, expelled some Jewish tribes from Medina, and massacred the men and enslaved the women and children of others. With Jewish opposition eliminated and control of Medina secured, Muhammad led an army against Mecca, which surrendered in 630.

Using force and negotiation, Muhammad drew many Arab tribes into his new religious community. His authority rested both on his ability as a military leader who raided caravans and defeated enemy tribes and on his reputation as a prophet. By the time he died, he had unified most of Arabia under Islam.

MUHAMMAD'S TEACHINGS Islam teaches that Allah (which means "God" in Arabic) revealed his message to Muhammad, the last in a line of prophets that included Abraham, Moses, and David, all pivotal biblical figures in the Jewish tradition, who transmitted divine instruction to humanity. Muslims also revere Jesus Christ as a prophet, but not as the son of God. Thus, Islam shares some of the beliefs of Judaism and Christianity.

Encounters and Transformations

Ships of the Desert:

CAMELS FROM MOROCCO TO CENTRAL ASIA

A remarkable thing happened when the Arab followers of the dynamic new religion of Islam encountered the humble camel, which had been the beast of burden in Arabia and the Near East for at least 2,000 years. The ancient caravan trade that transported goods on the backs of camels brought the Arabs into contact with a vast stretch of the world from Spain to China. In the exchanges that took place along the caravan routes, Islamic religious ideas were widely disseminated, and Arab merchants enriched Muslim cities. The camel also helped make Arab armies formidable in battle, which meant that Islam spread rapidly through conquest.

As the desert dwellers knew, camels were highly efficient for transporting people and goods, especially in arid regions, because of their bodies' capacity to conserve water. Able to drink as much as 28 gallons at a time, camels can last nine days without water and travel great distances. The fat in their humps allows them to survive for even longer without food. Camels are more efficient as pack animals than carts pulled by oxen or mules because they can traverse roadless rough terrain and cross rivers without bridges. They require fewer people to manage them on a journey than do wheeled vehicles.

Arabs developed the "North Arabian saddle," which enabled a rider to grasp the camel's reins with one hand while slashing downward at enemy troops with a sword in his other hand. Warriors on camels could attack infantry with speed and force. Camel-breeding Arab tribesmen, empowered by their new military technology, seized control of the lucrative spice trade routes and became an economic, military, and political force by exploiting and guarding the wealth of the caravans.

After Muhammad established his community in Mecca in 630, Islam literally "took off" on camelback. Tribesmen-warriors on camels spread Islam first throughout Arabia and the Middle East, and then to central Asia and across North Africa into Spain. Camels played a significant role in the expanding Islamic economy because they made long-distance trade extremely profitable. The transformations the camel brought were most evident in areas where the famous Roman roads had been a primary conduit of land trade. Thousands of miles of roads connected the provinces of the Roman Empire and let troops march easily from one front to another. However, the camels of Arabia changed that. Because these "ships of the desert" did not need paved roads, caravan routes did not have to stick to the Roman road systems, and merchants bypassed them altogether. New trade routes across the desert and other harsh terrains well suited to camels quickly developed from Morocco to central Asia, and paved roads started to disappear. Because camels could easily walk on narrow paths, the broad streets and wide markets suited to carts and wagons that typified Greek and Roman cities also fell out of use. Bazaars with narrow, winding lanes appropriate to camel traffic replaced them. Carts and wheeled vehicles all but vanished in these lands. There were also cultural consequences. In particular, caravan traffic linked China more closely to the Middle East and brought Chinese goods and ideas to the West.

For Discussion

How might the history of the West have differed if camel caravans had not replaced the system of Roman roads?

THE CAMEL CARAVAN This photograph shows a string of camels crossing sand dunes in the desert, carrying heavy loads, just as camel caravans would have in antiquity.

8.1 8.2

Pillars of Islam The five basic principles of Islam as taught by Muhammad.

Muhammad taught his followers basic principles that eventually came to be called the five **Pillars of Islam**. *Islam* means "submission," and by performing these acts of faith, Muslims ("those who submit to God") demonstrate obedience to the will of God. First, all Muslims must acknowledge that there is only one God and that Muhammad is his prophet. Second, they must state this belief in prayer five times a day. On Fridays, the noon prayers must be recited in the company of other believers if possible. Muslims may say their prayers anywhere. Third, Muslims must fast between sunrise and sunset during Ramadan, the ninth month of the Muslim calendar. Fourth, Muslims must donate money and food to the needy. Islam expects its followers to be kind to one another, especially to orphans and widows, and to work for the good of the entire Islamic community. Fifth, Muslims must make a pilgrimage to Mecca at least once in their lives if it is possible. As the focus of prayer and pilgrimage, Mecca quickly became the center of the Muslim world. The Qur'an affirmed Mecca's special role in Islam:

> Announce the Pilgrimage to the people. They will come to you on foot and riding along distant roads on lean and slender beasts, in order to reach the place of advantage (the Ka'aba) for them, and to pronounce the name of God on appointed days over cattle he has given them as food; then eat the food and feed the needy and the poor. (Qur'an 22:26)

With the spread of Islam to Persia, Asia, and parts of Europe in the seventh and eighth centuries, Muslims from different lands encountered one another in Mecca, developing a shared Islamic identity.

While the Qur'an contains many examples of proper behavior for the community to follow, Muslims also looked to Muhammad's example as a guide. Muhammad taught his followers to struggle for the good of the Muslim community. This struggle is called *jihad.* Islam teaches that the duty of *jihad* should be fulfilled by the heart, the tongue, the hand, and the sword. The *jihad* of the heart consists of a spiritual purification by battling the Devil and avoiding temptations to do evil. *Jihad* of the tongue requires believers to propagate the faith and of the hand to correct moral wrongs. *Jihad* of the sword is to wage holy war against unbelievers and enemies of Islam who can avoid attack by converting or paying special taxes, called the *jizya.* (See *Different Voices* in this chapter.) Most modern Muslim scholars understand *jihad* as waging war with one's inner self, the *jihad* of the heart, but some have revived the concept of *jihad* of the sword to support military struggle.

The Qur'an

THE SUCCESSION CRISIS AFTER MUHAMMAD: SUNNIS AND SHI'ITES Muhammad had demonstrated a talent for leadership during his lifetime, but he did not designate his successor. His death in 632 therefore caused a crisis. Would the Islamic community stay united under a single new leader? After many deliberations, Muslim elders chose the prophet's father-in-law, Abu Bakr, to lead them. Abu Bakr (r. 632–634) became the first caliph, or successor to Muhammad. The Islamic government that evolved under his leadership, the **caliphate**, combined religious and political responsibilities.

caliphate The Islamic imperial government that evolved under the leadership of Abu Bakr (r. 632–634), the successor of the prophet Muhammad. The sectarian division within Islam between the Shi'ites and Sunnis derived from a disagreement over how to determine the hereditary succession from Muhammad to the caliphate, which combined governmental and some religious responsibilities.

Most Muslims supported Abu Bakr, but a minority opposed him. One group claimed that Muhammad's son-in-law and cousin, Ali, should have become the first caliph. Other Arab tribes rejected Islam itself. They claimed their membership in the Islamic community had been valid only when Muhammad was alive. Abu Bakr crushed them in a struggle called the Wars of Apostasy (a word meaning "renunciation of a previous faith"). By the time he died in 634, Abu Bakr had brought most of Arabia back under his control, but disputes between his followers and those of Ali led to a permanent split within Islam between the minority Shi'ites, who followed Ali, and the majority Sunnis, who followed Abu Bakr. While the Shi'ites and Sunnis both considered

Different Voices

Christian and Muslim Justifications for Holy War

Augustine of Hippo (d. 430) was perhaps the most influential early Christian theologian. Early Christian thought was strongly pacifist as the New Testament clearly commands: "I say unto you, that you resist not evil: but if anyone strike you on the right cheek, turn to him the left also" (Luke 6:29). In contrast, Augustine developed a justification for Christian violence. Although he quoted biblical examples, his argument derives from the ancient Roman conception of just war. His case is a good example of the blending of biblical and Roman ideas characteristic of early Christianity.

Augustine of Hippo on Just War

[The] account of the wars of Moses will not excite surprise or abhorrence, for in wars carried on by divine command, he showed not ferocity but obedience; and God, in giving the command, acted not in cruelty, but in righteous retribution, giving to all what they deserved, and warning those who needed warning. What is the evil in war? Is it the death of some who will soon die in any case, that others may live in peaceful subjection? This is mere cowardly dislike, not any religious feeling. The real evils in war are love of violence, revengeful cruelty, fierce and implacable enmity, wild resistance, and the lust of power, and such like; and it is generally to punish these things, when force is required to inflict the punishment, that, in obedience to God or some lawful authority, good men undertake wars, when they find themselves in such a position as regards to conduct of human affairs, that right conduct requires them to act, or to make others act, in this way.

The sacred book of Islam, the Qur'an, consists of the prophet Mohammed's recitations of his visions of Allah. These excerpts about war and the relations of Muslims with other faiths have the status in Islam of the direct words of God.

The Qur'an on Religious War

Sura 2

190. You shall fight in the cause of god against those who attack you, but do not aggress. God does not love the aggressors.

191. You may kill those who wage war against you, and you may evict them whence they evicted you, for oppression is worse than murder. Do not fight them at the sacred mosque, unless they attack you therein. If they attack you, you may kill them. This is the just retribution for such disbelievers.

Sura 3

113. They are not all the same; among the followers of the scripture [that is, Jews and Christians as well as Muslims], there are those who are righteous. They recite God's revelations through the night, and they fall prostrate.

Sura 5

13. Also those who said, "We are Christians," we took their covenant. But they disregarded some of the commandments given to them. Consequently, we condemned them to animosity and hatred among themselves, until the day of resurrection. God will then inform them of everything they had done.

Sura 60

9. God enjoins you only from befriending those who fight you because of religion, evict you from your homes, and band together with others to banish you. You shall not befriend them. Those who befriend them are the transgressors.

SOURCE: S. J. Allen and Emilie Amt, eds. *The Crusades: A Reader.* 2003, 7, 10–13.

For Discussion

1. What makes war acceptable for a Christian or a Muslim?
2. How do Augustine's justifications for war compare with those of the Qur'an?
3. How does the Qur'an distinguish between Islam and Christianity?

the caliphate a hereditary office restricted to members of Muhammad's Hashimite clan of the Quraysh tribe, the Shi'ites believed that only direct descendants of Muhammad through his daughter Fatima and son-in-law Ali should rule the Islamic community. The Sunnis, in contrast, devised a more flexible theory of succession that allowed them later to accept even non-Arab caliphs.

During the wars among Muslims after the death of Muhammad, Abu Bakr created a highly trained Muslim army eager to spread the faith. Under the leadership of the second caliph, Umar (r. 634–644), Muslim forces invaded the rich territories of the Byzantine and Persian Empires. They seized Syria in 636. The next year they crushed the main Persian army, weakened from a long war with Byzantium, and captured the Persian capital,

Ctesiphon. Within a decade Islamic troops had conquered Egypt and all of Persia as far east as India. Meanwhile, Muslim fleets, manned by Egyptian and Syrian sailors, seized Cyprus, raided in the eastern Mediterranean. Muslim armies were racing across North Africa when civil war broke out among the Arabs in 655 and temporarily halted their advance.

Two groups struggled to control the caliphate during this six-year civil war. On one side were Muhammad's son-in-law Ali, who had become caliph in 656, and his supporters, the Shi'ites. On the other side was the wealthy Umayyad family, who opposed him and whose supporters were Sunnis. (See *Justice in History* in this chapter.) In 661 the Umayyads arranged Ali's assassination and took control of the caliphate, establishing a new dynasty, the Ummayads, that would last until 750. The Umayyads made Damascus in Syria their new capital city, which shifted Islamic power away from Mecca. The Shi'ites continued to oppose the Umayyads, but they remained a minority except in Persia and Iraq.

The Umayyad Caliphate

The Umayyad dynasty produced brilliant administrators and generals. At the end of the civil war, these talented leaders consolidated their control of conquered territories and established peace in the empire. Then they resumed wars of conquest; in less than a century, however, they built an empire that reached from Spain to central Asia.

THE "HOUSE OF WAR" As we saw in Chapter 6, the Romans distinguished themselves from uncivilized "barbarians" who had not yet come under Roman rule. In a similar fashion, Muslims viewed the world as consisting of two parts: the "House of Islam," which contained the territories they controlled, and the "House of War," which included all non-Muslim lands, which they hoped to conquer. By 700, Muslim armies had conquered North Africa as far as the Atlantic Ocean.

In 711, the Umayyads invaded Spain and easily overthrew the Arian Christian Visigothic kingdom. From Spain they attacked France, but in 732, Charles Martel "the Hammer," leading a Frankish army, stopped their advance at the Battle of Poitiers. After this defeat, the Umayyad armies retreated to their territories in Spain.

Umayyad caliphs also attempted to conquer the Christian kingdom of Nubia south of Egypt to obtain its gold and spread Islam. The Nubians repelled several Muslim invasions, however, and a peace treaty was signed between the Umayyad caliphate and Nubian kingdoms. This treaty was without parallel because the Nubians belonged to the "House of War." But what the Arabs failed to achieve through conquest, they gradually gained through immigration. By the fourteenth century, Muslim emigrants had Islamized Nubia. While struggling with the Nubians, Umayyad armies also attacked Byzantine territories, sometimes reaching as far as Constantinople, which they besieged but were never able to capture.

Umayyad armies moved eastward with equal speed and success. They reached modern Pakistan and India and captured the caravan city of Samarkand in central Asia, which was a hub on the trade route to China. In 751, just after the murder of the last Umayyad caliph, Muslim armies defeated Chinese troops at the Battle of Talas in central Asia. One consequence of this encounter between Arabs and Chinese was the introduction of paper from China into the Islamic world, from which it gradually spread to Christian Europe.

Like the Battle of Poitiers, which marked the limit of the Umayyads' expansion into western Europe, the Battle of Talas established the limit of Muslim military conquests into central Asia. For the next four centuries, these borders would define the Islamic world.

View the Map

Interactive Map: The Spread of Islam

Justice in History

"Judgment Belongs to God Alone": ARBITRATION AT SIFFIN

On a spring day in 657, two Muslim armies confronted each other at Siffin, a village on the Euphrates River in Mesopotamia. Men who had been long-time rivals, the Caliph Ali (r. 656–661) and Muawiya, the governor of Syria, commanded the armies. Their rivalry stemmed from Muawiya's refusal to accept Ali's authority as caliph. The Battle of Siffin became a defining moment in the development of the Islamic state. Basic Islamic ideas about divine judgment were put to the test, leading to passionate debate about how God makes his judgment known to Muslims.

Ali had taken power after the assassination of Caliph Uthman, in 656. The murder went unpunished, but many people considered Ali responsible because as caliph he appointed officials known to have taken part in the murder and because he had never disavowed the crime. Uthman belonged to the influential Umayyad clan, and his supporters and family felt obliged to avenge his death. Chief among Ali's opponents was Muawiya, a leading Umayyad, who had a strong army and powerful support in Syria.

Muawiya's and Ali's quarrel also involved tensions within the Muslim community. The earliest converts to Islam and their descendants believed that their association with Muhammad entitled them to greater status than the many new non-Arab converts to Islam, most of whom supported Ali, enjoyed. The early converts supported Muawiya as did tribal leaders who opposed the caliph's growing authority.

The newer converts to Islam also had complaints. In their view, the earliest Muslims, including the Umayyad clan, enjoyed unfair privileges in the Islamic community even though all Muslims were supposed to be equals.

When Ali and Muawiya confronted each other at Siffin, they hesitated to fight because many of their soldiers recoiled from shedding the blood of other Muslims. As one of Ali's followers said,

> It is one of the worst wrongs and most terrible trials that we should be sent against our own people and they against us. . . . Yet, if we do not assist our community and act faithfully toward our leader, we deny our faith, and if we do that, we abandon our honor and extinguish our fire.[1]

So for three months, the armies only skirmished.

Finally, in July 657, real fighting broke out. Ali encouraged his men with these words: "Be steadfast! May God's spirit descend on you, and may God make you firm with conviction so that he who is put to flight knows that he displeases his God. . . ."

The battle came to a sudden halt when Muawiya's soldiers held up pages of the Qur'an on the ends of their spears and appealed for arbitration. Ali's men demanded that their leader settle his differences with Muawiya peacefully through arbitration.

Arab tribes frequently used third-party arbitrators to mediate their conflicts. Muhammad himself had been a skilled mediator before Islam was revealed to him. However, the arbitration between Ali and Muawiya failed, and the two men and their armies separated without having reached an agreement. For the next four years, Ali continued to rule as caliph, but his authority declined because many Arabs interpreted his willingness to go to arbitration as a sign of the weakness of his cause.

In contrast, Muawiya's power grew. He claimed the caliphate for himself and began to make deals with the tribal leaders. In 661 the Ummayyads arranged Ali's assassination, and Muawiya became caliph.

That the arbitration at Siffin occurred at all had lasting consequences. A small but influential faction of Ali's followers argued that God was the only true arbitrator. They believed that Ali should have refused arbitration and submitted to God's judgment through battle. These Muslims wanted to fight Muawiya to find out what God wanted. This splinter group became known as the Kharijites or "secessionists" because they seceded from Ali's followers. The Kharijites expressed their view of justice in the phrase "Judgment belongs to God alone."

The Kharijites also maintained that Ali was not only wrong to accept human arbitration, but that he and his supporters had thereby committed an unpardonable sin and should no longer be considered Muslims. The Kharijites claimed that they were the only true Muslims. Although their numbers were small,

THE QUR'AN Muslim artists devised elaborate Arabic scripts to enhance the beauty of the Qur'an, the holiest text of their faith. This page of the Qur'an is an example of the ninth-century Islamic School script from Tunisia.

(continued on next page)

(continued from previous page)

8.1

8.2

they established independent communities within the Islamic Empire until they disappeared from the historical record in the tenth century.

Other Muslims who disagreed with the Kharijites proclaimed that neither the Kharijites nor any other human being could know whether sinners were still Muslims in the eyes of God. In their opinion, believers would discover God's judgment on these matters only at the End of Days, when God will judge all humanity.

For Discussion

During this early Islamic Empire, how did different beliefs about how God makes his judgment known influence the Islamic sense of the forms human justice should take?

Taking It Further

W. M. Watt. *The Formative Period of Islamic Thought.* 1973. This account discusses the formation of sects and political groups in early Islamic history.

GOVERNING THE ISLAMIC EMPIRE The Umayyads developed a highly centralized regime that changed the political character of the Muslim community. The first Umayyad caliph, Muawiya (r. 661–680), established a hereditary monarchy to ensure orderly succession of power. This was a major change in the caliphate. Unlike the first four caliphs, who ruled by virtue of their prestige (as did Arab tribal chiefs) and more importantly by the consent of the community, the Umayyads made the caliphate an authoritarian institution. Because of this, some soldiers protested that the Umayyads had turned "God's servants into slaves," corrupted the faith, and seized the property of God. A second civil war broke out (683–692) between these protestors and the Umayyads, but the Umayyads emerged victorious.

To control their vast empire, Umayyad rulers had to create a new administrative system that both borrowed from and supplanted Byzantine and Persian institutions. The Umayyads designed new provinces that replaced old Byzantine and Persian administrative units. The Umayyads also created a professional bureaucracy based in Damascus to meet their expanding financial needs and ensure that the taxes collected in the provinces reached the central treasury. Most of the administrators had served the Byzantine or Persian Empires and were non-Muslims, although many converted to Islam. These officials provided administrative continuity between the conquered empires and the caliphate.

After the Umayyads made Arabic the official language of their empire, it gradually replaced the languages of the conquered peoples. Only in Persia (now Iran) did Persian, which later evolved into modern Farsi, survive as a widely spoken language, and even there Arabic was the language of government. In the Umayyad caliphate, Arabic functioned as Latin had done in the Roman Empire: It provided a common language for diverse subject peoples. By 800 Arabic had become the essential language of administration and international commerce from Spain to central Asia.

The rapid expansion of Islam created problems for Umayyad rulers eager to consolidate their power. Arab armies had conquered enormous territories, but Arabs were only a small minority among the huge non-Muslim majority. The Umayyads established garrison cities to hold down local populations. Just as Greek colonists followed in the footsteps of Alexander the Great in the fourth century B.C.E., many Arab settlers from the Arabian peninsula migrated to newly conquered lands. They established themselves first in the garrison towns where government officials were based and then in major cities, such as Alexandria, Jerusalem, and Antioch. Some immigrants came from nomadic tribes that adopted a settled way of life for the first time. Others were farmers from the highlands of Yemen, who brought sophisticated irrigation systems and agricultural techniques to their new homes.

Arabs also founded new cities. In Egypt they built Fustat, which would later become Cairo. In North Africa, they established Kairouan in Tunisia. In Mesopotamia they created Basra, an important port on the Persian Gulf and Kufa on the Euphrates River. Though built on a smaller scale than the major urban centers of the Roman and Persian Empires, most new Arab cities drew from Hellenistic town planning. They

THE DOME OF THE ROCK IN JERUSALEM The Dome of the Rock, an eight-sided building with a gilded dome, dominates Jerusalem's skyline. Completed in 692 on the Temple Mount (the site of the Jewish Temple destroyed by the Romans in 69 C.E.), the building encloses a rock projecting from the floor. During the sixteenth century, the story began to circulate that when Muhammad ascended to heaven, his winged horse took one leap from Mecca to the rock and then sprang skyward.

had a square shape, walls with gates on all four sides, towers, and a central plaza. In the heart of these cities, Umayyad caliphs built a mosque to emphasize the central role of Islam in community life and to celebrate their own authority. The magnificent mosques in Damascus, Jerusalem, and other cities were intended to surpass the grand Christian churches in prestige.

Patterns of daily activity also changed under Muslim rule. With Islam now dominating public life, cities ceased to celebrate Greco–Roman culture. Theaters fell out of use because there was no Arabic tradition of publicly performed drama and comedy. The exercise fields, sports buildings, libraries, schools, and gymnasiums surviving from the Classical Age were also abandoned or adapted for other purposes. Revenues once earmarked for gymnasiums and public buildings now went to local mosques. These centers of Islamic urban culture replaced the forums and agoras of the Roman and Greek world as the chief public space for men. Mosque schools provided education for the community. Muslims gathered at mosques for public festivals and, of course, for religious worship. In their capacity as administrative centers, mosques provided courtrooms, assembly halls, and treasuries for the community. Judges, tax collectors, bureaucrats, and emissaries from the caliph conducted their affairs in the mosque precinct.

During the Umayyad caliphate, most Muslims were farmers and artisans who lived in prosperous villages. Many of these small communities stood on the vast estates of rich landowners who controlled the workers' labor. The caliphate also sponsored huge land reclamation projects on the edges of the desert in Syria and Mesopotamia.

8.1

8.2

Read the Document

Al-Farabi on the Perfect State

Officials of the imperial government drew revenues directly from the villages that sprang up in these new farmlands.

BECOMING MUSLIMS Islam sharply defined the differences between Muslims and their non-Muslim subjects. Muslim conquerors understood themselves as a community of faith. Only those who converted to Islam could fully participate in the Islamic community. Their ethnicity did not matter. The Qur'an states that "there is no compulsion in religion," meaning that monotheists (Jews, Christians, and Zoroastrians) cannot be forced to convert to Islam. These monotheists were required to accept Islamic political authority, pay a special tax, and accept other restrictions. But polytheists could not be tolerated and had the choice of conversion to Islam or death.

Under the Umayyads, 10 percent of the total population in the caliphate were Muslim. Most of the first converts had probably been Christians, Jews, and Zoroastrians who willingly accepted Islam. Other converts were slaves in the households of their Muslim owners whose willingness to convert is less easy to determine. Still others were villagers who migrated to garrison cities and converted to share in the spoils of conquest—and avoid the taxes non-Muslims had to pay. Their eagerness to convert so threatened the tax base that some Muslim officials refused to acknowledge their conversion and sent them back to their villages.

Conversion to Islam increased as Muslim armies fought their way across North Africa. In the huge area that stretches from Egypt to the Atlantic Ocean, the Muslims conquered many polytheist ethnic groups whom the Arab conquerors collectively called Berbers. Faced with the choice of conversion or death, many Berbers joined the victorious Muslim armies. Islam unified the Berber populations and brought them into a wider Islamic world. With the aid of these additional troops, Islamic power spread even more quickly across North Africa and into Spain.

PEOPLES OF THE BOOK How do empires govern subject peoples? Do subjects have the same privileges and obligations as their rulers? Can they freely enter into the society of their masters? Previous chapters showed how the Egyptians, Assyrians, Persians, Hellenistic Greeks, and Romans answered these questions. Though their solutions differed, none of these great empires considered the religions of their subjects when deciding their place in society.

By distinguishing their subjects on religious, not ethnic, grounds, the Umayyad caliphate took a different approach to governing their subject peoples. Jews, Christians, and Zoroastrians constituted the main religions among conquered peoples. Islamic law called them "Peoples of the Book" because each of these religious communities had a sacred book and they lived as *dhimmis*, non-Muslims protected by the Muslim state. They had lower status than Muslims, but they were free to practice their religion; however, they could not make converts. Islamic law forbade their persecution or forcible conversion. For this reason, large communities of Jews, Christians, and Zoroastrians lived peacefully under Muslim rule.

Several Christian communities, separated by old controversies about doctrinal issues, coexisted within the Islamic Empire because the caliphate was indifferent to which Christian doctrine they followed. Followers of the Chalcedonian Orthodox Church changed the language of prayer from Greek to Syriac and then to Arabic. Though these Christians had no direct political ties with Constantinople, they followed the Byzantine emperors' Chalcedonian Orthodoxy (see Chapter 7). Thus, their church was called the Melkite, or Royal, Church. The Melkite Church is still the largest Christian community in the Middle East today. Anti-Chalcedonian (Monophysite) Christians formed the Jacobite Church in the late sixth century. The Jacobite Bible and prayers are in Syriac. The Nestorian Church, comprising Christians who emphasized Jesus's humanity rather than the combination of his humanity and divinity, also flourished under Muslim rule. Nestorian missionaries established communities in India, central

Asia, and China. The variety of Christian communities in the caliphate was greater than in Byzantium and the Latin Christian kingdoms where laws enforced conformity to the dogmas of one particular Church, Orthodox or Catholic.

Jewish communities also flourished throughout Umayyad lands, notably in southern Spain and Mesopotamia. Jews found their subordinate but protected status under Islam preferable to the open persecution they suffered in many Christian kingdoms. In Persia, Zoroastrian communities fared less well under Islamic rule. As they were slowly forced into remote regions, their numbers dwindled. In the tenth century, many Zoroastrians migrated to India, where they are known today as *Farsis*, a word that means "Persians."

COMMERCIAL ENCOUNTERS To strengthen their rule, the Umayyads transformed the economic system of the empire. From the time of their first conquests, Muslim rulers derived revenues primarily from the huge amounts of gold and silver taken in war, taxes, and contributions Muslims made to support widows and orphans. To increase their revenues, Umayyad rulers introduced a land tax for Muslim landowners, in imitation of Byzantine and Persian taxation. Even the proud Arab tribesmen, for whom paying taxes was humiliating because it implied subordination, had to pay taxes, though less than non-Muslims paid. With land tax revenues, the Umayyads could afford a standing professional army. This further reduced the fighting role of Arab tribes, enabling caliphs to cement their authority more firmly.

The peace the empire brought led to the rapid expansion of long-distance trade. Although merchants could travel safely from Morocco to central Asia and earn great profits, such expeditions were expensive. The Qur'an approved of mercantile trading, and Islamic law permitted letters of credit, loans, and other financial instruments that made commerce over huge distances possible long before Christian Europe had such sophisticated commercial tools.

Umayyad rulers further stimulated international commerce by creating a new currency that imitated Persian and Byzantine coinage. The Persian silver *drahm* (a word derived from the Greek *drachma*) inspired the Umayyad *dirham,* which became the standard coin throughout the caliphate by the 780s. Muslim merchants, and businessmen as far away as western Europe, Scandinavia, and Russia, paid for goods with silver dirhams. For gold coinage the Umayyads minted the *dinar* (a word derived from a Roman coin, the *denarius*). Like the dirham, the dinar also became a standard coin in the caliphate and distant lands. Merchants could depend on the value of this currency wherever they did business.

Umayyad caliphs also encouraged maritime trade. Alexandria in Egypt became the chief Mediterranean port for Arab commercial shipping. The Umayyads maintained peace in the Persian Gulf and the Indian Ocean. Arab merchants sailed to India and the city of Guangzhou in southern China, following the sea routes Persian navigators had established. Arab traders also sailed down the coast of East Africa to obtain slaves and natural resources such as ivory and gold from the interior. In later centuries Muslim navigators reached Malaysia, Indochina, Indonesia, and the Philippines.

The Abbasid Caliphate

After the last Umayyad caliph died in a battle in 750, the Abbasid clan, who were descendants of Muhammad's uncle, seized the caliphate and tried to exterminate the Umayyad family. The only Umayyad to escape, Abd al-Rahman I (r. 756–788), fled to Spain where he founded what would later become the caliphate of Córdoba.

The Abbasid caliphate (750–945) quickly altered the character of the Muslim world. In 762–763, the Abbasids built a new capital in Baghdad where they were exposed to the ceremonial and administrative traditions of Persia, which helped expand the intellectual horizons of the caliphs, their courtiers, and bureaucrats.

The Abbasid caliphs expanded their control over society, but they were far from despots. The caliph was first and foremost an emir—that is, the commander of a professional army. He was also responsible for internal security, which meant suppressing rebellions, supervising officials, and making sure taxes were honestly collected. But he did not interfere with other public institutions, such as mosques, hospitals, and schools. The principal exception was the office of market inspector, through which the caliph guaranteed fair business practices. In this commitment to the integrity of markets and trade, the Islamic caliphate was more advanced than either Byzantium, where privileged monopolies dominated the economy, or the Latin states of Europe, where a market economy hardly existed.

The period of Abbasid greatness lasted about a century (754–861), and its literature reflects its eclectic nature. The famous *Arabian Nights,* stories written down for the caliph Harun al-Rashid (r. 786–809), were based on Hellenistic, Jewish, Indian, and Arab legends. The *Arabian Nights* and the rich tradition of Arabic poetry, which often recounted tales of thwarted love, in turn influenced the western Christian poetry of romantic love. Harun al-Rashid began the grand project of translating into Arabic the literature of ancient Greece and texts from Syria, India, and Persia.

Read the Document
Harun al-Rashid and the Zenith of the Caliphate

Philosophical and scientific inquiry thrived under Caliph al-Mamun (r. 813–833), who had an astronomical observatory built in Baghdad and appreciated the work of al-Kindi (d. ca. 870), the first outstanding Islamic philosopher. Al-Kindi grappled with questions specific to Islam but also with the works of Aristotle and problems in astrology, medicine, optics, arithmetic, cooking, and metallurgy. This made him well-known outside the Islamic world. The work of Arabic translators in the ninth and tenth centuries created a crucial cultural link between the ancient and medieval worlds. The Muslims supplied Arabic translations of ancient Greek and Syriac texts to a later generation of Jews and Christians in Spain, who translated them into Latin. These second- and third-hand Latin translations of ancient philosophy and science became the core of the university curriculum in western Europe during the twelfth century.

Abbasid political power ended in 945 when a clan of rough tribesmen from northwest Persia seized Baghdad. The Abbasid caliphs remained in office as religious and ceremonial figureheads; despite occasional attempts to reinvigorate the caliphate, its power as a ruling institution was over. However, the caliphate remained a vital symbol of Islamic unity and survived as a formal institution until 1924.

Islamic Civilization in Europe

During the eighth and ninth centuries, the Muslim armies chipped away at Christian territories in Europe. Unlike their fellow Muslims in the Middle East and North Africa, most of the Muslims in Europe conducted themselves more as raiders than conquerors. They plundered and pillaged but did not stay long or attempt a mass conversion of Christians to Islam. These raids, however, made urban life impossible, and many Mediterranean cities almost disappeared. To survive, populations fled into the countryside, where families could live off the land and find protection with one of the local lords who built castles for defense.

The significant exceptions to the pattern of raiding were in Sicily and Spain. Between 828 and 965, Muslim armies conquered Sicily. Arab farmers and merchants migrated there from North Africa, and Islam spread among the general population although most Sicilians remained Christian. In Spain, Muslim conquests in the early eighth century brought the peninsula into the orbit of Islam except for small Christian states in the extreme north.

Sicily and Spain became the principal borderlands through which Arabic learning and science filtered into Catholic Europe. These borderlands became zones of intense cultural interaction, where several languages were spoken and where Christians and

Jews were allowed to observe their own faiths. Although small, Muslim Sicily and Spain were among the most dynamic places in Europe during the eighth to early eleventh centuries. No Christian city in western Europe could rival Córdoba, capital of Muslim Spain, in size and prosperity. Even within the Muslim world, only Baghdad could compare to it. A German nun visiting Córdoba during the tenth century thought the city embodied "the majesty and adornment of the world, the wondrous capital . . . radiating in affluence of all earthly blessings."[2]

GREAT MOSQUE OF CÓRDOBA The great mosque of Córdoba was one of the wonders of the world during the tenth century. Because Islam prohibited the depiction of the human body, mosques were embellished with geometrical forms and quotations from the Qur'an. The repetition of multiple arches creates an intricate pattern that changes as the viewer moves about in the space.

The caliphate of Córdoba became the most important intellectual capital in western Europe, renowned for the learning of its Muslim and Jewish scholars. Córdoba's fame derived from the extensive authority and magnificent building projects encouraged by Caliph Abd al-Rahman III (r. 912–961) and his three successors. With an ethnically mixed population of more than 100,000, Córdoba boasted 700 mosques, 3,000 public baths, 5,000 silk looms, and 70 libraries. The caliph's library housed more than 400,000 volumes. The streets of the city were paved and illuminated at night, the best houses enjoyed indoor plumbing, and the rich had country villas as vacation retreats. (Rome did not erect streetlamps for another 1,000 years.) Besides the great mosque, which was one of the most famous religious monuments in Islam, the architectural centerpiece of the city was Madinat az-Zahra, a 400-room palace that Abd al-Rahman III built for his favorite concubine, Zahra. Adorned with marble and semiprecious stones from Constantinople, the palace took 20 years to build and housed 13,000 household servants in addition to the diplomats and courtiers who attended the caliph.

The influence of the golden age of Córdoba in the tenth century can be found in the legacy of the poets, scientists, physicians, astronomers, and architects who thrived under the caliphs' patronage. Despite tensions between Muslims and Jews, many of the intellectuals in the caliphs' court were Arabized Jews. Typical of the many non-Muslims who served Arab rulers, Hasdai ibn Shaprut (915–970), who was probably a Jew, became famous for his medical skills, in particular his antidotes for poisons. In the caliphs' court the demand for his cures was strong, because several princes had fallen victim to conspiracies hatched in the palace harem or had been poisoned by their lovers. The trust that Hasdai gained from his medical skills led the caliph to appoint him to deal with sensitive customs and diplomatic disputes. Both Muslim and Christian rulers considered Jews such as Hasdai politically neutral, making them prized as diplomatic envoys. The Jew Samuel ibn Nagrela (993–1055) became vizier (chief minister) of the neighboring Muslim kingdom of Granada. An able Hebrew poet, biblical commentator, and philosopher, he also commanded Muslim armies. Nagrela's career reflected the value Muslims placed on learning and talent.

Read the **Document**

Ibn Khaldun, from the *Muqaddimah*

During the early eleventh century, succession disputes led to the murder of several caliphs, and the caliphate of Córdoba splintered into small states. The disunity of Muslim Spain provided opportunities for the stubborn little Christian states of the north to push against the frontiers of their opulent Muslim neighbors. The kingdom of Navarre under Sancho III (r. 1004–1035) was the first to achieve dramatic success against the Muslims. After his death his conquests were divided into the kingdoms of Navarre, Aragon, and Castile. During the reign of Alfonso VI (r. 1065–1109), Castile became the dominant military power in Spain. Forcing Muslims to pay him tribute

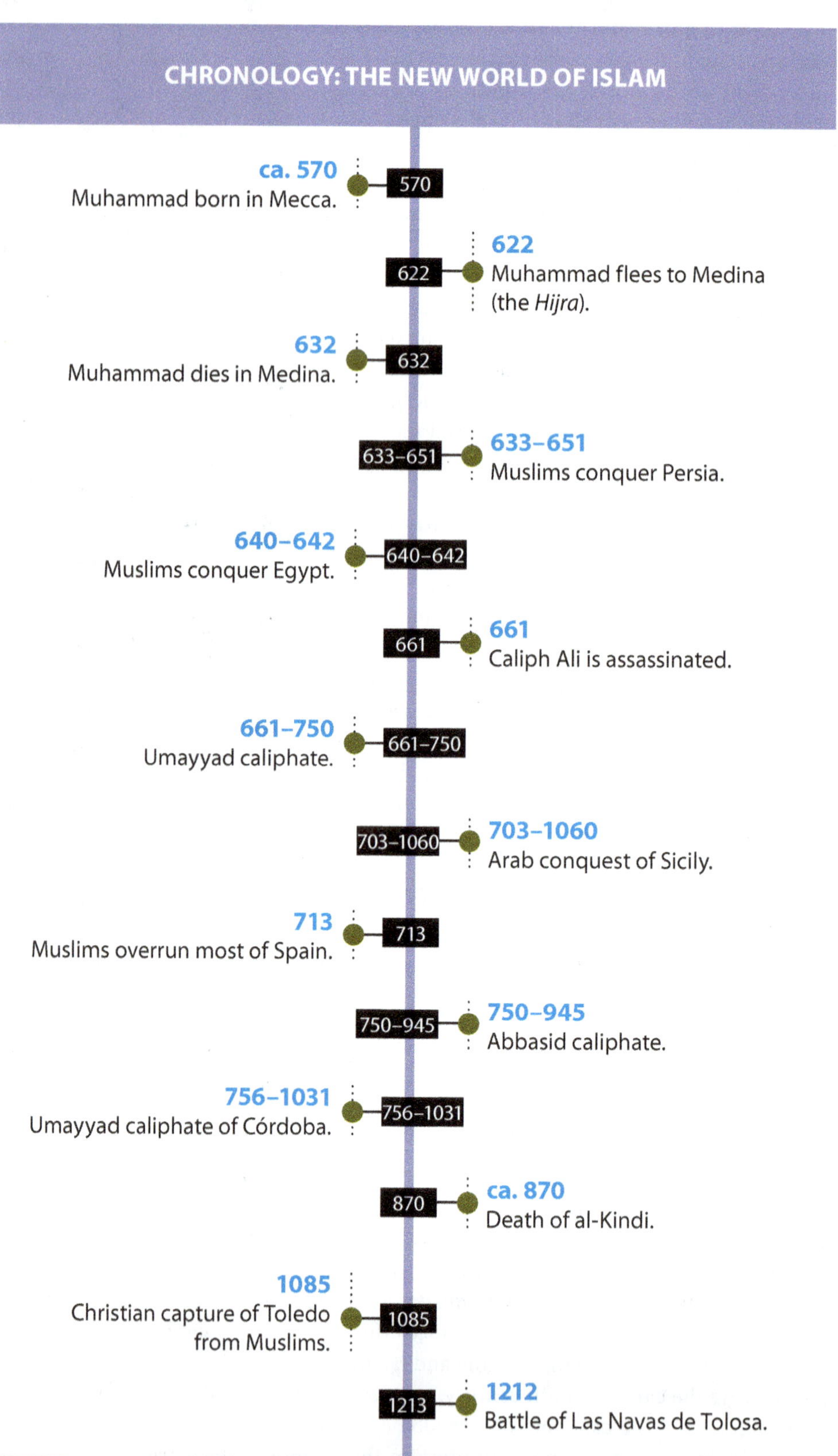

and helped by French knights eager for plunder and French monks ardent for converts, Alfonso launched a campaign known as the **Spanish Reconquest** that led to the capture of the city of Toledo in 1085. The center of Spanish Christianity before the Muslim conquests, Toledo provided Alfonso with a glorious prize that made him famous throughout Christian Europe (see **Map 8.3**).

The loss of Toledo so shocked the Muslim states in Spain that they asked for help from a sect of North African warriors called the Almoravids. The Almoravids defeated Alfonso VI and temporarily halted the Spanish Reconquest in 1086. But in 1212 at the Battle of Las Navas de Tolosa, the Christian kingdoms united to defeat the Muslims. Within two generations most Spanish Muslim cities, including Córdoba in 1236, fell to Christian armies. A few remnants of Muslim power hung on in Spain until 1492.

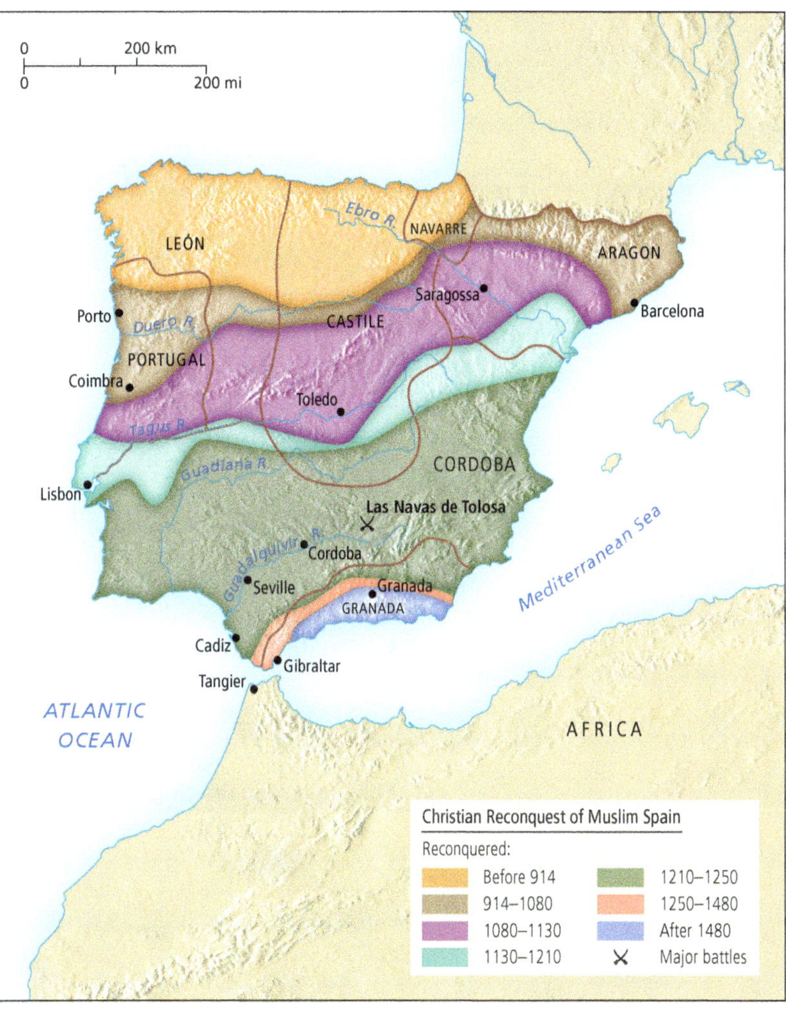

MAP **8.3** CHRISTIAN RECONQUEST OF MUSLIM SPAIN The Spanish Reconquest refers to the numerous military campaigns by the Christian kingdoms of northern Spain to capture the Muslim-controlled cities and kingdoms of southern Spain. This long, intermittent struggle began with the capture of Toledo in 1085 and lasted until Muslim Granada fell to Christian armies in 1492. What effects might this long series of engagement have had on the mentality of the Spanish Christians?

Spanish Reconquest Refers to the numerous military campaigns by the Christian kingdoms of northern Spain to capture the Muslim-controlled cities and kingdoms of southern Spain. This long, intermittent struggle began with the capture of Toledo in 1085 and lasted until Granada fell to Christian armies in 1492.

CONCLUSION

Three Cultural Realms

The death of the Byzantine Emperor Justinian I in 565 marked the last time one imperial ruler would control most of the territory from Spain to Syria. The Persian Empire still menaced Byzantium's eastern frontier, and except for Italy and some coastal areas of Spain, Germanic kings ruled western Europe. During the next two centuries, western Europe, the Mediterranean world, and the Middle East as far as India and central Asia were reconfigured politically and culturally. Part of that reconfiguration came about as new peoples migrated into central Europe and the Balkans from the steppe frontiers. As threatening as they were, these new arrivals were eventually absorbed into the civilizations of the West through conversions to Christianity. By ca. 750, three new realms had come into sharp focus: the Christian Byzantine Empire based at Constantinople; the vast Umayyad caliphate created by Muhammad's Islamic followers; and, as Chapter 9 examines, Latin Christendom in western Europe, which was fragmented politically but united culturally by Christianity. Each of these regions was constituted as a community of religious faith, which had, at best, a limited toleration of other faiths. The cultural foundations they established and the divisions that emerged among them still shape the West today.

These three cultural realms of the West each borrowed from the heritage of ancient Rome, especially its network of cities, which survived most completely in the Mediterranean and the Middle East in the Byzantine and Islamic Empires. The religious traditions of antiquity, especially the emphasis on monotheism in Judaism, influenced each of the three realms. They each adapted parts of Roman law and reshaped it to suit changing needs and new cultural influences. The heritage of Rome remained strongest in Byzantium. But between the sixth and eleventh centuries, these three cultural realms came to be distinguished by the language that dominated intellectual and religious life and by the forms of monotheism each practiced. In Byzantium the Greek language and Orthodox Christianity with its elaborate ceremonies defined the culture. By the end of the Umayyad caliphate in 750, the Arabic language and many Islamic beliefs and practices were becoming standard over a wide area. In western Europe, many languages were spoken, but Latin became the universal language of the Church and government.

The end of the Umayyad caliphate saw the limit of Muslim expansion in western Europe and central Asia. After that the Byzantine Empire struggled for survival. In Chapter 9 we will see how the kingdom of the Franks arrested Muslim incursions into western Europe. However, the very survival of many western European kingdoms was put to the test during the ninth and tenth centuries by yet more invasions and migrations from the Eurasian steppes and Scandinavia. By the end of the eleventh century, Latin Christianity had gathered sufficient cohesion and military strength to launch a vast counterstroke against Islam in the form of the Crusades.

MAKING CONNECTIONS

1. How did the Byzantine Empire manage to hold off so many enemies for so long?
2. Why did Islam split between Sunnis and Shi'ites?
3. Should Muslim countries be considered part of the West?

TAKING IT FURTHER

For suggested readings, websites, and films, see page R-1.

On MyHistoryLab

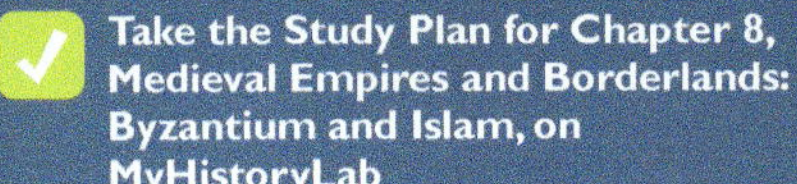

Chapter Review

Byzantium: The Survival of the Roman Empire

8.1 How did the Roman Empire's eastern provinces evolve into the Byzantine Empire?

Eastern and western Christians gradually grew apart until they were separate civilizations, one Byzantine and the other Latin. Besides difference of language, they held different opinions about religious matters, such as the rituals of the liturgy, the role of images in worship, and the authority of the pope. Eventually, the Byzantine Empire was reduced to a regional power struggling for survival against many enemies.

The New World of Islam

8.2 How did Islam develop in Arabia, and how did its followers create a vast empire so quickly?

Through forced conversion, negotiation, and by strictly regulating the internal affairs of the community and its relations with outsiders, Muhammad grew his new religious community and unified most of Arabia under Islam. After his death, the Umayyad dynasty's talented leaders consolidated their control of conquered territories and established peace in the empire before resuming wars of conquest. Immigration of Muslims throughout Arabia also contributed to the spread of Islam.

Chapter Time Line

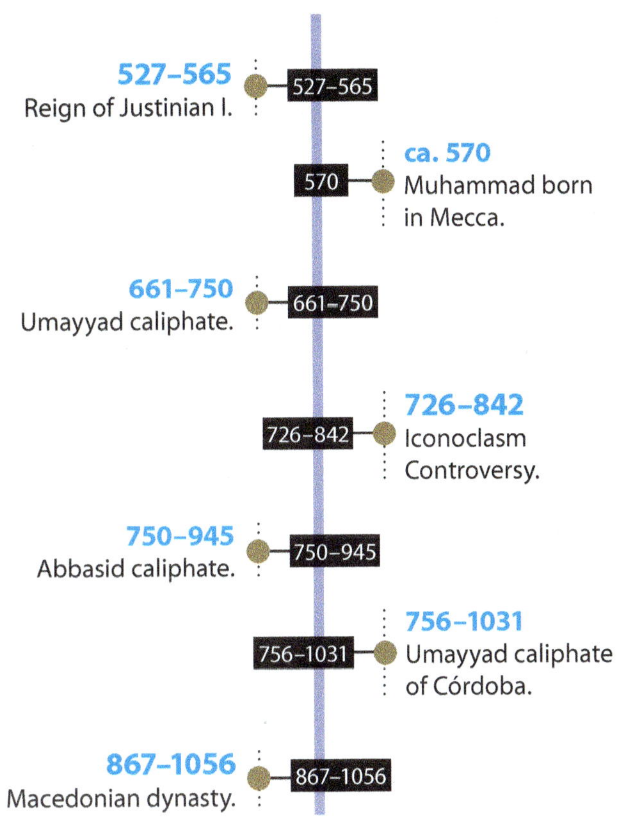

9 Medieval Empires and Borderlands: The Latin West

One gray day in central Germany in 740, an English monk named Boniface swung his axe at an enormous oak tree. This was the sacred Oak of Thor, where German men and women had prayed for centuries to one of their mightiest gods. Some local Christians cheered and applauded the monk. But an angry crowd of men and women gathered as well, cursing Boniface for attacking their sacred tree. Then something extraordinary occurred. Though Boniface had only taken one small chop, the entire tree came crashing down, split neatly into four parts. Boniface's biographer, a monk named Willibald, explained the strange event as God's judgment against "pagan" worshipers. In Willibald's account of the incident, the hostile crowd was so impressed by the miracle that they immediately embraced Christianity. As the news spread, more and more Germans converted, and Boniface's fame grew. According to Willibald, "The sound of Boniface's name was heard through the greater part of Europe. From the land of Britain, a great host of monks came to him—readers, and writers, and men trained in other skills."[1]

Boniface played a leading role in spreading Christianity among the peoples of northern Europe. The Christian

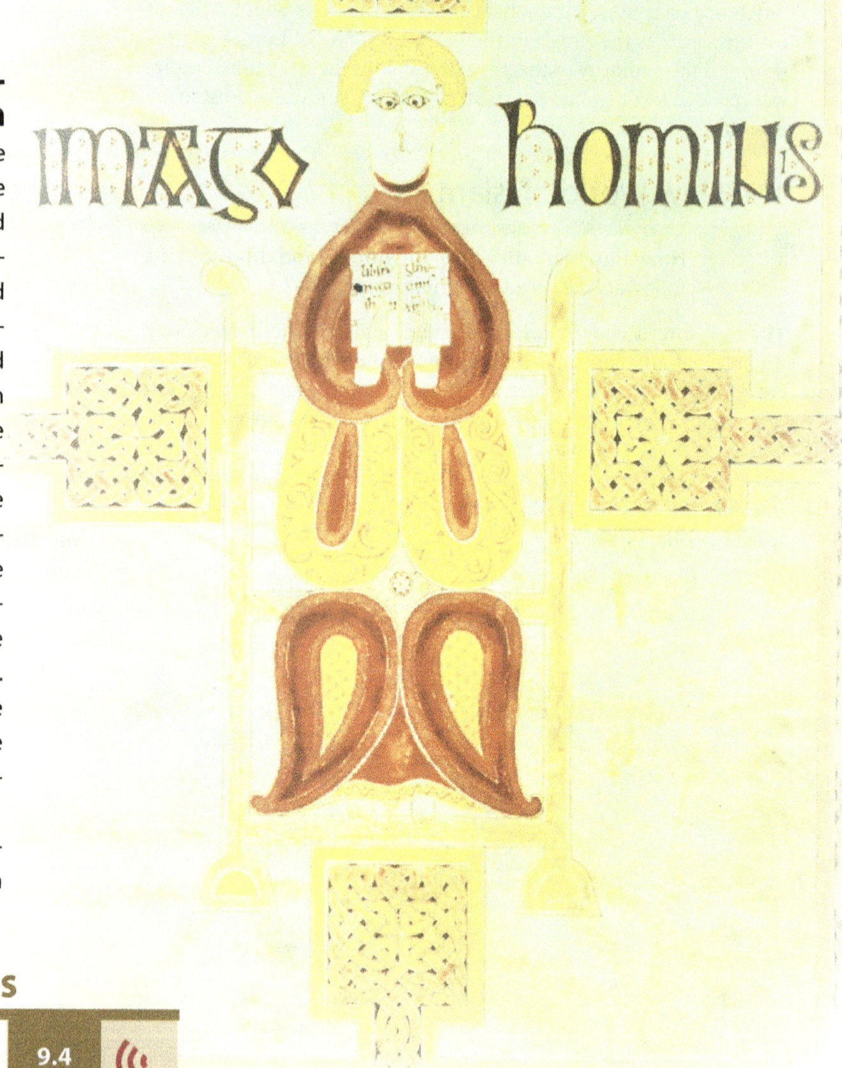

THE IMAGE OF A MAN (*IMAGO HOMINIS*) In this eighth-century manuscript, the image of a man symbolizes the evangelist Matthew. The other three evangelists, Mark, Luke, and John, were symbolized by a lion, bull, and eagle, all fixed signs of the zodiac, created by ancient polytheist astronomers. The adaptation of Christianity to pagan symbolism conveyed the message that Christianity represented the fulfillment of ancient wisdom.

LEARNING OBJECTIVES

9.1 How did Latin Christendom build on Rome's legacy and how did Christianity spread?

9.2 How did the Carolingian Empire contribute to establishing a distinctive western European culture?

9.3 How did Latin Christianity consolidate itself after the collapse of the Carolingian Empire?

9.4 What were the causes and consequences of the Crusades?

Listen to Chapter 9 on MyHistoryLab

Watch the Video Series on MyHistoryLab

Learn about some key topics related to this chapter with the *MyHistoryLab Video Series: Key Topics in Western Civilization*

missionaries who traveled to lands far beyond the Mediterranean world brought Latin books and established monasteries. Through Christianity and the literacy disseminated from these monastic centers, the monks established cultural ties among the new Germanic converts to Roman learning. Historians refer to the Christianized Germanic kingdoms on the continent and Britain as *Latin Christendom* because they celebrated the Christian **liturgy** in Latin and accepted the pope's authority in Rome. Even though they no longer celebrate the liturgy in Latin as they did in the Middle Ages, Roman Catholics today continue to revere the pope and the traditions of medieval Latin Christianity.

liturgy The forms of Christian worship, including the prayers, chants, and rituals to be said, sung, or performed throughout the year.

As discussed in Chapter 8, Latin Christianity and Orthodox Christianity gradually grew apart during the Middle Ages, primarily over theological differences and disputes about who held the ultimate authority in the Church. These two issues preoccupied the clergy and bishops. For most lay Christians, however, the crucial differences were over liturgy and language. The liturgy consists of the forms of worship—prayers, chants, and rituals. In the Middle Ages there was a great deal of variety in the Christian liturgy, and a number of languages were used, but followers of the Roman church gradually came to identify themselves with the Latin liturgy and the Latin language. As a result, the diverse peoples of medieval western Europe began to be called the "Latin people."

The Latin Christendom that came to dominate western Europe joined the Greek Orthodox and Arabic Muslim civilizations that constituted the three pillars of the West during the Middle Ages. Recurrently pressing across the frontiers of the Greek Orthodox and Latin Christian civilizations were wave after wave of barbarian peoples coming from the Eurasian steppes and Scandinavia. The Avars, Rus, most Slavs, and Bulgars who threatened Byzantium became Orthodox Christians. The raiders and invaders who entered the western half of the Roman Empire—the Germanic tribes, the Magyars, some Slavs, and the Vikings—eventually became Latin Christians. Their conversions took place through missionary efforts and military expeditions that forced the conquered to convert. By the end of the eleventh century few polytheists could still be found in Europe. With the exception of the Muslim pockets in Spain and Sicily and isolated communities of Jews, Christianity had become the dominant faith.

In this crucial phase in forming Western civilization from about 350–1100, new political formations in western Europe made possible greater political cohesion that brought together ethnically and linguistically diverse peoples under obedience to an emperor or king. As in Byzantium and the Islamic caliphates, the empires and kingdoms of the Latin West enforced or encouraged uniformity of religion, spread a common language among the ruling elite, and instituted systematic principles for governing. The Carolingian Empire, which lasted from 800 to 843 and controlled much of western Europe, reestablished the Roman Empire in the West for the first time in more than 300 years and sponsored a revival of interest in Roman antiquity called the Carolingian Renaissance. The Carolingian Empire's collapse was followed by a period of anarchy as Europe faced further incursions of hostile invaders. During the eleventh century, however, the Latin West recovered in dramatic fashion. By the end of the century the Latin kingdoms were strong enough to engage in a massive counterassault against Islam, in part in defense of fellow Christians in Byzantium. These campaigns against Islam, known as the Crusades, produced a series of wars in the Middle East and North Africa that continued throughout the Middle Ages. However, the consequences of the Crusades, which poisoned relations among Christians and Muslims, have lasted well into modern times, long after the active fighting ceased. The transformations in this period raised this question:

How did Latin Christianity help strengthen the new kingdoms of the Latin West so that they were eventually able to deal effectively with both barbarian invaders and Muslim rivals?

The Birth of Latin Christendom

9.1 How did Latin Christendom build on Rome's legacy and how did Christianity spread?

By the time the Roman Empire collapsed in the West during the fifth century, numerous Germanic tribes had settled in the lands of the former empire. These tribes became the nucleus for the new Latin Christian kingdoms that emerged by 750 (see **Map 9.1**).

Germanic Kingdoms on Roman Foundations

The new Germanic kingdoms of Latin Christendom created a new kind of society. They borrowed from Roman law while establishing government institutions, but they also relied on their own traditional methods of rule. Three elements helped unify these kingdoms. First, in the Germanic kingdoms personal loyalty rather than legal rights unified society. Kinship obligations to a particular clan of blood relatives rather than citizenship, as in the Roman Empire, defined a person's place in society and his or her relationship to rulers. Second, Christianity became the dominant religion in the kingdoms. The common faith linked rulers with their subjects. And third, Latin served as the language of worship, learning, and diplomacy in these kingdoms. German

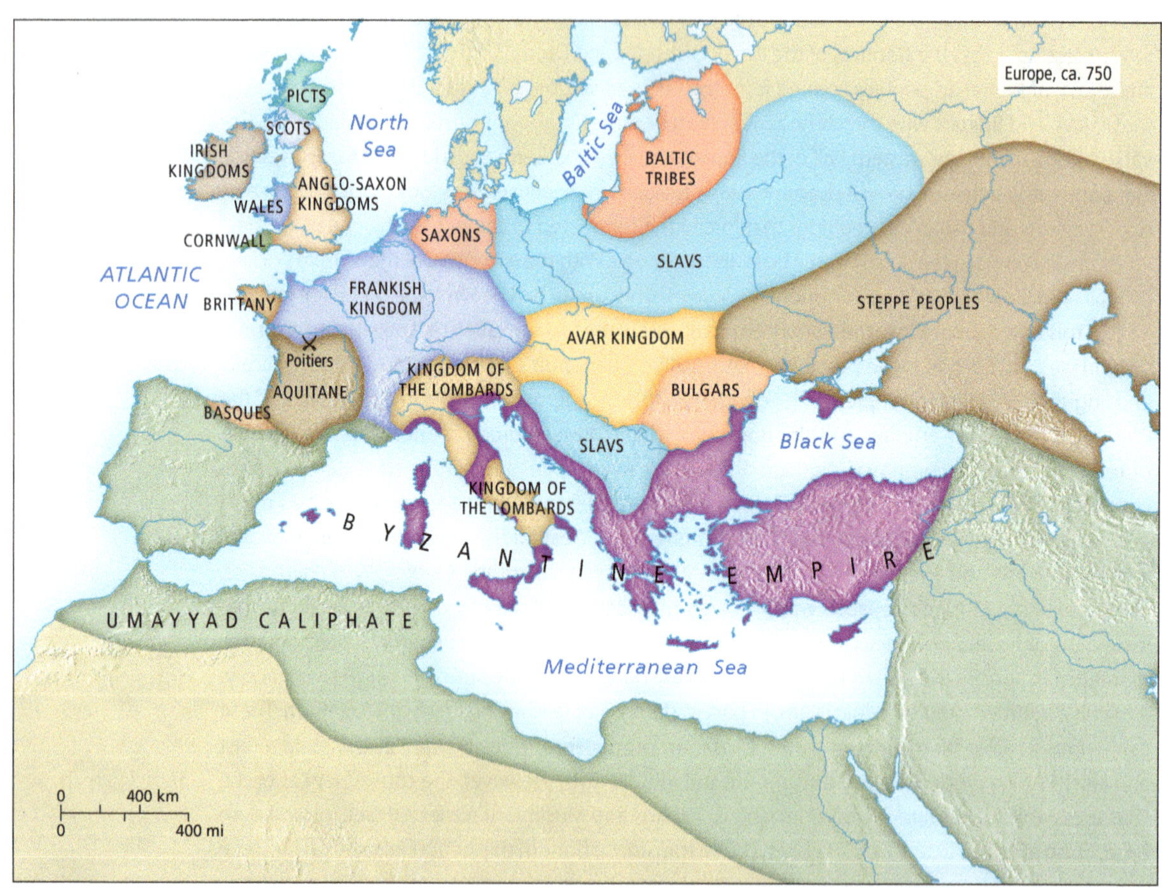

MAP **9.1** EUROPE, CA. 750 By about 750 the kingdom of the Franks had become the dominant power in western Europe. The Umayyad caliphate controlled Spain, and the Lombard kingdom governed most of Italy. The Byzantine Empire held power in Greece, as well as its core lands in Asia Minor. Based on this map, who were the dominant powers in the West: the Latin Christians of western Europe, the Greek Christians of the Byzantine Empire, or the Muslims of the Umayyad caliphate?

kingdoms based on Roman foundations appeared in Anglo-Saxon England, Frankish Gaul, Visigothic Spain, and Lombard Italy.

ANGLO-SAXON ENGLAND Roman civilization collapsed more completely in Britain during the fifth century than it did on the European continent, largely because of Britain's long distance from Rome and the small number of Romans who had settled there. About 400, the Roman economic and administrative infrastructure of Britain fell apart, and the last Roman legions left the island to fight on the continent. Raiders from the coast of the North Sea called Angles and Saxons (historians referred to them as Anglo-Saxons) took advantage of Britain's weakened defenses and launched invasions. They began to probe the island's southeast coast, pillaging the small villages they found there and establishing permanent settlements of their own.

Because the small bands of Anglo-Saxon settlers fought as often among themselves as they did against the Roman Britons, the island remained fragmented politically during the first few centuries of the invaders' rule. But by 750, three warring kingdoms managed to seize enough land to coalesce and dominate Britain: Mercia, Wessex, and Northumbria.

FRANKISH GAUL Across the English Channel from Britain lay the Roman province of Gaul. From the third to the seventh century the kingdom of the Franks, centered in Gaul, produced the largest and most powerful kingdom in western Europe. One family among the Franks, called the Merovingians, gradually gained preeminence. A crafty Merovingian war chief named Childeric ruled a powerful band of Franks from about 460 until his death in 481. With the support of his loyal soldiers, Childeric laid the foundation for the Merovingian kingdom. His energetic and ruthless son Clovis (r. 481–511) made the Franks one of the leading powers in the western provinces of the old Roman Empire. Clovis aggressively expanded his father's power base through the conquest of northern Gaul and neighboring territories. He murdered many of his relatives and other Frankish chieftains whom he considered rivals. In 486 Clovis overcame the last Roman stronghold in northern Gaul.

Around 500 the polytheist Clovis converted to Latin Christianity. About 3,000 warriors, the core of his army, joined their king in this change to the new faith. Clovis had a practical reason to convert. He intended to attack the Visigothic kingdom in southern Gaul. The Visigoths followed Arian Christianity, but their subjects, the Roman inhabitants of the region, were Latin Christians. By converting to Latin Christianity, Clovis won the support of many of the Visigoths' subjects. With their help, he crushed the Visigothic king Alaric II in 507. Clovis now controlled almost all of Gaul as far as Spain.

Gregory of Tours, Sixth Century

In the eighth century, however, the Merovingian kings became so ineffectual that real power passed to the man in charge of the royal household called the "Mayor of the Palace." One of these mayors, Charles Martel "the Hammer" (r. 719–741), established his personal power by regaining control over regions that had slipped away from Merovingian rule and by defeating an invading Muslim army at Poitiers in 732. Martel's son, Pepin the Short (r. 741–768), succeeded his father as Mayor of the Palace, but dethroned the last of the Merovingian monarchs and in 751 made himself king of the Franks. Pepin relied on the pope to legitimatize his coup; in exchange, the Franks guaranteed the pope's safety. Thus began the vital alliance between the Frankish monarchy and the popes in Rome.

VISIGOTHIC SPAIN The Franks were never able to conquer Spain, where a Visigothic kingdom emerged. As in all the Germanic kingdoms, religion was a unifying force. Originally Arians, Visigoth kings converted to Latin Christianity in the late sixth century, and Visigothic Spain became a Latin Christian kingdom. The kings began to imitate the Byzantine emperors with the use of elaborate court ceremonies and frequent church councils as assemblies that enforced their will. Thus, the key to their success was the ability to employ the Church's spiritual authority to enhance the king's secular authority. However, the autocratic instincts of the Visigoth kings alienated many of the substantial landowners who were easily lured by the promises of Muslim invaders to treat them more favorably.

In 711 invading armies of Muslims from North Africa vanquished the last Visigothic king. As a result, most of Spain became part of the Umayyad caliphate. Many Christians from the upper classes converted to Islam to preserve their property and offices. Some survivors of the Visigoth kingdoms held on in the northwest of Spain, where they managed to keep Christianity alive.

LOMBARD ITALY Between 568 and 774, a Germanic people known as the Lombards controlled most of northern and central Italy. They were called *Langobardi,* or "Long Beards," from which the name *Lombard* derives. The Lombard king, Alboin (r. ca. 565–572), took advantage of the weakness of the Byzantine Empire and invaded Italy in 569. Alboin's army contained soldiers of different ethnic backgrounds. That lack of unity made it impossible for Alboin to build a strong, lasting kingdom.

The Lombard kings also faced two formidable external enemies—the Byzantine forces who remained in the Exarchate of Ravenna and the Franks. In 751 the Lombards' ruler defeated the Exarchate, leading to the Byzantine abandonment of Ravenna. Internal political disputes, however, prevented the Lombards from capitalizing on their victory over the Byzantines. Just two decades later the Frankish king Charlemagne invaded Italy and crushed the Lombards.

Different Kingdoms, Shared Traditions

With the exception of England, where Anglo-Saxon invaders overwhelmed the Roman population, the leaders of the new Germanic kingdoms faced a common problem: How should the Germanic minority govern subject peoples who vastly outnumbered them? These rulers solved this problem by blending Roman and Germanic traditions. For example, kings served as administrators of the civil order in the style of the Roman emperor, issuing laws and managing a bureaucracy. They also served as war leaders in the Germanic tradition, leading their men into battle in search of glory and loot. As the Germanic kings defined new roles for themselves, they discovered that Christianity could bind all their subjects together into one community of believers. The merging of Roman and Germanic traditions could also be traced in the law, which eventually erased the distinctions between Romans and Germans, and in the ability of women to own property, a right far more common among the Romans than the Germans.

CIVIL AUTHORITY: THE ROMAN LEGACY In imitation of Roman practice, the monarchs of Latin Christendom designated themselves as the source of all law and believed that they ruled with God's approval. Kings controlled all appointments to civil, military, and religious office. Accompanied by troops and administrative assistants, they also traveled throughout their lands to dispense justice, collect taxes, and enforce royal authority.

Frankish Gaul provides an apt example of how these monarchs adopted preexisting Roman institutions. When Clovis conquered the Visigoths in Gaul, he inherited the nearly intact Roman infrastructure and administrative system that had survived the collapse of Roman imperial authority. Merovingian kings (as well as Visigoth rulers in Spain and Lombards in Italy) found it useful to maintain parts of the preexisting system and kept the officials who ran them. For instance, Frankish kings relied on the bishops and counts in each region to deal with local problems. Because Roman aristocrats were literate and had experience in Roman administration on the local level, they often served as counts. Based in cities, these officials presided in local law courts, collected revenues, and raised troops for the king's army. Most bishops also stemmed from the Roman aristocracy. In addition to performing their religious responsibilities, bishops aided their king by providing for the poor, ransoming hostages who had been captured by enemy warriors from other kingdoms, and bringing social and legal injustices to the monarch's attention. Finally, the kings used dukes, most of whom were Franks, to serve as local military commanders, which made them important patrons of the community. Thus, the civil and religious administration tended to remain the responsibility of the Roman counts and bishops, but military command fell to the Frankish dukes.

WAR LEADERS AND WERGILD: THE GERMANIC LEGACY The kingdoms of Latin Christendom developed from war bands led by Germanic chieftains. By rewarding brave warriors with land and loot taken in war, as well as with revenues skimmed from subject peoples, chieftains created political communities of loyal men and their families, called **clans or kin groups**. Though these followers sometimes came from diverse backgrounds, they all owed military service to the clan chiefs. Because leadership in Germanic society was hereditary, networks of loyalty and kinship expanded through the generations. The various political communities gradually evolved into distinct ethnic groups led by a king. These ethnic groups, such as the Lombards and the Franks, developed a sense of shared history, kinship, and culture.

clans or kin groups The basic social and political unit of Germanic society consisting of blood relatives obliged to defend one another and take vengeance for crimes against the group and its members.

Kinship-based clans stood as the most basic unit of Germanic society. The clan consisted of all the households and blood relations loyal to the clan chief, a warrior who protected them and spoke on their behalf before the king on matters of justice. Clan chieftains in turn swore oaths of loyalty to their kings and agreed to fight for him in wars against other kingdoms. The clan leaders formed an aristocracy among the Germanic peoples. Like the Roman elites before them, the royal house and the clan-based aristocracy consisted of rich men and women who controlled huge estates. The new Germanic aristocrats intermarried with the preexisting Roman elites of wealthy landholders, thus maintaining control of most of the land. These people stood at the very top of the social order, winning the loyalty of their followers by giving gifts and parcels of land. Under the weight of this new upper class, the majority of the population, the ordinary farmers and artisans, slipped into a deepening dependence. Most peasants could not enter into legal transactions in their own name, and they had few protections and privileges under the law. Even so, they were better off than the slaves who toiled at society's very lowest depths. Valued simply as property, these men, women, and children had virtually no rights in the eyes of the law.

Though this social hierarchy showed some similarities to societies in earlier Roman times, the new kingdoms' various social groups were defined by law in a fundamentally different way. Unlike Roman law, which defined people by citizenship rights and obligations, the laws of the new kingdoms defined people by their **wergild**. A Germanic concept, *wergild* referred to what an individual was worth in case he or she suffered some grievance at the hands of another. If someone injured or murdered someone else, wergild was the amount of compensation in gold that the wrongdoer's family had to pay to the victim's family.

wergild In Germanic societies, the term referred to what an individual was worth in case he or she suffered an injury. It was the amount of compensation in gold that the wrongdoer's family had to pay to the victim's family.

In the wergild system, every person had a price that depended on social status and perceived usefulness to the community. For example, among the Lombards service to the king increased a free man's worth—his wergild was higher than that of a peasant. In the Frankish kingdom, if a freeborn woman of childbearing age was murdered, the killer's family had to pay 600 pieces of gold. Noble women and men had higher wergild than peasants, while slaves and women past childbearing age were worth very little.

UNITY THROUGH LAW AND CHRISTIANITY Within the kingdoms of Latin Christendom, rulers tried to achieve unity by merging Germanic and Roman legal principles and by accepting the influence of the Church. Religious diversity among the peoples in their kingdoms made this unity difficult to establish. As discussed in Chapter 7, many of the tribes that invaded the Roman Empire during the fifth century practiced Arian Christianity. They kept themselves apart from the Latin Christians by force of law. For example, they declared marriage between Arian and Latin Christians illegal.

These barriers began to collapse when Germanic kings converted to the Latin Christianity of their Roman subjects. Some converted for reasons of personal belief or because their wives were Latin Christians. Others decided to become Latin Christians to gain wider political support. For instance, when Clovis converted about 500, laws against intermarriage between Arians and Latin Christians in Gaul disappeared. More and more Franks and Romans began to marry one another, blending the two formerly separate communities into one and reinforcing the strength of the Latin Church. By 750 most of the western European kingdoms had officially become Latin Christian, though substantial pockets of polytheist practice survived and communities of Jews were allowed to practice their faith.

Germanic kings adopted Latin Christianity, but they had no intention of abandoning their own Germanic law, which differed from Roman law on many issues, especially relating to the family and property. Instead, they offered their Roman subjects the opportunity to live under the Germanic law that governed the king. Clovis's *Law Code* or *Salic Law,* published sometime between 508 and 511, illustrated this development. The *Law Code* applied to Franks and to any other non-Roman peoples in his realm who chose to live according to Frankish law. Because the Romans dwelling in the Frankish kingdom technically still followed the laws of Byzantium, Clovis did not presume to legislate for them. Romans could follow their own law if they wished, or they could follow his laws and become Franks. By 750, however, most Romans had chosen to abandon their legal identity as Romans and live according to Frankish law, and the distinction between Roman and Frank lost all meaning. A similar process occurred in the other Germanic kingdoms. This unification of peoples under one law happened without protest, a sign that various groups had blended politically, religiously, and culturally.

GERMAN AND ROMAN WOMEN Roman law influenced more than just local administration in Latin Christendom. It also prompted Germanic rulers to reconsider the question of a woman's right to inherit land. In the Roman Empire, women had inherited land without difficulty. Indeed, perhaps as much as 25 percent of the land in the entire empire had been owned by women. In many Germanic societies, however, men could inherit land and property far more easily than women. Attitudes about female inheritance began to shift when the Germanic settlers established their homes in previously Roman provinces—and began to marry Roman women who owned property. However, the position of women varied a great deal among the Germanic tribes. Lombard law was much more restrictive for women than Frankish law where even a slave woman could become a queen.

By comparing the law codes of the new kingdoms over time, historians have detected the impact of Roman customs on Germanic inheritance laws. By the late eighth century, women in Frankish Gaul, Visigothic Spain, and even Lombard Italy could inherit land, though often under the restriction that they had to eventually pass it on to their sons. Despite these limitations, the new laws transformed women's lives. A woman who received an inheritance of land could live more independently, support herself if her husband died, and have a say in the community's decisions. Among the Merovingian Franks, women enjoyed especially high levels of respect. They participated in public assemblies and even appeared in law courts as advocates. They were so prominent that churchmen repeatedly admonished them to stay out of public affairs because it was unseemly. However, women's roles in household management, even of large estates and entire kingdoms, was unquestioned.

Most women, however, like most men, did not possess large estates or any landed property for that matter. Women managed and worked in the inner economy of the household; this included grinding grain with the hand-held rotary mill, cooking, baking, brewing, and especially making cloth. A number of crafts remained the exclusive preserve of women, as indicated by the Old English suffix "-ster," which indicated the feminine. A *webster* was a female weaver, a *brewster* a female brewer, for example. The term *spinster* survives in modern English to indicate an unmarried woman, who in the early Middle Ages would have worked at spinning.

The Spread of Latin Christianity in the New Kingdoms of Western Europe

As Latin Christianity spread as the official religion through the new kingdoms, churchmen decided that they had a moral responsibility to convert all the people of these kingdoms and beyond. They sent out missionaries to explain the religion to nonbelievers and challenge the worship of polytheist gods.

Meanwhile, bishops based in cities directed people's spiritual lives, instilling the moral and social conventions of Christianity through sermons delivered in church. Monks such as Boniface, who introduced this chapter, traveled from their home monasteries in Ireland, England, and Gaul to spread the faith to Germanic tribes east of the Rhine. Monasteries became centers of intellectual life, and monks replaced urban aristocrats as the keepers of books and learning.

THE GROWTH OF THE PAPACY In theory, the Byzantine emperors still had political authority over the city of Rome and its surrounding lands during this violent time. However, strapped for cash and troops, these distant rulers proved unequal to the task of defending the city from internal or external threats. In the resulting power vacuum, the popes stepped in to manage local affairs and became, in effect, princes who ruled over a significant part of Italy.

Gregory the Great (r. 590–604) stands out as the most powerful of these popes. The pragmatic Gregory wrote repeatedly to Constantinople, pleading for military assistance that never came. Without any relief from the Byzantines, Gregory had to look elsewhere for help. Through clever diplomacy, Gregory successfully cultivated the goodwill of the Christian communities of western Europe by offering religious sanction to the authority of friendly kings. He negotiated skillfully with his Lombard and Frankish neighbors to gain their support and establish the authority of the Roman Church. He encouraged Christian missionaries to spread the faith in England and Germany. In addition, he took steps to train educated clergymen for future generations, in this way securing Christianity's position in western Europe.

Gregory set the stage for a dramatic increase in papal power. As his successors' authority expanded over the next few centuries, relations between Rome

POPE GREGORY THE GREAT AND THREE SCRIBES In this tenth-century ivory depicting the influential sixth-century Pope Gregory, writing symbolizes his power and influence. During the early Middle Ages, the Church alone kept literacy and writing alive in the West.

SOURCE: St. Gregory writing with scribes, Carolingian, Franco-German School, ca. 850–875 (ivory). Kunsthistorisches Museum, Vienna, Austria/Bridgeman Art Library.

and the Byzantine emperors slowly soured, especially during the Iconoclastic Controversy discussed in Chapter 8. By the early eighth century the popes abandoned the fiction that they were still subject to the Byzantines and sought protection from the Frankish kings.

CONVERTING THE IRISH Though the Romans had conquered most of Britain during the imperial period, they never attempted to bring Ireland into their empire. Thus, the island off Britain's west coast had had only minimal contact with Christianity. Little is known of how Christianity came to Ireland. There were probably missionaries who traveled with traders from the Roman Empire, but the earliest firm date is 431 when Palladius was supposedly sent to administer to those in Ireland who were already Christians. The figure of Patrick (d. ca. 492 or 493) dominates the subsequent missionary history of Ireland, largely because his later biographers improbably gave him credit for converting all the Irish to Christianity. A ninth-century record describes Patrick's capture from a Roman villa in Britain by Irish raiders, who sold him into slavery in Ireland. He managed to escape and return to Britain, where he was ordained into the priesthood and sent back to Ireland as a missionary. A great deal of confusion exists regarding Patrick's life; some scholars argue that the traditional story of Patrick actually merges the experiences of the two missionaries Palladius and Patrick. Nevertheless, by the end of the fifth century, Christianity had a firm foothold in Ireland.

Read the Document

The Confession of Saint Patrick

THE BOOK OF KELLS The Book of Kells consists of an ornately illustrated manuscript produced by Irish monks about 800 C.E. The book contains the four Gospels of the New Testament in Latin and is one of the masterpieces of early medieval art. This highly decorated page shows the opening "Q" of *quoniam*, the first word in the Latin Gospel of Luke.

But Ireland was still an entirely rural place. Elsewhere in the West, Christianity spread out into the countryside from cities, with bishops administering the local church from their city cathedrals. Ireland, however, lacked cities in which to build churches and housing for bishops. No one living in Ireland knew Latin, Greek, or any of the other languages into which the Bible had been translated. And no schools existed where churchmen might teach the Gospel to new converts.

Irish churchmen found solutions to these problems in monasteries, places where priests could receive training and men and women from the surrounding homesteads and hamlets could learn to read Latin and absorb the basics of Christian education. The Irish scholars produced by these monasteries gained a high reputation for their learning across western Europe. They produced magnificently illustrated manuscripts in their libraries. These books brought Irish art to all the lands where Irish missionaries traveled.

CONVERTING THE ANGLO-SAXONS Irish missionaries established new monasteries in England and on the European continent. Columba (521–597), for instance, founded one on the island of Iona, off Scotland's western coast. From this thriving community missionaries began to bring Christianity to the peoples of Scotland. The offshoot monastery of Lindisfarne in northern England also became a dynamic center of learning and missionary activity. During the seventh century, missionaries based there carried Christianity to many other parts of England.

They also began converting the people of Frisia on the North Sea, in the area of the modern Netherlands.

Pope Gregory the Great (r. 590–604) understood that the first step in creating new Christian communities was to convert as many people as possible to the faith. Deep learning about the religion could come later. To that end he instructed missionaries to permit local variations in worship and to accommodate harmless vestiges of pre-Christian worship practices. "Don't tear down their temples," Gregory advised, "put a cross on the roofs!"

Following Gregory's pragmatic suggestion, missionaries in England accepted certain Anglo-Saxon calendar conventions that stemmed from polytheist worship. For example, in the Anglo-Saxon calendar, the weekdays took their names from old gods: Tuesday derived from Tiw, a war god; Wednesday from Woden, king of the gods; Thursday from Thor, god of thunder; and Friday from Freya, goddess of agriculture. Anglo-Saxon deities eventually found their way into the Christian calendar as well. Eostre, for example, a goddess whose festival came in April, gave her name to the Christian holiday Easter.

Despite their common commitment to Latin Christianity, the Irish and Roman monks working throughout England disagreed strongly about proper Christian practice. For instance, they argued over how to perform baptism, the ritual of anointing someone with water to admit him or her into the Christian community. They bickered about how monks should shave the tops of their heads to show their religious vocation, and they squabbled about the correct means of calculating the date of Easter. These disputes threatened to create deep divisions among England's Christians. The overall conflict finally found resolution in 664 in the Anglo-Saxon kingdom of Northumbria, where monastic life flourished. At a council of monks and royal advisers called the Synod of Whitby, the Northumbrian monarch commanded that the Roman rather than Irish version of Christianity would prevail in his kingdom. His decision eventually was accepted throughout England.

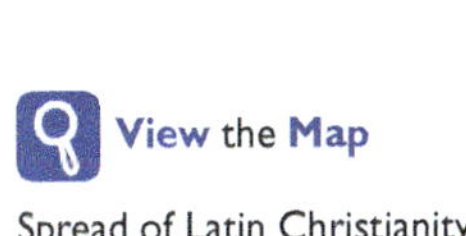

Spread of Latin Christianity in Western Europe

MONASTIC INTELLECTUAL LIFE The missionaries from Rome were members of the vigorous monastic movement initiated by Benedict of Nursia (ca. 480–547) from his monastery at Monte Cassino in Italy (see Chapter 7). These monks followed Benedict's *Rule*, a guidebook for the management of monastic life and spirituality. In the *Rule*, Benedict had written that individual monks should live temperate lives devoted to spiritual contemplation, communal prayer, and manual labor. So that their contemplations might not depart from the path of truth, Benedict had encouraged monks to seek guidance in the Bible, in the writings of the renowned theologians, and in works of spiritual edification. For Benedict, contemplative reading constituted a fundamental part of monastic life. Thus, monks had to be literate in Latin. They needed training in the Latin classics, which required books.

Medieval monasteries set aside at least two rooms—the **scriptorium** and the library—to meet the growing demand for books. In the scriptorium, scribes laboriously copied Latin and Greek manuscripts as an act of religious devotion. Monastery libraries were small in comparison with the public libraries of classical Rome, but the volumes were cherished and carefully protected. Because books were precious possessions, these libraries set forth strict rules for their use. Some librarians chained books to tables to prevent theft. Others pronounced a curse against anyone who failed to return a borrowed book. Nevertheless, librarians also generously lent books to other monasteries to copy.

scriptorium The room in a monastery where monks copied books and manuscripts.

Monks preferred to read texts with a Christian message, so these books were the most frequently copied. In many monasteries, however, monks preserved non-Christian texts as well. By doing so, they helped to keep knowledge of Latin and classical learning alive. Indeed, many of the surviving works by authors of the Classical Age were copied and passed on by monks in the sixth and seventh centuries. Without

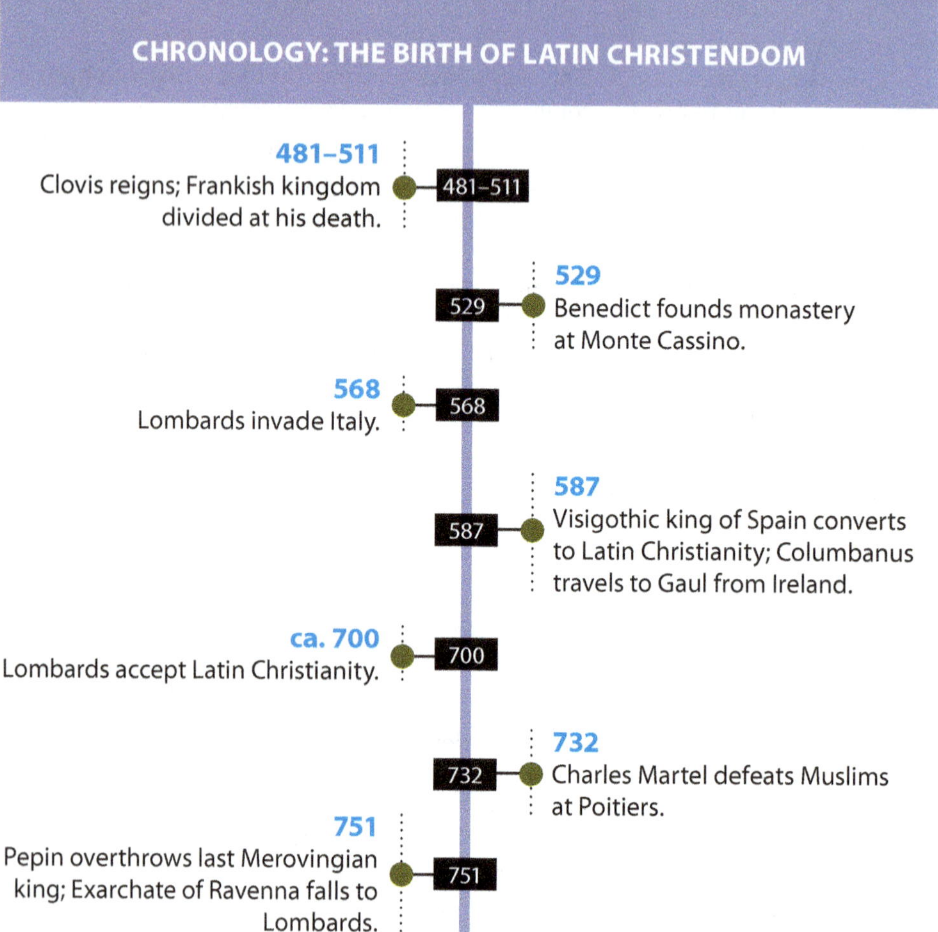

the monasteries and scriptoria, knowledge today of the literature of the classical world would be greatly reduced.

Monks did far more than merely copy ancient texts, however. Some wrote original books of their own. At the English monastery at Jarrow, for example, Bede (d. 735) became the most distinguished scholar in eighth-century Europe. He wrote many books, including the *History of the English Church and People*. This work provided an invaluable source of information about the early Anglo-Saxon kingdoms.

Bede, Conversion of England (582)

Monks carried books with them when they embarked on missionary journeys. They also acquired new books during their travels. For instance, Benedict Biscop, the founder of the monasteries of Wearmouth (674) and Jarrow (682) in England, made six trips to Italy. Each time he brought back crates of books on all subjects, including works written by classical authors whom monks studied with interest. Other Anglo-Saxon missionaries transported this literary heritage to the monasteries they founded in Germany during the eighth century. As monks avidly read, copied, wrote, and transported books of all sorts, knowledge and intellectual discourse flourished in the monasteries.

Monks shared their expanding knowledge with Christians outside the monastery walls. They established schools at monasteries where boys (and, in some places, girls) could learn to read and write. In Italy some public schools survived from antiquity, but elsewhere most of the very few literate people who lived between 550 and 750 gained their education at monastery schools. The men trained in these schools played an important role in society as officials and bureaucrats. Their skills in reading and writing were necessary for keeping records and writing business and diplomatic letters.

The Carolingians

9.2 How did the Carolingian Empire contribute to establishing a distinctive western European culture?

Among the successor kingdoms to the Roman Empire in the West, discussed in the previous section, none was more powerful militarily than the Merovingian kingdom of the Franks. The Merovingian dynasty, however, was plagued by factions, royal assassinations, and do-nothing kings. When Pepin the Short deposed the last of the Merovingian kings in 751, he made himself king of the Franks and inaugurated the Carolingian dynasty.

Both the weak Merovingians and the strong Carolingians illustrated how the problem of succession from one king to another could destabilize early medieval monarchies. The kingdom was considered the private property of the royal family, and according to Frankish custom, a father was obliged to divide his estates among all his legitimate sons. As a result, whenever a king of the Franks died, the kingdom was divided up. When Pepin died in 768, the kingdom was divided between his sons, Charlemagne and Carloman. When Carloman died suddenly in 771, Charlemagne ignored the inheritance rights of Carloman's sons and may even have had them killed, making himself the sole ruler of the Franks.

The Leadership of Charlemagne

Charlemagne's (r. 768–814) ruthlessness with his own nephews epitomized the leadership that made him the mightiest ruler in western Europe and gave him the nickname of Charles the Great. An unusually tall and imposing figure, Charlemagne was a superb athlete and swimmer, a lover of jokes and high living, but also a deeply pious Christian. One of his court poets labeled him "The King Father of Europe." No monarch in European history has enjoyed such posthumous fame.

During his reign, Charlemagne engaged in almost constant warfare, especially against polytheistic Germanic tribes that he compelled to accept Christianity after their defeat. He went to war 18 times against the Saxons, whose forced conversion only encouraged subsequent rebellions. Three factors explain Charlemagne's persistent warfare. He believed he had an obligation to spread Christianity. He also needed to protect his borders from incursions by hostile tribes. Perhaps most important, however, was his need to satisfy his followers, especially the members of the aristocracy, by providing them with opportunities for plunder and new lands. As a result of his many wars, Charlemagne established a network of subservient kingdoms that owed tribute to him (see **Map 9.2**).

The extraordinary expansion of the Carolingian Empire represented a significant departure from the small, loosely governed kingdoms that had prevailed after the Roman Empire's collapse. Charlemagne's empire covered all of western Europe except for southern Italy, Spain, and the British Isles. His military ambitions brought the Franks into direct confrontation with other cultures—the polytheistic German, Scandinavian, and Slavic tribes; the Orthodox Christians of Byzantium; and the Muslims in Spain. These confrontations were usually hostile and violent, characterized as they were by the imposition of Frankish rule and Latin Christian faith.

CORONATION OF CHARLEMAGNE AS EMPEROR On Christmas Day 800, in front of a large crowd at St. Peter's Basilica in Rome, Pope Leo III (r. 795–816) presided over a ceremony in which Charlemagne was crowned emperor. Historians have debated exactly what happened, but according to the most widely accepted account, the assembled throng acclaimed Charlemagne emperor, and the pope prostrated himself

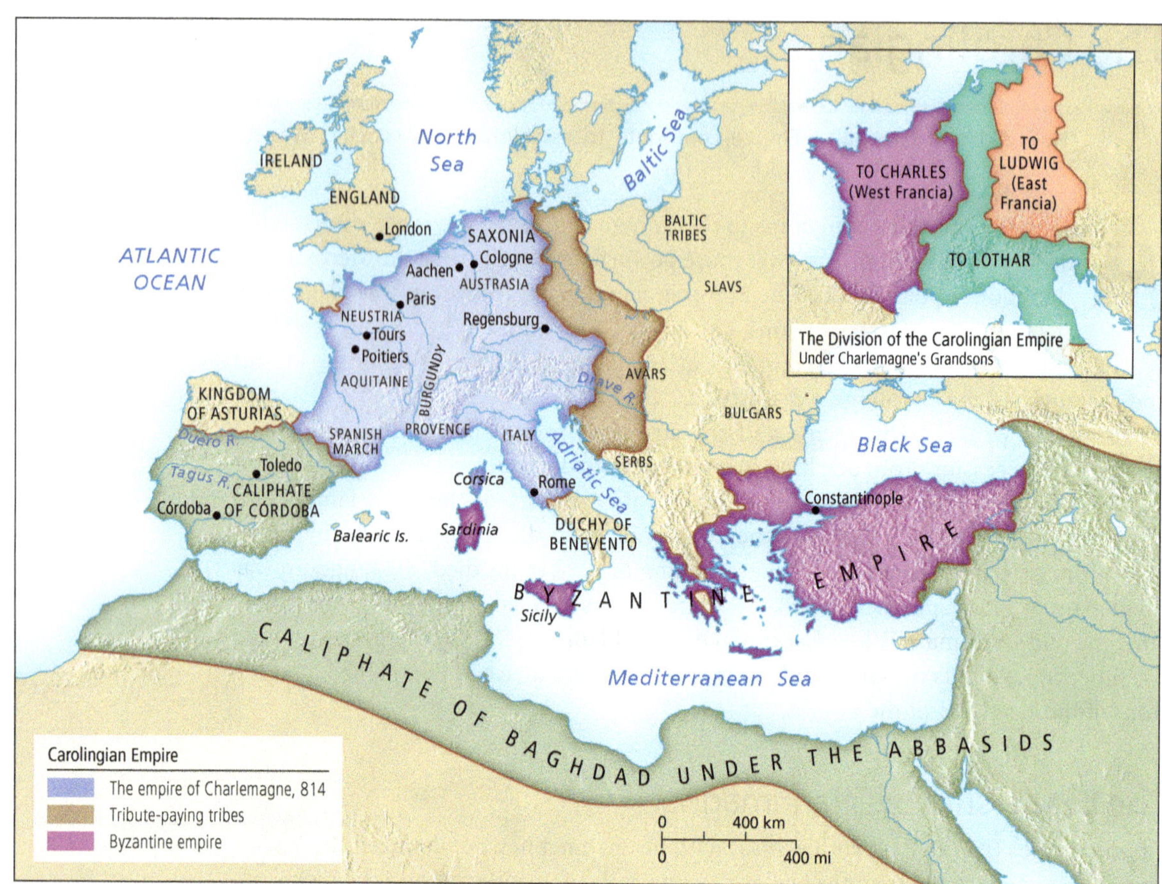

MAP **9.2** CAROLINGIAN EMPIRE Charlemagne's conquests were the greatest military achievement of the early Middle Ages. The Carolingian armies successfully reunified all western European territories of the ancient Roman Empire except for southern Italy, Spain, and Britain. However, the empire was fragile due to Frankish inheritance laws that required all legitimate sons to inherit lands from their fathers. By the time of Charlemagne's grandsons the empire began to fragment. By comparing this map with Map 9.1, determine what were the areas most under the influence of Latin Christianity as a result of the spread of the Carolingian Empire?

before the new emperor in a public demonstration of submission. Charlemagne's biographer Einhard later stated that the coronation came as a surprise to the king. Certainly there were dangers in accepting the imperial crown because the coronation was certain to antagonize Byzantium, where there already was a Roman emperor. To the Byzantines, Charlemagne was nothing more than a barbarian usurper of the imperial crown. In their minds the pope had no right to crown anyone emperor. Instead of reuniting the eastern and western halves of the ancient Roman Empire, the coronation of Charlemagne drove them further apart. Nevertheless, Charlemagne became the first Roman emperor in the West since the fifth century.

The coronation exemplified two of the most prominent characteristics of the Carolingians. The first was the conscious imitation of the ancient Roman Empire, especially the Christian empire of Constantine. Charlemagne conquered much of the former territory of the western Roman Empire, and the churches built during his reign were modeled after the fourth- and fifth-century basilicas of Rome. The second characteristic of Carolingian rule was the obligation of the Frankish kings to protect the Roman popes, an obligation that began under Charlemagne's father Pepin. In exchange for Frankish protection, the popes offered the Carolingian monarchs the legitimacy of divine sanction.

CAROLINGIAN RULERSHIP Even under the discerning and strong rulership of Charlemagne, the Carolingian Empire never enjoyed the assets that had united the ancient

Roman Empire for so many centuries. The Carolingians lacked a standing army and navy, professional civil servants, properly maintained roads, regular communications, and a money economy—a stark contrast with Byzantium and the Muslim caliphates, which could also boast the splendid capital cities of Constantinople, Damascus, Baghdad, and Córdoba. However, Charlemagne governed very effectively without a capital, spending much of his time ruling from the saddle.

Such a system of government depended more on personal than institutional forms of rule. Personal loyalty to the Carolingian monarch, expressed in an oath of allegiance, provided the strongest bonds unifying the realm, but betrayals were frequent. The Carolingian system required a monarch with outstanding personal abilities and unflagging energy, such as Charlemagne possessed; a weak monarch, however, threatened the collapse of the entire empire. Until the reign of Charlemagne, royal commands had been delivered orally, and there were few written records of what decisions had been made. As Charlemagne's decrees (called "capitularies") gradually came to be written out, they began to strengthen and institutionalize governmental procedures. In addition, Charlemagne's leading adviser, Alcuin, insisted that all official communications be stated in the appropriate Latin form, which would help prevent falsification because only the members of Charlemagne's court were well enough educated to know these proper forms.

One of the weaknesses of the previous Merovingian dynasty had been the decentralization of power, as local dukes appropriated royal resources and public functions for themselves. To combat this weakness, Charlemagne followed his father's lead in reorganizing government around territorial units called **counties**, each administered by a count. The counts were rewarded with lands from the king and sent to areas where they had no family ties to serve as a combined provincial governor, judge, military commander, and representative of the king. Traveling circuit inspectors reviewed the counts' activities on a regular basis and remedied abuses of office. On the frontiers of their sprawling kingdom, the Franks established special territories called **marches**, which were ruled by margraves with extended powers necessary to defend vulnerable borders.

counties Territorial units devised by the Carolingian dynasty during the eighth and ninth centuries for the administration of the empire. Each county was administered by a count who was rewarded with lands and sent to areas where he had no family ties to serve as a combined provincial governor, judge, military commander, and representative of the king.

marches Territorial units of the Carolingian Empire for the administration of frontier regions. Each march was ruled by a margrave who had special powers necessary to defend vulnerable borders.

In many respects, however, the Church provided the most vital foundations for the Carolingian system of rulership. As discussed in Chapter 7, the last years of the ancient Roman Empire the administration of the Church was organized around the office of the bishop. By the late seventh century this system had almost completely collapsed, as many bishoprics were left vacant or were occupied by royal favorites and relatives who lacked qualifications for church office. Because Carolingian monarchs considered themselves responsible for the welfare of Christianity, they took charge of the appointment of bishops and reorganized church administration into a strict hierarchy of archbishops who supervised bishops who, in turn, supervised parish priests. Pepin and Charlemagne also revitalized the monasteries and endowed new ones, which provided the royal court with trained personnel—scribes, advisers, and spiritual assistants. Most laymen of the time were illiterate, so monks and priests wrote the emperor's letters for him, kept government records, composed histories, and promoted education. All these tasks were essential for Carolingian rule.

THE CAROLINGIAN RENAISSANCE In addition to organizing an efficient political administration, Charlemagne sought to make the royal court an intellectual center. He gathered around him prominent scholars from throughout the realm and other countries. Under Charlemagne's patronage, these scholars were responsible for the flowering of culture that is called the Carolingian Renaissance.

The **Carolingian Renaissance** ("rebirth") was one of a series of revivals of interest in ancient Greek and Latin literature. Charlemagne understood that both governmental efficiency and the propagation of the Christian faith required the intensive study of Latin, which was the language of the law, learning, and the Church. The Latin

Carolingian Renaissance The "rebirth" of interest in ancient Greek and Latin literature and language during the reign of the Frankish emperor Charlemagne (r. 768–814). Charlemagne promoted the intensive study of Latin to promote governmental efficiency and to propagate the Christian faith.

of everyday speech had evolved considerably since antiquity. During Charlemagne's time, spoken Latin had already been transformed into early versions of the Romance languages of Spanish, Italian, Portuguese, and French. Distressed that the poor Latin of many clergymen meant they misunderstood the Bible, Charlemagne ordered that all prospective priests undergo a rigorous education and recommended the liberal application of physical punishment if a pupil was slow in his lessons. The lack of properly educated teachers, however, ensured that the Carolingian reforms did not penetrate very far into the lower levels of the clergy, who taught by rote the rudiments of Christianity to the illiterate peasants.

canon law The collected laws of the Roman Catholic Church. Canon law applied to cases involving the clergy, disputes about church property, and donations to the Church. It also applied to the laity for annulling marriages, legitimating bastards, prosecuting bigamy, protecting widows and orphans, and resolving inheritance disputes.

Charlemagne's patronage was crucial for the Carolingian Renaissance, which took place in the monasteries and the imperial court. Many of the heads of the monastic scriptoria wrote literary works of their own, including poetry and theology. The Carolingian scholars developed a beautiful new style of handwriting called the Carolingian minuscule, in which each letter was carefully and clearly formed. Texts collected by Carolingian librarians provided the foundation for the laws of the Church (called **canon law**) and codified the liturgy, which consisted of the prayers offered, texts read, and chants sung on each day of the year.

View the **Closer Look**

A Multicultural Book Cover

CAROLINGIAN RENAISSANCE ART This exquisite book cover for the Lindau Gospels is thought to have been produced at the Royal Abbey of St. Denis under the reign of Charles the Bald, grandson of Charlemagne, around 870. The images reflect several cultural influences, including Greek, Roman, Byzantine, Celtic, and Germanic, and they present a magnificent crucifixion iconography. Christ, true to Byzantine theology, is not shown suffering the agony of the cross but, instead, is depicted as serene, triumphant, and determined.

The man most fully responsible for the Carolingian Renaissance was the English poet and cleric Alcuin of York (ca. 732–804), whom Charlemagne invited to head the palace school in Aachen. Charlemagne himself joined his sons, his friends, and his friends' sons as a student, but Charlemagne struggled in his classes. Despite many years of practice he still could not learn to form letters. Nevertheless, under Alcuin's guidance the court became a lively center of discussion and exchange of knowledge. They debated issues such as the existence of Hell, the meaning of solar eclipses, and the nature of the Holy Trinity. After 15 years at court, Alcuin became the abbot of the monastery of St. Martin at Tours, where he expanded the library and produced a number of works on education, theology, and philosophy.

A brilliant young monk named Einhard (ca. 770–840), who studied in the palace school, quickly became a trusted friend and adviser to Charlemagne. Based on 23 years of service to Charlemagne and research in royal documents, Einhard wrote the *Life of Charlemagne* (830–833), which describes Charlemagne's family, foreign policy, conquests, administration, and personal attributes. In Einhard's vivid Latin prose, Charlemagne comes alive as a great leader, a lover of hunting and fighting, who unlike his rough companions possessed a towering sense of responsibility for the welfare of his subjects and the salvation of their souls. In Einhard's biography, Charlemagne appears as an idealist, the first Christian prince in medieval Europe to imagine that his role was not just to acquire more possessions but to better humankind.

Charlemagne's rule and reputation have had lasting significance for western Europe. Around 776 an Anglo-Saxon monk referred to the vast new kingdom of the Franks as the Kingdom of Europe, reviving the Roman geographical term *Europa*. Thanks to the Carolingians, Europe became more than a geographical expression. It became the geographical center of a new Christian civilization that supplanted the Roman civilization of the Mediterranean and transformed the culture of the West.

The Division of Western Europe

None of Charlemagne's successors possessed his personal skills, and without a permanent institutional basis for administration, the empire was vulnerable to fragmentation and disorder. When Charlemagne died in 814, the imperial crown passed to his only surviving son, Louis the Pious (r. 814–840). Louis's most serious problem was dividing the empire among his own three sons, as required by Frankish inheritance laws. Disputes among Louis's sons led to civil war, even before the death of their father; while they were fighting, the administration of the empire was neglected.

After years of fighting, the three sons—Charles the Bald (d. 877), Lothair (d. 855), and Louis the German (d. 876)—negotiated the Treaty of Verdun, which divided the Carolingian Empire. Charles the Bald received the western part of the territories, the kingdom of West Francia. Louis the German received the eastern portion, the kingdom of East Francia. Lothair obtained the imperial title as well as the central portion of the kingdom, the "Middle Kingdom," which extended from Rome to the North Sea (see Map 9.2). In succeeding generations, the laws of inheritance created further fragmentation of these kingdoms, and during the ninth and tenth centuries the descendants of Charlemagne died out or lost control of their lands. By 987 none were left.

The Carolingian Empire lasted only a few generations. Carolingian military power, however, had been formidable, providing within the Frankish lands an unusual period of security from hostile enemies, measured by the fact that few settlements were fortified. After the empire's collapse, virtually every surviving community in western Europe required fortifications, represented by castles and town walls. Post-Carolingian Europe became fragmented as local aristocrats stepped into the vacuum created by the demise of the Carolingians—and it became vulnerable, as a new wave of raiders from the steppes and the North plundered and carved out land for themselves.

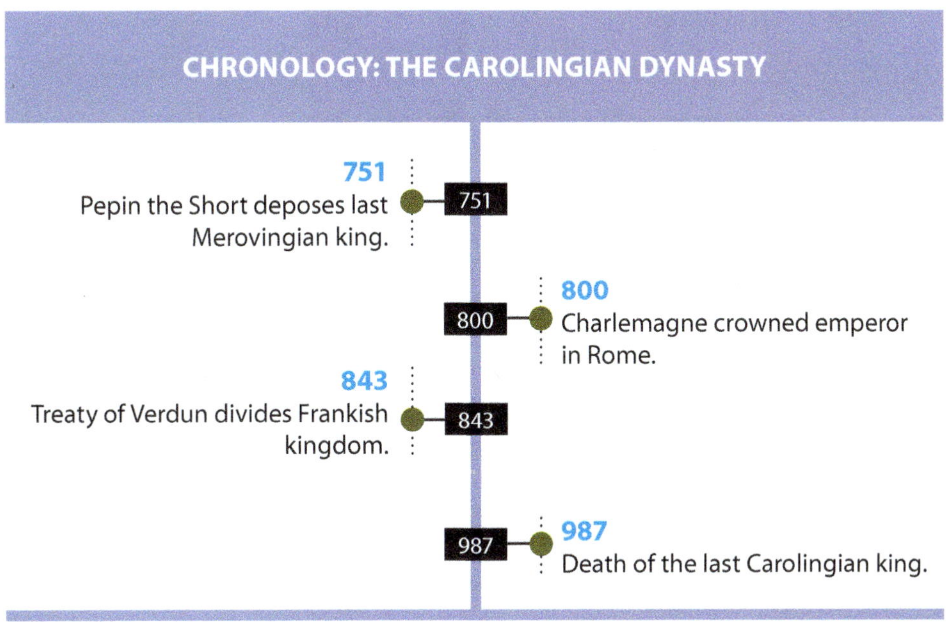

Invasions and Recovery in the Latin West

9.3 How did Latin Christianity consolidate itself after the collapse of the Carolingian Empire?

Despite Charlemagne's campaigns of conquest and conversion, the spread of Christianity throughout western Europe remained uneven and incomplete. By 900, Latin Christianity was limited to a few regions that constituted the heartland of western Europe—the Frankish lands, Italy, parts of Germany that had been under Carolingian rule, the British Isles, and a fringe in Spain. Moreover, the heartland was vulnerable because during the ninth and tenth centuries, hostile polytheistic tribes raided deep into the tightly packed Christian core of western Europe (see **Map 9.3**). Despite these attacks Christianity survived, and the polytheist tribes eventually accepted the Christian faith. These conversions were not always the consequence of Christian victories in battle, as had often been the case during late antiquity and the Carolingian period. More frequently, they resulted from organized missionary efforts by monks and bishops.

The Polytheist Invaders of the Latin West

Some of the raiders during the eighth to eleventh centuries plundered what they could from the Christian settlements of the West and returned home. Others seized lands,

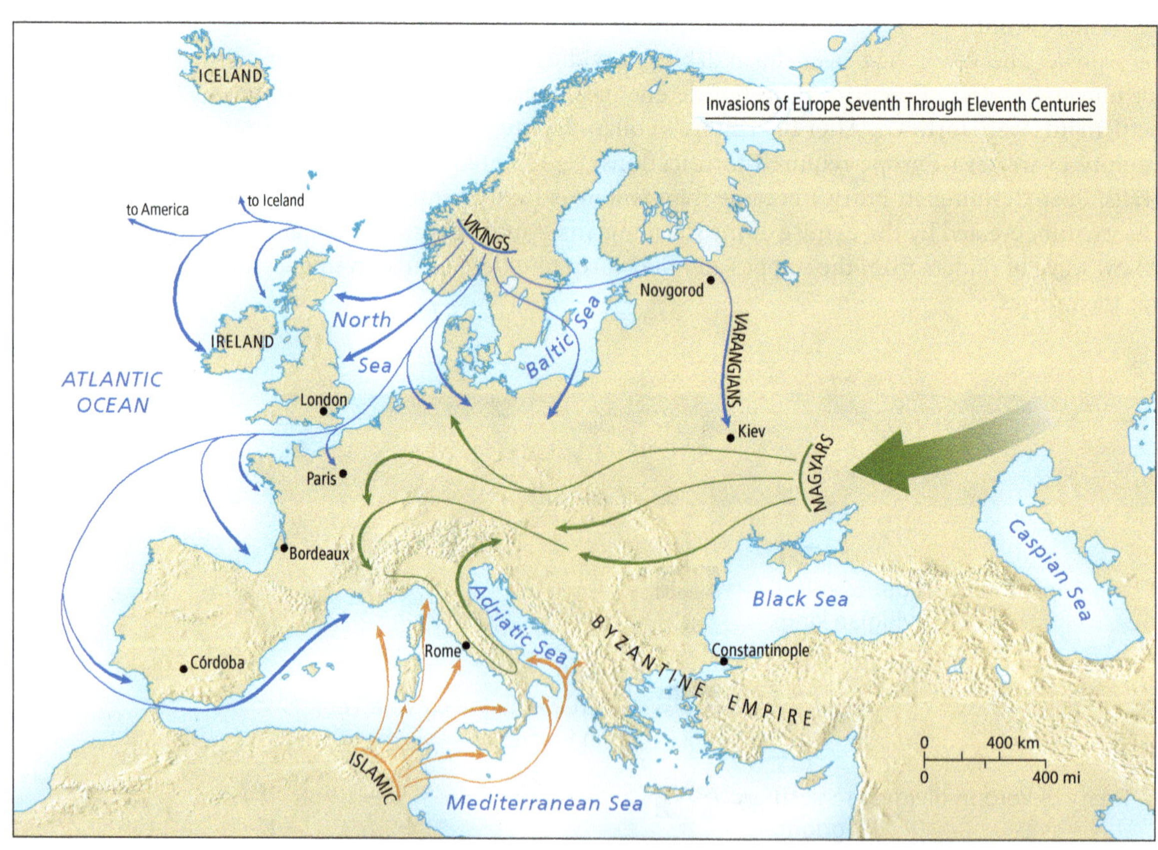

MAP **9.3** INVASIONS OF EUROPE, SEVENTH THROUGH ELEVENTH CENTURIES After the division of the Carolingian Empire, Britain and northern France, in particular, came under severe pressure from invading Viking bands from Scandinavia. The Varangians were a Viking tribe that invaded Kievan Rus and the territories of Novgorod. From the east came the Magyars, who eventually settled in the vast Hungarian plain. From the south there were persistent raids and conquests from various Islamic states, some of which established a rich Muslim civilization in Europe. (For these, see Chapter 8.) Which parts of Europe were most affected and which least affected by the invasions?

settled down, and established new principalities. The two groups who took advantage of the weakness of the Latin West most often during this period were the Magyars and Vikings.

The original homeland of the Magyars, later known as the Hungarians, was in the central Asian steppes. Gradually driven by other nomads to the western edge of the steppes, the Magyars crossed en masse in 896 into the middle of the Danube River basin, occupying sparsely settled lands that were easily conquered. Mounted raiding parties of Magyars ranged far into western Europe. Between 898 and 920 they sacked settlements in the prosperous Po River valley of Italy and then descended on the remnant kingdoms of the Carolingian Empire. Wherever they went they plundered for booty and took slaves for domestic service or sale. The kings of western and central Europe were powerless against these fierce raiders, who were unstoppable until 955 when the Saxon king Otto I destroyed a band of marauders on their way home with booty. After 955, Magyar raiding subsided.

The definitive end of Magyar forays, however, may have had less to do with Otto's victory than with the consolidation of the Hungarian plain into its own kingdom under the Árpád dynasty. Both Orthodox and Latin missionaries vied to convert the Magyars, but because of western political alliances they accepted Latin Christianity. On Christmas Day 1000, the Árpád king Stephen I (r. 997–1038) received the insignia of royalty directly from the pope and was crowned king. To help convert his people, King Stephen laid out a network of bishoprics and lavishly endowed monasteries.

The most devastating of the eighth- to eleventh-century invaders of western European settlements were the Vikings, also called Norsemen or Northmen. During this period, Danish, Norwegian, and Swedish Viking warriors sailed on long-distance raiding expeditions from their homes in Scandinavia. Every spring the long Viking dragon ships sailed forth, each carrying 50–100 warriors avid for loot. Propelled by a single square sail or by oarsmen when the winds failed or were blowing in the wrong direction, Viking ships were unmatched for seaworthiness and regularly sailed into the wild seas of the North Atlantic. The shallow-draft vessels could also be rowed up the lazy rivers of Europe to plunder monasteries and villages far into the interior.

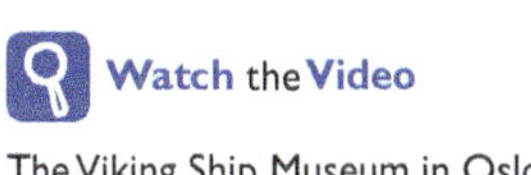

The Viking Ship Museum in Oslo

Historians continue to debate the causes for the enormous Viking onslaught. Higher annual temperatures in the North may have stimulated a spurt in population that encouraged raiding and eventually emigration. But the primary motive seems to have been an insatiable thirst for silver, which was deemed the essential standard of social distinction in Scandinavian society. As a result, monasteries and cathedrals with their silver liturgical vessels were especially prized sources of plunder for Viking raiding parties. In 793, for example, Vikings pillaged the great English monastery at Lindisfarne for its silver—and largely destroyed it in the process.

By the middle of the ninth century, the Vikings began to maintain winter quarters in the British Isles and on the shores of the Carolingian kingdoms—locations that enabled them to house and feed ever-larger raiding parties. These raiders soon became invading armies that took land and settled their families on it. As a result, the Vikings moved from disruptive pillaging to permanent occupation, which created a lasting mark on Europe. Amid the ruins of the Carolingian Empire, Viking settlements on the Seine River formed the beginnings of the duchy of Normandy ("Northman land"), whose soldiers in the eleventh century would conquer England, Sicily, and much of southern Italy.

Read the Document

Excerpt from the Annals of St. Vaast (882–886)

The most long-lasting influence of the Vikings outside Scandinavia was in the British Isles and North Atlantic. In 865 a great Viking army conquered large parts of northeastern England, creating a loosely organized network of territories known as the Danelaw. The Danish and Norse conquests in the British Isles left deep cultural residues in local dialects, geographical names, personal names, social structure, and literature. The most enduring example in Old English, the earliest form of spoken and written English, remains the epic of *Beowulf,* which recounts the exploits of a great Scandinavian adventurer in combat with the monster Grendel, Grendel's mother, and a fiery dragon.

VIKING SHIP This is a reconstructed Viking ship. It would have been propelled by a single square sail or rowed by oarsmen. Horses and warriors crowded into the ship. The tiller was mounted on the starboard side toward the stern. Stern-mounted rudders, which gave the helmsman much greater control of the direction of the ship, were gradually introduced during the twelfth century.

Read the Document

Saga of Erik the Red (985)

Read the Document

Speculum Princips, "The Animal Life of Greenland and the Character of the Land in Those Regions"

In the North Atlantic, Vikings undertook long voyages into the unknown across cold rough seas. Beginning about 870, settlers poured into unsettled Iceland. Using Iceland as a base, they ventured farther and established new colonies in Greenland. In Iceland the adventures of these Viking warriors, explorers, and settlers were celebrated in poetry and sagas; those of Erik the Red and the Greenlanders recount hazardous voyages to the coasts of Canada. These Europeans arrived in North America 500 years before Christopher Columbus. In 930 the fiercely independent Icelanders founded a national parliament, the *althing*, an institution at which disputes were adjudicated through legal procedures rather than combat. The *althing* still functions as the parliament of the Republic of Iceland.

After the mid-ninth century, the kings of Scandinavia (Norway, Denmark, and Sweden) began to assert control over the bands of raiders who had constituted the vanguard of the Viking invasions. By the end of the tenth century, the great age of Viking raiding by small parties ended. The Scandinavian kings established firm hold over the settled population and converted to Christianity, bringing their subjects with them into the new faith. Hence, the descendants of the Viking raiders settled down to become peaceable farmers and shepherds.

lord During the Middle Ages, a lord was someone who offered protection to dependents, known as vassals, who took an oath of loyalty to him. Most lords demanded military services from their vassals and sometimes granted them tracts of land known as fiefs.

vassals During the Middle Ages, men voluntarily submitted themselves to a lord by taking an oath of loyalty. Vassals owed the lord certain services—usually military assistance—and sometimes received in exchange a grant of land known as a fief.

The Rulers in the Latin West

As a consequence of the disintegration of the Carolingian order and the subsequent invasions, people during the ninth and tenth centuries began to seek protection from local warlords who assumed responsibilities once invested in royal authorities. Some of these warlords became the founders of what would become the kingdoms of the Latin West. They provided protection and a modicum of order in a period of anarchy caused by weak or failed governments.

LORDS AND VASSALS The society of warlords derived from Germanic military traditions in which a great chief attracted followers who fought alongside him. The relationship was voluntary and egalitarian. By the eighth century, however, the chief had become a **lord** who dominated others, and his dependents were known as **vassals**.

The bond of loyalty between lord and vassal was formalized by an oath. In the Carolingian period the vassal proved his loyalty to the lord by performing an act of homage, which made the vassal the "man" of the lord. The act of homage was a ritual in which the kneeling vassal placed his clasped hands between the hands of the lord and made a verbal declaration of intent, usually something such as, "Sir, I become your man." In return for the vassal's homage or *fealty*, as it came to be called, the lord swore to protect the vassal. The oath established a personal relationship in which the lord reciprocated the vassal's loyalty and willingness to obey the lord with protection and in some cases with a land grant called a **fief**. Lords frequently called on their vassals for military assistance to resist invaders or to fight with other lords. The fief supplied the vassal with an income to cover the expenses of armor and weapons and of raising and feeding horses, all of which were necessary to be an effective mounted soldier, known by the twelfth century as a **knight**. Historians called this connection between lord-vassal relations and the holding of a fief **feudalism**. The privileges for lords and vassals and their hold on fiefs lasted for many centuries, well into the eighteenth century in some parts of Europe. The long persistence of feudalism was one of the most important themes in the history of the West.

During the ninth and tenth centuries, after the collapse of public authority during the invasions and the dissolution of the Carolingian Empire, the lords often became the only effective rulers in a particular locality. Lords came to exercise many of the powers of a king, such as adjudicating disputes over property or inheritance and punishing thieves and murderers. (See *Justice in History* in this chapter.)

The mixture of personal lord-vassal obligations, property rights conveyed by the fief, and legal jurisdiction over communities caused endless complications. The king's vassals were also lords of their own vassals, who in turn were lords over lesser vassals down to the level of simple knight. In theory, such a system created a hierarchy of authority that descended down from the king, but reality was never that simple. In France, for example, many of the great lords possessed as much land as the king, which made it very difficult for the king to force them to enact his will. Many vassals held different fiefs from different lords, which created a confusion of loyalties, especially when two lords of the same vassal went to war against one another.

Women could inherit fiefs and own property of their own, although they could not perform military services. They often managed royal and aristocratic property when men were absent or dead, decided how property would be divided up among heirs, and functioned as lords when receiving the homage of male vassals. The lineage and accomplishments of prominent ladies enhanced their husbands' social prestige. A number of aristocratic families traced their descent from the female line, if it was more prestigious than the male line, and named their children after the wife's illustrious ancestors.

Lord-vassal relationships infiltrated many medieval social institutions and practices. Because most vassals owed military service to their lords, medieval armies were at least partially composed of vassal-knights who were obliged to fight for their lord for a certain number of days (often 40) per year. Vassals were required to provide their lord with other kinds of support as well. When summoned, they had to appear at the lord's court to offer advice or sit in judgment of other vassals who were their peers. When the lord traveled, his vassal was required to provide food and shelter in the vassal's castle, sometimes for a large entourage of family and retainers who accompanied the lord. Vassals were obliged to pay their lord certain fees on special occasions, such as the marriage of the lord's daughter. If the lord was captured in battle, his vassals had to pay the ransom.

THE WESTERN EUROPEAN KINGDOMS AFTER THE CAROLINGIANS At a time when the bonds of loyalty and support between lords and vassals were the only form of protection from invaders and marauders, lordship was a stronger social institution than the vague obligations all subjects owed to their kings. To rule effectively, a king was

fief During the Middle Ages, a fief was a grant of land or some other form of income that a lord gave to a vassal in exchange for loyalty and certain services (usually military assistance).

knight During the Middle Ages, a knight was a soldier who fought on horseback. A knight was a vassal or dependent of a lord, who usually financed the knight's expenses of armor and weapons and of raising and feeding horses with a grant of land known as a fief.

feudalism A term historians use to describe a social system common during the Middle Ages in which lords granted fiefs (tracts of land or some other form of income) to dependents, known as vassals, who owed their lords personal services in exchange. Feudalism refers to a society governed through personal ties of dependency rather than public political institutions.

Justice in History

Revealing the Truth: OATHS AND ORDEALS

No participant in a lawsuit or criminal trial today would dream of entering the courtroom without an accompanying pile of documents to prove the case. In modern society we trust written over oral evidence because we are aware of how easily our memories can be distorted. In an early medieval court, however, the participants usually arrived with nothing more than their own sworn testimony and personal reputations to support their cause. Papers alleging to prove one thing or another meant little in a largely illiterate society. Unable to read and perhaps aware that the few who could read might deceive them, most people trusted what they had personally seen and heard. Count Berthold of Hamm expressed the opinion of many when, after being presented with documents opposing his claim to a piece of land, he "laughed at the documents, saying that since anyone's pen could write what they liked, he ought not to lose his rights over it."

To settle disputes, medieval courts put much more faith in confession or in eyewitness testimony than in documents. In 1124 Pope Calixtus II pronounced that "we put greater faith in the oral testimony of living witnesses than in the written word."

Under normal trial procedures, a man would give his oath that what he was saying was true. If he was an established and respected member of the community, he would also have a number of "oath-witnesses" testify for his reliability, although not to the truth or falsehood of his evidence. The court would also hear from witnesses in the case. This system worked well enough when two local men, known in the community, were at odds. But what happened when there was a trial involving a person who had a bad reputation, was a known liar, or was a stranger? What would happen in a case with no witnesses?

In these instances, medieval courts sometimes turned to trial by ordeal—subjecting the accused to a painful test—to settle the matter. The judicial ordeal was used only as a last resort, as a German law code of 1220 declared: "It is not right to use the ordeal in any case, except that the truth may be known in no other way." The wide range of situations and people handed over to the ordeal makes clear that in the eyes of the medieval courts, the ordeal was a fallback method when all else failed to reveal the truth.

TRIAL BY ORDEAL This fifteenth-century painting by Dieric Bouts (ca. 1415–1475) was commissioned by the city of Louvain in 1468 for a large project on the theme of the Last Judgment. It shows the widow of a murdered count holding a hot iron in her left hand and her husband's severed head in her right. Emperor Otto III judges her guilt for the murder on the basis of her willingness to undergo the hot-iron ordeal.

There were several types of trial by ordeal. The most common was trial by fire. The accused would plunge his or her arm into a cauldron of boiling water to retrieve a coin or a jewel, or alternately would pick up a red-hot iron and walk nine paces. A variation of this method was to walk over hot coals or red-hot plowshares. After the accused suffered this ordeal, his or her hand or foot would be bound for three days and then examined. If the wound was healing "cleanly," meaning without infection, the accused was declared innocent. If not, he or she was adjudged guilty. Another common form of the ordeal was immersion in cold water, or "swimming," made famous in later centuries by its use in witch trials. The accused would be thrown into a river or lake. If the water "rejected" her and she floated, then she was guilty. If the water "embraced" her and she sank, then she was innocent. The obvious complication that a sinking person, even though innocent, may have also been a drowning person did not seem to deter use of trial by water.

The ordeal was especially widespread in judging crimes such as heresy and adultery and in assigning paternity. In 1218, Inga of Varteig carried the hot iron to prove that her son, born out of wedlock, was the son of deceased King Hakon III, which if true would change the line of succession in Norway. The ordeal was also used to decide much more pedestrian matters. In 1090, Gautier of Meigné claimed a plot of land from the monks of Saint Auban at Angers, arguing that he had traded a horse in return for the property. He too carried a hot iron to prove his claim.

The belief that an ordeal could effectively reveal guilt or innocence in a judicial matter was based on the widespread conviction that God constantly and actively intervened in earthly affairs and that his judgment could be seen immediately. To focus God's attention on a specific issue, the participants performed the ordeal in a ritual

(continued on next page)

(continued from previous page)

manner. A priest was usually present to invoke God's power and to bless the implements employed in the ordeal. In one typical formula, the priest asked God "to bless and sanctify this fiery iron, which is used in the just examination of doubtful issues." Priests would also inform the accused, "If you are innocent of this charge ... you may confidently receive this iron in your hand and the Lord, the just judge, will free you." The ritual element of the judicial ordeal emphasized the judgment of God over the judgment of men.

During the eleventh and twelfth centuries, the use of the ordeal waned. The recovery of Roman law, the rise of literacy and written documents in society at large, and a greater confidence in the power of courts to settle disputes all contributed to the gradual replacement of the ordeal with the jury trial or the use of torture to elicit a confession from the accused. In England the common law began to entrust the determination of the truth to a jury of peers who listened to and evaluated all the testimony. The jury system valued the opinions of members of the community over the reliability of the ordeal to reveal God's judgment. These changes mark a shift in medieval society toward a growing belief in the power of secular society to organize and police itself, leaving divine justice to the afterlife. But the most crucial shift came from within the Church itself, which felt its spiritual mission compromised by the involvement of priests in supervising ordeals. In 1215 the Fourth Lateran Council forbade priests from participating, and their absence made it impossible for the ordeal to continue as a formal legal procedure.

For Discussion

1. Why was someone's reputation in the community so significant for determining the truth in a medieval trial? How do reputations play a role in trials today?
2. What do oaths and the trial by ordeal reveal about the relationship between human and divine justice during the Middle Ages?

Taking It Further

Bartlett, Robert. *Trial by Fire and Water: The Medieval Judicial Ordeal.* 1986. Associates the spread of the trial by ordeal with the expansion of Christianity. The best study of the ordeal.

van Caenegen, R. C. *An Historical Introduction to Private Law.* 1992. A basic narrative from late antiquity to the nineteenth century that traces the evolution of early medieval trial procedures.

obliged to be a strong lord, in effect to become the lord of all the other lords, who in turn would discipline their own vassals. Achieving this difficult goal took several steps. First, the king had to establish a firm hand over his own lands, the royal domain. With the domain supplying food, material, and fighting men, the king could attempt the second step—establishing control over lords who lived outside the royal domain. To hold sway over these independent-minded lords, kings sometimes employed force but frequently offered lucrative rewards by giving out royal prerogatives to loyal lords. These prerogatives included the rights to receive fines in courts of law, to collect taxes, and to perform other governmental functions. As a result, some medieval kingdoms, such as France and England, began to combine in the hands of the same people the personal authority of lordship with the legal authority of the king, creating feudal kingship.

The final step in the process of establishing royal authority was to emphasize the sacred character of kingship. With the assistance of the clergy, kings emulated the great Christian emperors of Rome, Constantine and Justinian. Medieval kings became quasi-priests who received obedience from their subjects because commoners believed kings represented the majesty of God on Earth. The institution of sacred kingship gave kings an additional weapon for persuading the nobles to recognize the king's superiority over them.

Under the influence of ancient Roman ideas of rulership, some kings began to envision their kingdoms as something grander than private property. As the Germanic king and later emperor Conrad II (r. 1024–1039) put it, "If the king is dead the kingdom remains, just as the ship remains even if the helmsman falls overboard."[2] The idea slowly began to take hold that the kingdom had an eternal existence separate from the mortal person of the king and that it was superior to its component parts—its provinces, tribes, lords, families, bishoprics, and cities. This profound idea reached its fullest theoretical expression many centuries later. Promoting the sacred and eternal character of kingship required monarchs to patronize priests, monks, writers, and artists who could formulate and express these ideas.

EAST FRANCIA: THE GERMAN EMPIRE The kingdoms of East and West Francia, which arose out of the remnants of the Carolingian Empire, produced kings who attempted to expand the power of the monarchy and enhance the idea of kingship. East Francia largely consisted of Germanic tribes, each governed by a Frankish official called a duke. After 919 the dukes of Saxony were elected the kings of East Francia, establishing the foundations for the Saxon dynasty. With few lands of their own, the Saxon kings maintained their power by acquiring other duchies and controlling appointments to high church offices, which went to family members or loyal followers. The greatest of the Saxon kings, Otto I the Great (936–973), combined deep Christian piety with formidable military ability. More than any other tenth-century king, he supported the foundation of missionary bishoprics in polytheist Slavic and Scandinavian lands, thereby pushing the boundaries of Christianity beyond what they had been under Charlemagne. The pope crowned Otto emperor in 962, reviving the Roman Empire in the West, as Charlemagne had done earlier. Otto and his successors in the Saxon dynasty attempted to rule a more restricted version of the western empire than had Charlemagne. By the 1030s the Saxon kingdom had become the German Empire, consisting of most of the Germanic duchies, north-central Italy, and Burgundy. In later centuries these regions collectively came to be called the Holy Roman Empire.

As had been the case under Charlemagne, effective rulership in the new German Empire included the patronage of learned men and women who enhanced the reputation of the monarch. Otto and his able brother Bruno, the archbishop of Cologne, initiated a cultural revival, the **Ottonian Renaissance**, which centered on the imperial court. Learned Irish and English monks, Greek philosophers from Byzantium, and Italian scholars found positions there. Among the many intellectuals patronized by Otto, the most notable was Liutprand of Cremona (ca. 920–972), a vivid writer whose unabashed histories reflected the passions of the troubled times. For example, his history of contemporary Europe vilified his enemies and was aptly titled *Revenge*.

Ottonian Renaissance Under the patronage of the Saxon Emperor Otto I (936–973) and his brother Bruno, learned monks, Greek philosophers from Byzantium, and Italian scholars gathered at the imperial court, stimulating a cultural revival in literature and the arts. The writers and artists enhanced the reputation of Otto.

WEST FRANCIA: FRANCE Like East Francia, West Francia included many groups with separate ethnic and linguistic identities, but the kingdom had been Christianized much longer because it had been part of the Roman Empire. Thus, West Francia, although highly fragmented, possessed the potential for greater unity by using fully established Christianity to champion the king's authority.

Strengthening the monarchy became the crucial goal of the Capetian dynasty, which succeeded the last of the Carolingian kings. Hugh Capet (r. 987–996) was elevated as king of West Francia in an elaborate coronation ceremony in which the prayers of the archbishop of Reims offered divine sanction to the new dynasty. The archbishop's involvement established an important precedent for the French monarchy: Thereafter, the monarchy and the church hierarchy were closely entwined. From this mutually beneficial relationship, the king received ecclesiastical and spiritual support while the upper clergy gained royal protection and patronage. The term *France* at first applied only to Capet's feudal domain, a small but rich region around Paris, but through the persistence of the Capetians, West Francia became so unified that France came to refer to the entire kingdom.

The Capetians were especially successful in soliciting homage and services from the great lords of the land—despite some initial resistance. Hugh and his successors distinguished themselves by emphasizing that unlike other lords, kings were appointed by God. Shortly after his own coronation, Hugh had his son crowned—a strategy that ensured the succession of the Capetian family. Hugh's son, Robert II, the Pious (r. 996–1031), was apparently the first to perform the "king's touch": curing certain skin diseases with the power of his touch. The royal coronation cult and the king's touch established the reputation of French kings as miracle workers.

ANGLO-SAXON ENGLAND Anglo-Saxon England had never been part of the Carolingian Empire, but because it was Christian, England shared in the culture of the Latin West. England suffered extensive damage at the hands of the Vikings. After England was almost overwhelmed by a Danish invasion during the winter of 878–879, Alfred the

Great (r. 871–899) finally defeated the Danes as spring approached. As king of only Wessex (not of all England), Alfred consolidated his authority and issued a new law code. Alfred's successors cooperated with the nobility more effectively than the monarchs in either East or West Francia and built a broad base of support in the local units of government, the hundreds and shires. The Anglo-Saxon monarchy also enjoyed the support of the Church, which provided it with skilled servants and spiritual authorization.

During the late ninth and tenth centuries, Anglo-Saxon England experienced a cultural revival under royal patronage. King Alfred proclaimed that the Viking invasions had been God's punishment for the neglect of learning, without which God's will could not be known. Alfred accordingly promoted the study of Latin. He also desired that all men of wealth learn to read the language of the English people. Under Alfred a highly sophisticated literature appeared in Old English. This literature included poems, sermons, commentaries on the Bible, and translations of important Latin works. The masterpiece of this era was a history called the *Anglo-Saxon Chronicle*. It was begun during Alfred's reign but maintained over several generations.

During the late tenth and early eleventh centuries, England was weakened by another series of Viking raids and a succession of feeble kings. In 1066 William, the duke of Normandy and a descendant of Vikings who had settled in the north of France, defeated King Harold, the last Anglo-Saxon king. William seized the English throne. William the Conqueror opened a new era in which English affairs became deeply intertwined with those of the duchy of Normandy and the kingdom of France.

The Conversion of the Last Polytheists

As the core of the Latin West became politically stronger and economically more prosperous during the tenth and eleventh centuries, Christians made concerted attempts to convert the invaders, especially the polytheistic tribes in northern and eastern Europe. Through conversion, Latin Christianity dominated northern Europe up to the Kievan Rus border where Orthodox Christianity adopted from Byzantium triumphed.

CHRISTIAN CHURCH IMITATES POLYTHEIST TEMPLE The stave church was a type of wooden church built in northern Europe during the Middle Ages. Most of the surviving examples in Scandinavia are generally assumed to be modeled on polytheist temples. The Borgund church in Norway pictured here dates from about 1150.

Among the polytheistic tribes in Scandinavia, the Baltic Sea region, and parts of eastern Europe, the first Christian conversions usually took place when a king or chieftain accepted Christianity. His subjects were expected to follow. Teaching Christian principles and forms of worship required much more time and effort, of course. Missionary monks usually arrived after a king's conversion, but these monks tended to take a tolerant attitude about variations in the liturgy. Because most Christians were isolated from one another, new converts tended to practice their own local forms of worship and belief. Missionaries and Christian princes discovered that the most effective way to combat this localizing tendency was to found new bishoprics. Especially among the formerly polytheist tribes in northern and eastern Europe, the foundation of bishoprics created cultural centers of considerable prestige that attracted members of the upper classes. Those educated under the supervision of these new bishops became influential servants to the ruling families, further enhancing the stature of Christian culture.

Christian conversion especially benefited women through the abandonment of polygamous marriages, which were common among the polytheist peoples. As a result, aristocratic women played an important role in helping convert their peoples to Christianity. That role gave them a lasting influence in the churches of the newly converted lands, both as founders and patrons of convents and as writers on religious subjects. By the end of the fourteenth century organized polytheistic worship had disappeared in Scandinavia.

From the middle of the tenth century, a line of newly established Catholic bishoprics ensured that the Poles, Bohemians (Czechs), and Magyars (Hungarians) looked to the West and the pope for their cultural models and religious leadership. Poland,

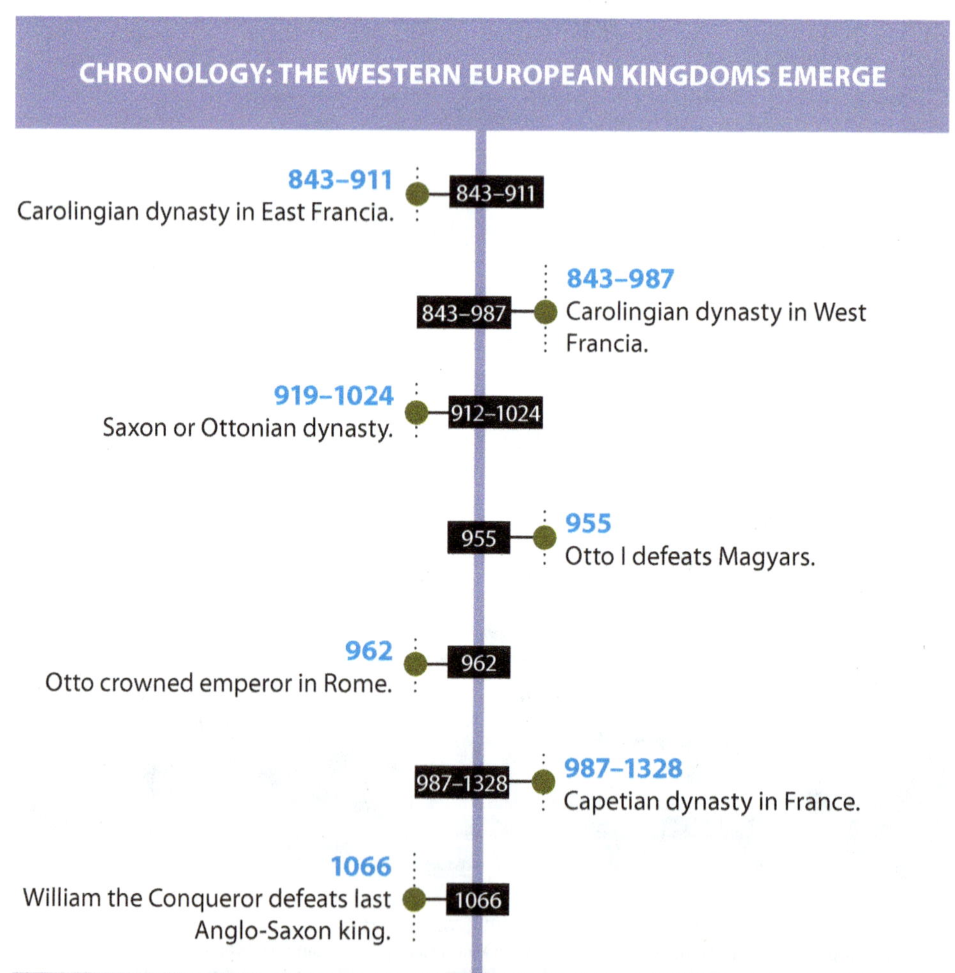

especially, favored Latin Christianity, an association that helped create strong political and cultural ties to western Europe. The Poles inhabited a flat plain of forested land with small clearings for farming. First exposed to missionaries tied to Saint Methodius, Poland resisted Christianity until Prince Mieszko (ca. 960–992) created the most powerful of the Slav states and accepted Latin Christianity in 966 in an attempt to build political alliances with Christian princes. Mieszko formally subordinated his country to the Roman pope with the Donation of Poland (ca. 991). Thus began Poland's long and special relationship with the papacy. At Mieszko's death, the territory of Poland approximated what it is today.

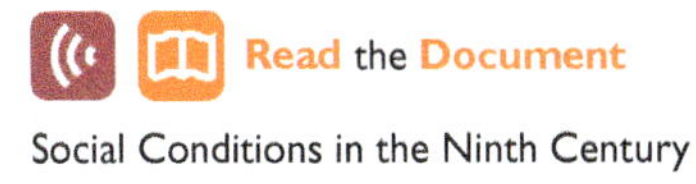

Social Conditions in the Ninth Century

The West in the East: The Crusades

9.4 What were the causes and consequences of the Crusades?

On a chilly November day in 1095 in a bare field outside Clermont, France, Pope Urban II (r. 1088–1099) delivered a landmark sermon to the assembled French clergy and laypeople eager to hear the pope. In stirring words Urban recalled that Muslims in the East were persecuting Christians and that the holy places in Palestine had been ransacked. He called upon the knights "to take up the cross" to defend their fellow Christians in distress.

Urban's appeal for a crusade was stunningly successful. When he finished speaking, the crowd chanted back, "God wills it." The news of Urban's call for a holy war in the East spread like wildfire. All across France and the western part of the German Empire knights prepared for the journey to Jerusalem. Unexpectedly and probably contrary to the pope's intentions, the poor and dispossessed also became enthused about an armed pilgrimage to the Holy Land. The zealous Peter the Hermit (ca. 1050–1115) preached the Crusade among the poor and homeless and gathered a huge unequipped, undisciplined army, which left for Jerusalem well in advance of the knights. Most of Peter the Hermit's People's Crusade starved or were enslaved long before they arrived in Constantinople. The Byzantine emperor was unwilling to feed the few who did arrive and shipped them off to Turkish territory where the Turkish army annihilated nearly all of them.

Urban's call for a crusade gave powerful religious sanction to the western Christian military expeditions against Islam. From 1095 until well into the thirteenth century, recurrent, large-scale crusading operations attempted to take, retake, and protect Christian Jerusalem (see **Map 9.4**), while the idea of going on a crusade lasted long after the thirteenth century into modern times.

The Origins of Holy War

The original impulse for the **Crusades** was the threat that Muslim armies posed to Christian peoples, pilgrims, and holy places in the eastern Mediterranean. By the middle of the eleventh century the Seljuk Turks, who had converted to Islam, were putting pressure on the Byzantine Empire. In 1071, after the Seljuks defeated the Byzantine army at Manzikert, all of Asia Minor lay open to Muslim occupation. Pope Urban's appeal for a crusade in 1095 came in response to a request for military assistance from the Byzantine emperor Alexius Comnenus, who probably thought he would get yet another band of Western mercenaries to help him reconquer Byzantine territory lost to the Seljuks. Instead, he got something utterly unprecedented—a massive volunteer army of perhaps 60,000 soldiers devoted less to cooperating with their Byzantine Christian brethren than to wresting as much territory as possible in the eastern Mediterranean from both Muslim and Byzantine hands.

Crusades Between 1095 and 1291, Latin Christians heeding the call of the pope launched eight major expeditions and many smaller ones against Muslim armies in an attempt to gain control of and hold Jerusalem.

MAP **9.4** THE MAJOR CRUSADES During the first three Crusades, Christian armies and fleets from western Europe attacked Muslim strongholds and fortresses in the Middle East in an attempt to capture and hold Jerusalem. The Fourth Crusade never arrived in the Middle East, as it was diverted to besiege Constantinople. Based on this map, where were the borders between Christian and Muslim populations?

Pope Urban made a special offer in his famous sermon at Clermont to remit all penance for sin for those who went on the Crusade. Moreover, a penitential pilgrimage to a holy site such as Jerusalem provided a sinner with a pardon for capital crimes such as murder. Urban's offer muddled the long-standing difference between a pilgrim and a crusader. Until this point, a pilgrim was always unarmed, while a crusader carried weapons and was willing not just to defend other pilgrims from attack, but to launch an assault on those he considered heathens. The innovation of the Crusades was to create the idea of armed pilgrims who received special rewards from the Church. The merger of a spiritual calling and military action was strongest in the knightly orders—Templars, Hospitallers, and Teutonic Knights. The men who joined these orders were soldiers who took monastic vows of poverty, chastity, and obedience. But rather than isolating themselves to pray in a monastery, they went forth, sword in hand, to conquer for Christ. These knightly orders exercised considerable political influence in Europe and amassed great wealth.

In the minds of crusader-knights, greed probably jostled with fervent piety. Growing population pressures and the spread of primogeniture (passing landed estates on to the eldest male heir) left younger sons with little to anticipate at home and much to hope for by seeking their fortunes in the Crusades. Nevertheless, crusaders testified to the sense of community they enjoyed by participating in "the common enterprise of all Christians." Fulcher of Chartres recalled the unity displayed by crusaders from so many different countries: "Who has ever heard of speakers of so many languages in one army. . . . If a Breton or a German wished to ask me something, I was utterly without words to reply. But although we were divided by language, we seemed to be like brothers in the love of God and like near neighbors of one mind." The exhilarating experience of brotherhood in the love of God motivated many crusaders.

Different Voices

Christian and Muslim Accounts of the Atrocities Crusaders Committed During the Fall of Jerusalem in 1099

Both Christians and Muslims were convinced that God was on their side during the Crusades. However, leaders on both sides had to find a way to convince people about the justness of their cause and the necessity to take up arms. The problem was to find a way to persuade people to risk their lives and fortunes on behalf of co-religionists and the abstract idea of holy war. One way to do that was to emphasize the atrocities of war. The Christian massacres of Muslims in Jerusalem after the city fell in 1099 became symbolic for both sides. Crusaders also burned Jews alive when they took refuge in their synagogue. Although even the Christian eyewitnesses did not deny the massacres, they indicated different things about God's will to the Christians than to the Muslims and Jews.

Raymond of Aguilers served as chaplain for a crusade and was an eyewitness of the siege and fall of Jerusalem. Abu L-Musaffar Al-Abiwardi was not in Jerusalem but was living in Baghdad at the time. His poem probably reflects the appeals for assistance that the Muslims living in Palestine sent to the caliphs of Baghdad.

A Christian Priest Reports and Interprets the Massacres

> [After the surrender of the walls and towers of Jerusalem] some of our men (and this was more merciful) cut off the heads of their enemies; others shot them with arrows, so that they fell from the towers; others tortured them longer by casting them into the flames. Piles of heads, hands, and feet were to be seen in the streets of the city. It was necessary to pick one's way over the bodies of men and horses. But these were small matters compared to what happened at the Temple of Solomon [the Al-Aqsa Mosque], a place where religious services are ordinarily chanted. What happened there? If I tell the truth, it will exceed your powers of belief. So let it suffice to say this much, at least, that in the Temple and porch of Solomon, men rode in blood up to their knees and bridle reigns. Indeed, it was a just and splendid judgment of God that this place should be filled with the blood of the unbelievers, since it had suffered so long from their blasphemies. The city was filled with corpses and blood. . . .
>
> Now that the city was taken, it was well worth all our previous labors and hardships to see the devotion of the pilgrims at the Holy Sepulcher. How they rejoiced and exulted and sang a new song to the Lord! For their hearts offered prayers of praise to God, victorious and triumphant, which cannot be told in words. A new day, new joy, new and perpetual gladness, the consummation of our labor and devotion, drew forth from all new words and new songs. This day, I say, will be famous in all future ages, for it turned our labors and sorrows into joy and exultation; this day, I say, marks the justification of all Christianity, the humiliation of paganism, and the renewal of our faith.

SOURCE: From *The First Crusade: The Accounts of Eyewitnesses and Participants*, trans. A. C. Krey (Princeton: Princeton University Press, 1921), pp. 257–262.

A Muslim Appeal for Jihad Against the Crusaders

> Sons of Islam, behind you are battles in which heads rolled at your feet.
>
> . . .
>
> Must the foreigners feed on our ignominy, while you trail behind you the
> train of a pleasant life, like men whose world is at peace?
> When blood has been spilt, when sweet girls must for shame hide their lovely
> faces in their hands?
> When the white swords' points are red with blood, and the iron of the brown
> lances is stained with gore!
> At the sound of sword hammering on lance young children's hair turns white.
> This is war, and the man who shuns the whirlpool to save his life shall grind
> his teeth in penitence.
> This is war, and the infidel's word is naked in his hand, ready to be sheathed
> Again in men's necks and skulls.
> This is war, and he who lies in the tomb at Medina [Muhammad] seems to raise his voice
> and cry: "O sons of Hasim! [Muhammad's great-grandfather, the "destroyer of evil"]
> I see my people slow to raise the lance against the enemy: I see the Faith
> resting on feeble pillars.
> For fear of death the Muslims are evading the fire of battle, refusing to believe
> that death will surely strike them." . . .

SOURCE: From E. J. Costello and F. Gabrieli, *Arab Historians of the Crusades*, ed. F. Gabrieli (Berkeley: University of California Press, 1969), p. 12.

For Discussion

1. How does Raymond of Aguilers justify the Christian atrocities on the Temple Mount? How does Abu L-Musaffar Al-Abiwardi appeal to his fellow Muslims?
2. What is more important in these appeals to war, serving God or defending co-religionists?
3. Since the Crusades, appeals for holy war have been a recurrent feature of relations between Muslims and Christians. How would you argue against these ideas of holy war?

Crusading Warfare

The First Crusade (1095–1099) was strikingly successful, but it was as much the result of Muslim weakness as Christian strength. Two factors depleted Arab Muslims' ability to resist the crusaders. First, the Arab states that controlled access to Jerusalem were already weakened from fighting the Seljuk Turks. Second, Muslims were divided internally. Theological divisions between Sunni and Shi'ite Muslims prevented the Muslim caliphs from uniting against the Christians.

In 1099, after a little more than a month's siege, the crusaders scaled the walls of Jerusalem and took possession of the city, which was also holy to Muslims and Jews and largely inhabited by them. (See *Different Voices* in this chapter.) The triumph of the First Crusade led to the establishment of the Latin principalities, which were devoted to maintaining a Western foothold in the Holy Land. The Latin principalities included all of the territory in contemporary Lebanon, Israel, and Palestine.

The subsequent crusades never achieved the success of the first. In 1144 Muslims captured the northernmost Latin principality, the county of Edessa—a warning to Westerners of the fragility of a defensive system that relied on a few scattered fortresses strung along a thin strip of coastline. In response to the loss of Edessa, Christians launched the Second Crusade (1147–1149). This ambitious offensive on several fronts failed in the East where the crusaders gained little ground. In the West, however, it was a great success because northern European crusaders helped the king of Portugal retake

JESUS CHRIST LEADING THE CRUSADERS The rider on the white horse is Jesus, who holds the Gospels in his right hand and the sword of righteousness in his teeth. The crusading knights bearing banners and shields emblazoned with the cross follow him. The figure in the upper left-hand corner represents St. John the Evangelist, whose writings were understood to prophesy the Crusades. This manuscript illumination dates from ca. 1310–1325.

SIDON CRUSADER SEA CASTLE, LEBANON This crusader castle survives on the coast of Lebanon in what was once a Latin Christian principality constructed to defend the Holy Land. The fortified port of Sidon anchored the thin strip of Christian territories along the Mediterranean coast of the Middle East.

Lisbon from the Muslims. In 1187, the sultan of Egypt and Syria, Saladin (1137–1193), recaptured Jerusalem for Islam. In response to this dispiriting loss, the Third Crusade (1189–1192) assembled the most spectacular army of European chivalry ever seen, led by Europe's three most powerful kings: German emperor Frederick Barbarossa, Philip Augustus of France, and Richard the Lion-Heart of England. Yet the Third Crusade's results were far from spectacular: After Frederick drowned wading in a river en route and Philip went home, Richard the Lion-Heart negotiated a truce with Saladin.

In 1199, Pope Innocent III called for the Fourth Crusade with the goal of recapturing Jerusalem. However, the Frankish knights and Venetian fleet diverted to intervene in a disputed imperial succession in Byzantium. Rather than fighting Muslims, Christian knights fought fellow Christians. In 1204 they besieged and captured Constantinople. The Westerners then divided the Byzantine Empire, set up a Latin regime that lasted until 1261, and neglected their oaths to reconquer Jerusalem. The Fourth Crusade dangerously weakened the Byzantine Empire by making it a prize for Western adventurers. None of the subsequent Crusades achieved lasting success in the Middle East. (See *Encounters and Transformations* in this chapter.)

The Significance of the Crusades

Despite the capture of Jerusalem during the First Crusade, the crusaders could not maintain control of the city. For more than two centuries, they wasted enormous efforts on what proved to be a futile enterprise. Neither did any of the Latin principalities in the Middle East survive for more than two centuries. The crusaders who resided in these principalities were obliged to learn how to live and trade with their Muslim neighbors, but few of them learned Arabic or took seriously Muslim learning. The strongest Islamic cultural and intellectual influences on Christian Europe came through Sicily and Spain rather than via returning crusaders.

9.1
9.2
9.3
9.4

Encounters and Transformations

Legends of the Borderlands:

ROLAND AND EL CID

From the eighth to the fifteenth centuries, Muslim and Latin Christian armies grappled with one another in the borderlands between their two civilizations in the Iberian peninsula, the territory now called Spain. The borderlands, however, were more than just places of conflict. During times of peace, Christians and Muslims traded with and even married one another, and in the confused loyalties typical of the times, soldiers and generals from both faiths frequently switched sides. These borderland clashes produced legends of great heroes, which once refashioned into epic poems created a lasting memory of Muslim and Christian animosity.

The Song of Roland, an Old French epic poem that dates from around 1100, tells a story about the Battle of Roncesvalles, which took place in 779. The actual historical battle had been a minor skirmish between Charlemagne's armies and some local inhabitants in Spain who were not Muslims at all, but *The Song of Roland* transformed this sordid episode into a great epic of Christian-Muslim conflict. In the climax of the poem, the Christian hero Roland, seeking renown for his valor, rejected his companion Oliver's advice to blow a horn to alert Charlemagne of a Muslim attack. The battle was hopeless; when the horn was finally sounded it was too late to save Roland or Oliver. Roland's recklessness made him the model of a brave Christian knight.

In the subsequent Spanish border wars, the most renowned soldier was Rodrigo Díaz de Vivar (ca. 1043–1099), known to history as El Cid (from the Arabic word for "lord"). He is remembered in legend as a heroic knight fighting for the Christian Reconquest of the peninsula, but the real story of El Cid was much more self-serving. El Cid repeatedly switched allegiances to the Muslims. Even when a major Muslim invasion from North Africa threatened the very existence of Christian Spain, El Cid did not come to the rescue and instead undertook a private adventure to carve out a kingdom for himself in Muslim Valencia.

THE DEATH OF ROLAND Here the dying Roland holds the horn he failed to blow in time to be rescued. No legend from the borderlands between Christianity and Islam had a greater influence on European Christian society than that of Roland.

Soon after El Cid's death and despite his inconstant loyalty to Castile and Christianity, he was elevated to the status of the great hero of Christian Spain. The popularity of the twelfth-century epic poem, *The Poem of My Cid,* transformed this cruel, vindictive, and utterly self-interested man into a model of Christian virtue and self-sacrificing loyalty.

The medieval borderlands created legends of heroism and epic struggles that often stretched the truth. The borderlands were a wild frontier, not unlike the American frontier, into which desperate men fled to hide or to make opportunities for themselves. However, the lasting significance of the violent encounters that took place in these borderlands was not the nasty realities but the heroic models they produced. Poetry transformed reality into a higher truth that emphasized courage and faithfulness. Because these poems were memorized and recited in the vernacular languages of Old French and Castilian (now Spanish), they became a model of aristocratic values in medieval society and over the centuries a source for a national literary culture. Thus, becoming French or Spanish meant, in some respects, rejecting Islam, which has created a lasting anti-Muslim strain in western European culture.

For Discussion

How did transforming the accounts of battles between Christians and Muslims into heroic poems change how these events would be remembered among Christians?

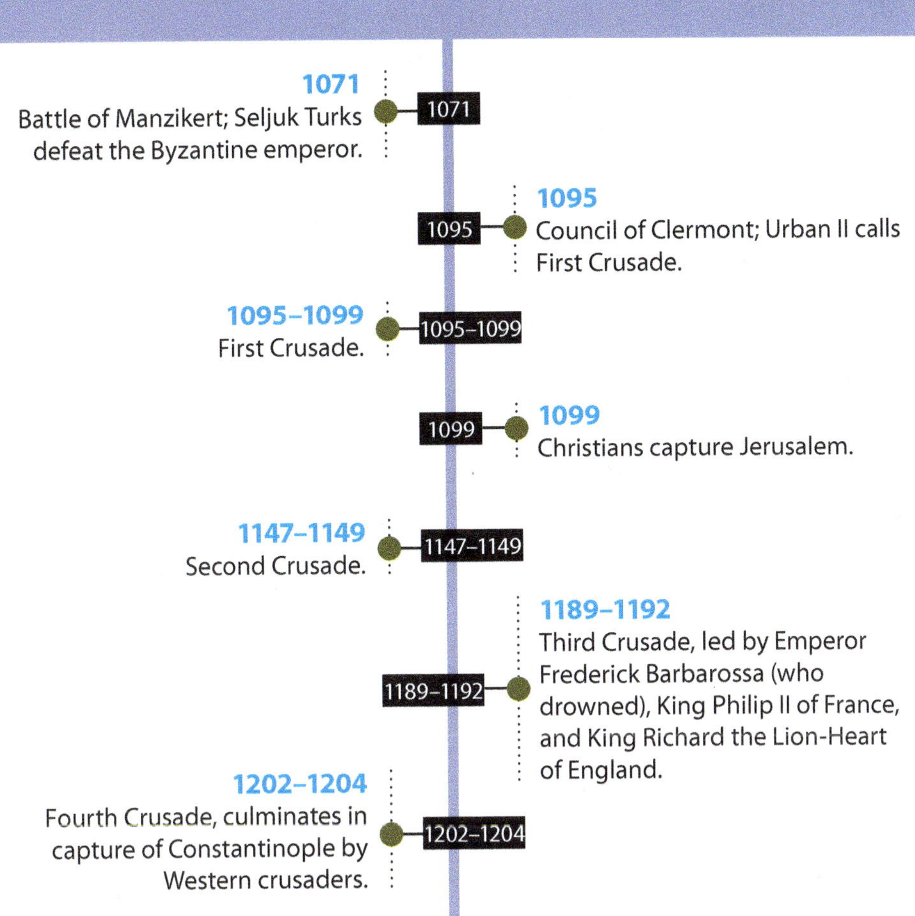

The most important immediate consequence of the Crusades was not the tenuous Western possession of the Holy Land, but the expansion of trade and economic contacts the expeditions facilitated. No one profited more from the Crusades than the Italian cities that provided transportation and supplies to the crusading armies. The Crusades helped transform Genoa, Pisa, and Venice from small ports of regional significance into hubs of international trade. Genoa and Venice established their own colonial outposts in the eastern Mediterranean, and both vied to monopolize the rich commerce of Byzantium. The new trade controlled by these cities included luxury goods such as silk, Persian carpets, medicine, and spices—all expensive, exotic consumer goods found in the bazaars of the Middle East. Profits from this trade helped galvanize the economy of western Europe, leading to an era of exuberant economic growth during the twelfth and thirteenth centuries.

The crusading ideal survived long after Europeans quit going on actual Crusades. When Columbus sailed west in 1492, he imagined he was engaged in a kind of Crusade to spread Christianity. Even as late as the twentieth century, some Latin American countries continued to collect a tax to finance Crusades.

CONCLUSION

An Emerging Unity in the Latin West

The most lasting legacy of the early Middle Ages was the distinction between western and eastern Europe, established by the patterns of conversion to Christianity. Slavs in eastern Europe, such as the Poles, who were converted to Latin Christianity looked to Rome as a source for inspiration and eventually considered themselves part of the West. Those who converted to Orthodox Christianity, such as the Bulgarians and Russians, remained Europeans certainly but came to see themselves as culturally distinct from their Western counterparts. The southern border of Christian Europe was defined by the presence of the Islamic caliphates, which, despite recurrent border wars with Christian kingdoms, greatly contributed to the cultural vitality of the West during this period.

During this same period, however, a tentative unity began to emerge among western European Christians, just as Byzantium fell into decline and Islam divided among competing caliphates. That ephemeral unity was born in the hero worship of Charlemagne and the resurrection of the Roman Empire in the West, symbolized by his coronation in Rome. The collapse of the Carolingian Empire created the basis for the European kingdoms that dominated the political order of Europe for most of the subsequent millennium. These new kingdoms were each quite distinctive, and yet they shared a heritage from ancient Rome and the Carolingians that emphasized the power of the law on the one hand and the intimate relationship between royal and ecclesiastical authority on the other. The most distinguishing mark of western Europe became the practice of Latin Christianity, a distinctive form of Christianity identifiable by the use of the Latin language and the celebration of the church liturgy in Latin.

In the wake of the Carolingian Empire, a system of personal loyalties associated with lordship and vassalage came to dominate the military and political life of Latin Christendom. All medieval kings were obliged to build their monarchies on the social foundations of lordship, which provided cohesion in kingdoms that lacked bureaucracies and sufficient numbers of trained officials. In addition to the lords and vassals, the Latin kingdoms relied on the support of the Church to provide unity and often to provide the services of local government. By the end of the eleventh century, emerging western Europe had recovered sufficiently from the many destructive invaders and had built new political and ecclesiastical institutions that enabled it to assert itself on a broader stage.

MAKING CONNECTIONS

1. Why were the kingdoms of Latin Christendom usually so weak?
2. How did the Carolingian Empire rise above those weaknesses? Why did it eventually fall prey to them?
3. Was military conflict between Christians and Muslims inevitable in the Crusades?

TAKING IT FURTHER

For suggested readings, see page R-1.

On MyHistoryLab

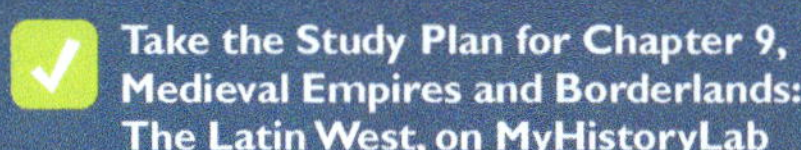

Chapter Review

The Birth of Latin Christendom

9.1 How did Latin Christendom build on Rome's legacy and how did Christianity spread?

Germanic kings acted as administrators in the style of Roman emperors by issuing laws and managing bureaucracy. The merging of Roman and Germanic traditions can also be traced in the law, and in the ability of women to own property, a right more common among the Romans than the Germans. Latin served as the language of worship, learning, and diplomacy. Conversion efforts on behalf of missionaries and intermarriage between Romans and Anglo-Saxons led to Christianity becoming the dominant religion in the kingdoms.

The Carolingians

9.2 How did the Carolingian Empire contribute to establishing a distinctive western European culture?

Charlemagne organized an efficient political administration that strengthened and institutionalized governmental procedures, and he also reorganized church administration into a strict hierarchy. Both new and revitalized monasteries provided the royal court with scribes, advisers, and spiritual assistants, and a revival of interest in ancient Greek and Latin literature marked the age.

Invasions and Recovery in the Latin West

9.3 How did Latin Christianity consolidate itself after the collapse of the Carolingian Empire?

Local warlords assumed responsibilities once invested in royal authorities and provided protection and order in a period of anarchy. Roman ideas of rulership influenced those leaders to expand the power of the monarchy and enhance the idea of kingship. The spread of Christianity to the edges of the continent was a result of organized missionary efforts by monks and bishops.

The West in the East: The Crusades

9.4 What were the causes and consequences of the Crusades?

The threat that Muslim armies allegedly posed to Christian peoples, pilgrims, and holy places in the eastern Mediterranean was the original cause of the Crusades; Pope Urban's appeal for a holy war in the east came as a response to the Byzantine emperor's request for military aid. Despite the successful capture of Jerusalem in the First Crusade, crusaders could neither maintain control of the city nor of the Latin principalities they established in the Middle East. Instead, for more than two centuries they wasted enormous efforts on a futile enterprise.

Chapter Time Line

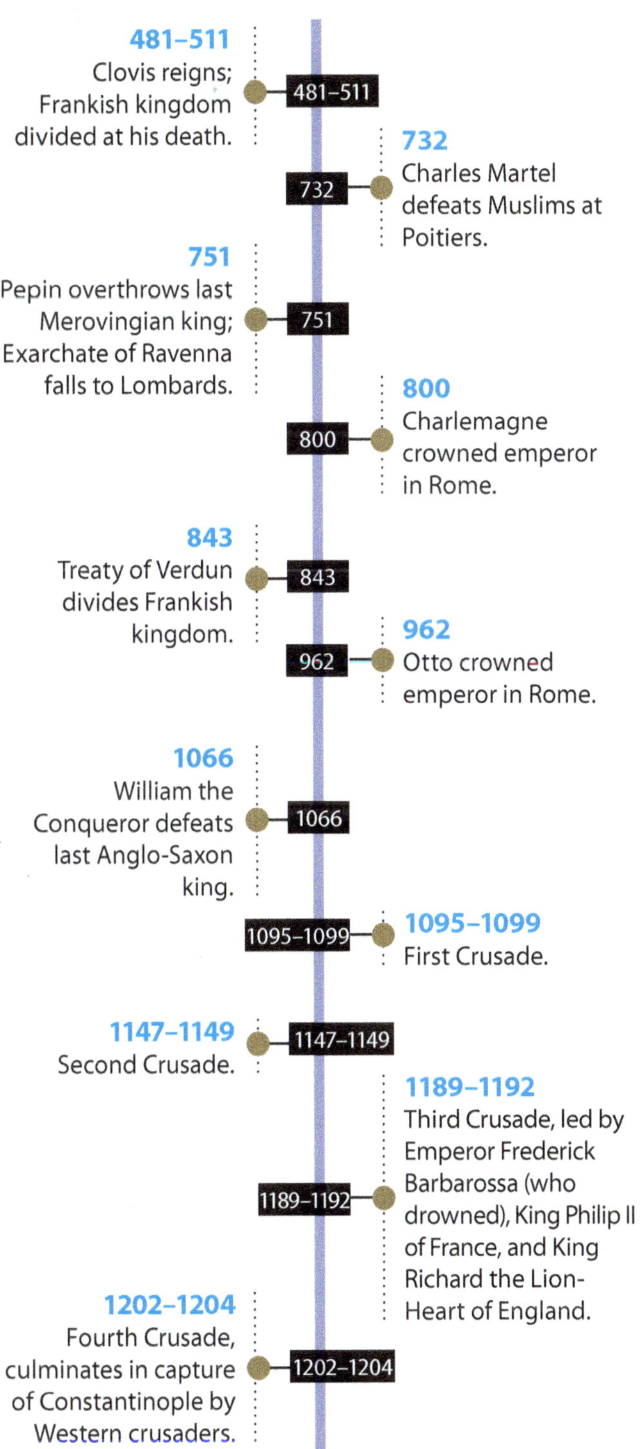

10 Medieval Civilization: The Rise of Western Europe

Francis of Assisi (ca. 1182–1226) was the son of a prosperous merchant in a modest-sized town in central Italy. As a young man of 20, Francis joined the Assisi forces in a war with the nearby town of Perugia. Taken prisoner, he spent nearly a year in captivity. After his release he became seriously ill, the first of many painful illnesses that afflicted him throughout his life. During a journey to join another army, he had the first of his many visions or dreams that led him to give up fighting and to convert to a life of spirituality and service to others. Initially he searched about for what to do. He went on a pilgrimage to Rome as a beggar, and although lepers personally disgusted him he gave them alms and kissed their hands as an act of charity and humility. Then, according to his earliest biographer, while praying in the dilapidated chapel of San Damiano outside the gates of Assisi, he

ST. FRANCIS RENOUNCES HIS WORLDLY GOODS St. Francis stripped off all his clothing in the town square and renounced his worldly possessions, a spiritual act signifying his rejection of the material world. Francis's angry father, the figure in left center, has to be restrained to prevent him from striking his son with his clenched fist. Meanwhile, the bishop covers Francis's nakedness.

LEARNING OBJECTIVES

10.1 How was the medieval western European economy and society organized around manors and cities?

10.2 How did the Catholic Church consolidate its hold over the Latin West?

10.3 How did the western European monarchies strengthen themselves?

10.4 What made western European culture distinctive?

Listen to Chapter 10 on MyHistoryLab

Watch the Video Series on MyHistoryLab

Learn about some key topics related to this chapter with the *MyHistoryLab Video Series: Key Topics in Western Civilization*

received a direct command from the crucifix above the altar: "Go Francis, and repair my house which, as you see, is nearly in ruins."

At first, Francis understood this command literally and began to repair churches and chapels. To raise money he took some of the best cloth from his father's shop and rode off to a nearby town where he sold the cloth and the horse. Angered by the theft of his cloth, his father denounced him to the town's authorities. When Francis refused the summons to court, his father had him brought to the bishop of Assisi for interrogation. Before his father could explain the situation to the bishop, Francis "without a word stripped off his clothing even removing his pants and gave them back to his father." Stark naked, Francis announced that he was switching his obedience from his earthly to his heavenly father. The astonished bishop gave him a cloak to cover his nakedness, but Francis renounced all family ties and worldly goods to live a life of complete poverty. Henceforth, he seemed to understand the command to "repair my house" as a metaphor for the entire Church, which he intended to serve in a new way.

Dressed in rags, Francis went about town begging for food, preaching repentance in the streets, and ministering to outcasts and lepers. Without training as a priest or license as a preacher, Francis at first seemed like a devout eccentric or even a dangerous heretic, but his rigorous imitation of Jesus began to attract like-minded followers. In 1210 Francis and 12 of his ragged brothers showed up in the opulent papal court of Pope Innocent III to request approval for a new religious order. A less discerning man than Innocent would have sent the strange band packing or thrown them in prison as a danger to established society, but Innocent was impressed by Francis's sincerity and his willingness to profess obedience to the pope. Innocent's provisional approval of the Franciscans was a brilliant stroke, in that it gave the papacy a way to manage the widespread enthusiasm for a life of spirituality and purity.

The life of Francis of Assisi and the religious order he founded, the Friars Minor (Lesser Brothers), known as the Franciscans, epitomized the strengths and tensions of medieval Europe. Francis was a product of the newly prosperous towns of Europe, which began to grow at an unprecedented rate after about 1050. In the streets of towns such as Assisi that thrived on profits from the international cloth trade, the extremes of wealth and poverty were always on display. Rich merchants such as Francis's father lived in splendid comfort and financed an urban building boom that had not been seen in the West for more than 1,000 years. The most lasting manifestations of that building boom were the vast new cathedrals, the pride of every medieval city. At the same time wretchedly poor people, many of them immigrants from the overpopulated countryside—starving and homeless—lined the steps into the great churches begging for alms. Francis abhorred the immorality of this contrast between wealth and poverty. His reaction was to reject all forms of wealth, to give away all his possessions, and to disdain money as poison. He and his followers devoted themselves to the poor and abandoned. They became traveling street preachers who relied entirely on the charity of others for food and shelter. Francis's rejection of the material world was not just a protest against the materialist values of his times. It was a total denial of the self. To put it in modern terms, it was a rejection of all forms of egotism and pride, combined with a revolutionary commitment to equality.

The late eleventh through thirteenth centuries were revolutionary in other ways. Based on the efforts of the knights who fought in the Crusades, the European merchants, and the great theologians of the Church, the Catholic West began to assert itself militarily, economically, and intellectually both in Byzantium and against the Muslim world. As a result, western Europeans more sharply distinguished themselves from the Orthodox and Muslim worlds. The West became more exclusively Latin and Catholic.

10.1

10.2

10.3

10.4

Internal developments within Europe made possible this consolidation of a distinctive Western identity and projection of Western power outside Europe. The agricultural revolution that began in the eleventh century stimulated population growth and urbanization. Fed by more productive farms, the expanding cities began to produce industrial goods, such as woolen cloth, that could be sold abroad in exchange for luxury goods from the Middle East and Asia. A number of vigorous kings created political stability in the West by consolidating their authority through financial and judicial bureaucracies. The most effective of these kings used a variety of strategies to force the most dangerous element in society, the landed aristocrats, to serve the royal interest. At the same time, the West experienced a period of creative ferment unequaled since antiquity. The Roman Catholic Church played a central role in encouraging intellectual and artistic activity, but there was also a flourishing literature in the vernacular languages such as French, German, and Italian. All these developments led to this question:

How did western European civilization mature during the eleventh through thirteenth centuries?

Two Worlds: Manors and Cities

10.1 How was the medieval western European economy and society organized around manors and cities?

agricultural revolution Refers to technological innovations that began to appear during the eleventh century, making possible a dramatic growth in population. The agricultural revolution came about through harnessing new sources of power with water and windmills, improving the pulling power of animals with better collars, using heavy plows to better exploit the soils of northern Europe, and employing a three-field crop rotation system that increased the amount and quality of food available.

After the end of the destructive Magyar and Viking invasions of the ninth and tenth centuries, the population of western Europe recovered dramatically. Technological innovations created the **agricultural revolution** that increased the supply of food. With more food available, people were better nourished than they had been in more than 500 years, and the population began to grow. In the seventh century all of Europe was home to only 14 million inhabitants. By 1300 the population had exploded to 74 million. From the seventh to the fourteenth centuries, then, the population grew many times over, perhaps as much as 500 percent.

The Medieval Agricultural Revolution

In the year 1000, the vast majority of people lived in small villages or isolated farmsteads. Peasants literally scratched out a living from a small area of cleared land around the village by employing a light scratch plow that barely turned over the soil. The farms produced mostly grain, which was consumed as bread, porridge, and ale or beer. Vegetables were rare; meat and fish, uncommon. Over the course of the century, the productivity of the land was greatly enhanced by a number of innovations that came into widespread use.

TECHNOLOGICAL INNOVATIONS The invention of new labor-saving devices ushered in the agricultural revolution. Farmers used water and windmills to grind grain, but others gradually adapted them to a wide variety of tasks, including turning saws to mill timber. In addition to these mechanical devices, the power of animals began to be used more efficiently. Metal horseshoes (until then, horses' hooves had been bound in cloth) gave horses better footing and traction. Perhaps even more important was the introduction of a new type of horse and ox collar. Older collars put pressure on the throat, which tended to choke the animal. The new collars transferred the pressure to the shoulders. With enhanced animal pulling power, farmers could plow the damp, heavy clay soils of northern Europe much more efficiently.

The centerpiece of the agricultural revolution was the heavy plow, called the *carruca.* It cut deeply and lifted the soil, aerating it and bringing minerals to the surface that were vital for plant growth. The *carruca*, however, required six or eight horses or oxen to pull it, and no single peasant family in the eleventh century could afford that many draft animals. Farmers had to pool their animals to create plow teams, a practice that required mutual planning and cooperation.

The introduction of the three-field system supplied the final piece in the agricultural revolution. In the three-field system farmers planted one field in the fall with grain and one in the spring with beans, peas, or lentils. The third field lay fallow. They harvested both fall and spring plantings in the summer, after which all the fields shifted. The three-field system produced extraordinary advantages: the amount of land under cultivation increased; beans planted in the spring rotation returned nitrogen to the soil; and the crop rotation combined with animal manure reduced soil exhaustion from excessive grain planting.

The agricultural revolution had a significant effect on society. First, villagers learned to cooperate—by pooling draft animals for plow teams, redesigning and elongating their fields to accommodate the new plow, coordinating the three-field rotation of crops, and timing the harvest schedule. To accomplish these cooperative ventures, they created village councils and developed habits of collective decision making that were essential for stable community life. Second, the system produced not only more food, but better food. Beans and other vegetables grown in the spring planting were rich in proteins.

A HEAVY CARRUCA PLOW At the center of the two-wheeled plow is a sturdy timber from which the coulter projects just in front of the plowshare, which is hidden by the earth. The surplus produced by the agricultural revolution made it possible for aristocrats to build huge and expensive castles such as the one in the background.

MANORS AND PEASANTS The medieval agricultural economy bound landlords and peasants together in a unit of management called the **manor**. The lord of the manor usually owned his own large house or stone castle and served as the presiding judge of the villagers in the manor court. His wife, the *chatelaine* or lady of the manor, was his partner in management, and when the lord was away at war, which was often the case, she ruled the manor.

The peasants who worked the land of manors fell into three categories: serfs, freeholders, and cottagers. Lords did not own **serfs**, who were not slaves, but lords tied their serfs to the manor, which they could not leave. Serfs had certain legal rights denied to slaves, such as the right to a certain portion of what they produced, but the lord's will was law. Freeholders worked as independent farmers, owned their land outright, and did not have to answer to a lord. At the bottom of rural peasant society struggled numerous impoverished cottagers who had no rights to the land and farmed small, less desirable plots, often as squatters.

No matter what their official status, each family worked the land together with all family members performing tasks suitable to their abilities, strength, and age. The rigors of medieval farm labor did not permit a fastidious division of labor between women and men. Women did not usually drive the heavy plow, but they toiled at

Watch the Video

The Big Picture: The World in 1000 C.E.

manor A medieval unit of agricultural management in which a lord managed and served as the presiding judge over peasants who worked the land.

serfs During the Middle Ages, serfs were agricultural laborers who worked and lived on a plot of land granted them by a lord to whom they owed a certain portion of their crops. They could not leave the land, but they had certain legal rights that were denied to slaves.

other physically demanding tasks. During the critical harvest times, women and children worked alongside men from dawn to dusk. Young girls typically worked as gleaners, picking up the stalks and kernels that the male harvesters dropped or left behind, and girls took responsibility for weeding and cleaning the fields. Nearly all women from peasant girls to the household servants of the manor engaged themselves in the tasks of fabricating clothing from spinning thread and yarn, to weaving cloth, to sewing and tailoring.

THE GREAT MIGRATIONS AND THE HUNGER FOR LAND After the eleventh century most peasant families were considerably better off than their ancestors had been before the new technological innovations. Due to the agricultural revolution, nutritional levels improved so that famines decreased, and a "baby boom" led to dramatic population growth.

The effect of the baby boom meant that the amount of land available to farm was insufficient to support the expanding population of the manors. As more and more young people entered the workforce, they either sought opportunities in the cities or searched for land of their own. Both options meant that many young people and whole families had to migrate. The modern phenomenon of mass immigration is hardly new.

Where did all these people go? Migrants seeking to clear new lands for agriculture moved in three directions: Germans into lands of the Slavic tribes to the east, Scandinavians to the far north and the North Atlantic islands, and Christian Spaniards to the south into previously Muslim territories on the Iberian peninsula, slowly creating the outlines of what would become modern Spain. Between 1100 and 1300, these migrants brought as much as 40 percent more land under cultivation in Europe. The vibrant civilization discussed in the rest of this chapter was the direct consequence of the European demographic success.

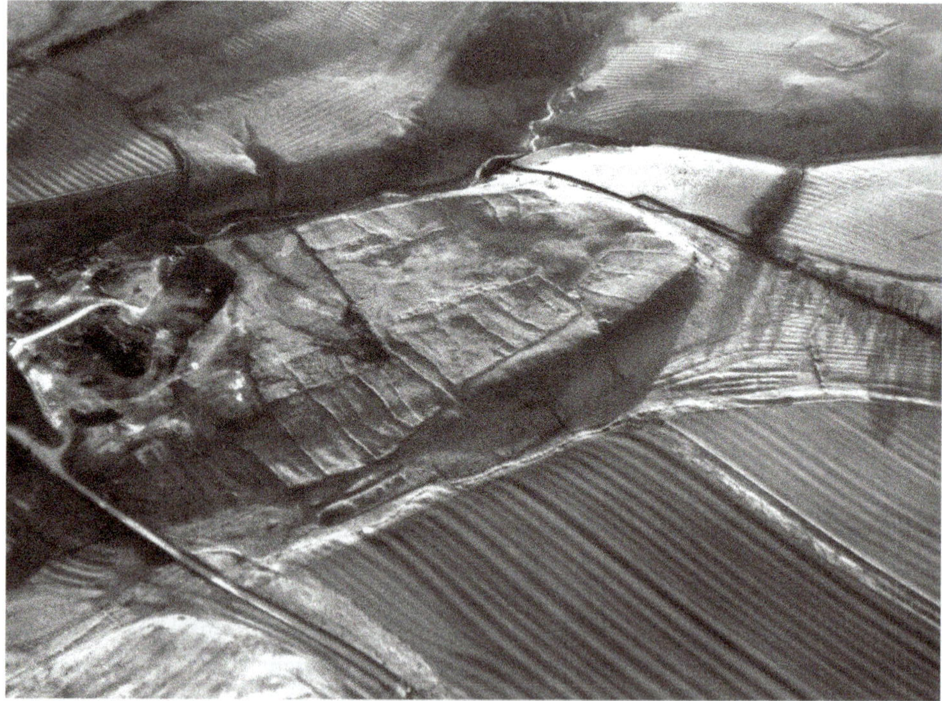

TWELFTH-CENTURY MANOR MADE POSSIBLE BY THE HEAVY PLOW Aerial photograph of the manor of West Whelpington North (England), which was settled in the twelfth century, but whose inhabitants died out during the Black Death of the fourteenth century (see Chapter 11). Outlines of the individual families' farm gardens can be seen in the left center. On the lower right are the ridges and furrows of the elongated fields created by the use of the heavy plow.

The Growth of Cities

All across Europe during the twelfth and thirteenth centuries, cities exploded in size. Exact population figures are difficult to determine, and by our own modern standards most of these cities were modest in size—numbering in the tens of thousands rather than hundreds of thousands—but there is ample evidence of stunning growth. Between 1160 and 1300 Ghent expanded its city walls five times to accommodate all its inhabitants. During the thirteenth century the population of Florence grew by an estimated 640 percent.

THE CHALLENGE OF FREE CITIES The newly thriving cities proved troublesome for the lords, bishops, and kings who had legal authority over them. As the population grew and urban merchants, such as Francis of Assisi's father, became increasingly rich, the cities in which they lived enjoyed even greater resources in people and money than those available to the rural lords. In many places the citizens of the new enlarged towns attempted to rid themselves of their lords to establish self-rule or, at least, substantial autonomy for their city. In the cities of north-central Italy, for example, townsmen formed sworn defensive associations called **communes** (from *communis* meaning "shared"), which quickly became the effective government of the towns. The communes evolved into city-states, which seized control of the surrounding countryside. Perhaps as many as 100 or more cities in north-central Italy formed communes after 1070.

communes Sworn defensive associations of merchants and workers that appeared in north-central Italy after 1070 and that became the effective government of more than a hundred cities. The communes evolved into city-states by seizing control of the surrounding countryside.

The Italian communes created the institutions and culture of self-rule. They were not fully democratic; nevertheless, in many of them a significant percentage of the male population, including artisans, could vote for public officials, hold office themselves, and have a voice in important decisions such as going to war or raising new taxes. They also emphasized the civic responsibilities of citizens to protect the weakest members of the community, to beautify the city with public buildings and monuments, and to defend it by serving in the militia and paying taxes. These cities created vital community institutions, some of which survive to this day. In the wake of the Crusades several north Italian communes, especially Venice, Genoa, and Pisa, became ports of international significance. Sailors from these cities had transported the crusading knights to the Holy Land, Egypt, Syria, and Byzantium. Even after the crusader kingdoms collapsed, these cities kept footholds in the eastern Mediterranean, some of which evolved into colonies. Through these trading cities western Europe became integrated into the international luxury trade, which they carried out with ships crisscrossing the Mediterranean Sea.

THE ECONOMIC BOOM YEARS The cities of the medieval West thrived on an economic base of unprecedented prosperity. What made possible the twelfth- and thirteenth-century economic boom? Four related factors explain the thriving medieval economy. We have already touched on the first two reasons: the agricultural revolution of the eleventh century, which enabled population growth; and the expansion of cities, which both facilitated the commercial boom and allowed city dwellers to be the primary beneficiaries of it.

The other two reasons were just as important: advances in transportation networks and the creation of new business techniques. Trade in grain, woolen cloth, and other bulk goods depended on the use of relatively cheap water transportation for hauling goods. Where there were neither seaports nor navigable rivers, drovers hauled goods cross-country by pack train, a very expensive enterprise. In Europe there were no land transportation routes or pack animals that rivaled the efficiency of the camel in the deserts of North Africa and the steppes of Asia. To address the problem and to facilitate transportation and trade, governments and local lords built new roads and bridges and repaired old Roman roads that had been neglected for 1,000 years.

A MEDIEVAL TOWN Carcassonne in southern France remains one of the best examples of a medieval walled city. Built on Roman foundations, the fortifications date from the eleventh to thirteenth centuries but were completely restored in the nineteenth century. In contrast to unfortified Roman cities, medieval towns required (as shown here) walls, fortified towers, and a moat for protection against bandits and the armies of rival towns and princes. The fortifications symbolized the insecurity of the prosperous towns. Carcassonne was a stronghold of the Cathars and subject to a long siege during the Albigensian Crusade (see the following text). After the defeat of the Cathars the walls were so effectively rebuilt that the city was considered impregnable.

The most lucrative trade was the international commerce in luxury goods. Because these goods were lightweight and high-priced, they could sustain the cost of long-distance transportation across land. Italian merchants virtually monopolized the European luxury trade. Camel caravans transported raw silk from China and Turkestan across Asia. Merchants sold the silk at trading posts on the shores of the Black Sea and in Constantinople to Italian merchants who shipped the goods across the Mediterranean, had the raw silk woven into cloth, and then earned enormous profits selling the shimmering fabrics to the ladies and gentlemen of the European aristocracy. Though small in quantity, the silk trade was of great value to international commerce because silk was so highly prized. One ounce of fine Chinese black silk sold on the London market for as much as a highly skilled mason would earn in a week's labor. Even the bulk commodities the Italians brought from the East were valuable enough to sustain the high transportation costs. Known by the generic term "spices," these included hundreds of exotic items: True spices such as pepper, sugar, cloves, nutmeg, ginger, saffron, mace, and cinnamon enhanced the otherwise bland cuisine; for dyeing cloth, blue came from indigo and red from madder root; for fixing the dyes the Genoese imported alum; and for pain relievers there were medicinal herbs including opiates. The profits from spices generated much of the capital in European financial markets.

Long-distance trade necessitated the creation of new business techniques. For example, the expansion of trade and new markets required a moneyed economy. Coins had almost disappeared in the West for nearly 400 years during the Early Middle Ages, when most people lived self-sufficiently on manors and bartered for what they could not produce for themselves. The few coins that circulated came from Byzantium or the Muslim caliphates. By the thirteenth century, Venice and Florence minted their own gold coins, which became the medium for exchange across much of Europe.

Merchants who engaged in long-distance trade invented the essential business tools of capitalism during this period. They created business partnerships, uniform accounting practices, merchants' courts to enforce contracts and resolve disputes, letters of credit (used like modern bankers' checks), bank deposits and loans, and insurance policies. The Italian cities established primary schools to train merchants' sons to write business letters and keep accounts—a sign of the growing professional character of business. Two centuries earlier an international merchant had been an itinerant peddler who led pack trains over dusty and muddy tracks to customers in small villages and castles. But by the end of the thirteenth century an international merchant could stay at home behind a desk, writing letters to business partners and ship captains and enjoying the profits from his labors in the bustling atmosphere of a thriving city.

At the center of the European market were the Champagne fairs in France, where merchants from northern and southern Europe met every summer to bargain and haggle (see **Map 10.1**). The Italians exchanged their silk and spices for English raw wool, Dutch woolen cloth, German furs and linens, and Spanish leather. From the Champagne fairs, prosperity spread into previously wild parts of Europe. Cities along the German rivers and the Baltic coast thrived through the trade of raw materials such as timber and iron, livestock, salt fish, and hides. The most prominent of the north German towns was Lübeck, which became the center of the Hanseatic League, a loose trade association of cities in Germany and the Baltic coast. Never achieving the level of a unified government, the league nonetheless provided its members mutual security and trading monopolies—which were necessary because of the weakness of the German imperial government.

Urban civilization, one of the major achievements of the Middle Ages, thrived from the commerce of the economic boom. From urban civilization came other achievements. All the cities built large new cathedrals to flaunt their accumulated wealth and to honor God. New educational institutions, especially universities, trained the sons of the urban, commercial elite in the professions. However, the merchants who commanded the urban economy were not necessarily society's heroes. The populace at large viewed them with deep ambivalence, despite the immeasurable ways in which they enriched society. Churchmen worried about the morality of making profits. Church councils condemned usury—the lending of money for interest—even though papal finances depended on it. Theologians promulgated the idea of a "just price," the idea that there should be a fixed price for any particular commodity. The just price was anathema to hardheaded merchants who were committed to the laws of supply and demand. Part of the ambivalence toward trade and merchants came from the inequities created in all market-based economies—the rewards of

MAP **10.1** EUROPEAN FAIRS AND TRADE ROUTES Trade routes crisscrossed the Mediterranean Sea and hugged the Atlantic Ocean, North Sea, and Baltic Sea coastlines. Land routes converged in central France at the Champagne fairs. Other trade routes led to the large market cities in Germany and Flanders. What parts of Europe benefited the most from the economic boom? From this map, what parts were left out?

the market were unevenly distributed, both socially and geographically, as St. Francis's protest demonstrated. The prosperous merchants symbolized disturbing social changes, but they were also the dynamic force that made possible the intellectual and artistic flowering of the High Middle Ages.

The Consolidation of Roman Catholicism

10.2 How did the Catholic Church consolidate its hold over the Latin West?

The late eleventh through thirteenth centuries witnessed one of the greatest periods of religious vitality in the history of Roman Catholicism. Manifest by the Crusades (discussed in Chapter 9), the rise of new religious orders, remarkable intellectual creativity, and the final triumph over the surviving polytheistic tribes of northern and eastern Europe, the religious vitality of the era was due in no small part to the effective leadership of a series of able popes. They gave the Church the benefits of the most advanced, centralized government in Europe.

The Task of Church Reform

As the bishops of the Church accepted many of the administrative responsibilities that in the ancient world had been performed by secular authorities, their spiritual mission sometimes suffered. They became overly involved in the business of the world. In addition, over the centuries wealthy and pious people had made large donations of land to the Church, making many monasteries, in particular, immensely wealthy. Such wealth tempted the less pious to corruption, and the Roman popes were unlikely to eliminate the temptations from which they benefited. Even those popes who wanted to were slow to assemble the administrative machinery necessary to enforce their will across the unruly lands of Roman Catholicism. The impulse for reform derived in many respects from the material success of the Church and the monasteries.

The slow but determined progress of the popes from the eleventh to thirteenth centuries to enforce moral reform is the most remarkable achievement of the medieval papacy. The movement for reform, however, did not begin with the popes. It came out of the monasteries. Monks thought the best way to clean up corruption in the Church was to improve the morals of individuals. If men and women conducted themselves with a sense of moral responsibility, the whole institution of the Church could be purified. Monks and nuns, who set an example for the rest of the Church, provided the model for self-improvement for society at large. The most influential of the reform-minded monasteries was **Cluny** in Burgundy, established in 910. Cluny itself sustained the reform movement through more than 1,500 Cluniac monasteries throughout Europe.

Cluny A monastery founded in Burgundy in 910 that became the center of a far-reaching movement to reform the Church that was sustained in more than 1,500 Cluniac monasteries, modeled after the original in Cluny.

From the very beginning Cluny was exceptional for several reasons. First, its aristocratic founder offered the monastery as a gift to the pope. As a result, the pope directed the activities of the Cluny monastery from Rome and kept it independent from local political pressures, which so often caused corruption. The Rome connection positioned Cluniacs to assist in reforming the papacy itself. Second, the various abbots who headed Cluny over the years closely coordinated reform activities of the various monasteries in the Cluniac system. Some of these abbots were men of exceptional ability and learning who had a European-wide reputation for their moral stature. Third, Cluny regulated the life of monks much more closely than did other monasteries, so the monks there were models of devotion. To the Cluniacs moral purity required complete renunciation of the benefits of the material world and a commitment to spiritual experiences. The elegantly simple liturgy in which the monks themselves sung the text of the mass and other prayers symbolized Cluniac purity. The beauty of the music enhanced the spiritual experience, and its simplicity clarified rather than obscured the meaning of the words. Because of these attractive traits, the Cluniac liturgy spread to the far corners of Europe.

The success of Cluny and other reformed monasteries provided the base from which reform ideas spread beyond the isolated world of monks to the rest of the Church. The first candidates for reform were parish priests and bishops. Called the *secular clergy* (in Latin *saeculum,* meaning "secular") because they lived in the secular world, they differed from the regular clergy (in Latin *regula,* those who followed a "rule") who lived in monasteries apart from the world. The lives of many secular clergy differed little from their lay neighbors. (*Laypeople* or *the laity* referred to all Christians who had not taken religious vows to become a priest, monk, or nun.) In contrast to celibate monks, who were sexually chaste, many priests kept concubines or were married and tried to bequeath church property to their children. In contrast to the Orthodox Church, in which priests were allowed to marry, the Catholic Church had repeatedly forbidden married priests, but the prohibitions had been ineffective until Cluniac reform stressed the ideal of the sexually pure priest. During the eleventh century bishops, church councils, and reformist popes began to insist on a celibate clergy.

The clerical reform movement also tried to eliminate the corrupt practices of simony and lay investiture. **Simony** was the practice of buying and selling church offices. **Lay investiture** took place when aristocrats, kings, or emperors installed churchmen and gave them their symbols of office ("invested" them). Through this practice, powerful lords controlled the clergy and usurped Church property. In exchange for protecting the Church, these laymen conceived of church offices as a form of vassalage and expected to name their own candidates as priests and bishops. The reformers saw as sinful any form of lay authority over the Church—whether the authority was that of the local lord or the emperor himself. As a result of this controversy, the most troublesome issue of the eleventh century became establishing the boundaries between temporal and spiritual authorities.

simony The practice of buying and selling church offices.

lay investiture The practice of nobles, kings, or emperors installing churchmen and giving them the symbols of office.

THE POPE BECOMES A MONARCH Religious reform required unity within the Church. The most important step in building unity was to define what it meant to be a Catholic. In the Middle Ages, Roman Catholicism identified itself in two ways. First, the Church insisted on conformity in rites. Rites consisted of the forms of public worship called the liturgy, which included certain prescribed prayers and chants, usually in Latin. Uniform rites meant that Catholics could hear the Mass celebrated in essentially the same way everywhere from Poland to Portugal, Iceland to Croatia. Conformity of worship created a cultural unity that transcended differences in language and ethnicity. When Catholics from far-flung locales encountered one another, they shared something meaningful to them all because of the uniformity of rites. The second thing that defined a Catholic was obedience to the pope. Ritual uniformity and obedience to the pope were closely interrelated because both the ritual and the pope were Roman. There were many bishops in Christianity, but as one monk put it, "Rome is . . . the head of the world."

Beginning in the late eleventh century the task of the popes became to make this theoretical assertion of obedience real—in short, to make the papacy a religious monarchy. Among the reformers who gathered in Rome was Hildebrand (ca. 1020–1085), one of the most remarkable figures in the history of the Church, a man beloved as saintly by his admirers and considered an ambitious, self-serving megalomaniac by many others. From 1055 to 1073 during the pontificates of some four popes, Hildebrand became the power behind the throne, helping enact wide-ranging reforms that enforced uniformity of worship and establishing the rules for electing new popes by the college of cardinals. In 1073 the cardinals elected Hildebrand himself pope, and he took the name Gregory VII (r. 1073–1085).

Gregory's greatness lay in his leadership over the internal reform of the Church. Every year he held a Church council in Rome where he decreed against simony and married priests. Gregory centralized authority over the Church itself by sending out papal legates, representatives who delivered orders to local bishops. He attempted to free the Church from external influence by asserting the superiority of the pope over all other authorities. Gregory's theory of papal supremacy led him into direct conflict with the German emperor, Henry IV (r. 1056–1106). The issue was lay investiture. During the eighth and ninth centuries weak popes relied on the Carolingian kings and emperors to name suitable candidates for ecclesiastical offices in order to keep them out of the hands of local aristocrats. At stake was not only power and authority, but also the income from the enormous amount of property controlled by the Church, which the emperor was in the best position to protect. During the eleventh century, Gregory VII and other reform-minded popes sought to regain control of this property. Without the ability to name his own candidates as bishops, Gregory recognized that his whole campaign for Church reform would falter. When Pope Gregory tried to negotiate with the emperor over the appointment of the bishop of Milan, Henry resisted and commanded Gregory to resign the papacy in a letter with the notorious salutation, "Henry, King not by usurpation, but by the pious ordination of God to Hildebrand now not Pope but false monk."

Investiture Controversy A dispute that began in 1076 between the popes and the German emperors over the right to invest bishops with their offices. The most famous episode was the conflict between Pope Gregory VII and Emperor Henry IV. The controversy was resolved by the Concordat of Worms in 1122.

excommunication A decree by the pope or a bishop prohibiting a sinner from participating in the sacraments of the Church and forbidding any social contact whatsoever with the surrounding community.

Gregory struck back in an escalating confrontation now known as the **Investiture Controversy**. He deposed Henry from the imperial throne and excommunicated him. **Excommunication** prohibited the sinner from participating in the sacraments and forbade any social contact whatsoever with the surrounding community. People caught talking, writing a letter, or even offering a drink of water to an excommunicated person could themselves be excommunicated. Excommunication was a form of social death, a dire punishment indeed, especially if the excommunicated person was a king. Both sides marshaled arguments from Scripture and history, but the excommunication was effective. Henry's friends started to abandon him, rebellion broke out in Germany, and the most powerful German lords called for a meeting to elect a new emperor. Backed into a corner, Henry plotted a clever counterstroke.

Early in the winter of 1077 Pope Gregory set out to cross the Alps to meet with the German lords. When Gregory reached the Alpine passes, however, he learned that Emperor Henry was on his way to Italy. In fear of what the emperor would do, Gregory retreated to the castle of Canossa, where he expected to be attacked. Henry surprised Gregory, however, by arriving not with an army, but as a supplicant asking the pope to hear his confession. As a priest Gregory could hardly refuse to hear the confession of a penitent sinner, but he nevertheless attempted to humiliate Henry by making him wait for three days, kneeling in the snow outside the castle. Henry's presentation of himself as a penitent sinner posed a dilemma for Gregory. The German lords were waiting for Gregory to appear in his capacity as the chief justice of Christendom to judge Henry, but Henry himself was asking the pope to act in his capacity as priest to grant absolution for sin. The priest in Gregory won out over the judge, and he absolved Henry.

Even after the deaths of Gregory and Henry, the Investiture Controversy continued to poison relations between the popes and emperors until the Concordat of Worms in 1122 resolved the issue in a formal treaty. The emperor retained the right to nominate high churchmen; however, in a concession to the papacy, the emperor lost the ceremonial privileges of investiture that conveyed spiritual authority. Without the ceremony of investiture, no bishop could exercise his office. By refusing to invest unsuitable nominees, the popes had the last word. Gregory VII's vision of papal supremacy over all kings and emperors persevered.

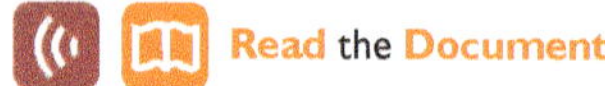

Letter of Pope Gregory VII to the Bishop of Metz, 1081

HOW THE POPES RULED The most lasting accomplishment of the popes during the twelfth and thirteenth centuries derived less from dramatic confrontations with emperors than from the humdrum routine of the law. Beginning with Gregory VII, the papacy became the supreme court of the Catholic world by claiming authority over a vast range of issues. To justify these claims, Gregory and his assistants conducted massive research among old laws and treatises. These were organized into a body of legal texts called canon law.

Canon law came to encompass many kinds of cases, including all those involving the clergy, disputes about church property, and donations to the Church. The law of the Church also touched on many of the most vital concerns of the laity including annulling marriages, legitimating bastards, prosecuting bigamy, protecting widows and orphans, and resolving inheritance disputes. Most of the cases originated in the courts of the bishops, but the bishops' decisions could be appealed to the pope and cardinals sitting together in the papal consistory. The consistory could make exceptions from the letter of the law, called dispensations, giving it considerable power over kings and aristocrats who wanted to marry a cousin, divorce a wife, legitimate a bastard, or annul a will. By the middle of the twelfth century, Rome was awash with legal business. The functions of the canon law courts became so important that those elected popes were no longer monks but trained canon lawyers, men very capable in the ways of the world.

The pope also presided over the **curia**, the administrative bureaucracy of the Church. The cardinals in the curia served as ministers in the papal administration and visited foreign princes and cities as ambassadors or legates. Because large amounts of revenue were flowing into the coffers of the Church, the curia functioned as a bank. Rome became the financial capital of the West.

curia The administrative bureaucracy of the Roman Catholic Church.

In addition to its legal, administrative, and financial authority, the papacy also made use of two powerful spiritual weapons against the disobedient. Any Christian who refused to repent of a sin could be excommunicated, as Emperor Henry IV had been. The second spiritual weapon was the **interdict**, the suspension of the sacraments in a locality or kingdom whose ruler had defied the pope. During an interdict the churches closed their doors, creating panic among the faithful who could not baptize their children or bury their dead. The interdict, which encouraged a public outcry, could be a very effective weapon for undermining the political support of any monarch who ran afoul of the pope.

interdict A papal decree prohibiting the celebration of the sacraments in an entire city or kingdom.

THE PINNACLE OF THE MEDIEVAL PAPACY: POPE INNOCENT III The most capable of the medieval popes was Innocent III (r. 1198–1216). To him, the pope was the overlord of the entire world. He recognized the right of kings to rule over the secular sphere, but he considered it his duty to prevent and punish sin, a duty that gave him wide latitude to meddle in the affairs of kings and princes.

Innocent's first task was to provide the papacy with a strong territorial base of support so that the popes could act with the same freedom as kings and princes. Historians consider Innocent the founder of the Papal State in central Italy, an independent state that lasted until 1870 and survives today in a tiny fragment as Vatican City.

Innocent's second goal was keeping alive the crusading ideal. He called the Fourth Crusade, which went awry when the crusaders attacked Constantinople instead of conquering Jerusalem. He also expanded the definition of crusading by calling for a crusade to eliminate heresy within Christian Europe. Innocent was deeply concerned about the spread of new heresies, which attracted enormous numbers of converts, especially in the growing cities of southern Europe. By crusading against Christian heretics—the Cathars and Waldensians (see the following discussion)—Innocent authorized the use of military methods to enforce uniformity of belief.

The third objective was to assert the authority of the papacy over political affairs. Innocent managed the election of Emperor Frederick II. He also assumed the right to veto imperial elections. He excommunicated King Philip II of France to force him to

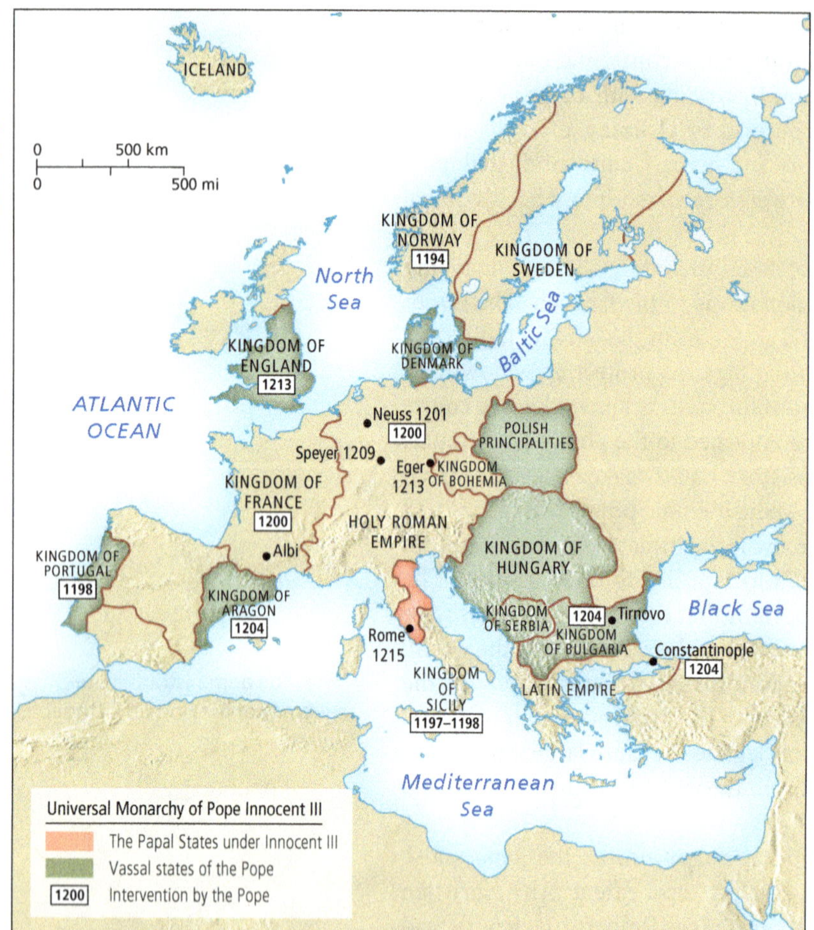

MAP **10.2** UNIVERSAL MONARCHY OF POPE INNOCENT III Besides his direct control of the Papal State in central Italy, Pope Innocent III made vassals of many of the kings of Catholic Europe. These feudal ties provided a legal foundation for his claim to be the highest authority in Christian Europe. Based on this map, what medieval countries were most influenced by the papal monarch?

take back an unwanted wife. And Innocent placed England under the interdict to compel King John to cede his kingdom to the papacy and receive it back as a fief, a transaction that made the king of England the vassal of the pope. Using whatever means necessary, he made papal vassals of the rulers of Aragon, Bulgaria, Denmark, Hungary, Poland, Portugal, and Serbia. Through the use of the feudal law of vassalage, Innocent brought the papacy to its closest approximation of a universal Christian monarchy (see **Map 10.2**).

Innocent's fourth and greatest accomplishment was to codify the rites of the liturgy and to define the dogmas of the faith. This monumental task was the achievement of the Fourth Lateran Council, held in Rome in 1215. This council, attended by more than 400 bishops, 800 abbots, and the ambassadors of the monarchs of Catholic Europe, issued decrees that reinforced the celebration of the sacraments as the centerpiece of Christian life. They included rules to educate the clergy, define their qualifications, and govern elections of bishops. The council condemned heretical beliefs, and it called for yet another Crusade. The council became the guidepost that has since governed many aspects of Catholic practice, especially with regard to the sacraments. It did more than any other council to fulfill the goal of uniformity of rites in Catholicism.

THE TROUBLED LEGACY OF THE PAPAL MONARCHY Innocent was an astute, intelligent man who in single-minded fashion pursued the greater good of the Church as he saw it. No one succeeded better than he in preserving the unity of the Catholic world in an era of chaos. His policies, however, were less successful in the hands of his less able successors. Their blunders undermined the pope's spiritual mission. Innocent's successors went beyond defending the Papal State and embroiled all Italy in a series of bloody civil wars between the Guelfs, who supported the popes, and the Ghibellines, who opposed them. The pope's position as a monarch superior to all others collapsed under the weight of immense folly during the pontificate of Boniface VIII (r. 1294–1303). His claims to absolute authority combined with breathtaking vanity and ineptitude corroded the achievements of Innocent III.

In 1302 Boniface promulgated the most extreme theoretical assertion of papal superiority over lay rulers. The papal bull, *Unam Sanctum*, decreed that "it is absolutely necessary for salvation that every human creature be subject to the Roman pontiff." Behind the statement was a specific dispute with King Philip IV of France (r. 1285–1314), who was attempting to try a French bishop for treason. The larger issue behind the dispute was similar to the Investiture Controversy of the eleventh century, but this time no one paid much attention to the pope. The loss of papal moral authority had taken its toll. In the heat of the confrontation, King Philip accused Pope Boniface of heresy, one of the few sins of which he was not guilty, and sent his agents to arrest the pope. Boniface died shortly after, and the papal monarchy died as well.

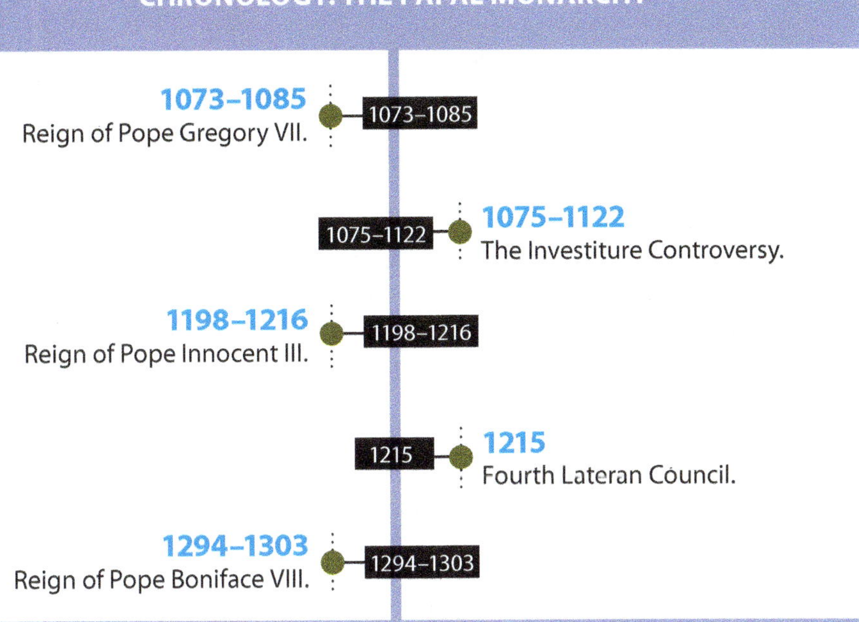

THE RELIGIOUS OUTCASTS: CATHARS AND WALDENSIANS In its efforts to defend the faith, the Church during the first half of the thirteenth century began to authorize bishops and other clerics to conduct inquisitions (formal inquiries) into specific instances of heresy or perceived heresy. The so-called heretics tended to be faithful people who sought personal purity in religion. During the thirteenth and early fourteenth centuries, inquisitions and systematic persecutions targeted the Cathars and Waldensians, who at first had lived peacefully with their Catholic neighbors and shared many of the same beliefs with them.

The name *Cathar* derives from the Greek word for purity. The Cathars were especially strong in northern Italy and southern France. Heavily concentrated around the French town of Albi, the Cathars were also known as Albigensians. They departed from Catholic doctrine, which held that God created the Earth, because they believed that an evil force had created all matter. To purify themselves, an elite few—known as "perfects"—rejected their own bodies as corrupt matter, refused to marry and procreate, and in extreme cases gradually starved themselves. These purified perfects provided a dramatic contrast to the more worldly Catholic clergy. For many, Catharism became a form of protest against the wealth and power of the Church. By the 1150s the Cathars had organized their own churches, performed their own rituals, and even elected their own bishops. Where they became deeply rooted, as in the south of France, they practiced their faith openly until Pope Innocent III authorized a crusade against them.

The Waldensians were the followers of Peter Waldo (d. ca. 1184), a merchant of Lyons, France, who like Francis of Assisi had abandoned all his possessions and taken a vow of poverty. Desiring to imitate the life of Jesus and live in simple purity, the Waldensians preached and translated the Gospels into their own language so that laypeople who did not know Latin could understand them. At first the Waldensians seemed similar to the Franciscans, but because of the Waldensians' failure to obtain licenses to preach as the Franciscans had done, they came to be depicted by Church authorities as heretics. In response, the Waldensians created an alternative church that became widespread in southern France, Rhineland Germany, and northern Italy.

Catholic authorities, who were often the objects of strong criticisms from the Cathars and Waldensians, grew ever more hostile to them. Bishops declared heretics liable to the same legal penalties as those guilty of treason, which authorized the political authorities to proceed against them. In 1208 Pope Innocent III called the Albigensian Crusade, the first of several holy wars launched against heretics in the south of France. The king of France was only too happy to fight the Albigensian Crusade because he saw it as a means of expanding royal power in a region of France where his authority was weak. To eradicate the remaining Cathars and Waldensians, several kings and popes initiated inquisitions. By the middle of the thirteenth century, Catholic authorities had either converted or exterminated the Cathars except for a few isolated pockets in the mountains. Inquisitorial campaigns nearly wiped out the Waldensians, but scattered groups have managed to survive to this day, mostly by retreating to the relative safety of the high Alps and later to the Americas. (See *Justice in History* in this chapter.)

Discovering God in the World

Even before the First Crusade, Catholic Europe began to experience an unprecedented spiritual awakening. The eleventh-century papal campaign to reform the morals of the clergy helped make priests both more respectable and better educated. A better-educated clergy in turn educated the laity more effectively. In large numbers Catholic Christians began to internalize the teachings of the Church. The most devout were drawn to dedicating their lives to religion. In England, for example, the number of monks increased tenfold from the late eleventh century to 1200. The newly expanding cities built loyalty and encouraged peaceable behavior through the veneration of civic patron saints. The most vital indication of spiritual renewal was the success of new religious orders, which satisfied a widespread yearning to discover the hand of God in the world.

THE PATRON SAINTS Saints are holy people whose moral perfection gives them a special relationship with the sacred. Ordinary Christians venerated saints to gain access to supernatural powers, protection, and intercession with God.

The relationship between Christian believers and the saints was profoundly intimate and intertwined with many aspects of life: Parents named their children after saints who became special protectors; every church dedicated itself to a saint; every town and city adopted a patron saint. And even entire peoples cherished a patron saint. For example, the Irish adopted Saint Patrick, who supposedly brought Christianity to the island.

A city gained protection from a patron saint by obtaining the saint's relics: the corpse, skeleton, part of the skeleton, or some object associated with the saint. These relics, verified by miracles, served as contacts between Earth and Heaven. The belief in the miraculous powers of relics created an enormous demand for them in the thriving medieval cities. But because the remains of the martyrs and early saints of the Church were spread across the Middle East and Mediterranean from Jerusalem to Rome, someone first had to discover the saint's relics and then transfer them to new homes in the churches of the growing western and northern European cities. Relics were bought or stolen, and there was ample room for fraud in passing off unauthentic bones to gullible buyers. During the Crusades the supply of relics greatly increased because the knights had access to the tombs of early Christian saints and martyrs.

During the twelfth and thirteenth centuries public veneration of saints began to undergo a subtle shift away from the cults of the local patron saints toward more universal figures such as Jesus and the Virgin Mary. The patron saints had functioned almost like the family deities of antiquity who served the particular needs of individuals and communities, but the papal monarchy encouraged uniformity throughout Catholicism.

Christians had always honored the Virgin Mary, but beginning in the twelfth century her immense popularity provided Catholics with a positive female image that contradicted the traditional misogyny and mistrust associated with Eve. Clerics and monks had long depicted women as deceitful and lustful in luring men to their moral ruin. In contrast, the veneration of the Virgin Mary promoted the image of a loving mother who would intervene with her son on behalf of sinners at the Last Judgment. Theologians still taught that the woman Eve had brought sin into the world, but the woman Mary offered help in escaping the consequences of sin.

The popularity of Mary was evident everywhere. The burgeoning cities of Europe dedicated most of the new cathedrals to her. Mary became a model with whom women could identify, presenting a positive image of femininity. In images of her suckling the Christ child, she became the perfect embodiment of the virtue of charity, the willingness to give without any expectation of reward. In contrast to the early Christian saints who were predominantly martyrs and missionaries, during the twelfth and thirteenth centuries saints exhibited sanctity more through nurturing others, especially by feeding the poor and healing the sick. Women embodied the capacity to nurture, and many more women became saints during this period than during the entire first millennium of Christianity. In 1100 fewer than 10 percent of all the saints were female. By 1300 the percentage had increased to 24 percent. During the fifteenth century about 30 percent were women.

MOSAICS IN THE BASILICA OF ST. MARK IN VENICE Pilgrims learned of Venice's intimate association with its patron, St. Mark, from the magnificent mosaics that adorned the basilica's ceilings and walls. This scene shows a miracle that occurred after St. Mark's body was lost during a fire in the basilica. The leaders of Venice, shown on the left, spent days in prayer. In response, St. Mark opened a door in a column shown at the far right to reveal the place where his body was hidden. In between these two scenes, those who witnessed the miracle turn to one another in amazement. The leaders of Venice derived considerable prestige and political authority from their veneration of St. Mark.

THE NEW RELIGIOUS ORDERS By the eleventh century many men attracted to the religious life found the traditional orders too lax in their discipline and too worldly. In 1098 a small group of Benedictine monks removed themselves to an isolated wasteland to establish the Cistercian Order. The Cistercians practiced a very strict discipline. They ate only enough to stay alive. Each monk possessed only one robe. Unlike other orders, such as the Cluniacs, which required monks to attend frequent and lengthy services, the Cistercians spent more time in private prayer and manual labor. Their churches were bare of all decoration. Under the brilliant leadership of Bernard of Clairvaux (1090–1153), the Cistercians grew rapidly, as many men disillusioned with the sinful and materialistic society around them joined the new order. Bernard's asceticism led him to seek refuge from the affairs of the world, but he was also a religious reformer and activist, engaged with the important issues of his time. He even helped settle a disputed papal election and called for a crusade.

The Cistercians established their new monasteries in isolated, uninhabited places where they cleared forests and worked the land so that they could live in complete isolation from the troubled affairs of the world. Their hard work had an ironic result. By bringing new lands under the plow and by employing the latest technological innovations, such as water mills, many of the Cistercian monasteries produced more than was needed for the monks, and the sale of excess produce made the Cistercians rich. The economic success of the Cistercians helped them expand even more rapidly, especially into places previously untouched by monasticism in northeastern Europe. The rapid Cistercian push beyond the frontiers of Latin Europe helped disseminate the culture of Catholic Christianity through educating the local elites and attracting them to join

THE TWO MARYS: THE MOTHER OF GOD AND THE REPENTANT PROSTITUTE Medieval thinking about women began with the fundamental dichotomy between Eve, the symbol of women as they are, and Mary, the ideal to which all women strived. Eve brought sin and sex into the world through her disobedience to God. Mary, the Virgin Mother, kept her body inviolate. Into the gap between the two natures of women emerged Mary Magdalene, who was considered in the twelfth century to have been a repentant prostitute even though there is no biblical evidence that she was. In contrast to the perpetually virginal ideal of Mary, the mother of Christ, the idea of Magdalene as a prostitute offered the possibility of redemption to all women. In this painting, the Virgin Mary suckles the Christ child in the middle, while Magdalene, shown on the left, makes an offering of her devotion.

the Cistercians. By recruiting lay brothers, known as *converses,* the Cistercians made important connections with the peasants.

More than a century after the foundation of the Cistercians in France, the Spaniard Dominic and the Italian Francis formulated a new kind of religious order composed of mendicant **friars**. From the very beginning the friars wanted to distinguish themselves from monks. As the opening of this chapter indicated, instead of working in a monastery to feed themselves as did the Cistercians, friars ("brothers") wandered from city to city and throughout the countryside begging for alms (*mendicare* means "to beg"; hence, *mendicant friars*). Unlike monks who remained in a cloister, friars tried to help ordinary laypeople with their problems by preaching and administering to the sick and poor.

friars "Brothers" who wandered from city to city and throughout the countryside begging for alms. Unlike monks who remained in a cloister, friars tried to help ordinary laypeople with their problems by preaching and administering to the sick and poor.

The Spaniard Dominic (1170–1221) founded the Dominican Order to convert Muslims and Jews and to combat heresy among Christians against whom he began his preaching mission while traveling through southern France. The ever-perceptive Pope Innocent III recognized Dominic's talents while he was visiting Rome and gave his new order provisional approval. Dominic believed the task of conversion could be achieved through persuasion and argument. To hone the Dominicans' persuasive skills, they created the first multigrade, comprehensive educational system. It connected schools located in individual friaries with more advanced regional schools that offered specialized training in languages, philosophy, and especially theology. Most Dominican friars never studied at a university but enjoyed, nevertheless, a highly sophisticated education that made them exceptionally influential in European intellectual life. Famed for their preaching skills, Dominicans were equally successful in exciting the illiterate masses and debating sophisticated opponents.

The Franciscan Order enjoyed a similar success. Francis of Assisi (1182–1226), whose story opened this chapter, deeply influenced Clare of Assisi (1194–1253), who founded a parallel order for women, the Poor Clares. Like the Franciscans, she and her followers enjoyed the "privilege of perfect poverty," which forbade the ownership of any property even by the community itself.

Both the Dominican and Franciscan Orders spread rapidly. Whereas the successful Cistercians had founded 500 new houses in their first century, the Franciscans established more than 1,400 in their first 100 years. Liberated from the obligation to live in a monastery, the mendicant friars traveled wherever the pope ordered them, making them effective agents of the papal monarchy. They preached crusades. They pacified the poor. They converted heretics and non-Christians through their inspiring preaching revivals. Even more effectively than the Cistercians before them, they established Catholic colonies along the frontiers of the West and beyond. They became missionary scouts looking for opportunities to disseminate Christian culture. In 1254 the Great Khan in Mongolia sponsored a debate on the principal religions of the world. There, many thousands of miles from Catholic Europe, was a Franciscan friar ready to debate the learned men representing Islam, Buddhism, and Confucianism.

THE FLOWERING OF RELIGIOUS SENSIBILITIES During the twelfth and thirteenth centuries, the widespread enthusiasm for religion exalted spiritual creativity. Experimentation pushed Christian piety in new directions, not just for aristocratic men, who dominated the Church hierarchy and the monasteries, but for women and laypeople from all social levels.

Catholic worship concentrated on the celebration of the Eucharist. The **Eucharist**, which was the crucial ritual moment during the Mass, celebrated Jesus's last meal with his apostles. The Eucharistic rite consecrated bread and wine as the body and blood of Christ. After the consecration, the celebrating priest distributed to the congregation the bread, called the host. Drinking from the chalice of wine, however, was a special privilege of the priesthood. More than anything else, belief in the miraculous change from bread to flesh and wine to blood, along with the sacrament of baptism, distinguished Christian believers from others. The Fourth Lateran Council in 1215 obligated all Christians to partake of the Eucharist at least once a year at Easter.

As simple as it was as a ritual observance, belief in the Eucharistic miracle presented a vexing and complex theological problem—why the host still looked, tasted, and smelled like bread rather than flesh, and why the blood in the chalice still seemed to be wine rather than blood. After the Fourth Lateran Council, Catholics solved this problem with the doctrine of **transubstantiation**. The doctrine rested on a distinction between the outward appearances (the "accidents" in theological terms) of the object, which the five senses could perceive, and the substance of an object, which they could not. When the priest spoke the words of consecration during the Mass, the bread and wine changed into the flesh and blood of Christ in substance ("transubstantiated"), but not in outward appearances. Thus, the substance of the Eucharist literally became God's body, but the senses of taste, smell, and sight perceived it as bread and wine.

Veneration of the Eucharist enabled the faithful to identify with Christ because believers considered the consecrated Eucharistic wafer to be Christ himself. By eating the host, they had literally ingested Christ, making his body part of their bodies.

Eucharist Also known as Holy Communion or the Lord's Supper, the Eucharistic rite of the Mass celebrates Jesus's last meal with his apostles when the priest-celebrant consecrates wafers of bread and a chalice of wine as the body and blood of Christ. In the Middle Ages the wafers of bread were distributed for the congregation to eat, but drinking from the chalice was a special privilege of the priesthood. Protestants in the sixteenth century and Catholics in the late twentieth century began to allow the laity to drink from the chalice.

transubstantiation A doctrine promulgated at the Fourth Lateran Council in 1215 that explained by distinguishing between the outward appearances and the inner substance how the Eucharistic bread and wine changed into the body and blood of Christ.

Justice in History

Inquiring into Heresy: THE INQUISITION IN MONTAILLOU

In 1208 Pope Innocent III issued a call for a crusade against the Cathars or Albigensians. Fighting on behalf of French King Philip II, Simon de Montfort decisively defeated the pro-Cathar barons of southern France at Muret in 1213. Catharism retreated to the mountains, where a clandestine network of adherents kept the faith alive. The obliteration of these stubborn remnants required methods more subtle than the blunt instrument of a crusade. It required the techniques of inquisitors adept at interrogation and investigation.

Against the Cathar underground, the inquisition conducted its business through a combination of denunciations, exhaustive interrogations of witnesses and suspects, and confessions. Because its avowed purpose was to root out doctrinal error and to reconcile heretics to the Church, eliciting confessions was the preferred technique. But confessed heretics could not receive absolution until they informed on their friends and associates.

One of the last and most extensively documented inquisition cases against Catharism took place in Montaillou, a village in the Pyrenees Mountains, near the border of modern France and Spain. The Montaillou inquisition began in 1308, a century after the launch of the Albigensian Crusade and long after the heyday of Catharism.

BURNING OF THE HERETICAL BOOKS OF THE CATHARS In this fifteenth-century painting, St. Dominic, the figure with a halo on the left, gives a Catholic book to a Cathar priest dressed in blue. The Cathars attempt to burn the book, which miraculously floats unharmed above the flames.

However, the detailed records of the Montaillou inquisitors provide a revealing glimpse into Catharism and its suppression as well as the procedures of the inquisition. The first to investigate Montaillou was Geoffrey d'Ablis, the inquisitor of Carcassone. In 1308 he had every resident over age 12 seized and imprisoned. After the investigation, the villagers suffered the full range of inquisitorial penalties for their Cathar faith. The inquisitor's court sentenced some to life in prison, others to be burned at the stake. It forced many of those who were allowed to return to Montaillou to wear a yellow cross, the symbol of a heretic, sewn to the outside of their garments.

Unfortunately for these survivors, the most fearsome inquisitor of the age, Jacques Fournier, who was later elected Pope Benedict XII, investigated Montaillou again from 1318 to 1325. Known as an efficient, rigorous opponent of heresy, Fournier forced virtually all the surviving adults in Montaillou to appear before his tribunal. When the scrupulous Fournier took up a case, his inquiries were notoriously lengthy and rigorous. Both witnesses and defendants spoke of his tenacity, skill, and close attention to detail in conducting interrogations. If Fournier and his assistants could not uncover evidence through interrogation and confession, they did not hesitate to employ informers and spies to obtain the necessary information. When Pierre Maury, a shepherd the inquisitors sought for many years, returned to the village for a visit, an old friend received him with caution: "When we saw you again we felt both joy and fear. Joy, because it was a long time since we had seen you. Fear, because I was afraid lest the Inquisition had captured you up there: if they had they would have made you confess everything and come back among us as a spy in order to bring about my capture."[1]

Fournier's success in Montaillou depended on his ability to play local factions against each other by encouraging members of one clan to denounce the members of another. Fournier's persistence even turned family members against one another. The clearest example of this convoluted play of local alliances and animosities, family ties, religious belief, and self-interest is the case of Montaillou's wealthiest family, the Clergues.

Bernard Clergue was the count's local representative, which made him a kind of sheriff; his brother Pierre was the parish priest. Together they represented both the secular and religious arms of the inquisition in Montaillou. In his youth, Pierre had Cathar sympathies, and he allegedly kept a heretical book or calendar in his home. Nevertheless, at some time before 1308, he and Bernard betrayed the local Cathars to the inquisition. In the proceedings that followed, they had the power to either protect or expose their neighbors and family members. When the inquisition summoned one of his relatives, Bernard warned her to "say you fell off the ladder in your house; pretend you

(continued on next page)

(continued from previous page)

have broken bones everywhere. Otherwise it's prison for you."[2] Pierre relentlessly used his influence for his own and his family's benefit. A notorious womanizer, Pierre frightened women into sleeping with him by threatening to denounce them to the inquisition. Those he personally testified against were primarily from other prominent Montaillou families who represented a challenge to the Clergues' power. As one resident bitterly testified, "The priest himself cause[s] many inhabitants of Montaillou to be summoned by the Lord Inquisitor of Carcassone. It is high time the people of the priest's house were thrust as deep in prison as the other inhabitants of Montaillou."[3]

Despite the Clergues' attempted misuse of the inquisitorial investigation for their own purposes, the inquisitor Fournier persevered according to his own standards of evidence. In 1320 he finally had Pierre Clergue arrested as a heretic. The sly priest died in prison.

For Discussion

1. How did the methods of the inquisition help create outcasts from Catholic society? How did these methods help consolidate Catholic identity?
2. The primary function of the inquisition was to investigate what people believed. What do you think the inquisitors thought justice to be?

Taking It Further

Lambert, Malcolm. *The Cathars.* 1998. The best place to investigate the Cathar movement in the full sweep of its troubled history.

Le Roy Ladurie, Emmanuel. *Montaillou: The Promised Land of Error.* Translated by Barbara Bray. 1978. The best-selling and fascinating account of life in a Cathar village based on the records of Fournier's inquisition.

Moore, R. I. *The Formation of a Persecuting Society: Power and Deviance in Western Europe, 950–1250.* 1987. Places the harassment of heretics in the broader context of medieval persecutions.

Eucharistic veneration became enormously popular in the thirteenth century and the climax of dazzling ritual performance. Priests enhanced the effect of the miracle by dramatically elevating the host at the moment of consecration, holding it in upraised hands. Altar screens had special peepholes so that many people could adore the host at the elevation, and the faithful would rush from altar to altar or church to church to witness a succession of host elevations.

Many Christians became attracted to mysticism, the attempt to achieve union of the self with God. To the mystic, complete understanding of the divine was spiritual, not intellectual, an understanding best achieved through *asceticism*, the repudiation of material and bodily comforts. Both men and women became mystics, but women

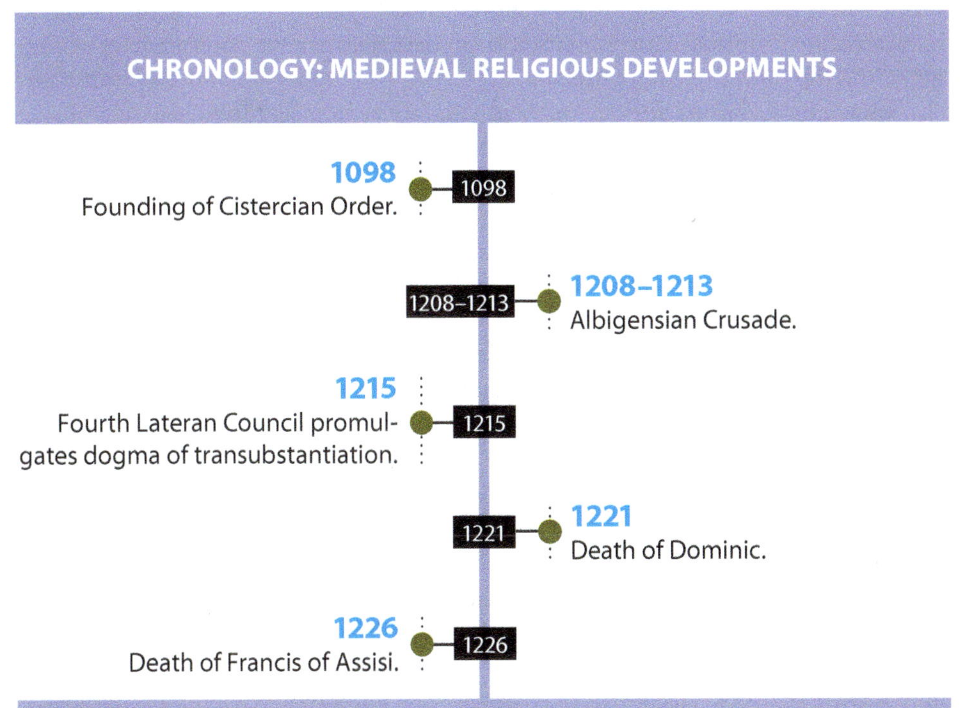

concentrated on the more extreme forms of asceticism. For example, some women allowed themselves to be walled up in dark chambers to achieve perfect seclusion from the world and avoid distractions from their mystical pursuits. Others had themselves whipped, wore painful scratching clothing, starved themselves, or claimed to survive with the Eucharist as their only food. Female mystics, such as Juliana of Norwich (1342 to ca. 1416), envisioned a holy family in which God the Father was almighty, but the Mother was all wisdom. Some female mystics believed that Christ had a female body because he was the perfect nurturer, and they ecstatically contemplated spiritual union with him.

Mystics, however, were exceptional people. Most Christians contented themselves with the sacraments, especially baptism, penance, and the Eucharist; perhaps a pilgrimage to a saint's shrine; and a final attempt at salvation by making a pious gift to the Church on their deathbed.

Strengthening the Center of the West

10.3 How did the western European monarchies strengthen themselves?

During the twelfth and thirteenth centuries, the kingdoms of Catholic western Europe became the supreme political and economic powers in the Christian world, eclipsing Byzantium—an achievement that made them potent rivals to the Islamic states. One reason was stronger political unity. These kingdoms laid the foundations of the modern nation-states, which remain to this day the dominant forms of government around the globe. What happened in France and England during the twelfth and thirteenth centuries, therefore, represents one of the most important and lasting contributions of the West to world history.

The Monarchies of Western Europe

During the High Middle Ages, France and England began to exhibit the fundamental characteristics of unified kingdoms. Stable borders, permanent bureaucracies, sovereignty, and the rule of law were the foundations on which they became the most powerful kingdoms in Europe during the twelfth and thirteenth centuries (see **Map 10.3**).

The kings of France achieved unity through military conquests and shrewd administrative reforms. In the turbulent Middle Ages, dynastic continuity was a key ingredient in building loyalty and avoiding chaos. From Philip I (r. 1060–1108) to Philip IV (r. 1285–1314), France enjoyed not only a succession of extremely effective kings but a consistent policy that guaranteed the borders, built a bureaucracy, expanded the idea of royal sovereignty, and enforced the rule of law. By securing complete military and judicial control of the royal domain, the Ile-de-France, these kings provided the dynasty with a dependable income from the region's abundant farms and the thriving trade of Paris. To administer the domain and lands newly acquired by conquest, the French monarchy introduced new royal officials, the *baillis,* who were paid professionals, some trained in Roman law. Directly responsible to the king, they had full administrative, judicial, and military powers in their districts. The *baillis* laid the foundation for a bureaucracy that centralized French government. Louis IX (r. 1226–1270), who was canonized St. Louis in 1297 for his exemplary piety and justice, introduced a system of judicial appeals that expanded royal justice and investigated the honesty of the *baillis.* Philip IV, the Fair (r. 1285–1314), greatly expanded the king's authority and also managed to bring the Church under his personal control, making the French clergy largely exempt from papal

MAP **10.3** WESTERN EUROPEAN KINGDOMS IN THE LATE TWELFTH CENTURY The kings of England occupied Ireland as well as much of western France. France itself was consolidated around the Ile-de-France, the area around Paris. The kingdoms of Germany, Bohemia, Burgundy, and Italy were ruled by the German emperors. Based on this map, which countries had the potential for the greatest power in the twelfth century?

supervision. To pay for his frequent wars, Philip expelled the Jews after stripping them of their lands and goods and then turned against the rich Order of the Knights Templar, a crusader order that had amassed a fortune as the papal banker and creditor of Philip. He confiscated the Templars' lands and tortured the knights to extort confessions to various crimes in a campaign to discredit them. (See *Different Voices* in this chapter.) Philip was perhaps most effective in finding new ways to increase taxation. Under Philip, royal revenues grew tenfold from what they had been in the saintly reign of Louis IX.

England was even better unified than France. When the Duke of Normandy, William I the Conqueror (r. 1066–1087), seized England in 1066, he claimed the crown and all the land for himself. The new king kept about one-fifth of the land under his personal rule and parceled out the rest to the loyal nobles, monasteries, and churches. This policy ensured that every landholder in England held his property as a fief, directly or indirectly, from the king, a principle of lordship enforced by an oath of loyalty to the crown required of all vassals. About 180 great lords from among the Norman aristocracy held land directly from the king, and hundreds of lesser nobles were vassals of these great lords. William accomplished what other kings only dreamed about: He had truly made himself the lord of all lords. William's hierarchy of nobles transformed the nature of the English monarchy, giving the Norman kings far greater authority over England than any of the earlier Anglo-Saxon kings had enjoyed.

The Battle of Hastings, 1066

Building on the legacy of the conquest, King Henry II (r. 1154–1189) reformed the judiciary. His use of sheriffs to enforce the royal will produced the legends of Robin Hood, the bandit who resisted the nasty sheriff of Nottingham on behalf of the poor. But in reality the sheriffs probably did more good than harm in protecting the weak against the powerful. In attempting to reduce the jurisdiction of the nobles, Henry made it possible for almost anyone to obtain a writ that moved a case to a royal court. Henry introduced a system of itinerant **circuit court** judges who visited every shire

circuit court Established by King Henry II (r. 1154–1189) to make royal justice available to virtually anyone in England. Circuit court judges visited every shire in England four times a year.

in the land four times a year. When this judge arrived, the sheriff assembled a group of men familiar with local affairs to report the major crimes that had been committed since the judge's last visit. These assemblies were the origins of the **grand jury** system, which persists to this day as the means for indicting someone for a crime. To resolve disputes over the possession of land, sheriffs collected a group of 12 local men who testified under oath about the claims of the disputants, and the judge made his decision based on their testimony. These assemblies began **trial by jury**. Judges later extended to criminal cases trial by jury, which remains the basis for rendering legal verdicts in common-law countries, including Britain, the United States, and Canada.

Henry also subjected priests alleged to have committed crimes to the jurisdiction of the royal courts. The king wanted to apply a principle of universal justice to everyone in the realm, a principle fiercely opposed by Thomas Becket, the archbishop of Canterbury. Becket insisted the Church must be free of interference from secular authorities. When four knights—believing they were acting on the king's wishes—murdered Becket before the altar of the Canterbury cathedral, the public was outraged and blocked Henry's plan to subject the Church to royal justice. The Church soon canonized Becket, revered as England's most famous saint.

The royal authority Henry asserted foundered under King John (r. 1199–1216), who lost to King Philip II of France, the duchy of Normandy, which had been one of the foundations of English royal power since William the Conqueror. The barons of England grew tired of John's requests to pay for wars he lost. In 1215 English barons forced John to sign the **Magna Carta** ("great charter," in reference to its size), in which the king pledged to respect the traditional feudal privileges of the nobility, towns, and clergy. Contrary to widespread belief, Magna Carta had nothing to do with asserting the liberty of the common people or guaranteeing universal rights. It addressed only the privileges of a select few rather than the rights of the many. Subsequent kings, however, swore to uphold it, thereby accepting the fundamental principle that even the king must respect the law. After the Magna Carta the lord of all lords became less so. King Edward I (r. 1272–1307) began to call the **English Parliament** (from the French "talking together") in order to raise sums of money for his foreign wars. The English Parliament differed from similar assemblies on the Continent. It usually included representatives of the "commons," which consisted of townsmen and prosperous farmers who lacked titles of nobility, but whom the king summoned because he needed their money. As a result, a broader spectrum of the population joined parliament than in most other medieval kingdoms.

To the east the Holy Roman Empire suffered from the division between its principal component parts in Germany and northern Italy. Germany itself was an ill-defined region, subdivided by deep ethnic diversity and powerful dukes who ruled their lands with a spirit of fierce independence. As a result, emperors could not rule Germany directly, but only by demanding homage from the dukes who became imperial vassals. These feudal bonds were fragile substitutes for the kinds of monarchic institutions that evolved in France and England. The emperor's best asset was the force of his personality and his willingness to engage in a perpetual show of force to prevent rebellion. In northern Italy, the other part of the emperor's dominion, he did not even enjoy these extensive ties of vassalage and could rely only on vague legal rights granted by the imperial title and his ability to keep an army on the scene.

The century between the election of Frederick I (r. 1152–1190), known as Barbarossa or "red-beard," and the death of his grandson Frederick II (r. 1212–1250) represented the great age of the Holy Roman Empire, a period of relative stability preceded and followed by disastrous phases of anarchy and civil war. In the case of both of these emperors, lofty ambitions contrasted with the flimsy base of support and the failure to sustain judicial reforms, which prevented the centralization that took place in France and England. After Frederick II's death, his successors lost their hold on both Italy and Germany.

During the twelfth and thirteenth centuries, Spain and Poland, both of which would later become major European powers, were broken into small, weak principalities.

grand jury In medieval England after the judicial reforms of King Henry II (r. 1154–1189), grand juries were called when the circuit court judge arrived in a shire. The sheriff assembled a group of men familiar with local affairs who constituted the grand jury and who reported to the judge the major crimes that had been committed since the judge's last visit.

trial by jury When disputes about the possession of land arose after the late twelfth century in England, sheriffs assembled a group of 12 local men who testified under oath about the claims of the plaintiffs, and the circuit court judge made his decision on the basis of their testimony. The system was later extended to criminal cases.

Magna Carta In 1215 some English barons forced King John to sign the "great charter," in which the king pledged to respect the traditional feudal privileges of the nobility, towns, and clergy. Subsequent kings swore to uphold it, thereby accepting the fundamental principle that even the king was obliged to respect the law.

English Parliament Assembly usually consisting of representatives of the "commons," which consisted of townsmen and prosperous farmers who lacked titles of nobility, but whom the king summoned because he needed their money.

The Magna Carta

Different Voices

The Trial of the Knights Templar

The Knights Templar had been one of the most successful crusading orders, but after the end of the Crusades, their popularity declined. Nevertheless, they retained extensive properties given to finance their crusading expeditions. Deeply indebted to the Knights and in need of cash to finance his wars against England, King Philip IV of France seized upon rumors about a secret Templar initiation rite to justify arresting the prominent French Templars and confiscating their properties. Some Templars confessed under torture but later reversed themselves. The following documents describe the alleged secret rites of the Templars and summarize the testimony of some of those arrested. This notorious case not only illustrates how a ruthless king financed his kingdom, but how unsubstantiated rumors of homosexual practices could be used to destroy personal reputations and the order itself. The Crown burned many Templars at the stake, dissolved their order, and seized their property.

Royal Order for the Arrests of the Templars (September 14, 1307)

By the testimony of a great number of reliable witnesses, the brothers of the order of Knights Templar have been behaving as though they were wolves under sheep's clothing, and villainously trampling on the religion of our faith under the dress of religion.

They are again crucifying in these days our Lord Jesus Christ, by bringing him wounds more grievous than those he bore on the cross. For on initiation into their order, his image is presented to them, and they deny him three times with wretched and miserable blows, and with horrific cruelty spit three times in his face.

Then taking off their everyday clothes, they line up in the presence of the visitor or deputy who is receiving them for initiation. Next he kisses them; first at the bottom of the spine, secondly on the navel, and finally on the mouth, in accordance with the profane rite of their Order—but for shame on human dignity. Not fearing to break human law, they bind themselves with a vow of initiation to give themselves over, one to another, to that disgusting and terrifying vice of sexual intercourse—when asked and without excuse.

SOURCE: *Chronicles of the Crusades: Eyewitness Accounts of the Wars between Christianity and Islam,* trans. E. Hallam (London: Orion Publishing Co., 1989), p. 286. Reprinted by permission.

Pope Clement V Suppresses the Templars (March 22, 1312)

Many of the Templars accused of participating in the initiation rites, including the prominent knights Geoffrey of Charney and the Grand Master of the Templars James of Molay, denied under oath any homosexual practices among the knights. Nevertheless, Pope Clement V decided to condemn them. But it is evident from the papal bull that they still had supporters among the cardinals who were not convinced of the Templars' guilt.

There were therefore two opinions: some said that sentence should immediately be pronounced, condemning the order for the alleged crimes, and others objected that from the proceedings taken up to now the sentence of condemnation against the order could not justly be passed. After long and mature deliberation, having in mind God alone and the good of the Holy Land, without turning aside to right or to left, we elected to proceed by way of provisions and ordinance; in this way scandal will be removed, perils avoided, and property saved for the help of the Holy Land. We have taken into account the disgrace, suspicion, vociferous reports, and other attacks mentioned above against the order, also the secret reception into the order, and the divergence of many of the brothers from the general behavior, way of life and morals of other Christians. . . . We observe in addition that the above have given rise to grave scandal against the order, scandal impossible to allay as long as the order continues to exist. We note also the danger to faith and to souls, the many horrible misdeeds of so many brothers of the order, and many other just reasons . . .

SOURCE: *Decrees of the Ecumenical Councils,* trans. N.P. Tanner (Washington, D.C.: Georgetown University Press, 1990), Vol. 1, pp. 336-343.

For Discussion

1. Historians now consider the charges against the Templars fabrications. Why would these accusations of denying Christ and homosexual practices rather than others be fabricated to destroy the Templars?
2. In his suppression of the order, Pope Clement is especially concerned about causing scandal. Why might covering up a scandal be more important for the Church than finding out the truth of the allegations?

Medieval Culture: The Search for Understanding

10.4 What made western European culture distinctive?

Medieval intellectuals vastly expanded the range of Western culture. The most important cultural encounters came when thinkers read the books of ancient philosophers and faced challenging ideas that did not fit easily into their view of the world. The greatest medieval thinkers attempted to reconcile the reason of the ancients and the faith of the Christians by creating new philosophical systems. Lawyers began to look back to ancient Roman law for guidance about how to settle disputes, adjudicate crimes, and create governmental institutions. Muslim influences reinvigorated the Christian understanding of the sciences. Themes found in Persian love poetry found their way into the Christian notion of courtly love. Catholic western Europe experienced a cultural flowering through the spread of education, the growing power of Latin learning, and the invention of the university. Distinctively western forms developed in literature, music, drama, and above all the Romanesque and Gothic architecture of Europe's great cathedrals.

Revival of Learning

Some simple statistics reveal the magnitude of the educational revolution in medieval western Europe. In 1050 less than 1 percent of the population of Latin Christian Europe could read, and most of these literate people were priests who knew just enough Latin to recite the offices of the liturgy. Four hundred years later, as much as 40 percent of men living in cities were literate. Europeans embraced learning on a massive scale. How did this come about?

In 1050 only monasteries and cathedral schools provided an education. The curriculum was very basic, usually only reading and writing. Monastic education trained monks to read the books available in their libraries as an aid to contemplating the mysteries of the next world. In contrast, the cathedral schools, which trained members of the ecclesiastical hierarchy, emphasized the practical skills of rational analysis that would help future priests, bishops, and royal advisers solve the problems of this world.

By 1100 the number of cathedral schools had grown significantly and the curriculum expanded to include the study of the ancient Roman masters, Cicero and Virgil, who became models for clear Latin composition. These schools met the demand for trained officials from various sources—the thriving cities, the growing church bureaucracy, and the infant bureaucracies of the western kingdoms.

scholasticism A term referring to a broad philosophical and theological movement that dominated medieval thought and university training. Scholasticism used logic learned from Aristotle to interpret the meaning of the Bible and the writings of the Church Fathers, who created Christian theology in its first centuries.

SCHOLASTICISM: A CHRISTIAN PHILOSOPHY In the cathedral schools, the growing need for training in logic led to the development of scholasticism. **Scholasticism** refers to the use of logic learned from Aristotle to interpret the meaning of the Bible and the writings of the Church Fathers, who formulated Christian theology in its first centuries. The principal method of teaching and learning in the cathedral schools was the lecture. In the classroom the lecturer recited a short passage in Latin, presented the comments of other authorities on it, and drew his own conclusions. He then moved on to another brief passage and repeated the process. In addition to listening to lectures, students engaged in disputations in which they presented oral arguments for or against a particular thesis, a process called dialectical reasoning. The lecturers evaluated student disputants on their ability to investigate through logic the truth of a thesis. Disputations required several skills—verbal facility, a prodigious memory to produce apt citations on the spot, and the ability to think quickly. The process we know today as debate originated with these medieval disputations. Lectures and disputations became the core activities of the scholastics, who considered all subjects, however sacred, as appropriate for reasoned examination.

None of the scholastic teachers was more influential than the acerbic, witty, and daring Peter Abelard (1079–1142). Students from all over Europe flocked to hear Abelard's lectures at the cathedral school of Paris. Abelard's clever criticisms of the ideas of other thinkers delighted students. In *Sic et Non* ("Yes" and "No"), Abelard boldly examined some of the foundations of Christian truth. Employing the dialectical reasoning of a disputation, he presented both sides of 150 theological problems discussed by the Church Fathers. He left the conclusions open in order to challenge his students and readers to think further, but his intention was to point out how apparent disagreements among the experts masked a deeper level of agreement about Christian truth.

UNIVERSITIES: ORGANIZING LEARNING From the cathedral schools arose the first universities. The University of Paris evolved from the cathedral school where Abelard once taught. Initially the universities were little more than guilds (trade associations), organized by either students or teachers to protect their interests. As members of a guild, students bargained with their professors, as would other tradesmen, over costs and established minimum standards of instruction. The guild of the law students at Bologna received a charter in 1158, which probably made it the first university. Some of the early universities were professional schools, such as the medical faculty at Salerno, but true to their origins as cathedral schools, most emphasized theology over other subjects.

The medieval universities formulated the basic educational practices still in place today. They established a curriculum, examined students, conferred degrees, and conducted graduation ceremonies. Students and teachers wore distinctive robes, which are still worn at graduation ceremonies. Teachers were clergymen—that is, they "professed" religion, hence, the title of *professor* for a university instructor. In their first years students pursued the liberal arts curriculum, which consisted of the *trivium* (grammar, rhetoric, and logic) and the *quadrivium* (arithmetic, geometry, astronomy, and music). Arts and sciences faculties and distribution requirements in modern universities are vestiges of the medieval liberal arts curriculum.

Medieval universities did not admit women because the Church barred women from the priesthood and most university students trained to become priests. (Women did not attend universities in significant numbers until the nineteenth century.) The few women who did receive advanced educations relied on a parent or a private tutor, such as Abelard who tutored the young Heloise. But tutoring had its own dangers. The relationship of Abelard and Heloise resulted in a love affair, a pregnancy, and Abelard's castration at the hands of Heloise's relatives.

THE ANCIENTS: RENAISSANCE OF THE TWELFTH CENTURY The scholastics' integration of Greek philosophy with Christian theology represented a key facet of the **Twelfth-Century Renaissance**, a revival of interest in the ancients comparable in importance to the Carolingian Renaissance of the ninth century and the Italian Renaissance of the fifteenth. Between about 1140 and 1260, new Latin translations of the Greek classics arrived from Sicily and Spain, where Christians had close contacts with Muslims and Jews. Muslim philosophers translated into Arabic the Greek philosophical and scientific classics, which were readily available in the Middle East and North Africa. Jewish scholars who knew both languages then translated these Arabic versions into Latin. Later a few Catholic scholars traveled to Byzantium, where they learned enough Greek to make even better translations from the originals.

Twelfth-Century Renaissance
An intellectual revival of interest in ancient Greek philosophy and science and in Roman law in western Europe during the twelfth and early thirteenth centuries. The term also refers to a flowering of vernacular literature and the Romanesque and Gothic styles in architecture.

As they encountered the philosophy of the ancients, Muslim, Jewish, and Christian thinkers faced profoundly disturbing problems. The philosophical methods of reasoning found in Greek works, especially those by Aristotle, were difficult to reconcile with the principles of faith revealed in the Qur'an of Islam and the Hebrew and Christian Bibles. Religious thinkers recognized the superiority of Greek thought and worried that the power of philosophical reasoning undermined religious truth. As men of faith they challenged themselves to demonstrate that philosophy did not, if properly understood, contradict religious teaching. Some of them went even further to employ philosophical reasoning to demonstrate the truth of religion. They always faced opposition within their own religious faiths, however, especially from people who thought philosophical reason was an impediment to religious faith.

View the Image

Illustration from the Properties of Things

The most perceptive Muslim thinker to confront the questions raised by Greek philosophy was Averroës (1126–1198), who rose to become the chief judge of Córdoba and an adviser to the caliph. In *The Incoherence of the Incoherence* (1179–1180), Averroës argued that the aim of philosophy was to explain the true, inner meaning of religious revelations. This inner meaning, however, was not to be disclosed to the unlettered masses, who had to be told only the simple, literal stories and metaphors of Scripture. Although lively and persuasive, Averroës's defense of philosophy failed to stimulate additional philosophical speculation within Islam. Once far superior to that of the Latin Christian world, Islamic philosophy and science declined as Muslim thinkers turned to mysticism and rote learning over rational debate. In fact, Averroës received a more sympathetic hearing among Jews and Catholics than among Muslims.

Within Judaism, Moses Maimonides (1135–1204)—a contemporary of Averroës, also from Córdoba—was the most prominent thinker. His most important work in religious philosophy, *The Guide for the Perplexed* (ca. 1191), synthesized Greek philosophy, science, and Judaism. Widely read in Arabic, Hebrew, and Latin versions, the book stimulated both Jewish and Christian philosophy.

Thomism A branch of medieval philosophy associated with the work of the Dominican thinker, Thomas Aquinas (1225–1274), who wrote encyclopedic summaries of human knowledge that confirmed Christian faith.

For medieval Catholic philosophers, one of the most difficult tasks was reconciling the biblical account of the divine creation with Aristotle's teaching that the universe was eternal. Even in this early clash between science and religion, creationism was the sticking point. Thomas Aquinas (1225–1274), whose philosophy is called **Thomism**, most effectively resolved the apparent conflict between faith and philosophy. A Dominican friar, Aquinas spent most of his career developing a school system for the Dominicans in Italy, but he also spent two short periods teaching at the University of Paris. Aquinas avoided distracting controversies and academic disputes to concentrate on his two great summaries of human knowledge—the *Summary of the Catholic Faith Against the Gentiles* (1261) and the *Summary of Theology* (1265–1274). In both of these massive scholastic works, reason fully confirmed Christian faith. Encyclopedias of knowledge, both books rigorously examined whole fields through dialectical reasoning.

Building on the works of Averroës, Aquinas solved the problem of reconciling philosophy and religion by drawing a distinction between *natural truth* and *revealed truth*. For Aquinas, natural truth meant the kinds of things anyone can know through the operation of human reason. Revealed truth referred to the things that one can know only through revelation, such as the doctrines of the Trinity and the incarnation of Christ. Aquinas argued that these two kinds of truths could not possibly contradict one another because both came from God. Apparent contradictions could be accommodated by an understanding of a higher truth. On the issue of Creation, for example, Aquinas argued that Aristotle's understanding of the eternal universe was inferior to the higher revealed truth of the Bible that God created the universe in seven days.

The most influential of the scholastic thinkers, Aquinas asserted that to achieve religious truth one should start with faith and then use reason to reach conclusions. He was the first to understand theology systematically in this way, and in doing so he raised a storm of opposition among Christians threatened by the difficulty of philosophical thinking. The theological faculties in universities at first prohibited Aquinas's writings. Nevertheless, his method remains crucial for Catholic theology to this day.

Just as scholastic theologians looked to ancient Greek philosophy as a guide to reason, jurists revived ancient Roman law, especially at the universities of Bologna and Pavia in Italy. In the law faculties, students learned the legal work of Emperor Justinian—the text of the *Corpus Juris Civilis*, together with the commentaries on it. The systematic approach of Roman law provided a way to make the legal system less arbitrary for judges, lawyers, bureaucrats, and advisers to kings and popes. Laws had long consisted of a contradictory mess of municipal regulations, Germanic customs, and feudal precepts. Under Roman law, judges had to justify their verdicts according to prescribed standards of evidence and procedure. The revival of Roman law in the twelfth century made possible the legal system that still guides most of continental Europe.

Courtly Love

In addition to the developments in philosophy, theology, and the law, the Twelfth-Century Renaissance included a remarkable literary output of romances in the vernacular languages, the tongues spoken in everyday life. Poets called **troubadours** wrote romances—poems of love, meant to be sung to music—which reflected an entirely new sensibility about the relationships between men and women. Their literary movement is called **courtly love** or chivalry. The troubadours composed their poems in Provençal, one of the languages of southern France, and the princely courts of southern France provided the first audience. These graciously elegant poems show influences from Arabic love poetry and from Muslim mystical literature in which the soul, depicted as feminine, seeks her masculine God/lover. The troubadours secularized this theme of religious union by portraying the ennobling possibilities of the love between a woman and a man. In so doing, they popularized the idea of romantic love, one of the most powerful concepts in all of Western history, an ideal that still dominates popular culture to this day.

troubadours Poets from the late twelfth and thirteenth centuries who wrote love poems, meant to be sung to music, which reflected a new sensibility, called courtly love, about the ennobling possibilities of the love between a man and a woman.

courtly love An ethic first found in the poems of the late twelfth- and thirteenth-century troubadours that portrayed the ennobling possibilities of the love between a man and a woman. Courtly love formed the basis for the modern idea of romantic love.

The ideal male depicted in courtly love poems was the knight-errant, a warrior who roamed in search of adventure. He was poor and free of ties to home and family, a man who lived a life of perfect freedom, but whose virtue led him to do the right thing. Knights took vows in the name of ladies, revealing that the courtly love ideal included a heavy dose of erotic desire. Besides self-denial, the most persistent chivalric fantasy was the motif of the young hero who liberates a virgin, either from a dragon or from a rioting mob of peasants.

The courtly love poems of the troubadours idealized women. The male troubadours, such as Chrétien de Troyes (1135–1183), placed women on a pedestal and treated men as the "love vassals" of beloved women to whom they owed loyalty and service. Female troubadours, such as Marie de France (dates unknown), did not place women on a pedestal but idealized emotionally honest and open relationships between lovers. From southern France, courtly love spread to Germany and elsewhere throughout Europe.

View the Closer Look The Joys and Pains of the Medieval Joust

THE MEDIEVAL JOUST This scene from a manuscript from ca. 1300–1340 idealizes the medieval joust, which served to keep the warring skills of noblemen sharp and provide popular entertainment.

The Center of Medieval Culture: The Great Cathedrals

When tourists visit European cities today, they usually want to see the cathedrals. Mostly built between 1050 and 1300, these imposing structures symbolize the soaring ambitions and imaginations of their largely unknown builders. During the great medieval building boom, cities built hundreds of new cathedrals and thousands of other churches, sparing no expense and reflecting the latest experimental techniques in architectural engineering and

ROMANESQUE ARCHITECTURE The rounded arches, the massive columns, the barrel vaults in the ceilings, and the small windows were characteristic of the Romanesque style. Compare the darkness of this interior of a Romanesque monastery in Tuscany, Italy, with the Gothic style of the Abbey Church of St. Denis, France, in the next illustration.

GOTHIC VAULTS The delicately ribbed ceiling vaults and vast expanses of stained glass in the Abbey Church of St. Denis, France, brings light into the church, in contrast with the obscurity of the Romanesque monastery in the previous illustration.

artistic fashion. These buildings became multimedia centers for the arts—incorporating architecture, sculpture, stained glass, and painting and providing a setting for the performance of music and drama. The medieval cathedrals took decades, sometimes centuries, to build at great cost and sacrifice.

Romanesque A style in architecture that spread throughout western Europe during the eleventh and the first half of the twelfth centuries and was characterized by arched stone roofs supported by rounded arches, massive stone pillars, and thick walls.

The **Romanesque** style of cathedral-building spread throughout western Europe during the eleventh century and the first half of the twelfth century because the master masons who understood sophisticated stone construction techniques traveled from one building site to another, bringing with them a uniform style. The principal innovation of the Romanesque was the arched stone roofs, which were more aesthetically pleasing and less vulnerable to fire than the flat roofs they replaced. The rounded arches of these stone roofs, called *barrel vaults*, looked like the inside of a barrel. Romanesque churches employed transepts, which fashioned the church into the shape of a cross if viewed from above, the vantage point of God. The high stone vaults of Romanesque churches and cathedrals required the support of massive stone pillars and thick walls. As a result, windows were small slits that imitated the slit windows of castles.

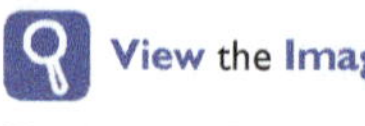

The Leaning Tower of Pisa

The religious experience of worshiping in a Romanesque cathedral had an intimate, almost familiar quality to it. In such a building, God became a fellow townsman, an associate in the grand new project of making cities habitable and comfortable.

During the late twelfth and thirteenth centuries, the **Gothic** style replaced the Romanesque. The innovation of this style was the ribbed vault and pointed arches, which superseded the barrel vault of the Romanesque. These narrow pointed arches drew the viewer's eye upward toward God and gave the building the appearance of weightlessness that symbolized the Christian's uplifting reach for heaven. The neighborly solidity of the Romanesque style disappeared for a mystical appreciation of God's utter otherness, the supreme divinity far above mortal men and women. The Gothic style also introduced the innovation of the flying buttress, an arched construction on the outside of the walls that redistributed the weight of the roof. This innovation allowed for thin walls pierced by windows much bigger than possible with Romanesque construction techniques.

Gothic A style in architecture in western Europe from the late twelfth and thirteenth centuries, characterized by ribbed vaults and pointed arches, which drew the eyes of worshipers upward toward God. Flying buttresses, which redistributed the weight of the roof, made possible thin walls pierced by large expanses of stained glass.

The result was stunning. The stonework of a Gothic cathedral became a skeleton to support massive expanses of stained glass, transforming the interior spaces into a mystical haven from the outside world. At different times of the day, the multicolored windows converted sunlight into an ever-changing light show that offered sparkling hints of the secret truths of God's creation. The light that passed through these windows symbolized the light of God. The windows themselves contained scenes that were an encyclopedia of medieval knowledge and lore. In addition to Bible stories and the lives of saints, these windows depicted common people at their trades, animals, plants, and natural wonders. Stained-glass windows celebrated not only the promise of salvation, but all the wonders of God's creation. They drew worshipers out of the busy cities in which they lived and worked toward the perfect realm of the divine.

View the **Image**

Mont Saint Michel at Night

In France, Germany, Italy, Spain, and England, cities made enormous financial sacrifices to construct new Gothic cathedrals during the economic boom years of the thirteenth century. Because costs were so high, many cathedrals, such as the one in Siena, Italy, remained unfinished, but even the incomplete ones became vital symbols of local identity.

Watch the **Video**

The Big Picture: The World in 1200 C.E.

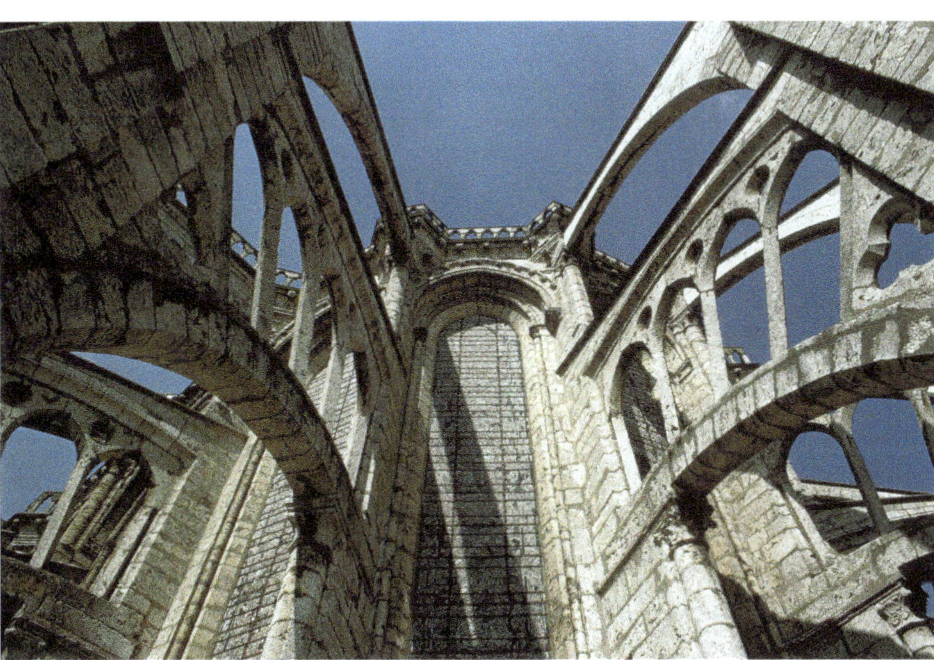

FLYING BUTTRESSES OF CHARTRES CATHEDRAL The flying buttress did more than hold up the thin walls of Gothic cathedrals. The buttress created an almost lacelike appearance on the outside of the building, magnifying the sense of mystery evoked by the style.

CONCLUSION

Asserting Western Culture

During the twelfth and thirteenth centuries, western Europe matured into its own self-confident identity. Less a semi-barbarian backwater than it had been even in the time of Charlemagne, western Europe cultivated modes of thought that revealed an almost limitless capacity for creative renewal and critical self-examination. That capacity, first evident during the Twelfth-Century Renaissance, especially in scholasticism, is what has most distinguished the West ever since. These critical methods repeatedly caused alarm among some believers. However, this tendency to question basic assumptions is among the greatest achievements of Western civilization. The western European university system, which was based on teaching methods of critical inquiry, differed from the educational institutions in other cultures, such as Byzantium or Islam, that were devoted to passing on received knowledge. This distinctive critical spirit connects the cultures of the ancient, medieval, and modern West.

MAKING CONNECTIONS

1. What was the role of theology and philosophy in allowing the West to assert itself more forcefully?
2. Why was kingship the most effective form of political organization in the Middle Ages?
3. By the end of the thirteenth century, what distinguished Christian from Muslim culture?

TAKING IT FURTHER

For suggested readings, websites, and films, see page R-1.

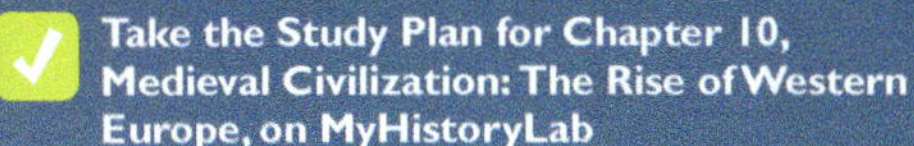

Chapter Review

Two Worlds: Manors and Cities

10.1 How was the medieval western European economy and society organized around manors and cities?

The medieval agricultural economy bound landlords and peasants together in a unit of management called the manor, a system where the lord of the manor presided over the villagers, including serfs, freeholders, and cottagers. The population growth that was a result of the agricultural revolution and its food surplus led to migrations to urban centers; at the same time, new transportation networks spurred the creation of business techniques that supported trade, including a moneyed economy. The population explosion in cities supported this commercial boom.

The Consolidation of Roman Catholicism

10.2 How did the Catholic Church consolidate its hold over the Latin West?

A movement toward reform against worldly pursuits required unity within the Church, which included building a Catholic identity based on conformity of religious rites and obedience to the pope. Monastic orders flourished as Catholic Christians internalized the teachings of the Church and devoted their lives to religion. The economic success of the monasteries encouraged expansion, as well as new traveling orders, which facilitated the spread of Catholic Christianity into the far corners of the Latin West.

Strengthening the Center of the West

10.3 How did the western European monarchies strengthen themselves?

During the High Middle Ages, France and England began to exhibit the fundamental characteristics of unified kingdoms when extremely effective kings instituted reforms to stabilize borders, build permanent bureaucracies, expand the concept of sovereignty, and enforce the rule of law.

Medieval Culture: The Search for Understanding

10.4 What made western European culture distinctive?

The invention of the medieval university established educational practices still in place today, and the integration of the ancient reason and Christian faith created new philosophical systems. Ancient Roman law provided guidance about how to settle disputes and create governmental institutions, while Muslim influences reinvigorated the Christian understanding of the sciences. Distinctively Western forms developed in literature, music, drama, and in the architecture of Europe's great cathedrals.

Chapter Time Line

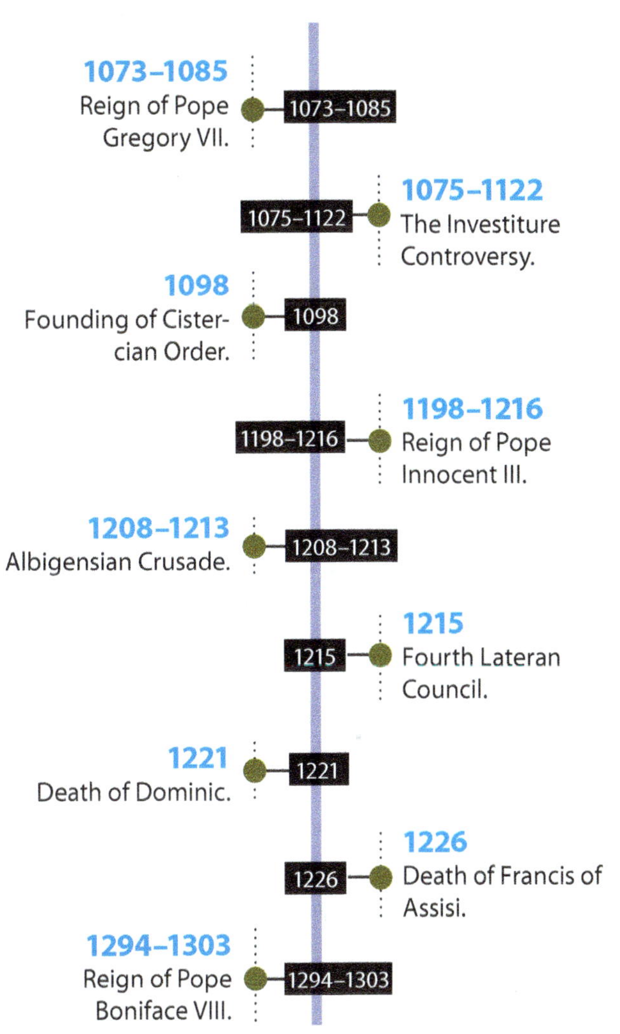

11

The Medieval West in Crisis

THE OTTOMAN SULTAN In 1478 the Venetian painter, Gentile Bellini, went to Constantinople to paint the portrait of Sultan Mehmet II, who had conquered the Byzantine Empire. Hence, encounters between Christian Europe and the Turks became one of the most important themes in the history of the West. Although Islam prohibited the depiction of the human image, the Sultan apparently did not object to a Christian painting his portrait.

The fourteenth century dawned with a chill. In 1303 and then again during 1306–1307, the Baltic Sea froze over. No one had ever heard of that happening before, and the freezing cold foretold worse disasters. The cold weather spread beyond its normal winter season, arriving earlier in the autumn and staying later into the summer. Then it started to rain and did not let up. The Caspian Sea began to rise, flooding villages along its shores. In the summer of 1314 all across Europe, crops rotted in sodden fields. The meager harvest came late, precipitating a surge in prices for farm produce and forcing King Edward II of England to impose price controls. But capping prices did not grow more food.

In 1315 the situation got worse. In England during that year, the price of wheat rose 800 percent.

LEARNING OBJECTIVES

11.1 What caused the deaths of so many Europeans?

11.2 How did forces outside Europe, in particular the Mongol and Ottoman Empires, influence conditions in the West?

11.3 How did disturbances in the rudimentary global economy of the Middle Ages precipitate almost complete financial collapse and widespread social discontent in Europe?

11.4 How did incessant warfare transform the most powerful medieval states?

11.5 Why did the Church fail to provide leadership and spiritual guidance during these difficult times?

11.6 How did European culture offer explanations and solace for the otherwise inexplicable calamities of the times?

Listen to Chapter 11 on MyHistoryLab

Watch the Video Series on MyHistoryLab

Learn about some key topics related to this chapter with the *MyHistoryLab Video Series: Key Topics in Western Civilization*

Preachers compared the ceaseless rains to the great flood in the Bible, and floods did come, overwhelming dikes in the Netherlands and England, washing away entire towns in Germany, turning fields into lakes in France. Everywhere crops failed.

Things got much worse. Torrential rains fell again in 1316, and for the third straight year the crops failed, creating the most severe famine in recorded European history. The effects were most dramatic in the far north. In Scandinavia agriculture almost disappeared, in Iceland peasants abandoned farming and turned to fishing and herding sheep, and in Greenland the European settlers began to die out. Already malnourished, the people of Europe became susceptible to disease and famine. Desperate people resorted to desperate options. They ate cats, rats, insects, reptiles, animal dung, and tree leaves. Stories spread that some ate their own children. In Poland the starving were said to cut down criminals from the gallows for food.

By the 1340s, nearly all of Europe west of Poland was gripped by a seemingly endless cycle of disease and famine. Then came the deadliest epidemic in European history, the Black Death, which killed at least one-third of the total population. The economy collapsed. Trade disappeared. Industry shriveled. Hopeless peasants and urban workers revolted against their masters, demanding relief for their families. Neither state nor Church could provide it. The two great medieval kingdoms of France and England became locked in a struggle that depleted royal treasuries and wasted the aristocracy in a series of clashes that historians call the Hundred Years' War. The popes left the dangerous streets of Rome for Avignon, France, where they were obliged to extort money to survive. After the pope returned to Rome, a group of French cardinals refused to go and elected a second pope, leading to the Great Schism when Europe was divided by allegiances to two different popes.

During the twelfth and thirteenth centuries the West had asserted itself against Islam through the Crusades and spread Catholic Christianity to the far corners of Europe. During the fourteenth and early fifteenth centuries, however, the West drew into itself due to war, epidemics, and conflicts with the Mongol and Ottoman Empires. As an additional shock, the Byzantine Empire, once the bastion of Orthodox Christianity, fell to the Muslim armies of the Ottomans. This chapter explores these encounters with death and turmoil, and asks this question:

How did the death and turmoil of fourteenth- and fifteenth-century Europe transform the identity of the West?

A Time of Death

11.1 What caused the deaths of so many Europeans?

The magnitude of Europe's demographic crisis is evident from the raw numbers. In 1300 the population of Europe was about 74 million—roughly 15 percent of its current population and about double the population of California today. Population size can be an elementary measure of the success of an economy to keep people alive; by this measure, Europe had been very successful up to about 1300. It had approximately doubled its population over the previous 300 years. After the 1340s, however, Europe's ability to sustain its population evaporated. Population fell to just

52 million. The demographic crisis of the fourteenth century was the greatest natural disaster in Western civilization since the epidemics of antiquity. How did it happen?

Famine

Widespread famine, caused by a crisis in agricultural production, began during the decade of 1310–1320. The agricultural revolution of the eleventh century had made available more food and more nutritious food, triggering the growth of the population during the Middle Ages. During the twelfth and thirteenth centuries, vast tracks of virgin forests were cleared for farming, especially in eastern Europe. After all the good bottomland was cleared, farmers moved to clear the more marginal land on hills and mountainsides. These clearings created soil erosion that contributed to the devastating floods of the 1310s. Thus, human actions facilitated the ecological catastrophe. By the fourteenth century no more virgin land was available for clearing, which meant that a still-growing population tried to survive on a fixed amount of farming land. Because of the limitations of medieval agriculture, the ability of farmers to produce food could not keep up with unchecked population growth. The propensity for famine was especially acute in heavily populated western Europe. In eastern Europe, the lower population and better balance between agriculture, animal husbandry, and fishing meant the population remained better fed and less susceptible to famine and disease.

At the same time there was probably a change in climate, known as the "Little Ice Age." The mean annual temperatures dropped just enough to make it impossible to grow crops in the more northerly parts of Europe and at high elevations such as the Alps. Before the fourteenth century, for example, grapes were grown in England to produce wine; however, with the decline in temperatures, the grape vineyards ceased to produce. Growing grapes in England became possible again only with global warming in the twenty-first century. The result of the Little Ice Age was twofold. First, there was less land available for cultivation as it became impossible to grow crops in marginal areas. Second, a harsher climate shortened the growing season, which meant that even where crops could still grow, they were less abundant.

The imbalance between food production and population set off a dreadful cycle of famine and disease. Insufficient food resulted in either malnutrition or starvation. Those who suffered from prolonged malnutrition were particularly susceptible to epidemic diseases, such as typhus, cholera, and dysentery. By 1300, children of the poor faced the probability of extreme hunger once or twice during the course of their childhood. In Pistoia, Italy, priests kept the *Book of the Dead,* which recorded the pattern: famine in 1313, famine in 1328–1329, famine and epidemic in 1339–1340 that killed one-quarter of the population, famine in 1346, famine and epidemic in 1347, and then the killing hammer blow—the Black Death in 1348 (see **Map 11.1**).

The Black Death

Black Death An epidemic disease, possibly bubonic plague, that struck Europe between 1348 and the 1350s killing at least one-third of the total population.

Following on the heels of the Great Famine, the **Black Death** arrived in Europe in the spring of 1348 with brutal force. In the lovely hilltop city of Siena, Italy, all industry stopped, carters refused to bring produce and cooking oil in from the countryside, and on June 2 the daily records of the city council and civil courts abruptly ended, as if the city fathers and judges had all died or rushed home in panic. A local chronicler, Agnolo di Tura, wrote down his memories of those terrible days:

> Father abandoned child, wife husband, one brother another; for this illness seemed to strike through the breath and sight. And so they died. And none could be found to bury the dead for money or friendship. Members of a household brought their dead to a ditch as best they could, without priest, without divine offices. Nor did the [death] bell sound. And in many places in Siena great pits were dug and piled deep with the multitude of dead. . . . And I,

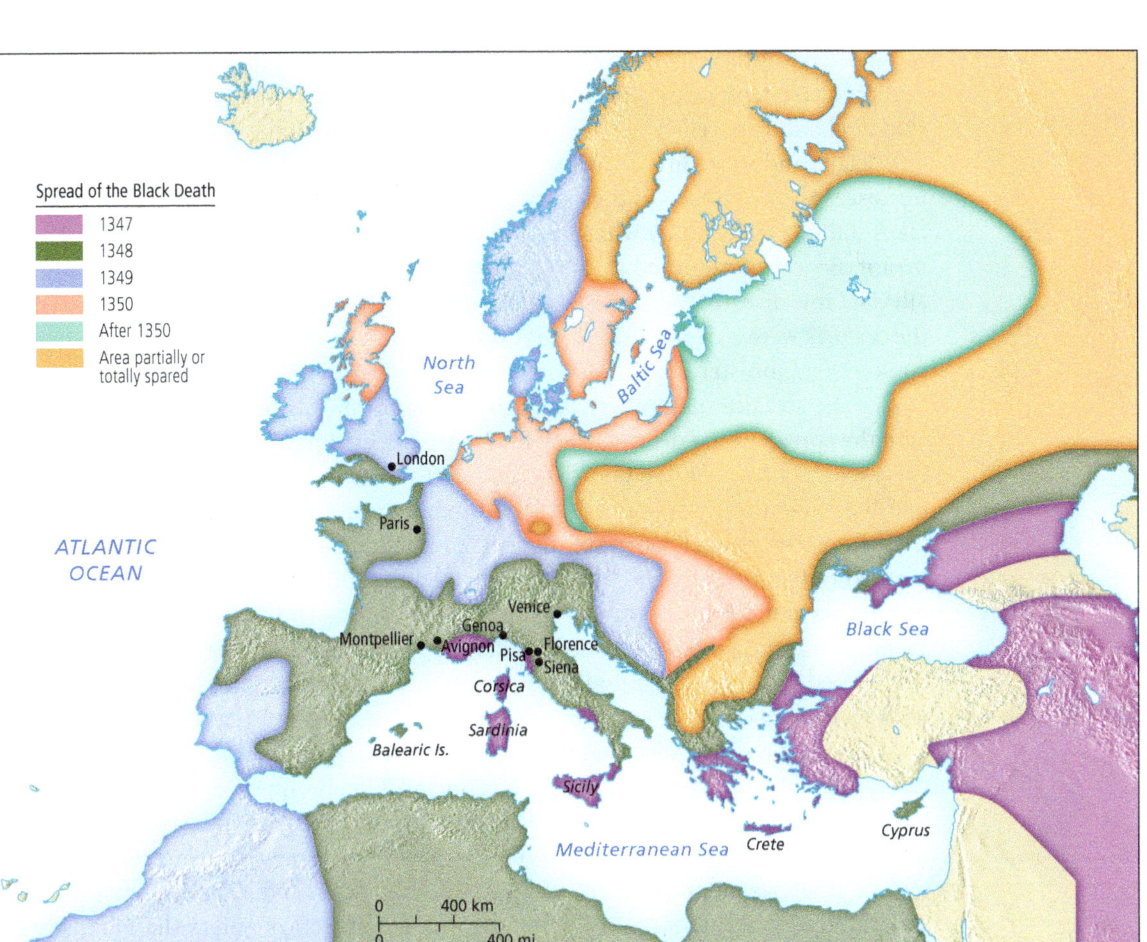

MAP **11.1** SPREAD OF THE BLACK DEATH After the Black Death first appeared in the ports of Italy in 1347, it spread relentlessly throughout most of Europe, killing at least 20 million people in Europe alone. What does this map show about how rapidly the Black Death spread?

> Agnolo di Tura, called the Fat, buried my five children with my own hands. And there were also those who were so sparsely covered with earth that the dogs dragged them forth and devoured many bodies throughout the city.[1]

During the summer of 1348 more than half of the Sienese died. The construction of Siena's great cathedral, planned to be the largest in the world, stopped and was never resumed due to a lack of workers. In fact, Siena, once among the most prosperous cities in Europe, never fully recovered and lost its economic preeminence.

No disease left more distinctive and disturbing signs on the body than the Black Death. According to one quite typical contemporary description: "all the matter which exuded from their bodies let off an unbearable stench; sweat, excrement, spittle, breath, so fetid as to be overpowering; urine turbid, thick, black or red. . . . "[2] In the introduction to *The Decameron,* Giovanni Boccaccio described what he had witnessed of the symptoms:

> In the year 1348 after the fruitful incarnation of the Son of God, that most beautiful of Italian cities, noble Florence, was attacked by deadly plague. . . . The symptoms . . . began both in men and women with certain swellings in the groin or under the armpit. They grew to the size of a small apple or an egg, more or less, and were vulgarly called tumors. In a short space of time these tumors spread from the two parts named [to] all over the body. Soon after this the symptoms changed and black or purple spots appeared on the arms or thighs or any other part of the body, sometimes a few large ones, sometimes many little ones. These spots were a certain sign of death, just as the original tumor had been and still remained.[3]

11.1

11.2

11.3

11.4

11.5

11.6

The fear of the Black Death and the inability to discern its causes focused the attention of contemporaries on the bodies of the sick. Almost any discoloration of the skin or glandular swellings could be interpreted as a sign of the Black Death's presence. Physicians and surgeons, of course, were the experts in reading the signs of the body for disease. As victims and their distraught families soon discovered, however, physicians did not really know what the glandular swellings and discolorations of the skin meant. Boccaccio reported that "No doctor's advice, no medicine could overcome or alleviate this disease. . . . Either the disease was such that no treatment was possible or the doctors were so ignorant that they did not know what caused it, and consequently could not administer the proper remedy."[4]

In the absence of an alternative, government officials resorted to quarantines to stop the spread of the disease. They locked up infected households for 40 days, which was especially hard on the poor who needed to work to eat. To maintain quarantines and bury the dead, city councils created public health bureaucracies, complete with their own staff physicians, grave diggers, and police force. The extraordinary powers granted to the public health authorities helped expand the authority of the state over its citizens in the name of pursuing the common good. The expansion of governmental bureaucracy that distinguished modern from medieval states was partly the result of the need to keep human bodies under surveillance and control—a need that began with the Black Death.

Experts have long disputed the cause of the Black Death, but DNA evidence has now verified that the bubonic plague was the most likely culprit, even if the epidemiological characteristics of the disease have mutated over the past 700 years. The bubonic plague can appear in two forms. In the first form it is usually transmitted to humans by a flea that has bitten a rodent infected with the *Yersinia pestis* bacillus, usually a rat. The infected flea then bites a human victim. The infection enters the bloodstream, causing inflamed swellings called buboes (hence, "bubonic" plague) in the glands of the groin or armpit, internal bleeding, and discoloration of the skin, symptoms similar to those Boccaccio described. The second form of plague was the pneumonic type, which infected the lungs and spread by coughing and sneezing. Either form could be lethal, but the complex epidemiology of bubonic plague meant that the first form could not be transmitted directly from one person to another. After being infected, many victims probably developed pneumonia as a secondary symptom, which then spread quickly to others. As one contemporary physician put it, one person could seemingly infect the entire world. In some cases, the doctor caught the illness and died before the patient did.

The visitations of the bubonic plague in the late nineteenth and twentieth centuries, which have been observed by physicians trained in modern medicine, formed the basis for the theory linking the Black Death to the bubonic plague. Alexandre Yersin discovered the bubonic plague bacillus (*Yersinia pestis*) in Hong Kong in 1894 and traced its spread through rats and fleas. Most historians and epidemiologists think that something similar to this must have happened in 1348, but there are differences between the fourteenth- and twentieth-century plagues. The Black Death spread much more rapidly from person to person and place to place than the bubonic plague does in modern epidemics. For example, rats do not travel very far very fast, and in modern examples the bubonic plague has rarely spread more than 12 miles per year. In 1348, however, the Black Death traveled as far in a day as rat-borne bubonic plague does in a year. Many of the reported symptoms from the fourteenth century do not match the symptoms observed in modern plague victims. Moreover, the Black Death, unlike the bubonic plague, seems to have had a long incubation period before the first symptoms appeared. Because of the long incubation, those who had the disease transmitted it to others before they knew they were sick, which helps explain why the disease was so lethal despite attempts to quarantine those afflicted with it.

Thus, the bacillus has probably mutated, changing the epidemiology, or the bubonic plague that appeared during the Black Death was often confused with other epidemics that had other characteristics.

In Europe about 20 million people died, which would have been more than the combined populations of the six largest cities (New York, Los Angeles, Chicago, Houston, Philadelphia, and Phoenix) in the United States today. Across Europe life expectancy decreased from 43 years in 1300 to only 24 years by 1400. The deaths usually clustered in a matter of a few weeks or months after the disease first appeared in a particular locale. The death toll, however, varied erratically from place to place, ranging from about 20 to 90 percent. So great was the toll in southern and western Europe that entire villages were depopulated or abandoned. Paris lost half its population, Florence as much as four-fifths, and Venice two-thirds. In the seaport of Trapani, Italy, everyone apparently died or left. Living in enclosed spaces, monks and nuns were especially hard hit. All the Franciscans of Carcassonne and Marseille in France died. In Montpellier, France, only 7 of the 140 Dominicans survived. In isolated Kilkenny, Ireland, Brother John Clyn found himself left alone among his dead brothers, and he began to write a diary of what he had witnessed because he was afraid he might be the last person left alive in the world. (See *Different Voices* in this chapter.)

The Black Death kept coming back. In the Mediterranean basin where the many port cities formed a network of contagion, the plague reappeared between 1348 and 1721 in one port or another about every 20 years. Some of the later outbreaks were just as lethal as the initial 1348 catastrophe. Florence lost half its population in 1400; Venice lost a third in 1575–1577 and a third again in 1630–1631. Less exposed than the Mediterranean, northern Europe suffered less and saw the last of the dread disease in the Great Plague of London of 1665–1666. Most of Poland escaped without any signs of the disease, and east-central Europe in general was far less severely hit than western Europe, probably because the sparse population made the spread of contagion less likely.

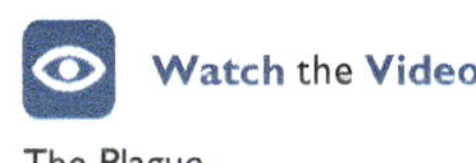

The Plague

THE TRIUMPH OF DEATH This detail from Francesco Traini's fresco, *The Triumph of Death,* in the Camposanto, Pisa, ca. 1350, depicts an elegant cavalcade of aristocrats on horseback peering in horror at the bodies of plague victims.

SOURCE: Cemetery, Pisa, Italy/Canali PhotoBank, Milan/SuperStock.

FLAGELLANTS During the Black Death many people believed God was punishing them for their sins. In order to expiate those sins, some young men performed flagellation, a practice once reserved for monks who whipped themselves as a form of penance. In order to control the practice among laymen, confraternities were formed in which collective flagellation was organized. The flagellants depicted here are formed into a procession displaying a holy banner and crucifix while one brother flogs two others.

A Cold Wind from the East

11.2 How did forces outside Europe, in particular the Mongol and Ottoman Empires, influence conditions in the West?

During the same period the West was suffering from deadly microbes, it also faced the mounted warriors of the distant Mongol tribes, whose relentless conquests drove them from Outer Mongolia across central Asia toward Europe. The Mongols and Turks were nomadic peoples from central Asia. Closely related culturally but speaking different languages, these peoples exerted an extraordinary influence on world history despite a rather small population. **Map 11.2** shows the place of origin of the Mongols and Turks and where they spread across a wide belt of open, relatively flat steppe land stretching from the Yellow Sea between China and the Korean peninsula to the Baltic Sea and the Danube River basin in Europe. Virtually without forests and interrupted only by a few easily traversed mountain ranges, the broad Eurasian steppes have been the great migration highway of world history from prehistoric times to the medieval caravans and the modern trans-Siberian railway.

As the Mongols and Turks charged westward out of central Asia on their fast ponies, they put pressure on the kingdoms of the West. Mongol armies hobbled Kievan Rus, and Turks destroyed Byzantium. As a consequence, the potential Orthodox allies in the East of the Catholic Christian West were weakened or eliminated. Converts to Islam, the Ottomans pushed into the Balkans. In contrast to the era of the twelfth-century Crusades, Catholic Europe found itself on the defensive against a powerful Muslim foe.

The Mongol Invasions

Whereas the Europeans became successful sailors because of their extensive coastlines and close proximity to the sea, the Mongols became roving horsemen because they needed to migrate several times a year in search of grass and water for their ponies and livestock. They also became highly skilled warriors because they competed persistently with other tribes for access to the grasslands.

Between 1206 and 1258, the Mongols transformed themselves from a collection of disunited tribes with a vague ethnic affinity to create the most extensive empire in the history of the world. The epic rise of the previously obscure Mongols was the work of a Mongol chief named Temujin, who succeeded in uniting the various quarreling tribes and transforming them into a world power. In 1206 Temujin was proclaimed Genghis Khan (ca. 1162–1227) ("Very Mighty King"), the supreme ruler over all the Mongols. Genghis broke through the Great Wall of China, destroyed the Jin (Chin) Empire in northern China, and occupied Beijing. His cavalry swept across Asia as far as Azerbaijan, Georgia, northern Persia, and Kievan Rus. Genghis Khan ordered that after his death his empire would be divided into four principalities or khanates for his sons and grandsons. They continued Mongol expansion. Eventually, Mongol armies conquered territories that stretched from Korea to Hungary and from the Arctic Ocean to the Arabian Sea.

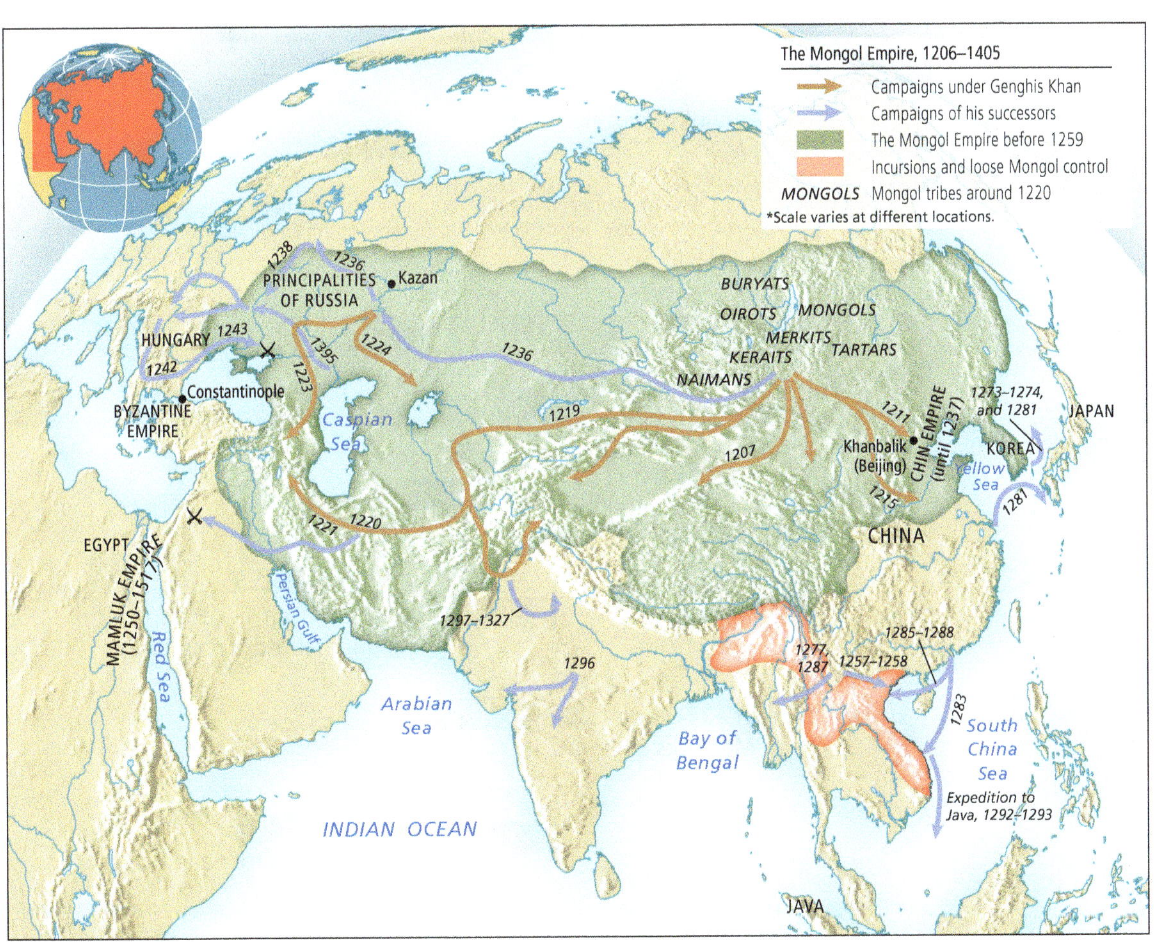

MAP **11.2** THE MONGOL EMPIRE, 1206–1405 The Mongols and Turks were nomadic peoples who spread out across Asia and Europe from their homeland in the region of Mongolia. The Mongol armies eventually conquered vast territories from Korea to the borders of Hungary and from the Arctic Ocean to the Arabian Sea. From the dates shown, how rapidly did the Mongol armies spread their rule?

MONGOL HORSEMAN Unlike the fourteenth-century European representations of the Mongols, this contemporary Chinese illustration accurately depicts the appearance, dress, and equipment of a Mongol Archer on horseback.

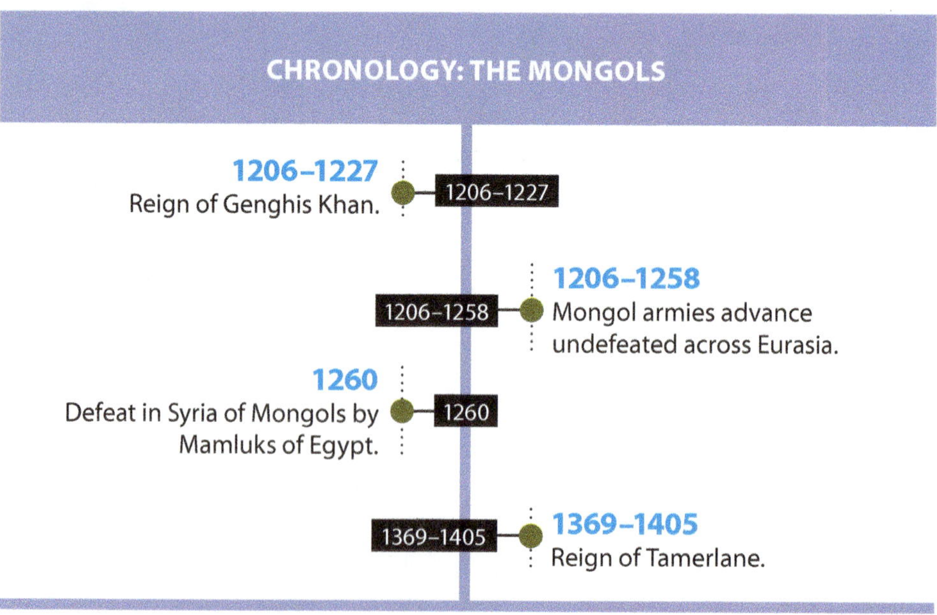

The Mongol success was accomplished through a highly disciplined military organization, tactics that relied on extremely mobile cavalry forces, and a sophisticated intelligence network. During the campaign against the Rus in the winter of 1223, the Mongol cavalry moved with lightning speed across frozen rivers. Although the Rus forces outnumbered the Mongol armies and had superior armor, they were crushed in every encounter with the Mongols.

The Mongol armies employed clever tactics. First, they unnerved enemy soldiers with a hail of arrows. Then they appeared to retreat, only to draw the enemy into false confidence before the Mongol horsemen delivered a deadly final blow. European chroniclers at the time tried to explain their many defeats at the hands of the Mongols by reporting that the Mongol "hordes" had overwhelming numbers, but evidence clearly shows that their victories were the result not of superior numbers, but of superior discipline and the sophistication of the Mongol intelligence network. Once they had conquered a territory the Mongols secured the caravan routes across Asia, known as the Silk Road, creating the Mongol Peace. (See *Encounters and Transformations* in this chapter.) However, the Mongol Peace came at an enormous human cost. It is estimated that Ghenghis Khan's armies were responsible for the deaths of 40 million people or about 11.1 percent of the world's population, a death toll second only to World War II, which killed 66 million people. And Mongol armies may have been responsible for spreading the *Yersinia pestis* bacillus from its home in China, making the Mongols indirectly responsible for the Black Death.

Mongol power climaxed in 1260. In that year the Mongols suffered a crushing defeat in Syria at the hands of the Mamluk rulers of Egypt, an event that ended the Mongol reputation for invincibility. Conflicts and succession disputes among the various Mongol tribes made them vulnerable to rivals and to rebellion from their unhappy subjects. The Mongol Empire did not disappear overnight, but its various successor khanates never recaptured the dynamic unity forged by Genghis Khan. During the fourteenth century the Mongol Peace sputtered to an end.

In the wake of these upheavals, a warrior of Mongol descent known as Tamerlane (r. 1369–1405) created an army composed of Mongols, Turks, and Persians, which challenged the established Mongol khanates. Tamerlane's conquests rivaled those of Genghis Khan, but with very different results. His armies pillaged the rich cities that supplied the caravan routes. Thus, in his attempt to monopolize the lucrative trans-Eurasian trade, Tamerlane largely destroyed it. The collapse of the Mongol Peace broke the thread of commerce across Eurasia and stimulated the European search for alternative routes to China that ultimately resulted in the voyages of Christopher Columbus in 1492.

Read the Document

The Mongols: An Excerpt from the *Novgorod Chronicle*, 1315

The Rise of the Ottoman Turks

The Mongol armies were never very large, so the Mongols had always augmented their numbers with Turkish tribes. The result was that outside Mongolia, Turks gradually absorbed the Mongols. Turkish replaced Mongolian as the dominant language, and the Turks took over the government of the central Asian empires that had been scraped together by the Mongol conquests. In contrast to the Mongols, many of whom remained Buddhists, the Turks became Muslims and created an exceptionally dynamic, expansionist society of their own (see **Map 11.3**).

Among the Turkish peoples, the most successful state builders were the Ottomans. Named for Osman I (r. 1281–1326), who brought it to prominence, the Ottoman dynasty endured for more than 600 years, until 1924. The nucleus of the Ottoman state was a small principality in Anatolia (a portion of present-day Turkey), which in the early fourteenth century began to expand at the expense of its weaker neighbors, including the Byzantine Empire. The Ottoman state was built not on national, linguistic, or ethnic unity, but on a purely dynastic network of personal and military loyalties to the Ottoman prince, called the sultan. Thus, the vitality of the empire depended on the energy of the individual sultans. The Ottomans thought of themselves as *ghazis,* warriors for Islam devoted to destroying polytheists, including Christians. (To some Muslims, the Christian belief in the Trinity and veneration

Encounters and Transformations

The Silk Road

Nothing better facilitated encounters between East and West than the Silk Road. The label actually refers to a network of caravan trails connecting China with western Asia and Europe through the Taklimakan, one of the most inhospitable deserts on Earth. Travelers had little choice but to pick their way from oasis to oasis across central Asia. On the eastern and western edges of this vast territory the civilizations of China and the West developed, and the Silk Road connected them.

Many highly valuable commodities were transported along these routes besides silk, including ivory, gold, jewels, iron, furs, and ceramics (hence, the term "fine China" for the most precious ceramics). None of these commodities, however, captured the imagination of the West as much as silk, which had been transported from China across the Silk Road since Roman times (see Chapter 6). The importance of the Silk Road required peaceful political conditions to thrive, lest caravans be plundered. Perhaps the greatest era for the Silk Road came under the Chinese T'ang dynasty (618–907), which provided stability that allowed commerce to flower along the road. After the T'ang dynasty collapsed, the road was unsafe until the Mongol invasions in the thirteenth century.

The Mongol invasions completely altered the composition of Asia and much of eastern Europe—economically, politically, and ethnically. Once the Mongols had conquered new territories, they established the Mongol Peace by reopening the Silk Road across the Asian steppes, making trans-Eurasian trade possible and guaranteeing the safety of merchants. Thanks to the Mongols, European Christians began to traverse the Silk Road to China and to encounter directly the civilizations of the East. The Mongols were tolerant of religious diversity and welcomed the first Christian missionaries into China. A Roman Catholic archbishopric was founded in Beijing in 1307.

The most famous of the many merchants who traversed the Silk Road during the Mongol Peace were the Venetians from the Polo family, including Marco Polo, who arrived at the court of the Great Khan in China in 1275. Marco Polo's book about his travels offers a vivid and often remarkably perceptive account of the Mongol Empire during the Mongol Peace. It also illustrates better than any other source the cultural engagement of the Christian West with the Mongol East during the late thirteenth century. Although Marco Polo was a merchant who traveled

(continued on next page)

 **View the Closer Look** Mongols and Trade on the Silk Road

MARCO POLO TRAVELING BY CAMEL CARAVAN ON THE SILK ROAD This illustration is likely from a late fourteenth-century atlas. A Mongol escort provides security for the travelers.

(continued from previous page)

to make a profit, his book brought a great store of cultural information—some accurate, some fanciful—that stimulated the Western imagination about the East. Perhaps most revealing were his discussions of religion. Marco classified peoples according to their religion and evaluated religions with the eye of a western European Catholic. He was harshest about Muslims, but seemed more tolerant of "idolaters"; that is, Buddhists and Hindus, whose practices he found intriguing. He also reported on magical practices and reports of miracles. Because of the popularity of his book, Marco Polo's views of Asia became the principal source of knowledge in the West about the East until the sixteenth century.

For Discussion

What were the advantages and disadvantages of the Mongol Peace for the West?

MAP **11.3** THE OTTOMAN EMPIRE The Ottoman state expanded from a small principality in Anatolia, which is south of the Black Sea. From there the Ottomans spread eastward into Kurdistan and Armenia. In the West they captured all of Greece and much of the Balkan peninsula. From this map, what was the strategic significance for trade and military power of the location of the Ottoman Empire?

of numerous saints demonstrated that Christians were not true monotheists.) During the fourteenth century, incessant Ottoman guerilla actions gradually chipped away at the Byzantine frontier.

The Byzantine Empire in the middle of the thirteenth century was emerging from a period of domination by Frankish knights and Venetian merchants who had conquered Constantinople during the Fourth Crusade in 1204. In 1261, the Byzantine emperor, Michael VIII Palaeologus (r. 1260–1282), recaptured the great city. The revived Byzantine Empire, however, was a pale vestige of what it once had been, and the Palaeologi emperors desperately sought military assistance from western Europe to defend themselves from the Ottomans. Dependent on mercenary armies and divided by civil wars, the Byzantines offered only pathetic resistance to the all-conquering Ottomans.

From their base in Anatolia, the Ottomans raided far and wide, launching pirate fleets into the Aegean and gradually encircling Constantinople after they crossed over into Europe in 1308. By 1402 Ottoman territory had grown to 40 times its size a century earlier. During that century of conquests, the frontier between Christianity and Islam shifted. The former subjects of the Byzantines in the Balkans fell to the Ottoman Turks. Fragile Serbia, a bastion of Orthodox Christianity in the Balkans, broke under Ottoman pressure. First unified in the late twelfth century, Serbia established political independence from Byzantium and autonomy for the Serbian church. Although the Serbs had taken control over a number of former Byzantine provinces, they fell to the invincible Ottomans at the Battle of Kosovo in 1389. Lamenting the Battle of Kosovo has remained the bedrock of Serbian national identity to this day.

Serbia's western neighbors, the kingdoms of Bosnia and Herzegovina, deflated under Ottoman pressure during the late fifteenth century. Unlike Serbia, where most of the population remained loyal to the Serbian Orthodox Church, in Bosnia and Herzegovina the Serbian-speaking land-holding classes converted to Islam to preserve their property. The subjugated peasants, also Serbian-speaking, remained Orthodox Christians who turned over one-third of everything they raised to their Muslim lords, which created considerable resentment and religious tensions. The Ottomans allowed the Bosnians to keep their territorial identity and name, a unique situation among conquered provinces of the Ottoman Empire.

When Mehmed II, "The Conqueror" (r. 1451–1481), became the Ottoman sultan, he began to obliterate the last remnants of the Byzantine Empire. During the winter of 1451–1452, the sultan ordered the encirclement of Constantinople, a city that had once been the largest in the world but now was reduced from perhaps a million people to fewer than 50,000. The Ottoman siege strategy was to bombard Constantinople into submission with daily rounds from enormous cannons. The largest was a monster cannon, 29 feet long, that could shoot 1,200-pound stones. It required a crew of 200 soldiers and 60 oxen to handle it, and each firing generated so much heat that it took hours to cool off before it could be fired again. The siege was a gargantuan task because the walls of Constantinople, which had been built, repaired, and improved over a period of 1,000 years, were formidable. However, the new weapon of gunpowder artillery had rendered city walls a military anachronism. Brought from China by the Mongols, gunpowder had gradually revolutionized warfare. Breaching city walls in sieges was merely a matter of time as long as the heavy metal cannons could be dragged into position. Quarrels among the Christians also hampered the defense of Constantinople's walls. Toward the end, the Byzantine emperor was forced to melt down church treasures so "that from them coins should be struck and given to the soldiers, the sappers and the builders, who selfishly cared so little for the public welfare that they were refusing to go to their work unless they were first paid."[5]

The final assault came in May 1453 and lasted less than a day. When the city fell, the Ottoman army spent the day plundering, raping, and enslaving the populace. The last Byzantine emperor, Constantine XI, was never found amid the multitude of the dead. The fall of Constantinople ended the Christian Byzantine Empire, the continuous remnant of the ancient Roman Empire. But the idea of Rome was not so easily snuffed out. The first Ottoman sultans residing in Constantinople continued to be called "Roman emperors."

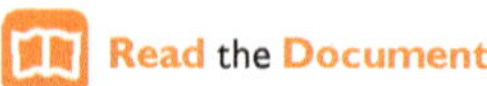

Mehmed II (15th Century) Kritovoulos

Although the western European princes had done little to save Byzantium, its demise shocked them. Now they were also vulnerable to the Ottoman onslaught. For the next 200 years the Ottomans used Constantinople as a base to threaten Christian Europe. Hungary and the eastern Mediterranean empire of Venice remained the last

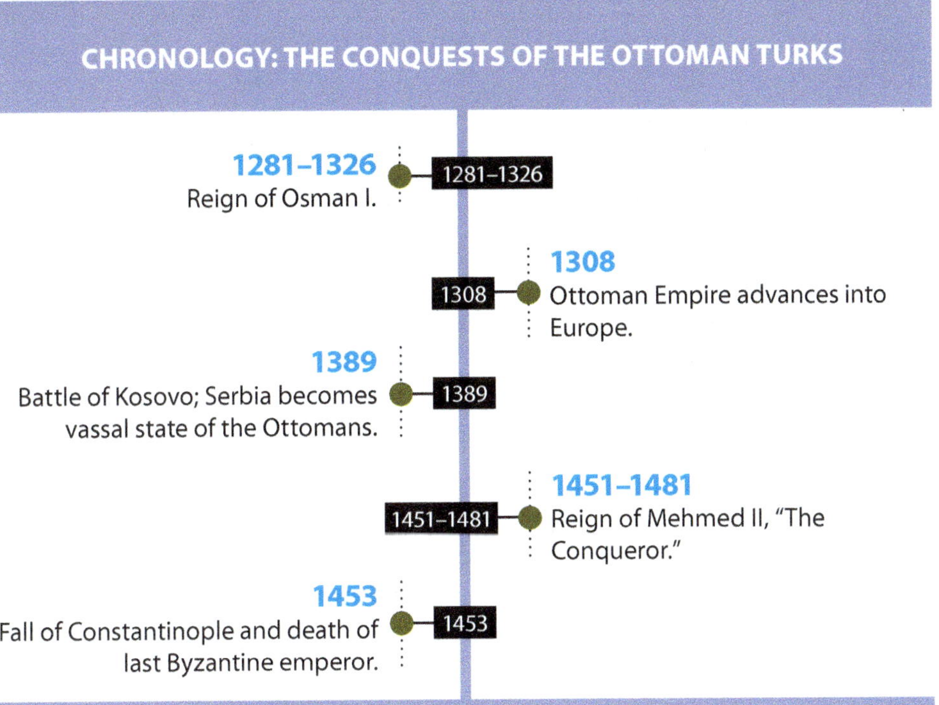

lines of defense for the West, and at various times in succeeding centuries the Ottomans launched expeditions against Europe, including two sieges of Vienna (1529 and 1683) and several invasions of Italy.

Hundreds of years of attacks by the Mongol and Ottoman Empires redrew the map of the West. Events in Europe did not and could not take place in isolation from the eastern pressures and influences. The Mongol conquest finished off Kievan Rus. Although Mongols burned down Moscow in the winter of 1238 and pillaged it in 1293, its remote, forested location offered some security from further attacks and occupation. As a result, Moscow and the Republic of Novgorod, which escaped the Mongol attacks entirely, replaced Kiev as the centers of power in what would become Russia. The Ottoman conquests also created a lasting Muslim presence within the borders of Europe, especially in Bosnia and Albania. In succeeding centuries Christian Europe and the Muslim Ottoman Empire would be locked in a deadly competitive embrace, but they also benefited from innumerable cultural exchanges and regular trade. Hostility between the two sides was recurrent but never inevitable and was broken by long periods of peaceful engagement. In fact, the Christian kingdoms of western Europe went to war far more often with one another than with the Turks.

Read the Document

An Ambassador's Report on the Ottoman Empire (1555) Ogier Ghiselin de Busbecq

Read the Document

Venetian Observations on the Ottoman Empire Late Sixteenth Century

Economic Depression and Social Turmoil

11.3 How did disturbances in the rudimentary global economy of the Middle Ages precipitate almost complete financial collapse and widespread social discontent in Europe?

Adding insult to injury in this time of famine, plague, and conquest, the West began to suffer a major economic depression during the fourteenth century. The economic boom fueled by the agricultural revolution and the revitalization of European cities during the eleventh century and the commercial prosperity of the twelfth and thirteenth centuries petered out in the fourteenth. The causes of this economic catastrophe were complex, but the consequences were obvious. Businesses went bust, banks collapsed, guilds were in turmoil, and workers rebelled.

At the same time, the effects of the depression were unevenly felt. Eastern Europe, which was less fully integrated into the international economy, fared better than western Europe. The economic conditions for many peasants actually improved because there was a labor shortage in the countryside due to the loss of population. Forced to pay their peasants more for their labor and crops, landlords saw their own fortunes decline. Finding it harder to pay the higher prices for food, urban workers probably suffered the most because their wages did not keep up with the cost of living.

The Collapse of International Trade and Banking

After the breakup of the Mongol Empire and the conquests of Tamerlane, trade between Europe and Asia dwindled. The entire financial infrastructure of medieval Europe was tied to this international trade in luxury goods. The successful, entrepreneurial Italian merchants who dominated the luxury trade deposited their enormous profits in Italian banks. The Italian bankers lent money to the aristocracy and royalty of northern Europe to finance the purchases of exotic luxuries and to fight wars. The whole system was mutually reinforcing, but it was very fragile. With the disruption of supply sources for luxury goods, the financial networks of Europe collapsed, precipitating a major depression. By 1346, all the banks in Florence, the banking center of Europe, had crashed.

The luxury trade that brought exotic items from Asia to Europe represented only half of the economic equation. The other half was the raw materials and manufactured goods that Europeans sold in exchange, principally woolen cloth. The production of woolen cloth depended on a sophisticated economic system that connected shepherds in England, the Netherlands, and Spain with woolen cloth manufacturers in cities. The manufacture of cloth and other commodities was organized by **guilds**, which were professional associations devoted to protecting the special interests of a particular trade or craft and to monopolizing production and trade in the goods the guild produced. The rise of the guilds marked a shift from household manufactures performed by women, as was common in the early Middle Ages, to industrial production performed mostly by men in shops. Over time, many guilds attempted to restrict or prohibit female membership.

guilds Professional associations devoted to protecting the special interests of a particular trade or craft and to monopolizing production and trade in the goods the guild produced.

There were two types of guilds. The first type, merchant guilds, attempted to monopolize the local market for a particular commodity. There were spice guilds, fruit and vegetable guilds, and apothecary guilds. The second type, craft guilds, regulated the manufacturing processes of artisans such as carpenters, bricklayers, woolen-cloth manufacturers, glass blowers, and painters. These guilds were dominated by master craftsmen, who ran their own shops. Working for wages in these shops were the journeymen, who knew the craft but could not yet afford to open their own shops. Under the masters and journeymen were apprentices, who usually worked without pay for a specific number of years to learn the trade.

In many cities the guilds expanded far beyond the economic regulation of trade and manufacturing to become the backbone of urban society and politics. The masters of the guilds constituted part of the urban elite, and guild membership was often a prerequisite for holding public office. One of the obligations of city government was to protect the interests of the guildsmen, who in turn helped stabilize the economy through their influence in city hall. Guilds often organized festivals and sports competitions, endowed chapels, and provided funeral insurance for their members and welfare for the injured and widows of masters.

When the economy declined during the fourteenth century, the urban guilds became lightning rods for mounting social tension. Guild monopolies produced considerable conflict, provoking anger among those who were blocked from joining guilds, young journeymen who earned low wages, and those who found themselves unemployed due to the depression. These tensions exploded into dangerous revolts.

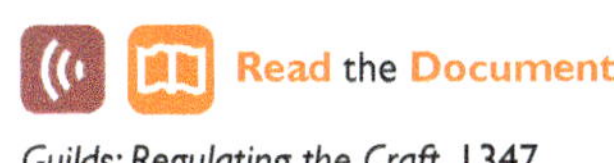

Guilds: Regulating the Craft, 1347

Workers' Rebellions

Economic pressures erupted into rebellion most dramatically among woolen-cloth workers in the urban centers in Italy, the Netherlands, and France. The most famous revolt involved the Ciompi, the laborers in the woolen-cloth industry of Florence, Italy, where guilds were the most powerful force in city government. The Ciompi, who performed the heaviest jobs such as carting and the most noxious tasks such as dyeing, had not been allowed to have their own guild and were therefore deprived of the political and economic rights of guild membership.

Fueling the Ciompi's frustration was the fact that by the middle of the fourteenth century woolen-cloth production in Florence dropped by two-thirds, leaving many workers unemployed. In 1378 the desperate Ciompi rebelled. A crowd chanting, "Long live the people, long live liberty," broke into the houses of prominent citizens, released political prisoners from the city jails, and sacked the rich convents that housed the pampered daughters of the wealthy. Over the course of a few months, the rebels managed to force their way onto the city council, where they demanded tax and economic reforms and the right to form their own guild. The Ciompi revolt is one of the earliest cases of workers demanding political rights. The disenfranchised workers did not want to eliminate the guilds' monopoly on political power. They merely wanted a guild of their own so that they could join the regime. That was not to be, however. After a few weeks of success, the Ciompi were divided and defeated.

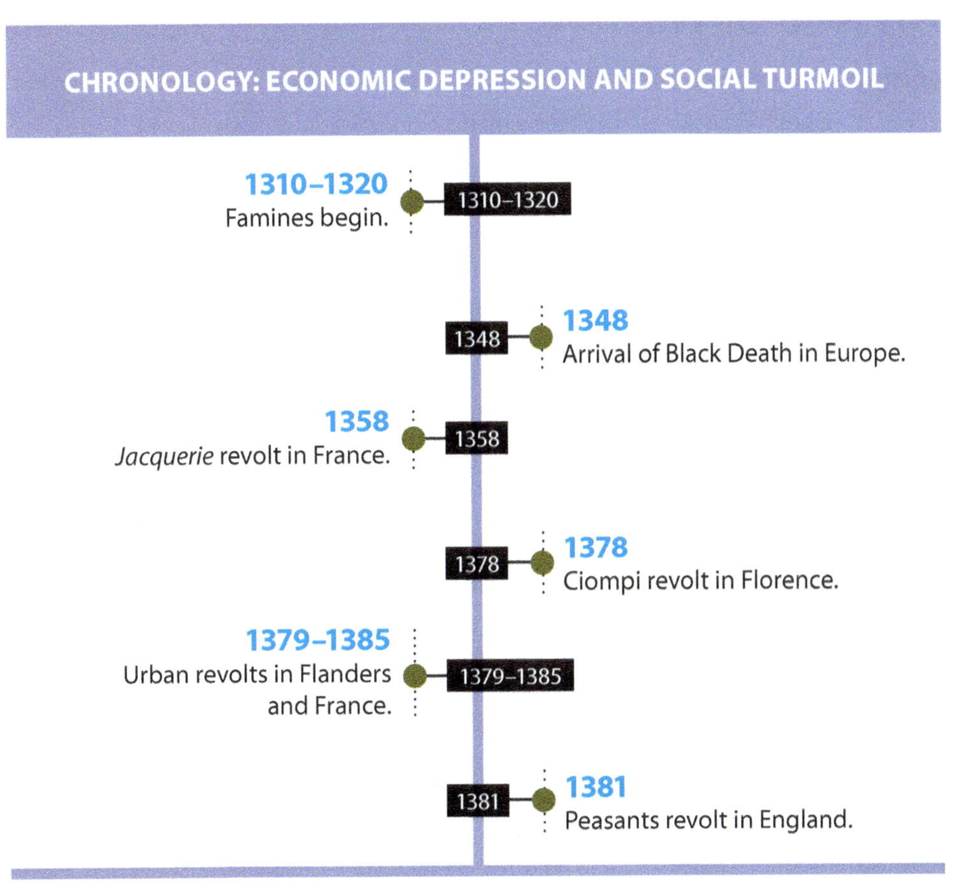

Shortly after the Ciompi revolt faded, troubles broke out in the woolen-cloth centers of Ghent and Bruges in Flanders and in Paris and Rouen in France. In these cases, however, the revolt spread beyond woolen-cloth workers to voice the more generalized grievances of urban workers. In Ghent and Bruges the weavers attempted to wrest control of their cities from the local leaders who dominated politics and the economy. In Paris and Rouen in 1380, social unrest erupted in resistance to high taxes and attacks by the poor on the rich.

Like urban workers, many rural peasants also rebelled during the troubled fourteenth century. In France in 1358 a peasant revolt broke out called the *Jacquerie*. Filled with hatred for the aristocracy, the peasants indulged in pillaging, murder, and rape, but they offered no plan for an alternative social system or even for their own participation in the political order, so their movement had no lasting effects. They were quickly defeated by a force of nobles.

Unlike the French *Jacquerie*, the peasants who revolted in England in 1381 had a clear political vision for an alternative society. The English rebels demanded the abolition of new taxes, lower rents, higher wages, and the end of serfdom, but to these they added a class-based argument against the aristocracy. Influenced by popular preachers, who told them that in the Garden of Eden there had been no aristocracy, the English rebels imagined an egalitarian society without ranks or hierarchy. However, the greatest peasant rebellion in medieval English history ended with broken promises and no tangible achievements.

None of the worker or peasant revolts of the fourteenth century met with lasting success. However, the rebellions revealed for the first time in the West a widespread impulse among the lower classes to question and protest the existing social and economic order. The tradition of worker protest became common and recurrent during subsequent centuries.

An Age of Warfare

11.4 How did incessant warfare transform the most powerful medieval states?

Prolonged war between its two largest and previously most stable kingdoms, England and France, further weakened western Europe during the fourteenth century. The **Hundred Years' War** (1337–1453) was a struggle over England's attempts to assert its claims to territories in France. The conflict drained resources from the French and English aristocracies, deepening and lengthening the economic depression.

Hundred Years' War Refers to a series of engagements (1337–1453) between England and France over England's attempts to assert its claims to territories in France.

The Fragility of Monarchies

Medieval monarchies depended on the king to maintain stability. Despite the remarkable legal reforms and bureaucratic centralization of monarchies in England and France during the twelfth and thirteenth centuries (see Chapter 10), weak or incompetent kings were all too common during the fourteenth. Weak kings created a perilous situation made worse by disputed successions. The career of Edward II (r. 1307–1327) of England illustrates the peril. Edward was unable to control the vital judicial and financial mechanisms of royal power. He continued the policy of his father, Edward I, by introducing resident justices of the peace who had replaced the inadequate system of itinerant judges who traveled from village to village to hear cases. In theory, these justices of the peace should have prevented the abuses of justice typical of aristocratic jurisdictions, but even though they were royal officials who answered to the king, most of those appointed were also local landowners who were deeply implicated in many of the disputes that came before them. As a result, justice in England became notoriously corrupt and the cause of discontent. Edward II was so incompetent to deal with the consequences of corrupted justice that he provoked a civil war in which his own queen joined his aristocratic enemies to depose him.

The French monarchy was no better. In fact, the French king was in an even weaker constitutional position than the English monarch. In France the king had effective jurisdiction over only a small part of his realm. Many of the duchies and counties of France were quasi-independent principalities paying only nominal allegiance to the king, whose will was ignored with impunity. In these regions the administration of justice, the collection of taxes, and the recruitment of soldiers all remained in the hands of local lords. To explain why he needed to raise taxes, Philip IV, "The Fair" (r. 1285–1314), created a representative assembly, the Estates General, which met for the first time in 1302. Even so, he still had to negotiate with each region and town individually to collect the taxes. Given the difficulty of raising taxes, the French kings resorted to makeshift solutions that hurt the economy, such as confiscating the property of vulnerable Jewish and Italian merchants and debasing the coinage. Such a system made the finances of the kingdom of France especially shaky because the king lacked a dependable flow of revenue.

The Hundred Years' War

The Hundred Years' War revealed the fragility of the medieval monarchies. The initial cause of the war involved disputes over the duchy of Aquitaine. The king of England inherited the title of duke of Aquitaine, who was a vassal of the French crown, which meant that the English kings technically owed military assistance to the French kings whenever they asked for it. A long succession of English kings had reluctantly paid homage as dukes of Aquitaine to the king of France, but the unusual status of the duchy held by the king of England was a continuing source of contention.

The second cause of the war derived from a dispute over the succession to the French crown. When King Charles IV died in 1328, his closest surviving relative was none other than the archenemy of France, Edward III (r. 1327–1377), king of England. To the barons of France, the possibility of Edward's succession to the throne was unthinkable, and they excluded him because his relation to the French royal family was through his mother. Instead the barons elected to the throne a member of the Valois family, King Philip VI (r. 1328–1350). At first Edward reluctantly accepted the decision. However, when Philip started to hear judicial appeals from the duchy of Aquitaine, Edward changed his mind. He claimed the title of king of France for himself, sparking the beginning of more than a century of warfare (see **Map 11.4**).

The Hundred Years' War (1337–1453) was not a continuous formal war, but a series of occasional pitched battles, punctuated by long truces and periods of general exhaustion. Nineteenth-century historians invented the term *Hundred Years' War* to describe the prolonged time of troubles between the two countries. France, far richer and with three times the population, held the advantage over sparsely populated England, but the English were usually victorious because of superior discipline and the ability of their longbows to break up cavalry charges. As a rule, the English avoided open battle, preferring raids, sieges of isolated castles, and capturing French knights for ransom. For many Englishmen the objective of fighting in France was to get rich by looting. Because all the fighting took place on French soil, France suffered extensive destruction and significant civilian casualties from repeated English raids.

FROM ENGLISH VICTORIES TO FRENCH SALVATION In the early phases of the war, the English enjoyed a stunning series of victories. At the Battle of Sluys in 1340, a

1337
(before the Battle of Crécy)
English holdings
French holdings

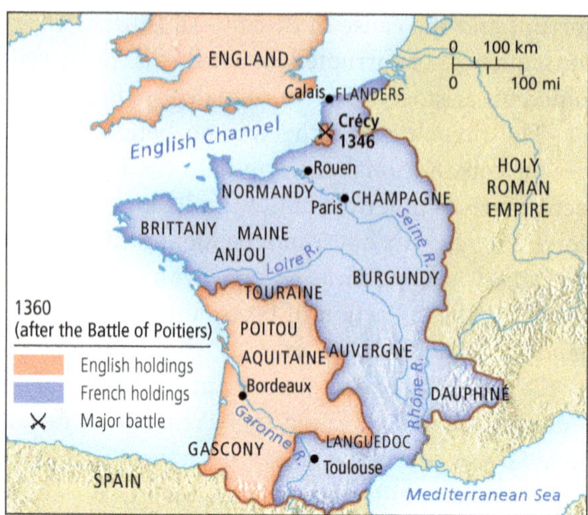

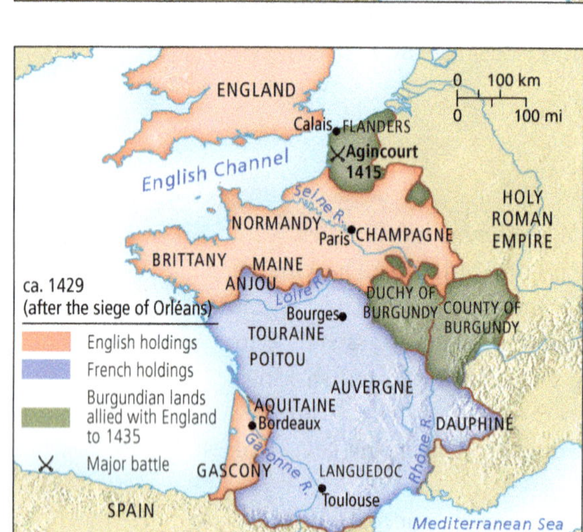

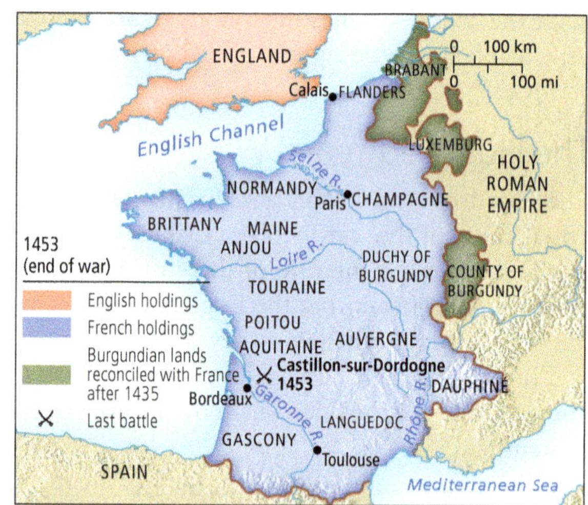

MAP **11.4** THE HUNDRED YEARS' WAR This map illustrates four phases of the Hundred Years' War. In the first phase (1337), England maintained a small foothold in the southwest of France. In the second phase (1360), England considerably expanded the territory around Aquitaine and gained a vital base in the north of France. In the third phase (ca. 1429), England occupied much of the north of France, and England's ally Burgundy established effective independence from French authority. In the fourth phase at the end of the war (1453), England had been driven from French soil except at Calais, and Burgundy maintained control over most of its scattered territories. What were the likely effects of the frequent changes of rulership for France?

small English fleet of 150 ships carrying the English invasion forces ran into a French blockade of more than 200 ships. In the heavy hand-to-hand combat, the English captured 166 French ships and killed some 20,000 men, so many that it was later said, "If fish could talk, they would speak French." At Agincourt in 1415, King Henry V (r. 1413–1422) and England's disease-racked army of 6,000 were cut off by a French force of about 20,000, yet in the ensuing battle the English archers repelled a hasty French cavalry charge and the fleeing, terrified horses trampled the French men-at-arms as they advanced. The English lost only a few hundred, but the French suffered nearly 10,000 casualties. After Agincourt, the French never again dared challenge King Henry in open battle, and were forced to recognize him as the heir to the French throne.

English victory appeared complete, but by 1422 Henry V was dead, leaving two claimants to the French throne. The English asserted the rights of the infant King Henry VI of England, son of King Henry V. Most of the French defended the claim of the Dauphin (the title of the heir to the throne) Charles, the only surviving son of the late King Charles VI of France. The Hundred Years' War entered a new phase with factions of the French aristocracy supporting the two rivals in a bloody series of engagements. The war was now as much a civil war as one between kingdoms.

ENGLISH LONGBOW ARCHERS English archers use the longbow at the Battle of Crecy in 1346. The English longbow archers on the right are massacring the French crossbowmen on the left. Because of the cumbersome process of cranking back the bowstring between shots, the crossbow had a much slower shooting rate than a longbow.

By 1429 the English were again on the verge of final victory. They occupied Paris and Rheims, and their army was besieging Orleans. The Dauphin Charles was penniless and indecisive. Even his own mother denied his legitimacy as the future king. At this point, a 17-year-old illiterate peasant from Burgundy, Joan of Arc (Jeanne d'Arc, ca. 1412–1431), following "divine voices," went to Orleans to lead the French armies. Under her inspiration Orleans was relieved, French forces began to defeat the English, much of the occupied territory was regained, and the Dauphin was crowned King Charles VII (r. 1429–1461) in the cathedral of Rheims. After Joan failed to recapture Paris, however, her successes ceased. (See *Justice in History* in this chapter.) The final victory of the French came from the leadership of King Charles and the general exhaustion of the English forces.

Charles VII reorganized the French army and gradually chipped away at the English holdings in France, eventually taking away Aquitaine in 1453. The English lost all their possessions in France except Calais, which was finally surrendered in 1558. There was no peace treaty, just a fading away of war in France, especially after England stumbled into civil war—the War of the Roses (1455–1485).

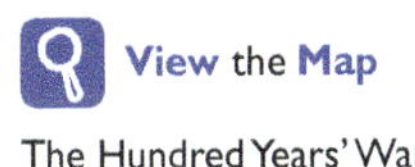

The Hundred Years' War

THE HUNDRED YEARS' WAR IN PERSPECTIVE The Hundred Years' War had broad consequences. First, nearly continuous warfare between the two most powerful kingdoms in the West exacerbated other conflicts as well. Scotland, the German princes, Aragon, Castile, and most importantly Burgundy were drawn into the conflict, making the English-French brawl a European-wide war at certain stages. The squabble between France and England also made it much more difficult to settle the Great Schism that split the Church during the same period. Second, the war devastated France, which

Justice in History

The Trial of Joan of Arc

After only 15 months as the inspiration of the French army, Joan of Arc fell into the hands of the English, who brought her to trial at Rouen in 1431 for witchcraft. The English needed to stage a show trial to demonstrate to their own demoralized forces that Joan's remarkable victories resulted from witchcraft rather than military superiority. In the English trial, Joan testified that she was merely responding to spiritual voices she heard that commanded her to wear men's clothing. On the basis of her cross dressing, the ecclesiastical tribunal declared her a witch and a relapsed heretic. The court sentenced her to be burned at the stake.

From the beginning of her emergence onto the political scene, the voices Joan heard guided her every move. Joan claimed that she heard the voices of St. Catherine, St. Margaret, and the Archangel Michael. To Joan, these voices carried the authority of divine commands. The problem the English judges faced was to demonstrate that the voices came from the Devil rather than from God. If they could prove that, then they had evidence of witchcraft and sorcery. Following standard inquisitorial guidelines, the judges knew that authentic messages from God would always conform to church dogma. Any deviation from official doctrines would constitute evidence of demonic influence. Thus, during Joan's trial the judges demanded that she make theological distinctions that were alien to her. When they wanted to know if the voices were those of angels or saints, Joan seemed perplexed and responded, "This voice comes from God. . . . I am more afraid of failing the voices by saying what is displeasing to them than answering you."[6] The judges kept pushing, asking if the saints or angels had heads, eyes, and hair. Exasperated, Joan simply replied, "I have told you often enough, believe me if you will."

The judges reformulated Joan's words to reflect their own rigid scholastic categories and concluded that her "veneration of the saints seems to partake of idolatry and to proceed from a pact made with devils. These are less divine revelations than lies invented by Joan, suggested or shown to her by the demon in illusive apparitions, in order to mock at her imagination while she meddled with things that are beyond her and superior to the faculty of her condition."[7] In other words, Joan was just too naive and uneducated to have authentic visions. But the English judges were on dangerous ground because during the previous 50 years there had been a number of notable female mystics, including St. Catherine of Siena and St. Bridget of Sweden, whose visions the pope had accepted as authentic. The English could not take the chance that they were executing a real saint. So they changed tactics.

JOAN OF ARC Arrival of Joan of Arc at the Château de Chinon, March 6th 1428.

If they could not convict her for bad theology, the English needed evidence for superstitious practices. In an attempt to do that, they drew up 70 charges against Joan. Many of these consisted of allegations of performing magic, such as chanting spells, visiting a magical tree at night, and invoking demons. They attempted to prove bad behavior by insinuating that a young man had refused to marry her on account of her immoral life. They asserted that her godmother was a notorious witch who had taught her sorcery. None of these ploys worked, however, because Joan consistently denied the charges. She did, however, admit to one allegation: she dressed as a man.

Some of the charges against her and many of the judges' questions concerned how she dressed:

> The said Joan put off and entirely abandoned women's clothes, with her hair cropped short and round in the fashion of young men, she wore shirt, breeches, doublet, with hose joined together, long and fastened to the said doublet by twenty points, long leggings laced on the outside, a short mantle reaching to the knee, or thereabouts, a close-cut cap, tight-fitting boots or buskins, long spurs, sword, dagger, breastplate, lance and other arms in the style of a man-at-arms.[8]

The judges explained to her that "according to canon law and the Holy Scriptures" a woman dressing as a man or a man as a woman is "an abomination before God."[9] She replied simply and consistently that "everything that I have done, I did by command of the voices" and that wearing male dress "would be for the great good of France."[10] When they asked her to put on a woman's dress in order to take the Eucharist on Easter Sunday, she refused, saying the miracle of the Eucharist did not depend on whether she wore a man's or a woman's clothing. On many occasions she had been asked to put on a woman's dress and refused. "And as for womanly duties, she said there were enough other women to do them."[11]

(continued on next page)

(continued from previous page)

After a long imprisonment and psychological pressure from her inquisitors, Joan confessed to charges of witchcraft, signed a recantation of her heresy, and agreed to put on a dress. She was sentenced to life imprisonment on bread and water. Why did she confess? Some historians have argued that she was tricked into confessing because the inquisitors really wanted to execute her but could not do so unless she was a *relapsed* heretic. To be relapsed she had to confess and then somehow return to her heretical ways. If that were the inquisitors' intention, Joan soon obliged them. After a few days in prison, Joan threw off the women's clothes she had been given and resumed dressing as a man.

Joan was willing to be burned at the stake rather than disobey her voices. Why? Historians will never know for sure, but dressing as a man may have been necessary for her to fulfill her role as a military leader. In her military career, Joan had adopted the masculine qualities of chivalry: bravery, steadfastness, loyalty, *and* a willingness to accept pain and death. She made herself believable by dressing as a knight. Joan's condemnation was much more than another example of men's attempt to control women. Joan's transgressive gender identity threatened the whole system of neat hierarchical distinctions upon which Christian theology rested. To the theologians, everything in God's Creation had its own proper place and anyone who changed his or her divinely ordained position in society presented a direct affront to God.

For Discussion

1. In medieval ecclesiastical trials such as this one, what kinds of evidence were presented and what kind of justice was sought?
2. What did Joan's claim that she heard voices reveal about her understanding of what constituted the proper authority over her life?

Taking It Further

Joan of Arc. *In Her Own Words*, Translated by Willard Trask. 1996. The record of what Joan reputedly said at her trials.

Warner, Marina. *Joan of Arc: The Image of Female Heroism*. 1981. A highly readable feminist reading of the Joan of Arc story.

eventually regained control of most of its territory but still suffered the most from the fighting. During the century of war, the population dropped by half, due to the ravages of combat, pillage, and plague. Third, the deaths of so many nobles and destruction of their fortunes diminished the international luxury trade. Merchants and banks as far away as Italy went broke. In addition, the war disrupted the Flemish woolen industry causing further economic damage. Finally, the war helped make England more English. Before the war the Plantagenet dynasty in England was more French than English. The monarchs possessed extensive territories in France and were embroiled in French affairs. English aristocrats also had business in France, spoke French, and married their French cousins. After 1450 the English abandoned the many French connections that had stretched across the English Channel since William the Conqueror sailed from Normandy to England in 1066. Henceforth, the English upper classes cultivated English rather than French language and culture.

The Military Revolution

The "military revolution" first became evident during the Hundred Years' War but lasted well into the seventeenth century. It refers to changes in warfare that marked the transition from the late medieval to the early modern state. The heavily armored mounted knights, who had dominated European warfare and society since the Carolingian period, were gradually supplanted by foot soldiers as the most effective fighting unit in battle. Infantry units were composed of men who fought on foot in disciplined ranks, which allowed them to break up cavalry charges by concentrating firepower in deadly volleys. Infantry soldiers could fight on a greater variety of terrains than mounted knights, who needed level ground and plenty of space for their horses to maneuver. The effectiveness of infantry units made battles more ferocious but also more decisive, which was why governments favored them. Infantry, however, put new requirements on the governments that recruited them. Armies now demanded large numbers of well-drilled foot soldiers who could move in disciplined ranks around a battlefield. Recruiting, training, and drilling soldiers made armies much more complex organizations than they had been, and officers needed to possess a wide range of management skills. Governments faced added expenses as they needed to arrange and pay for the logistical support necessary to feed and transport those large numbers. The creation of the highly centralized modern state resulted in part from the necessity to maintain a large army in which infantry played the crucial role.

Infantry used a variety of weapons. The English demonstrated the effectiveness of longbowmen during the Hundred Years' War. Capable of shooting at a much more rapid rate than the French crossbowmen, the English longbowmen at Agincourt protected themselves behind a hurriedly erected stockade of stakes and rained a shower of deadly arrows on the French cavalry to break up charges. In the narrow battlefield, which was wedged between two forests, the French cavalry had insufficient room to

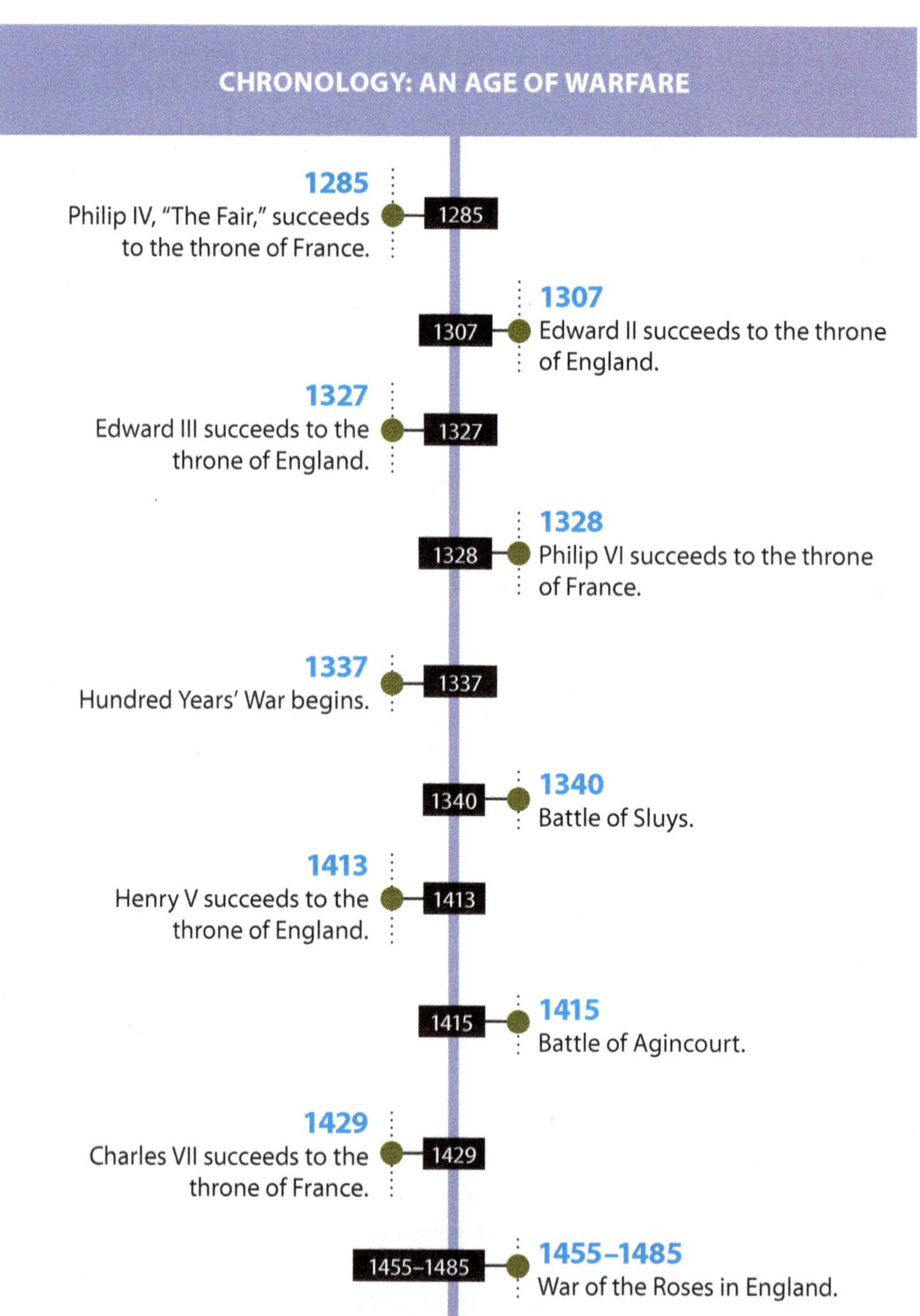

maneuver; when some of them dismounted to create more room, their heavy armor made them easy to topple over and spear through the underarm seam in their armor. Some English infantry units deployed ranks of pikemen who created an impenetrable wall of sharp spikes.

The military revolution of the fourteenth and fifteenth centuries also introduced gunpowder to European warfare. Arriving from China with the Mongol invasions, gunpowder was first used in the West in artillery. Beginning in the 1320s, besieging armies shot stone or iron against fortifications from huge wrought-iron cannons. By the early sixteenth century bronze muzzle-loading cannons were used in field battles. With the introduction during the late fifteenth century of the handgun and the harquebus (a predecessor to the musket), properly drilled and disciplined infantrymen could deliver destructive firepower. Gunshots pierced plate armor, whereas arrows bounced off. The slow rate of fire of these guns, however, necessitated carefully planned battle tactics. Around 1500 the Spanish introduced mixed infantry formations that pursued "shock" and "shot" tactics. Spanish pikemen provided the shock, which was quickly followed by gunshot or missile fire. This combination of technology and technique enabled Spanish infantry formations to defeat cavalry even in the open field without defensive fortifications, an unprecedented feat. By the end of the fifteenth century, every army included trained infantry.

The military revolution precipitated a major shift in European society. The successful states were those that created the financial base and bureaucratic structures necessary to field a professional army composed of infantry units and artillery. Superior armies required officers capable of drilling infantry or understanding the science of warfare to serve as an artillery officer.

A Troubled Church and the Demand for Religious Comfort

11.5 Why did the Church fail to provide leadership and spiritual guidance during these difficult times?

In reaction to the suffering and widespread death during the fourteenth century, many people turned to religion for spiritual consolation and for explanations of what had gone wrong. But the spiritual authority of the Church was so dangerously weakened during this period that it failed to satisfy the popular craving for solace. The moral leadership that had made the papacy such a powerful force for reform during the eleventh through thirteenth centuries evaporated in the fourteenth. Many laypeople found their own means of religious expression, making the Later Middle Ages one of the most religiously creative epochs in Christian history.

The Babylonian Captivity of the Church and the Great Schism

Faced with anarchy in the streets of Rome as local aristocrats engaged in incessant feuding, seven consecutive popes chose to reside in the relative calm of Avignon, France. This period of voluntary papal exile is known as the **Babylonian Captivity of the Church** (1305–1378), a biblical reference recalling the captivity of the Jews in Babylonia (587–539 B.C.E.). The popes' presumed subservience to the kings of France during this period dangerously politicized the papacy, destroying its ability to rise above the petty squabbles of the European princes and to serve as a spiritual authority to all. Even though these French popes residing in France were never the French kings' lackeys,

Babylonian Captivity of the Church Between 1305 and 1378 seven consecutive popes voluntarily chose to reside in Avignon, France, in order to escape anarchy in the streets of Rome. During this period the popes became subservient to the kings of France.

Different Voices

The Struggle over the Papal Monarchy

The most extreme assertion of papal authority during the Middle Ages came from Pope Boniface VIII (1294-1303). In his decree Clericis Laicos *of 1296, he asserted that any secular ruler whether emperor, king, or even minor officials of towns who taxed the Church or seized its property would incur a sentence of excommunication. In 1302 in the midst of a bitter conflict with the King of France, Boniface expanded that bold rejection of any jurisdictional claims by secular princes over the Church in the decree* Unam Sanctam *excerpted below.*

From Pope Boniface VIII, *Unam Sanctam*

We are taught by the words of the Gospel that in this church and in her power there are two swords, a spiritual one and a temporal one. . . . But both then are in the power of the church, the material sword and the spiritual. But the one is exercised for the church, the other by the church, the one by the hand of the priest, the other by the hand of kings and soldiers, though at the will and sufferance of the priest. One sword ought to be under the other and the temporal authority subject to the spiritual power. . . . Therefore we declare, state, define and pronounce that it is altogether necessary to salvation for every human creature to be subject to the Roman Pontiff.

SOURCE: *The Middle Ages*, ed. Brian Tierney. 3rd ed. (New York: Alfred A. Knopf, 1978), vol. 1, pp. 321–22. © The McGraw-Hill Companies, Inc. Reprinted by permission.

Boniface's radical claim did not sit well with medieval princes any more than it would with governments today. Not only did King Philip IV of France send troops to Boniface's hideout in Anagni in an attempt to force his resignation, but within a few years of the pope's death, the papacy itself moved to France. During the fourteenth century several theologians and political thinkers attempted to refute Boniface and to assert the authority of autonomous secular states. In this passage William of Ockham (1299–1350) defends the liberty of the emperor to act without papal interference and even questions the authority of a heretical or immoral pope over the Church itself. This passage is from Ockham's Dialogus.

From William of Ockham, *Dialogus*

Every people and every community and every body which can make law for itself without the consent or authority of anyone else can without the authority of anyone else elect certain persons to represent the whole community or body. . . . Moreover, if men so elected come together at one time, they constitute a general council, since a general council seems to be nothing else than an assembly of certain men who represent the whole of Christendom. Therefore, a general council can be convened without the authority of anyone whatever who is not a catholic and a believer, and, consequently, without the authority of a heretical pope.

SOURCE: *The Middle Ages*, ed. Brian Tierney. 3rd ed. (New York: Alfred A. Knopf, 1978), vol. 1, pp. 328. © The McGraw-Hill Companies, Inc. Reprinted by permission.

For Discussion

1. How does Boniface interpret the two swords metaphor of authority for the benefit of the clergy and the papacy? Does he leave any wiggle room for his opponents?
2. How does Ockham attack the claims of the popes that "it is altogether necessary to salvation for every human creature to be subject to the Roman Pontiff?" Is Ockham advocating democracy in this passage?

indulgences Certificates that allowed penitents to atone for their sins and reduce their time in purgatory. Usually these were issued for going on a pilgrimage or performing a pious act, but during the Babylonian Captivity of the Church (1305–1378) popes began to sell them, a practice Martin Luther protested in 1517 in an act that brought on the Protestant Reformation.

the enemies of the kings of France did not trust them. The loss of revenues from papal lands in Italy lured several popes into questionable financial schemes, which included accepting kickbacks from appointees to church offices, taking bribes for judicial decisions, and selling **indulgences**, certificates that allowed penitents to atone for their sins and reduce their time in Purgatory.

When Pope Urban VI (r. 1378–1389) announced his intention to reside in Rome, a group of disgruntled French cardinals returned to Avignon and elected a rival French pope. The Church was then divided over allegiance to Italian and French claimants to the papal throne, a period called the **Great Schism** (1378–1417). Toward the end of the schism there were actually three rival popes. During the Great Schism the kings, princes, and cities of Europe divided their allegiances between the rival candidates. Competing political alliances, not doctrinal differences, split the Church.

The Great Schism

Great Schism The division of the Catholic Church (1378–1417) between rival Italian and French claimants to the papal throne.

The **Conciliar Movement** attempted to create a mechanism for ending the Schism. The conciliarists, however, also sought to restrict the theoretical and practical authority of the papacy. They argued that a general meeting or *council* of the bishops of the Church had authority over the pope. A king could call such a council to undertake reforms, pass judgment on a standing pope, or order a conclave to elect a new one. Several general councils convened during the early fifteenth century to resolve the Schism and initiate reforms, but the intertwining of political and Church affairs made solutions difficult to achieve. The Council of Constance (1414–1417) finally succeeded in restoring unity to the Church and also in formally asserting the principle that a general council was superior to the pope and should be called frequently. The Council of Basel (1431–1449) approved a series of necessary reforms, but Pope Eugene IV (r. 1431–1447), who opposed conciliarism, never implemented them. The failure of even the timid reforms of the Council of Basel opened the way for the more radical rejection of papal authority during the Protestant Reformation of the sixteenth century.

Conciliar Movement A fifteenth-century movement that advocated ending the Great Schism and reforming church government by calling a general meeting or council of the bishops, who would exercise authority over the rival popes.

The Search for Religious Alternatives

The popes' loss of moral authority during the Babylonian Captivity and the Great Schism opened the way for a remarkable variety of reformers, mystics, and preachers. Most of these movements were traditional in their doctrines, but some were heretical. The weakened papacy was unable to control them, as it had successfully done during the thirteenth-century Crusade against the Albigensians.

PROTESTS AGAINST THE PAPACY: NEW HERESIES For most Catholic Christians during the fourteenth century, religious life consisted of witnessing or participating in the seven sacraments, the formal rituals celebrated by duly consecrated priests usually within the confines of churches. After baptism, which was universally performed on infants, the most common sacraments for lay adults were penance and communion. Both of these sacraments emphasized the authority of the clergy over the laity and therefore were potential sources for resentment. The sacrament of penance required the layperson to confess his or her sins to a priest, who then prescribed certain penalties to satisfy the sin. At communion, it was believed, the priest changed the substance of an unleavened wafer of bread, called the Eucharist, into the body of Christ and a chalice of wine into Christ's blood, a miraculous process of transubstantiation (see Chapter 10). Priests and lay recipients of communion both ate the wafer, but the chalice was reserved for the priest alone. More than anything else, the reservation of the chalice for priests profoundly symbolized the privileges of the clergy. Because medieval Catholicism was primarily a sacramental religion, reformers and heretics tended to concentrate their criticism on sacramental rituals.

The most serious discontent about the authority of the popes, the privileges of the clergy, and the efficacy of the sacraments appeared in England and Bohemia (a region in the modern Czech Republic). An Oxford professor, John Wycliffe (1320–1384), criticized the power and wealth of the clergy, played down the value of the sacraments for encouraging ethical behavior, and exalted the benefits of preaching, which promoted a sense of personal responsibility. During the Great Schism, Wycliffe rejected the authority of the rival popes and asserted instead the absolute authority of the Bible, which he wanted to make available to the laity in English rather than in Latin, which most laypeople could not understand.

Outside England Wycliffe's ideas found their most sympathetic audience among a group of reformist professors at the University of Prague in Bohemia, where Jan Hus (1369–1415) regularly preached to a large popular following. Hus's most revolutionary act was to offer the chalice of consecrated communion wine to the laity, thus symbolically diminishing the special status of the clergy. When Hus also preached against indulgences, which he said converted the sacrament of penance into a cash transaction, Pope John XXIII excommunicated him. Hus attended the Council of Constance to defend his ideas. Despite the promise of a safe-conduct from the Holy Roman emperor (whose jurisdiction included Bohemia and Constance) that should have made him immune from arrest, Hus was imprisoned, his writings were condemned, and he was burned alive as a heretic.

Wycliffe and Hus started movements that survived their own deaths. In England Wycliffe's followers were the Lollards and in Bohemia the Hussites carried on reform ideas. Both groups were eventually absorbed into the Protestant Reformation in the sixteenth century.

IMITATING CHRIST: THE MODERN DEVOTION In the climate of religious turmoil of the fourteenth and fifteenth centuries, many Christians sought deeper spiritual solace than the institutionalized Church could provide. By stressing individual piety, ethical behavior, and intense religious education, a movement called the **Modern Devotion** built on the existing traditions of spirituality and became highly influential. Promoted by the Brothers of the Common Life, a religious order established in the Netherlands, the Modern Devotion was especially popular throughout northern Europe. In the houses for the Brothers, clerics and laity lived together without monastic vows, shared household tasks, joined in regular prayers, and engaged in religious studies. (A similar structure was devised for women.) The lay brothers continued their occupations in the outside world, thus influencing their neighbors through their pious example. The houses established schools that prepared boys for church careers through constant prayer and rigorous training in Latin. Many of the leading figures behind the Protestant Reformation in the sixteenth century had attended schools run by the Brothers of the Common Life.

Modern Devotion A fifteenth-century religious movement that stressed individual piety, ethical behavior, and intense religious education. The Modern Devotion was promoted by the Brothers of the Common Life, a religious order whose influence was broadly felt through its extensive network of schools.

The Modern Devotion also spread through the influence of the best-seller of the late fifteenth century, the *Imitation of Christ*, written about 1441 by a Common Life brother, probably Thomas à Kempis. By emphasizing frequent private prayer and

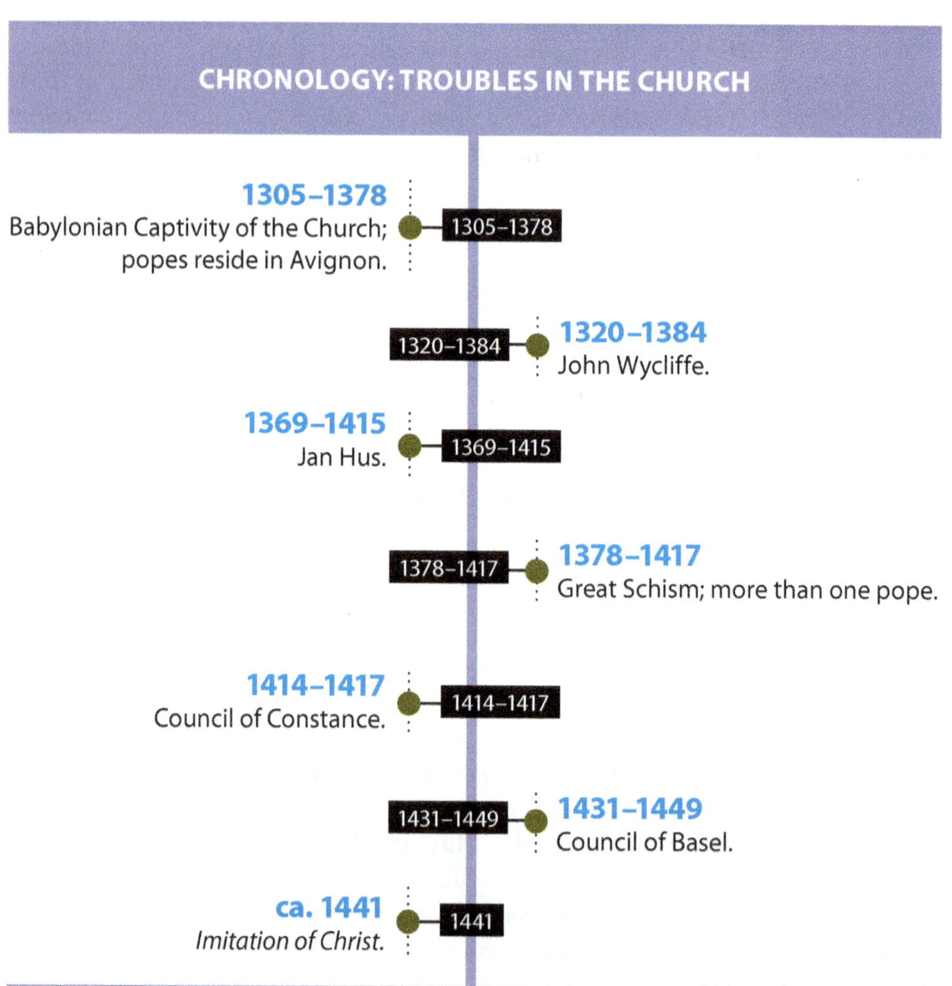

moral introspection, the *Imitation* provided a manual to guide laypeople in the path toward spiritual renewal that had traditionally been reserved for monks and nuns. There was nothing especially reformist about the *Imitation of Christ*, which emphasized the need for regular confession and communion. However, its popularity helped prepare the way for a broad-based reform of the Church by turning the walls of the monastery inside out, spilling out a large number of lay believers who were dedicated to becoming living examples of moral purity for their neighbors.

The Culture of Loss

11.6 How did European culture offer explanations and solace for the otherwise inexplicable calamities of the times?

During the fourteenth and early fifteenth centuries, the omnipresence of violence and death provoked widespread anxiety. This anxiety had many manifestations. Some people went on long penitential pilgrimages to the shrines of saints or to the Holy Land. During the fourteenth century the tribulations of the pilgrim's travels became a metaphor for the journey of life itself, stimulating creative literature. Still others tried to find someone to blame for calamities. The search for scapegoats focused on minority groups, especially Jews and Muslims.

Reminders of Death

In no other period of Western civilization has the idea of death so pervaded popular cultures as during the fourteenth and fifteenth centuries. The Reminders of Death was a theme found in religious books, literary works, and the visual arts. A contemporary book of moral guidance advised the reader that "when he goes to bed, he should imagine not that he is putting himself to bed, but that others are laying him in his grave."[12] Reminders of Death became the everyday theme of preachers, and popular woodcuts represented death in simple but disturbing images. The Reminders of Death tried to encourage ethical behavior in this life by showing that in everyone's future was neither riches, nor fame, nor love, nor pleasure, but only the decay of death.

The most famous Reminder of Death was the Dance of Death. First appearing in a poem of 1376, the Dance of Death evolved into a street play, performed to illustrate sermons that called for repentance. It also appeared in church murals, depicting a procession led by a skeleton that included representatives of the social orders, from children and peasants to pope and emperor. All danced to their inevitable deaths. At the Church of the Innocents in Paris, the inscription that accompanies the mural depicting the Dance of Death reads:

> Advance, see yourselves in us, dead, naked, rotten and stinking. So will you be. . . . To live without thinking of this risks damnation. . . . Power, honor, riches are nothing; at the hour of death only good works count. . . . Everyone should think at least once a day of his loathsome end [in order to escape] the dreadful pain of hell without end which is unspeakable.[13]

In earlier centuries, tombs had depicted death as serene: On top of the tomb rested an effigy of the deceased, dressed in the finest clothes with hands piously folded and eyes open to the promise of eternal life. In contrast, during the fourteenth century, tomb effigies began to depict putrefying bodies or naked skeletons, symbols of the futility of human status and achievements. These tombs were disturbingly graphic Reminders of Death. Likewise, poems spoke of the disgusting smell of rotting flesh, the livid color of plague victims, and the cold touch of the dead.

DANCE OF DEATH This late-fifteenth century painted engraving illustrates the fascination with death during the period. The skeletons dance and play musical instruments. The cadaver on the right holds his own entrails.

Late medieval society was completely frank about the unpleasant process of dying, unlike modern societies that hide the dying in hospitals and segregate mourning to funeral homes. Dying was a public event, almost a theatrical performance. The last rites of the Catholic Church and the Art of Dying served to assist souls in their final test before God and to separate the departed from their kin. According to the Art of Dying, outlined in numerous advice books and illustrations, the sick or injured person should die in bed, surrounded by a room full of people, including children. Christians believed that a dying person watched a supernatural spectacle visible to him or her alone as the heavenly host fought with Satan and his demon minions for the soul. The Art of Dying compared the deathbed contest to a horrific game of chess in which the Devil did all he could to trap the dying person into a checkmate just at the moment of death. In the best of circumstances, a priest arrived in time to hear a confession, offer words of consolation, encourage the dying individual to forgive his or her enemies and redress any wrongs, and perform the last rites.

Pilgrims of the Imagination

During the Middle Ages, a pilgrimage offered a religiously sanctioned form of escape from the omnipresent suffering and peril. Pious Christians could go on a pilgrimage to the Holy Land, Rome, or the shrine of a saint, such as Santiago de Compostela in Spain, Canterbury in England, or Częstochowa in Poland. The usual motive for a pilgrimage was to fulfill a vow or promise made to God, or to obtain an indulgence, which exempted the pilgrim from some of the time spent in punishment in Purgatory after death. The pilgrimage became the instrument for spiritual liberation and escape from difficulties. As a result, going on a pilgrimage became a compelling model for creative literature, especially during the fourteenth century. Not all of these great works of literature were fictional pilgrimages, but many evoked the pilgrim's impulse to find a refuge from the difficulties of daily life or to find solace in the promise of a better life to come.

DANTE ALIGHIERI AND *THE DIVINE COMEDY* In *The Divine Comedy* an Italian poet from Florence, Dante Alighieri (1265–1321), imagined the most fantastic pilgrimage ever attempted, a journey through Hell, Purgatory, and Paradise. A work of astounding originality, *The Divine Comedy* remains the greatest masterpiece of medieval literature. Little is known about Dante's early life except that somehow he acquired expertise in Greek philosophy, scholastic theology (the application of logic to the understanding of Christianity, discussed in Chapter 10), Latin literature, and the newly fashionable poetic forms in Provençal, the language of southern France. Dante's involvement in the dangerous politics of Florence led to his exile under pain of death if he ever returned. During his exile Dante wandered for years, suffering grievously the loss of his home: "Bitter is the taste of another man's bread and . . . heavy the way up and down another man's stair" (*Paradiso,* canto 17). He sustained himself by writing his great poetic vision of human destiny and God's plan for redemption.

In the poem Dante himself travels into the Christian version of the afterlife. Dante's trip, initially guided by the Latin poet Virgil, the epitome of ancient wisdom, starts in Hell. As he travels deeper into Hell's harsh depths, a cast of sinful characters who inhabit the world of the damned warn Dante of the harmful values of this world. In Purgatory his guide becomes Beatrice, Dante's deceased beloved, who stands for the Christian virtues. In this section of the poem, he begins the painful process of spiritual rehabilitation

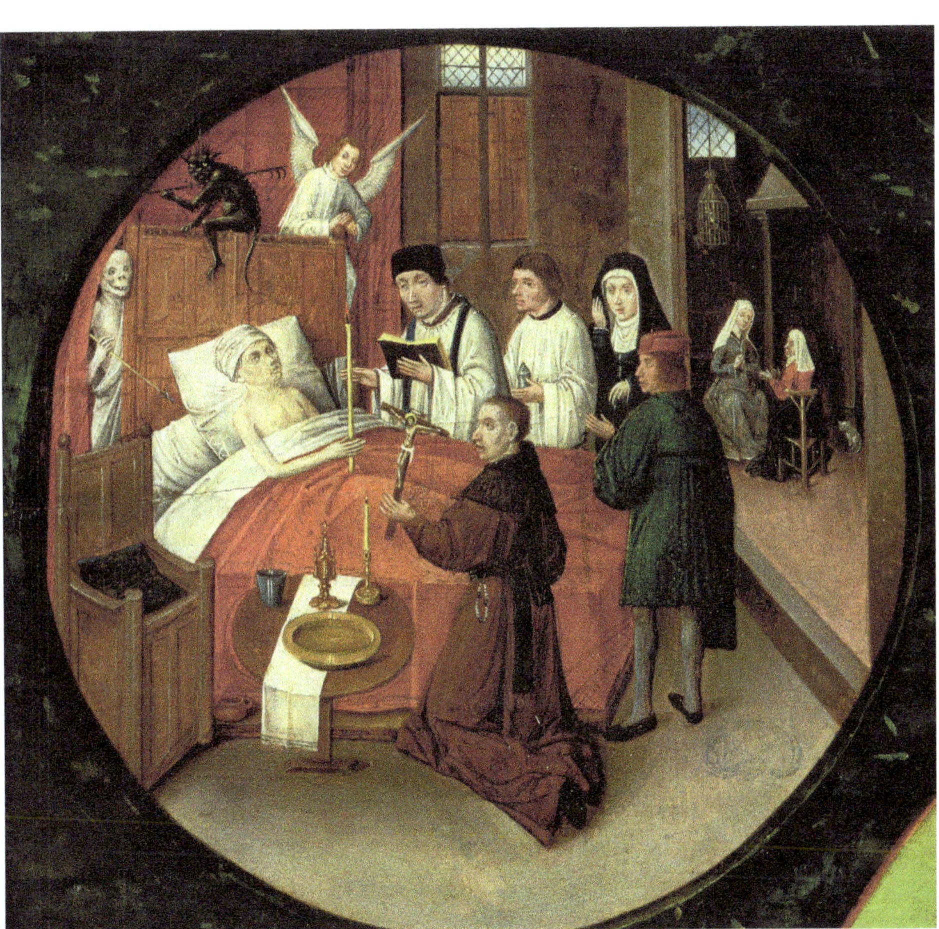

THE ART OF DYING In this death scene, the dying man receives extreme unction (last rites) from a priest. A friar holds a crucifix for him to contemplate. Above his head a devil and angel compete for his soul, while behind him Death lurks waiting for his moment.

in which he comes to accept the Christian image of life as a pilgrimage. In Paradise he achieves spiritual fulfillment by speaking with figures from the past who have defied death. Although the poem is deeply Christian, it displays numerous non-Christian influences. The passage through Hell, for example, derived from a long Muslim poem reconstructing Muhammad's *miraj*, a night journey to Jerusalem and ascent to heaven.

The lasting appeal of this long and difficult poem is a wonder. Underlying the appeal of *The Divine Comedy* is perhaps its optimism, which expresses Dante's own cure to his depressing condition as an exile. The power of Dante's poetry established the form of the modern Italian language. Even in translation the images and stories can intrigue and fascinate.

GEOFFREY CHAUCER AND *THE CANTERBURY TALES* Geoffrey Chaucer (ca. 1342–1400) was the most outstanding English poet prior to William Shakespeare. As a courtier and diplomat, Chaucer was a trusted adviser to three successive English kings. But he is best known for his literary output, including *The Canterbury Tales.*

In *The Canterbury Tales* a group of 30 pilgrims tell stories as they travel on horseback to the shrine at Canterbury. Chaucer's use of the pilgrimage as a framing device for telling the stories allowed him to bring together a collection of people from across the social spectrum, including a wife, indulgence hawker, miller, town magistrate, clerk, landowner, lawyer, merchant, knight, abbess, and monk. The variety of characters who told the tales allowed Chaucer to experiment with many kinds of literary forms, from a chivalric romance to a sermon. The pilgrimage combined the considerations of religious morality with the fun of a spring vacation. Many pilgrims were more concerned with the pleasures of this world than preparing for the next, which was the avowed purpose of going on a pilgrimage. In this intertwining of the worldly and the spiritual, Chaucer brought the abstract principles of Christian morality down to a level of common understanding.

CHRISTINE DE PISAN AND THE DEFENSE OF FEMALE VIRTUE The work of the poet Christine de Pisan (1364–1430) was not a spiritual pilgrimage like Dante's or Chaucer's but a thoughtful and passionate commentary on the tumultuous issues of her day. At age 15 Pisan married a notary of King Charles V of France, but by age 25 she was a widow with three young children. In order to support her family, she turned to writing and relied on the patronage of the royalty and wealthy aristocrats of France, Burgundy, Germany, and England.

Christine de Pisan championed the cause of women in a male-dominated society. Following the fashion of the times, she invented a new chivalric order, the Order of the Rose, whose members took a vow to defend the honor of women. She wrote a defense of women for a male readership and an allegorical autobiography. But she is most famous for the two books she wrote for women readers, *The Book of the City of Ladies* and *The Book of Three Virtues* (both about 1407). In these she recounted tales of the heroism and virtue of women and offered moral instruction for women in different social roles. In 1415 she retired to a convent where in the last year of her life she wrote a masterpiece of ecstatic lyricism that celebrated the early victories of Joan of Arc. Pisan's book turned the martyred Joan into the heroine of France.

Defining Cultural Boundaries

During the Later Middle Ages, systematic discrimination against certain ethnic and religious groups increased markedly in Europe. As European society enforced ever-higher levels of religious uniformity, intolerance spread in the ethnically mixed societies of the European periphery. Intolerance was marked in three areas: Spain with its mixture of Muslim, Jewish, and Christian cultures; the German borderlands in east-central

Europe, where Germans mingled with Slavs; and Ireland and Wales, where Celts came under the domination of the English. Within the heartland of Europe were other areas of clashing cultures—Switzerland, for example, where the folk culture of peasants and shepherds living in the isolated mountains collided with the intense Christian religiosity of the cities.

RELIGIOUS COMMUNITIES IN TENSION The Iberian peninsula was home to thriving communities of Muslims, Jews, and Christians. Since the eleventh century the aggressive northern Christian kingdoms of Castile and Aragon had engaged in a protracted program of Reconquest (*Reconquista*) against the Muslim states of the peninsula. By 1248 the Reconquest was largely completed, with only a small Muslim enclave in Granada holding out until 1492. The Spanish Reconquest placed former enemies in close proximity to one another. Hostilities between Christians and Muslims ranged from active warfare to tense stalemate, with Jews working as cultural intermediaries between the two larger communities.

During the twelfth and thirteenth centuries Muslims, called the Mudejars, who capitulated to the conquering Christians, received guarantees that they could continue to practice their own religion and laws. During the fourteenth century, however, Christian kings gradually reneged on these promises. In 1301 the king of Castile decreed that the testimony of any two Christian witnesses could convict a Jew or Muslim, notwithstanding any previously granted privileges that allowed them to be tried in their own courts. The Arabic language began to disappear in Spain as the Mudejars suffered discrimination on many levels. By the sixteenth century, the practice of Islam became illegal, and the Spanish state adopted a systematic policy to destroy Mudejar culture by prohibiting Muslim dress, customs, and marriage practices.

The Jews also began to feel the pain of organized, official discrimination. Christian preachers accused Jews of poisonings, stealing Christian babies, and cannibalism. When the Black Death arrived in 1348, the Jews of Aragon were accused of having poisoned the wells, even though Jews were dying just like Christians. Beginning in 1378, a Catholic prelate in Seville, Ferrant Martínez, commenced an anti-Jewish preaching campaign by calling for the destruction of all 23 of the city's synagogues, the confinement of Jews to a ghetto, the dislodging of all Jews from public positions, and the prohibition of any social contact between Christians and Jews. His campaign led to an attack on the Jews of Seville in 1391. Violence spread to other cities throughout the peninsula and the nearby Balearic Islands. Jews faced a stark choice: conversion or death. After a year of mob violence, about 100,000 Jews had been murdered and an equal number had gone into hiding or fled to more tolerant Muslim countries. The 1391 pogroms led to the first significant forced conversions of Jews in Spain. A century later in 1492, on the heels of the final Christian victory of the Reconquest, all remaining Jews in Spain were compelled to either leave or convert.

Violence against religious minorities occurred in many places, but besides Spain it was most systematic in German-speaking lands. Between November 1348 and August 1350, violence against Jews occurred in more than 80 German towns. Like the allegations in Aragon, the fear that Jews poisoned the wells led to massacres in German lands even *before* plague had arrived in these communities. The frequent occurrence of violence on Sundays or feast days suggests that preachers consciously or unconsciously encouraged the rioting mobs.

Jews had already been expelled from England in 1290 and France in 1306. The situation for Jews was better in Italy where the small population of Jews signed contracts with local towns offering them protection. This pattern of friction among ethnic communities was largely absent in Poland, however, where King Casimir III the Great (1333–1370) granted Jews special privileges and welcomed Jewish immigrants, many of them fleeing persecution elsewhere.

ETHNIC COMMUNITIES IN TENSION Other regions with diverse populations also witnessed discrimination and its brutal consequences. During the population boom of the twelfth and thirteenth centuries, German-speaking immigrants had established colonial towns in the Baltic and penetrated eastward, creating isolated pockets of German culture in Bohemia, Poland, and Hungary. During the fourteenth and fifteenth centuries, hostilities between the native populations and the colonizing Germans arose, particularly in Bohemia. One Czech prince offered 100 silver marks to anyone who brought him 100 German noses. The Teutonic Knights, who had been the vanguard of the German migrations in the Baltic, began to require German ancestry for membership. In German-speaking towns along the colonized borderlands of east-central Europe, city councils and guilds began to use ethnicity as a qualification for holding certain offices or joining a guild. The most famous example was the "German Paragraph" in guild statutes, which required candidates for admission to a guild to prove German descent. As the statutes of a bakers' guild put it, "Whoever wishes to be a member must bring proof to the councilors and the guildsmen that he is born of legitimate, upright German folk." Others required members to be "of German blood and tongue," as if language were a matter of biological inheritance.[14] German guildsmen were also forbidden to marry non-Germans.

In the Celtic fringe of the British Isles, too, discrimination became far more evident in the fourteenth century. In Ireland the ruling English promulgated laws that attempted to protect the cultural identity of the English colonists. The English prohibited native Irish from citizenship in town or guild membership. The Statutes of Kilkenny of 1366 attempted to legislate ethnic purity: They prohibited intermarriage between English and Irish and required English colonists to speak English, use English names, wear English clothes, and ride horses in the English way. They also forbade the English to play Irish games or listen to Irish music. A similar pattern appeared in Wales, where the lines dividing the Welsh and English communities hardened as the English community attempted to prevent its absorption into the majority culture.

CONCLUSION

Looking Inward

Unlike the more dynamic, outward-looking thirteenth century, Europeans during the fourteenth and early fifteenth centuries turned their attention inward to their own communities and their own problems. Europe faced one calamity after another, each crisis compounding the misery. The process of changing Western identities during this period can be seen in two ways.

First, as a result of the Western encounters with the Mongol and Ottoman Empires, the political and religious frontiers of the West shifted. These two empires redrew the map of the West by ending the Christian Byzantine Empire. With the Mongol invasions, the eastward spread of Christianity into Asia ended. The Ottoman conquests left a lasting Muslim influence inside Europe, particularly in Bosnia and Albania. The Ottoman Empire remained hostile to and frequently at war with the Christian West for more than 200 years.

Second, most Europeans reinforced their identity as Christians and became more self-conscious of the country in which they lived. At the same time Christian civilization was becoming eclipsed in parts of the Balkans, however, it revived in the Iberian peninsula, where the Muslim population (once the most extensive in the West) suffered discrimination and defeat. The northern Spanish kingdoms, for example, began to unify their subjects around a militant form of Christianity that was overtly hostile to Muslims and Jews. In many places in the West, religious and ethnic discrimination against minorities increased. A stronger sense of self-identification by country can be most dramatically seen in France and England as a consequence of the Hundred Years' War.

Except for the very visible military conquests of the Mongols and the Ottomans, the causes of most of the calamities of the fourteenth century were invisible or unknown. No one recognized a climate change or understood the dynamics of the population crisis. No one understood the cause of the epidemics. Only a few merchants grasped the role of the Mongol Empire in the world economy or the causes for the collapse of banking and trade. Unable to distinguish how these forces were changing their lives, Europeans only witnessed their consequences. In the face of these calamities, European culture became obsessed with death and with finding scapegoats to blame for events that could not be otherwise explained. However, calamity also bred creativity. The search for answers to the question, "Why did this happen to us?" produced a new spiritual sensibility and a rich literature. Following the travails of the fourteenth century, moreover, there arose in the fifteenth a new, more optimistic cultural movement—the Renaissance. Gloom and doom were not the only responses to troubles. As we will see in the next chapter, during the Renaissance some people began to search for new answers to human problems in a fashion that would transform the West anew.

MAKING CONNECTIONS

1. Many of the responses to the calamities of the fourteenth century seem "irrational" to modern eyes. Why might people have reacted in these ways? If one-third of the population of the United States were to die from a mysterious disease in a matter of a few months, how do you think people would react today?
2. Calamities provoked fear. Who were the most likely victims of widespread fear?
3. How could the Church have better helped Christians deal with their suffering during this period?

TAKING IT FURTHER

For suggested readings, websites, and films, see page R-1.

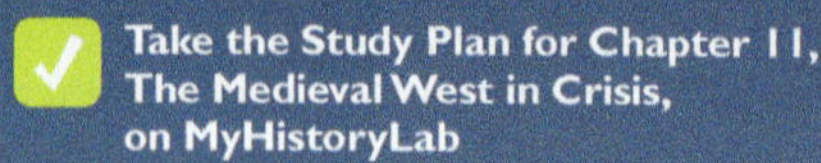
Take the Study Plan for Chapter 11, The Medieval West in Crisis, on MyHistoryLab

Chapter Review

A Time of Death

11.1 What caused the deaths of so many Europeans?

A crisis in food production, caused by a combination of the limitations of medieval agriculture and climate change, resulted in widespread famine and a population susceptible to disease. Weakened and starving, 20 million people died in Europe from the Black Death, which, historians suspect, was a variation of the modern bubonic plague.

A Cold Wind from the East

11.2 How did forces outside Europe, in particular the Mongol and Ottoman Empires, influence conditions in the West?

Hundreds of years of attacks allowed the Mongol and Ottoman Empires to redraw the map of the West. The Ottoman conquests created a lasting Muslim presence within the borders of Europe. Consequently, the potential Orthodox allies in the East of the Catholic Christian West were weakened or eliminated.

Economic Depression and Social Turmoil

11.3 How did disturbances in the rudimentary global economy of the Middle Ages precipitate almost complete financial collapse and widespread social discontent in Europe?

Since the fragile financial system of medieval Europe was tied to the international trade for luxury goods, the trade's collapse, due to disrupted supply sources, caused a major depression. As the economy declined, social unrest spread when those with grievances ranging from low wages to unemployment targeted the urban guilds. These tensions exploded into dangerous revolts that eventually spread to rural areas.

An Age of Warfare

11.4 How did incessant warfare transform the most powerful medieval states?

Continuous war between England and France, its two most powerful kingdoms, further weakened western Europe and revealed the fragility of the medieval monarchies. The conflict drained resources from the French and English aristocracies, worsening the economic depression by diminishing the international luxury trade.

A Troubled Church and the Demand for Religious Comfort

11.5 Why did the Church fail to provide leadership and spiritual guidance during these difficult times?

Unrest in Rome prompted the voluntary exile to France of several popes, and this in turn caused many to view the papacy as beholden to France's kings. One result was the Great Schism, which led to first two and then three claimants to the papal throne, with rulers of Europe dividing their loyalty among them. The papacy was unable to rise above the squabbles of the European princes and serve as a spiritual and moral authority to all. Instead, an anxious populace turned to a variety of reformers, mystics, and preachers.

The Culture of Loss

11.6 How did European culture offer explanations and solace for the otherwise inexplicable calamities of the times?

European culture became obsessed with death and searched for meaning during a time of famine, plague, and unrest. This search for answers bred a new spiritual sensibility that included penitential pilgrimages, which in turn spawned a rich literature. Others looked for someone to blame for events that could not be otherwise explained, and the search for scapegoats focused on minority groups, especially Jews and Muslims.

On MyHistoryLab

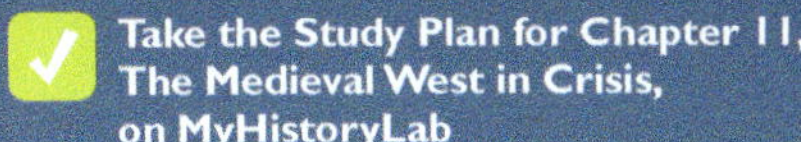
Take the Study Plan for Chapter 11, The Medieval West in Crisis, on MyHistoryLab

Chapter Time Line

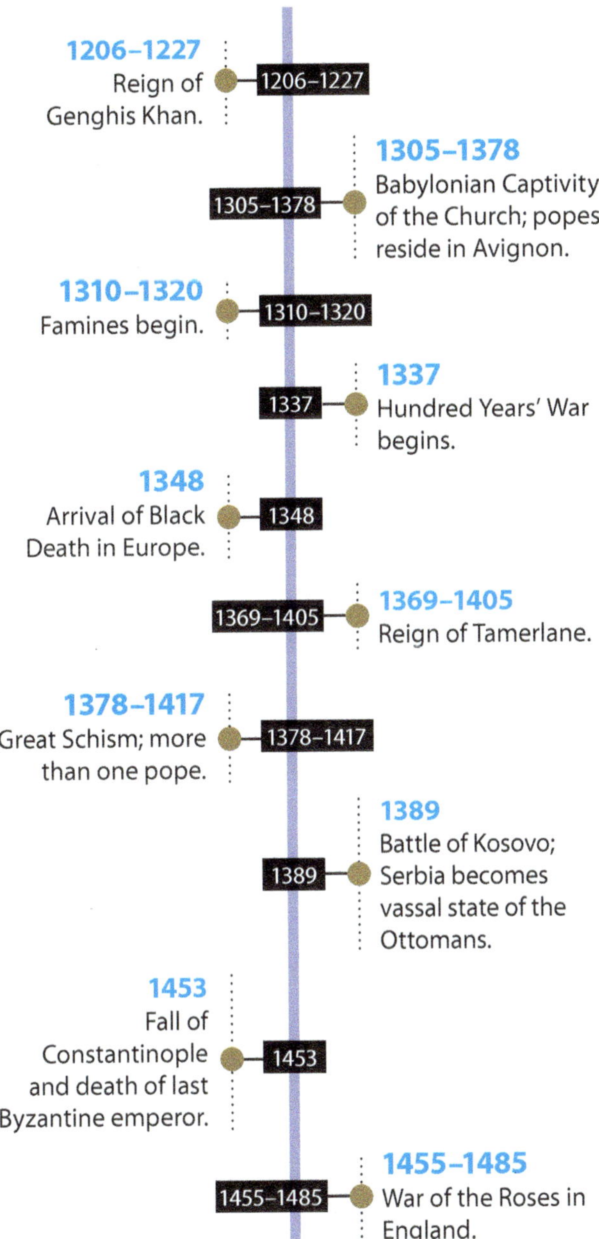

GLOSSARY

absolutism (p. 493) A theory and form of government in the seventeenth and eighteenth centuries in which a ruler claimed unrivaled power.

acropolis (p. 80) The defensible hilltop around which a polis grew. In classical Athens, the Acropolis was the site of the Parthenon (Temple of Athena).

agora (p. 81) An open area in the town center of a Greek polis that served as a market and a place for informal discussion.

agricultural revolution (p. 298) Refers to technological innovations that began to appear during the eleventh century, making possible a dramatic growth in population. The agricultural revolution came about through harnessing new sources of power with water and windmills, improving the pulling power of animals with better collars, using heavy plows to better exploit the soils of northern Europe, and employing a three-field crop rotation system that increased the amount and quality of food available.

alchemy (p. 531) The practice, rooted in a philosophical tradition, of attempting to turn base metals into precious ones. It also involved the identification of natural substances for medical purposes. Alchemy was influential in the development of chemistry and medicine in the sixteenth and seventeenth centuries.

aldeias (p. 412) Settlements for natives who had converted to Christianity in Brazil. In these settlements the Jesuit fathers protected the natives from enslavement.

Alexandrianism (p. 131) A style of Hellenistic poetry that demonstrated a command of meter and language and appealed more to the intellect than the emotions.

Allies (p. 779) During World War I, the states allied against the Central Powers of Germany and Austria-Hungary. During World War II, the states allied against the regimes of Nazi Germany, fascist Italy, and imperial Japan.

Anabaptism (p. 447) Meaning "to rebaptize"; refers to those Protestant radicals of the sixteenth century who rejected infant baptism and adopted adult baptism. Anabaptists treated the Bible as a blueprint for reforming not just the church but all of society, a tendency that led them to reject the authority of the state, to live in self-governing "holy communities," and in some cases to practice a primitive form of communism.

anarchism (p. 732) Ideology that views the state as unnecessary and repressive and rejects participation in parliamentary politics in favor of direct, usually violent, action.

anticlericalism (p. 759) Opposition to the political influence of the Roman Catholic Church.

Antonine Age (p. 172) Almost one hundred years of political stability in the Roman Empire, inaugurated when Nerva adopted Trajan as his son and heir.

Antonine Decree (p. 180) In 212 C.E. the emperor Aurelius Antoninus, called Caracalla, issued a decree that granted citizenship to all the free inhabitants of the Roman Empire. The decree enabled Roman law to embrace the entire population of the empire.

Apocalypse (p. 439) In the language of the Bible, the end times which would lead into Christ's Second Coming.

appeasement (p. 849) British diplomatic and financial efforts to stabilize Germany in the 1920s and 1930s and so avoid a second world war.

Arians (p. 212) Christians who believe that God the Father is superior to Jesus Christ his Son. Most of the Germanic settlers in western Europe in the fifth century were Arians.

aristocracy (p. 587) A term that originally applied to those who were considered the most fit to rule and later identified the wealthiest members of society, especially those who owned land.

asceticism (p. 214) The Christian practice of severely suppressing physical needs and daily desires in an effort to achieve a spiritual union with God. Asceticism is the practice that underlies the monastic movement.

auto-da-fé (p. 468) Meaning literally a "theater of faith," an *auto* was practiced by the Catholic Church in early modern Spain and Portugal as an extended public ritual of penance designed to cause physical pain among the sinful and promote fear of God's judgment among those who witnessed it.

auxiliary (p. 176) Soldiers in the Roman imperial army who were drawn from subject peoples. Auxiliaries received Roman citizenship after their term of service.

Babylonian Captivity of the Church (p. 352) Between 1305 and 1378, seven consecutive popes voluntarily chose to reside in Avignon, France, in order to escape anarchy in the streets of Rome. During this period the popes became subservient to the kings of France.

Babylonian Exile (p. 69) The period of Jewish history between the destruction of Solomon's temple in Jerusalem by Babylonian armies in 587 B.C.E., and 538 B.C.E, when Cyrus of Persia permitted Jews to return to Palestine and rebuild the temple.

balance of power (p. 501) An arrangement in which various countries form alliances to prevent any one state from dominating the others.

Balfour Declaration (p. 809) Declaration of 1917 that affirmed British support of a Jewish state in Palestine.

barbarians (p. 112) A term used by Greeks to describe people who did not speak Greek and who were therefore considered uncivilized.

baroque (pp. 129, 498) A dynamic style in art, architecture, and music that was intended to elicit an emotional response.

Baroque buildings were massive, imposing structures with sweeping façades. The baroque style represented a development of Greek classicism in the Hellenistic period. In the seventeenth century the baroque style was closely associated with royal absolutism.

Berlin Wall (p. 897) Constructed by the East German government, the wall physically cut the city of Berlin in two and prevented East German citizens from access to West Germany; stood from 1961 to 1989.

Big Three (p. 883) Term applied to the British, Soviet, and U.S. leaders during World War II: until 1945, Winston Churchill, Joseph Stalin, and Franklin Roosevelt; by the summer of 1945, Clement Attlee, Joseph Stalin, and Harry Truman.

Black Death (p. 330) An epidemic disease, possibly Bubonic plague, that struck Europe between 1348 and the 1350s, killing at least one-third of the total population.

blitzkrieg (p. 851) "Lightning war"; offensive military tactic making use of airplanes, tanks, and motorized infantry to punch through enemy defenses and secure key territory. First demonstrated by the German army in World War II.

boers (p. 557) Dutch settlers, most of them farmers, who settled in the Dutch colony established at the Cape of Good Hope in southern Africa.

Bolsheviks (p. 803) Minority group of Russian socialists, headed by Vladimir Lenin, who espoused an immediate transition to a socialist state. It became the Communist Party in the Soviet Union.

boule (p. 85) A council of 400 male citizens established by Solon in Greece in the sixth century B.C.E. It served as an advisory body for the general assembly of all male citizens.

Bourbon reforms (p. 559) Measures introduced by the Bourbon kings of Spain in the eighteenth century to make the Spanish Empire more manageable and profitable.

bourgeoisie (p. 594) A social group, technically consisting of those who were untitled people living in the towns, that included prosperous merchants and financiers, members of the professions, and some skilled craftsmen known as "petty bourgeoisie." In later centuries, synonymous with "middle class."

boyars (p. 487) Upper-level nobles who dominated Russian society until the tsars began to supplant them in the fifteenth and sixteenth centuries.

Bretton Woods Agreement (p. 884) Agreement signed in 1944 that established the post-World War II economic framework in which the U.S. dollar served as the world's reserve currency.

brinkmanship (p. 894) Style of Cold War confrontation in which each superpower endeavored to convince the other that it was willing to wage nuclear war.

Byzantine Empire (p. 225) The eastern half of the Roman Empire, which lasted from the founding of Constantinople in 324 to its conquest by the Ottoman Turks in 1453.

caliphate (p. 248) The Islamic imperial government that evolved under the leadership of Abu Bakr (r. 632–634), the successor of the prophet Muhammad. The sectarian division within Islam between the Shi'ites and Sunni derived from a disagreement over how to determine the hereditary succession from Muhammad to the caliphate, which combined governmental and some religious responsibilities.

calling (p. 443) The Calvinist doctrine that God calls the Elect to perform his will on Earth. God's calling gave Calvinists a powerful sense of personal direction.

canon law (p. 276) The collected laws of the Roman Catholic Church. Canon law applied to cases involving the clergy, disputes about church property, and donations to the Church. It also applied to the laity for annulling marriages, legitimating bastards, prosecuting bigamy, protecting widows and orphans, and resolving inheritance disputes.

capital (p. 661) All the physical assets used in production, including fixed capital, such as machinery, and circulating capital, such as raw materials; more generally, the cost of these physical assets.

caravels (p. 397) Hybrid three-masted ships developed about 1450 in the Iberian peninsula by combining the rigging of square with triangular lateen sails. These ships could be sailed in a variety of winds, carry large cargoes, be managed by a small crew, and be defended by guns mounted in the castle superstructure.

Carolingian Renaissance (p. 275) The "rebirth" of interest in ancient Greek and Latin literature and language during the reign of the Frankish emperor Charlemagne (r. 768–814). Charlemagne promoted the intensive study of Latin to promote governmental efficiency and to propagate the Christian faith.

Catholic Reformation (p. 451) A series of efforts during the sixteenth century to purify the Church that evolved out of late medieval spirituality and that included the creation of new religious orders, especially the Society of Jesus.

Central Powers (p. 779) Germany and Austria-Hungary in World War I.

Chalcedonians (p. 213) Christians who followed the doctrinal decisions and definitions of the Council of Chalcedon in 451 C.E. stating that Christ's human and divine natures were equal, but entirely distinct and united in one person "without confusion, division, separation, or change." Chalcedonian Christianity came to be associated with the Byzantine Empire and is called Greek Orthodoxy. In western Europe it is known as Roman Catholicism.

Chartists (p. 698) A British group of workers and middle-class radicals who drafted a People's Charter in 1837 demanding universal male suffrage and other political reforms.

chinoiserie (p. 576) A French word for an eighteenth-century decorative art that combined Chinese and European motifs.

Christian Democracy, Christian Democratic parties (p. 905) Conservative and confessionally based (Roman Catholic) political parties that dominated much of western European politics after World War II.

Christian humanists (p. 429) During the fifteenth and sixteenth centuries these experts in Greek, Latin, and Hebrew subjected the Bible to philological study in an attempt to understand the precise meaning of the founding text of Christianity.

Church Fathers (p. 219) Writers in late antiquity from both the Greek- and Latin-speaking worlds who sought to reconcile Christianity with classical learning.

circuit court (p. 317) Established by King Henry II (r. 1154–1189) to make royal justice available to virtually anyone in England. Circuit court judges visited every shire in England four times a year.

civic humanism (p. 376) A branch of humanism introduced by the Florentine chancellor Leonardo Bruni, who defended the republican institutions and values of the city. Civic humanism promoted the ethic of responsible citizenship.

civic virtue (p. 167) The belief that the success of a republic depended on its citizens' possession of personal traits that contributed to the common good.

civilization (p. 11) The term used by archaeologists to describe a society differentiated by levels of wealth and power, and in which religious, economic, and political control are based in cities.

civil society (p. 925) Public organizations and activities separate from the state, commerce, or the family that help to create community life and a sense of identity.

clans or kin groups (p. 267) The basic social and political unit of Germanic society consisting of blood relatives obliged to defend one another and take vengeance for crimes against the group and its members.

class (p. 588) A social group with similar economic and political interests.

class consciousness (p. 670) The awareness of people from different occupations that they belonged to a class.

classicism (p. 591) A style in art, architecture, music, and literature that emphasizes proportion, adherence to traditional forms, and a rejection of emotion and enthusiasm.

Cluny (p. 304) A monastery founded in Burgundy in 910 that became the center of a far-reaching movement to reform the Church that was sustained in more than 1,500 Cluniac monasteries, modeled after the original in Cluny.

Cold War (p. 883) Struggle for global supremacy between the United States and the Soviet Union, waged from the end of World War II until 1990.

collectivization (p. 828) The replacement of private and village farms with large cooperative agricultural enterprises run by state-employed managers. Collectivization was a key part of Joseph Stalin's plans for modernizing the Soviet economy and destroying peasant opposition to communist rule.

Columbian exchange (p. 417) The trade of peoples, plants, animals, microbes, and ideas between the Old and New Worlds that began with Columbus.

Columbian question (p. 420) The debate among historians and epidemiologists about whether syphilis or its ancestor disease originated in the Americas and was brought to the Old World after Columbus's voyages.

communes (p. 301) Sworn defensive associations of merchants and workers that appeared in north-central Italy after 1070 and that became the effective government of more than a hundred cities. The communes evolved into city-states by seizing control of the surrounding countryside.

communism (p. 686) The revolutionary form of socialism developed by Karl Marx and Friedrich Engels that promoted the overthrow of bourgeois or capitalist institutions and the establishment of a dictatorship of the proletariat.

Companions (p. 113) Elite regiments of cavalrymen armed with heavy lances formed by Philip of Macedon in the fourth century B.C.E.

Concert of Europe (p. 693) The joint efforts made by Austria, Prussia, Russia, Britain, and France during the years following the Congress of Vienna to suppress liberal and nationalist movements throughout Europe.

Conciliar Movement (p. 352) A fifteenth-century movement that advocated ending the Great Schism and reforming church government by calling a general meeting or council of the bishops, who would exercise authority over the rival popes.

confessions (p. 460) The formal sixteenth-century statements of religious doctrine: the Confession of Augsburg for Lutherans, the Helvetic Confessions for Calvinists, the Thirty-Nine Articles for Anglicans, and the decrees of the Council of Trent for Catholics.

Congress of Vienna (p. 647) A conference of the major powers of Europe in 1814–1815 to establish a new balance of power at the end of the Napoleonic Wars.

conquistadores (p. 407) Spanish adventurers in the Americas who explored and conquered the lands of indigenous peoples, sometimes without legal authority but usually with a legal privilege granted by the king of Spain who required that one-fifth of all things of value be turned over to the crown. The conquistadores extended Spanish sovereignty over new lands.

conservatism (p. 683) A nineteenth-century ideology intended to prevent a recurrence of the revolutionary changes of the 1790s and the implementation of liberal policies.

corporatism (p. 819) The practice by which committees (or "corporations") made up of representatives of workers, employers, and the state direct the economy.

Cortes (p. 494) Legislative assemblies in the Spanish kingdoms.

cosmology (p. 134) A theory concerning the structure and nature of the universe such as those proposed by Aristotle in the fourth century B.C.E. and Copernicus in the sixteenth century.

counties (p. 275) Territorial units devised by the Carolingian dynasty during the eighth and ninth centuries for the administration of the empire. Each county was administered by a count who was rewarded with lands and sent to areas where he had no family ties to serve as a combined provincial governor, judge, military commander, and representative of the king.

courtly love (p. 323) An ethic first found in the poems of the late twelfth- and thirteenth-century troubadours that portrayed the ennobling possibilities of the love between a man and a woman. Courtly love formed the basis for the modern idea of romantic love.

creoles (p. 559) People of Spanish descent who had been born in Spanish America.

Crusades (p. 287) Between 1095 and 1291, Latin Christians heeding the call of the pope launched eight major expeditions and many smaller ones against Muslim armies in an attempt to gain control of and hold Jerusalem.

Cubism (p. 756) Modernist artistic movement of the early twentieth century that emphasized the fragmentation of human perception through visual experiments with geometric forms.

Cubists (p. 756) Followers of the early twentieth century modernist artistic movement that emphasized the fragmentation of human perception through visual experiments with geometric forms.

cultural relativism (p. 421) A mode of thought first explored during the sixteenth century to explain why the peoples of the New World did not appear in the Bible. Cultural relativism recognized that many (but not necessarily all) standards of judgment are specific to particular cultures rather than the fixed truths established by natural or divine law.

culture (p. 11) The knowledge and adaptive behavior created by communities that helps them to mediate between themselves and the natural world through time.

cuneiform (p. 24) A kind of writing in which wedge-shaped symbols are pressed into clay tablets to indicate words and ideas. Cuneiform writing originated in ancient Sumer.

curia (p. 307) The administrative bureaucracy of the Roman Catholic Church.

Cynics (p. 133) Followers of the teachings of Antisthenes (ca. 445–360 B.C.E.) who rejected pleasures, possessions, and social conventions to find peace of mind.

Darwinian theory of evolution (p. 747) Scientific theory associated with the nineteenth-century scientist Charles Darwin that highlights the role of variation and natural selection in the evolution of species.

D-Day (p. 861) Common term for June 6, 1944, when 150,000 Allied troops landed on the shores of northern France to open an effective second front against German-occupied Europe.

Decembrists (p. 694) Russian liberals who staged a revolt against Tsar Nicholas I on the first day of his reign in December 1825.

de-Christianization (p. 633) A program inaugurated in France in 1793 by the radical Jacobin and former priest Joseph Fouché that closed churches, eliminated religious symbols, and attempted to establish a purely civic religion.

decolonization (p. 893) The retreat of Western powers from their imperial territories.

deduction, deductive reasoning (p. 533) The logical process by which ideas and laws are derived from basic truths or principles.

Defenders (p. 581) Irish Catholic peasants who joined the United Irishmen in the rebellion against Britain in 1798.

deism (p. 597) The belief that God created the universe and established immutable laws of nature but did not subsequently intervene in the operation of nature or in human affairs.

deists (p. 543) Seventeenth- and eighteenth-century thinkers who believed that God created the universe and established immutable laws of nature but did not subsequently intervene in the operation of nature or in human affairs.

Delian League (p. 94) The alliance among many Greek cities organized by Athens in 478 B.C.E. in order to fight Persian forces in the eastern Aegean Sea. The Athenians gradually turned the Delian League into the Athenian Empire.

demand (p. 662) The desire of consumers to acquire goods and the need of producers to acquire raw materials and machinery.

democracy (p. 84) A form of government in which citizens devise their own governing institutions and choose their leaders; began in Athens, Greece, in the fifth century B.C.E.

de-Stalinization (p. 901) Nikita Khrushchev's effort to decentralize political and economic control in the Soviet Union after 1956.

détente (p. 919) During the 1970s, a period of lessened Cold War hostilities and greater reliance on negotiation and compromise.

dialectic (p. 686) The theory that history advanced in stages as the result of the conflict between different ideas or social groups.

dialectical materialism (p. 686) The socialist philosophy of Karl Marx according to which history advanced as the result of material or economic forces and would lead to the creation of a classless society.

Diaspora (p. 195) Literally "dispersion of population"; usually used to refer to the dispersion of the Jewish population after the Roman destruction of the Temple in Jerusalem in 70 C.E.

diets (p. 494) Legislative assemblies in German territories.

divination (p. 23) The practice of discerning the future by looking for messages imprinted in nature.

divine right (p. 494) The theory that rulers received their power directly from God.

division of labor (p. 657) The assignment of one stage of production to a single worker or group of workers to increase efficiency and productive output.

domestic system (p. 656) An economic arrangement developed in the sixteenth century in which capitalist entrepreneurs employed families in rural areas to spin and weave cloth and make nails and cutlery.

Dreyfus Affair (p. 725) The trials of Captain Alfred Dreyfus on treason charges, which dominated French political life in the decade after 1894 and revealed fundamental divisions in French society.

dualistic (pp. 88, 534) A term used to describe a philosophy or a religion in which a rigid distinction is made between body and mind, good and evil, or the material and the immaterial world.

Dutch Revolt (p. 479) The rebellion against Spanish rule of the seven northern provinces of the Netherlands between 1579 and 1648, which resulted in the independence of the Republic of the United Provinces.

Edict of Nantes (p. 476) Promulgated by King Henry IV in 1598, the edict allowed the Huguenots to build a quasi-independent state within the kingdom of France, giving them the right to have their own troops, church organization, and political autonomy within their walled towns, but banning them from the royal court and the city of Paris. King Louis XIV revoked the edict in 1685.

empires (pp. 19, 554) Large political formations consisting of different kingdoms or territories outside the boundaries of the states that control them.

empiricism (p. 532) The practice of testing scientific theories by observation and experiment.

enclosure (p. 660) The consolidation of scattered agricultural holdings into large, compact fields which were then closed off by hedges, bushes, or walls, giving farmers complete control over the uses of their land.

encomienda (p. 409) The basic form of economic and social organization in early Spanish America, based on a royal grant awarded to a Spaniard for military or other services that gave the grantee and his successors the right to gather tribute from the Indians in a defined area.

English Parliament (p. 318) King Edward I (r. 1272–1307) began to call the English Parliament in order to raise sums of money for his foreign wars. The English Parliament differed from similar assemblies in Europe. It usually included representatives of the "commons," which consisted of townsmen and prosperous farmers who lacked titles of nobility, but whom the king summoned because he needed their money. As a result, a broader spectrum of the population joined Parliament than in most other medieval kingdoms.

enlightened despots (p. 611) The term assigned to absolute monarchs who initiated a series of legal and political reforms in an effort to realize the goals of the Enlightenment.

Enlightenment (p. 595) An international intellectual movement of the eighteenth century that emphasized the use of reason and the application of the laws of nature to human society.

Epicureans (p. 132) Followers of the teachings of the philosopher Epicurus (341–271 B.C.E.). Epicureans tried to gain peace of mind by choosing pleasures rationally.

Estates General (p. 494) The legislative assembly of France in the Old Regime.

ethnic cleansing (p. 936) A term introduced during the wars in Yugoslavia in the 1990s; the systematic use of murder, rape, and violence by one ethnic group against members of other ethnic groups in order to establish control over a territory.

Eucharist (p. 313) Also known as Holy Communion or the Lord's Supper, the Eucharistic rite of the Mass celebrates Jesus's last meal with his apostles when the priest-celebrant consecrates wafers of bread and a chalice of wine as the body and blood of Christ. In the Middle Ages the wafers of bread were distributed for the congregation to eat, but drinking from the chalice was a special privilege of the priesthood. Protestants in the sixteenth century and Catholics in the late twentieth century began to allow the laity to drink from the chalice.

eugenics (p. 835) The effort to improve the physical and intellectual capacities of the population by encouraging individuals with "desirable" traits to reproduce and/or by discouraging those individuals designated as "undesirable" from reproducing.

Euro-Islam (p. 942) The identity and belief system being forged by European Muslims who argue that Islam does not contradict or reject European values.

European Economic Community (EEC) (p. 906) Originally comprising West Germany, France, Italy, Belgium, Luxembourg, and the Netherlands, the EEC was formed in 1957 to integrate its members' economic structures and so foster both economic prosperity and international peace. Also called the Common Market.

European Union (EU) (p. 937) A successor organization to the EEC; the effort to integrate European political, economic, cultural, and military structures and policies.

excommunication (p. 306) A decree by the pope or a bishop prohibiting a sinner from participating in the sacraments of the Church and forbidding any social contact whatsoever with the surrounding community.

existentialism (p. 814) Twentieth-century philosophy that emerged in the interwar era and influenced many thinkers and artists after World War II. Existentialism emphasizes individual freedom in a world devoid of meaning or coherence.

Expressionism (p. 756) Modernist artistic movement of the early twentieth century that used bold colors and experimental forms to express emotional realities.

factories (p. 415) Trading posts established by European powers in foreign lands.

fanatic (p. 474) Originally referring to someone possessed by a demon, during the sixteenth century a fanatic came to mean a person who expressed immoderate enthusiasm in religious matters or who pursued a supposedly divine mission, often to violent ends.

fascism (p. 818) Twentieth-century political ideology that rejected the existing alternatives of conservatism, communism, socialism, and liberalism. Fascists stressed the authoritarian power of the state, the efficacy of violent action, the need to build a national community, and the use of new technologies of influence and control.

feminism, feminist movement (p. 737) International movement that emerged in the second half of the nineteenth century and demanded broader political, legal, and economic rights for women.

Fertile Crescent (p. 13) Also known as the Levantine Corridor, this 25-mile-wide arc of land stretching from the Jordan River to the Euphrates River was the place where food production and settled communities first appeared in southwest Asia (the Middle East).

feudalism (p. 281) A term historians use to describe a social system common during the Middle Ages in which lords granted fiefs (tracts of land or some other form of income) to dependents, known as vassals, who owed their lords personal services in exchange. Feudalism refers to a society governed through personal ties of dependency rather than public political institutions.

fief (p. 281) During the Middle Ages a fief was a grant of land or some other form of income that a lord gave to a vassal in exchange for loyalty and certain services (usually military assistance).

Final Solution (p. 868) Nazi term for the effort to murder every Jew in Europe during World War II.

fin-de-siecle (p. 751) French term for the "turn of the century"; used to refer to the cultural crisis of the late nineteenth century.

firestorm (p. 864) Human-made catastrophe: incendiary bombs cause fires, which combine with winds to suck the oxygen out of the air and raise temperatures to combustible levels. First experienced during the British bombing of the German city of Hamburg in World War II.

First Triumvirate (p. 163) The informal political alliance made by Julius Caesar, Pompey, and Crassus in 60 B.C.E. to share power in the Roman Republic. It led directly to the collapse of the Republic.

Forms (p. 103) In the philosophical teachings of Plato, these are eternal, unchanging absolutes such as Truth, Justice, and Beauty that represent true reality, as opposed to the approximations of reality that humans encounter in everyday life.

Fourteen Points (p. 806) The principles outlined by U.S. President Woodrow Wilson as the basis for a new world order after World War I.

freemasons (p. 609) Members of secret societies of men and women that flourished during the Enlightenment, dedicated to the creation of a society based on reason and virtue and committed to the principles of liberty and equality.

French Wars of Religion (p. 475) A series of political assassinations, massacres, and military engagements between French Catholics and Calvinists from 1560 to 1598.

friars (p. 312) "Brothers" who wandered from city to city and throughout the countryside begging for alms. Unlike monks who remained in a cloister, friars tried to help ordinary laypeople with their problems by preaching and administering to the sick and poor.

Gaullism (p. 913) The political ideology associated with twentieth-century French political leader Charles de Gaulle. Gaullism combined the advocacy of a strong, centralized state with social conservatism.

general strike (p. 732) Syndicalist tactic that called for every worker to go on strike and thus disrupt the capitalist economy and force a political revolution.

genocide (p. 800) The murder of an entire people.

German-Soviet Non-Aggression Pact (p. 849) Signed by Joseph Stalin and Adolf Hitler in 1939, the agreement publicly pledged Germany and the Soviet Union not to attack each other and secretly divided up Poland and the Baltic states between the two powers.

Girondins (p. 625) The more conservative members of the Jacobin party who favored greater economic freedom and opposed further centralization of state power during the French Revolution.

glasnost (p. 928) Loosely translated as openness or honesty; Gorbachev's effort after 1985 to break with the secrecy that had characterized Soviet political life.

globalization (p. 950) The process by which global systems of production, distribution, and communication link together the peoples of the world.

Gnostic (p. 197) Religious doctrine that emphasizes the importance of *gnosis*, or hidden truth, as a way of releasing spiritual reality from the prison of the essentially unreal or evil material world.

Gothic (p. 325) A style in architecture in western Europe from the late twelfth and thirteenth centuries, characterized by ribbed vaults and pointed arches, which drew the eyes of worshipers upward toward God. Flying buttresses, which redistributed the weight of the roof, made possible thin walls pierced by large expanses of stained glass.

grand jury (p. 318) In medieval England after the judicial reforms of King Henry II (r. 1154–1189), grand juries were called when the circuit court judge arrived in a shire. The sheriff assembled a group of men familiar with local affairs who constituted the grand jury and who reported to the judge the major crimes that had been committed since the judge's last visit.

Great Depression (p. 819) Calamitous drop in prices, reduction in trade, and rise in unemployment that devastated the global economy in 1929.

Great Persecution (p. 206) An attack on Christians in the Roman Empire begun by the emperor Galerius in 303 C.E. on the grounds that their worship was endangering the empire. Several thousand Christians were executed.

Great Purge (p. 831) Period of mass arrests and executions particularly aimed at Communist Party members in the Soviet Union.

Great Schism (p. 352) The division of the Catholic Church (1378–1417) between rival Italian and French claimants to the papal throne.

Green movement, Green politics (p. 923) A new style of politics and set of political ideas resulting from the confluence of environmentalism, feminism, and anti-nuclear protests of the 1970s.

guilds (p. 343) Professional associations devoted to protecting the special interests of a particular trade or craft and to monopolizing production and trade in the goods the guild produced.

Gulag (p. 829) Term for the network of forced labor and prison camps in the Soviet Union.

habiru (p. 55) Peasants who existed outside the palace system of the Late Bronze Age; often seen as bandits.

haciendas (p. 409) Large landed estates that began to be established in the seventeenth century and replaced encomiendas throughout much of Spanish America.

Hallstatt culture (p. 124) The first Celtic civilization in central Europe; from about 750 to about 450 B.C.E., Hallstatt Celts spread throughout Europe.

Hellenistic (p. 112) The word used to describe the civilization, based on that of Greece, that developed in the wake of the conquests of Alexander the Great.

helots (p. 84) The brutally oppressed subject peoples of the Spartans. Tied to the land they farmed for Spartan masters, they were treated little better than beasts of burden.

Helsinki Accords (p. 923) Signed by representatives of 32 European states, Canada, the United States, and the Soviet Union in 1975; often regarded as the apex of détente.

heresy (p. 196) A teaching or belief not considered orthodox.

hetairai (p. 98) Elite courtesans in ancient Greece who provided intellectual as well as sexual companionship.

hieroglyphs (p. 31) Ancient Egyptian system of writing that represented both sounds and objects.

Holocaust (p. 867) Adolf Hitler's effort to murder all the Jews in Europe during World War II.

Homo sapiens sapiens (p. 12) Scientific term meaning "most intelligent people"; applied to physically and intellectually modern human beings that first appeared between 200,000 and 100,000 years ago in Africa.

hoplites (p. 82) Greek soldiers in the Archaic Age who could afford their own weapons. Hoplite tactics made soldiers fighting as a group dependent on one another. This contributed to the internal cohesion of the polis and eventually to the rise of democracy.

Huguenots (p. 474) The term for French Calvinists, who constituted some 10 percent of the population by 1560.

humanists (p. 374) During the Renaissance, writers and orators who studied ancient Latin and sometimes Greek texts. Their principal interests were grammar, rhetoric, poetry, history, and ethics.

Hundred Years' War (p. 345) A series of engagements (1337–1453) between England and France over England's attempts to assert its claims to territories in France.

hyperinflation (p. 821) Catastrophic price increases and currency devaluation, such as that which occurred in Germany in 1923.

iconoclasm (p. 241) The destruction of religious images in the Byzantine Empire in the eighth century.

icons (p. 240) The Christian images of God and saints found in Byzantine art.

ideologies (p. 682) Theories of society and government that form the basis of political programs.

Indo-European (p. 45) Parent language of a majority of modern European languages as well as modern Armenian and Persian; sometimes used to refer to the people who spoke this language.

induction (pp. 24, 532) The process of reasoning that formulates general hypotheses and theories on the basis of specific observation and the accumulation of data.

indulgences (p. 352) Certificates that allowed penitents to atone for their sins and reduce their time in purgatory. Usually these were issued for going on a pilgrimage or performing a pious act; however, during the Babylonian Captivity of the Church (1305–1378) popes began to sell them, a practice Martin Luther protested in 1517 in an act that brought on the Protestant Reformation.

industrial capitalism (p. 669) A form of capitalism characterized by the ownership of factories by private individuals and the employment of wage labor.

inheritance of acquired characteristics (p. 749) Now discredited scientific theory of evolutionary change, which was powerful in the nineteenth century.

intendants (p. 496) French royal officials who became the main agents of French provincial administration in the seventeenth century.

interdict (p. 307) A papal decree prohibiting the celebration of the sacraments in an entire city or kingdom.

Investiture Controversy (p. 306) A dispute that began in 1076 between the popes and the German emperors over the right to invest bishops with their offices. The most famous episode was the conflict between Pope Gregory VII and Emperor Henry IV. The controversy was resolved by the Concordat of Worms in 1122.

Iron Age (p. 57) Historical period following the Bronze Age; marked by the prevalent use of iron.

Iron Curtain (p. 883) Metaphor for the Cold War division of Europe after World War II.

Islamism (p. 939) Ideology that insists that Islam demands a rejection of Western values and that violence in this struggle against the West is justified.

Jacobins (p. 621) A French political party supporting a democratic republic that found support in political clubs throughout the country and dominated the National Convention from 1792 until 1794.

Jim Crow (p. 770) Series of laws mandating racial segregation throughout the American South.

Julio-Claudian dynasty (p. 172) Established by Octavian Augustus, this hereditary monarchy drawn from members of his extended family ruled Rome until 68 C.E.

Junkers (p. 508) The traditional nobility of Prussia.

justification by faith (p. 432) Refers to Martin Luther's insight that humanity is incapable of performing enough religious good works to earn eternal salvation. Salvation is an unmerited gift from God called grace. Those who receive grace are called the Elect.

Keynesian economics (p. 833) Economic theories associated with the British economist John Maynard Keynes that advocate using the power of the democratic state to ensure economic prosperity.

knight (p. 281) During the Middle Ages a knight was a soldier who fought on horseback. A knight was a vassal or dependent of a lord, who usually financed the knight's expenses of armor and weapons and of raising and feeding horses with a grant of land known as a fief.

Koine (p. 127) The standard version of the Greek language spoken throughout the Hellenistic world.

kulak (p. 828) Russian term for a peasant who was relatively prosperous.

laissez-faire (p. 683) The principle that governments should not regulate or otherwise intervene in the economy unless it is necessary to protect property rights and public order.

late antiquity (p. 202) The period between about 250 and 600, which bridged the classical world and the Middle Ages.

Late Bronze Age (p. 44) The period from 1500 to 1100 B.C.E., characterized by an unprecedented degree of international trade and diplomatic exchange.

La Tène culture (p. 125) A phase of Celtic civilization that lasted from about 450 to 200 B.C.E. La Tène culture became strong especially in the regions of the Rhine and Danube Rivers.

Latin Christendom (p. 214) The parts of medieval Europe, including all of western Europe, united by Christianity and the use of Latin in worship and intellectual life. Latin served as an international language among the ruling elites in western Europe, even though they spoke different languages in their daily lives.

Latin War (p. 145) A war that the Latin peoples of Italy waged against the Roman Republic between 340 and 338 B.C.E.

Law of the Twelve Tables (p. 142) A body of written law inscribed on 12 bronze tablets and published in 451 B.C.E. This written summary of existing law was the first body of written law in Rome.

lay investiture (p. 305) The practice of nobles, kings, or emperors installing churchmen and giving them the symbols of office.

League of Nations (p. 806) Association of states set up after World War I to resolve international conflicts through open and peaceful negotiation.

Lend-Lease Act (p. 858) Passed in March 1941, the act gave Britain and later the Soviet Union access to U.S. industrial products during World War II, with payment postponed for the duration of the war.

Levantine Corridor (p. 13) Also known as the Fertile Crescent, this arc of land stretching from the Jordan River to the Euphrates River was the place where food production and settled communities first appeared in southwest Asia (the Middle East).

liberalism (p. 682) An ideology based on the conviction that individual freedom is of supreme importance and the main responsibility of government is to protect that freedom.

"Linear B" (p. 49) The earliest written form of Greek, used by the Mycenaeans.

linear perspective (p. 382) In the arts, the use of geometrical principles to depict a three-dimensional space on a flat, two-dimensional surface.

liturgy (p. 263) The forms of Christian worship, including the prayers, chants, and rituals to be said, sung, or performed throughout the year.

lord (p. 280) During the Middle Ages, a lord was someone who offered protection to dependents, known as vassals, who took an oath of loyalty to him. Most lords demanded military services from their vassals and sometimes granted them tracts of land known as fiefs.

lustration (p. 935) Implemented in many former communist states in the 1990s, this policy banned former communists and communist collaborators from public office.

ma'at (p. 30) Ancient Egyptian concept of the fundamental order established by the gods.

Macedonian Renaissance (p. 242) During the Macedonian dynasty's rule of Byzantium (867–1056), aristocratic families, the Church, and monasteries devoted their immense riches to embellishing Constantinople with new buildings, mosaics, and icons. The emperors sponsored historical, philosophical, and religious writing.

Mafia (p. 706) Organizations of armed men who took control of local politics and the economy in late nineteenth-century Sicily.

magic (p. 470) Learned opinion described two kinds of magic: natural magic, which involved the manipulation of occult forces believed to exist in nature, and demonic magic, which called upon evil spirits to gain access to power. This was widely accepted as a reality until the middle of the seventeenth century.

Magisterial Reformation (p. 440) Refers to Protestant churches that received official government sanction.

Magna Carta (p. 318) In 1215 some English barons forced King John to sign the "great charter," in which the king pledged to respect the traditional feudal privileges of the nobility, towns, and clergy. Subsequent kings swore to uphold it, thereby accepting the fundamental principle that even the king was obliged to respect the law.

Malthusian population trap (p. 668) The theory of Thomas Malthus (1766–1834) that the natural tendency of population to grow faster than the food supply would eventually drive the size of populations back to sustainable levels and end periods of economic expansion that usually accompany the growth of population.

Manhattan Project (p. 864) Code name given to the secret Anglo-American project that resulted in the construction of the atom bomb during World War II.

manor (p. 299) A medieval unit of agricultural management in which a lord managed and served as the presiding judge over peasants who worked the land.

marches (p. 275) Territorial units of the Carolingian Empire for the administration of frontier regions. Each march was ruled by a margrave who had special powers necessary to defend vulnerable borders.

Marshall Plan (p. 886) The use of U.S. economic aid to restore stability to Europe after World War II and so undercut the appeal of communist ideology.

martyr (p. 199) In Christian tradition, believers who chose to die rather than to renounce or deny their Christian beliefs.

mass politics (p. 717) A political culture characterized by the participation of non-elites.

matriarchy/matriarchal (p. 48) A social or cultural system in which family lineage is traced through the mother and/or in which women hold significant power.

mechanical philosophy (p. 534) The seventeenth-century philosophy of nature, championed by René Descartes, holding that nature operated in a mechanical way, just like a machine made by a human being.

megalith (p. 16) A very large stone used in prehistoric European monuments between 5000 and 1500 B.C.E.

mercantilism (p. 499) The theory that the wealth of a state depended on its ability to import fewer commodities than it exported and thus acquire the largest possible share of the world's monetary supply. The theory encouraged state intervention in the economy and the regulation of trade.

meritocracy (p. 640) The practice of appointing people to office solely on the basis of ability and performance rather than social or economic status.

mesmerism (p. 610) A pseudoscience developed by Franz Anton Mesmer in the eighteenth century that treated sickness by massaging or hypnotizing the patient to produce a crisis that restored health.

mestizos (p. 573) People of mixed white and Indian ancestry.

metropolis (p. 553) The parent country of a colony or imperial possession; the "mother state" that controlled an empire.

Middle Kingdom (p. 32) In ancient Near Eastern history, refers to the period of Egyptian history from 2040 to 1720 B.C.E.

Middle Passage (p. 569) The journey taken by European ships bringing slaves from Africa to the Americas.

Mishnah (p. 195) Completed around 220, a collection of homilies and decisions to explain Jewish law.

Modern Devotion (p. 354) A fifteenth-century religious movement that stressed individual piety, ethical behavior, and intense religious education. The Modern Devotion was promoted by the Brothers of the Common Life, a religious order whose influence was broadly felt through its extensive network of schools.

modernism, modernist (pp. 752, 754) Term applied to artistic and literary movements from the late nineteenth century through the 1950s. Modernists sought to create new aesthetic forms and values.

monastic movement (p. 215) In late antiquity, Christian ascetics organized communities where men and women could pursue a life of spirituality through work, prayer, and asceticism. Called the monastic movement, this spiritual quest spread quickly throughout Christian lands.

Monophysites (p. 214) Christians who do not accept the Council of Chalcedon (see Chalcedonians). Monophysites believe that Jesus Christ has only one nature, equally divine and human.

monotheism (p. 39) The belief in only one god, first attributed to the ancient Hebrews. Monotheism is the foundation of Judaism, Christianity, Islam, and Zoroastrianism.

mosque (p. 246) A place of Muslim worship.

Mountain, the (p. 625) Members of the radical faction within the Jacobin party during the French Revolution who advocated the centralization of state power and instituted the Reign of Terror.

mulattos (p. 565) People of mixed white and black race.

Munich Agreement (p. 849) The agreement in 1939 between the governments of Nazi Germany, Britain, and France that granted Germany sovereignty over the Sudetenland; part of the effort to appease the Nazi government and avoid a second total war in Europe.

nabobs (p. 575) Members of the British East India Company who made fortunes in India and returned to Britain, flaunting their wealth.

Napoleonic Code (p. 639) The name eventually given to the Civil Code of 1804, promulgated by Napoleon, which gave France a uniform and authoritative code of law.

nation (p. 687) A large community of people who possess a sense of unity based on a belief that they have a common homeland and share a similar culture.

national consciousness (p. 688) The awareness or belief of people that they belong to a nation.

nationalism (p. 687) The belief that the people who form a nation should have their own political institutions and that the interests of the nation should be defended and promoted at all costs.

nationalist-racist politics (p. 732) Anti-liberal politics that appeal to race-based identities and fears.

national self-determination (p. 687) The doctrine advanced by nationalists that any group that considers itself a nation has the right to be ruled only by the members of their own nation and to have all members of the nation included in that state.

nation-state (p. 687) A political structure sought by nationalists in which the boundaries of the state and the nation are identical, so that all the members of a nation are governed by the same political authorities.

natural law (p. 144) A law that is believed to be inherent in nature rather than established by human beings.

nawabs (p. 573) Native provincial governors in eighteenth-century India.

Nazism (p. 820) Twentieth-century political ideology associated with Adolf Hitler that adopted many fascist ideas but with a central focus on racism and particularly anti-Semitism.

neoclassicism (p. 591) The revival of the classical art and architecture of ancient Greece and Rome in the eighteenth century.

Neolithic Age (p. 11) The New Stone Age, characterized by the development of agriculture and the use of stone tools.

Neoplatonism (pp. 221, 536) A philosophy based on the teachings of Plato and his successors that flourished in late antiquity, especially in the teachings of Plotinus. Neoplatonism influenced Christianity in late antiquity. During the Renaissance Neoplatonism was linked to the belief that the natural world was charged with occult forces that could be used in the practice of magic.

New Conservatism (p. 923) Political ideology that emerged at the end of the 1970s combining the free market approach of nineteenth-century liberalism with social conservatism.

New Economic Policy (NEP) (p. 827) Vladimir Lenin's economic turnaround in 1921 that allowed and even encouraged small private businesses and farms in the Soviet Union.

new feminism (p. 922) Reemergence of the feminist movement in the 1970s.

new imperialism (p. 760) The third phase of modern European imperialism, which occurred in the late nineteenth and early twentieth centuries and extended Western control over almost all of Africa and much of Asia.

New Kingdom (p. 35) In ancient Near Eastern history, the period in Egyptian history from 1550 to 1150 B.C.E. During the New Kingdom, Egyptian kings first took the title of pharaoh and established an empire that reached to the Euphrates River.

New Left (p. 915) Left-wing political and cultural movement that emerged in the late 1950s and early 1960s; sought to develop a form of socialism that rejected the overcentralization, authoritarianism, and inhumanity of Stalinism.

New Testament (p. 196) The collection of texts that together with the Hebrew Bible, or Old Testament, comprise the Christian Bible. New Testament texts include the Epistles (letters of Paul of Tarsus to early Christians), the Gospels (stories of Jesus Christ's life, death, and resurrection), and other early Christian documents.

95 theses (p. 434) Propositions about indulgences Martin Luther announced he was willing to defend in debate. The publication of the 95 theses in 1517 started the Protestant Reformation.

nobility (p. 588) Members of the aristocracy who received official recognition of their hereditary status, including their titles of honor and legal privileges.

nobility of the robe (p. 588) French noblemen whose families acquired their status by appointment to office.

no-man's-land (p. 786) The area between the combatants' trenches on the Western Front during World War I.

North Atlantic Treaty Organization (NATO) (p. 889) Defensive anti-Soviet alliance of the United States, Canada, and the nations of western Europe established in 1949.

northern Renaissance (p. 430) A movement in northern Europe that built on the foundations of the Italian Renaissance, especially to subject the Bible and the sources of Christianity to critical scrutiny.

Nuremberg trials (p. 870) Post-World War II trials of members of the Nazi Party and German military; conducted by an international tribunal.

Old Kingdom (p. 29) In ancient Near Eastern history, the period in Egyptian history from ca. 2680–2200 B.C.E., formed by the unification of the kingdoms of Upper Egypt and Lower Egypt.

Old Regime (p. 611) The political order of eighteenth-century France, dominated by an absolute monarch and a privileged nobility and clergy.

oligarchy (p. 84) A government consisting of only a few people rather than the entire community.

Olympic Games (p. 81) Greek athletic contests held in Olympia every four years between 776 B.C.E and 217 C.E.

orthodox, orthodoxy (p. 196) In Christianity, the term indicates doctrinally correct belief.

Ottonian Renaissance (p. 284) Under the patronage of the Saxon Emperor Otto I (936–973) and his brother Bruno, learned monks, Greek philosophers from Byzantium, and Italian scholars gathered at the imperial court, stimulating a cultural revival in literature and the arts. The writers and artists enhanced the reputation of Otto.

pagan (p. 210) The Christian term for polytheist worship (worshiping more than one god). In the course of late antiquity, the Christian Church suppressed paganism, the traditional religions of the Roman Empire.

palace system (p. 53) Late Bronze Age social system that concentrated religious, economic, political, and military power in the hands of an elite, who lived apart from most people in monumental fortified compounds.

pan-Arabism (p. 839) Nationalist ideology that called for the political unification of all Arabs, regardless of religious affiliation.

papacy (p. 209) The bishop of the city of Rome, sometimes referred to as "Father." The papacy refers to the administrative and political institutions controlled by the Pope. The papacy began to gain strength in the sixth century in the absence of Roman imperial government in Italy.

papal infallibility (p. 759) The doctrine of the Roman Catholic Church proclaimed at the First Vatican Council in 1870 that the pope could not err when making solemn declarations regarding faith or morals.

paradigm (p. 536) A conceptual model or intellectual framework within which scientists conduct their research and experimentation.

parlements (p. 496) The highest provincial courts in France, the most important of which was the Parlement of Paris.

patriarchy (p. 28) A social or cultural system in which men occupy the positions of power; in a family system, a father-centered household.

patricians (p. 141) In ancient Rome, patricians were aristocratic clans with the highest status and the most political influence.

patrons and clients (p. 156) In ancient Roman society, a system in which a powerful man (the patron) would exercise influence on behalf of a social subordinate (the client) in anticipation of future support or assistance.

Pax Romana (p. 170) Latin for "Roman Peace," this term refers to the Roman Empire established by Augustus that lasted until the early third century C.E.

Pentateuch (p. 73) The first five books of the Hebrew Bible.

perestroika (p. 928) Loosely translated as "restructuring"; Gorbachev's effort to decentralize, reform, and thereby strengthen Soviet economic and political structures.

personal rule (p. 515) The period from 1629 to 1640 in England when King Charles I ruled without Parliament.

phalanx (p. 82) The military formation favored by hoplite soldiers. Standing shoulder-to-shoulder in ranks often eight men deep, hoplites moved in unison and depended on one another for protection.

pharaoh (p. 35) Title for the Egyptian king, used during the New Kingdom period.

philology (p. 374) A method reintroduced by the humanists during the Italian Renaissance devoted to the comparative study of language, especially to understanding the meaning of a word in a particular historical context.

philosophes (p. 596) The writers and thinkers of the Enlightenment, especially in France.

pilgrimages (p. 217) Religious journeys made to holy sites in order to encounter relics.

Pillars of Islam (p. 248) The five basic principles of Islam as taught by Muhammad.

plantation colony (p. 398) First appearing in the Cape Verde Islands and later in the tropical parts of the Americas, these colonies were established by Europeans who used African slave labor to cultivate cash crops such as sugar, indigo, cotton, coffee, and tobacco.

plebeians (p. 141) The general body of Roman citizens.

plebiscite (p. 631) A popular vote for or against a form of government or rule by a particular person.

pogroms (p. 735) An organized and often officially encouraged riot or attack to persecute a particular ethnic or religious group, especially associated with eastern European attacks against Jews.

polis (p. 80) A self-governing Greek city-state.

polytheistic (p. 23) The belief in many gods.

pop art (p. 908) Effort by artists in the 1950s and 1960s both to utilize and to critique the material abundance of post-World War II popular culture.

Popular Front (p. 833) A political coalition of liberals, socialists, and communists designed to defeat fascist and racist-nationalist political rivals.

positivism (p. 689) The philosophy developed by August Comte in the nineteenth century according to which human society passed through a series of stages, leading to the final positive stage in which the accumulation of scientific data would enable thinkers to discover the laws of human behavior and bring about the improvement of society.

positivist (p. 751) The emphasis on the use of the scientific method to reach truth; a stress on observable fact.

postindustrialism, postindustrial society (p. 946) A service-based, rather than manufacturing-based, economy characterized by an emphasis on marketing and information and by a proliferation of communications technologies.

postmodernism (p. 943) Umbrella term covering a variety of artistic styles and intellectual theories and practices; in general, a rejection of a single, universal, Western style of modernity.

Potsdam Conference (p. 885) The meeting in July 1945 of the Allied leaders of Britain, the Soviet Union, and the United States in the German city of Potsdam.

Pragmatic Sanction of Bourges (p. 387) An agreement in 1438 that guaranteed the virtual autonomy of the French Church from papal control, enabling the French king to interfere in religious affairs and exploit Church revenues for government purposes.

Prague Spring (p. 904) Short-lived popular effort in 1968 to reform Czechoslovakia's political structures; associated with the phrase "socialism with a human face."

predestination (p. 442) The doctrine promoted by John Calvin that since God, the all-knowing and all-powerful being, knew everything in advance and caused everything to happen, then the salvation of any individual was predetermined.

prerogative (p. 515) The set of powers exercised by the English monarch alone, rather than in conjunction with Parliament.

Price Revolution (p. 464) The period between about 1540 and 1640 in which Europe, after a long period of falling or stable prices that stretched back to the fourteenth century, experienced sustained price increases. This caused widespread social and economic turmoil.

priesthood of all believers (p. 435) Martin Luther's doctrine that all those of pure faith were themselves priests, a doctrine that undermined the authority of the Catholic clergy over the laity.

primogeniture (p. 513) The legal arrangement by which the eldest son inherits the entire estate upon the death of the father.

proletariat (p. 686) The word used by Karl Marx and Friedrich Engels to identify the class of workers who received their income from wages.

prophetic movement (p. 72) An important phase in the development of what became Judaism. In the ninth century B.C.E., Hebrew religious reformers, or prophets, demanded the transformation of religious and economic practices to reflect ideals of social justice and religious purity.

protectionism (p. 561) The policy of shielding domestic industries from foreign competition through a policy of levying tariffs on imported goods.

Protestant Reformation (p. 427) Period that dominated European affairs between 1517 and 1560 when the movement for religious reform begun by Martin Luther led Germany, Britain, and most of northern Europe to break away from the Catholic Church.

Radical Reformation (p. 440) Refers to Protestant movements that failed to gain official government recognition and were at best tolerated, at worst persecuted, during the sixteenth century.

Radical Right (p. 820) Refers to extremist ideologies on the far right of the political spectrum, such as fascism and Nazism.

rationalism (p. 533) The theory that the mind contains rational categories independent of sensory observation; more generally that reason is the primary source of truth.

Realpolitik (p. 707) The adoption of political tactics based solely on their realistic chances of success.

redistributive economies (p. 19) Type of economic system characteristic of ancient Mesopotamian societies. The central political authority controls all agricultural resources and their redistribution.

regency (p. 496) Rule by relative of a monarch during a period when the monarch was too young to rule or otherwise incapacitated.

Reign of Terror (p. 627) A purging of alleged enemies of the French state between 1793 and 1794, superintended by the Committee of Public Safety, that resulted in the execution of 17,000 people.

relativity, theory of (p. 750) Albert Einstein's revolutionary model of the physical universe as four-dimensional.

relics (p. 217) In Christian belief, relics are sacred objects that have miraculous powers. They are associated with saints, biblical figures, or some object associated with them. They served as contacts between Earth and Heaven and were verified by miracles.

Religious Peace of Augsburg (p. 440) In 1555 this peace between Lutherans and Catholics within the Holy Roman Empire established the principle of *cuius regio, eius religio*, which means "he who rules determines the religion of the land." Protestant princes in the Empire were permitted to retain all church lands seized before 1552 and to enforce Protestant worship, but Catholic princes were also allowed to enforce Catholic worship in their territories.

Renaissance (p. 365) A term meaning "rebirth" used by historians to describe a movement that sought to imitate and understand the culture of antiquity. The Renaissance generally refers to a movement that began in Italy and then spread throughout Europe from about 1350 to 1550.

reparations (p. 807) Payments imposed upon Germany after World War I by the Versailles Treaty to cover the costs of the war.

republic (p. 141) A state in which political power resides in the people or their representatives rather than in a monarch.

republicanism (p. 366) A political theory first developed by the ancient Greeks, especially the philosopher Plato, but elaborated by the ancient Romans and rediscovered during the Italian Renaissance. The fundamental principle of republicanism as developed during the Italian Renaissance was that government officials should be elected by the people or a portion of the people.

Republic of Letters (p. 596) An international community of Enlightenment writers and thinkers in the eighteenth century.

Republic of Virtue (p. 625) The ideal form of government proposed by Maximilien Robespierre and other Jacobins during the French Revolution. Its proponents wished to make the republic established in 1792 more egalitarian and secular and inspire civic pride and patriotism in the people.

requerimiento (p. 407) A document read by conquistadores to the natives of the Americas before making war on them. The document briefly explained the principles of Christianity and commanded the natives to accept them immediately along with the authority of the pope and the sovereignty of the king of Spain. If the natives refused, they were warned they would be forced to accept Christian conversion and subjected to Spain anyway.

Resistance, the (p. 870) Label given to the many different underground political and partisan movements directed against Nazi rule in German-occupied Europe during World War II.

revisionism, socialist revisionism (p. 731) The belief that an equal society can be built through participation in parliamentary politics rather than through violent revolution.

rhetoric (p. 374) The art of persuasive or emotive speaking and writing, which was especially valued by the Renaissance humanists.

Romanesque (p. 324) A style in architecture that spread throughout western Europe during the eleventh and the first half of the twelfth centuries and was characterized by arched stone roofs supported by rounded arches, massive stone pillars, and thick walls.

Romanization (p. 177) The process by which conquered peoples absorbed aspects of Roman culture, especially the Latin language, city life, and religion.

romanticism (p. 690) An artistic and literary movement of the late eighteenth and nineteenth centuries that involved a protest against classicism, appealed to the passions rather than the intellect, and emphasized the beauty and power of nature.

Rome-Berlin Axis (p. 848) Alliance between Benito Mussolini's Italy and Adolf Hitler's Germany formed in 1936.

Russification (p. 727) Tsarist policy from the 1890s until the outbreak of World War I that imposed the use of Russian language and emphasized Russian Orthodox religious and cultural practices.

salons (p. 609) Private sitting rooms or parlors of aristocratic French women where discussions of philosophy, science, literature, and politics took place in the eighteenth century.

sans-culottes (p. 621) The militant citizens of Paris who refused to wear the pants worn by noblemen and provided support for the Jacobins during the French Revolution; literally, those without breeches.

satraps (p. 117) Persian provincial governors who collected taxes and oversaw the bureaucracy.

Schlieffen Plan (p. 783) German military plan devised in 1905 that called for a sweeping attack on France through Belgium and the Netherlands.

scholasticism (p. 320) A term referring to a broad philosophical and theological movement that dominated medieval thought and university training. Scholasticism used logic learned from Aristotle to interpret the meaning of the Bible and the writings of the Church Fathers, who created Christian theology in its first centuries.

Scramble for Africa (p. 765) The frenzied imposition of European control over most of Africa that occurred between 1870 and 1914.

scriptorium (p. 271) The room in a monastery where monks copied books and manuscripts.

Sea Peoples (p. 55) Name given by the Egyptians to the diverse groups of migrants whose attacks helped bring the International Bronze Age to an end.

Second Industrial Revolution (p. 718) A new phase in the industrialization of the processes of production and consumption, which was underway in Europe in the 1870s.

Second Triumvirate (p. 166) In 43 B.C.E. Octavian (later called Caesar Augustus), Mark Antony, and Lepidus made an informal alliance to share power in Rome while they jockeyed for control. Octavian emerged as the sole ruler of Rome in 31 B.C.E.

secularization (p. 545) The reduction of the importance of religion in society and culture.

seigneur (p. 593) The lord of a French estate who received payments from the peasants who lived on his land.

separate spheres (p. 607) The theory that men and women should conduct their lives in different social and political environments, confining women to the domestic sphere and excluding them from the public sphere of political involvement.

sepoys (p. 574) Indian troops serving in the armed forces of the British East India Company.

Septuagint (p. 127) The Greek translation of the Hebrew Bible (Old Testament).

serfs (p. 299) During the Middle Ages serfs were agricultural laborers who worked and lived on a plot of land granted them by a lord to whom they owed a certain portion of their crops. They could not leave the land, but they had certain legal rights that were denied to slaves.

settler colony (p. 398) A colony authorized when a private person obtained a license from a king to seize an island or parcel of land and occupied it with settlers from Europe who exported their own culture to the new lands. Settler colonies first appeared among the islands of the eastern Atlantic and portions of the Americas.

simony (p. 305) The practice of buying and selling church offices.

skepticism (p. 541) A tendency to doubt what one has been taught or is expected to believe.

Social Darwinism (p. 748) The later-nineteenth-century application of the theory of evolution to entire human societies.

social democracy (p. 831) Political system in which a democratically elected parliamentary government endeavors to ensure a decent standard of living for its citizens through both economic regulation and the maintenance of a welfare state.

socialism (p. 684) An ideology calling for the ownership of the means of production by the community with the purpose of reducing inequalities of income, wealth, opportunity, and economic power.

socialist revisionism (p. 731) The belief that an equal society can be built through participation in parliamentary politics rather than through violent revolution.

Social War (p. 160) The revolt of Rome's allies against the Republic in 90 B.C.E. demanding full Roman citizenship.

Solidarity (p. 925) Trade union and political party in Poland that led an unsuccessful effort to reform the Polish communist state in 1981; survived to lead Poland's first non-communist government since World War II in 1989.

Sophists (p. 103) Professional educators who traveled throughout the ancient Greek world, teaching many subjects. Their goal was to teach people the best ways to lead better lives.

soviets (p. 801) Workers' and soldiers' councils formed in Russia during the Revolution of 1917.

Spanish Armada (p. 478) A fleet of 132 ships, which sailed from Portugal to rendezvous with the Spanish army stationed in the Netherlands and launch an invasion of England in 1588. The English defeated the Armada as it passed through the English Channel. The defeat marked a shift in the power balance from Spain to England.

Spanish Reconquest (p. 259) Refers to the numerous military campaigns by the Christian kingdoms of northern Spain to capture the Muslim-controlled cities and kingdoms of southern Spain. This long, intermittent struggle began with the capture of Toledo in 1085 and lasted until Granada fell to Christian armies in 1492.

spiritualists (p. 448) A tendency within Protestantism, especially Lutheranism, to emphasize the power of personal spiritual illumination, called the "inner Word," a living form of the Scriptures written directly on the believer's soul by the hand of God.

stagflation (p. 920) Term coined in the 1970s to describe an economy troubled by both high inflation and high unemployment rates.

standing armies (p. 494) Trained and equipped military forces that were not disbanded after the conclusion of war. Standing armies often helped maintain order and enforce governmental policy at home.

states (p. 553) Consolidated territorial areas that have their own political institutions and recognize no higher political authority.

Stoics (p. 133) Followers of the philosophy developed by Zeno of Citium (ca. 335–ca. 263 B.C.E.) that urged acceptance of fate while participating fully in everyday life.

structuralism (p. 909) Influential post-World War II social theory that explored the common structures of language and thought.

Struggle of the Orders (p. 142) The political strife between patrician and plebeian Romans beginning in the fifth century B.C.E. The plebeians gradually won political rights and influence as a result of the struggle.

suffragettes (p. 742) Feminist movement that emerged in Britain in the early twentieth century. Unlike the suffragists, who sought to achieve the national vote for women through rational persuasion, the suffragettes adopted the tactics of violent protest.

suffragists (p. 742) Feminists who sought to achieve the national vote for women through rational persuasion and parliamentary politics.

supply (p. 662) The amounts of capital, labor, and food that are needed to produce goods for the market as well as the quantities of those goods themselves.

syncretism (p. 70) The practice of blending foreign religious beliefs with an indigenous religious system; a common practice throughout the Roman Empire.

syndicalism (p. 732) Ideology of the late nineteenth and early twentieth century that sought to achieve a working-class revolution through economic action, particularly through mass labor strikes.

Talmud (p. 216) Commentaries on Jewish law. Rabbis completed the Babylonian Talmud and the Jerusalem Talmud by the end of the fifth century C.E.

tetrarchy (p. 204) The government by four rulers established by the Roman emperor Diocletian in 293 C.E. that lasted until 312. During the tetrarchy many administrative and military reforms altered the fabric of Roman society.

Third Estate (p. 618) The component of the Estates General in Old Regime France that technically represented all the commoners in the kingdom.

Third Reich (p. 854) Term for Adolf Hitler's Germany; articulates the Nazi aim of extending German rule across Europe.

Third World (p. 898) Term coined in 1955 to describe nations that did not align with either the Soviet Union or the United States; commonly used to describe the industrially underdeveloped nations.

Thomism (p. 322) A branch of medieval philosophy associated with the work of the Dominican thinker, Thomas Aquinas (1225–1274), who wrote encyclopedic summaries of human knowledge that confirmed Christian faith.

Time of Troubles (p. 489) The period from 1604 to 1613 when Russia fell into chaos, which ended when the national assembly elected Tsar Michael Romanov, whose descendants ruled Russia until they were deposed in 1917.

Torah (p. 73) Most commonly, the first five books of the Hebrew Bible; also used to refer to the whole body of Jewish sacred writings and tradition.

total war (p. 779) A war that demands extensive state regulation of economic production, distribution, and consumption; a war that blurs (or erases entirely) the distinction between civilian and soldier.

trading posts (p. 400) Areas built by European traders along the coasts of Africa and Asia as a base for trade with the interior. Trading posts or factories were islands of European law and sovereignty, but European authority seldom extended very far beyond the fortified post.

transubstantiation (p. 313) A doctrine promulgated at the Fourth Lateran Council in 1215 that distinguished the difference between the outward appearances and the inner substance of how the Eucharistic bread and wine changed into the body and blood of Christ.

Treaty of Brest-Litovsk (p. 791) Treaty between Germany and Bolshevik-controlled Russia, signed in March 1918, that ceded to Germany all of Russia's western territories.

trial by jury (p. 318) When disputes about the possession of land arose after the late twelfth century in England, sheriffs assembled a group of 12 local men who testified under oath about the claims of the plaintiffs; the circuit court judge then made his decision on the basis of their testimony. The system was later extended to criminal cases.

Triple Alliance (p. 781) Defensive alliance of Germany, Austria-Hungary, and Italy, signed in 1882.

Triple Entente (p. 781) Informal defensive agreement linking France, Great Britain, and Russia before World War I.

triremes (p. 91) Greek warships with three banks of oars. Triremes manned by the poorest people of Athenian society became the backbone of the Athenian Empire.

troubadours (p. 323) Poets from the late twelfth and thirteenth centuries who wrote love poems, meant to be sung to music, which reflected a new sensibility, called courtly love, about the ennobling possibilities of the love between a man and a woman.

Truman Doctrine (p. 886) Named after U.S. president Harry Truman, the doctrine that in 1947 inaugurated the Cold War policy of resisting the expansion of communist control.

Twelfth-Century Renaissance (p. 321) An intellectual revival of interest in ancient Greek philosophy and science and in Roman law in western Europe during the twelfth and early thirteenth centuries. The term also refers to a flowering of vernacular literature and the Romanesque and Gothic styles in architecture.

tyrants (p. 83) Rulers in Greek city-states, usually members of the aristocracy, who seized power illegitimately rather than acquiring it by heredity or election. Tyrants often gained political support from the hoplites and the poor.

Unitarians (p. 449) A religious reform movement that began in the sixteenth century and rejected the Christian doctrine of the Trinity. Unitarians (also called Arians, Socinians, and Anti-Trinitarians) taught a rationalist interpretation of the Scriptures and argued that Jesus was a divinely inspired man, not God who became a man, as other Christians believed.

United Kingdom (p. 688) The name of the British state formed by the union of England and Scotland in 1707. In 1801 Ireland became part of the United Kingdom, but after the establishment of the Irish Free State in 1922, only the six Irish counties in the northern province of Ulster remained united to Britain.

universal law of gravitation (p. 530) A law of nature established by Isaac Newton in 1687 holding that any two bodies attract each other with a force that is directly proportional to the product of their masses and indirectly proportional to the square of the distance between them. The law was presented in mathematical terms.

universal male suffrage (p. 624) The granting of the right to vote to all adult males.

vassals (p. 280) During the Middle Ages, men voluntarily submitted themselves to a lord by taking an oath of loyalty. Vassals owed the lord certain services—usually military assistance—and sometimes received in exchange a grant of land known as a fief.

Vatican II (p. 912) Popular term for the Second Vatican Council that convened in 1963 and introduced a series of changes within the Roman Catholic Church.

vernacular languages (p. 480) The native spoken languages of Europe, which became literary languages and began to replace Latin as the dominant form of learned expression during the sixteenth century.

Versailles Treaty (p. 807) Treaty between Germany and the victorious Allies after World War I.

Vichy, Vichy regime, Vichy government (p. 852) Authoritarian state established in France after its defeat by the German army in 1940.

vizier (p. 36) The chief minister of state in New Kingdom Egypt, the vizier supervised the administration of the entire kingdom.

Vulgate (p. 213) The Latin translation of the Bible produced about 410 by the monk Jerome. It was the standard Bible in western Christian churches until the sixteenth century.

Wahhabism (p. 840) A religious reform and revival movement founded by Muhammad Abd al-Wahhab (1703–1787) in the eighteenth century to purify Islam by returning to a strict interpretation of the *Sharia,* or Islamic law. Revived during the 1920s in Saudi Arabia.

Warsaw Pact (p. 889) Military alliance of the Soviet Union and its eastern European satellite states in the Cold War era.

Weimar Republic (p. 820) The democratic German state constructed after defeat in World War I and destroyed by the Nazis in 1933.

wergild (p. 267) In Germanic societies, the term referred to what an individual was worth in case he or she suffered an injury. It was the amount of compensation in gold that the wrongdoer's family had to pay to the victim's family.

witch-hunt (p. 470) Refers to the dramatic increase in the judicial prosecution of alleged witches in either church or secular courts from the middle of the sixteenth to the middle of the seventeenth centuries.

Yahwism (p. 70) The worship of Yahweh ("Jehovah"); the form of early Israelite religious belief.

Yalta Conference (p. 884) Meeting in 1945 of the leaders of the Allied states of Britain, the Soviet Union, and the United States to devise plans for postwar Europe.

ziggurat (p. 23) Monumental tiered or terraced temple characteristic of ancient Mesopotamia.

Zionism (p. 736) Nationalist movement that emerged in the late nineteenth century and sought to establish a Jewish political state in Palestine (the Biblical Zion).

Zoroastrianism (p. 88) The monotheistic religion of Persia founded by Zoroaster that became the official religion of the Persian Empire.

SUGGESTIONS FOR FURTHER READING

CHAPTER 1 THE BEGINNINGS OF CIVILIZATION, 10,000–1150 B.C.E.

Andrews, Anthony P. *First Cities.* 1995. An excellent introduction to the development of urbanism in Southwest Asia, Egypt, India, China, and the Americas.

Crawford, Harriet. *Sumer and the Sumerians.* 2004. A comprehensive study of the interplay between the physical environment, emerging political structures, and technological change. Clearly illustrated.

Dalley, Stephanie. *Mari and Karana: Two Old Babylonian Cities.* 1984. Despite the rather forbidding title, a delightful exploration of daily life in the eighteenth century B.C.E., using excavations of two small kingdoms in northwest Mesopotamia.

Fagan, Brian. *People of the Earth: An Introduction to World Prehistory.* 1998. A comprehensive textbook that introduces basic issues with a wealth of illustrations and explanatory materials.

Hornung, Erik. *History of Ancient Egypt: An Introduction,* trans. David Lorton. 1999. A concise and lucid overview of Egyptian history and life.

Kuhrt, Amélie. *The Ancient Near East, ca. 3000–330 B.C.,* 2 vols. 1995. A magisterial overview, with an excellent bibliography. The place to start for a continuous historical narrative of the region.

Redford, Donald B. *Egypt, Canaan, and Israel in Ancient Times.* 1993. A distinguished Egyptologist discusses 3,000 years of uninterrupted contact between Egypt and southwestern Asia.

Sasson, Jack M, ed. *Civilizations of the Ancient Near East,* vol. 2. 1995. Contains a number of very helpful essays, particularly on Egypt.

Schmandt-Besserat, Denise. *How Writing Came About.* 1996. A highly readable and groundbreaking argument that cuneiform writing developed from a method of counting with tokens.

Schulz, Regine, and Matthias Seidel, eds. *Egypt: The World of the Pharaohs.* 1999. A sumptuously illustrated collection of essays on all aspects of Egyptian society and life by leading experts.

Snell, Daniel C. *Life in the Ancient Near East.* 1997. A concise account of the major developments over 5,000 years.

Spindler, Konrad. *The Man in the Ice: The Discovery of a 5,000-Year-Old Body Reveals the Secrets of the Stone Age.* 1994. A leader of the international team of experts interprets the corpse of a Neolithic hunter found in the Austrian Alps.

Stiebing, William H. *Ancient Near Eastern History and Culture.* 2008. Clear and comprehensive survey of important political and cultural events.

Trigger, Bruce G. *Early Civilizations: Ancient Egypt in Context.* 1995. A leading cultural anthropologist examines Old and Middle Kingdom Egypt through comparison with the early civilizations of China, Peru, Mexico, Mesopotamia, and Africa.

Van De Mieroop, Marc. *A History of the Ancient Near East ca. 3000–323 B.C.* 2007. Authoritative and up-to-date history.

Wenke, Robert J. *Patterns in Prehistory: Humankind's First Three Million Years,* 4th ed. 1999. An often witty, highly readable account.

CHAPTER 2 THE AGE OF EMPIRES: THE INTERNATIONAL BRONZE AGE AND ITS AFTERMATH, CA. 1500–550 B.C.E.

Bryce, Trevor. *Life and Society in the Hittite World.* 2002. A lively look at Hittite customs, laws, and social structures.

Bryce, Trevor. *The Letters of the Great Kings of the Ancient Near East: The Royal Correspondence of the Late Bronze Age.* 2003. Bryce explores the Club of the Great Powers through their surviving correspondence.

Bryce, Trevor. *The Trojans and Their Neighbors.* 2005. An up-to-date examination of the historical Troy.

Cohen, Raymond, and Raymond Westbrook, eds. *Amarna Diplomacy: The Beginnings of International Relations.* 2000. An intriguing collaboration of archaeologists, linguists, and specialists in international diplomacy, this book looks at the Amarna Letters from the context of modern international relations.

Dever, William G. *What Did the Biblical Writers Know and When Did They Know It?: What Archaeology Can Tell Us About the Reality of Ancient Israel.* 2001. A clear and often entertaining account of the writing of the Hebrew Bible.

Dever, William G. *Who Were the Early Israelites and Where Did They Come From?* 2003. A clear and lively account that takes the reader step-by-step through the various historical, archaeological, and political controversies that bedevil the study of ancient Israel.

Dickinson, Oliver. *The Aegean Bronze Age.* 1994. Now the standard treatment of the complex archaeological data.

Dothan, Trude, and Moshe Dothan. *People of the Sea: The Search for the Philistines.* 1992. A survey of the archaeological material, written for non-specialists.

Finkelstein, Israel, and Neil Asher Silberman. *David and Solomon: In Search of the Bible's Sacred Kings and the Roots of the Western Tradition.* 2006. An important, if controversial, archaeological interpretation that views David and Solomon as tribal chieftains and the "United Monarchy" as a fiction, this elegantly written study also explores the impact of the biblical story on Western identity.

Fitton, J. Lesley. *Minoans: Peoples of the Past.* 2002. Accessible account of recent research and conclusions.

Fitton, J. Lesley. *The Discovery of the Greek Bronze Age.* 1996. A lucid and well-illustrated study of the archaeologists who brought the Greek Bronze Age to light in the nineteenth and early twentieth centuries.

Kuhrt, Amélie. *The Ancient Near East, ca. 3000–330 B.C.,* 2 vols. 1995. A magisterial overview, with an excellent bibliography. The place to start for a continuous historical narrative of the region.

Latacz, Joachim. *Troy and Homer: Towards a Solution of an Old Mystery.* 2004. One of the most recent efforts to solve the puzzle of the historicity of Homer's account of the Trojan War.

Markoe, Glenn. *Phoenicians.* 2000. An important treatment of Phoenician society by a noted expert.

Miller, Patrick D. *Chieftains of the Highland Clans: A History of Israel in the 12th and 11th Centuries B.C.* 2003. Uses not only archaeological and textual evidence but also anthropological methodology to explore the history of the early Israelites.

Redford, Donald B. *Egypt, Canaan and Israel in Ancient Times.* 1992. An excellent, detailed synthesis of textual and archaeological evidence that emphasizes interconnections among cultures.

Stiebing, William H. *Ancient Near Eastern History and Culture.* 2008. A comprehensive survey that also pays close attention to historiographical and archaeological controversies. The chapter on the end of the International Bronze Age is particularly well done.

van de Mieroop, Marc. *A History of the Ancient Near East ca. 3000–323 B.C.* 2007. An excellent survey, with clear maps and useful time lines.

Walker, Christopher, ed. *Astronomy Before the Telescope.* 1996. A fascinating collection of essays about astronomy in the premodern period, which makes clear Western civilization's enormous debt to the Babylonians.

CHAPTER 3 GREEK CIVILIZATION

Boardman, John. *Persia and the West: An Archaeological Investigation of the Genesis of Achaemenid Art.* 2000. A brilliantly illustrated study that stresses intercultural influences in every aspect of Persian art.

Boyce, Mary. *A History of Zoroastrianism,* vol. 2. 1975. This authoritative examination provides a masterful overview of the religion of the Persian Empire.

Burkert, Walter. *The Orientalizing Revolution: Near Eastern Influence on Greek Culture in the Early Archaic Age,* trans. Margaret Pinder and Walter Burkert. 1993. Explains how the Semitic East influenced the development of Greek society in the Archaic Age.

Cohn, Norman. *Cosmos, Chaos, and the World to Come: The Ancient Roots of Apocalyptic Faith.* 1993. Expert critical analysis of apocalyptic religions in the West, including Zoroastrianism, ancient Judaism, Christianity, and other faiths.

Finkelstein, Israel, and Neil Asher Silberman. *The Bible Unearthed: Archaeology's New Vision of Ancient Israel and the Origin of the Sacred Texts.* 2001. An important archaeological interpretation that challenges the narrative of the Hebrew Bible and offers a reconsideration of biblical history.

Gottwald, Norman K. *The Hebrew Bible: A Socio-Literary Introduction.* 1985. Combines a close reading of the Hebrew Bible with the latest archaeological and historical evidence.

Just, Roger. *Women in Athenian Law and Life.* 1989. Provides an overview of the social context of women in Athens.

Kuhrt, Amélie. *The Ancient Near East, ca. 3000–330 B.C.,* vol. 2. 1995. This rich and comprehensive bibliography is a remarkably concise and readable account of Persian history with excellent discussion of ancient textual evidence. Many important passages appear in fluent translation.

Lindberg, David C. *The Beginnings of Western Science: The European Scientific Tradition in Philosophical, Religious, and Institutional Context, 600 B.C. to A.D. 1450.* 1992. This highly readable study provides an exciting survey of the main developments in Western science.

Markoe, Glenn. *Phoenicians.* 2000. The best and most up-to-date treatment of Phoenician society by a noted expert.

Murray, Oswyn. *Early Greece.* 1983. A brilliant study of all aspects of the emergence of Greek society between the Dark Age and the end of the Persian Wars.

Osborne, Robin. *Greece in the Making, 1200–479 B.C.* 1996. An excellent narrative of the development of Greek society with special regard to the archaeological evidence.

Stewart, Andrew. *Art, Desire, and the Body in Ancient Greece.* 1997. A provocative study that examines Greek attitudes toward sexuality and art.

Walker, Christopher, ed. *Astronomy Before the Telescope.* 1996. A fascinating collection of essays about astronomy in the premodern period, which makes clear our enormous debt to the Babylonians.

Wieshöfer, Josef. *Ancient Persia from 550 B.C. to A.D. 650,* trans. Azizeh Azodi. 1996. A fresh and comprehensive overview of Persian cultural, social, and political history that relies on Persian evidence more heavily than on biased Greek and Roman sources.

CHAPTER 4 HELLENISTIC CIVILIZATION

Auatin, Michel. *The Hellenistic World from Alexander to the Roman Conquest: A Selection of Ancient Sources in Translation,* 2nd ed. 2006. A major collection of more than 325 documents from this period.

Boardman, John, Jasper Griffin, and Oswyn Murray, eds. *Greece and the Hellenistic World. The Oxford History of the Classical World.* 1988. A synthesis of all aspects of Hellenistic life, with excellent illustrations and bibliography.

Bosworth, A. B. *Alexander and the East: The Tragedy of Triumph.* 1997. A negative interpretation of Alexander as a totalitarian ruler.

Bugh, Glenn R. *The Cambridge Companion to the Hellenistic World.* 2006. A collection of essays on 15 different aspects of Hellenistic politics and culture.

Cartledge, Paul, Peter Garnsey, and Erich Gruen, eds. *Hellenistic Constructs: Essays in culture, history and historiography.* 1997. Emphasizes the cultural interaction between Greek and non-Greek societies during this period.

Cohen, Getzel M. *The Hellenistic Settlements in Europe, the Islands, and Asia Minor.* 1996. The standard reference work on the cities founded in these areas during the Hellenistic period.

Cohn, Norman. *Cosmos, Chaos, and the World to Come: The Ancient Roots of Apocalyptic Faith.* 1993. This brilliant study explains the development of ideas about the end of the world in the cultures of the ancient world.

Cunliffe, Barry. *The Ancient Celts.* 1997. This source analyzes the archaeological evidence for the Celtic Iron Age, with many illustrations and maps.

Cunliffe, Barry, ed. *The Oxford Illustrated Prehistory of Europe.* 1996. A collection of well-illustrated essays on the development of European cultures from the end of the Ice Age to the Classical period.

Fox, Robin Lane. *Alexander the Great.* 1994. Shows that the myth Alexander created is as influential today as it was in the ancient world.

Freeman, Philip. *Alexander the Great.* 2011. A highly readable study based on sound scholarship.

Green, Peter. *Alexander to Actium: The Historical Evolution of the Hellenistic Age.* 1990. A vivid interpretation of the world created by Alexander until the victory of Augustus.

Gruen, Erich S. *The Hellenistic World and the Coming of Rome.* 1984. An important study of how Rome entered the eastern Mediterranean world.

Kuhrt, Amélie, and Susan Sherwin-White, eds. *Hellenism in the East: The Interaction of Greek and Non-Greek Civilizations from Syria to Central Asia After Alexander.* 1987. These studies help us understand the complexities of the interaction of Greeks and non-Greeks in the Hellenistic world.

Momigliano, Arnaldo. *Alien Wisdom: The Limits of Hellenization.* 1975. A study of Greek attitudes toward the contemporary civilizations of the Romans, Celts, Jews, and Persians.

Onians, John. *Art and Thought in the Hellenistic Age: The Greek World View, 350–50 B.C.* 1979. Amply illustrated study of Hellenistic artistic and intellectual history.

Pollitt, J. J. *Art in the Hellenistic Age.* 1986. A brilliant interpretation of the development of Hellenistic art. Discusses the freedom of aristocratic Greek women in Egypt during this period.

Pomeroy, Sarah B. *Women in Hellenistic Egypt: From Alexander to Cleopatra.* 1984. Describes the lives of women in different strata of society.

Steele, James. *Hellenistic Architecture in Asia Minor.* 1992. Challenges the belief that Hellenistic architecture represented a degradation of the Greek classical style.

CHAPTER 5 THE ROMAN REPUBLIC

Bringmann, Klaus. *A History of the Roman Republic.* 2007. A useful survey that not only provides a detailed narrative but also challenges some of the traditional interpretations.

Cornell, T. J. *The Beginnings of Rome: Italy and Rome from the Bronze Age to the Punic Wars (ca. 1000–264 B.C.).* 1996. A synthesis of the latest evidence with many important new interpretations.

Crawford, Michael, *The Roman Republic*, 2nd ed. 1992. An overview by a leading scholar.

Flower, Harriet I., ed. *The Cambridge Companion to the Roman Republic.* 2004. Includes essays on political and military history, Roman society, republican territorial expansion, culture, and the influence of the Republic on the French and American revolutions.

Gardner, Jane F. *Women in Roman Law and Society.* 1986. Explains the legal position of women in the Roman world.

Goldsworthy, Adrian. *The Fall of Carthage: The Punic Wars, 265–146 B.C.* 2003. A sweeping history of one of the great military conflicts of the ancient world.

Gruen, Erich S. *The Last Generation of the Roman Republic.* 1995. An exhaustive study of a crucial period of the republic.

Lintott, Andrew. *The Constitution of the Roman Republic.* 2003. An authoritative and well-written treatment of the subject.

Orlin, Eric. *Temples, Religion and Politics in the Roman Republic.*1997. A study of Roman religion focusing on the building and dedication of new temples.

Sherwin-White, A. N. *Roman Citizenship.* 1980. A comprehensive treatment of the subject.

Stein, Peter. *Roman Law in European History.* A superb overview, beginning with the Law of the Twelve Tables.

Wiseman, T. P. *Remembering the Roman Republic: Essays on Late Republican Politics and Literature.* 2009. Explores different aspects of the popular, democratic tradition of political ideology in the Roman Republic.

CHAPTER 6 ENCLOSING THE WEST: THE EARLY ROMAN EMPIRE AND ITS NEIGHBORS: 31 B.C.E.–235 C.E.

Barrett, Anthony A. *Livia: First Lady of Imperial Rome.* 2002. Biography of one of the most intriguing figures in the Roman Empire.

Beard, Mary, John North, and Simon Price. *Religions of Rome.* 1995. The first volume contains essays on polytheist religions, and the second contains translated ancient sources.

Chancey, Mark. *Greco-Roman Culture and the Galilee of Jesus.* 2005. A concise but broad-ranging survey of the title topic.

Crossan, J. D. *The Birth of Christianity.* 1998. Lively account of the Roman context of this new religious force.

Futrell, Alison. *Blood in the Arena: The Spectacle of Roman Power.* 1997. Explores the role of violent spectacle in creating and sustaining Roman rule.

Gardner, Jane F. *Women in Roman Law and Society.* 1987. Discusses issues pertaining to women in Rome.

Isaac, Benjamin. *The Creation of Racism in Classical Antiquity.* 2004. A highly readable discussion of ancient social prejudices and discriminatory stereotypes that influenced the development of modern racism.

Mattingly, David. *Imperialism, Power, and Identity: Experiencing the Roman Empire.* 2010. A critical look at the concept of "Romanization," with an emphasis on the experience of the ruled rather than the ambitions of the rulers.

Nickelsburg, George W. E. *Ancient Judaism and Christian Origins. Diversity, Continuity, and Transformation.* 2003. Innovative study of the emergence of Christianity from Judaism.

Ramage, Nancy H., and Andrew Ramage. *Roman Art,* 4th ed. 2005. An excellent, beautifully illustrated introduction to Roman art and architecture.

Romm, James. *The Edges of the Earth in Ancient Thought: Geography, Exploration, and Fiction.* 1992. An exciting introduction to the Roman understanding of real and imaginary peoples.

Scott, Sarah, and Jane Webster, eds. *Roman Imperialism and Provincial Art.* 2003. A collection of essays that explores new approaches to the cultural interconnections between the Romans and the peoples they ruled.

Talbert, Richard, ed. *The Barrington Atlas of the Classical World.* 2000. Contains excellent maps.

Webster, Graham. *The Roman Imperial Army,* 3rd ed. 1985. Discusses military organization and life in the empire.

Wells, Peter S. *The Battle That Stopped Rome.* 2003. A lively account of the Battle of Teutoburg Forest that provides a clear and comprehensive demonstration of the way archaeological evidence helps shape our understanding of the past.

Wolfram, Herwig. *The Roman Empire and Its Germanic Peoples.* 1997. Examines the interrelation of Romans and Germans over several centuries.

Woolf, G., ed. *The Cambridge Illustrated History of the Roman World.* 2003. Richly illustrated and comprehensive.

Woolf, Greg. *Becoming Roman: The Origins of Provincial Civilization in Gaul.* 1998. An acclaimed study of Romanization.

CHAPTER 7 LATE ANTIQUITY: THE AGE OF NEW BOUNDARIES, 250–600

Bowersock, G. W. *Hellenism in Late Antiquity.* 1990. Explains the important role of traditional Greek culture in shaping late antiquity.

Bowersock, G. W., Peter Brown, and Oleg Grabar, eds. *Late Antiquity: A Guide to the Postclassical World.* 1999. An indispensable handbook containing synthetic essays and shorter encyclopedia entries.

Brown, Peter. *The Cult of the Saints: Its Rise and Function in Late Antiquity.* 1981. A brilliant and highly influential study.

Brown, Peter. *The Rise of Western Christendom: Triumph and Diversity.* 1997. An influential and highly accessible survey.

Brown, Peter. *The World of Late Antiquity.* 1971. A classic treatment of the period.

Cameron, Averil. *The Later Roman Empire.* 1993. *The Mediterranean World in Late Antiquity.* 1997. Excellent textbooks with bibliography and maps.

Clark, Gillian. *Women in Late Antiquity: Pagan and Christian Life-Styles.* 1993. The starting point of modern discussion; lucid and reliable.

Harries, Jill. *Law and Empire in Late Antiquity.* 1999. Explores the presence and practice of law in Roman society.

Lee, A. D. *Information and Frontiers: Roman Foreign Relations in Late Antiquity.* 1993. An exciting and original investigation.

Maas, Michael. *The Cambridge Companion to the Age of Justinian.* 2005. A collection of 20 chapters by different experts on all aspects of the Mediterranean world in the sixth century.

Maas, Michael. *Readings in Late Antiquity: A Sourcebook.* 2000. Hundreds of ancient sources in translation illustrating all aspects of late antiquity.

Markus, Robert. *The End of Ancient Christianity.* 1995. Excellent introduction to the transformation of Christianity in late antiquity.

Pagels, Elaine. *The Origin of Satan: How Christians Demonized Jews, Pagans, and Heretics.* 1996. The award-winning historian Elaine Pagels tells the griping story of how early Christians transformed the gospel of love into the irrational hatred of others.

Rich, John, ed. *The City in Late Antiquity.* 1992. Important studies of changes in late antique urbanism.

Thompson, E. A. *The Huns,* rev. Peter Heather. 1997. The best introduction to major issues.

CHAPTER 8 MEDIEVAL EMPIRES AND BORDERLANDS: BYZANTIUM AND ISLAM

Bowersock, Glen, Peter Brown, and Oleg Grabar, eds. *Late Antiquity: A Guide to the Post-Classical World.* 1999. Interpretive essays combined with encyclopedia entries make this a starting point for discussion.

Brown, Thomas S. *Gentlemen and Officers: Imperial Administration and Aristocratic Power in Byzantine Italy, A.D. 554–800.* 1984. The basic study of Byzantine rule in Italy between Justinian and Charlemagne.

Bulliet, Richard W. *The Camel and the Wheel.* 1990. A fascinating investigation of the importance of the camel in history.

Cook, Michael. *Muhammad.* 1996. A short, incisive account of Muhammad's life that questions the traditional picture.

Cormack, Robin. *Writing in Gold: Byzantine Society and Its Icons.* 1985. An expert discussion of icons in the Byzantine world.

Donner, Fred M. *The Early Islamic Conquests.* 1981. Discusses the first phases of Islamic expansion.

Fletcher, Richard. *Moorish Spain.* 1992. Highly readable.

Franklin, Simon, and Jonathan Shepard. *The Emergence of Rus: 750–1200.* 1996. The standard text for this period.

Hawting, G. R. *The First Dynasty of Islam: the Umayyad Caliphate, AD 661–750.* 2000. The most up-to-date study of the Umayyads.

Herrin, Judith. *The Formation of Christendom.* 2001. An exceptionally learned and lucid book; Herrin sees Byzantium as crucial both for the development of Christianity and Islam.

Hourani, George. *Arab Seafaring in the Indian Ocean in Ancient and Early Medieval Times.* 1995. The standard discussion of Arab maritime activity.

King, Charles. *The Black Sea: A History.* 2004. A comprehensive history of the Black Sea region from antiquity to the present. It is especially useful for anyone interested in this borderland among cultures.

Lings, Martin. *Muhammad: His Life Based on the Earliest Sources.* 2006. This readable biography is based exclusively on the eighth- and ninth-century Arabic sources. The view of Muhammad is sympathetic, but the book strips away many of the later Muslim pieties and anti-Muslim rhetoric that has distorted the historical Muhammad.

Moorhead, John. *The Roman Empire Divided, 400–700.* 2001. A reliable and up-to-date survey of the period.

Norwich, John Julius. *A Short History of Byzantium.* 1998. The most readable short account. Norwich is a born storyteller, making the book a joy to read.

Petry, Carl F. *The Cambridge History of Egypt, vol. 1: Islamic Egypt, 640–1517.* 2008. The most comprehensive and up-to-date study of how Egypt became Muslim and one of the dominant powers in the Islamic world.

The Qu'ran (Oxford World Classics). Trans. Haleem, Muhammad Abdel. 2008. The best new translation of the founding text of Islam.

Robinson, Francis, ed. *The Cambridge Illustrated History of the Islamic World.* 1978. Many excellent and well-illustrated articles that will be useful for beginners.

Treadgold, Warren. *A History of the Byzantine State and Society.* 1998. A reliable narrative of Byzantine history.

Treadgold, Warren T. *A Concise History of Byzantium.* 2001. A reliable and insightful short survey.

CHAPTER 9 MEDIEVAL EMPIRES AND BORDERLANDS: THE LATIN WEST

Asbridge, Thomas. *The Crusades: The Authoritative History of the War for the Holy Land.* 2011. A sweeping study that captures the spiritual motivations behind the warfare. It is the only account that is thoroughly based on sources from both Christian and Muslim sides.

Bachrach, Bernard S. *Early Medieval Jewish Policy in Western Europe.* 1977. A significant revisionist view of the history of the Jews in Latin Christian Europe.

Bartlett, Robert. *The Making of Europe: Conquest, Colonization and Cultural Change: 950–1350.* 1993. The best, and often greatly stimulating, analysis of how Latin Christianity spread in post-Carolingian Europe.

Brown, Peter. *The Rise of Western Christendom: Triumph and Diversity A.D. 200–1000.* 2001. A brilliant interpretation of the development of Christianity in its social context.

Cohen, Jeremy. *Living Letters of the Law: Ideas of the Jew in Medieval Christianity.* 1999. A masterful investigation of early medieval Judaism.

Geary, Patrick J. *The Myth of Nations: The Medieval Origins of Europe.* 2003. Debunks the widespread idea that the European nations can trace their origins back to ethnic groups from the early Middle Ages. Geary convincingly undermines the nationalist ideologies of modern nationalist movements.

Geary, Patrick J. *The Peoples of Europe in the Early Middle Ages.* 2002. Discusses the emergence of the new kingdoms of Europe, stressing the incorporation of Roman elements.

Hollister, C. Warren. *Medieval Europe: A Short History.* 1997. This concise, crisply written text presents the development of Europe during the Middle Ages by charting its progression from a primitive rural society, sparsely settled and impoverished, to a powerful and distinctive civilization.

Jones, Gwyn. *A History of the Vikings.* 2001. A comprehensive, highly readable analysis.

Keen, Maurice, ed. *Medieval Warfare: A History.* 1999. Lucid specialist studies of aspects of medieval warfare.

Lawrence, C. H. *Medieval Monasticism.* 2001. A fine introduction to the phenomenon of Christian monasticism.

Maalouf, Amin. *The Crusades Through Arab Eyes.* 1984. Based on the works of Arab chroniclers, this book depicts a culture nearly destroyed both by internal conflicts and the military threat of the alien Christian culture.

Madden, Thomas F. *The New Concise History of the Crusades.* 2005. This crisp account helps explain the lasting legacy of the Crusades among Muslims today.

Mayr-Harting, Henry. *The Coming of Christianity to Anglo-Saxon England.* 1991. How a Germanic people were converted to Christianity.

McKitterick, Rosamond. *The Early Middle Ages.* 2001. The best up-to-date survey for the period 400–1000. It is composed of separate essays by leading specialists.

Moorhead, John. *The Roman Empire Divided, 400–700.* 2001. The best recent survey of the period.

Reuter, Timothy. *Germany in the Early Middle Ages, c. 800–1056.* 1991. A lucid explanation of the complexities of German history in this period.

Reynolds, Susan. *Fiefs and Vassals: The Medieval Evidence Reinterpreted.* 1994. The most important reexamination of the feudalism problem.

Riché, Pierre. *Education and Culture in the Barbarian West, Sixth Through Eighth Centuries,* translated from the third French edition by John J. Contreni. 1975. Demonstrates the rich complexity of learning during this period, once thought to be the Dark Ages of education.

Riché, Pierre. *The Carolingians: A Family Who Forged Europe.* 1993. Translated from the 1983 French edition, this book traces the rise, fall, and revival of the Carolingian dynasty, and shows how it molded the shape of a post-Roman Europe that still prevails today. This is basically a family history, but the family dominated Europe for more than two centuries.

Riley-Smith, Jonathan Simon Christopher. *The Crusades: A Short History.* 1987. Exactly what the title says.

Riley-Smith, Jonathan Simon Christopher. *The Oxford Illustrated History of the Crusades.* 2001. An utterly engaging, comprehensive study.

Stenton, Frank M. *Anglo-Saxon England.* 2001. This classic history covers the period ca. 550–1087 and traces the development of English society from the oldest Anglo-Saxon laws and kings to the extension of private lordship.

Strayer, Joseph B., ed. *Dictionary of the Middle Ages.* 1986. An indispensable reference work.

Webster, Leslie, and Michelle Brown, eds. *The Transformation of the Roman World, A.D. 400–900.* 1997. A well-illustrated synthesis with maps and bibliography.

Wickham, Chris. *Early Medieval Italy: Central Government and Local Society, 400–1000.* 1981. Examines the economic and social transformation of Italy.

CHAPTER 10 MEDIEVAL CIVILIZATION: THE RISE OF WESTERN EUROPE

Bony, Jean. *French Gothic Architecture of the Twelfth and Thirteenth Centuries.* 1983. With many beautiful illustrations, this is a good way to begin an investigation of these magnificent buildings.

Colish, Marcia L. *Medieval Foundations of the Western Intellectual Tradition, 400–1400.* 1997. The best general study.

Gimpel, Jean. *The Medieval Machine: The Industrial Revolution of the Middle Ages.* 1976. A short, lucid account of the power and agricultural revolutions.

Keen, Maurice. *Chivalry.* 1984. Readable and balanced coverage of this sometimes misunderstood phenomenon.

Lambert, Malcolm. *Medieval Heresy: Popular Movements from the Gregorian Reform to the Reformation*, 2nd ed. 1992. The best general study of heresy.

Lawrence, C. H. *The Friars: The Impact of the Early Mendicant Movement on Western Society.* 1994. The best general study of the influence of Dominicans and Franciscans.

Moore, R. I. *The Formation of a Persecuting Society: Power and Deviance in Western Europe, 950–1250.* 1987. A brilliant analysis of how Europe became a persecuting society.

Morris, Colin. *The Papal Monarchy: The Western Church from 1050 to 1250.* 1989. A thorough study that should be the beginning point for further investigation of the many fascinating figures in the medieval Church.

Mundy, John H. *Europe in the High Middle Ages, 1150–1309*, 3rd ed. 1999. A comprehensive introduction to the period.

Panofsky, Erwin. *Gothic Architecture and Scholasticism.* 2005. A learned and thoughtful book by one of the twentieth century's most influential art historians. It is not an easy read, but it is enormously stimulating.

Peters, Edward. *Europe and the Middle Ages.* 1989. An excellent general survey.

Pieper, Joseph, Clara Winston, and Richard Winston. *Scholasticism: Personalities and Problems of Medieval Philosophy.* 2001. This concise book clearly explains the principal Christian thinkers of the Middle Ages and gives proper credit to the Jewish and Muslim influences.

Strayer, Joseph R. *On the Medieval Origins of the Modern State.* 1970. Still the best short analysis.

CHAPTER 11 THE MEDIEVAL WEST IN CRISIS

Aberth, John. *The Black Death: The Great Mortality of 1348–1350: A Brief History with Documents.* 2005. A useful source for research papers.

Carmichael, Ann G. *Plague and the Poor in Renaissance Florence.* 1986. An innovative study that both questions the traditional theory of the bubonic plague as the cause of the Black Death and examines how fear of the disease led to regulation of the poor.

Cohn, Samuel Kline. *The Black Death Transformed: Disease and Culture in Early Renaissance Europe.* 2003. A well-argued case that the Black Death was not caused by the bubonic plague.

Cohn, Samuel Kline. *Lust for Liberty: The Politics of Social Revolt in Medieval Europe, 1200–1425.* 2008. Challenging many of the common assumptions about medieval revolts, Cohn shows that most involved workers and artisans tried to gain political rights.

Cohn, Samuel Kline. *Popular Protest in Late Medieval Europe: Italy, France, and Flanders.* 2005. The volume presents more than 200 documents translated for the first time showing the wide range of protest over two centuries. A good source for research papers.

Duby, Georges. *France in the Middle Ages, 987–1460: From Hugh Capet to Joan of Arc.* 1991. Traces the emergence of the French state.

Gordon, Bruce, and Peter Marshall, eds. *The Place of the Dead: Death and Remembrance in Late Medieval and Early Modern Europe.* 2000. A collection of essays that shows how the placing of the dead in society was an important activity that engendered considerable conflict and negotiation.

Herlihy, David. *The Black Death and the Transformation of the West.* 1997. A pithy, readable analysis of the epidemiological and historical issues surrounding the Black Death.

Holmes, George. *Europe: Hierarchy and Revolt, 1320–1450.* 1975. Excellent examination of rebellions.

Huizinga, Johan. *The Autumn of the Middle Ages*, trans. Rodney J. Payton and Urlich Mammitzsch. 1996. A new translation of the classic study of France and the Low Countries during the fourteenth and fifteenth centuries. Dated and perhaps too pessimistic, Huizinga's lucid prose and broad vision still make this an engaging reading experience.

Imber, Colin. *The Ottoman Empire, 1300–1481.* 1990. The basic work that establishes a chronology for the early Ottomans.

Jordan, William C. *The Great Famine: Northern Europe in the Early Fourteenth Century.* 1996. The most comprehensive book on the famine.

Lambert, Malcolm. *Medieval Heresy: Popular Movements from the Gregorian Reform to the Reformation.* 1992. Excellent general study of the Hussite and Lollard movements.

Le Roy Ladurie, Emmanuel. *Times of Feast, Times of Famine: A History of Climate Since the Year 1000,* trans. Barbara Bray. 1971. The book that introduced the idea of the Little Ice Age and promoted the study of the influence of climate on history.

Lynch, Joseph H. *The Medieval Church: A Brief History.* 1992. A pithy, elegant survey of ecclesiastical institutions and developments.

Morgan, David O. *The Mongols.* 1986. Best introduction to Mongol history.

Nirenberg, David. *Communities of Violence: Persecution of Minorities in the Middle Ages.* 1996. An important analysis of the persecution of minorities that is deeply rooted in Spanish evidence.

Scott, Susan, and Christopher Duncan. *Biology of Plagues: Evidence from Historical Populations.* 2001. An analysis by two epidemiologists who argue that the Black Death was not the bubonic plague but probably a virus similar to Ebola.

Sumption, Jonathan. *The Hundred Years' War: Trial by Battle.* 1991. First volume goes only to 1347. When it is completed, it will be the best comprehensive study.

Swanson, R. N. *Religion and Devotion in Europe, c. 1215–c. 1515.* 1995. The best up-to-date textbook account of late medieval religious practice.

NOTES

CHAPTER 1

1. Robert J. Wenke, *Patterns in Prehistory: Humankind's First Three Million Years* (1999), 404.
2. Ibid.
3. Marc van de Mieroop, *A History of the Ancient Near East, ca 3000–323 B.C.E.* (2007), 23.
4. Wenke, *Patterns in Prehistory,* 404.
5. Quoted in Stephen Bertman, *Handbook to Life in Ancient Mesopotamia* (2003), 65.
6. Ibid., 179.
7. Quoted in van de Mieroop, *A History of the Ancient Near East,* 113.
8. Ibid.
9. Quoted in Bertman, *Handbook to Life in Ancient Mesopotamia,* 172–173.
10. Jean Bottero, *Mesopotamia: Writing, Reasoning, and the Gods,* translated by Zainab Bahrani and Marc van de Mieroop (1992), 33, 127, 129.
11. *Code of Hammurabi,* translated by J. N. Postgate, 55–56. Cited in Postgate, *Early Mesopotamia: Society and Economy at the Dawn of History* (1992), 160.
12. Samuel Greengus, "Legal and Social Institutions of Ancient Near Mesopotamia," in *Civilizations of the Ancient Near East,* ed. Jack M. Sasson, vol. 1 (1995), 471.
13. Ibid., 474.
14. *A Dispute of a Man with His Ba,* probably composed ca. 2180–2040 B.C.E. Quoted in W. Stiebing, *Ancient Near Eastern History and Culture* (2008), 153.
15. *The Admonitions of Ipuwer,* quoted in Stiebing, *Ancient Near Eastern History and Culture,* 164.

CHAPTER 2

1. Quoted in Carlo Zaccagnini, "The Interdependence of the Great Powers," in *Amarna Diplomacy: The Beginnings of International Relations,* eds. Raymond Cohen and Raymond Westbrook (2000), 149.
2. Quoted in Michael Roaf, *Cultural Atlas of Mesopotamia and the Ancient Near East* (2004), 136.
3. Quoted in Trevor Bryce, *Life and Society in the Hittite World* (2002), 113.
4. Quoted in William H. Stiebing, Jr., *Ancient Near Eastern History and Culture* (2008), 229.
5. Quoted in Marc van de Mieroop, *A History of the Ancient Near East ca. 3000–323 B.C.* (2007), 194.
6. Ibid., 195.
7. A. Kirk Grayson, in *Assyrian and Babylonian Chronicles* (1975).
8. Quoted in Stiebing, *Ancient Near Eastern History and Culture,* 281.
9. Micah 6: 6–8, Revised Standard Version.
10. Ezekiel 34: 15–20. Revised Standard Version.

CHAPTER 3

1. Demosthenes, *Orations,* 59.122.
2. From Euripides, *The Trojan Women,* translated by Peter Levi, in John Boardman, Jasper Griffith, and Oswyn Murray, eds., *The Oxford History of the Classical World* (1986), 169.
3. Plato, *Phaedo,* 1.118.

CHAPTER 4

1. Athenaios, 253 D; cited and translated in J. J. Pollitt, *Art in the Hellenistic Age* (1986), 271.

CHAPTER 5

1. From *Selected Works* by Cicero, translated by Michael Grant (Penguin Classics 1960, second revised edition 1971). Copyright © Michael Grant 1960, 1965, 1971. Reproduced by permission of Penguin Books Ltd.

CHAPTER 7

1. John Helgeland, *Christians in the Military: The Early Experience* (1985), 64–65.

CHAPTER 8

1. Al-Tabari, *The History of Al-Tabari,* vol. 17: *The First Civil War,* translated and annotated by G. R. Hawting (1985), 50.
2. Quoted in Jane S. Gerber, *The Jews of Spain: A History of the Sephardic Experience* (1992), 28.

CHAPTER 9

1. Willibald, *The Life of Boniface,* in Clinton Albertson, trans., *Anglo-Saxon Saints and Heroes* (1967), 308–310.
2. Quoted in Edward Peters, *Europe and the Middle Ages* (1989), 159.

CHAPTER 10

1. Cited in Emmanuel Le Roy Ladurie, *Montaillou: Promised Land of Error,* translated by Barbara Bray (1978), 130.
2. Ibid., 56.
3. Ibid., 63.

CHAPTER 11

1. Quoted in William Bowsky, "The Impact of the Black Death," in Anthony Molho (ed.), *Social and Economic Foundations of the Italian Renaissance* (1969), 92.
2. Cited in Philip Ziegler, *The Black Death* (1969), 20.
3. Giovanni Boccaccio, *The Decameron,* translated by Richard Aldington (1962), 30.
4. Ibid.
5. Quoted in Mark C. Bartusis, *The Late Byzantine Army: Arms and Society, 1204–1453* (1992), 133.
6. Trial record as quoted in Marina Warner, *Joan of Arc* (1981), 122.
7. Ibid., 127.
8. Ibid., 143.
9. *The Trial of Joan of Arc,* translated by W. S. Scott (1956), 134.
10. Ibid., 106.
11. Ibid., 135.
12. Johan Huizinga, *The Autumn of the Middle Ages,* translated by Rodney J. Payton and Ulrich Mammitzsch (1996), 156.
13. Quoted in Barbara W. Tuchman, *A Distant Mirror: The Calamitous 14th Century* (1978), 505–506. Translation has been slightly modified by the authors.
14. Cited in Bartlett, *The Making of Europe,* 238.

PHOTO CREDITS

Page 2: Galina Mikhalishina/Alamy; page 3: GSO Images/Getty Images; page 4: National Maritime Museum, London, UK/The Bridgeman Art Library; page 10: Prehistoric/National Museum of Art of Romania, Bucharest, Romania/Giraudon/The Bridgeman Art Library; page 14: DK Images; page 17: desfa24/Fotolia; page 20: Tim Parmenter/DK Images; page 23: World Religions Photo Library/The Bridgeman Art Library; page 25: Mesopotamian (4th century BC)/Iraq Museum, Baghdad/Giraudon/The Bridgeman Art Library; page 27: Art Resource, NY; page 31: Geoff Brightling/DK Images; page 37: Head from Osiride Statute of Hatshepsut. Egyptian; Thebes, Deir el-Bahri, New Kingdom Dynasty 18, Joint reign of Hatshepsut and Thutmose III, ca. 1473–1458 BCE. Painted limestone, H 124.4 cm (49 in). Rogers Fund, 1931 (31.3.157). The Metropolitan Museum of Art, New York, NY, U.S.A. Image copyright © The Metropolitan Museum of Art. Image Source: Art Resource, NY; page 37: AP Photo/Discovery Channel/Brando Quilici; page 38: Egyptian 19th Dynasty (c. 1297–1185 BC)/ Egyptian National Museum, Cairo, Egypt/The Bridgeman Art Library; page 39: bpk, Berlin/Aegyptisches Museum, Staatliche Museen, Berlin, Germany/Art Resource, NY; page 43: Erich Lessing/Art Resource, NY; page 46: Cindy Miller Hopkins/ DanitaDanita Delimont Photography/Newscom; page 48: Nimatallah/Art Resource, NY; page 51: Universal History Archive/ UIG/The Bridgeman Art Library; page 54: Imagestate Media Partners Limited-Impact Photos/Alamy; page 54: Joe Cornish/DK Images; page 60: Ancient Art & Architecture/DanitaDelimont; page 61: RMN-Grand Palais/Art Resource, NY; page 62: DeA Picture Library/The Granger Collection, NYC; page 64: DK Images; page 64: Erich Lessing/Art Resource, NY; page 68: Erich Lessing/Art Resource, NY; page 71: The Israel Museum, Jerusalem, Israel/The Bridgeman Art Library; page 78: Bettmann/Corbis; page 83: Corinth: Citadel at the Crossroads (gouache on paper), Payne, Roger (b. 1934)/Private Collection/© Look and Learn/The Bridgeman Art Library; page 91: SEF/Art Resource, NY; page 93: Vanni/Art Resource, NY; page 94: RMN-Grand Palais/Art Resource, NY; page 98: Foto Marburg/Art Resource, NY; page 104: The Trustees of the British Museum/Art Resource, NY; page 105: Scala/Art Resource, NY; page 107: Roy Rainford/Robert Harding; page 108: Scala/Ministero per i Beni e le Attività culturali/Art Resource, NY; page 111: Scala/Ministero per i Beni e le Attività culturali/Art Resource, NY; page 115: Roman (1st century BC)/ Museo Archeologico Nazionale, Naples, Italy/Giraudon/The Bridgeman Art Library; page 121: RMN-Grand Palais/Art Resource, NY; page 122: The Granger Collection, NYC; page 128: Erich Lessing/Art Resource, NY; page 129: Erich Lessing/Art Resource, NY; page 130: Jeremy Lightfoot/Robert Harding; page 131: RMN-Grand Palais/Art Resource, NY; page 132: Erich Lessing/Art Resource, NY; page 133: Musei Capitolini, Rome, Italy/ Giraudon/The Bridgeman Art Library; page 138: John Miller/ Robert Harding; page 140: Mike Dunning/DK Images; page 145: DeA Picture Library/Art Resource, NY; page 152: Scala/Art Resource, NY; page 154: kompasstudio/Shutterstock; page 154: Vanni/Art Resource, NY; page 155: bpk, Berlin/Museo Archeologico Nazionale, Naples, Italy/Alfredo Dagli Orti/Art Resource, NY; page 160: Dea Picture Library/Age Fotostock; page 161: Scala/Art Resource, NY; page 164: Scala/White Images/Art Resource, NY; page 165: Romancoins.info; page 165: Romancoins.info; page 169: Scala/Art Resource, NY; page 172: Scala/Art Resource, NY; page 175: Forum of Trajan, Rome, Italy/Bildarchiv Steffens/Ralph Rainer Steffens/The Bridgeman Art Library; page 179: Erich Lessing/Art Resource, NY; page 184: Travel Pix/Robert Harding; page 185: Alinari/Art Resource, NY; page 190: Erich Lessing/Art Resource, NY; page 193: Erich Lessing/Art Resource, NY; page 194: Scala/Art Resource, NY; page 195: Werner Forman/Art Resource, NY; page 198: Scala/Art Resource, NY; page 201: John Heseltine/ DK Images; page 203: steve estvanik/Shutterstock; page 204: James McConnachie/DK Images; page 207: Vanni Archive/Encyclopedia/ Corbis; page 210: Zvonimir Atletic/Shutterstock; page 211: V&A Images, London/Art Resource, NY; page 213: akg-images; page 217: Art Resource, NY; page 226: Scala/Art Resource, NY; page 229: Giraudon/SuperStock; page 232: Mikhail Markovskiy/ Shutterstock; page 238: Plate with the Battle of David and Goliath. Constantinople, Early Byzantine, 629–630. Silver. verall: 19 7/16 × 2 5/8 in., 203.9 oz. (49.4 × 6.6 cm, 5780 g) foot: 8 1/8 × 3/4 in. (20.6 × 1.9 cm). Gift of J. Pierpont Morgan, 1917 (17.190.396). The Metropolitan Museum of Art, New York, NY, U.S. Image copyright © The Metropolitan Museum of Art. Image source: Art Resource, NY; page 241: Cretan School (16th century)/Benaki Museum, Athens, Greece/Gift of Helen Stathatos/The Bridgeman Art Library; page 242: Byzantine Master (10th century)/Pushkin Museum, Moscow, Russia/The Bridgeman Art Library; page 246: RULHAN ARIKAN/Science Source; page 247: Tom Hollyman/ Science Source; page 251: Islamic School (9th century)/ Bibliotheque Nationale, Tunis, Tunisia/Giraudon/The Bridgeman Art Library; page 253: Magnus Rew/DK Images; page 257: Vittoriano Rastelli/Terra/Corbis; page 262: Bridgeman Art Library, London/SuperStock; page 269: St. Gregory writing with scribes, Carolingian, Franco-German School, c. 850–875 (ivory). Kunsthistorisches Museum, Vienna, Austria/Bridgeman Art Library; page 270: Photos.com/Thinkstock; page 276: Front cover of the Lindau Gospels. Court School of Charles the Bald, France. Ca. 880 CE. Repousse gold and jewels. M.1, front cover. The Pierpont Morgan Library, New York, NY, USA. Photo Credit: The Pierpont Morgan Library/Art Resource, NY; page 280: iStockphoto/Thinkstock; page 282: Scala/Art Resource, NY; page 285: GavinHellier/naturepl.com; page 290: British Library/ HIP/Art Resource, NY; page 291: iStockphoto/Thinkstock; page 292: bpk, Berlin/Staatsbibliothek zu Berlin, Stiftung Preussicher Kulturbesitz/Ruth Schacht/Art Resource, NY; page 296: Alinari/Art Resource, NY; page 299: Ancient Art & Architecture/DanitaDelimont; page 300: Copyright reserved Cambridge University Collection of Aerial Photography; page 302: Aispix by Image Source/Shutterstock; page 311: Cameraphoto Arte,Venice/Art Resource, NY; page 312: Scala/Art Resource, NY; page 314: The Coronation of the Virgin, detail of St. Dominic giving back the book to the Albigensians, c. 1430–32 (tempera on panel), Angelico,Fra (Guido di Pietro) (c. 1387–1455)/ Louvre, Paris, France/Giraudon/The Bridgeman Art Library; page 323: Album/Art Resource, NY; page 324: AJancso/ Shutterstock; page 325: Dean Conger/Corbis; page 324: Interior view looking down the nave towards the east end (photo), French School (12th century)/Basilique Saint-Denis, France/Giraudon/ The Bridgeman Art Library; page 328: National Gallery, London/ Art Resource, NY; page 333: Canali PhotoBank Milan/SuperStock; page 334: Interfoto/Alamy; page 337: Mongol archer on horseback, from seals of the Emperor Ch'ien Lung and others, 15th–16th century (ink & w/c on paper), Chinese School, Ming Dynasty (1368–1644)/ Victoria & Albert Museum, London, UK/The Bridgeman Art Library; page 338: The Art Gallery Collection/Alamy; page 347: Fr 2643 f.165v Battle of Crecy from the Hundred Years War, from 'Froissart's Chronicle', 24th August 1346 (vellum) (detail of 42253), French School (15th century)/Bibliotheque Nationale, Paris, France/The Bridgeman Art Library; page 349: Classic Image/ Alamy; page 356: Sheila Terry/Science Source; page 357: Death, detail from The Table of the Seven Deadly Sins and the Four Last Things (oil on panel) (detail of 68744), Bosch, Hieronymus (c. 1450–1516)/Prado, Madrid, Spain/Giraudon/The Bridgeman Art Library; page 364: Scala/Art Resource, NY; page 369: Scala/Art Resource, NY; page 370: Erich Lessing/Art Resource, NY; page 371: Dea/M. Carrieri/De Agostini/Getty Images; page 379: Snark/Art Resource, NY; page 381: Scala/Art Resource, NY; page 382: Erich Lessing/Art Resource, NY; page 382: Scala/Art Resource, NY; page 383: Pietro Basilico/Shutterstock; page 384: Erich Lessing/Art Resource, NY; page 388: Erich Lessing/Art Resource, NY; page 394: GL Archive/Alamy; page 401: Michel Zabe/DK Images; page 404: Bridgeman-Giraudon/Art Resource, NY; page 406: Library of Congress, Prints & Photographs Division, [LC-USZ62-43536]; Cortes meets Montezuma, from 'Homenaje a Cristobal Colon' by Alfredo Chavero, 1892 (colour litho), Mexican School (19th century)/British Library, London, UK/© British Library Board. All Rights Reserved/The Bridgeman Art Library; page 409: Ritual drinking vessel (kero), with Inca-Spanish colonial decoration/ Werner Forman Archive/The Bridgeman Art Library; page 410: The Art Gallery Collection/Alamy; page 411: Snark/Art Resource, NY; page 419: The Granger Collection, NYC; page 423: bpk, Berlin/ Art Resource, page 426: bpk, Berlin/Alte Pinakothek, Bayerische Staatsgemaeldesammlungen, Munich, G/Art Resource, NY; page 430: Album/Art Resource, NY; page 433: bpk, Berlin/ Kupferstichkabinett, Staatliche Museen, Berlin, Germany/Joerg P. Anders/Art Resource, NY; page 435: akg-images; page 436: Schongauer, Martin (1435–1491) Saint Anthony Tormented by Demons. Engraving, sheet: 11 13/16 × 8 9/16 in. (30 × 21.8 cm). Rogers Fund, 1920 (20.5.2). The Metropolitan Museum of Art, New York, NY, USA. The Metropolitan Museum of Art. Image source: Art Resource, NY; page 438: Foto Marburg/Art Resource, NY; page 443: Destruction of relics and statues in churches, April 1566, engraving by Franz Hogenberg (1535–1590), Wars of Religion, France, 16th century/De Agostini Picture Library/ G. Dagli Orti/The Bridgeman Art Library; page 453: David Sutherland/DK Images; page 454: Scala/Art Resource, NY; page 455: The Death of the Virgin, 1605–06 (oil on canvas) (detail of 3678), Caravaggio, Michelangelo Merisi da (1571–1610)/ Louvre, Paris, France/Giraudon/The Bridgeman Art Library; page 459: Erich Lessing/Art Resource, NY; page 462: bpk, Berlin/ Alte Pinakothek, Bayerische Staatsgemaeldesammlungen, Munich, G/Art Resource, NY; page 467: akg-images; page 468: A Woman Peeling Apples, c. 1663 (oil on canvas), Hooch, Pieter de (1629–84)/© Wallace Collection, London, UK/The Bridgeman Art Library; page 469: Erich Lessing/Art Resource, NY; page 471: The Torture of a Witch, Anne Hendricks, in Amsterdam in 1571 (engraving) (b/w photo), French School (16th century)/Private Collection/The Bridgeman Art Library; page 477: Dea/G.Dagli Orti/De Agostini Picture Library/Getty Images; page 482: Credit: Queen Elizabeth I (1533–1603) being carried in Procession (Eliza Triumphans) c. 1601 (oil on canvas), Peake, Robert (fl. 1580–1626) (attr. to)/Private Collection/The Bridgeman Art Library; page 484: Erich Lessing/Art Resource, NY; page 487: JTB Photo Communications/Age Fotostock; page 488: Wojtek Buss/Age Fotostock; page 492: HIP/Art Resource, NY; page 496: Triple Portrait of the Head of Richelieu, 1642 (oil on canvas), Champaigne, Philippe de (1602–74)/National Gallery, London, UK/The Bridgeman Art Library; page 498: Erich Lessing/Art Resource, NY; page 501: Erich Lessing/Art Resource, NY; page 503: Erich Lessing/Art Resource, NY; page 506: bpk, Berlin/ Kunstbibliothek, Staatliche Museen, Berlin, Germany/Knud Petersen/Art Resource, NY; page 514: View of the Neva, the Harbour and the Exchange at St. Petersburg, illustration for June from 'A Year in St. Petersburg' etched by John H. Clark, coloured by M. Dubourg, pub. 1815 in London by Edward Orme (coloured engraving), Mornay (19th century) (after)/Private Collection/The Stapleton Collection/The Bridgeman Art Library; page 518: Trial of Charles I, 4th January 1649 (engraving), English School (17th century)/Private Collection/The Stapleton Collection/The Bridgeman Art Library; page 521: Mary Evans Picture Library/ Alamy; page 522: bpk, Berlin/Rijksmuseum, Amsterdam, The Netherlands/Hermann Buresch/Art Resource, NY; page 525: SuperStock/SuperStock; page 527: Library of Congress Prints and Photographs Division [LC-USZ62-44642]; page 527: Bettmann/ Corbis; page 528: Bettmann/Corbis; page 528: Scenographia: Systematis Copernicani Astrological Chart (c. 1543) devised by Nicolaus Copernicus (1473–1543), from 'The Celestial Atlas, or the Harmony of the Universe', 1660 (hand-coloured engraving), Cellarius, Andreas (c. 1596–1665)/British Library, London, UK/ © British Library Board. All Rights Reserved/The Bridgeman Art Library; page 529: Bridgeman-Giraudon/Art Resource, NY; page 531: Interfoto/Alamy; page 533: The Art Gallery Collection/ Alamy; page 539: Jean-Baptiste Colbert (1619–1683) Presenting the Members of the Royal Academy of Science to Louis XIV (1638–1715) c. 1667 (oil on canvas), Testelin, Henri (1616–95)/ Chateau de Versailles, France/Giraudon/The Bridgeman Art Library; page 542: Benedict Spinoza (1632–77) (oil on canvas), Dutch School (17th century)/Herzog August Bibliothek, Wolfenbuttel, Germany/The Bridgeman Art Library; page 544: RMN-Grand Palais/Art Resource, NY; page 547: Bettmann/Corbis.

INDEX

Abbasid caliphate, 255–256
Abbey Church (St. Denis), *324* (illus)
Abd al-Rahman III (caliph), 257
Abelard, Peter, 320, 321
Abortion, 218
Abraham (biblical)
  Muslims and, 246
  sacrifice of Isaac, 381–382, *382* (illus)
Absolutism, 492–524
  in central and Eastern Europe, 505–513
  defined, 493
  Dutch Republic and, 513–523
  England and, 513–523
  in France, 495–497
  of Louis XIV (France), 498–500
  practice of, 494
  in Prussia, 507–509
  royal, 513
  in Spain, 495, 502–505
  theory of, 493–494
  warfare and, 494–495
Abu Hureyra, Syria (settlement), 14
Académie des Sciences (France), 500
Académie Française, 500
Academies in France, 480. *See also specific academies*
Academy of Experiment (Florence), 539
Academy of Fine Arts (France), 500
Academy of Music (France), 500
Academy of Sciences (France), 539, *539* (illus), 546. *See also* French Academy of Sciences
Academy of the Lynx-Eyed (Rome), 537, 539
Achilles (Greek hero), *108* (illus)
Acosta, Joseph de, 420
Acropolis (hilltop), 80
  temple built on, 107
Actium, Battle of, 166
Acts of Supremacy and Succession (England), 450
Adam and Eve (Bible), 216. *See also* Eve (Bible)
Administration. *See also* Government(s)
  of Babylonia, 47
  Byzantine, 236–238, 243
  of Egypt, 36
  of Neo-Assyrian Empire, 61
  Roman, 177–178
Adrianople, Battle of, 223
Aegean region, Greek colonization in, 81
Aegospotami, Battle of, 96
Aeneid (Camões), 481
Aeneid (Virgil), 182, 183, 192
Aeschylus, 101
Africa. *See also* North Africa; Sub-Saharan Africa, before Europeans
  colonialism in, 397–398
  European voyages along, 397–400
  Europeans in, 395–400
  gold from, 399
  Portugal and, 400
  Roman provinces of, 187–188
Africans. *See* Slaves and slavery
Against the Thieving, Murderous Hordes of Peasants (Luther), 439
Agamemnon (Mycenae), "Death Mask of Agamemnon", *51* (illus)
"Age of Pericles", 95
Aggression. *See specific countries*
Agincourt, battle at, 346, 350
Agora, 81
Agricola (Tacitus), 191
Agricola, Gnaeus Julius (Rome), 178, 182–183
Agricultural revolution, in Middle Ages, 298–300
Agriculture
  in Abu Hureyra, 14
  development of, 42
  in Europe, 16, 462
Ahab (Israel), 67
Ahmose I (Egypt), 35
Ahriman (god), 88
Ahura Mazda (god), 88, 90
Air pump (Boyle), *531* (illus), 531–532
Airplane, Leonardo's invention of, *379* (illus)
Akhenaten (Egypt), 39, *39* (illus). *See also* Amenhotep IV (Egypt)
Akkad and Akkadians, 19–21, 44, 62, 65
  culture of, 75–76
Akkadian language, 19, 25, 45, 65
Alaric II (Visigoths), 265
Alba, Duke of, 479
Alberti, Leon Battista (Italy), 372, 376, 380
Albigensian Crusade, 310, 315
Albrecht of Mainz, 434
Alchemy, 531
Alcibiades, 95
Alcuin of York (poet and cleric), 276
Aldeias, 412
Alexander, Severus (Rome), 203
Alexander the Great (Macedon), 90, 109, 111–119
  conquests by, 114–119, *116* (map)
  kingdoms after, 119
  kingdoms after (map), *120* (map)
  mosaic of, *115* (illus)
Alexander VI (pope), 372, 403, *435* (illus)
Alexandria, Egypt, 116, 121
Alexandrianism, 131
Alfred the Great (Wessex), 284–285
Ali (caliph), 251
Ali (Muhammad's son-in-law), 250
Alighieri, Dante, 357–358
Allah, 246
Alliances. *See also specific alliances*
al-Mamun (caliph), 256
Alphabet
  in Greece, 80
  Phoenician, 59, 80, *80* (illus)
  "Proto-Canaanite", 59, 76
  tablet and parchment, *60* (illus)
Amarna Letters, 44–45
Amarna Period, in Egypt, 39
Ambassadors, 387

Amenemhet (Egypt), 33
Amenhotep III (Egypt), 36, 38–39. *See also* Akhenaten (Egypt)
Amenhotep IV (Egypt), 38–39. *See also* Akhenaten (Egypt)
America. *See also* England (Britain); *specific countries and regions*
American Indians, 422
Americas, Europeans in, 400–414
Ammon, 59, 69
Amorites, 21
Amos (Hebrew prophet), 72
Amphitheaters, *179* (illus)
Amsterdam, stock exchange in, 521, *521* (illus)
Amun, temple of (Karnak), 36
Anabaptists, 447–448
Anasazi people, 400
Anatolia (Turkey). *See also* Turkey
  in Byzantine Empire, *237* (map)
  Cyrus conquering of, 87
  economic hardship and political fragmentation, 40
  Egypt and, 36, 40
  fall of, 60
  food production in, 13, 15
  Hittite Empire in, 45–47
  International Bronze Age and, 50, 54
  Medes and, 87
  Ottomans in, 337–339, *339* (map)
  Pergamum in, *111* (illus), *120* (map), 129, *129* (illus)
  Troy/Wilusa, 50
Anatomy
  chronology of publication, 380
  dissection and, *533* (illus)
  first handbook on, 134
  Vesalius and, 379
Anaximander, 102
Anaximenes, 102
Andes Mountains regions, Inca Empire in, 402
Anglo-Saxon Chronicle, 285
Anglo-Saxons
  conversion to Christianity, 270–271
  in England, 284–285
Angra Mainyu (god), 88
Anguissola, Sofonisba, 383
Animals
  agriculture and, 42
  in Columbian Exchange, 420
  domestication of, 42
Annals of Assurbanipal II, 70
Anne of Austria, 497
Anti-Chalcedonian (Monophysite) Christians, 214, 254
Antigone (Sophocles), 101
Antigonus, 119
Antioch, Syria
  Christianity in, 208
  Persia and, 228
  sack of, 228
Antiochus IV Epiphanes and Jews, 124
Antiquity and Renaissance arts, 380–383
Anti-semitism. *See also* Jews and Judaism
Antisthenes, 133
Antonine Age (Rome), 172
Antonine Decree, 180
Antonius, Marcus (Mark Antony), 181
Antwerp, 462, 479
Anu (god), 23, 26
Anubis (god), *193* (illus)
Anxiety, Price Revolution and, 464–465
Aphrodite (goddess), 154
Aphrodite, Temple of, *130* (illus)
Aphrodite of Melos (statue), *128* (illus)
Apocalypse, 439
Apopis (god), 30
Apuleius (writer), 193
Aquinas, Thomas, 322
Aquitaine and Hundred Years' War, 345, *346* (maps)
Arab world: Islamic caliphates in, 250, 252–255
Arabian Nights, 256
Arabian Peninsula, Midian and, 70
Arabs
  Arameans and, 57
  before Islam, 245
  in Sicily, 256–259
Aragon
  Castile joined with, 389–390
  Castile united with, 502–503
Aramaic language, 57
Aram-Damasus, 57
Arameans, 57
Arch of Titus (Rome), *195* (illus)
Archaic Age, in Greece, 79–86
Archbishops, in Western church, 208
Archers, *347* (illus)
Archimedes, 536
Archimedes of Syracuse, 134
Architecture
  Brunelleschi and, 381
  of Egyptian pyramids, 30–31
  Gothic, *324* (illus)
  Hellenistic, 128–129
  in Rome, 153
  of St. Petersburg, 514
  Sumerian, 23
Arcimboldo, Giuseppe, *484* (illus)
Ares (god), 154
Arian Christianity, 212
  of Germanic tribes, 224
Aristarchus of Samos, 134, 535
Aristides, Aelius (writer), 169–170
Aristocracy. *See also* Nobility
Aristocrats, 26
Aristophanes of Athens, 101
Aristotelianism and education, 540–541
Aristotle, 106
  geocentric theories of, 134, 526–527
  impetus theory and, 535
  on physics, 527, 535
Ark of the Covenant, 72
Armada, Spanish, 478
Armed forces
  charioteers in, 20–21, 35, 49, 52
  of Mongols, 337
  in Sparta, 84, 85
  standing armies and, 494–495
Armenian language, 211, 213
Arminius (Germany), 186
Armor and military revolution, 349–350, 372
Art of Dying, 356, *357* (illus)
"Art of Love, The" (Ovid), 191
Artemis (goddess), 154
Arthur (legendary English king), 223–224
Art(s)
  in Carolingian Renaissance, 275–276, *276* (illus)
  in Classical Greece, 100–101
  in Egypt, 32
  Greek, 80
  in Hellenistic cities, 128–129
  icons and, 240
  Minoan, 48
  in Rome, 153
Asceticism and Antony, 214–215
Asherah (goddess), 60
Ashtart (goddess), 60
Ashurbanipal (Neo-Assyrian Empire), library of, 62–63
Ashurbanipal III (Neo-Assyrian Empire), cavalry, *62* (illus)
Ashurnasirpal II (Neo-Assyria Empire), 61

Asia. *See also* Middle East; Southwest Asia; *specific countries*
Egypt and, 35
before Europeans, 414
Europeans and, 414
missionaries to, 415–416
Mongols in, 337
Portugal and, 416
Aspasia, 98
Assassinations. *See specific individuals*
Assayer, The (Galileo), 544
Assemblies. *See* Diet (assembly); Parliament (England); Parliament, French Estates General as; *specific assemblies*
Assimilation, in Roman provinces, 177
Assur, 53, 61
Assurbanipal (Assyrian king), 62–63
Assurbanipal II (Assyrian king), 70
Assur-Ubalit I (Assyria), 52
Assyria and Assyrians, 21–22. *See also* Neo-Assyrian Empire
Arameans in, 57
Empire of, *58* (map)
Great Power cultures and, 52–53, 57
International Bronze Age and, 44, 47, 50, 51–52
in Iraq, 47
Israelites and, 57, 67
Kassites in, 47
kingdom of, 47
rule over Babylonia, 62
torture, *68* (illus)
Astarte (god), *71* (illus)
Astronomy
Babylonian, 65
cosmology, 134
Galileo and, 379
Hellenistic, 134
Neo-Babylonian, 65
Stonehenge and, 17
Sumerian, 24
Atahuallpa (Incas), 408
Aten (god), 38–39, *39* (illus)
Athena (goddess), 98, 107
Athenian Empire, 94–96
Athens, 81–82
battle at Thermophylae and, 92
democracy in, 85–86, 95
Hellenistic Age philosophy, 133
Peloponnesian War and, 93
slavery in, 99
Athletics, Greek, 81
Atlantic Ocean region, Phoenicians in, 57–59
Atoms, Boyle on, 536
Attalus I, 129
Attica, 85
August, Sigismund (king), 450
Augustine of Hippo (Saint), 219–220
Augustus (Octavian, Rome), 112, 136
army and, 176
conquests of, 170–171, 183
death of, 172
imperial power under, 170–171, 172
in Second Triumvirate, 166
Senate and, 172, 176
Spain and, 171
statue of, *172* (illus)
Augustus, Caesar, 136
Augustus, Philip (France), 291
Aurelian and Roman wall, 203
Aurelius, Marcus (Rome), 172, 185, *185* (illus)
Austrian Habsburg Monarchy, 507
Authority, of popes, 209
Autobiography (Teresa of Avila), 452
Auto-da-fé
defined, 467, 468
in Lisbon, *467* (illus)
Auxiliary, 176
Avar peoples
Byzantine Empire and, 235
empire of, 235
Averroës, 321–322
Avesta, 88
Avignon, papacy in, 352
Azores, 398
Aztecs, before European arrival, 400–402

Ba'al (god), 60, *61* (illus), 70
Baby boom, in Middle Ages, 300
Babylon and Babylonia, 21–22
Alexander the Great in, 116
Arameans in, 57
Assyrians and, 62
breakdown of, 22
creation epic in, 62
during the Dark Age, 57
Hammurabi in, 22, 23, 28
International Bronze Age and, 47
kingdom of, 21–22, 65
Neo-Babylonian Empire, 63–65
Persian conquest of, 65, 87
Babylonian Captivity of the Church, 351–353, 428
Babylonian exile of Hebrews, 67–69, 73, 74
Bacon, Francis (philosopher), 532–533, 540, 546
Baghdad
city of Agade under, 19
Muslim capital at, 256
Bahamas, Columbus in, 394
Baillis (French royal officials), 316–317
Baker, Abu (Muhammad's father-in-law), 248
Balance of power, 501
Balkan region, Celts in, 124, 126
"Ballad of East and West, The" (Kipling), 1
Banks and banking, collapse of, 342–343
Baptism and Anabaptists, 447–448
Baptism of the Indians by the Dominicans, *410* (illus)
Baptistery (Florence)
chronology, 385
doors designed by Ghiberti, 381–382
doors of, 381–382, *382* (illus)
Barbarians, 112
Barbarossa, Frederick, 291
Barca, Hamilcar (Carthage), 147
Barca, Hannibal (Carthage), 148
Baroque, 129, 498
Baroque style, in Spanish painting, 505
Basel, Council of, 352–353
Basil I (Byzantium), 242
Basil II (Byzantium), 243
Bathsheba, 74–75
Battle of the Books, 541
Battles. *See specific battles and wars*
Becket, Thomas, 318
Bede (scholar), 272
Belisarius (general), 227
Benedict of Nursia (Saint), 215, 271
Benedict XII (Pope), 314
Beowulf, 279
Bernard of Clairvaux, 311
Bernini, Gianlorenzo, sculpture of St. Teresa, *453* (illus)
Berosus (Babylonian priest), 123
Bessarion, John, 368
Bible (Christian). *See also* Bible (Hebrew)
Christian humanists and, 429–431
Jerome and, 220
language, 213
on motion of sun, 537

Bible (Christian) *(continued)*
New Testament, 196
science and, 537
Vienna Genesis and, *213* (illus)
Vulgate, 213
Bible (Hebrew). *See also* Bible (Christian)
Book of Numbers, 70–71
The Epic of Gilgamesh, recorded in, 25
Exodus, 66
in Greek, 127
justice and, 28
King Solomon, 58
legacy, 74
Old Testament, 65
sacred objects in "high places", 60
Septuagint as, 127, 214
Torah and, 73
Bill of Rights (England), 519
Biological exchange, in Columbian Exchange, *419* (illus), 419–420
Biology, 532
Birds, The (Aristophanes), 101
Bireme, 58
Birth control, Christian attitudes toward, 218
Biscop, Benedict (missionary), 272
Black Death, 330–334
Boccaccio and, 331–332
causes of, 332
deaths from, 329
defined, 330
European population and, 329, 333
spread by Mongols, 337
spread of, *331* (map)
symptoms, 331
Black Sea region, Greek colonization in, 81
Blacks and African slave trade, 418
Blood circulation, 532
Blue Prussians (Giants of Potsdam), 509
Boccaccio, Giovanni (writer), 454
Bodin, Jean, 472, 493
Body of the Civil Law (Justinian), 144
Bohemia. *See also* Czech Republic
diet in, 506
under Habsburgs, 506
religious toleration in, 449–450, 483
Boleyn, Anne
marriage to Henry VIII, 445
trial of, 445
Boniface (monk), 262
Boniface VIII (Pope), 308
Book of Ceremonies (Constantine VII Porphyrogenitus), 243
Book of Common Order (Knox), 447
Book of Kells, *270* (illus)
Book of the City of Ladies, The (Christine de Pisan), 358
Book of the Courtier, The (Castiglione), 371, 372, 373
Book of the Dead, 330
Book of the Law, 72
Book of the Three Virtues, The (Christine de Pisan), 358
Books
burning of Cathar heretical books, *314* (illus). *See also* Libraries
in monasteries, 271
printing of, 379
Bora, Katherine Von, 437
Borgia family
Alexander VI (Pope) and, 372
Cesare, 372
Lucrezia, 372
Borgund church, *285* (illus)
Boris I (Bulgarian Khan), 235
Boudicca (Britain), in revolt against Romans, 177, 181
Boule, 85
Boundaries
of Roman Empire, 183–188
of Russian Empire, 512–513
Bourbon, Henry. *See* Henry IV (France)
Bourgeoisie. *See also* Middle class
Bouts, Dieric (painting by), *282* (illus)
Boyars (Russia), 487
Boyle, Robert, *531* (illus), 531–532, 535–536
Bradshawe, John, 518, 519
Brahe, Tycho (astronomer), 484, 527–528
Brandenburg, 507–508
Brandenburg-Prussia, *508* (map)
Bravo, The (Titian), *388* (illus)
Brazil, Portugal and, 412
Brenz, Johann, 472
Brief Relation of the Destruction of the West Indies, The (Las Casas), 422
Britain. *See* England (Britain)
Bronze
in Assyria, 52
change to iron from, 56–57
military technology, 35
weapons, 52
Bronze Age. *See* International Bronze Age
Bruges, 344
Brunelleschi, Filippo, 380, 381, 385
Bruni, Leonardo, 376, 380
Bruno, Giordano, 484
Bubonic plague, as Black Death, 332. *See also* Black Death
Bulgars, 235
Bull (Minoan mural), *48* (illus)
Buonarroti, Michelangelo, 383, 385
King David statue, *364* (illus)
Bureaucracy, in Egypt, 35, 36
Burgundy
Charles V and, 389
in Hundred Years' War, *346* (illus), 347
Burials
in Egypt, 30–31, 36
Mycenaean, 53
Business. *See* Commerce; Trade
Byblos, 58
Byzantine Empire (Byzantium). *See also specific emperors*
civilization of, 236–242
at the death of Justinian, *227* (map), 259
defined, 225
dynastic succession disputed in, 242
fall of, 340
in Greece, 236–238
Islam and, 233, 238, 242
Justinian and, 225–226
map, *237*
in Middle Ages, 233
Muslim invasion of, 239
Orthodox Christianity in, 233, 239–240
Ottomans and, 340
Persia and, 228
plague in, 227
Roman Empire and, 225, 234

Cabral, Pedro, 412
Caesar, Gaius Julius, 162
Caesar, Julius (Rome)
in Gaul, 164
Roman Republic under, 163–166
Caesarius, Bishop of Arles, 218
Calais, France, in Hundred Years' War, *346* (map), 347
Caliphs and caliphates
Abbasid caliphate, 255–256
defined, 248

religions under, 254–255
in Spain, *245* (map)
Umayyad, 250, 252–255
Callicrates (architect), 107–108
Callimachus (poet), 131
Calling, 443
Calvin, John, and Calvinism
challenge by Catholic Cardinal, 444
in France, 474–475
French Huguenots and, 474–475, 497
in Geneva, 442–443
predestination and, 442
in Scotland, 446–447
spread of, 474–475
Cambyses II, 87
Camel caravans, 57, 247
Camões, Luis Vaz de, 481
Canaan
cultures and continuities, 59
diplomatic revolution, 49
Egypt and, 33, 35, 36, 55
fall of, 60–61
Hebrews in, 65, 66, 69–70
during International Bronze Age, 50
Proto-Canaanite alphabet, 59
religion in, 59–60
Syria, Mesopotamia and, 46
Canaanites
bronze and, 35
Iron Age, 60
religion and, 59–60
Canals in Egypt, 36
Canary Island and Portugal, 398
Cannons for war, 340
Canon law, 276
Canterbury Tales, The (Chaucer), 358
Capac, Huayna (Inca), 402
Cape of Good Hope, 405, 416
Cape Verde Islands, 398, 399, 403
Capet, Hugh, 284
Capetian dynasty (France), 284
Capital punishment, Thomas More on, 445–446
Capitalism, science and, 540
Capitoline Hill, 139
Caracalla (Aurelius Antoninus, Rome) and Antonine Decree, 180
Caravaggio, *455* (illus)
Caravans
camel, *247* (illus)
long-distance trade by, 52
Ugarit trade and, 50
Caravels, 397
Carcassonne, France, *302* (illus)
Carolingian Empire, 273–277, *274* (map)
division of Western Europe, 277
Carolingian minuscule, 276
Carolingian Renaissance, 275–276, 321
Carruca plow, *299* (illus)
Carthage. *See also* Punic Wars
Exarchate of, 234
Muslim conquest of, 244
Phoenician colonies in, 59, 147
Roman conquest of, 147–149
trade in, 59
Castiglione, Baldassare, 371–372
Castile, Aragon united with, 389–390, 502–503
Çatal Hüyük, *14* (illus), 14–15
Cathars
heresy of, 309–310, 314–315
Montaillou inquisition and, 314–315
Cathedrals
Gothic, 323–325, *324* (illus)
Haghia Sophia, *232* (illus)
medieval culture in, 323–325
Romanesque, *324* (illus)
Catholic League, procession of, *459* (illus)
Catholic Reformation
arts in, 451–456
defined, 451
Paul III (Pope) in, 452, 454
religious orders in, 311–313, 451–452
Catholicism. *See* Christianity; Roman Catholicism
Catiline Conspiracy, 161
Cavaliers. *See* Royalists, in England
Cavalry
Assyrians and, 61, *62* (illus)
Companions, 113–114
of Mongols, 335, *336* (illus)
Parthian Empire and, 184
Cavendish, Margaret, 547
Cecil, William, 446
Cellarius, Andreas, *528* (illus)
Celts
expansion of, 124–126, *125* (map)
Halstatt culture of, 124–126
hellenistic world and, 124–126
La Tène culture of, 125
Rome and, 126, 145
urban society, 126–127
Censorship, by *Index of Forbidden Books*, 452, 454
Central America. *See* Latin America
Cereta, Laura, 377, 380
Cervantes, Miguel de, 505
Cesi, Federico, 539
Chaeronea, Battle of, 114
Chalcedon, Council of, 220
Chalcedonian Christianity
defined, 213
Islam and, 254
Chaldean Empire, 63. *See also* Neo-Babylonian Empire
Champagne fairs (France), 303
Chariots
Hittites and, 49
military, 35, 49, 52
Mycenaean, 53
Charlemagne (Franks)
administration under, 274–275
biography of, 273
Carolingian Renaissance and, 275–276
coronation of, 273–274
division of empire after, *274* (map)
as Roman emperor, 273–274
Charles I (England)
absolutism and, 515
chronology, 516
Parliament and, 518–519
trial of, *518* (illus), 518–519
Charles II (Spain), 501
Charles the Bald (Carolingian), 277
Charles V (emperor), 435, 437, 438, 440
capture of Rome, 445
Charles V (Holy Roman Empire), 389, 483
inflation and, 465
Charles V (Spain), 391
Charles VII (France), 347, 387, 390, 391
Charney, Geoffrey of (Templar), 319
Chartres Cathedral, flying buttresses of, *325* (illus)
Chaucer, Geoffrey, 358
Chemistry, 531
Cheops. *See* Khufu (Cheops, Egypt)
Cherubim, 70
Childeric (Franks), 265
Children. *See* Families
China
Mongols in, 351
Portugal and, 416
Rome and, 186–187
Chosroes I (Persia), 228
Christ. *See* Jesus Christ (Jesus of Nazareth)

Christian Church, 208. *See also* Christianity; Roman Catholicism
Christianity. *See also* Bible (Christian); Jesus Christ (Jesus of Nazareth); Latin Christianity; Orthodox Christianity; Roman Catholicism
in Anglo-Saxon England, 265
Arians, 212
bishops in, 208–209
Calcedonian, 213
chronology, 220
communities and identities of, 211–221
Constantine and, 206–208
conversions to, 240, 359, 407
division in West by 1555, *441* (map)
doctrine, heresy and, 196, 212–213, 353
emergence of, 195–198
in Ethiopia, 399
Gnosticism and, 221
Great Persecution of, 206, 220
growth of, 208
in Islamic Empire, 254–255
Jews, Judaism, and, 194–195, 216–217, 240
under Justinian, 225–226
languages and, 213–214
in Middle Ages, 233, 262
Neoplatonism and, 221
orthodoxy in, 196
paganism and, 210–211, 228–229
persecution of, 206, 210–211
pilgrimages in, 217–219
in Roman Empire, 195–198, 206–211
scholasticism and, 320–321
in Spain, 358–359
Spanish Reconquest and, 259, 358–359
spread of, 208–211
Trinity in, 212
Chronology
absolutism and state building, 524
Age of Empires, 77–78
Age of Warfare, 350
Alexander the Great and the Greek East, 117
ancient culture, influence of, 380
arts, antiquity and nature in the, 385
beginnings of civilization, 42
Byzantine Empire, 244
Byzantium and Islam, 261
Carolingian dynasty, 277
Catholic Reformation, 456
Celts, 126
Christianity, polytheism, and Judaism, 220
Church troubles, 354
Classical Greece, 97
Confessional division, 491
Crusades, 293
Eastern Europe, states and confessions in, 489
Egyptian civilization, 40
England, century of revolution, 516
European state system, early modern, 391
Europeans in Africa, 399
Europeans in Asia, 416
Europeans in the Americas, 413
foundations of civilization, 15
France in the Age of Absolutism, 497
French wars of religion, 477
Greece rebuilds, 86
Greek Civilization, 110
Hebrew Kingdoms, 69
Hellenistic civilization, 137
Hellenistic literature, science, and philosophy, 135
Imperial Carthage, 148
International Bronze Age, 56
international conflict in the seventeenth century, 504
Islam, 258
Italian city-states, 373
Italian Renaissance, 393
Late Antiquity, 231
Latin Christendom, birth of, 272
Latin West, 295
Lutheran Reformation, 442
medieval civilization, rise of Western Europe, 327
medieval religious developments, 315
Medieval West economic depression and social turmoil, 343
Medieval West in crisis, 363
Mesopotamian civilization, 28
Mongols, 336
Neo-Assyrian Empire, 63
Neo-Babylonian Empire, 63
Netherlands, 480
Ottoman Turk conquests, 341
papal monarchy, 309
Persia, 92
Protestantism, diversity of, 450
Reformations, 458
Roman dynasties, 173
Roman Empire, early, 200
Roman Empire, East and West, 225
Roman political and military events, 181
Roman Republic, 168
Rome and Italy, social and political conflict, 163
Rome's rise to power, 146
Scientific Revolution, 530, 541, 551
Scientific Societies, 539
Scotland, century of revolution, 516
Spain, 480
West and the world, 425
Western European kingdoms, 286
Church Fathers, 219
Church of England, 446, 450
Church(es). *See also* Roman Catholicism
in Constantinople, 239–240
in France, 387
Cicero
attacking Catiline, *161* (illus)
First Oration Against Catiline, 162
Petrarch and, 375, 380
prosecution of Verres and, 153
Cicero, Marcul Tullius, 143
Ciompi revolt, 343–344
Circuit court, English origins of, 317–318
Circular temple, *152* (illus)
Circumnavigation of globe, 416
Cistercian Order, 311–312
Cities and towns. *See also* City-states; *specific locations*; Villages
agricultural revolution and, 301–304
economic boom and, 301–304
in Egypt, 29, 57
Greek, 78
growth of, 301–304, 463–464
Hellenistic, 126–127
in Mediterranean region, 57
in Roman Empire, 178–179
in Sumer, *18* (map), 18–19, *28* (illus)
wealthy and poor in, 463
Citizens and citizenship
in ancient Greece, 80
Antonine Decree and, 180
Bruni on, 376, 380
of freedmen in Rome, 151, 189
City of God, The (Augustine), 221

City walls around Rome, *204* (illus)
City-states
Greek polis as, 78
in Italy, 366
Civic humanism, 376
Civic virtue, 167
Civil authority, in Latin Christendom, 266–267
Civil war(s)
in England, 474, 515–517
French Wars of Religion as, 474–477
War of the Roses (England) as, 347, 350
Civilization(s). *See also specific civilizations*; Western world (the West)
beginnings of, 11–12, *12* (map)
Byzantine, 236–242
defined, 11
Egyptian, 12, 29–41
Hebrew, 44, 57, 65–74
Hellenistic, 111–137
in Mesopotamia, 12, 18–22, 24, 28, 44, 46–47
Minoan Crete as, 47–49
Mycenaean Greece as, 47–49
Phoenician, 57–59, 64
in Southwest Asia, 45, 54–55
in Sumer, 18–19, 22, 28, 44
Western. *See* Western civilizations
Clans, Germanic, 267
Clare of Assisi, 313
Classes. *See also* Elites; Society; *specific groups*
lord and vassals as, 280–281
in Rome, 188–189
Classical Age, in Greece, 73–108. *See also* Greece (ancient); Hellenistic Age
Cleisthenes (Athens), 85–86, 95
Clement VII (pope), 445
Cleopatra VII, 120, 166
Clients, 156
Cloth and clothing, of Otzi the Ice Man, 10–11
Clovis (Merovingian)
Law Code (Salic Law) of, 268
reign of, 272
Club of the Great Powers and client-states, 51–52
Cluny, reform-minded monastery at, 304–305
Clyn, John, 333
Coins
Celtic, 125
Greek, 81–82
Roman, *164* (illus), 190
solidus, 206
Colbert, Jean-Baptiste, 499, 505
Collections of Wonders of the World (Callimachus), 131
Colleges. *See* Universities and colleges
Colonies and colonization. *See also* Empire(s); Imperialism
Greek, 81–82
in Mediterranean region, 57–59
in North America, 412–414
Colosseum (Rome), *179* (illus)
Columbanus (missionary), 272
Columbian Exchange, 417–423
cultural diversity and, 420–421, 423
syphilis and, 420
Columbian question, 420
Columbus, Christopher
arrest by Bobadilla, *404* (illus)
arrival in the Bahamas, 394
Bobadilla and, 404–405
chronology, 413
financing the voyage, 389
portrait of, *394* (illus)
"trial" of, in Honduras, 404–405
voyage to the Americas, 402–403
Comédie Française, 500
Comedy mosaic from Pompeii, *132* (illus)
Commentaries on the Gallic War (Caesar), 164
Commerce. *See also* Trade
Akkadian revenues from, 20
Egyptian, 29
in Mesopotamia, 19
Muslims in, 255
Mycenaean, 48
Phoenician, 59
in Ugarit, 50
Commercial agriculture, 462
Commodus (Rome), 172
Common market. *See also* European Economic Community (EEC)
Communes, 301
in cities, 301
Italian republics as, 301, 373
Communications(s). *See* Transportation and Industrial Revolution; Writing
Communion, 432–433, *433* (illus). *See also* Eucharist
Communities
of faith, Christian, 213–214
food-producing, 13
Companions (Macedonian army), 113–114
Compass, 397
Conciliar Movement, 352–353
Confession of Augsburg, 465
Confessions
confessional states, 473–482
defined, 460
divine justice, 130
in Eastern Europe, 483–489
Confessions (Augustine), 220
Conquest and client states, 52
Conquistadores, 7, 400–402
Conservative party (Britain). *See also* Tories (England)
Constance, Council of, 353
Constantine (Rome)
Christian bishops and, 208–209
Christianity and, 206–208
Council of Nicaea and, 220
as emperor, 206–208
statue of, *207* (illus)
Constantine VII Porphyrogenitus (Byzantium), *242* (illus)
Constantinople (Istanbul). *See also* Byzantine Empire (Byzantium)
besieged by Muslims, 244
as Byzantine capital, 225
characteristics of, 232
as Christian center, 228
fall to Ottomans (1453), 340
founding of, 225
Haghia Sophia in, *232* (illus)
Justinian as emperor, 225
under Macedonian dynasty, 242–243
Ottoman sultans as Roman emperors in, 340
as Roman capital, 224
Turkish conquest of, 341
Consular diptych, *226* (illus)
Convents. *See* Nuns, Modern Devotion and
Conversations on the Plurality of Worlds (Fontenelle), 541
Conversion (to Christianity)
of Anglo-Saxons, 270–271
Augustine of Hippo (Saint), 220, 249
of Clovis, 265
of Constantine, 208, 210–211, 219, 220
of Irish, 270

Conversion (to Christianity) *(continued)*
of Jews, 240, 312–313, 359
of Magyars, 279
to Orthodox Christianity, 240
of polytheists, 285–287
Spanish Jews and, 359, 409
in trading post empires, 415–416
Copernicus, Nicolaus
chronology, 380
heliocentric theory of, 134, 378, 527–528, 538
motion laws, 529
Neoplatonism, 536
papacy and, 538
Coptic language, 213
Copts, 213
Córdoba
caliphate of, 257
great mosque of, *257* (illus)
Islamic civilization, 257
Corinth, Greece, 81, 83, *83* (illus), 138
Corpus Juris Civilis (Corpus of Civil Law, Justinian), 144, 226, 322
Cortes (Spanish assembly), 494
Cortés, Hérnan, 407
Cosmology, 134
Council of Blood, 479
Council of Florence, 396
Council of Trent, 454–455, 456, 465
Council of Troubles, 479
Councils (Christian)
of Basel, 352–353
of Constance, 353
of Nicaea, 220
Counter Reformation. *See* Catholic Reformation
Court (royal)
of Rudolf II (Holy Roman Empire), 483–484
at Versailles, 498
Court Chamber (Austria), 509
Court of Star Chamber (England), 390
Courtiers, Italian Renaissance, 370–372, *371* (illus)
Courtly love, poetry of, 323
Covenant, of Hebrews with God, 72
Craft guilds, 342
Craft(s) in Sumer, 18–19
Cranach, Lucas (the Elder), *433* (illus)
Cranmer, Thomas (Archbishop), 445
Crassus, Marcus Licinius, 162, 164
Crates of Thebes, 133
Creation epic, in Babylonia, 62
Crecy, Battle of, *347* (illus)
Crete
International Bronze Age and, 47–49
Minoan Crete as, *45* (map)
Crime
auto-da-fé and, 467–468
Hammurabi's Code and, 26, 28
Croesus (Lydia), 101–102
Cromwell, Oliver, 516, 517
Cromwell, Thomas (minister), 445
Crops. *See* Agriculture
Crusades, 287–293
Albigensian, 310, 315
appeal for jihad against, 289
atrocities of, 289
chronology of, 293
defined, 287
major, *288* (map)
origins of, 287–288
significance of, 291, 293
Urban II's call for, 287
warfare, 290–291
Cult(s) of Cybele, 155
Cultural imperialism, in Egypt, 35
Cultural relativism, 421, 423
Culture(s). *See also* Art(s); Renaissance; Society
after Roman Empire, 152–153
Akkadian, 19–21
in Archaic Greece, 79–80
Babylonian, 22–26, 44, 64–65
cathedrals and, 323–325
defined, 11
Egyptian, *45* (map)
European, 319–325
foundations of Western, 74
Greek, 52–53
Greek vs. Roman, 151
Hellenistic, 126–131
Minoan, 48, 49
Mycenaean, 52–53
Reminder of Death and, 355–356
scientific, 101–102
of Spanish America, 409–410
Sumerian, 18–19
use of term, 11
Cuneiform writing, *25* (illus), *60* (illus)
correspondence of pharaohs, 44
Sumerian, 24
Curia, in Catholic Church, 307
Cybele (goddess), 155
Cynics, 133
Cypselus, 83
Cyrus of Persia, 87, 89–90
Czech Republic. *See also* Bohemia; Poland-Lithuania

Dacia (Romania), conquest by Romans, *175* (illus), 181
Damascus, Syria
during Iron Age, 57
Second Crusade and, *288* (map)
Dance of Death, 355, *356* (illus)
Danelaw, 279
D'Anghiera, Peter Martyr (priest and historian), 421, 423
Darius I (the Great, Persia), 90–91
Darius III, 115–116
Dark Age
characteristics of, 57
in Greece, 79, 81
years of, 79
David (Hebrew Biblical King)
Court History, 74–75
Divided Monarchy, 67
Muslims and, 246
silver plates and, *238* (illus)
succession to Saul, 66
David (Michelangelo), *364* (illus), 383, 385
de Sepúlveda, Juan Ginés, *The Second Democrates*, 422
"Death Mask of Agamemnon", *51* (illus)
Death of the Virgin, The (Caravaggio), *455* (illus)
Death(s)
in famines of fourteenth century, 330, 341–342, 344
from infectious disease, 330–333
Decameron, The (Boccaccio), 331, 454
Declaration of Rights, 519
Decline and Fall of the Roman Empire (Gibbon), 222
Deductive reasoning, 533–534
Dee, John, 484
Defender of the Peace, The (Marsilius of Padua), 366, 373
Defenestration of Prague, 506, *506* (illus)
Deification, of kings, 39
Deists, 543
Deities. *See* Gods and goddesses; Religion(s); *specific deities*
Delian League, 94, 107
Demand
elastic, 464
inelastic, 464
Demeter (goddess), 130, 147
Demetrius (Antigonid king), 121

Democracy
in Athens, 85–86
defined, 84
Democritus of Abdera (Greece), 535
Demonic magic, 470
Demosthenes, 114
Demotic Chronicle, The, 124
Dentière, Marie, 437
Depression (economic) in the Middle Ages, 341–344
Descartes, René
control of nature, 546
deductive reasoning, 533–534
Discourse on the Method, 541
dualism of, 534
d'Este, Isabella, 370, *370* (illus), 373
Deuteronomy, 72–73
Devil and witchcraft, 471, 473
Devourer (god), 32
Diabolism, 470
Dialogue Concerning the Two Chief World Systems (Galileo), 528, 544
Diana (goddess), 154
Dias, Bartholomew, 405, 416
Diaspora (Jewish), 194, 195, 216
Dictator, Sulla as, 162
Diet (assembly)
of Brandenburg, 509
defined, 494
Imperial Diet, 435
of Worms, 435, 438–439
Digenes Akritas (Poem), 239
Dinar (Umayyad coin), 255
Diocles (doctor), 134
Diocletian (Rome), 203–206
Christianity and, 206
reforms by, 203–206
resignation of, 206
tetrarchy and, 204, 225
Diogenes, 133
Dionysos (god), 80, 155
Diplomacy
after International Bronze Age, 55
Egyptian, 36, 49, 56
in Late Bronze Age, 49, 51, 56
Mycenaean, 49
Discipline
of children, 470
confessional identities and, 465–466
Discourse on the Method (Descartes), 533, 541, 544
Discrimination
against Jews, 216
in Middle Ages, 358–360
Disease, in Africa, 419. *See also* Black Death
Disputations and scholasticism, 320–321
Disquisition on the Spiritual Condition of Infants, 470
Dissection, *533* (illus)
Dissenters, in American colonies. *See* Puritans
Dissidents. *See also* Revolts and rebellions
Divided Monarchy (Hebrew), 67
Divination, 23–24
Divine Comedy, The (Dante), 357–358
Divine right
Charles I (England) and, 517
theory of, 494, 517, 518
Divorce, 437
Djoser (Egypt), 30
Doctors. *See* Medicine
Dominic (Saint), 312
Dominican Order, 312–313
Dominicans, 434
Domitian (Rome), 172
Don Quixote (Cervantes), 481, 505
Donatello, 380, 385
Donation of Constantine, 376, 380
Donation of Poland, 287
Drake, Sir Francis (privateer), 478
Drama
in Classical Greece, 100–101
Comédie Française as, 500
Drebbel, Cornelius, 484
Dualism
defined, 88
of Descartes, 534
Dubois, François (painter), 477
Duels, in Italian Renaissance, 388–389
Dürer, Albrecht
The Knight, Death, and The Devil, *430* (illus), 431
self-portrait, *426* (illus), 428
Dutch. *See also* Dutch Republic (United Provinces of the Netherlands); Holland; Netherlands
revolt against Spain by, 478–479, *479* (map)
trading companies of, 520
Dutch Reformed Church, 521
Dutch Republic (United Provinces of the Netherlands), 520–522. *See also* Dutch; Holland; Netherlands
chronology, 480
map, *479*
Dynastic Prophecy, 124
Dynasties. *See also specific dynasties*
marriages among, 389
of Rome, 172–173

Early Bronze Age, 35
Early Dynastic period (Egypt), 29
Early Modern Europe, peoples of, 461–464
Earth
Aristotle on, 134, 527
size of, 134
East Francia
German Empire and, 283–284
kingdom of, 283–284
kingship in, 283–284
East Germany. *See also* Germany; West Germany
Eastern Christianity. *See* Orthodox Christianity
Eastern Europe. *See also specific countries*
in Early Middle Ages, 234–235
Ottoman Empire in, 341
peoples from, 234
religious freedom in, 449–450
Roman Catholicism vs. Orthodox Christianity in, 234
states and confessions in, 483–489
Eastern Roman Empire. *See also* Byzantine Empire (Byzantium); Western Roman Empire
chronology, 225
Diocletian in, 225
separation from West, 224–225
"East/West Poem" (Lum), 2
Eating habits and table fork, 469, *469* (illus)
Eck, Johann (professor), 434
Economy and economics. *See also* Industrial Revolution; Industrialization
in Babylon, 47, 64, 65
Byzantine, 236–238
of Rome, 186–188
Sumerian, 18–19
of Ugarit, 50
Edessa, county of, 290
Edict of Nantes, 476–477, 497, 499
Edom, 59

Education. *See also* Schools
Dominican, 312–313
humanism and, 540
Jesuits and, 451–452
Scientific Revolution and, 540–541
Edward II (England), 344–345, 350
Edward III (England), 345, 350
Edward VI (England), 446
Egypt (ancient), 29–41. *See also* Gods and goddesses
Amarna Period in, 39
Antony in, 220
in Byzantine Empire, 244
empire of (map), *30*
Hatshepsut in, 37, *37* (illus), 37–38
Hyksos people in, 33, 35
International Bronze Age and, *45* (map), 45–46, 54–55
Middle Kingdom in, 29, *30* (map), 32–33
mummies in, *37* (illus), *38* (illus)
New Kingdom in, 29, *30* (map), 35–40, *45* (map), 45–47, 49
Nubia and, 36
Old Kingdom in, 12, 29, 32, 34, 39
periods in, 29
Persia and, 91
pyramids in, 30–31
religion in, 29–30, 33, 34
slavery in, 32, 66, 418
split into separate kingdoms, 29–30
trade by, 29, 33, 42
women in, 31, 36–37
Egyptian Empire in Late Bronze Age, 40, 44, 52, 59
Egyptians and Great Power Cultures, 52–53
EI (god), 60, 70
Einhard (monk), 276
El Cid, 292
Electors, of Brandenburg, 507–508
Elegies (Callimachus), 131
Elements (Euclid), 134
Elijah, 72
Elisabeth of Bohemia, 547
Elites. *See also* Aristocracy; Nobility
in Rome, 157, 158, 188
in Sumer, 26
Elizabeth I (England). *See also* Elizabethan Renaissance (England)
Elizabethan Renaissance, 482
inflation and, 465
literature and, *482* (illus)
as Queen, 412–413
Elizabethan Renaissance (England), 481–482
Elizabethan Settlement (England), 446, 450
Elmina, Ghana, 400
Emigration after 1870. *See also* Slave trade
Emir, Abbasid caliphs as, 256
Emperors. *See also specific empires and emperors*
Byzantine, 340
Charlemagne as, 273–274
Roman, tetrarchy and, 204, 225
Empire(s). *See also* Byzantine Empire (Byzantium); Colonies and colonization; Roman Empire; *specific empires*
Akkadian, 19–21, 25, 28, 34
Assyrians and, 47
Athenian, 94–96
Carthaginian, 147
characteristics of, 19
defined, 19
in eastern Europe, 234–235
Egyptian, 29–41, 54–55
fall of Aztec, 407
Hittite, *45* (map), 45–47, 49, 55
of Huns, *224* (map)
of International Bronze Age, 51–52
medieval, 262–295
Mongol, 334
Neo-Assyrian, 44, *58* (map), 61–63, 65
Neo-Babylonian, 44, *58* (map), 63–65, 67–68
Persian, 87–88, *88* (map), 90, 228
Roman, *171* (map)
of Ur III, 28
Empirical observation, 532
Employment of children. *See also* Labor; Workers
Encomienda system, 409
Encounters, 7–8
England (Britain)
absolutism and, 517–520
Elizabethan Renaissance in, 481–482
Glorious Revolution in, 516, 517–520
in late twelfth century, 316
monarchy in, 317, 515
polytheistic Germanic invaders in, 223
Price Revolution in, 464–465
Reformation in, 444–447
Romans and, 225
Stonehenge in, 16–17, *17* (illus)
in United Kingdom, 516
William the Conqueror in, 285, 349
English language, 349
Enki (god), 23
Enkidu (Sumerian character), 25
Enlil (god), 23, 26
Enquiries into Plants (Theophrastus), 134
Entertainment. *See specific types*
Enuma Elish (Babylonian creation epic), 62
Epic literature. *See also specific works*
in Babylonia, 24–26
by Homer, 50, 80
Epic of Erra, The, 55
Epic of Gilgamesh, The
Babylonia and, 24–26
final edition, 62
Hittite adoption of, 47
as verbal version of archaeological site, 51
Epicureans, 132
Epicurus of Samos, 132, 134
Epidemics. *See also* Black Death; Disease
in Columbian Exchange, 419–420
in Middle Ages, 329–330
Episcopalian Church. *See* Church of England
Equestrian class (Rome), 157, 188
Erasmus, Desiderius, 430–431
Eratosthenes of Cyrene, 134
Erechtheum, *107* (illus)
Estates General (France), 345, 494
Ethiopia
before Europeans, 396
Europeans in, 399
Ethnic diversity, in Middle Ages, 360
Ethnic groups and ethnicity
Statues of Kilkenny and, 360
in Venice, 368–369
Etruscans and Rome, 139–141
Eucharist, 313, 315–316. *See also* Communion
defined, 313
illustration, *433*
Zwingli on, 442
Euclid, 134
Eudoxus, 122
Eugene IV (pope), 353
Euphrates River region, 18, 20, 35, 61, 64

Eurasia, migrations from, 334
Euripides, 101
Europa, use of term, 277
Europe. *See also* Europe and Europeans
Europe and Europeans
  in Africa, 395–400
  Americas and, 400–414
  Black Death in, 330, 337
  ca. 750, *264* (map)
  Celts in, 124–125
  culture of, 319
  food producing-revolution in, 15–16
  invasions of (seventh–eleventh centuries), *278* (map)
  Islamic civilization in, 256–259
  Neolithic cultures in, *16* (map)
  overseas empires of, *399* (map)
  voyages along African coast, 397–400
European Economic Community (EEC). *See also* Common Market
Eve (Bible), 310–311. *See also* Adam and Eve (Bible)
Evil in ancient times, 34
Exarchates (administrative units), 234
  of Carthage, 234
  of Ravenna, 234, 272
Exchange Bank (Amsterdam), 521
Exchanges, 51–52
Excommunication
  defined, 306
  of Henry IV (Germany), 306
  of Leo (Byzantium), 241
Expansion. *See also* Empire(s)
  of Persia, 89–90
  Phoenician, 58, *59* (map)
  by Rome, 144–151, *147* (map)
Experimentation, scientific, 532–533
Exploration and discovery
  astrolabe and, 397
  by Columbus, 389, 413
  Hellenistic, 121–123
  Portuguese in Africa, 398–400
Ezekiel, 73

Factors and factories (trading posts), 415
Fairs, European, *303* (map)
Faith. *See* Confessions; Justification by faith; Theology
Falloppio, Gabriele, 379, 380
Families
  patriarchal, 372–374
  Roman patron-client relations and, 156
Famine. *See also* Starvation
  in fourteenth century, 330
Fanatic and fanaticism
  assassination of Henry IV (France) and, 477, 496, 497
  in Poland-Lithuania, 486
  use of term, 474
Far East. *See specific countries*
Farms and farming. *See also* Agriculture; Peasants
  agricultural revolution and, 298–300
Father of History, Herodotus as, 102–103
Fathers. *See* Families
Faust (Goethe), 483
Fealty, by vassals, 281
Feminism, of Christine de Pisan, 358. *See also specific rights*; Women
Ferdinand II (Aragon)
  Isabella of Castile and, 389–390, 502–503
  succeeds to the throne, 391
Ferdinand II (Bohemia, Hungary, Holy Roman Empire), 509
Fertile Crescent, 13. *See also* Levantine Corridor
Feudalism
  defined, 281
  vassalage under, 281
Fiefs, 281
Finances and sale of indulgences, 434. *See also* Taxation
First and Second Book of Maccabees, 118, 124
First Crusade, 290
First Intermediate Period (Egypt), 32
First Macedonian War, 149
First Punic War, 147
First Triumvirate (Rome), 163
Fisher, John (bishop), 445–446, 450
Five Pillars of Islam, 248
Flagellation
  defined, *334* (illus)
  self-flagellation, 411
  in Spanish America, 411
Flanders
  market cities in, *303* (map)
  worker rebellions in, 344
Flavian dynasty (Rome), 172
Flooding, in Sumer, 18
Florence
  Baptistery in, 381–382, 385
  Black Death in, 333
  Ciompi revolt in, 343–344
  Italian Renaissance in, 366
  Machiavelli in, 364–365
  vendettas in, 388–389
Flying buttresses, 325, *325* (illus)
Fontenelle, Bernard de, 541, 546
Food
  first food-producing communities, 13–15
  production in communities, *13* (map)
  revolution in production of, 13
Forms, 103
Forts. *See* Trading posts
Forum. *See* Roman Forum
Four Books on the Family (Alberti), 372
Fournier, Jacques. *See* Benedict XII (Pope)
Fourth Crusade, 291, 307
Fourth Lateran Council, 308, 313
  Eucharist requirements, 313
  Jews and, 308, 313
  on trial by ordeal, 283
France
  absolutism in, 495–497
  academies in, 480
  Black Death in, 333
  boundaries of, 500 i (map)
  dynastic marriage encircling, 389, *390* (map)
  Estates General in, 345
  Huguenots in, 474–475
  Jews and, 316–317
  in late twelfth century, 316
  use of term, 284
  worker rebellions in, 344
France, Marie de (troubadour), 323
Francis I (France), 384, 391, 475
Francis of Assisi (saint), *296* (illus), 296–297, 313
Franciscan Order, 313
Franciscans, 297
  in Mexico, 411
Franks, 265. *See also* Carolingian empire
Frederick I (Barbarossa, Germany), 291, 318
Frederick II (German emperor), 307
Frederick the Wise (Elector of Saxony), 434, 435, 438–439
Free Egyptians, 32
Freedman, in Rome, 189
Freedom of a Christian, The (Luther), 435
Freedom of the Sea, The (Grotius), 521
Freethinking, of Spinoza, 542–543
French Academy of Sciences, 500, 539, *539* (illus)

French language, 480, 500
French Revolution (1789 and 1792), end of, 493
French Wars of Religion, 474–477
Frescoes, 53
Friars, 312
Friars Minor (Lesser Brothers). *See* Franciscans
Fronde (France), 497
Fur trade, Russian immigration to, 417

Galatia, Celts in, 126
Galen (physician), 192
Galerius (Rome), 206
Galilei, Galileo
  astronomy of, 379, 380
  as Catholic, 537
  mathematics and, 534
  moons of Jupiter, 537
  physics and, 528–529
  responsibility for creating Western civilization, 7
  on separation of religion and science, 543
  telescope, 525–526
Gama, Vasco da, 405, 415, 416
Gas, Boyle on, 531–532
Gaugamela, battle at, 115–116
Gaul
  Frankish attacks on, 265
  Germanic tribes in, 224
  Merovingians in, 265
  Visigoths in, 223, 224
Gay marriage, 5
Gender and gender issues, in Greece, 97–99. *See also* Women
Geneva, Calvin in, 442–443
Genghis Khan, 335, 337
Genoa, Black Death in, *331* (map)
Geoffrey of Charney (Templar), 319
Geography (Ptolemy), 192
Germanic kingdoms, *264* (map)
  civil authority in, 266–267
  of Franks, 265
  German legacy in, 267
  Jews in, 268
  Roman legacy, 264, 266–267
  unifying forces in, 264, 267–268
  of Visigoths in Spain, 265–266
  wergild in, 267
  women in, 268–269
Germanic peoples and Rome, 184–185
Germanic tribes, in Gaul, 224. *See also* *specific tribes*
Germany. *See also* Holy Roman Empire; Nazi Germany
  borderlands of, 360
  market cities in, 303
  peasant's revolt in, 437, 439–440
  Romans and, 184–185
  Thirty Years' War and, 474, 506–507
Ghazis (warriors for Islam), 337
Ghent, 301, 344
Ghibellines, 308
Ghiberti, Lorenzo, 381–382, 385
Gibbon, Edward, 222
Gilbert, Humphrey, 412–413
Gilgamesh (Sumerian character), 25
Giza, Great Pyramid at, 30
Glorious Revolution (England), 516, 517–520
Gnosticism, 197–198, 221
Gods and goddesses. *See also* Religion(s); *specific deities*
  Egyptian, 29–30
  Greek, 99–100, 154
  Hebrews and, 70
  Hittite, 46–47
  Mesopotamian justice and, 23, 26
  Roman, 154, *156* (table)
  Sumerian, 19, 23
Gods on Parade, *46* (illus)
"God's Wife" (Egypt). *See also* Hatshepsut (Egypt)
"God's Wife of Amun" (Egypt), 37
Goethe (poet), 483
Gold
  in Africa, 396–397, 400
  coins in Rome, Umayyad dinar as, 255
  Egypt as source of, 52
  Umayyad dinar as Roman coin. *See also* Coins
Golden Age (Dutch), 521–522
Golden Age, in Spanish literature, 257, 481
Golden Ass, The (Apuleius), 193
Gothic style of architecture, 325
Goths, Arian Christianity of, 265
Government(s). *See also specific countries*
  of Egypt, 31–32
  of Greece, 80–81
  Hobbes on, 494
  of Incan Empire, 402
  of Italian city-states, 366
  Locke on, 519
  of Persian Empire, 87–88
  Price Revolution and, 464–465
  standing armies of, 494–495
  of Ur, 21
Gracchi (Rome), 159–160
  Gaius, 159–160
  Marius, 159–160
  Tiberius, 159–160
Granada
  defeat by Isabella and Ferdinand, 389, 391
  Jewish vizier in, 257
  Muslims in, 257, 387, 389
Grand Alliance, 501
Grand jury, English origins of, 318
Granicus River, Battle of the, 115
Gravitation, 528–530
  Newton on, 530
Great Britain. *See* England (Britain)
Great Famine, 330
Great Kings, Egyptian, 29–30
Great Northern War, 504, 514
Great Persecution (Rome), 206, 220
Great Plague (London), 333
Great Power Cultures, 52–53
  Assyrian society and, 52–53
  collapse of, 76
  during the Dark Age, 57
  Egyptian society and, 52–53
  habiru and, 55
  Hittite society and, 52–53
  Minoan-Mycenean society and, 52–53
Great Pyramid (Giza), 30
Great Schism, 351–353
Great Temple at Abu Simbel, 36
Greece
  ancient. *See* Greece (ancient)
  Byzantine control of, *237* (map)
Greece (ancient). *See also* Hellenistic Age
  alphabet in, 80
  Archaic Age in, 79
  Classical Age in, 93–108
  coins from, 81–82
  colonization and settlements by, 81–82
  culture of, *45* (map)
  Dark Age in, 79, 81, 86
  democratic traditions from, 93
  hoplites in, 82–83
  intellectual thought in, 85, 98, 99, 100–102
  International Bronze Age and, 47
  Ionia and, 81

Minoan Crete and, 47–49
Mycenaean, *45* (map), 55
Persia and, 79, 87, 91–92
Persians and, 79
Philip II (Macedon) and, 113–114
polis in, 80
slavery in, 99
Greek language
endurance at end of International Bronze Age, 54
Koine and, 127
Linear B and, 49
Greek Orthodox, 241
Gregory I (the Great, Pope), 269, *269* (illus), 271
Gregory III (Pope), 241
Gregory of Nyssa and Neoplatonism, 221
Gregory VII (pope), 305–306, 307
Gritti, Andrea, 368–369, 373
Grotius, Hugo, 521
Guelfs, 308
Guestworkers. *See also* Immigrants and immigration
Guicciardini, Francesco, 386
Guide for the Perplexed, The (Maimonides), 322
Guilds, "German Paragraph," in statutes of, 360
Guion, Francois, 459
Guise family, 475–476
Gunpowder, 340, 351, 495
Gutenberg, Johannes, 380, 429

Habiru, 55–56
Habsburg Empire. *See also* Austrian Habsburg Monarchy; Habsburg Monarchy; Holy Roman Empire; *specific rules*
Treaty of Utrecht and, 501
Habsburg Monarchy, 509–510. *See also* Austrian Habsburg Monarchy
Philip II (Spain) and, 477–478
Haciendas, 409
Hadrian (Rome), 172, 183
Hadrian's Wall, *184* (illus)
Haghia Sophia (Constantinople), *232* (illus)
Hall of Mirrors, Versailles, paintings in, 498
Hallstatt culture, 124–125
Hals, Franz, 522
Hammer of Witches, The, 471
Hammurabi (Babylon), *18* (map), 22, 26, 28
Hammurabi, empire of, *18* (map), 22, 23, 26
Hammurabi, Stele of, 27
Hammurabi's Code, 22, 26, 27–28
Handbook for the Militant Christian (Erasmus), 431
Hanging Gardens of Babylon, 64
Hannibal (Carthage), 155
Hanseatic League, 303
Hapiru people. *See* Hebrews
Harbor town, *169* (illus)
Harold (Anglo-Saxon, England), 285
Harun al-Rashid (caliph), 256
Harvey, William, 532, 534
Hasdai ibn Shaprut, 257
Hashemites, 245
Hashimite clan, of Quraysh tribe, 245
Hatshepsut (Egypt), *37* (illus), 37–38
Hattushas (Hittite capital), *45* (map)
Hattusili III, 46, 49, 52, 76
Heavy plow, 299, *299* (illus)
Hebrews. *See also* Bible (Hebrew); Jews and Judaism
Babylonian exile of, 69, 73
civilization of, 57, 65–74
during the Dark Age, 57
in Egypt, 66
Epic of Gilgamesh and, 25
foundational ethic of Western civilization, 41
Hammurabi's Code and, *27* (illus), 27–28
history of, 65–66
monotheism of, 44, 72–73
prophets of, 72
Western civilization and, 44, 74
Hecataeus of Abdera, 123
Helen, queen of Sparta, 50
Heliocentric theory. *See* Sun-centered theory
Hell, in Dante's *The Divine Comedy*, 357–358
Hellenism and Jews, 119–121, 124
Hellenistic Age, 111–137
Celts and, 124–126
contacts with foreign peoples in, 121–126
defined, 112
exploration of, 121, *123* (map)
Greek vs. Roman culture and, 153
Jews and, 124, 127
philosophy and, 132–133
urban society, 126–127
women in, 128
Helots, 84
Helvetic Confessions, 465
Helwys, Thomas, 448
Henry II (France), 474
Henry IV (France), 476, 496
Henry IV (Germany and Holy Roman Empire), pope and, 306
Henry the Navigator (Portugal), 398, 400
Henry V (England), 345–347
Henry VII (England), 390, 391
Henry VIII (England)
Anne Boleyn and, 445, 481
More and, 445
Reformation and, 444–446
security of kingdom, 391
Hera (goddess), *2* (illus)
Heraclides of Pontus, 134
Heraclitus of Ephesus, 102
Hercules (god), 47, 113
Hereditary social status, abolition of privileges in France. *See also* Aristocracy
Heresy. *See also* Crusades; Inquisition(s)
auto-da-fé and, 467–468
as Christian outcasts, 309–310
defined, 196
Galileo and, 544–545, 546
of Joan of Arc, 348–349
in later Middle Ages, 353
Montaillou inquisition and, 314–315
Roman Inquisition and, 544
of Waldensians, 309–310
Herod the Great, 193–194
Herodotus, 89, 102–103
Hetairai, 98
Hevelius, Elisabetha and Johannes, *547* (illus)
Hezekiah, 68, 72
Hieroglyphs
defined, 31
Minoan, 48
scribes and, 31–32
writing, 59
Hijra, 246
Hildebrand. *See* Gregory VII (Pope)
Hipparchia, 133
Hipparchus of Nicaea, 134
Hispaniola, 403
Histories (Polybius), 131

History and historians. *See also specific individuals*
Augustine and, 220–221
concept of history, 47
Gibbon and, 222
origins of modern thought and, 386
Polybius and, 131
Tacitus and, 172, 182–183, 191
History of Italy, The (Guicciardini), 386
History of the English Church and People (Bede), 272
History of the Peloponnesian War (Thucydides), 103
Hitler, Adolf. *See also* Nazi Germany
Hittites
after Battle of Kadesh, 46
culture and, 46–47
Great Power Cultures and, 52–53
history and, 47
imperial practice, 61
International Bronze Age and, *45* (map), 55
Kingdom of Hatti and, 46
mathematics and, 47
religion, 46
Storm God (Weather God), 46
warfare and, 55
Hobbes, Thomas, *Leviathan* by, *492* (illus), 493
Holland. *See* Dutch; Dutch Republic (United Provinces of the Netherlands); Netherlands
Holy communities, Anabaptist, 447–448
Holy Office of the Inquisition
chronology, 456
function of, 452
Jews and, 452
trial of Galileo, 544–545
Holy Roman Empire, 506. *See also* Crusades; Inquisition(s)
Charles V and, 389, 483
East Francia, 284
Imperial Diet in, 484
Italian Wars and, 385
monarchy of Pope Innocent III, *308* (map)
Prussia, 508
Holy wars
in the ancient world, 70–71
Crusades as, 287–288
justifications for, 249
Homer, 50
epic poems by, 50, 80
on Trojan War, 50
Homo sapiens sapiens, 12
Homosexuals and homosexuality, gay marriage, 5
Hooch, Pieter de, *468* (illus)
Hoplites, 82–83, 85
Horace (poet), 191–192
Horus (god), 30
Hosea (Israel), 72
Hoshea (Israel), 67
Hosius, Stanislaus, 486
"House of Islam", 250
House of the Admiral, *43* (illus)
"House of War", 250
How question, 7–8
Huguenots
Edict of Nantes and, 477, 497, 499
in France, 474–475
Huitzilopochtli (god), 401
Human body, Harvey on, 532, 534, 536. *See also* Medicine
Human sacrifice, by Aztecs, *401* (illus), 401–402
Humanists and humanism
battle of the sexes, 378
Christian, 429–431
civic, 376
defined, 374
education and, 376–377
in Italian Renaissance, 374–377
Renaissance science and, 377–379
women and, 377
Humors (bodily fluids) and Galen, 532, 534, 536
Hundred Years' War, 344–351, *346* (maps)
consequences of, 347, 349
defined, 344
Hungary
in Hapsburg Empire, 509
religious toleration in, 450
royal absolutism in, 513
Huns
empire of, *224* (map)
raids of, 222
Visigoths and, 222–223
Hunter-gatherers, 13, 29
Hus, Jan, 353
Hussite movement, 449–450
Hyadaspes River, Battle of the, 116
Hybrid religion, in Mexico, 411
Hyksos, 33, 35

I Will Praise the Lord of Wisdom, 34
Iberian peninsula. *See* Portugal; Spain
Ice Age, 13
Ice Man. *See* Otzi (Ice Man)
Iconoclasm, 241
Byzantine, *241* (illus)
controversy in Byzantine Empire, 241, 244
Netherlands, *443* (illus)
Iconoclastic Controversy, 241, 244
Icons, 240–241
Ictinus (architect), 107–108
Iliad (Homer), 50, 51, 80, *108* (illus)
Illuminated manuscripts
of Crusades, *290* (illus)
Irish, *270* (illus)
Image of a Man (Imago Hominis), 262
Images (religious). *See* Iconoclasm
Imitation of Christ (Thomas à Kempis), 354–355, 428
Immigrants and immigration, to Spanish America, 409. *See also* Slave trade
Imperial Diet, 435
in Holy Roman Empire, 484
of Speyer, 437
Imperialism, Roman model for, 170. *See also* Empire(s)
Imports. *See* Trade
Inanna (goddess), 23
Inca Empire, 402, 407–409
Incoherence of the Philosophers, 322
Index of Forbidden Books, 452, 454
Index of Prohibited Books, 537
India
Alexander the Great in, 114, 116
Europeans in, 415
Portugal and, 403, 416
Indians. *See* American Indians; Native Americans
Indo-European languages, 45, 48
Indonesia, trading post empires, 415
Induction, 532
Inductive reasoning, 24
Indulgences (certificates), 352, 433–434
Industrial Revolution. *See also* Industrialization
Industrialization. *See also* Industrial Revolution
Industry. *See also* Industrial Revolution
Infantry. *See* Armed forces; Military; Soldiers; Wars and warfare
Innocent III (Pope), 307–308
Albigensian Crusade and, 310, 314
Crusade and, 291
monarchy of, 307–308

Inquisition(s)
art criticized by, 454
against Cathars and Waldensians, 309–310, 314–315
in Montaillou, 314–315
in Spain, 389, 503
Institutes of the Christian Religion (Calvin), 443, 450
Instructions for Merikare, The, 34
Intellectual thought. *See also* Italian Renaissance; Jews and Judaism; Philosophy
in Carolingian Renaissance, 275–277
Christian, 219–221
cultural relativism in, 421, 423
Dominican, 312–313
Hellenistic science and, 131–132, 133–134, 136
medieval, 319
monastic preservation of, 271–272
Unitarians and, 449
Intelligence network, of Mongols, 337
Intendants (France), 496
Interdict, in Catholic Church, 307
Interior Castle (Teresa of Avila), 452
International Bronze Age, 43–77
chronology of, *56* (illus)
collapse of, 41, 54–56, 64, 65, 75
gift exchanges, 51–52
international monumental style, *54* (illus)
Israel and collapse of, 66
"Sea Peoples" and, 55–56
zones of power, 45–51
International organizations. *See specific organizations*
Inventions. *See specific inventors and inventions*
Investiture Controversy, 306
Invincible Armada, Spanish, 480
Ionia
during the Dark Age, 79
science in, 86, 101–102
Iran. *See also* Persia
Iraq. *See also* Mesopotamia
Ireland, conversion to Christianity in, 270
Irene (Byzantium), 242
Ireton, Henry, 519
Iron Age, 57
Canaanites in, 59–60
Damascus in, 57
defined, 57
Iron and iron industry, 57
Iroquois people, 400
Irrigation
Babylonian, 64
Sumerian, 29
Isabella (Castile)
chronology, 391
Columbus and, 389, 402
Ferdinand II or Aragon and, 389–390, 502–503
Isaiah (Hebrew prophet), 72
Ishtar Gate, *64* (illus), 64–65
Isis (goddess), 193
Islam. *See also* Crusades; Muslims; Ottoman Empire
Byzantium and, 233
Europe and, 248
expansion of, 233, *245* (map), 247
growth of, 233
mosque, 246
rise of, 245–250
in Spain, 233, 256–259, 478
Islamic Empire
Abbasid caliphate in, 255–256
Europe and, 248, 256–259
government of, 252–254
trade in, 255
Umayyad caliphate in, *245* (map), 252–255
Israel. *See also* Zionism
ancient kingdom of, 57, 59, 66, 67
in Canaan, 57
divided monarchy of, 67
Egyptian trade with, 33
united monarchy of, 66–67
Israelite kingdoms, 66–67, 72–73
Issus, battle at, 115
Istanbul. *See* Constantinople (Istanbul)
Italian peninsula, Roman expansion into, 145–147
Italian Renaissance, 364–393
ancient culture in, 374–385
in Florence, 366
humanists in, 374–377
in northern Italy, *367* (map)
patriarchal families in, 372–374
princes and courtiers in, 369–372
vendettas in, 388–389
Italian Wars, 385, 386, 391
Italy. *See also* Roman Empire; Rome (ancient)
Black Death in, 330, 333
communes in, 301, 373
French invasion of, 389
Lombards in, 266, 272
Odovacar in, 224
Ravenna exarchate in, 234, 272
Ivan III ("the Great," Russia), 487
Ivan IV ("the Terrible," Russia), 488–489

Jacquerie revolt, 344
James I (England), 515, 516
James II (England), 517, 519
James of Molay, 319
James VI (Scotland). *See* James I (England)
Jamestown, 413
Jarrow, 272
Jerome (Saint), 220
Jerusalem
built by Saul, 66
as capital of Judah, 67
Dome of the Rock in, *253* (illus)
Jews and Judaism, 66, 72–73, 194
Persian conquest of, 68
temple built by Solomon, 66
Jesuits
in Catholic Reformation, 451–452
in Poland, 486
in South America, 412
Jesus Christ (Jesus of Nazareth), 195–198. *See also* Christianity
End of Days and, 221
Muslims and, 246
nature of, 213–214
Socinus on, 449
trial of, 196–197
Jews and Judaism. *See also* Anti-semitism; Bible (Hebrew)
in Babylon, 67–69
in Byzantine Empire, 240
Christianity and, 216–217
in Córdoba, 257
Diaspora and, 216
forced conversions and, 240, 359, 389
Fourth Lateran Council decrees and, 308, 313
in France, 344–345
Hebrews and, 57, 69, 73–74
Hellenism and, 119–121
Inquisition and, 389, 409
in Islamic empire, 246, 255
in Middle Ages, 240
Mishnah and, 195, 216
Muhammad and, 246
in Palestine, 193–194
rabbis and, 193–195, 216
resistance to slave trade by, 418
slavery in ancient Egypt and, 418

Jews and Judaism *(continued)*
in Spain, 359
Spanish expulsion of, 359, 389, 409
Spinoza and, 542
Temple in Jerusalem and, 72–73, 194–195
in Transylvania, 450
women and, 216–217
Jihad, 248
against Crusaders, 289
requerimiento and, 407
Joan of Arc (France), 7, 348–349, 358
Joanna ("The Mad," Spain), 483
John (Evangelist), *290* (illus)
John II (Portugal), 403
John of Leiden, 448
Jordan, 33
Josiah, 72–73
Journal des savants, 500
Joust, medieval, *323* (illus)
Judah, kingdom of, 59
during the Dark Age, 57
Divided Monarchy, 67
Neo-Babylonian Empire and, 67
prophetic movement, 72
Judaism. *See* Jews and Judaism
Judea, 69, 194. *See also* Jews and Judaism
Judgment Day (Egypt), *38* (illus)
Judiciary, Montesquieu on. *See also* Court (royal)
Juliana of Norwich, 316
Julio-Claudian dynasty (Rome), 172
Julius (Christian soldier), trial of, 228–229
Julius II (Pope), 372
Junkers (Prussia), 508
Jupiter (god), 138, 154
Justice, in Mesopotamia, 26–28
Justification by faith, 432
Justinian I (Byzantine Empire)
Christianity and, 225–226
death of, 259
forced conversions and, 211
legal code of, 225–226
map, *227*
Persian Empire and, 228
reforms of, 228
reign of, 244
wars with Persia, 228
western provinces and, 226–228
Juvenal (poet), 192

Kadesh, Battle of, 46, 49
Kalhu, *62* (illus)
Kanesh, 22
Karnak, temple of Amun at, 36
Kassite Babylonian Empire, *45* (map), 47–49
Kassites, *28* (illus), 47–49
Keepers of the Gateway of the South, 33
Kepler, Johannes, 484, 528, 546
Khadija (Muhammad's wife), 245
Khufu (Cheops, Egypt), 30
Kievan Rus, 236, 334, 335
King Cyrus of Persia, 69
King Hiram of Tyre, 58
Kings and kingdoms. *See also* Absolutism; Monarchs and monarchies; *specific rulers*
of Assyria, 59
of Babylonia, 28, 47
divinity of, 39
in Egypt, 29–30
Germanic, 267
Israelite, 66–67
Mesopotamian justice and, 26–28
modern state system and, 385
in Sumer, 18–19
Ugarit, 55
Western European after Carolingians, 281, 283
Kipling, Rudyard, 1
Kneller, Godfrey, *529* (illus)
Knights
defined, 281
in Hundred Years' War, 345, 359
Teutonic, 359
Knolles, Richard, 511–512
Knossos, palace at, 47, 53
Knox, John, 447
Koine language, 127
Kore (goddess), 130
Kosovo, Battle of (1389), 340
Kremlin (Moscow), *488* (illus)
Kuhn, Thomas, 536

La Tène Celts, 125
Labor. *See also* Industrial Revolution; Slaves and slavery; Workers
encomienda system and, 409
slave trade and, 399, 418
Labyrinth, 47
Language(s). *See also* Alphabet; *specific languages*; Writing
Akkadian, 19, 45, 60, 65
Arabic, 19
Aramaic, 57, *60* (illus), 65
Armenian, 45
English, 349
French, 349, 480, 500
Hebrew, 19
Hittite, 45
Indo-European, 45, 48
Koine, 127
Latin, 213–214, 234, 320
Persian, 45
Provençal, 357
in Roman Empire, *178* (map)
Sumerian, 19
vernacular, 480
Las Casas, Bartolomé de, 421–423
Last rites, 356, *357* (illus)
Late antiquity, 201–231
Christianity in, 201–202
defined, 202
Jews in, 216–217
Roman Empire in, *205* (map)
Sasanian dynasty in, 228
Late Bronze Age
in Canaan, 35
capital cities and, *54* (illus)
characteristics of, 43–44
collapse of, 75
defined, 44
Egyptian Empire in, 40, 57
Hebrews after, 65
Mediterranean civilizations and, 47
palace system and, 53, 55
Ugarit, 50
Later Middle Ages
Babylonian Captivity and Great Schism in, 351–353
cultural boundaries in, 358–360
discrimination against ethnic and religious groups in, 358–360
plague and famine in, 330
warfare in, 344–351
Latin (language), 213–214, 320
Latin America. *See also* Americas, Europeans in; Spanish America; *specific regions and countries*
Latin Christendom, 214
Latin Christianity. *See also* Roman Catholicism; Western Christianity, division by 1555
Byzantines and, 241
conversions to, 272
Germanic kingdoms and, 267–268
Irish-Roman disagreements over, 270
kingdoms in Middle Ages, 269
Lombards and, 272

in Spain, 272
spread in Western Europe, 222, 264, 269
in Visigoth Spain, 272
Latin language
Carolingian Renaissance and, 275–276
Italian Renaissance and, 375
poetry in, 191–192
Vulgate Bible and, 213
Latin War, 145, 151
Latium, 145
Laud, William (archbishop), 515
Law codes
of Alfred the Great (Wessex), 284–285
of Hammurabi, 22, 26, 28
of Justinian, 226
Law of the Twelve Tables (Rome), 142, 144, 167
Law of War and Peace, The (Grotius), 521
Law(s). *See also* Law codes
canon, 276
corrupt Romans and, 143
Germanic, 268
Mishnah (Jewish law), 195, 216
Roman, 268
Ten Commandments as, 74
Lay investiture, 305. *See also* Investiture Controversy
Learning, medieval revival of, 320–322. *See also* Intellectual thought
Lebanon
Egyptian trade with, 33
Phoenicians in, 57
Legends of Gilgamesh, 24–26
Leningrad, in Second World War. *See also* Saint Petersburg, Russia
Leo (Byzantium), 240
Leo X (pope), 372, 433–434, 435
Leonidas (Sparta), 92
Letter to the Genevans (Sadoleto), 444
Levant, Phoenician contact with, 57
Levantine Corridor
after the Great Powers, 57
defined, 13
Neo-Assyrian imperialism, 61
trade and, 15, 33
Levellers (England), 517
Leviathan (Hobbes), 493
Libraries
in Alexandria, *122* (illus)
in Rome, 243
in Venice, 369
Library (Photius), 243
Life of Antony, 215
Life of Charlemagne (Einhard), 276
Lincoln, Abraham, 6
Linear A writing, 48
Linear B writing, 49, 79
Linear perspective
chronology, 385
defined, 382
Ghiberti panels, *383* (illus)
in painting, 379
Literature. *See also* Bible (Christian); Bible (Hebrew); *specific works*
of Abbasid caliphate, 256
courtly love in, 323
in Elizabethan England, 481–482
epic, 24–26, 50, 51, 80
in France, 480–481
Hellenistic, 129, 131
monasteries and classical literature, 271–272
Roman, 191–192
Lithuania. *See also* Poland-Lithuania
Little Ice Age and food production, 330
Liturgy, 263
Catholic, 305
codification of Catholic, 305
conformity in, 305
Slavic, 234
Livy (historian), 191
Locke, John
on Glorious Revolution, 519–520
reason, religion and, 543
Lombards, 266, 272
London
agricultural crops sold in, 462
Great Plague in, 333
Long Parliament (England), 515–516, 517
Longbow, *347* (illus), 350
Lord, 280
Lorenzo the Magnificent. *See* Medici family
Lost Ten Tribes of Israel, 67
Lothair (Carolingian), 277
Louis IX (Saint Louis, France), 316
Louis the German (Carolingian), 277
Louis the Pious (Carolingian), 277
Louis XI (France), 387, 391
Louis XIII (France), 495–496
Louis XIV (France)
absolutism and, 500
Mazarin and, 497, 499
mercantilism and, 499
portrait of, *501* (illus)
revocation of Edict of Nantes by, 497, 499
standing army of, 494–495
warfare by, 500–502, 504
Lower classes, 188–189
Lower Egypt, 29, 36
Loyola, Ignatius, 451, 456
Lucius Varus (Rome), Germanic revolt and, 186
Lucretius (poet), 153
Lum, Wing Tek, 1
Lusiads, The (Camões), 481
Luther, Martin
beliefs of, 431
break with Rome, 432–435
Diet of Worms and, 435, *438* (illus), 438–439
Erasmus and, 430–431
Freedom of a Christian, The, by, 435
justification by faith, 432
Ninety-Five Theses of, 426–427, 433–434
print culture and, 429
on sale of indulgences, 434
Lutheran Reformation, 431–440
women and, 437
Zwinglian Reformation and, 441–442
Lutherans and Lutheranism, 431
confessional identity of, 466
in Poland-Lithuania, 450
Luxury goods
medieval trade in, 342–343
trade and, 396–397
Lyceum, of Aristotle, 106
Lysander (Sparta), 96

Ma'at, 30–32, 38, 39
Maccabees, 118, 124
Macedon, kingdom of, 113–114
Alexander the Great and, 117
Macedonian Renaissance, 242–243
Macedonian Wars, 149–151
Machiavelli, Niccolò, 364–365, 386
Machine age. *See* Industrialization
Machinery. *See also* Industrialization
Madeira, 398
Madinat az-Zahra (palace), 257
Magellan, Ferdinand (Portugal), 406, 416
Maghreb region, North Africa
before Europeans, 397
in fourteenth century, *396* (map)

Magic, 470
Magisterial Reformation, 440
Magna Carta (England), 318
Magyars
conversion to Christianity, 286
European invasions by, 279
Maimonides, Moses (scholar), 322
Malabar Coast, 405, 416
Maleficia, 470–471
Mali, 396–397
Mamluks (Egypt), 337
Manassah, 72
Manetho (Egyptian priest), 123
Manifest destiny, 74
Manors, medieval, 298–304
Mantua, d'Este family in, 370, 373
Manzikert, Battle of, 287
Marathon, battle at, 91–92
Marciana Library (Venice), 369, *369* (illus)
Marcomanni (Germanic tribal confederation), 185
Marcus Antonius (Mark Antony), 166
Marduk (god), 23, 65, 89
Marguerite of Angoulême, 475
Marguerite of Navarre, 475
Mariner's Compass, *4* (illus)
Maritime technology, 397
Marriage
in Early Modern Europe, 466
European dynastic, 389
in Italian Renaissance, 372–373
in Mesopotamia, 26
patriarchy, 28
Mars (god), 154
Marsilius of Padua, 366, 373
Martel, Charles (France), 250, 265, 272
Martínez, Ferrant, 359
Martyrs, Christian, 198, 199, 217
Mary (mother of Jesus), 310–311, *312* (illus)
Mary I (England) and Phillip II (Spain), 478
Mary II (England). *See* William and Mary (England)
Mary Magdalene, *312* (illus)
Mary of Modena, 519
Masaccio
fresco by, 381, *381* (illus)
Renaissance painter, 381
Massachusetts Bay, English settlement in, 414
Massacres
St. Bartholomew's Day, 476–477
at Vassy, France, 476
Mathematical Principles of Natural Philosophy (Newton), 530, 534
Mathematics
deductive reasoning and, 533
Euclid and, 134
Hittites and, 47
nature and, 534
Newton and, 534
Sumerian, 24
value of *pi*, 134
Matriarchal system, 48
Maxentius (Rome), *207* (illus)
Maximian (Rome), 204, 206
Maximus (prefect), 228–229
Mayans, hybrid religion, 411
Mayas, 400
Mazarin, Jules, 497, 499
Measure for Measure (Shakespeare), 482
Mecca
Ka'aba in, 245, *246* (illus)
rise of Islam in, 245–246
Mechanics, 528–529
Archimedes on, 536
Descartes on, 534–535
Medicean Age (Florence), 367
Medici, Catherine de', 474, 475
Medici, Cosimo II de', 373
Medici, Marie de', 496
Medici family
Cosimo II de', 367, 539
in Florence, 367–368, 373
Lorenzo the Magnificent, 368, 373
Medicine
dissection and, *534* (illus)
Galen and, 192
Medieval joust, *323* (illus)
Medina, 246
Mediterranean region
economic hardship and political fragmentation, 40
International Bronze Age, collapse of, 54–55
Minoan civilization of, 47–49
Mycenaeans in, 47–49, 52–53
Raiders, 55
Megabyzus, 89
Megalith, 16–17
Megara, 81
Megasthenes, 123
Mehmed II (The Conqueror, Ottomans), 340
Mehmed the Conqueror (sultan), 510
Melania the Younger, 215–216
Memphis, Egypt, 29, 36, 39
Menander of Athens (play wright), 131
Mentuhotep II (Egypt), 32, 33
Mercantilism. *See also* Colonies and colonization; Empire(s); *specific empires*
Dutch, 520–521, 522
in France, 499
Merchant guilds, 342
Merikare (Egypt), 34
Merovingian dynasty, 265
Mesoamerica, before European arrival, 400
Mesopotamia. *See also* Iraq
Akkadians in, 19–21, 34
Amorites in, 21
Arameans in, 57
Assyria and, 21–22, 63
civilization in, 17–26, *28* (illus), 42, 44, 46–47, 57
conquest by Romans, 184
divination in, 23–24
economic hardship and political fragmentation, 40
economy of, 21–22
Egypt and, 29, 36
empires of, 17–22, 44, 47
flood control in, 18, 22–23
food production in, 13
International Bronze Age and, 44, 45–47, 57
Jews in, 57
justice in, 26–28
Kassites in, 22, 47–49
religion in, 22–23
Sumer in, 18–19
Messenia, 84
Messiah, 195
Mestizos, 409, 412
Metals and Phoenician commerce, 58. *See also specific metals*
Metamorphoses (Ovid), 191
Mexico
Aztecs in, 400–402
Cortés in, 407–408, *408* (illus)
epidemics in, 419
religion in, 411
Micah (Israel), 72
Michael VIII Palaeologus (Byzantine Empire), 339
Michelangelo. *See* Buonarroti, Michelangelo

Microscope, 379, 532
Middle Ages
Black Death in, 330–334
cities and towns in, 301–304
defined, 233
manors in, 298–304
papacy in, 353
science in, 535
trials by ordeal in, 282–283
Middle Bronze Age, 35
Middle class. *See also* Bourgeoisie
Middle East
Egyptian conquest of, 35–36
history of Western civilization, 12
Middle Kingdom (Egypt)
defined, 32
map, *30*
rise to empire, 32–33
span of years, 29
trade in, 32
Midian, 70
Mieszko, Prince (Latin west), 287
Military. *See also* Armed forces; Soldiers; Wars and warfare
Byzantine, 238–239, 242, 243
Egyptian, 35–36
Mongols in, 337
Mycenaean, 52
Scientific Revolution and, 540
Military revolution, 349–351
Millennium, Protestant belief in, 537
Millones (Spanish tax), 503
Milvian Bridge, Battle of the, 206
Mind-body dualism
Descartes on, 534
Spinoza on, 542
Ming China, 414
Minoan Crete, 47–49
Egypt and, 33
International Bronze Age and, *45* (map)
Mycenaeans and, 48
women in, 48
Minoans
Great Power Cultures and, 52–53
International Bronze Age and, 47–49, 56
Mishnah (Jewish law), 195, 216
Missions and missionaries
Jesuits and, 412, 416, 451–452
in Latin America, 410
in Mexico, 410, 411
Mithras (god), 193, *194* (illus)
Moab, 59, 69
Modern Devotion, 354–355, 428
Molay, James of (Grand Master, Templar), 319
Molière, Jean Baptiste, 500
Monarchs and monarchies. *See also* Carolingian Empire; Empire(s); Holy Roman Empire; Kings and kingdoms; Ottoman Empire; *specific rulers and empires*
absolutism and, 494
Church and, 387
in France, 387, 494
of Innocent III, 307–308, *308* (map)
medieval weaknesses of, 344–345
modern state system and, 386–391
pope as, 305–306
of western Europe, 316–318
Monasteries, 214–216
books in, 271
in Byzantium, 239–240
Cistercian, 311
Irish-Roman disagreements over, 270
Modern Devotion and, 354–355
scriptorium, 271
Monastic movement, 215
Monasticism, 215–216. *See also* Monasteries; Monks
asceticism and, 214
Benedict of Nursia and, 215, 220, 271
Franciscan order and, 313
intellectual life of, 271–272
women, sexuality, and, 215–216
Mongol Empire, 334
from 1206–1405, *335* (map)
European invasions by, 335–337
Mongol Peace, 337, 338–339
Monks. *See also* Monasteries; Monasticism; *specific monks*
Black Death and, 333
Cistercian Order of, 311
Monophysites, 214
Monotheism, 39, 44, 72–73
Montaigne, Michel de, 480
Montaillou inquisition, 314–315
Monte Cassino, monastery at, 215, 220, 271
Montefeltro, Federico II da (Urbino), 369–370, 373
Montezuma II (Aztecs), and Cortés, *408* (illus)
Monuments, 36
Moravia, 236
More, Thomas, 431, 445–446
Moriscos, 480
Moscow, Kremlin in, *488* (illus)
Moses (Bible), 66, 72, 246
Motion, 528–530
Galileo's theory of, 529
Movement. *See* Immigrants and immigration
Mudejar culture, 359
Muhammad (prophet), 259
after death of, 233
background, 245–246
Jews and, 246
Sunni-Sh'ite succession crisis after, 248, 250
teachings of, 246, 248
Mummius, Lucius (Roman general), 138
Mummy, *193* (illus)
in Egypt, 38, *38* (illus)
Münster, Anabaptists in, 448, 450
Muses (goddess), 134
Museums, in Alexandria, 133–134
Muslims. *See also* Islam; Islamic Empire
conversion and, 312–313
Ethiopia attacked by, 399
expulsion from Spain, 480
in Middle Ages, 254
Ottomans and, 337–339
Peoples of the Book and, 254–255
perception of Western world by, 254–255
Qur'an and, 245–246
in Spain, 359
Spanish Reconquest and, 259, 359
Muwatalli II, 49
Muwatallis (Hittites), 49
Mycenaean Greece
International Bronze Age and, 47–49, 54–55
lifestyle of, 52–53, 54–55
palace system in, 56, 79, 86
trade by, 48–49
Troy and, 50–51
writing, 49
Mycenaeans
fortress gate of, *54* (illus)
Great Power Cultures and, 52–53
Minoan Crete and, 47–49
Mysticism
Christian, 315, 316
of Teresa of Avila, 452

Nabonidus (Babylon), 65, 89
Nabopolassar (Neo-Babylonian Empire), 63
Nabu (god), 89

Nagrela, Samuel ibn, 257
Naples (Neapolis), chronology, 391
Napoleon, responsibility for creating Western civilization, 7
Nathan (prophet), 75
National Covenant (Scotland), 515
Nationalism, Hebrew, 74
Nations(s). *See* State (nation)
Native Americans. *See also* American Indians
  encomienda system and, 409
  Europeans and, 409–410
  Las Casas on, 421–422
  mutilation of, *423* (illus)
Native peoples. *See specific groups*
Natural law, defined, 144
Natural magic, 470
Nature
  control of, 546
  mechanical philosophy of, 534–535
  Neoplatonists and, 536
  universal laws of, 530
  women, men, and, 547–548
Navarre
  Bourbon family in, 475
  Huguenots in, 475
  kingdom of, 475
Navies
  Minoan, 48
  warfare and, 94
Navigation
  astrolabe and, 397
  maritime technology and, 397
Nazi Germany. *See also* Hitler, Adolf
Near East
  Arameans in, 57
  Hebrews, 65
  Persia, 87
  Phoenicians and, 59
  social structure in, 16
Nebuchadnezzar II (Neo-Babylonian Empire), 64
Necho II (Egypt), 58
Nefertiti (Egypt), 39, *39* (illus)
Neo-Assyrian Empire
  after International Bronze Age collapse, 44
  collapse of, 63
  imperialism and, 61
  in the Iron Age, *58* (map)
  Israel and, 67
  kings, 65
  libraries, 76
  record keeping in, 62–63
  resurgence of, 65
Neo-Babylonian Empire, 63–65
  after International Bronze Age collapse, 44
  Hebrew exile, 67–69
  in the Iron Age, *58* (map)
  irrigation system, 64
  kings, 65
  libraries, 76
  resurgence of, 65
Neolithic (New Stone) Age
  defined, 11
  European cultures in, *16* (map)
  technology and social change in, 15
  trade networks in, 15
Neoplatonism
  Christianity and, 221
  defined, 536
  Renaissance science, 536
Nero, 172
Nerva (Rome), 172
Netherlands. *See also* Dutch; Dutch Republic (United Provinces of the Netherlands); Holland
  iconoclasm in, *443* (illus)
  painting in, 522
New Astronomy (Kepler), 528
New Comedy, 153
New Comedy in Greece, 131
New Kingdom (Egypt), 37–40
  competition with Hittites, 46
  defined, 35
  diplomatic revolution, 49
  economic hardship and political fragmentation, 40
  map, *30*
  power of, 47
  span of years, 29
New Model Army (England), 517, 518
New Organon (Bacon), 532–533
New Spain, 408
New Stone Age. *See* Neolithic (New Stone) Age
New Testament, 196. *See also* Bible (Christian)
New World. *See also* Americas, Europeans in; *specific regions*
  cosmology and, 420
  use of term, 403
New Year, 70
Newton, Isaac
  background, 530
  mathematics and, 534
  portrait of, *529* (illus)
Nicaea, Council of, 220
Nike of Samothrace (sculpture), 129, *131* (illus)
Nile River region
  Egypt and, 29–40
  history of, 2
  Neo-Assyrian Empire in, 61
Niña (ship), 403
Ninety-Five Theses (Luther), 433–434
Nineveh, library and, 63
Noah, 421
Nobility. *See also* Aristocracy
Nogarola, Isotta, 377, 380
Nomads, Arabs as, 247
North Africa, Vandals in, 225. *See also* Carthage
North America
  colonization of, 412–414
  Spanish missionaries in, 410, 411
Northern Renaissance
  Christian humanists and, 429–430
  defined, 430
Northwest Palace (Assyria), *62* (illus)
Novels. *See* Literature; *specific works*
Novgorod, 488
Nubia
  Egypt and, 33, 36
  Great Temple at Abu Simbel, 36
  Umayyad caliphs and, 250
Numerals, in Sumer, 24, 42
Nunneries. *See* Convents
Nuns, Modern Devotion and, 354–355

Oaths, in medieval trials, 282–283
Observation, empirical, 532
Obsidian trade, 15
Octavian. *See* Augustus (Octavian, Rome)
Odovacar (Italy), 224
Odyssey (Homer), 80
Oedipus the King, 101
Old Kingdom (Egypt)
  architecture, 36
  collapse of, 32
  defined, 29
  kings as divine beings, 39
  map, *30*
  trade in, 32
Old Stone Age. *See* Paleolithic (Old Stone) Age
Old Testament. *See* Bible (Hebrew)
Oligarchy, 84

Olivares, Count-Duke of, 503
Olympic games in Greece, 81, 86
Omri (Israel), 67
On Disciplining Children: How the Disobedient, Evil, and Corrupted Youth of These Anxious Last Days Can Be Bettered, (Calvin), 470
On the Fabric of the Human Body (Vesalius), 379
On the Nature of the Universe (Lucretius), 153
On the Nature of Things (Anaximander), 102
On the Revolution of the Heavenly Spheres (Copernicus), 527, 530, 538
Optics, 379, 529
Oracle of the Potter, The, 124
Ordeals, trials by, 282–283
Oresteia, 101
Orthodox Christianity, 196
  in Byzantine Empire, 239–240
  Latin Christianity and, 241
  in Russia, 487, 512
  Slavic liturgy in, 234
  in Transylvania, 450
Osiris (god), 29–30, *193* (illus)
Osman I (Ottoman dynasty), 337
Ostrogoths, Theodoric and, 224
Otanes, 89
Otto I (the Great), 279, 284
Ottoman Empire, *339* (map)
  converts to Islam, 334
  between East and West, 510, 512
  in Eastern Europe, 341
  Hungary and, 510, 512
  Turks, 510–512
Ottoman Turks
  Byzantine fall to, 340
  conquest of Constantinople, 341
  rise of, 337, 339–341
Ottonian Renaissance, 285
Otzi (Ice Man), 10–11, 40
Overseas empire. *See* Empire(s)
Ovid (poet), 191–192

Pacific Ocean region and Magellan, 406
Paganism and Christianity, 210–211, 228–229
Painting
  Greek, 107
  linear perspective in, 379, 382
  optics, perspective, and, 379
  portraits in, 385
Palace of the Popes (Avignon), 352
Palace system and Late Bronze Age, 53, 54–55
Palaces
  Assyrian, 53, *62* (illus)
  Minoan, 47, 53
  Mycenaean, 53, 79, 86
  at Versailles, *498* (illus)
Paleolithic (Old Stone) Age, 12
Palestine
  Egypt and, 35
  during International Bronze Age, 50
  Jews and, 193–194, 216
  origin of, 59
  Peleset as name origin, 59
  under Roman rule, *194* (map)
Pallavicino, Ferrante, letter addressed to "Ungrateful Woman", 378
Pantheon (Rome), 155, *175* (illus)
Papacy. *See also* Pope(s); *specific popes*
  Babylonian Captivity and Great Schism, 351–353
  canon law and, 307
  Conciliar Movement and, 352–353
  Council of Trent and, 454–455
  defined, 209
  growth of, 269–270
  Innocent III and, 307–308
  in Italy, 241
  legacy of, 308
  protests against, 353–354
  science and, 538
Papal decree against heliocentrism, 538
Papal States, 307, 372
Papyrus, *60* (illus)
Paracelsus, 531
Parachute, Leonardo's invention of, *379* (illus)
Paradigms, collapse of scientific, 536
Paris
  Black Death in, 333
  University of, 321
Paris of Troy, 50
Parlement of Paris (court), 496, 497
Parliament (England), 318
  Charles I and, 517
  Charles II and, 517
  defined, 318
  purpose of, 318
Parliament, French Estates General as, 345
Parthenon (Athens), 94, 99, 107
  Green and Doric order in, *154* (illus)
Parthians
  Rome and, 184
  warriors, 184
Pascal, Blaise, 545
Patriarchy, 466
  defined, 28
  in Italian Renaissance, 372–374
Patriciate, in Florence and Venice, 366–367
Patrick (Saint), 218, 270, 310
Patron saints, 310–311
Patronage
  artists and, 383–384
  of Renaissance arts, 383–384
  science and, 537, 539
Patrons, 156
Paul II (pope), 538
Paul III (Pope), 452, 454
Paul of Tarsus, 196
Pax Romana, 167, 170, 182
Peace (Roman). *See Pax Romana*
Peace of Augsburg, 440, 484
Peasants. *See also* Serfs
  Jacquerie revolt and, 344
  manors and, 299–300
  revolt in England, 344
  serfs, 299
Peasants' Revolt (Germany), 437, 439–440
Peisistratus, 85, 91
Peloponnese, 48, 49, 84
Peloponnesian War, 93, 95–96, *96* (map), 113
Penance
  Luther on, 432
  pain and suffering as, 467
Pentateuch, 73
Peoples of the Book, 254–255
Peoples Republic of China. *See* China
Pepin the Short (Franks), 273
Pepin the Short (Gaul), 265
Pergamum, *111* (illus), *120* (map), 129, *129* (illus)
  Alter of Zeus, 129 (illus)
  Celt and Wife, 111 *(illus)*, 129
Periander, 83
Pericles (Athens), democracy in, 95
Persecution. *See also* Anti-semitism
  of Christians, 206, 211
  of Jews, 409
Persepolis, Persia, 116
  Alexander in, 116
  palace at, *91* (illus)

Persia. *See also* Iran; Persian Empire
Abbasid caliphate and, 256
Cyrus the Great and, 69, 89–90
despotism, 89
Greece and, 87
Zoroastrianism in, 88, 90
Persian Empire, 87, *88* (map), 90
under Sasanian dynasty, 228
Zoroastrianism in, 88, 90
Persian Gulf region, 20, 22
Persian Wars, 91–93
Macedonia, 113
Marathon and, 91–92
Personal rule, 515
Perspective, 379
linear, 379
in painting, 379
Peru
Incan Empire in, 408–409
Pizarro in, 408–409
Peter I ("the Great," Russia), 2, 512
Peter the Hermit, 287
Petrarch (Francesco Petrarca), 374–377, 380
Petrograd, Russian Revolution in. *See also* Saint Petersburg, Russia
Phalanx, 82
Pharaohs (Egypt)
change in New Kingdom, 37–40
cuneiform tablets, 44
defined, 35
in Egypt, 35
Egyptian empires under, 35
use of title, 29, 35
worship of, 39
Phidias, 108
Philip II (France), 307–308, 477–478
Philip II (Macedonia), 113–114
Philip II (Spain), and inflation, 465
Philip IV (The Fair, France), 316–317, 345, 350
Philip of Anjou. *See* Philip V (Spain)
Philip V (Spain), 501
Philip VI (France), 345, 350
Philippi, Battle of, 166
Philippines, Magellan's death in, 406
Philistines, 59, 66
cultures and continuities, 59
Philology, in Renaissance, 374
Philosophy. *See also* Science
Greek, 93, 103–104, 106
Hellenistic, 132–133, 153–155
Neoplatonism, 536
origins of, 103
scholasticism, 320–321
Phocas (Constantinople aristocrat), trial of, 228–229
Phoenicians, 57–59. *See also* Carthage
alphabet from, 59, 80
Byblos and, 58
as maritime power, 57–59
Sidon and, 58
trade and, 58–59
Tyre and, 58
Photius (Patriarch), 243
Physicians. *See* Disease; Medicine
Pilgrims and pilgrimages
Christian, 218–219
to Mecca, 248
in medieval literature, 356–358
in Middle Ages, 356–358
Pinta (ship), 403
Pisan, Christine de, 358
Pizarro, Francisco, 408–409
Plague. *See also* Black Death
bubonic, 332
in Byzantine Empire (542), 227
Planets. *See* Astronomy; Universe
Plantation colony, 398
Plantation crops, 420
Plataea, Battle of, 78, 92–93
Plato (Athens), 103–104
Academy of, 97, 103, 221
philosophy, 103
The Republic, 104
Platonic thought and Copernicus, 536
Plautus (playwright), 153
Plays. *See* Drama
Plebeian Assembly (Rome), 144, 146, 147
Gracchi and reforms through, 159–160
Plebeians (Rome), 141–142
Plotinus (philosopher), 221, 536
Plows, 16
Plutarch, on Alexander the Great, 118
Poem of My Cid, The, 292
Poets and poetry
Digenes Akritas as, 239
The Divine Comedy (Dante), 357–358
Homer and, 80
Horace and, 191–192
Latin, 191–192
Roman, 191–192
troubadours and, 323
Virgil and, 182, 183, 192
Poitiers, Battle of (732), 250, 265, 272
Poland, Jews in, 359, 486
Poland-Lithuania
Commonwealth of, 489
religious toleration in, 450
Renaissance, 485–487
royal absolutism in, 513
Russia and, *485* (map)
Polis (Greek city-state), 80
Political parties. *See specific parties*
Politics
in Athens, 81–82
iconoclasm controversy and, 240–242
modern thought about, 386
papacy and, 241
in Renaissance, 385–386
Roman Senate and, 176
Polo, Marco, 338, *338* (illus)
Polybius (Greek historian), 138, 142
Polybius (Rome), 131
Polyclitus, Spear-Carrier by, *108* (illus)
Polytheism and polytheists
chronology, 220
defined, 23
Roman, 193
Pompeius, Gnaeus, 162–165
Pompey (Gnaeus Pompeius, Rome), 162
Pontifex Maximus (High Priest, Rome), 173
Poor. *See* Poverty
Pope(s). *See also* Papacy; Roman Catholicism; *specific popes*
authority of, 209
Conciliar Movement and, 352–353
divorce of Henry VIII and, 445
Great Schism and, 351–353
as monarch, 305–306
in Renaissance, 372
Population
of Early Modern Europe, 461–462
epidemic disease and, 329–330
of fourteenth-century Europe, 461–462
of slaves in Rome, 189
Poros, King, 116
Portolanos, 397
Portrait of the Prince Baltasar Carlos… (Velazquez), *503* (illus)
Portraits, in Renaissance painting, *384* (illus)
Portugal
Africa and, 398–400
Asia and, 403
Brazil and, 412
colonies of, 398–400

exploration by, 403
India and, 403, 416
slave trade and, 412
Spain and, 504
trading post empire of, 400, 405
Treaty of Tordesillas and, 403
West Africa and, 400
Portuguese Empire, 400, 480
Potosí, 408
Pottery, in Sumer, 24
Poverty
Benedict of Nursia and, 215
of religious orders, 297
Power (political) in Rome, 157
Pragmatic Sanction of Bourges, 387
Prague, Czechoslovakia, defenestration of, 506, *506* (illus)
Praise of Folly, The (Erasmus), 431
Praxagoras of Cos, 134
Predestination, 442
Predynastic period (Egypt), 29
Prerogative, 515
Price Revolution, 464–465
inflation and, 464–465
Priesthood of all believers, 435
Primogeniture, 513
Prince, The (Machiavelli), 364–365, 386
Princeps (First Citizen), Octavian (Augustus) as, 171
Princes
Fronde of (France), 497
in Italy, 369–372
Principalities
defined, 366
ideal courtier, 370
in Italy, 369, 372
in Rome, 366
Printing and Erasmus, 430–431
Printing press, 379
Scientific Revolution and, 540
Private justice, 388–389
Procession of the Catholic League, *459* (illus)
Production of food, 13–15. *See also* Industrialization
Professors, in medieval universities, 321
Prophetic movement (Hebrews), 72
Prophets
Hebrew, 72
Muhammad as, 245
Proselytizing by Christians, 198. *See also* Conversion (to Christianity)
Protectionism, mercantilism and, 499
Protectorate (England), 517
Protestant Reformation. *See also* Protestants and Protestantism
causes of, 427–431
Charles V and, 445
defined, 427
duration of, 426
in England, 445–446
print revolution and, 428–429
spread of, 426–427
women and, 437
Protestants and Protestantism. *See also* Huguenots; Puritans; *specific countries*
in Austrian Habsburg lands, 509
Council of Trent and, 454–455
diversity of, 440–450
in Poland-Lithuania, 450
in Prussia, 509
science and, 537
St. Bartholomew's Day Massacre and, 476–477, *477* (illus)
Proto-Canaanite alphabet, 59
Provençal language, 357
Provinces (Rome)
loss of, 221
Romanization of, 178
Prussia
absolutism in, 507–509
growth of, 507–509
Hohenzollerns in, 508
Junkers in, 508
Ptolemaic universe, *527* (illus)
Ptolemies (Egypt), Ptolemy VI, *121* (illus)
Ptolemy, Claudius (astronomer, scientist), 119, 192, 526–527, 536
calculation of Earth's circumference, 402–403
Ptolemy I, 133–134
Ptolemy II, 120–121
Punic Wars, 147–148
Punt (Somalia), 33
Puritans, 515
in England, 446
Pyramids, in Egypt, 30–31
Pyrrhus of Epirus, 147
Pytheas of Marseilles, 122, 135

Quarantines, Black Death and, 332
Queen Anne's War. *See* War of the Spanish Succession
Quinta, Claudia, 155
Qur'an, 245–246, 248, 249, *251* (illus)
Rabbinic Judaism, 193–194, 216
Rabbis, 216
Rabelais, François, 480
Race and racism. *See also* Discrimination; Immigrants and immigration
Racine, Jean (writer), 500
Radical Reformation, 440, 447–449
Raleigh, Walter, 412–413
Ramesses II (Egypt), 36, *38* (illus), 46, 49, 76
Rape of the Sabine Women (by Pietro da Cortona), *140* (illus)
Rational deduction, 24
Rationalism, 533
Ravenna, Exarchate of, 234, 272
Re (god), 30, 37, 39
Realism, in Dutch Painting, 522
Reason and reasoning
deductive, 533–534
independent, 541–543
Rebaptism. *See* Anabaptists
Reconquest (Spain), *259* (map), 359
Red Sea, 22
Redistributive economies, 19
Reformation(s). *See also* Catholic Reformation; Protestant Reformation
Magisterial, 440
Radical, 440, 447–449
Reform(s). *See also* Reformation(s)
of Catholic Church, 304–310
by Diocletian (Rome), 203–206
Puritans and, 446
Quakers and, 448–449
Regency, 496
Reichstag (Germany), 506
Relajados (sinners), 467
Relics (sacred), of saints and martyrs, 217, 310
Relief, Neo-Assyrian, *60* (illus)
Religion(s). *See also* Bible (Christian); Bible (Hebrew); Catholic Reformation; Gods and goddesses; Protestant Reformation; *Qur'an*; *specific religions*; Toleration under Islam
in Classical Greece, 99–100
confessional identities and, 465–466
in Egypt, 34
flagellation in, *334* (illus)
Gnosticism and, 221
Hebrew Bible and, 73

Religion(s) *(continued)*
Hebrew temple of Jerusalem and, 69, 72–73, 194–195
Hellenistic world, 127
Hittite, 46
Islamism and, 246, 248
in Judah, 69–70, 72
in Mexico, 411
Minoan, 49
Persians and, 88, 90
pilgrimages and, 218–219
in Poland-Lithuania, 450
in Rome, 153–155, 192–198
spiritual creativity of, 313
in Sumer, 19, 22–23
Religious divisions in Europe about 1600, *475* (map)
Religious orders. *See also specific orders*
in Catholic Reformation, 311–313, 451–452
of women, 452
Religious Peace of Ausburg (1555), 440, 473
Religious wars, 249
Rembrandt (van Rijn), 522
Reminders of Death, 355–356
Renaissance
defined, 365
in Italy, 364–393
Machiavelli and, 364–365
of Poland-Lithuania, 485–487
science in, 377–379
Twelfth-Century, 321–322
Republic of the United Provinces, 479
Republicanism, 366
Requerimiento (document), 407
Research. *See* Scientific Revolution
Resistance. *See* Revolts and rebellions
Responsible citizenship, Bruni on, 376, 380
Revenge (Liutprand of Cremona), 284
Revenue, Akkadian, 20
Revolts and rebellions
Ciompi, 343–344
Dutch Revolt against Spain, 478–479
by German peasants, 437, 439, 440
Jacquerie, 344
by Jews, 124, 194
by peasants, 343–344
against Roman Empire, 176
by Roman slaves, 189
Revolutions of the Heavenly Spheres, The (Copernicus), 530, 538
Rheims, 347
Rhetoric, 374
humanists and, 374
Petrarch and, 374
in Rome, 155–156
Rhine River and Roman Empire, 225
Rich. *See* Wealth
Richard I (the Lion-Hearted, England), 291
Richelieu, Cardinal (Armand Jean du Plessis de Richelieu), 496, *496* (illus), 499
Rivers and river regions. *See specific rivers and river regions*
Roads and highways, in western Europe, 301
Roanoke Island, English settlement at, 413
Robin Hood, legends of, 317
Roman Catholicism. *See also* Catholic Reformation; Missions and missionaries; Protestant Reformation
anti-Catholic propaganda and, *435* (illus)
auto-da-fé in, 467–468
Babylonian Captivity of the Church, 351–353
consolidation of, 304–316
conversions to, 499
Eucharist and, 313, 315–316
Great Schism and, 351–353
Inquisition and, 389
James II (England) and, 519
of Mary I (England), 446
vs. Orthodox Christianity, 241
Philip II and, 477–478
St. Bartholomew's Day Massacre and, 476–477
uniform rites of, 305
Roman Empire, 169–200. *See also* Eastern Roman Empire; Roman Republic; Western Roman Empire
administration of, 177–178
African contacts with, 187–188
agriculture in, *178* (map)
Anglo-Saxon England and, 284–285
Antonine age, 172
army in, 176
assimilation of conquered peoples in, 177
breakdown of, 203
breakup of, 222–228
Britain and, 183
Celts in, 126
China and, 186–187
chronology, 200
citizenship in, 180, 182
commerce in, 177–178
control of provinces in, 177–178
culture after, 188
Diocletian's reforms in, 203–206
division of, 222
extent of, *171* (map)
Flavian dynasty of, 172
freedmen in, 189
frontiers of, 183
Germanic invasions of, *204* (illus)
Germanic peoples and, 184–185
Huns and, 222
invasions of, 203
Julio-Claudian dynasty of, 172
languages in, *178* (map)
in late antiquity, *205* (map)
Latin Christianity and, 222
laws in, 180, 182
literature and, 191–192
loss of western provinces by, 222–224
medieval empires and, 262–295
Parthian Empire and, 184
provinces in, 178–179, 222, 226–228, 234
roads in, 301
Senate in, 170, 171
Severan dynasty, 172–173
slaves in, 189
tetrarchy in, 204, 225
in third century, 202–206
women and property in, 190
Roman Forum, *138* (illus), 174
Roman Inquisition, trial of Galileo, 528. *See also* Holy Office of the Inquisition
Roman law, 142, 144
Roman Republic, 138–168. *See also* Roman Empire; Rome (ancient)
Caesar and, *150* (map)
classes in, 157–158
conquest of Carthage by, 147–149, *150* (map)
culture of, 152–153
First Triumvirate and, 162–164
government of, 138
Gracchi in, 159–160
lifestyle in, 157–158
Mediterranean conquests by, *150* (map)

Social War in, 160
warship, *160* (illus)
Roman Theater (Aosta, Italy), *145* (illus)
Romanesque style of architecture, 324
Romanization
defined, 177
Roman law and, 178
Romanov, Michael (Russia), 489. *See also specific tsars*
Romantic love, in troubadour poetry, 323
Rome (ancient), 174–175, *175* (map). *See also* Gods and goddesses; Punic Wars
expansion by, 144–151
Greek culture and, 152
Hellenistic world and, 152–153
origins of, 139–141
Rome (city)
Christianity and, 209–210
churches in, 209
lifestyle of slaves in, 189
popes in, 209
sacks of, 147
Romulus Augustulus (Rome), 223, 225
Roncesvalles, Battle of, 292
Rosh Hashanah, 70
Roundheads (England), 516–517
Royal absolutism, 513
Royal Academy of Sciences (France), 539
Royal Navy. *See* England (Britain); Navies
Royal Road, in Persian Empire, 87
Royal roads, 61
Royal Society (England), 539, 540, 547
Royalists, in England, 517, 519
Rudolf II (Holy Roman Empire), 483–484
portrait of, *484* (illus)
Rule (Benedict), 271
Rural areas. *See* Peasants
Rus people
Byzantium and, 232–233
conversion to Christianity, 236
Russia. *See also* Soviet Union
Ivan the Terrible in, 488–489
West and, 512–513
westernization in, 512–514
Russian Empire
expansion of, 512–513
in Pacific region, 416
Ryswick, Treaty of, 501, 504

Saavedra, Miguel de Cervantes, 481
Sabaea (Sheba), 67
Sacks, of Antioch, 228
Sacraments (Catholic), 410
Sacred Band, 99
Sadoleto, Jacop (Cardinal), Letter to the Genevans, 444
Sailing and sailors, Phoenician, 58. *See also* Navigation; Ships and shipping
Saint Anthony, *436* (illus)
Saint Bartholomew's Day Massacre, 476–477, *477* (illus)
Saint Denis, Gothic church at, *324* (illus)
Saint Mark (Basilica, Venice), *311* (illus)
Saint Paul Outside the Walls, 209, *210* (illus)
Saint Peter's Basilica (Rome), 372
Saint Petersburg, Russia, *514* (illus)
as new capital, 513
West and, 514
Saladin (Egypt and Syria), 291
Salamis, battle at, 78, *78* (Illus)
Salic Law, 268
Sancho III (Navarre), 258
Sansovino, Jacopo, 369, *369* (illus)
Santa Maria (ship), 403
Saqqara, pyramids at, 30
Sargon (Akkad)
chronology, *28* (illus)
empire of, *18* (map), 19–21, 25
government of, 22
history of, 19
Sasanian dynasty (Iran), 228
Satan. *See* Devil and witchcraft
Satellite states (Soviet). *See* Eastern Europe; *specific countries*
Satraps, 90, 117, 376
Saul (Hebrews), 66
Savior. *See* Messiah
Savorgnan, Antonio, 388
Saxons
Charlemagne and, 273
invading Britain, 223, 224
Scandinavia, Vikings from, 279
Scapegoats, minority groups as, 355, 360
Scarab, 33
Schliemann, Heinrich, *51* (illus)
Schmalkaldic League, 440
Scholarship. *See* Intellectual thought
Scholasticism, religion and science, 320–325
Schongauer, Martin (artist), *436* (illus)
Schools. *See also* Education
Schwenckfeld, Casper (Spiritualist), 448
Science. *See also* Scientific Revolution; Technology
Babylonian, 65
collapse of paradigms in, 536
coming of millennium and, 537
intellectual development outside, 537–540
in Ionia, 86
in later medieval period, 535
patronage and, 537, 539
printing press and, 540
Protestantism and, 537
religion and, 537, 538
in Renaissance, 377–379, 535–536
in Roman Empire, 192
Scientific Revolution, 525–551
in astronomy, 526–528
in biology, 532, 534, 536
causes of, 535–540
chemistry and, 531–532
intellectual consequences of, 540–545
natural law and, 545–548
in physics, 528–530
search for scientific knowledge in, 532–535
Scotland
Calvinism in, 446–447
Charles I and, 517
England and, 517
in United Kingdom, 517
Scots Confession (1560), 450
Scribes
Babylonian, 47, 63
in Carolingian Renaissance, 275–276
in Egypt, 32
functions of, 44
schooling for writing, 32
in Sumer, 24
tablet and parchment, *60* (illus)
Script, Sumerian, 24
Scriptorium, 271
Scripture and heliocentrism, 538
Sculpture
Aprodite of Melos as, *128* (illus)
David, 383
Greek, 106–107
Hellenistic, *111* (illus), *128* (illus)
by Michelangelo, *364* (illus), 385
Nike of Samothrace, 129
"Sea Peoples", 55
Egypt and, 66
Philistines as, 59
as rebels, 56
Second Crusade, 290–291

Second Intermediate Period (Egypt), 33
Second Punic War, 147–148
Second Triumvirate, 166
Secretism, 193
Secular clergy, 305
Secularization, 545
Seleucids, 119
Self-flagellation, *334* (illus), 467
Seljuk Turks, 287
Senate (Rome), 176
  Augustus and, 170–171
  as social order, 188
Seneca (philosopher), 191
Sennacherib, 62, 68
Separation of church and state, Anabaptists and, 447–448
Separatist revolts, in Spanish territories, 503–504
Septuagint (Hebrew Bible), 127, 214
Serapis (Osiris) (god), 193
Serbia, Ottomans and, 340
Serfs, 84, 299
Servetus, Michael (Spain), 449
Seth (god), 30
Settlement(s)
  Celtic, 127
  food-producing, 14
Settler colony, 398
Severan dynasty (Rome), 172–173
Sex and sexuality, in early Christianity, 218
Sforza, Lodovico, 384
Shaftesbury, Earl of, 517
Shakespeare, William, 482
Shamash (god), 26, *27* (illus)
Sheba, Queen of. *See* Sabaea (Sheba)
Shechem, 67
Shi'ites, 248–250
Ships and shipping
  maritime technology and, 397
  Phoenician, 57–58
  slave ships and, 418
  spread of Black Death and, 333
  Viking, *280* (illus), 280–281
Short Account of the Destruction of the Indies, The (Las Casas), 421
Sic et Non (Abelard), 320
Sicily
  Islam in, 256–259
  Peloponnesian War and, 95–96
Sidon, 58
Sidon Crusader Sea Castle, Lebanon, *291* (illus)
Siffin, battle at, 251–252
Silk Road, *187* (map), 337, 338–339
Silver
  discovery of at Potosí, 408
  trading by factories, 415
Simons, Menno, 448
Simony, 305
Sin (goddess), 65
Sin, Luther on penance and, 432
Six Books of a Commonwealth (Bodin), 493–494
Skepticism
  defined, 541
  and independent reasoning, 541–543
  of Spinoza, 542
Slave trade, 417–419
  Portugal and, 399
  in Roman Empire, 400
  through trading posts, 400
Slaves and slavery
  in Egypt, 32, 66
  in Greece, 99
  peasants unable to pay debts, 55
  in Rome, 158
Slavic liturgy in, 234
Slavic peoples, 234–236
  Celts and, 126
  conversion to Christianity, 235
Sluys, Battle of, 345–346
Smallpox epidemic, 419
Smith, Thomas, 511–512
Social War (Rome), 160
Socialist parties. *See* Socialists and socialism; *specific parties*
Socialists and socialism. *See also specific parties*
Society. *See also* Classes
  Babylonian, 47
  in Classical Greece, 96–100
  guilds in, 342
  in Roman Republic, 156–158
  urban, 126–127
Society of Jesus, 451, 456. *See also* Jesuits
Socinus, Faustus, 449
Socrates, *105* (illus)
  philosophy, 103
  trial and execution of, 105–106
Soldiers
  in Hundred Years' War, 349–351
  infantry, 349–351
Solomon (Hebrews), 58, 66–67, 75
Solon (Athens), 85, 142
Somalia as Punt, 33
Somnium (Lunar Astronomy) (Kepler), 546
Song of Roland, The, 292
Sophists, 103
Sophocles, 101
South Africa. *See also* Africa
South America
  Magellan and, 406
  Spain and, 410
South Pacific region. *See* Pacific Ocean region and Magellan
Southwest Asia. *See also* Middle East
  civilizations in, 45, 54–55, 56
  Hammurabi's Code and, 22
  in Iron Age, *59* (map)
  Western civilization and, 18
Soviet Union. *See also* Russia
Spain
  Aztec fall to, 407
  Columbus' voyages and, 389
  conquistadores from, 400, *406* (illus), 407
  decline of, *502* (map)
  Inquisition in, 389, 503
  Italian Wars and, 385, 386
  Jews and, 359, 389, 409
  overseas empire of, 501
  Phoenician colonies in, 58–59
  Phoenician trade and, 59
  precious metals for, *59* (map)
  Treaty of Tordesillas and, 403
  Umayyad caliphate and, 250, 252
  Visigoths in, 244, 265–266, 272
Spanish America, culture of, 409–410. *See also* Spain; *specific locations*
Spanish Armada, 478
Spanish Inquisition
  conversions to Christianity, 389
  purpose of, 479
Spanish Reconquest (Reconquista), *259* (map)
Sparta
  Athens and, 85
  Battle at Thermopylae and, 92–93
  Battle of Marathon and, 91–92
  Peloponnesian War and, 93
  society of, 84
Spartacus (gladiator), slave uprising and, 157, 162
Spice Islands, 405
  Portugal and, 477
  trading post empires, 415
Spinoza, Baruch, 521, 541–543, *542* (illus)
Spiritual Exercises (Loyola), 451, 456

Spiritualists and spiritualism
defined, 448
Quakers, 448–449
Schwenckfeld on, 448
Stadholder (United Provinces), 479
Standard of living and industrialism. *See also* Economy and economics
"Standard of Ur", 20
Standing armies, after Thirty Years' War, 494–495
Starkey, Thomas (theorist), 445
Starvation. *See* Famine
State (nation)
confessional, 473–482
in Prussia, 507–509
Statues
Augustus (Octavian, Rome), *172* (illus)
Cybele, 155
King David, *364* (illus)
Marcus Aurelius, 185, *185* (illus)
The Tetrarchs, *201* (illus)
Steen, Jan, 522
Step Pyramid (Egypt), 30–31, *31* (illus)
Stock exchange, in Amsterdam, *521* (illus)
Stoics and stoicism
defined, 133
philosophy, 133
Romans and, 133
Stonehenge, 16–17, *17* (illus)
Struggle of the Orders (Rome), 142
Stuart, Mary (Scotland), 446
Stuart dynasty (England)
Glorious Revolution and, 517–520
later absolutism of, 517–520
Students, in medieval universities, 321
Sub-Saharan Africa, before Europeans, 396. *See also* Africa
Succoth, 70
Sugar cane, 398
Sugar industry, in Brazil, 412
Sulla, Lucretia Conelius, 160
Sultan (Ottoman Empire), *328* (illus). *See also specific rulers*; Turks
Sumer and Sumerians (Mesopotamia), 18–19
cultural inheritance of, 75–76
Neo-Assyria and, 62
religion in, 22–23
restoration of, 65
Summary of the Catholic Faith Against the Gentiles (Thomas Aquinas), 322
Summary of Theology (Thomas Aquinas), 322
Sun-centered theory, 527
Sunni Muslims, 290
Sunnis, 248–250
Supernatural and magic, 470–472. *See also* Magic; Religion(s)
Supper in the House of Levi (Veronese), *454* (illus)
Supply, demand, and inflation, 464
Surinam, 418
Surrender of Breda, The (Velázquez), 505
Switzerland, Protestant Reformation and, 441–443
Symposia, 104
Syncretism, 69–70
Syndics of the Clothmakers of Amsterdam (Rembrandt), 522, *522* (illus)
Syphilis, 420
Syria
after International Bronze Age collapse, 65
Arab control of, 244
Arameans in, 57
Assyria and, 47
Canaan and, 46, 50
diplomatic revolution, 49
Egypt and, 46, 55
end of independence of, 60
fall of, 60
Hittites and, 46
Muslim seizure of, 244
Phoenicians in, 57
Syriac language, 214
Arab translations from, 254
for prayer, 254
Szlachta (Polish nobility), 485–486

Tablet and Parchment, Cuneiform and Alphabet, *60* (illus)
Tacitus (historian), 172, 182–183, 191
Taille (tax), 387
Taille in France, 496
Talas, Battle of, 250
Talmud, 216, 220
Tamerlane (Mongols), 337, 342
Tarabotti, Arcangela, 378
Tauret (god), 30
Taxation. *See also* Revenue, Akkadian
in Babylonia, 22
Byzantine, 255
for maintaining armies, 61, 495
in Persia, 255
taille, 387, 496
Technology. *See also* Science
agricultural revolution and, 298–299
bronze and, 35
Hyksos, 35
Otzi the Ice Man and, 10–11
Telescope, 379, 380, *525* (illus), 525–526
Tell el-Amarna, 39, 45
Templars, 319
Temple(s). *See also* Pyramids, in Egypt
on Capitoline Hill, *138* (illus), 139
circular, *152* (illus)
in Jerusalem (temple of Solomon), 66, 72–73
in Rome, *152* (illus)
Sumerian, 19, 23
in Ur, 21
Temujin (chief), 335
Ten Commandments, 74
Tenochtitlán, 400
Terence (playwright), 153
Teresa of Avila (St. Teresa), 452
Test Act of 1673, 519
"Tetrarchs, The" (statue), *201* (illus)
Tetrarchy (Rome), 204, 225
Tetzel, John, 434
Teutoburg Forest, Battle of, 186
Teutonic Knights, 360
Thales of Miletus, 102
The Republic (Plato), 104
Theater. *See* Drama
Thebes, Egypt, 32, 36, 39
Themes (military districts), 238–239
Theocritus (poet), 131
Theodora (Byzantium), 225, 242
Theodoric the Ostrogoth, 224
Theodosius I, 81
Theology
Byzantine icons and, 240–241
Christian, 74
Hebrew, 74
of Orthodox Christianity, 240
science and, 535–536
Trinity in, 212
Theophrastus, 134
Theory of motion, of Galileo, 529
Thera (island), 48
Thera, painting from, *43* (illus)
Thermophylae, Battle of, 92–93
Thinker of Cernevoda, *10* (illus)
Third Crusade, 291
Third Punic War, 149
Thirty Years' War
Germany and, 474, 485, 506–507
religious conflicts, 483
standing armies after, 492, 494–495
Treaty of Westphalia, 507

Thirty-Nine Articles, 465
Thomism, 322
Three Romes, Russian theory of, 488
Thucydides, 103
Thutmose I (Egypt), 36
Thutmose II (Egypt), 37
Thutmose III (Egypt), 36, 37–38
Tiberius (Rome), 172, 186
Tiglath-Pileser III (Neo-Assyria), 61, 67
Tigris River region, 18, 61
Time of Troubles (Russia), 489
Timeline. *See* Chronology
Titian, *The Bravo*, *388* (illus)
Titus (Rome), *195* (illus)
To the Christian Nobility of the German Nation (Luther), 435
Toledo, Spanish Reconquest of, 259
Toleration under Islam, 246. *See also* Religion(s)
Toltecs, 400
Tombs, Egyptian pyramids as, 30
Tools of Otzi the Ice Man, 10–11
Torah, 73. *See also* Bible (Hebrew)
Tordesillas, Treaty of, 403, 412
Tories (England), 519
Torture
  Assyrian, 68
  in *auto-da-fè*, 467–468
Trade. *See also* Commerce; Slave trade
  Akkadian, 20
  Assyrian, 21–22
  Black Death and, 333
  bronze and, 35, 44, 51–52
  camel caravans and, 57, 247
  in Carthage, 59
  cities and towns in, 301–302
  collapse of, 342–343
  fairs for, 303
  guilds in, 342
  Hellenistic, 121–122, *123* (map)
  in International Bronze Age, 44, 51–52, 56–57
  in Islamic Empire, 246
  maritime, 121–122
  in minerals, 33, 56–57
  Minoan, 48
  during Mongol Peace, 337
  obsidian, 15
  in Roman Empire, 233
  Sumerian, 18–19
  in Ugarit, 50
Trade associations, Hanseatic League as, 303
Trade routes
  control by Solomon, 67
  Egyptian, 64
  European, *303* (map)
  in Roman Empire, 233
Trading companies, Dutch, 520
Trading posts. *See also* Factors and factories (trading posts)
  empires, 415–417
  Portuguese, 400
Traini, Francesco, *333* (illus)
Trajan (Rome)
  conquests of, 172, 184
  empire under, *171* (map)
Transformations, 7–8
Transportation and Industrial Revolution. *See also specific types*
Transubstantiation, 313
Transylvania, religious toleration in, 450
Travel by Marco Polo, 338
Treaties. *See specific treaties*
Treatise on Religion and Political Philosophy, A (Spinoza), 542
Treatises on the Plurality of Worlds (Fontenelle), 546
Trials
  of Anne Boleyn, 445
  of Charles I (England), *518* (illus), 518–519
  of Galileo, *544* (illus), 544–545
  of Jesus Christ, 196–197
  of Joan of Arc, 348–349
  of Julius, 228–229
  of Knights Templar, 319
  by ordeal, 282–283
  of Socrates, 105–106
  for witchcraft, 470–473
Tribunes (Rome), 142, 146, 162
Tribute, Akkadian, 20
Tribute Money, The (Masaccio), 381, *381* (illus)
Triemes, 91
Trinity, Unitarians and, 449
Triumph of Death, The (Traini), *333* (illus)
Triumvirates (Rome), 162–164
Trivium
  as classical curriculum, 321
  as university curriculum, 321
Trojan War, Homer on, 50. *See also Iliad* (Homer)
Trojan Women, The (Euripides), 101
Troubadours, 323
Troy, a city of legend, 50–51
Troyes, Chrétien de, 326
Truth, Thomas Aquinas on, 322
Tsars (Russia). *See* Russia; *specific rulers*
Tudor dynasty (England), 390–391. *See also specific rulers*
  Reformation and, 444–446
Tukulti-Ninurta I (Assyria), 47
Tura, Agnolo di, (chronicler), 330–331
Turkey. *See also* Anatolia (Turkey); Ottoman Empire
Turks. *See also* Ottoman Empire; Ottoman Turks
  absolutism and, 511
  Byzantine fall to, 340
Tutankhamen (Egypt), 39
Twelfth-Century Renaissance, 321–322
Two Treatises of Government (Locke), 519
Tyrants, in Greece, 83, 84, 100
Tyre, 58, 115

Ugarit
  destruction of, 55
  during International Bronze Age, 50
  kingdom of, 50
Ulpian (jurist and legal scholar), 180
Uluburun, merchant ship at, 43, 44
Umayyad caliphate, *245* (map), 252–255, 260
  Spain in, 244, 266
Unitarianism, 449
United Kingdom. *See also* England (Britain)
  formation of, 516
  Scotland in, 517
United Monarchy (Hebrew), 66–67, 70
United Provinces of the Netherlands. *See* Dutch Republic (United Provinces of the Netherlands)
Universal Law of Gravitation, 530
Universe
  Aristotle on, 134, 527
  Democritus on, 535
  geocentric theory of, 545–546
  heliocentric theory of, 134, *528* (illus), 545–546
  humans in, 545–546
  Neoplatonists on, 536
  pre-Copernican, *527* (illus)
Universities and colleges
  Jesuits and, 451–452
  in Middle Ages, 321
  women in, 377
Upper classes, Roman, 188–189

Upper Egypt, 29, 36
Ur (city), 21, 65
Ur III Dynasty, 21, *28* (illus)
Urban II (Pope), 287, 288
Urban society, growth of, 126–127
Urban VI (Pope), 352
Urban VIII (Pope), 528
Urbino, Federico II da Montfeltro of, 373
Ur-Nammu (Sumer), 21, 22, 23, *28* (illus)
Uruk, Mesopotamia
  bevel-rimmed bowls in, 19
  cuneiform writing from, 24
  economy of, 19
  history of, 18
  religion in, 24
Uthman (caliph), 251
Utopia (More), 431, 445–446
Utrecht, Treaty of, 501, 504

Valerian (Rome), Persian capture of, 203, *203* (illus)
Valla, Lorenzo, 374, 376, 380, 429
Valois, Marguerite of (France), 475, 476
Valois family, during Hundred Years' War, 345
Vandals
  Justinian and, 226
  in North Africa, 225
  Roman Empire and, 223, 225
Vassals and vassalage, 280–281
Vassy, France, massacre at, 476
Vatican and Vatican City, 209
Velázquez, Diego de, 505
Vendetta as private justice, 388–389
Venice
  Black Death in, 333
  in Italian Renaissance, 366, 368–369
Venus (goddess), 154
Venus de Milo (goddess), *128* (illus)
Venus di Milo. *See* Aphrodite of Melos (statue)
Vercingetorix Surrenders to Caesar (painting by L. Royer), *164* (illus)
Verdun, Treaty of, 277
Vernacular languages, 480
Veronese, Paolo, *454* (illus)
Verres, Gaius, 143, 153
Versailles, Louis XVI and, 498–499
Vesalius, Andreas, 379, 380
Vespasian (Titus Flavius Vespasianus), 172
Vespucci, Amerigo, 403
Vestal Virgins, in Rome, 141
Viceroys and viceroyalties, in Spanish Empire, 410
Vienna Genesis (manuscript), *213* (illus)
Villages. *See also* Cities and towns; *specific communities*
  agricultural revolution and, 299
  food-producing, 14
Vinci, Leonardo da, *379* (illus), 385
  Renaissance patron, 384
Virgil (poet)
  Aeneid, 182, 183, 192
  Divine Comedy, The (Dante) and, 358
Virgin Mary. *See* Mary (mother of Jesus)
Visigoths
  in Balkans, 222–223
  in Gaul, 223, 224
  Huns and, 222–223
  Rome and, 222–223, 224
  in Spain, 244, 272
Viziers, in Egypt, 36
Vladimir the Great (Rus), 236
Voyage Around the Red Sea (author unknown), 186
Voyages
  along African coast, 397–400
  of Columbus, 391
  European, 405–406
Vulgate Bible, 213

Waldensians, heresy of, 309–310
Waldo, Peter, 309
Wales, ethnic tension in, 360
Walter of Brienne (Duke of Athens), 388
War gallery, *94* (illus)
War of the Roses (England), 347, 350, 390, 391
War of the Spanish Succession, 501, 504
Warriors
  on camels, 247
  in Europe, 16
  Mycenaean warrior graves, 53
Wars and warfare. *See also specific wars*; Weapons
  camels in, 247
  chariots and, 21, 35, 49, 52, 53, 61
  in Crusades, 287–293
  Egyptian, 35–36
  flowery war, 400
  Germanic, 267
  gunpowder and, 340, 351, 495
  Hittites, 55, 61
  in Hundred Years' War, 345, 349
  in Later Middle Ages, 344–351
  military revolution and, 349–351, 386–387
  Persian Wars, 91–93
  at sea, 94
  in Sumer, 19, *20* (illus)
Wars of Apostasy, 248
Warsaw Confederation (1573), 486
Water and sanitation, 53
Wealth. *See also* Aristocracy; Elites
  from Anatolian trade, 21–22
  in Mali, 396, 397
  in Rome, 157
Weapons. *See also specific weapons*
  bronze in, 35, 52
  cannons, 340
  gunpowder and, 340, 351, 495
  in Hundred Years' War, 351
Wearmouth, 272
Wergild, 267
West Africa, in fourteenth century, *396* (map)
West Francia, kingdom of, 284. *See also* France
  Capetian dynasty in, 284
  crusades, 287
West Germany. *See also* East Germany; Germany
West Whelpington North (England), manor of, *300* (illus)
Western Christianity, division by 1555, *441* (map). *See also* Roman Catholicism
Western civilizations
  characteristics of, 12
  economic connections, 59
  ethical framework, 44
  geographical and cultural designation, 40
  Hebrew religious legacy, 69
  Hebrews and, 74
  Hittites, 46–47
  Jesus, impact of trial, 196–197
  Proto-Canaanite alphabet, 76
  Roman Republic and, 166–167
  Rome's influence on, 199
  writing, 24
Western Europe
  kingdoms in, *317* (map)
  Latin Christianity in, 242, 264
  monarchies of, 387, 494
  rulers in, 280–281, 283–285
  table fork in, 469

Western Roman Empire. *See also* Eastern Roman Empire
Byzantium and, 234
under Constantine, 225
reconquering provinces, 226–228
separation from East, 222–223
Western values, 5
Western world (the West). *See also* America; Americas, Europeans in; Europe and Europeans; *specific countries*
core lands of, *6* (map)
in Hellenistic Age, 136
Saint Petersburg and, 512–514
satellite photo, *3* (illus)
science in, 65
Westernization, of Russia, 512–514
Westphalia, Treaty of
chronology, 504
Europe after, *507* (map)
ito end Thirty Years' War, 507
Weyer, Johann, 472
What question, 5–6
When question, 6–7
Where question, 7
Whigs (England), 517, 519
White Mountain, Battle of, 504, 509
Who question, 7
Why question, 8–9
William, Frederick (Great Elector), 508–509
William and Mary (England), 519
William I (the Conqueror, England), 317, 318
William III (Orange), 519
William the Silent (House of Orange), 459–460, 479, 480
Willibald (Boniface biographer), 262
Wilusa (site of Troy), 50. *See also* Troy, a city of legend
Winterthur, Johann von, 334–335
Witchcraft
burning of a witch, *471* (illus)
Dutch Republic and, 473
ordeals in witch trials, 473
were there really witches?, 472
Witch-hunt, 470
Wittenberg, Germany
Luther in, 432
Ninety-Five Theses in, 433–434
Wittenberg Cathedral, 434
Women. *See also* Feminism
Anabaptists on, 447
asceticism and, 215
as Christian saints, 310–311
Christianity and, 215–216, 452
courtly love and, 323
in Egypt, 32, 36–37
in food-producing communities, 14
gender boundaries and, 97–99
in Greece, 98–99
Hebrews and, 73
in Hellenistic world, 128
humanists, 377
in Italian Renaissance, 377
Jewish, 216–217
medieval universities and, 377
in Mesopotamia, 14, 28
monasticism and, 215–216
nature and, 547–548
patriarchal family, 372–373
as pharaoh, 37
property in Germanic kingdoms, 268–269
religious orders of, 452
in Roman Catholicism, 310–311
in Rome, 178–179, 189–191
and their hairdresser, *190* (illus)
as troubadours, 323
in Turkey, 378
witchcraft and, 471, 473
Women's movement, international. *See also* Feminism
Woolley, Sir Leonard, *23* (illus)
Workers. *See also* Labor
rebellions in Middle Ages, 343–344
Writing
Carolingian minuscule, 276
express mail, 61
in Greece, 49, 79–80
hieroglyphs as, 31–32, 59
Minoan, 48
Phoenician, 59
Sumerian, 24, 42
Wycliffe, John, 353

Xerxes I (Persia), 78, 92–93

Yahweh, 70, 72–73
Yazilikaya, *46* (illus)
"Year of Four Emperors" (Rome), 172
Yemen, Sheba in, 67
Yersin, Alexandre, 332

Zagros Mountains, 15, 21
Zama, Battle of, 149
Zamosc, *487* (illus)
Zamoyski, Jan (Count), 486
Zarathustra. *See* Zoroaster and Zoroastrianism
Zedekiah, 68–69
Zeno of Citium, 133, *133* (illus)
Zeus (god), 81, 113, 154
Ziggurat of Ur, 23, *23* (illus)
Zionism. *See also* Jews and Judaism
Zodiac, Greek in synagogue, *217* (illus)
Zoroaster and Zoroastrianism
in Islamic Empire, 255
in Persian Empire, 88, 90
Zürich
Anabaptists in, 448
Zaingli in, 450
Zwingli in, 441–442
Zwingli, Ulrich, 441–442